First Published in 2016 by Victory Belt Publishing Inc.

PAPERBACK ISBN 13: 978-1-628600-00-1

HARDCOVER ISBN 13: 978-1-628600-02-5

The information included in this book is for educational purposes only. It is not intended or implied to be a substitute for professional medical advice. The reader should always consult his or her health-care provider to determine the appropriateness of the information for his or her own situation or if he or she has any questions regarding a medical condition or treatment plan. Reading the information in this book does not create a physician-patient relationship.

Victory Belt ® is a registered trademark of Victory Belt Publishing Inc.

Book design by Joan Olkowski, Graphic D-Signs, Inc. and Justin-Aaron Velasco
Illustrations by Alex Boake, Yordan Terziev, and Boryana Yordanova
Photography by Diane Sanfilippo (recipes, additional), Bill Staley (recipes),
Kelty Luber (additional)

Cover and inside portraits by Michelle Lange
Kitchen provided by Valerie Zaloom-Buccino

Printed in Canada

TC0519

UPDATED & EXPANDED SECOND EDITION

PRACTICAL PALEO

a customized approach to health and a whole-foods lifestyle

Diane Sanfilippo, BS, NC

Victory Belt Publishing Inc.

Contents

Foreword

By Robb Wolf, *New York Times* bestselling author of
The Paleo Solution

It was an enormous honor to write the foreword for the first edition of *Practical Paleo* several years ago, but that feeling honestly pales in comparison to adding a few words to this, the second edition of *Practical Paleo*. This book was not only one of the very first on the Paleo scene, it was— and still is—easily one of the best. Diane was one of the first people to give the Autoimmune Paleo Protocol a solid treatment, and it's hard to estimate how many people have benefitted from the accessibility of this information. This second edition updates not just the science of the Paleo / ancestral health concepts but also expands heavily on the coaching insights Diane has gained by helping literally millions of people change their lives. The remainder of this foreword appears largely as it did in the original. I'm hard pressed to improve my small contribution to this work, but rest assured, as good as the first edition of *Practical Paleo* was, this second edition shows a remarkable degree of evolution and insight on the part of the author. You will love it.

I've been researching and studying this Paleo concept for almost twenty years, and the evolution and reach of the information has been nothing short of remarkable. Years ago you had to hunt (and gather?) to find information on Paleo in general, to say nothing of how to alter your approach for specific problems such as gastrointestinal issues or autoimmunity.

People often come to me saying that Paleo worked for them, but they're unsure of how to tread with loved ones—how to best help their type 2 diabetic mom, or their dad/friend/(insert other loved one here) with a specific condition. While I've personally answered these questions for thousands of people through my own website, blog, podcast, and book, *Practical Paleo* takes all of the concepts that we know will help people and provides clear plans, laid out in an easy-to-understand way. It takes the guesswork out of how to move forward and take your health into your own hands—from lifestyle to diet to smart supplementation. All this with amazing recipes to boot!

Once, it was tough to find this information, and if you were fortunate enough to find what you needed, it was in a dry, unaesthetic format. Those days are gone. My good friend, Diane Sanfilippo, has made *Practical Paleo* a work of art that is as useful as it is beautiful. Are you an athlete? Suffer from digestive distress? Been diagnosed with an autoimmune condition? Maybe you just want to live a long life and look good naked? Whatever your goals, Diane has done the heavy lifting by condensing the science and a lot of practical how-tos into bite-sized pieces.

You don't need a pocket protector to read this book. In easy-to-understand language, you will learn the science behind the original human diet and how it can unlock the door to better health. Science, recipes, customization, and beautiful, easy-to-read graphics—*Practical Paleo* has it all.

—Robb Wolf

Dedication and Gratitude

I'd be remiss if I didn't make the initial dedication of this updated version of the book to all of you, dear readers.

I've traveled the country and landed in countless cities to meet and interact with you all, and what a blessing that has been. I never could have imagined the response that you all have had to this book, and I want you to know that I'm immensely proud of all of you for the time, energy, and effort you've put into your own journeys of healing.

Countless numbers of you have expressed to me that I, and this book, changed—or even saved—your lives. What I want you to know is that I have simply followed my passion and you, the strong and powerful humans reading this book, have done the work. Writing a book is difficult, sure, but taking responsibility for your own health and committing to that path is work that not everyone is willing to do. I am consistently humbled by you all, and I'm grateful to hold a place in your lives as support along your paths.

When I wrote the first edition of this book, it was through the motivation of my grandmother, Barbara Frank, who was turning ninety that year—and who has since passed. Not only did my grandmother push me to write a "real" book instead of an e-book, since that concept was lost on her, but I'm not kidding when I tell you she also said to me, not too long ago, "Oh, you'll need to update that book soon, won't you?" I can't make this stuff up. It's as if my grandmother had some kind of sixth sense about these things. She was really something special.

In any event, while Grandma wasn't the primary reason I wanted to update this book, she remained a cheerleader up until her last days, proud as ever to put copies of my latest books into her wheeling walker to show all of her bridge cronies.

To my grandfather, Bill, who passed away before ever knowing this book was in creation, for his confidence in me as a well-intentioned person and a businesswoman. His support through every phase of my life and career was unwavering. Whatever path I was on, he was confident that it was the right one for me . . . and if it wasn't the right path, he was confident that I'd blaze a trail for myself to make it that way.

To my parents, who raised me with the words "do what makes you happy." Some may think those words will lead a child into an adult life that is hedonistic and irresponsible, but I have experienced firsthand how important that value has been in my life. After working several jobs that I didn't wake up with a burning passion to tackle, their words to "do what makes you happy" still resonate. I feel lucky to wake up every day to a life I am choosing, and I thank them for their 100 percent support. I can't tell you how many times my father has texted me a photo of this book in stores (mostly Costco, his favorite place to shop), and the pride I imagine he beams when he does that is pretty awesome.

To my love, my life, my better half, my grounding, my family, my husband, Scott Mills. I feel lucky every single day that we met. I don't know how you can possibly put up with all that is me and my crazy ideas, but I'm glad you do. There's no one with whom I'd rather spend all of my days. You're my favorite.

To my nutrition instructors at Bauman College, Nori Hudson and Laura Knoff, for not looking at me like I had a third eye when, early in my nutritional education, I showed up to classes with newfound passion for a Paleo lifestyle, and for being supporters and promoters of the teachings of Dr. Weston Price, so that traditional and well-raised animal foods were consistently discussed as health-promoting options in a classroom where the curriculum was clearly created with a vegetarian slant.

To Robb Wolf, Chris Kresser, and Chris Masterjohn: Robb, for igniting my vigor and passion for sharing the profoundly powerful message of Paleo nutrition; Chris K., for your levelheaded approach to dissecting literature and disseminating information; and Chris M., for digging in and researching to find the answers (and often more questions) about human nutrition and health to bring to the public in a useful and practical way. All of you have unrelenting motivation to help people and spread the word about how profoundly what we eat can affect our entire lives, and that continues to motivate and inspire me.

To my trainer and friend, Dave Engen, who was the first person to tell me that I should be eating coconut oil and *not* to fear fat. You patiently waited while I figured out for myself that you were right. I still credit you every time I talk about my journey, and I hope that my expression of gratitude is always felt by you.

To my former boss, Dan Antonelli at Graphic D-Signs, Inc. in New Jersey, for teaching me the skill to turn information into a piece of graphic art that people can use over and over to make their lives healthier.

To my friend and teaching/podcasting partner in crime, Liz Wolfe, for allowing me to drag you deeper into this whole nutty world of helping folks in a very public and visible way. You shine brightly with integrity, humility, knowledge, and caring in a noisy world of advice-slinging. I'm eternally grateful for our connection.

To Caitlin Weeks, Brittany Angell, Jenny Castaneda, and Tony Kasandrinos, for being not only amazing colleagues—always ready to listen to my ideas, give advice, or tell me I'm crazy—but also some of the most die-hard loyal and caring friends a girl could ask for.

To the entire Victory Belt family, you all have supported me and this book endlessly and tirelessly, and there aren't enough ways to say thank you for that.

To Team Balanced Bites: April, Holly, Lindsey, Moriah, Kate, Niki, Amanda B., Amanda S., Rebekah, and Tonja P., for making this entire operation run smoothly and having the most amazing attitudes. I am so honored to have you all along for this ride with me for as long as you want to be on it.

Last, but certainly not least, to Bill Staley and Hayley Mason. Without the two of you, the recipes in this book would likely have originally been accompanied by iPhone photos tweaked with a ninety-nine-cent app. Your friendship and support has meant *the world* to me, and this book would absolutely not be what it is without the two of you.

Thank you.

A Note on the Second Edition

When I wrote this book in 2011/2012, I had a feeling it would fill a void in the collection of books that were already out there on the subject of Paleo, but I honestly couldn't have expected what would happen next. From the book's appearance in the *New York Times* bestseller list in October 2012 as the first book ever with "Paleo" in the title to be printed on that list (Robb Wolf's *The Paleo Solution* made the list but only online, never printed in the paper), to the reach it had thereafter (the sixth-bestselling cookbook in 2014!), I've been consistently amazed.

I'm amazed not only at the response of the Paleo community, which has embraced this book as their own, referring every friend, family member, coworker, and stranger to it as their number-one resource, but also at how people have taken the information in these pages and used it to transform their lives from the inside out.

This book has remained the bestselling Paleo book since its release, so I felt it was extremely important that it remain as relevant and comprehensive today as it was when it was originally published. There are lots of new conversations in the Paleo community, new topics to discuss, and new questions to answer. While the vast majority of what I originally wrote remains relevant and holds true today, I'd be remiss if I didn't address the questions we see popping up now so that you can continue to feel confident that this is the best go-to resource for anyone interested in Paleo.

What's New: The Small Stuff

This book has been more than a little bit updated. It's an entirely new edition, with some major content additions as well as expansions upon the original content. Most of what I wrote in the first edition remains as it was, with some small changes and refinements here and there. For example, the USDA's *Dietary Guidelines for Americans* was updated in 2015, so I've made some changes to the discussion of the government's nutritional recommendations. I've also, given the ever-increasing popularity of low-carb diets, explained more about carbohydrates and their role in a healthy diet: why some people may need more carbs and how to tell if you've actually gone *too* low-carb, how to easily include more healthy carbs in your diet, and how a higher-carb Paleo meal may affect blood sugar regulation.

I've also expanded the FAQs to address hot topics like white rice and white potatoes, alcohol, baking with nut flours, and more on the pros and cons of counting calories.

What's New: The Big Stuff

Part 1: The Why—Food and Your Body has been revised and now includes two entirely new chapters: "Getting Started with Paleo" and "Living a Paleo Lifestyle." In the chapter on getting started, I tackle the question of whether to ease into this new way of eating or to dive in headfirst, and a new two-page guide that provides a road map for starting Paleo can be used either way: you can follow it step by step over several weeks or months to make a gradual transition to Paleo, or you can use it to prepare for the switch during the few days leading up to an all-in approach.

I've also expanded the discussion of whether it's necessary to follow a strict Paleo diet for life in order to enjoy optimal health, or if some people may find they do quite well eating some non-Paleo real foods. The question "Is it Paleo?" is also addressed at length, as well as what to do if you currently eat a vegetarian or vegan diet and want to make the switch—because it's not an overnight change for most people.

In the chapter on the Paleo lifestyle, I tackle at length some of the most common topics I've received questions about: inviting friends and family to give Paleo a shot, dealing with unsupportive friends and family, eating Paleo with kids, and what to do about the ever-growing abundance of recipes for "Paleo" baked goods.

In Part 2: 30-Day Meal Plans, I've added three new plans on several health challenges I often field questions about: Adrenal Health (to support stress management), Healthy Hormones (to support a healthy balance for both men and women), and Liver Detox Support (to support the liver and its work in removing toxins from the bloodstream). Like the plans in the first edition, each new plan is much more than just notes on meals to eat for the month; they also include lifestyle recommendations and diet and supplement suggestions. You'll also find a new guide to selecting a meal plan that's designed to help you choose a plan that offers the most benefit with the least restrictions. Furthermore, all of the meal plans have been updated to include new recipes added in this edition, for increased variety and new flavor profiles.

In Part 3: Recipes, I've added nearly 50 new recipes, most of which are entrées that utilize affordable protein sources, since these are the types of recipes you all asked for the most! You'll also find lots of all-in-one meals (meat and vegetables in one dish) that help keep things simple, some easy new breakfast options, recipes that come together quickly using my signature Practical Paleo Spice Blends (recipes for the spice blends are in the book, but they're also available premade at www.practicalpaleospices.com), and some creative new salad ideas to keep up the excitement around your dinner table. Many of your favorite recipes have new photos in this edition, from Spaghetti Squash Bolognese (page 338) to Balsamic Braised Short Ribs (page 332) and lots in between, so be ready to see them in a whole new light—literally and figuratively!

All these changes have been made with the goal of making this book even more helpful, keeping it up to date with the latest information on nutrition and health, and answering the questions I'm asked most frequently. My hope is that this new edition will continue to act as a guide to all of you who are doing the hard work of changing your life for the better. I can't wait to hear even more success stories from you!

Diane

OUT WITH THE OLD...
I've removed only a handful of less-popular recipes from the first edition to make room for as many new recipes as possible. To download a PDF of those recipes for free, visit balancedbites. com/practicalpaleo and click the button for the book resource files!

Introduction

Let food be thy medicine, and medicine be thy food.
—Hippocrates

I grew up playing soccer, volleyball, and softball, but like most kids, I never thought about nutrition. In fact, it never crossed my mind that I might need to change my eating habits. I ate whatever I liked, I was always in pretty good shape, and I considered myself to be healthy and strong.

Then, during high school, I began to have disruptive bouts of digestive distress, to the extent that I took Imodium A-D several times a week. I also suffered from repeated sinus infections throughout the year. The infections became so old-hat that I simply demanded antibiotics when I visited the doctor. After all, I had been taught that pills were the best way to handle symptoms.

My close friends struggled with the same health issues. All of us had a range of chronic ailments, like acne, pharyngitis, heartburn, headaches, dental cavities, and deteriorating vision, in addition to sinus and digestive discomfort. It never occurred to any of us that we had the power to prevent these problems.

After eighteen years as an active youth, I became much less active in college, and my weight started to rise. My late nights with pizza and Buffalo wings meant that "the freshman fifteen" didn't end after freshman year. I continued to eat like an athlete even though I had all but abandoned that aspect of my life. By the time I finished college, I had put on thirty pounds. There is a photo from my graduation dinner that shows my bloated midsection—it's one I use as a "before" picture when I tell my story at seminars. At the time, I had no idea my body had fallen completely apart.

Like many people who gain weight during their college years, I thought, "This is just what happens when people get older." I learned later, of course, that it's what happens when people stop exercising and eat foods that do not support a healthy body. My symptoms may have been common, but what I didn't realize until later is that "common" doesn't necessarily mean "normal."

In the year after college, I gained yet another ten pounds, and a nurse practitioner brought up my weight during a routine checkup. She talked to me about food portion sizes and I suddenly realized how out of control my eating had become. Even though everyone around me ate the same way, I couldn't deny that I didn't feel or look good.

That winter, I joined a gym and tried to watch what I ate, but I had no clue what that meant. I dined out on burgers and fries (on large seedy buns, of course) and washed it all down with Coke. I did know that soda wasn't healthy, so I sometimes substituted water instead. At home, I made dinners of pasta with red sauce and analyzed the meal in my head. "Well, that's just some pasta and tomatoes," I'd think, "so it's healthy." I gave myself a bit less than I served my boyfriend, and I sweated away on the cardio machines at the gym. You probably aren't surprised to hear that my weight *did not budge*.

Months later, I started a new job and found myself surrounded by middle-aged women on Weight Watchers. "Okay," I thought, "if they can do it, I can do it." So I started the diet and stayed on it . . . until the end of each workday, when I found myself still hungry and with no points left. I knew that going home and not eating anything for the rest of the evening wasn't an option, so I bent the rules on the points system. But I had started to work out and, in spite of my rule-bending, the diet began to work. I was losing weight.

What Weight Watchers taught me more than anything was to read food labels. Granted, I now teach people to read labels more for nutritional information to discover the quality of the item in their hand, but paying attention to calories, fat, and fiber was a start for me. I lost twelve pounds from simply watching my diet and working out on the elliptical machine for thirty minutes several times a week. The initial weight loss gave me the confidence to exercise at the gym more often, and I started lifting weights again for the first time in four years.

Days turned into weeks and months, and before I knew it, I had lost thirty pounds. In many ways, I felt amazing. My body was finally getting back to a size that was more comfortable for me, but the rest of my system was the same as it had always been—riddled with digestive distress, chronic sinus infections, and deteriorating vision. I even had a new ailment to add to the mix: hypoglycemia (low blood sugar), which caused me to nearly pass out at times. When I became shaky, sweaty, and light-headed, a friend usually said, "Get her a granola bar!" Of course, that was the last thing I needed.

What I Didn't Know About Proper Nutrition Was Hurting Me (And May Be Hurting You!)

It wasn't until several years later that I discovered the root cause of my chronic symptoms of low blood sugar. I was eating close to 300 grams of carbohydrates a day, reaching for bread with olive oil if my dinner wasn't filling enough, but I thought it was crazy that bread—innocent old bread—could be the source of such hefty problems. When I finally came to terms with the long list of conditions associated with gluten intolerance, it *still* took me a year to finally give it up. It took reading books on the topic (*Dangerous Grains*, to name one), attending seminars for health-care practitioners on gluten sensitivity, and tuning in to how my body was truly reacting when I ate pasta (indigestion) or whole-wheat bread (digestive distress). Then there was a big turning point for me.

Not long after converting to a 90 percent gluten-free way of eating, I attended Robb Wolf's "Paleo Solution" seminar. By then I had already studied nutrition for many years, but there were two big takeaways for me that day:

1. Avoid gluten like the plague!

2. Managing blood sugar, insulin levels, and systemic inflammation is critical for health and can be done fairly easily by avoiding the modern, processed foods we've come to rely on as staples in our diet: grains, legumes, poor-quality dairy, and sugar-laden foods.

I went home and gutted my house, cleaning it of every grain—quinoa, buckwheat, rice, millet, gluten-free oats, and more. I prepared meat and vegetables with some fat and spices, and I cooked eggs and bacon in the mornings, packing them in a glass container to take to work so I could eat at my desk. My coworkers were jealous as they chowed on bagels and granola bars and downed bowls of cereal, all of which were always well stocked in the office kitchen. When it was time for our lunch orders, I designed mine to provide me with as much protein and as many veggies as possible. When a last-minute work meeting over breakfast offered only pastries and fruit, I took a short walk to the corner deli for hard-boiled eggs to eat alongside the fruit for a much more satisfying meal.

When I couldn't get enough healthy fare from a restaurant or deli, I brought extra food with me. That took a bit of planning, of course, but it was easier than you'd think.

The results were dramatic. I stopped suffering from the chronic ailments that had plagued me for most of my life. My digestion works predictably well now, I rarely get sinus infections, and the hypoglycemia is long gone. I no longer worry that I might pass out without a snack or that I might have to run to the bathroom when it isn't convenient. The vision deterioration I had experienced for years has halted, and I have not had a cavity in a long time. On the very rare occasion that I experience heartburn or a bit of digestive upset, I can quickly identify the food that caused it. At most, I get sick once or twice a year, usually after air travel or too little rest. When that happens, I no longer have to take prescription antibiotics, and the bug passes through my system within three to five days. While my acne took a bit longer to alleviate, using natural skin care techniques instead of harsh cleansers, discovering additional food allergies and eliminating those foods, and avoiding seed oils like soybean, corn, and canola oils (primarily from restaurant food) as often as possible eventually did the trick.

Changing my diet resolved all of the ailments that had haunted me for years. It was a matter of healing my gut, which, in turn, healed my entire body, and balancing my blood sugar levels.

After these two main issues were addressed, I simply fine-tuned my diet and lifestyle practices to optimize my health. I had suffered needlessly for many years, but the health I now enjoy with this new lifestyle is extraordinarily liberating. I said good-bye to urgent trips to the bathroom and frequent doctor visits, and I no longer need to carry sugary snacks like granola bars to keep myself from feeling like I might pass out.

Your Health Requires That You Help Yourself

Not long after I discovered how to become and stay healthy, I found that I wanted to share my knowledge with others and help them feel the same freedom from pain and illness. I started an organic meal delivery business, but after just a few months of providing meals to clients, I realized I was doing the work for them rather than actually transforming their lives. I had to teach them how to create new lifestyle habits. So I decided to go back to school to study nutrition and become a Certified Nutrition Consultant.

It has been very rewarding to share my passion for nutritious food with others and help them create dietary plans for healthier, happier lives. I first began my practice with small group talks and one-on-one consulting, then expanded into teaching seminars all over the country to anywhere from 20 to 120 people. I started educating people through a weekly podcast, *The Balanced Bites Podcast,* my blog (dianesanfilippo.com), and social media channels like Facebook, Instagram, and Twitter. The natural progression was to reach even more people and provide a comprehensive body of work by writing a book.

I realize there is a lot of information out there about how and what to eat, but it's often difficult to understand. So this book is designed to be easy to follow and use, whether you are totally new to the Paleo way of eating and living or have been on this path for a while. My aim is to provide you with a resource that is practical and useful in your

everyday life by explaining the basics of how food works in your body and showing you how to create a customized meal plan for your personal nutritional needs. When you finish this book, you will have the tools you need to shop for and cook delicious meals that give your body what it requires to stay healthy and energized.

But if you're looking for detailed scientific writing filled with jargon and citations, you won't find it here. Hence, the word "practical" in the title. My goal is to distill my years of education and experience into a guide that's easy to understand and just plain useful.

This Is Not a Diet

Remember that a "diet" is temporary. *Practical Paleo*, on the other hand, offers a way to change your lifestyle, leading to long-term health benefits that reach far beyond the coming weeks or months. This book will show you how food works so that you can design a plan that's right for *your* body.

If you're entirely new to this way of living, you may find it helpful to start by following one of the 30-Day Meal Plans in Part 2 (starting on page 162). If that feels too overwhelming, simply follow the one-page guides throughout the book on how to select real, whole foods and start cooking the recipes. This will take you most of the way to a healthier you, and you won't need to follow a specific plan.

Practical Paleo serves not just the average person looking for improved health but also those who have been diagnosed with a medical condition and perhaps told they'd suffer with those symptoms for life. If you fall into this group, this book was particularly created for *you*. I want you to know that there is a better way; pills and pain are not always the final stop. For many, it *is* possible to feel better, despite what you have been told, even perhaps by doctors. **You, not your doctor, get to choose what you eat and how you nourish your body with the raw materials it needs to thrive, and that can often be the most powerful medicine of all.**

Finding Health in a Modern World

When I first told my then ninety-year-old grandmother that I was becoming a nutrition consultant, she had difficulty understanding how teaching people what to eat could be a job, let alone a career. She was born in a different time, when food was still whole and unprocessed and made a short trip from the farm to the table. She fondly recounted the days she spent milking cows, collecting eggs, and feeding the animals.

When refined foods were introduced, my grandmother and her peers strayed from real food in favor of what was faster and more convenient. Grandma didn't need a lesson in how and what to eat when she was growing up, but today, we *all* do.

Modern grocery stores are enormous and filled with aisle after aisle of packaged, processed "foods" that your grandmother never saw in the kitchen of her youth. Those of us in subsequent generations were raised on pasteurized milk products, refined grains, and sugar-laden foods like macaroni and cheese, soda, and breakfast cereal. Even health-conscious families scooped up instant oatmeal, whole-grain breads, and nonfat yogurt.

When we began to eat foods created in factories rather than grown on farms, we moved steadily away from health-promoting nutrition and toward building our bodies' tissues from synthetic, nutrient-poor foodlike substances. Isn't it obvious that problems would arise? It's pretty clearly seen in the declining health of the people around us.

Your constitution

Your foundational state of physical health and robustness can make it easier or harder to maintain or achieve optimal health. For example, a person who was born to a healthy and robust mother, birthed naturally, breast-fed until self-weaned, and transitioned to whole food is likely to have a more robust constitution than someone who was fed an unhealthy diet of cereals and refined foods during his or her formative years.

When I started writing this book, medication was keeping my grandmother alive as her body suffered the consequences of decades of processed foods and undiagnosed food allergies. It's sad that the majority of her severe health conditions could have been avoided by shunning factory foods. Still, my grandmother was lucky. A foundation of better childhood nutrition allowed her to develop a much sturdier constitution than that of most children today, who not only are born to mothers who were raised on processed foods but are also fed commercially prepared infant formula that is not as nutrient-dense and naturally healthy as breast milk. If Grandma had been raised on the foods that most people today consume, she likely wouldn't have made it into her nineties.

I explained to Grandma that most food today isn't produced the way it was when she was a kid and that it's important to seek out and support the rare individuals who produce food with traditional values in mind. But she spent so many decades relying on processed food that many of those discussions failed to stick. She remembered my "cookie monster" days and offered me some when I visited her, forgetting that I no longer ate grains or sugar. When I reminded her that I feel better when I don't eat those foods, I always asked her, "Do I look hungry?" It's a cheeky question, but it proved the point that you can get sufficient nourishment from foods that aren't conventionally considered staples.

Grandma was intrigued when I told her that my profession is needed because people are quite confused about what to eat, and a change in nutrition—yes, a simple change in *food*—can help people feel better, even those who have taken multiple medications for years to manage symptoms. This concept befuddled my grandmother partly because doctors, in her mind, are the final word, and they never offered dietary solutions. She lived with medical issues ranging from gallbladder disease to thyroid and other autoimmune complications, as well as diverticulitis and intense sciatic pain. I'm confident that she also had undiagnosed celiac disease (a condition caused by gluten intolerance).

After her bout with colon cancer a few years ago, I told my grandmother that she had an allergy to gluten. I thought that she might more readily accept a dietary explanation for a disease of the digestive system than for problems that seemed to her to be unrelated to food. When she arrived home from the hospital, I stocked her kitchen with gluten-free bread and other prepackaged gluten-free foods. Even though I don't recommend these for most people, this ninety-year-old was hardly about to give up her morning toast or afternoon cookies. I simply hoped for at least a small change in her routine.

A few days after she got home from the hospital, I asked how she was feeling. She reported that she no longer had the pain in her abdomen that she had experienced every day for as long as she could remember. Other food-related issues aside, what appeared to be a lifelong gluten allergy—constantly aggravated by continuous exposure to it—had subsided for reasons that escaped her. I cannot help but wonder if this had affected other aspects of her health as she aged. Hearing her say that she didn't feel the same pain was enough to solidify in my mind that she had suffered needlessly—likely for decades.

Why Paleo Is So Powerful

I fully recognize that there are certain conditions for which a prescription or medical intervention may be necessary and even lifesaving. Most chronic conditions, however, are rooted in our overall level of immune health, which is directly affected by food. These conditions *can* and *will* be improved by dietary and lifestyle changes. So how can we circle back toward the idea that health is a natural state for humans and that relying on medications to relieve symptoms is not usually a real solution?

While we've forgotten what "real food" is over the last few decades, there is hope. Although the low-fat and low-cholesterol mentality still has a stronghold in conventional nutritional wisdom, mainstream media outlets like *Time* magazine have retracted previous statements against dietary cholesterol and fat. The public is beginning to question conventional wisdom and recognize that doctors may not be the best source of information on nutrition. From where I stand, this palpable shift has made it easier to explain that butter is healthy while Crisco is not.

Still, many people who are ready and willing to change lack the information that will help them put their chronic symptoms in remission. Luckily, the health movement that has arisen from disillusionment has gained extraordinary momentum for a reason: it has helped countless individuals overcome what were seemingly insurmountable, chronic, and even unrecognized health problems.

People are beginning to realize that they are no longer destined to suffer from diseases—or even minor ailments—that are caused by modern food and unhealthy lifestyles. We have found a better way. I want to share with you, as I shared with my grandmother, that we can indeed return to food that comes from properly raised animals and well-tended plants. You don't have to rely on factory-derived, packaged calories stamped with unfounded health claims that are nothing more than marketing spin. You can find extraordinary health in beautifully simple, unprocessed, whole foods.

WHAT IS THIS THING CALLED GLUTEN?
The word "gluten" is often used as an umbrella term for gliadin proteins and a number of other constituents in grains to which people can react negatively. Gluten is found in grains and by-products of wheat, barley, rye, triticale, oats (typically from cross-contamination), and other grains, as well as in some other foods where these grains are used in production, such as soy sauce, which is typically fermented with wheat to speed up the process. For more on gluten and its effects, see page 99.

PART 1
THE WHY:
FOOD & YOUR BODY

What Is Paleo?

CHAPTER 1

"Paleo" is short for "Paleolithic," but the name is less important than the power of the overall approach.

While the term "Paleo" has gained traction in the mainstream media and on bookstore shelves everywhere due to the improved health of those who follow the lifestyle, you could also call this way of eating "primal," "grain-free," "real food," "whole food," "nutrient-dense," or "ancestral." Whatever name you choose, the Paleo way of eating is simple: mimic our ancestors, who suffered from fewer chronic diseases than we do today. This doesn't mean that you'll re-create a caveman's food landscape, of course. Our food supply and our environment are different from our ancestors', so we must adapt as new information comes to light.

The Paleo lifestyle is simply about (1) eating whole foods that provide better fuel for your body and (2) avoiding processed, refined, nutrient-poor factory foods. This means avoiding grains, legumes (beans), refined sugar, and poor-quality dairy products (see page 63 for more on food quality).

When we eat a food in the whole form provided by nature, it promotes health, healing, and immunity against future ailments. On the other hand, if a food is not in its whole, natural form, chances are that it has been refined and is a less-than-optimal choice. When we remove ourselves from the complex food web that exists in nature, we fight against our birthright of health. Processed and refined foods—including grains, pasteurized dairy products, industrial seed oils (such as corn, cottonseed, soybean, canola, and rapeseed oils), and artificial or refined sugar and sweeteners (especially high fructose corn syrup)—are damaging to health. If it has to pass through a factory before it is edible, reconsider whether or not it is actually food. More likely, it is an "edible product" or "foodlike substance."

The reason Paleo works so well for so many people—the reason so many of us simply feel better when we eat a Paleo diet—is that these basic guidelines help resolve digestive problems and stabilize blood sugar, and those two things alone are at the root of most diet-related health problems.

Digestion: The ability to fight chronic and even acute diseases begins in the gut. In fact, 60 to 80 percent of the immune system is within the gut, following the entire length of the small intestine. If your digestive system is constantly irritated, it sets the stage for autoimmune conditions and disrupted immune function. This can result in a problem as innocuous as seasonal allergies or one that's much more aggressive, such as diverticulitis, eczema, psoriasis, or a number of other inflammatory and autoimmune conditions. And when it comes to problems with the digestive system itself, such as irritable bowel syndrome, inflammatory bowel disease, and celiac disease, what we eat can make all the difference. The Paleo diet eliminates foods that cause inflammation and irritation, helping to heal the gut and promote overall health.

BEYOND YOUR BELLY
Digestive disruption may appear as any form of chronic inflammatory condition, even those that aren't associated with digestion. It does not always manifest with upper or lower GI symptoms such as belching, burping, gas, bloating, diarrhea, or constipation, though all of these are surefire signs that your digestive process has gone awry.

Check out the guide to digestion on page 91 for a complete list of chronic inflammatory conditions associated with impaired digestive function.

Blood sugar: If you're often hungry, eating every two to three hours, or feeling shaky, weak, or starving entering into each meal or snack, you are probably not eating the right balance of food for you. Eating the right amount of protein, fat, and good carbs will help you to maintain well-balanced blood sugar throughout the day while comfortably eating roughly every four to six hours. The Paleo diet eliminates unhealthy foods that can send you on a blood sugar roller coaster (especially processed and refined foods, which are often full of sugar) and helps stabilize blood sugar instead, keeping you feeling energized throughout the day.

The improvement in digestion and blood sugar will benefit anyone who tries Paleo. In addition, the Paleo template can and should be adjusted to meet your own needs. In fact, the most important part of Paleo—-or any dietary plan—is figuring out what works best for *you.* You need to understand what to do to reach your own personal health goals, whether you want to treat a particular health condition, lose weight, or tackle another health concern. Paleo is not a one-size-fits-all approach, but it *is* a way of eating that is appropriate for all human animals. Since you are a human animal, there is a Paleo plan that is right for you.

PALEO IS NOT AN RX
Paleo is a template, not a dietary prescription. There isn't one cookie-cutter "Paleo diet." If you are eating solely chicken breasts, broccoli, and olive oil, you're missing the point entirely.

Recommended reading

The quantity and quality of scientific research behind the Paleo way of eating is astounding and shows that an ancestral diet promotes excellent health. If you're interested in learning more about the science behind Paleo, I recommend the works of these leading experts:

- Dr. Loren Cordain, *New York Times* bestselling author of *The Paleo Diet*

- Dr. Staffan Lindeberg, author of *Food and Western Disease: Health and Nutrition from an Evolutionary Perspective*

- Dr. Alessio Fasano, leading researcher on the effects of gluten on the small intestine and author of *Gluten Freedom*

- Robb Wolf (www.robbwolf.com), biochemist and *New York Times* bestselling author of *The Paleo Solution*

- Chris Kresser, LAc (www.chriskresser.com), integrative medicine practitioner and *New York Times* bestselling author of *Your Personal Paleo Code* (in paperback as *The Paleo Cure*)

- Stephan Guyenet (wholehealthsource.blogspot.com), obesity researcher, neurobiologist, and author of *Why Do We Gain Fat, and How Do We Lose It? An Introduction to the Science of Body Fat*

- Chris Masterjohn (cholesterol-and-health.com), cholesterol, fat, and nutrition researcher and assistant professor of health and nutrition sciences at Brooklyn College

The term "Paleo" can be misleading, though—the Paleo diet is not about eating exactly what people ate in the Paleolithic era. Some have wondered if they could try to create a nutritional plan based on what their ancestors ate in a particular part of the world. If every one of your ancestors was born and grew up in that region, you could try this, but it would still be challenging to find the same foods that were eaten so long ago because plants and animals have both evolved since then. We can guess what animal and plant foods would have been available in different climates on different terrain and with varied access to bodies of water. If we were to attempt to re-create early diets with 100 percent accuracy, though, we would have difficulty finding the indigenous plants and animals that were available in the past. More importantly, so much time has passed since the end of the Paleolithic era (12,000 years!) that it's impossible to know where *all* of our ancestors are from. Instead, the Paleo concept is based on estimations of what humans from that era ate, as well as the nutritional and dietary history of many parts of the world.

While I propose that there are certain foods that are nutritionally optimal and should be part of your dietary landscape, you may very well experience vibrant, long-term, and exemplary health eating foods outside of these recommendations. Eating processed foods and maintaining excellent health is hardly the norm, however. And unfortunately, exemplary health is far from what most people are experiencing in the modern world.

Ask Yourself These Questions

Evaluate your upbringing and foundational nutrition (or lack thereof), as well as your genetic predispositions to health or disease, to the best of your ability. Then answer these questions regarding your current health status:

- How do you feel most of the time?
- What is the status of your physical fitness or athletic performance?
- What is your body composition? How much fat do you have compared to muscle?
- How are your moods?
- Does your energy level fluctuate throughout the day?
- How is your appetite?
- Do you have food cravings? For sugar? For carbs? For salty or fatty foods?
- Does your skin look healthy, clear, and glowing?
- How is your vision?
- How is your dental health?
- Do you have regular bowel movements?
- Have you been diagnosed with a specific health condition?

If you answered all of these questions positively, congratulations! You're in a very small minority, and you can skip ahead to the recipes later in the book. But if you're like most people, you didn't give a positive answer to all of the questions, which means you would benefit from evaluating your current approach to health and nutrition. Read on to learn more about how food works in your body and how you can personalize the way you eat to optimize your health.

Didn't cavemen only live to 30?

While the Paleo way of eating is not a replication of a caveman diet, let's shatter the myth about the life span of primitive humans. Their life span was based on several factors:

1. In the absence of modern medicine, infant mortality rates were high, and estimated life span is based on the overall average—including the life spans of those who died at birth as well as those who lived to old age. It doesn't mean that every human alive in the Paleolithic era dropped dead by age thirty. In fact, those who lived to about age twenty had an estimated life span closer to sixty years.

2. Deaths from infectious diseases were more common in the absence of modern medicine.

3. They were more vulnerable to predatory animals.

4. They were more vulnerable to the elements due to inferior shelter.

If You're Ready to Get Started, Jump on In, the Water's Fine

If you simply want to improve your overall health, reading the next chapter on the truth about nutrition, reviewing the one-page guides throughout the book, and following the recipes will get you well on your way. If you have an existing health condition, a particular set of symptoms, or a specific health goal, check out chapters 6 through 9 (pages 77 to 122) to learn about how food may be affecting your health and what you can do to treat your health concerns and reach your goals. Then, proceed to the 30-Day Meal Plans (pages 162 to 243) to find recommended meal plans for different health conditions that use the recipes in this book.

Everything We've Been Taught About Good Nutrition Is Wrong

We live in a time when up is down and black is white. We have been taught to believe that the foods coming out of factories are safer and healthier than the foods our great-grandmothers ate.

Think about it a minute. If Food A has gone through a factory and been processed from what it once was in nature into something else entirely, and Food B is identical to what it was in nature (with the exception of having been cooked, of course), which food is healthier? It's a no-brainer, isn't it?

More packaged "foods" than ever are out there touting health claims, yet we're less healthy with each passing generation. It just doesn't add up. Obesity is on the rise in children, who also frequently suffer from behavioral disorders, early-onset puberty, and autoimmune conditions, and they're receiving those diagnoses at younger and younger ages.

Unfortunately, the broad, sweeping claims about health and nutrition that we hear from so-called authorities are more likely to represent the interests of giant food corporations, which spend millions on lobbying and campaign contributions and whose hands are deep in our pockets. It isn't the goal of the food industry to keep us healthy, so relying on Big Food to tell us the truth about nutrition would be foolish and misguided.

Did you know that doctors are typically given less than a week of training in nutritional biochemistry? Yet people who are suffering as a result of poor diet and lifestyle choices end up in their offices on a daily basis. And most dietitians are unable to help because they have been taught to promote and support the USDA recommendations, which have led us down a path of declining health for more than three decades.

The guidelines set forth by the USDA are not based on sound scientific theories or conclusive proof. They are based on illogical and potentially dangerous hypotheses that simply don't hold water. So we're left to take dietary advice from the media, which inundate us with contradictions. We're barraged by recommendations that don't help, while people remain sick.

Know this: We are not smarter than nature. We cannot make better food than nature. We need to eat real, whole food—period.

A responsible individual won't trust the status quo, the media, the government, or even a well-intentioned but likely ill-informed health-care professional for information on how to achieve health. We must self-educate, never accept conventional wisdom at face value, and seek thorough information that we find sensible, helpful, and intuitive. Heck, if what I recommend in this book doesn't make sense to you based on your intuition and how it feels when you actually follow my advice, then try something else. Insanity is doing the same thing over and over again while expecting different results each time. Let's try to break this cycle. The first step is to recognize what we've been fed.

CHAPTER 2

What the Government Is Feeding You

Let's look at how the United States government tells us to eat in its latest recommendations, which are revised and published every five years as the *Dietary Guidelines for Americans*, a joint USDA-FDA venture. (The famous USDA Food Pyramid, which was recently rebranded as MyPlate, is based on these guidelines.)

The key recommendations in the *2015 Dietary Guidelines for Americans* state:

> Consume a healthy eating pattern that accounts for all foods and beverages within an appropriate calorie level.
>
> A healthy eating pattern includes:
>
> - A variety of vegetables from all of the subgroups—dark green, red and orange, legumes (beans and peas), starchy, and other
> - Fruits, especially whole fruits
> - Grains, at least half of which are whole grains
> - Fat-free or low-fat dairy, including milk, yogurt, cheese, and/or fortified soy beverages
> - A variety of protein foods, including seafood, lean meats and poultry, eggs, legumes (beans and peas), and nuts, seeds, and soy products
> - Oils
>
> A healthy eating pattern limits:
>
> - Saturated fats and trans fats, added sugars, and sodium

In previous editions of the *Dietary Guidelines*, the USDA also recommended limiting cholesterol to less than 300 mg per day. However, that recommendation was dropped from the 2015 edition. Here's how the report released by the *Guidelines* advisory committee in advance of the actual guidelines addressed the change:

> Previously, the *Dietary Guidelines for Americans* recommended that cholesterol intake be limited to no more than 300 mg/day. The 2015 [Dietary Guidelines Advisory Committee] will not bring forward this recommendation because available evidence shows no appreciable relationship between consumption of dietary cholesterol and serum cholesterol.... Cholesterol is not a nutrient of concern for overconsumption.

Did you catch that? The USDA is finally saying that the amount of cholesterol that we obtain from our diet is not of concern! This is a huge step in the right direction. But because myths about the health effects of cholesterol are still widespread, we'll explore why there's no need to be concerned about cholesterol on page 31.

In the guidelines above, it seems at first glance that the USDA is trying to get people to eat more real food, right? Well, while many of the recommendations are a step in the right direction, some are still misguided, and, as with many things, the details are what matter most.

Eating a variety of vegetables and sources of protein and increasing seafood consumption make sense, but the remaining recommendations are flawed from the standpoint of nutritional biochemistry and health. And, unfortunately, these are the biggest points of contention when trying to get people to open their minds up to a new possibility—that what we think we know about nutrition is wrong.

Let's take a closer look at these questionable USDA recommendations.

What We've Been Fed: The Recommendation for Grains

"A healthy eating pattern includes grains, at least half of which are whole grains."

When most people replace "refined" grains with "whole" grains, how do you think this translates on the plate? Do you think it means they begin eating bulgur wheat and wheat berries instead of white bread, cereal, and pasta? (Not that I regard either bulgur or wheat berries as healthy, but they are more "whole" than standard supermarket fare.) No, it simply means that people read packages of bread, cereal, and pasta for those shiny, happy words, "whole grain." They buy the same brands, just the versions with a different label. Nobody in the food production industry loses money, and nothing on the business end changes. Only now people think that the bread they're buying is healthy, and they can't wait to tell their doctor, neighbors, and friends that they've switched to whole-grain bread.

As nutritionist Radhia Gleis says, "If it's popped, puffed, flaked, floured, shredded, or instant, it's refined." This includes gluten-free rolls, gluten-free oats, whole- and sprouted-grain breads, quinoa pasta, puffed cereals, and corn chips, to name a few. They are no longer in their natural state, no matter how "whole" the grains may have been before the factory got hold of them.

Know this: Whole-grain products are still refined foods.

Whole-grain foods simply include more parts of the grain than are found in foods like white bread, standard cereal, or pasta. They're all still refined, and refined foods will never promote health more than whole foods, not even if the word "whole" is tacked onto them.

Consumption of grains in particular—even so-called whole grains—causes a host of problems for many people, and we'll discuss the whys and hows in great detail in the chapter on autoimmunity (page 93). For now, it is worth noting that the basis for the USDA recommendation to eat whole grains is supported by what is termed "moderate evidence," which the USDA says "reflects somewhat less evidence or less consistent evidence. The body of evidence may include studies of weaker design and/or some inconsistency in results. The studies may be susceptible to some bias, but not enough to invalidate the results, or the body of evidence may not be as generalizable to the population of interest."

In other words, the science on which they base their claims is not entirely sound, nor can it be completely trusted. And they know it.

What We've Been Fed:
The Recommendation for Legumes

"A healthy eating pattern includes a variety of vegetables [including] legumes (beans and peas)."

"A healthy eating pattern includes a variety of protein foods, including . . . legumes (beans and peas)."

The USDA categorizes legumes (beans, including soy, peas, and lentils) as both vegetables *and* a source of protein, but legumes are truly neither of these. Nutritionally speaking, legumes are a lot more like grains than they are like any vegetable or true protein source. A quick look at the nutritional breakdown of some commonly consumed beans and lentils compared to some common vegetables and protein sources shows exactly what I mean.

LEGUMES VS. VEGETABLES AND PROTEINS									
	Black Beans	Garbanzo Beans	Lentils	Broccoli	Sweet Potatoes	Amaranth	Quinoa	Chicken Breast	Salmon
CALORIES	132	164	116	35	76	102	120	165	184
FAT (grams)	1	3	0	0	0	2	2	4	8
CARBS (grams)	24	27	20	7	18	19	21	0	0
FIBER (grams)	9	8	8	3	3	2	3	0	0
PROTEIN (grams)	9	9	9	2	1	4	4	31	27
VITAMIN A (% daily value)	0	1	0	31	315	0	0	0	2
VITAMIN C (% daily value)	0	2	2	108	21	0	0	0	2
CALCIUM (% daily value)	3	5	2	4	3	5	2	1	5
IRON (% daily value)	12	16	19	4	4	12	8	6	4

Source: Nutritiondata.com. All data is per 100 grams.

As you can see, while beans and legumes do have *slightly* more protein than vegetables like broccoli and sweet potatoes, they have nowhere near the protein density that chicken and salmon deliver.

Legumes should be treated much more like a grain than either a protein source or a vegetable in terms of their recommended consumption. And, in my estimation, this means that they should either be eliminated entirely (to follow a strict Paleo diet) or limited to *very* small portions, since they're not as significant a source of vitamins and minerals as vegetables, nor as significant a source of protein as animal foods.

But there's a study that says . . .

In nutritional research, most studies are epidemiological, which means they look at patterns and correlative information in groups of people. Discovering a correlation does not provide evidence of any causation, though. It simply means that two factors seem to be related, but it doesn't take into account every other variable involved. For example, while you may see people carrying umbrellas when you also see rain falling, you'd never say that carrying an umbrella *causes* rain to fall.

Unlike epidemiological nutrition studies, randomized, controlled trials in metabolic wards—where all food given to test subjects is carefully measured and recorded—*can* be used to discover direct cause and effect. That's the solid scientific evidence that nutritional advice should be based on. The problem is that most studies that result in broad, sweeping (and often sensationalized) nutrition news headlines are epidemiological, not randomized, controlled trials.

An even bigger problem is that epidemiological studies are based on "dietary recall," in which subjects remember and record their daily diets, going as far back as several years. Let's get real! Do you remember what you ate last year? Last month? Last week? Even yesterday? Obviously, claims based on dietary recall are far from science.

When you see broad nutritional recommendations without actual biological explanations, you can assume that they're derived from evidence reported in an epidemiological study using dietary recall as the source. Run the other way.

What We've Been Fed: The Recommendation for Dairy

"A healthy eating pattern includes fat-free or low-fat dairy, including milk, yogurt, cheese, and/or fortified soy beverages."

Following this recommendation could mean increasing your consumption of pasteurized, processed milk and dairy products from cows raised in concentrated animal feeding operations (CAFOs) or even more highly processed milk substitutes made from legumes (soy), none of which are what's best for your health.

You will be hard-pressed to find a producer of high-quality, raw, grass-fed milk selling low-fat or fat-free cow's milk (or yogurt, for that matter). Why? Because they know that vitamins A, D, and K2 are fat-soluble—meaning that we need to consume them alongside fat for proper absorption. What's more, that straight-from-the-farm beverage is richer in these vitamins because cows grazing on pasture produce more nutrient-rich milk. We need these vitamins for proper growth, strong immune systems, and the integrity of our bones (often referred to as "bone density"). In fact, many people who ingest extra calcium from low-fat dairy products or supplements in the hope of building bone strength aren't getting enough of these vitamins for the calcium to be properly assimilated. Skimming and processing raw milk is a waste of beautiful nutrients.

REAL MILK INFO
Visit realmilk.com to find out where you can buy raw milk.

Fact #1: Calcium is abundantly present in more than just dairy foods. Did you know that sardines (with the bones in, of course), sesame seeds, and dark green leafy vegetables are good sources of calcium? What's more, these whole, unprocessed foods are also fantastic sources of magnesium, a mineral that your body needs to help to assimilate calcium. Boom. Right there you have a great way of getting calcium *and* magnesium into your diet.

Fact #2: To absorb and utilize calcium appropriately, we need other nutrients, too. Simply consuming calcium as a mineral isn't enough to make stronger bones! We also need fat-soluble vitamin D, which helps your body absorb the calcium you eat, and vitamin K2, which helps direct the show—it actually orchestrates the placement of calcium into our bones, where we want it, and not into our soft tissues. In other words: it's not just how much calcium you *eat* but how much you *absorb*, and where it goes when you absorb it. If you want to build strong bone matrix, be sure you're getting enough sun exposure, which is one of the best ways to get vitamin D (just don't overdo it and get sunburned!), and eating foods rich in vitamin D—like liver, egg yolks, and grass-fed dairy, if you tolerate it—and vitamin K2, primarily found in fermented cod liver oil and fermented grass-fed dairy (think kefir or yogurt that's fermented for twenty-four hours), grass-fed butter, chicken breast, ground beef, and fermented meats like salami. Vitamin K2 will likely be undetectable in pasteurized, grain-fed milk.

Fact #3: Grain consumption can inhibit calcium absorption. Grain products all contain antinutrients called phytates. Phytates bind to minerals we eat and keep them from being absorbed by our bodies. So when we sit down to a bowl of cereal with milk, we're actually eating a food that blocks the absorption of calcium right along with calcium-rich milk!

Fact #4: Not all dairy is created equal. The dairy nature produces *isn't* the problem. The primary problem is that we think we have to process dairy to be "healthier" for us to consume, and we muck it all up! If you can find a great local source of raw, grass-fed milk or other dairy products and you feel good eating dairy, I say go right on ahead. Many of the studies that have found problems with dairy are examining either isolated dairy proteins like casein or whey, not the whole foods that contain whey and casein together, or processed and reduced-fat forms of dairy foods.

Note that while dairy products are not considered part of a strict Paleo diet, I recommend testing them in your reintroduction phase (see page 46) to discover your own personal tolerance. If you find that your body does well with dairy products, then consuming high-quality forms will not only provide great nutrition but also broaden your list of available foods for maintaining a real foods–based lifestyle after your initial strict Paleo phase.

Yet the USDA recommends that we eat fat-free or low-fat milk and milk products. Why? Do they mean that milk straight from the cow isn't recommended, and milk that has been processed and had its most valued nutrients removed is actually healthier? Perhaps in addition to forgetting how real, nutritious milk should be produced and consumed, they have also misinterpreted epidemiological data yet again. Is the government smarter than Mother Nature?

Know this: Real milk is raw (unpasteurized), comes from grass-fed/pasture-raised cows, and is not low-fat or fat-free.

If you are lactose-intolerant, you may be able to drink raw milk without a problem, as the lactase enzyme necessary for the digestion of lactose is still present in raw milk. Raw milk is a good dietary source of protein, fat, carbohydrates, calcium, and fat-soluble vitamins A, D, and K2, all of which are important for bone density. If you find that you tolerate dairy well, without sinus congestion, sneezing, digestive upset, or signs of chronic inflammation (see page 91), find a trustworthy source and enjoy your milk in its whole, full-fat, natural state.

If you don't tolerate dairy products well, even after trying raw milk, you may still be well-served by incorporating grass-fed butter, which contains fewer of the commonly irritating dairy proteins, into your diet. You could also use ghee, which contains virtually no dairy proteins (learn how to make it at home on page 261), or a butter oil supplement (I recommend the Green Pasture brand), which has the lowest potential for containing any trace of dairy proteins. Typically, an allergic or inflammatory response to dairy does not occur with pure butter oil because it lacks the milk protein constituents, such as casein and whey, and sugars, like lactose, that are the underlying problem. (See page 63 for more information about choosing dairy products responsibly.)

What We've Been Fed: The Recommendation for Cholesterol

"Individuals should eat as little dietary cholesterol as possible while consuming a healthy eating pattern."

Although the 2015 *Guidelines* no longer recommends limiting dietary cholesterol to 300 mg per day, the idea that cholesterol is bad for your health remains pervasive—in fact, the government itself spread fear of cholesterol in the previous editions of the *Guidelines*.

The fear of dietary cholesterol is based on the notion that cholesterol in the bloodstream causes heart disease, and therefore by avoiding dietary cholesterol, we can avoid heart disease. The few studies that introduced this idea are problematic, however. They were primarily based on research done on rabbits, whose natural diet does not include cholesterol-containing foods! How can we expect human cholesterol metabolism to mimic that of a rabbit that isn't supposed to eat cholesterol in the first place? Studies that are more reliable show that dietary cholesterol raises the level of cholesterol in the bloodstream by less than 1 percent. In other words, eating cholesterol doesn't raise the level of cholesterol in your blood.

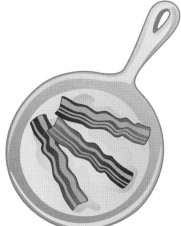

While the idea that dietary cholesterol is unhealthy was pushed as truth as early as the 1950s in an effort to sell more factory-made vegetable oil products, it wasn't until more recently that we were inundated with frightening claims about the cholesterol in real, whole foods. A 1984 *Time* magazine article entitled "Hold the Eggs and Butter" was among the most influential pieces of propaganda that molded the modern food landscape that we know today. The article claimed that "cholesterol is proved deadly, and our diet may never be the same." But it went on to say:

> For decades, researchers have been trying to prove conclusively that cholesterol is a major villain in this epidemic [of heart disease]. It has not been easy. Cholesterol is, after all, only one piece in a large puzzle that also includes obesity, high blood pressure, smoking, stress, and lack of exercise. All of these play their part in heart disease "like members of an orchestra," explains pathologist Richard Minick of the New York Hospital-Cornell Medical Center. . . . Despite its bad reputation, cholesterol is essential to life: it is a building block of the outer membrane of cells, and it is a principal ingredient in the digestive juice bile, in the fatty sheath that insulates nerves, and in sex hormones such as estrogen and androgen.

Even within the article itself, the facts about cholesterol contradict the title and claim that it's bad for you. Unfortunately, what people remembered were headlines and cover images like the one used with the article—a plate of eggs and bacon arranged to form a frowning face. The biology and the science, or lack thereof, behind the idea became secondary to the striking image, and the article created a massive fear of dietary cholesterol and reinforced the idea that heart disease risk is drastically increased when blood levels of cholesterol are high.

There is just one problem. As physician Mike Eades has said, "Only about half the people who have heart attacks have elevated cholesterol levels." The *Time* article itself stated, "The experts were still not quite able to pin the blame on cholesterol, however. Explains Fred Mattson, a leading researcher at the University of California at San Diego, 'We were missing a key piece of evidence: No one had ever shown that reducing the level of cholesterol in the blood did any good.'"

The entire country, for better or worse and despite conflicting ideas about cholesterol and heart health, was encouraged to stop eating natural foods like butter, cream, egg yolks, and fatty meats—all based on science that didn't exist. And we bought it hook, line, and sinker. Egg substitutes appeared on the market, and eggs were made out to be bad for us, even though they are rich in essential nutrients, including choline, selenium, vitamin B2, and vitamin B12.

Finally, the 2015 *Dietary Guidelines* have acknowledged that there's no need to fear dietary cholesterol. But they still recommend avoiding it because cholesterol tends to be found in the foods that also have saturated fats. Speaking of which . . .

What We've Been Fed:
The Recommendation for Saturated Fats

"A healthy eating pattern limits saturated fats."

The USDA recommends avoiding saturated fats because they say there is evidence that eating less saturated fats "is associated with reduced risk of cardiovascular disease," especially higher blood cholesterol levels. The truth about saturated fat consumption is that it's never been shown to *cause* cardiovascular disease (CVD). What we have seen is that there seems to be a correlation between a diet higher in saturated fat and incidence of CVD. But this correlation appears in observational studies, not randomized, controlled trials, which are truly the only way to determine cause and effect. Recall that correlation does not equal causation (see page 29). This is so critical to understand when talking about broad-sweeping claims regarding nutrition and health and the bold, often fear-based headlines we see in the media.

While it's true that naturally occurring saturated fat—from sources like egg yolks and coconut oil—can raise "good" (HDL) cholesterol, this is not cause for alarm. These fats may actually help prevent coronary artery disease, according to a 2004 study. Furthermore, increasing HDL is generally understood as a good thing, since higher HDL may mean a lower risk of CVD. And eating foods that support cholesterol production actually helps your body, which needs the fuel to manufacture cholesterol.

Furthermore, as we discussed briefly in the previous section on cholesterol, high blood cholesterol levels have not been proven to cause heart disease. In fact, many who experience CVD have *low* cholesterol! Dr. William Castelli, a former director of one of the longest-running dietary studies in existence, the Framingham Heart Study, reported that "people with low cholesterol (lower than 200) suffer nearly 40 percent of all heart attacks." According to Dr. Castelli, "In Framingham, Mass., the more saturated fat one ate, the more cholesterol one ate, the more calories one ate, the lower the person's serum cholesterol.... We found that the people who ate the most cholesterol, ate the most saturated fat, ate the most calories, weighed the least and were the most physically active."

THE SKINNY ON FAT
Check out the guide to fats and oils on page 64 for more information.

A fat update!

You may have seen that *Time* magazine ran an article in June 2014 that responded to its own historical statement on the topic of fat—complete with a large swirl of butter prominently featured on the cover. Essentially, the article exonerated natural saturated fat and encouraged us not to be afraid of butter anymore.

Despite this update, the long-held, fear-based beliefs about fat seem to run deep for a lot of people. In an era when plant-based-diet devotees are growing in numbers, seemingly right alongside those of us who ascribe to a Paleo-based, omnivorous way of eating, this update may be too little, too late.

Many are still scared and are convinced that animal fat can't possibly be healthy to eat.

But there's good news here as well! We *are* seeing more and more well-raised animal-based products and brands that align with a Paleo lifestyle. Brands like EPIC and Fatworks, which provide jarred fats made from pastured animals (among other products), are growing in response to consumer demand. EPIC was even acquired by General Mills in early 2016, a sign of the times for sure. Big Food knows to go where the money is, and that is a very good sign for Paleo eaters who aren't fearing the fat.

And here's some more good news about saturated fat: the more saturated fat you eat, the less likely you are to suffer a stroke. Your risk of stroke decreases by 15 percent for every 3 percent increase in your saturated fat intake.

So then, what does the USDA consider a healthy source of fats? Oils! Specifically, they encourage the use of oils high in polyunsaturated fats (PUFAs), such as corn, soybean, and cottonseed oils, as well as those high in monounsaturated fats (MUFAs), such as olive, canola, peanut, sunflower, and safflower oils. We'll talk in more detail about why these oils are often problematic on pages 58 to 59, but in a nutshell, highly processed oils, especially those high in PUFAs, are less stable and more prone to becoming damaged (oxidized and rancid), particularly during cooking. Fatty acids from the foods we eat are incorporated into our cell membranes, so avoiding poor-quality or damaged oils can help prevent cellular damage.

The *Guidelines* also recommend seeking out "lean or low-fat versions of meats, poultry, and dairy products." We've already talked about the problem with low-fat dairy products—vitamins A, D, and K2 are fat-soluble, so we actually need fat in order to absorb them, and processing raw milk into low-fat or fat-free products simply wastes these nutrients. What's even worse is that getting rid of fat means getting rid of flavor, and to compensate, food companies add sugar to low-fat and fat-free foods.

The first *Dietary Guidelines for Americans* was created in the late 1970s, nearly twenty years after initial claims were made that dietary fat and cholesterol are harmful to our health. At the same time, an even more exciting development arose: the amount of fat used in many processed products could be *reduced* while still preserving flavor and palatability through the use of (you guessed it) high fructose corn syrup! Oh boy.

The number of low-fat and fat-free profit-earning products began to snowball. Fat-free cookies, "light" yogurts loaded with sweeteners, fat-free puddings, and low-fat "buttery spreads" hit their stride, filling our cupboards and refrigerators and crowding out the natural foods that could be made from scratch in every kitchen in America. We fell prey to the desire for convenience and sweet taste, helped along by food companies' marketing, and as a nation, our waistlines grew and our internal, metabolic physiology became unbalanced.

Sadly, the recommendation to avoid saturated fat is likely a result of massive lobbying by the vegetable oil industry, which benefits whenever we use their industrial products rather than natural animal fats.

Know this: The science does not support the demonization of saturated fat. The USDA is wrong, and their recommendations have made the refined seed oil industry lots of money while we've run scared from eggs, bacon, and butter.

What may be more accurately associated with CVD are trans fats, which are often lumped together with saturated fats in dietary recall studies. We know man-made trans fats are dangerous, but why must natural saturated fats like those in egg yolks, well-raised meats, coconut oil, and grass-fed dairy products take equal blame when their chemical structures and origins are entirely different? People all too often assume that the naturally occurring forms of saturated fats are also harmful—quite possibly due to media reporting that continues to promote these notions. The reality is that the chemical structure of a short- or medium-chain saturated fat—from butter or coconut oil, for example—is easier for your body to break down and digest than artificial and even natural polyunsaturated fats. Why? Because they place less demand on bile salts, which the body uses to break down and utilize fats.

Know this: Man-made trans fats and refined seed and vegetable oils (canola, soybean, corn, and cottonseed oils, to name a few) are not healthful and may even be considered toxins.

We Cannot Improve What Nature Provides

Refining foods to "improve" them is oxymoronic at worst and nonsensical at best. We can only hope the government will step aside and allow proven nutritional science and common sense—not food industry lobbyists or alarmist health claims—to prevail in the field of public health. If you're curious about how governmental entities come to a consensus on dietary guidelines, Marion Nestle's book *Food Politics* is an interesting resource. Though Nestle's overall dietary recommendations are, in my opinion, lacking, she is certainly respected as an authority on the complexities of how politics affect both U.S. food policy and what's on your plate every day.

Regarding changes that have been made to the *Dietary Guidelines* over the years, Nestle informs us that not only did government nutrition authorities and researchers get together to discuss the implications of the new guidelines, food industry and agricultural commodity groups were also invited to these meetings. It was well-known that these

If cholesterol and saturated fat intake aren't good markers of heart disease risk, then what is?

There is strong evidence to suggest that your ratio of triglycerides to HDL cholesterol is a much better predictor of your risk for cardiovascular disease than your cholesterol level or saturated fat intake. This ratio is quite simple to calculate, since both triglycerides and HDL are measured in most standard lipid panels as part of a blood test. Both measures should be taken after you've fasted for at least 12 hours and when your weight is stable, since testing them while your body is undergoing fat loss can lead to skewed and inaccurate results.

To find your ratio, divide your total triglycerides by your HDL. Generally speaking, a ratio between 0 and 2.5 is good (some say that under 2.0 is ideal), between 2.5 and 3 may be cause for some lifestyle changes, and over 3 may indicate insulin resistance and increased risk for CVD and heart attacks.

$$\frac{\text{triglycerides}}{\text{HDL}} = \begin{cases} \text{0–2.5} & \text{good} \\ \text{2.5–3} & \text{make some lifestyle changes} \\ \text{3+} & \text{may indicate insulin resistance and increased risk for heart disease} \end{cases}$$

special-interest groups would have a vested interest in any nutritional guidelines created by the government, and they were there to weigh in.

Of course the food industry and agricultural commodity groups are interested in the content of population-wide nutrition guidelines! It is their bottom line that takes a hit when a major government report indicates that their products are undesirable or, worse, pose a major public health risk.

Changes must be made, though, each time the guidelines are revisited, and over the years the recommended amounts of certain food groups have been reduced. Nestle says:

> The AMA [American Medical Association] also noted that "the recommendations carry with them the underlying potential for . . . discouraging the agricultural production of certain food products which may not in the view of the government be supportive of the dietary goals." . . .
> Although opposition to the *Dietary Goals* often was expressed as skepticism about the quality of the underlying science, it derived more directly from the profound economic implications of the advice.

In other words, the opposition to changes to the *Dietary Guidelines* and *Dietary Goals* (one and the same, for our purposes) from food companies and agricultural groups is often not based on science but on how the guidelines would affect their bottom line.

The more you follow the USDA's recommendations, the more processed foods you'll have to buy. You can't possibly eat all of those servings of grains and low-fat dairy without eating breakfast cereal, low-fat milk, or low-fat yogurt, can you? When you follow those suggestions, many large corporations make lots of money from your dietary "choices," and they don't have to spend much to produce the stuff. In fact, many USDA-compliant items are made with the cheapest and most subsidized commodity food items, such as corn, wheat, and soy. Sometimes you're the one eating these commodities, sometimes it's the dairy cow. Either way, you're the end consumer.

Yes, this includes that innocent-looking light yogurt with the alluring ads describing fantastically indulgent flavors and high fructose corn syrup in the list of ingredients. (I should know because I used to down those puppies like crazy.)

No wonder everyone is confused about what to eat! But don't worry. After you finish this book, you'll have the tools you need to navigate the modern food landscape.

What We Talk About When We Talk About Nutrient Density

So much for what the government's nutritional guidelines say. What they *don't* talk about is one of the most important factors we should consider when choosing what to eat: nutrient density.

Nutrient density refers to the micronutrient (vitamin and mineral) and macronutrient (protein, fat, and carbohydrate) value of food per a standard number of calories. We can compare the quantity of nutrients in specific foods to determine the most and least nutrient-dense options. The foods that deliver the most vitamins and minerals in a set number of calories are considered the most nutrient-dense.

You can see why nutrient density matters: the more nutrients we feed our bodies, the healthier we are, and getting the most nutrients possible per a set number of calories only makes sense. It's the most efficient way to nourish our bodies.

That said, comparing nutrient density across equal calorie portions isn't very practical for everyday nutritional choices. In order to get the same number of calories and protein from broccoli as from grass-fed ground beef, for example, you'd need to eat around 600 grams of broccoli and only 100 grams of beef. This would mean you need to eat about 6 1/2 cups of broccoli (a typical portion is 1/2 to 1 cup) to get the same amount of protein that you can get from about 3.2 ounces of the beef (a typical portion is 3 to 6 ounces).

Also, a significant factor in determining nutrient density is how readily the nutrients are absorbed and used by the body—their bioavailability. For example, carrots are often touted as being rich in vitamin A, but the source of the vitamin A in carrots is beta-carotene, which humans can't use directly. We need vitamin A in the form of retinol in order for our bodies to put the nutrient to work. This doesn't mean that the beta-carotene is worthless, but it *does* mean that our bodies have to convert it into retinol before we can use it. This conversion process isn't 1:1, however—we don't get one unit of retinol for every unit of beta-carotene. The ratio is actually around 15:1—for every fifteen units of beta-carotene, we get one unit of retinol. But even that ratio depends on a number of variables: the amount of fat consumed in the meal, efficiency of digestive function, and amount of body fat—higher body fat may mean lower conversion rates. In other words, simply eating 1 cup of chopped carrots won't deliver 428 percent of the recommended daily value of vitamin A, as the nutrition facts panel suggests it will. When the conversion ratio is taken into account, you're looking at closer to 28.5 percent of the recommended amount of vitamin A (if you're converting the beta-carotene that efficiently) from that cup of carrots.

It turns out, you can get 62 percent of the recommended daily amount of vitamin A as retinol in just one ounce of chicken liver. The moral of the story? It's not always obvious what the most nutrient-dense option is. But there's good news. Eating a wide variety of real, whole foods is the best way to maximize the nutrients you consume, and that's the essence of the Paleo diet.

The foods that *aren't* nutrient-dense in any sense are the ones the Paleo diet recommends avoiding: processed, refined foods. These offer empty calories without the essential nutrients that we need for good health.

For a comprehensive guide to the nutrient density of Paleo foods, please visit balancedbites.com/practicalpaleo.

Getting Started with Paleo

People often believe eating whole foods is difficult and limiting, but it isn't. Sure, it may be an adjustment at first, but it's simply a matter of eliminating foods that don't promote health in your body and then creating habits that make it easier to choose healthier foods over time.

If you're new to Paleo, this chapter will help guide you through the practical steps of starting a Paleo diet. We'll also look at the importance of having the right mindset toward food. Eating a Paleo diet isn't about rigid adherence to a set of rules. It's about figuring out what works for you and how you can promote health and healing in your body.

PALEO EATING BASICS

[+] eat whole, nutrient-dense foods

It's always best to seek out grass-fed, pasture-raised meat; wild-caught, sustainable seafood; and organic vegetables. For examples of the wide variety of all these foods, see page 61.

+ **Meat, seafood, & eggs**

+ **Vegetables & fruit**

+ **Nuts & seeds**

+ **Healthy fats & oils** (see page 64)

[–] eliminate grains, legumes, dairy, processed sugars and refined foods

For more on how and why to get these foods out of your diet, see pages 50 to 51.

– **Refined grains**

– **Whole grains**

– **Legumes**

– **Packaged snacks**

– **Dairy products**

– **Sweetened beverages**

– **Alcohol & caffeine** (see page 150)

– **Sweeteners** (see page 73)

Going Paleo: All-In or Taking It Slow?

Going Paleo can be approached in one of two ways: you can decide to go all-in and strictly eliminate all non-Paleo foods all at once, or you can make the transition to Paleo slowly, step by step and little by little.

There are pros and cons to both approaches. Which approach you prefer and which works best for you will depend largely on your personality, what you've found to be most effective in changing your habits and lifestyle in the past, and your own desire and commitment to change.

	ALL-IN	TAKING IT SLOW
PROS [+]	[+] Figure out food swaps fast. [+] Push past the painful part quickly. [+] Strict elimination diets *work*.	[+] Slowly roll in the swaps. [+] Manage expectations. [+] Ease others in along with you.
CONS [–]	[–] Instant overwhelm can lead to instant failure. [–] Unresolved whys. [–] A household uprising. [–] An added challenge for you. [–] Mind (and mindset) games.	[–] Potentially prolonged pain. [–] Identifying problem foods takes longer.

All-In

If you do best with an all-in plan, one that you commit to completely starting on a specific day, and you prefer to follow rules with little flexibility, then committing to a thirty-day plan is a good idea. Sixty or even ninety days on a strict Paleo plan would provide an even greater benefit—it would allow more time for the new eating habits to take hold and is better for your physical health—but many changes in your health can be felt within the first month, so a thirty-day commitment is enough for many people to kick-start a new lifestyle.

The Squeaky Clean Paleo 30-Day Meal Plan (page 234) is a perfect place to begin, whether or not you have any health condition or other goal (fat loss or improved athletic performance, for example) specified in the other meal plans.

PROS

[+] **Figure out food swaps fast.** By going all-in, you essentially rip the bandage off quickly and cram any and all potential suffering (more emotional than physical, if we're being honest here) into the first couple of weeks. After that, you can coast through the second half of the month—you'll almost be an old pro at eating Paleo. Most of what's difficult at first is simply finding replacements for old favorites, and the guide to starting Paleo (page 50) has you covered there. Shopping for and preparing food will get easier as the days go on, and learning how to order at your favorite restaurants, what to choose at parties, and how to navigate office-snack minefields, well, it'll all come in time.

[+] **Push past the painful part quickly.** By roughly the second week, most of the physical discomfort that may accompany the dietary change—largely from a reduction in overall carbohydrate intake and increase in fat intake—will begin to subside. "Carb flu," flu-like symptoms you may experience for a short time when you first start eating low-carb, is a very real side effect of this change in nutrition. Carb flu doesn't typically last more than a few days to a couple of weeks, and once those symptoms fade, your energy and vitality will be much higher than they were before the dietary change.

[+] **Strict elimination diets *work*.** When you give your body an extended amount of time without *any* potentially inflammatory foods, you create a clean slate for your immune system. Your body heals and resets in the absence of potential gut irritants and blood sugar–spiking foods. This way of eating is often referred to in holistic nutrition as an "elimination diet." While the term "Paleo" is an easy way to identify this way of eating today, the concept isn't new, and its beneficial effects have been widely known for many years.

CONS

[–] **Instant overwhelm can lead to instant failure.** Unless you've taken sufficient time to prepare yourself, your mindset, your kitchen and pantry, your office (desk drawers!), and even your car (I know what kinds of snacks you're keeping in there), pulling the trigger to go Paleo right away can be overwhelming. Suddenly you realize exactly how much your diet—and life!—revolves around not just eating but eating foods that are no longer part of your plan. The smallest activity, like a coffee break with a coworker, can become a stressful conundrum when you realize that your usual coffee shop doesn't have nondairy creamer without sweeteners. Your workplace meeting that's always catered—this week it's bagels, and there you are, left without an alternative. Or you remember at the last minute that you'd planned to go for happy hour drinks to celebrate a friend's birthday. Without spending adequate time ramping up to a new eating plan, you may be instantly derailed in situations like these, leading to rapid burnout. For many people, this is a setup for failure.

[–] **Unresolved whys.** When you dive headfirst into a dietary change, you may not have taken the time to find answers to all of the questions that may arise for you. If you miss this step or rush through it, you may find that your resolve isn't strong when you're faced with doubts, whether your own or from your from family, friends, or coworkers. Easing into the change can give you time to seek answers first, so that challenges that arise can be handled smoothly.

[-] **A household uprising.** If you decide to change everything about the way you eat overnight, those around you, especially those who rely on you to feed them, can feel like they're being ignored or forced along with your desire for change. Going Paleo is a big change for most households! This can cause a lot of arguments for which you may not be prepared. Additionally, if your family, spouse, or children are not onboard with the change, it can be harder for you to maintain your healthy choices. Often, slowly swapping foods over time can prevent this type of revolt. (For more on dealing with non-Paleo family or friends, see page 126.)

[-] **An added challenge for you.** As if changing your food weren't enough, going all-in means you're also faced with explaining the big changes you've decided to make to those around you. This is often an unforeseen challenge, as we somehow expect others around us not to be so interested in what we're doing. The problem is, when you change what you're eating, the people around you often feel as if you disapprove of their way of doing things (which was the way you did things not long ago). While you may wish they'd change with you, the reality is that no one can change anyone else. (Of course, the exception to that rule is small children, who are not able to procure or prepare their own food.) When you make small changes little by little, it's more likely to go unnoticed and may be easier on you and those around you.

[-] **Mind (and mindset) games.** Going hard-core overnight can create a diet mentality: you commit to the change for a certain amount of time, but when that time period ends, you return to your previous way of eating. While there may be elements of a Paleo diet that you do not want to maintain for the long haul, going into it as if it's all or nothing "for now" often leads to a full-on backlash after the designated time period ends.

taking it slow

If you're more of a "slow and steady wins the race" type, then the guide to starting Paleo (page 50) will be your road map. Plan to incorporate each change on its own for anywhere from one to three weeks before moving on to the next change, speeding up or slowing down based on how you're feeling, how easily you are able to incorporate the change into your everyday life, and how manageable it feels for you. At that pace, your lifestyle changeover will take anywhere from five weeks to about four months.

PROS

[+] **Slowly roll in the swaps.** Allowing more time to figure out what food swaps you need to make can take some of the pressure for perfection off of your shoulders. It's often tough to anticipate every challenging food decision that will arise. If you give yourself more time to make changes, when you hit some bumps in the road, you can learn how to address them next time without beating yourself up for not being perfect the first time.

[+] **Manage expectations.** Often we expect that making changes will be easy simply because we feel ready for them, but that's not the case in practice. Taking baby steps can empower you with small wins day after day and let you escape the added pressure of winning every potential food battle that crosses your path. The wins will add up and eventually become habits, allowing the decision-making effort to lessen over time.

[+] **Ease others in along with you.** You can imagine how it would feel for someone you live with to suddenly change everything about the way they eat. What if you used to share milk? Or a loaf of bread? How will the people you live with finish these items up before they go bad if you're not eating them? As you can see, while you may think that the changes you're making only impact you, it simply isn't true. Small steps can help others as much as they help you by allowing them to acclimate to each change little by little, so they don't feel as alienated by your desire for change. And perhaps some of the early steps will motivate them to change as well, since those steps can be a bit easier to incorporate, even for someone who holds deep-rooted nutritional dogmas. Swapping oils used in cooking or salads and ditching foods with added sweeteners are also steps that others can easily get onboard with, since so much in the mainstream media circles around the dangers of trans fats and sugar. If you're single and not living with family or roommates, then this won't be quite the same challenge as it will be for those sharing living (and cooking/eating) space with lots of others—lucky you!

CONS

[–] **Potentially prolonged pain.** If you're struggling with health issues and hope that going Paleo will resolve them, then taking a slow approach will only make you wait longer for healing. That's not to say that removing one unhealthy kind of food at a time won't provide great benefit, or even possibly give you some relief for what ails you, but it may take longer for you to feel your best.

[–] **Identifying problem foods takes longer.** As you'll see in the guide to starting Paleo (page 50), I've prioritized the removal of certain foods and food groups that will give you the biggest health bang for your buck. But your personal trigger food may not be one that's removed first. For you, perhaps removing dairy will be the biggest needle-mover, and it may be frustrating if you wait to do that until several weeks into the process. Additionally, you may not feel any ill effects from something like organic corn, and it will take longer to discover that if you take the slower elimination timeline.

The Long-Term Plan: Finding Your Personal Food Tolerances

Once you've eliminated all of the non-Paleo foods from your diet, whether all at once or gradually over time, is that it? Do you simply eat strictly Paleo forever?

You certainly *can* follow a strict Paleo plan for the long term if you want to; there is no harm in doing so from a nutritional standpoint. That said, unless you discover that you need to keep all of those foods out of your diet for your own health, you'd be better served to find a balance that works some of the eliminated foods back in, perhaps with cameo appearances instead of their previous starring roles.

How do you determine which foods are okay for you to enjoy now and then and which are best avoided? Allow me to introduce you to the 4R Protocol.

The 4R Protocol is a step-by-step process by which you can discover exactly which foods work for you and which don't. The cool thing here is that, once you've eliminated the non-Paleo foods, you've already crossed the first R—"remove"—off the list. Just don't do what so many do when they're new to Paleo: jump from completing the first step, "remove," to the fourth step, "reintroduce," without ever completing the steps between. Completing the first three steps before reintroducing foods will truly create a more accurate picture of which foods are problematic for you and which aren't.

Step 1: REMOVE | Step 2: REPAIR | Step 3: REINOCULATE | Step 4: REINTRODUCE

The 4R Protocol

Step 1: Remove
Minimum of 1 month, without overlapping other steps

Remove common dietary irritants, such as processed and refined foods, alcohol, grains, legumes, dairy, and sugar, from your diet.

Avoid refined seed and vegetable oils (see page 64) and restaurant-made fried foods as much as possible.

Avoid anti-inflammatory medications, especially NSAIDs (such as aspirin, ibuprofen, and naproxen), as they can promote leaky gut (see page 93). Working on reducing stress is also highly recommended in this step.

Note: If you have removed the foods listed above for thirty days and are still experiencing digestive distress, acne, skin irritation, headaches, joint pain, allergies, autoimmune flares, or other inflammatory conditions, you can add two weeks to this step and remove nuts, seeds, nightshades (such as potatoes, tomatoes, eggplant, and peppers), and eggs.

Step 2: Repair

2 to 12 weeks; after 2 weeks, may overlap with Step 3: Reinoculation

Now that you've removed potential irritants, it's important to work on repairing the gut! This can begin to happen as a benefit of removing damaging foods, but that doesn't do it all. To repair the gut, it's best to follow these guidelines:

Eat

- A *minimum* of two to three 4-ounce servings of fatty cold-water fish (such as salmon, mackerel, and sardines) per week. This provides anti-inflammatory omega-3 fatty acids to balance out the high amounts of pro-inflammatory omega-6 that most of us eat in our regular diet.
- At least 1 cup per day of starchy vegetables and fruits like sweet potatoes, butternut squash, and plantains. The soluble fiber in these foods supports healthy gut bacteria.
- 1 cup or more per day of homemade bone broth (page 259), either in soups or stews or on its own.

Drink

- 1 to 4 cups per day of herbal teas (such as peppermint and licorice root) and/or fresh aloe vera juice. These aid in repairing the mucosal lining of your gut.
- A minimum of 32 ounces (4 cups) per day of water. The exact amount you'll need will vary, but it's important to get plenty of water to prevent constipation and dehydration. This amount should be consumed in addition to the herbal tea recommended above—caffeinated beverages do not count toward water intake.

Supplement with

- 5 to 8 g per day of L-glutamine, a gut-healing amino acid, in water between meals
- Quercitin, a powerful antioxidant that helps with inflammation
- Deglycerized licorice (DGL), slippery elm, or marshmallow extract to promote the repair of the mucosal lining of the gut

Note: You may find a gut-healing supplement that includes many of these together in powder form.

Step 3: Reinoculate

At least 2 weeks; may overlap with Step 2: Repair

Now that you've worked on repairing your gut lining, it's time to make sure that you've got plenty of good gut bacteria in there fighting for a healthy balance. That means consuming probiotics! To reinoculate the gut, it's best to follow these guidelines:

Eat probiotic foods like raw sauerkraut (page 262) and other fermented vegetables.

Drink probiotic beverages like kombucha and water kefir.

Supplement with probiotics in pill or powder form. I recommend a soil-based version such as Prescript-Assist brand (available at balancedbites.com/shop).

Step 4: Reintroduce

3 days per food tested; may overlap with Step 2: Repair and Step 3: Reinoculate

This is the part that you've been waiting for since you started, right? Now that you've been living without so many of your old favorite foods and you've repaired and reinoculated your gut to get it strengthened and ready for whatever you have to throw at it, it's time to figure out what's truly going on under the hood for you.

To reintroduce foods back into your diet, it's best to follow these guidelines:

1. Eat *one* of the eliminated foods (or items from that food group) at each of your meals on the day you're ready to do so.

2. Note any changes to your mood, energy, mental clarity, digestive function, and skin.

3. Reintroduce one eliminated food every three days to discover which are causing problems and which are not.

SAMPLE NOTES FOR BEFORE AND AFTER REINTRODUCTION

Food/Food group: goat cheese Date: May 14, 2016	Before adding this food (poor, fair, good, great; add description/detail)	After adding this food (poor, fair, good, great; add description/detail)
ENERGY	Good; tired after lunch most days	Great; still tired after lunch but not every day
MOOD/EMOTIONS	Good; nothing out of the ordinary here	no change
SKIN/HAIR/NAILS	Good; clear skin, some random breakouts	Poor; broke out afterward
DIGESTION	Good	Good
ELIMINATIONS	Good	Good
ALLERGIES	n/a	n/a
SLEEP	Fair; not the best in general	Fair; no change here
HORMONES	Good; nothing notable here	Good; no change here

Need help deciding what to reintroduce first? You can either test the food you miss most first or follow this list of foods, presented in order of least problematic to most problematic:

- Rice: I recommend trying white rice first, then brown. (For more on white rice, see page 146.)

- Beans/legumes: Try some hummus, lentils, or black beans, for example.

- Sweeteners: Add 1 teaspoon of sweetener to coffee or tea, or see what happens when you make a Paleo-friendly baked item.

- Gluten-free grains: Organic corn, oats, quinoa, amaranth, or any others you may want to try

- Yogurt or other fermented dairy: Try items made from goat or sheep's milk before those made from cow's milk.

- Soft cheeses: Goat cheese and feta are examples of soft cheeses.

- Hard cheeses: Cheddar, Parmesan, and Gouda are examples of hard cheeses.

- Gluten-containing grains: Wheat, barley, rye

Is It Paleo?

Here's a question I get all the time from people who are new to Paleo: "How can I figure out if a specific ingredient, food, or premade item is Paleo or not?"

But here's the thing: Paleo isn't a religion, and eating Paleo isn't about being so rigid that you end up fearful of foods, militant about your choices, or dogmatic about the lifestyle. That kind of mindset is an unhealthy one when it comes to food, and it can be extremely damaging to your morale when you're faced with a less-than-ideal food situation. It can also unnecessarily alienate a lot of your friends and loved ones who aren't interested in eating the way that you do.

The point of eating Paleo is to provide your body with the most nutritious foods to support your health. As we talk about which foods are truly going to do that, there is a lot of myth-busting that has to be done to dispel common fears about (gasp!) eating whole eggs and bacon, and to correct misguided advice about whole grains so you can let go of that whole-grain muffin or breakfast bar. But now that you know there are far better choices for you, you can loosen your grip and use the information you've learned, your logic, and your intuition to decide whether or not a food is right for you. For example, many find that they don't need to completely eliminate organic corn from their diets with other grains because they don't experience ill health effects when they eat it occasionally.

Of course, if you have food allergies or intolerances that have serious implications for your own health, then it's *warranted* to uphold your perhaps non-negotiable eliminations. It isn't dogmatic to strictly avoid foods you can't tolerate! And if you're struggling with health challenges or are in an autoimmune flare, then you may need to take a more restrictive approach to your nutrition for a time. But make sure that your goal isn't to eliminate as many foods as possible for as long as possible.

Your goal should always be to include as many foods as possible in your diet in a balanced way, a way that feels good for you and supports your health goals, so that your life isn't about limits and you're making thoughtful, reasonable decisions about what to eat. As you make those decisions over an extended period of time, they'll become habits and you won't have to make an active, concentrated effort each time you eat or go grocery shopping. In other words, making that effort for a period of time helps you create healthy habits that will turn into a consistent lifestyle pattern that supports your goals. Boom!

This is how we take the concept of Paleo and apply it to our lives for the maximum benefit while minimizing dietary dogma. What we do the majority of the time is what has the most profound impact on our health. This is especially important to keep in mind after you've followed a strict Paleo plan, or one of the meal plans in this book, for one to three months. At that point, you're ready to find a balance that will work for you permanently, rather than simply follow a strict diet plan that someone else has created. To live by a set of rules that this food is "Paleo" and therefore "good" and will make me healthy, while that food is "not Paleo" and therefore "bad" and will not make me healthy, is possibly dangerous and certainly overly stringent.

With that in mind, back to the question at hand: is it Paleo?

It seems like answering that question should be super simple—just ask if it's meat, eggs, seafood, vegetables, fruit, nuts, or seeds; if not, then no, it's not Paleo. But it's not always that clear. News flash: we aren't living in Paleolithic times! We're constantly faced with new and novel combinations of these foods and ingredients made from these foods, so we need to think a bit here. We need to apply a better filter to our food choices,

What's the deal with guar gum?

Guar gum is a perfect example of an additive that's well tolerated by many people but causes problems for others. Guar gum is derived from a legume (the guar bean) and is commonly added to coconut milk products as an emulsifier, blending the high fat content of the coconut milk with the watery part to create a consistent, creamy texture. Many Paleo recipes, including those in this book, call for full-fat coconut milk, and most brands that are widely available do contain guar gum. For the vast majority of people, this additive is completely safe and doesn't cause problems. However, some people have a reaction to it.

If you use full-fat coconut milk that includes guar gum and feel you may be reacting to the additive, try an additive-free brand or make homemade coconut milk. The reaction to guar gum may indicate a FODMAP intolerance (see page 149) because it's a concentrated source of a specific type of carbohydrate. But coconut is also high in FODMAPs, so you may be reacting to the coconut itself. Trying an additive-free brand or homemade coconut milk should clarify that for you.

one that's a bit more well-rounded than simply "Is it Paleo?" Try asking these questions instead:

Is it processed and/or factory-made?

Does it contain grains or legumes?

Does it contain dairy?

Does it contain sugar or sweeteners?

Does it contain additives, preservatives, colors, or other questionable ingredients?

Or, regarding specific ingredients:

Is it a food additive that is derived from a grain, legume, or dairy?

Is it sugar in some form or an artificial sweetener?

Is it an additive about which I'm unsure?

But even if you answered "no" to all of the above questions, you may still find yourself unsure. And there will be times when you are traveling or simply don't have your homemade food with you to enjoy. In those cases, you need to do some research and make the most educated decision you can—for you. Remember, what works for one person may not work for another.

My hope is that you'll seek to consistently fill your plate with the most nutrient-dense foods possible that support your goals. That's it. Once you've learned that protein, vegetables, and healthy fats should build the bulk of your diet, it's up to you to find the wiggle room where you can.

Guide to: Starting Paleo

In the pages to come, we'll talk about how going Paleo can help you improve your health. But right now, you may be sitting at home, looking at your fridge, pantry, and even your current grocery list, and thinking, *Where do I start?!*

The five steps here will walk you through getting started with Paleo. These practical steps are listed in order of importance, starting with what I consider to be the most critical. If going straight to a strict Paleo diet seems overwhelming, try following each step for one or two weeks before moving on to the next. Once you've completed all of the steps, I recommend following a strict Paleo diet for at least 30 days to give your body a chance to heal. After that, you can slowly reintroduce some foods to see if they adversely affect you (guidelines for reintroducing foods are on page 46).

1. Opt for an oil change.

WHY? Healthy fats and oils are critical for good health: they're incorporated into our body cells and help create their structure. Building cells from healthy, natural fats is ideal, but unfortunately, man-made, highly processed, unhealthy fats are pervasive. I recommend this step for *everyone* who wants to get healthier, not just those who want to go Paleo!

HOW? Look through your pantry, cabinets, and refrigerator and toss the following oils, along with any product that lists one of these as an ingredient.

· Vegetable oil
· Canola oil
· Corn oil
· Cottonseed oil
· Soybean oil
· Crisco and other butter-like spreads
· Anything hydrogenated or partially hydrogenated

NOW WHAT?

REPLACE	WITH
Liquid oils for cooking, baking, and eating	Real butter, preferably grass-fed (or ghee, page 261, if you need to remain strictly dairy-free), extra-virgin olive oil, avocado oil, animal fats from pastured animals (like bacon fat or schmaltz), or coconut oil (melt or store near heat to use as a liquid)
Solid fats for cooking and baking	Real butter, preferably grass-fed (or ghee, page 261, if you need to remain strictly dairy-free), coconut oil (room temperature), lard or tallow from pasture-raised pigs or grass-fed cows, or palm shortening, organic and sustainably sourced

2. Say goodbye to gluten, grains, and soy.

WHY? Gluten and antinutrients in grains can disrupt normal, healthy digestive function for many people (see pages 96 to 100), and the products that contain them are typically highly processed. Soy may disrupt normal endocrine function and is often found in highly processed foods. Foods that contain grains and soy often have a lot of sugar as well, so you'll naturally ditch a lot of added sugars in the process of eliminating these items! How's that for a win-win?

HOW? Look through your pantry, cabinets, and refrigerator and toss the following items. Be sure to check ingredient lists and get rid of products containing any of these!

· Wheat flour, whole wheat flour, enriched wheat flour, hydrolyzed wheat protein, tempeh
· Barley, rye, oats, quinoa, corn, spelt, einkorn, and any other grains
· Pastas, breads, cereals, pastries, crackers, cookies
· Soy sauce, soy protein, hydrolyzed soy protein

NOW WHAT?

REPLACE	WITH
Pasta and noodles	Squash noodles! Spaghetti squash (page 338) and zucchini cut with a spiral slicer (page 380) work well.
Bread	Lettuce wraps for burgers and deli meats, portobello mushroom slices as buns (page 340)
Cereal	N'Oatmeal (page 288) or grain-free granola
Crackers	Nut- or seed-based crackers, such as Jillz or GoRaw brands
Granola bars	Bars made from meats and/or nuts, seeds, and dried fruits, such as Primal Kitchen or EPIC brands, or jerky and nuts with dried fruit
Soy sauce	Coconut aminos (liquid aminos, a soy-based product, is not the same as coconut aminos)
Rice	Cauliflower rice (pages 412 to 413) or shredded potatoes

3. Sideline the sweet stuff.

WHY? Blood sugar regulation is a critical element of overall health—it plays a role in everything from hormones to cholesterol and energy levels. Added sugars, refined foods, and sweets will derail your efforts to keep your blood sugar stable.

*See the guide to sweeteners on page 76 for all the different kinds of sugar and artificial sweeteners found in food products.

HOW? Look through your pantry, cabinets, and refrigerator and toss the following items. Be sure to check ingredient lists and get rid of products containing any of these!

· Refined white sugar in any form, including granulated white sugar, agave, and corn syrup

· Artificial/man-made sweeteners, such as aspartame and sucralose

NOW WHAT?

Replace sugary, sweetened goods with fruit!
You have lot of options:

· Whole, fresh fruit

· Dried fruit

· Smoothies made with fresh fruit

· Cooked fruit, such as applesauce made from just apples and spices

· Date paste: use 1:1 for any liquid sweetener

It's important to steer away from sweeteners entirely for the first 30 days on Paleo to give your body time to heal. After that, a very small amount of one of the following sweeteners—once in a while, not daily!—isn't likely to adversely affect you in the long term. Try to use organic versions.

· Raw honey

· Maple syrup

· Molasses

· Coconut sugar

· Green leaf stevia

4. Ditch the dairy.

WHY? Many people don't tolerate dairy well or find that certain types of dairy (like yogurt or soft cheeses) are easier to digest than others (like milk or hard cheeses). Eliminating all dairy for at least 30 days lets your body heal; after that, you can try reintroducing it slowly (see page 46).

HOW? Look through your refrigerator and toss the following items. Be sure to check ingredient lists and get rid of products containing any of these!

· Milk, cream, sour cream

· Cheese, cream cheese, cottage cheese

· Yogurt

· Whey protein

· Casein

· Lactose

· Powdered milk/ milk powder

· Butter

NOW WHAT?

REPLACE	WITH
Milk	Coconut milk or almond milk
Cheese	For cooking, depending on the recipe: nutritional yeast, roasted garlic, or dairy-free savory white sauce (see the béchamel sauce on page 304)
Yogurt	Homemade coconut milk yogurt (there are many recipes available online; most store-bought brands have too many additives). You can also try getting probiotics in other forms, such as sauerkraut (page 262).
Whey protein	Egg white protein powder, beef-based protein powder, or collagen peptides (see page 462 for recommended brands)

5. Leave the legumes.

WHY? Most people think of legumes as a source of protein, but they're much higher in carbohydrates! The type of carbohydrates in legumes can cause digestive distress, gas, and bloating.

HOW? Look through your refrigerator, cabinets, and pantry and toss the following items. Be sure to check ingredient lists and get rid of products containing any of these!

· Beans, including black beans, garbanzo beans (chickpeas), lentils, navy beans, and red beans

· Bean flours

· Hummus made from garbanzo beans

NOW WHAT?

REPLACE	WITH
Beans	Diced vegetables with a soft, lightly starchy texture, such as cauliflower, squash, potatoes, and sweet potatoes
Hummus	Cauliflower hummus (page 428)

Try filling your plate with more nutrient-dense vegetables.

PLATE BUILDING OPTIONS
(as percentages of food):

- - protein
- - starchy carbs or fruit
- - non-starchy vegetables

Add fat as needed or eat meat with fat.

If you are moderately active or are unsure of how to go, build your plate this way to start. See how you feel and adjust from there.

If you are very active or athletic (or are pregnant/nursing), build your plate this way to start. See how you feel and adjust from there.

If you are not very active or are active in ways that require fewer carbohydrates, build your plate this way to start. See how you feel and adjust from there.

GENERAL PORTION SIZE GUIDELINES

FOOD TYPE	AMOUNT TO EAT
PROTEINS	**WOMEN: 3-8 ounces for meals, 2-4 ounces for snacks** **MEN: 8-12 ounces for meals, 3-6 ounces for snacks** The higher end of the range is recommended for more active or larger individuals, and the lower end for more sedentary or smaller individuals.
NON-STARCHY VEGGIES	**EVERYONE:** **Eat non-starchy veggies to satiety; do not limit them.** If they are drowning in fats or oils, you may need to monitor your intake for certain goals as outlined in the 30-Day Meal Plans (see pages 156 to 243).
STARCHY VEGGIES	**WOMEN: about 1/2 to 1 cup** **MEN: about 1 to 1 1/2 cups or more** Portions may vary based on your activity level and overall size/calorie needs. Starchy veggies can be found on page 75.
FRUITS	**EVERYONE: In general, 1 piece of fruit is a serving.** **For larger pieces of fruit, 1/2 piece is a serving.** **Around 1/2 to 1 cup of berries is a good serving size.** Again, these portion sizes may be modified and increased or decreased per the recommendations in any 30-Day Meal Plan. See the guide to food quality (page 63) for more information.
FATS & OILS	**WOMEN: 1 tablespoon of a fat or oil** **MEN: 2 to 3 tablespoons of a fat or oil** A good portion of oil for a salad is around 2 tablespoons, while 1 tablespoon may be adequate for melting over steamed vegetables. This also varies by size and activity level; being larger and/or more active warrants additional fat intake. Coincidentally, adding fat to meals is one of the easiest ways to add good calories and satiety if you do need to eat more.

Eat Whole Foods

The Paleo approach to eating can seem daunting when you realize that you are no longer going to rely on the cheap filler ingredients you may have been eating for decades.

No more rice and beans. No more bread, pasta, or cereal. These are all cheap foods, and rightfully so, since they provide little nutritional value when you compare them to vegetables, meats, fruits, nuts, seeds, and quality fats and oils.

While much of the grocery store is filled with processed items you could—and likely used to—buy, your mission is now entirely different. Seek out as much whole food as possible. This means foods without health claims on the packages or, better yet, foods that aren't even in packages. Instead, buy produce, butcher-counter meats, and seafood.

At the Grocery Store: Walk the Perimeter

If you are currently eating foods primarily from the center aisles of the grocery store, you are most likely purchasing refined, processed food. Instead, I suggest shopping the perimeter of the store. This is where you'll find produce, meat, seafood, and eggs. (It's also where you'll find the bakery, but just pretend it's not there.) The outer sections of the store are where you'll find most fresh foods because it's where the store can easily supply power to the displays to keep food cool, damp, and unspoiled. Real food does not have a long shelf life and usually spoils within a couple of weeks at most (except for frozen vegetables or meats).

Round out your grocery trip by cruising down just a few of the inner aisles, where you can stock up on items like cooking fats and oils, vinegars, mustards, "clean" sauces, spices, and certain canned or jarred items (see page 62).

Read Before You Eat

When you purchase from the inner aisles, *read the labels carefully!* If you aren't accustomed to checking ingredients, you'll be surprised how many seemingly innocent items are loaded with hidden sweeteners, preservatives, and artificial fats.

Become a label detective. If you don't recognize a listed ingredient—especially if it has a scientific name—put the item back on the shelf, not in your cart. There are some very common additives to avoid even in a few so-called healthy items. Look for any of the sweeteners listed on page 76 and any of the forms of hidden gluten described on page 107. Use the guide to stocking a Paleo pantry on page 62 to navigate the interior aisles of the store.

LABEL CRAZED?
Check out the guide to food quality on page 63 for more information.

By the same token, do not trust anything written on the front of the package. Please! The word "natural" on a food package essentially means nothing. According to the FDA food-labeling regulations, anything that originated from nature at one time can be called "natural" on a food label, no matter what has been done to it since it was in its natural state. Here is what the FDA has to say about it:

> From a food science perspective, it is difficult to define a food product that is "natural" because the food has probably been processed and is no longer the product of the earth. That said, the FDA has not developed a definition for use of the term "natural" or its derivatives. However, the agency has not objected to the use of the term if the food does not contain added color, artificial flavors, or synthetic substances.

What about your breakfast cereal, which says on the box that it contains 100 percent of the daily recommended value of essential vitamins and minerals? The truth is that your cereal has been *fortified* with those vitamins and minerals. When it was refined and processed, it was stripped of its natural nutrients, and now nutrients have to be added back into the product. What's the problem? The nutrients added to these foods are synthetic, and their quantities are not in balance, as they would be in natural, whole foods. We don't know exactly *how* or *why* some vitamins and minerals work, but we do know that the human body needs to use them in certain combinations and in certain proportions, the way nature provides them in whole foods. Adding nutrients in isolation, simply because there is media hype around one specifically, ignores this natural balance.

When we try to outsmart Mother Nature and add synthetic nutrients to foods in a factory, we make serious missteps. Manufacturers often add the trendiest, most hyped nutrient to foods that wouldn't contain it naturally. The most recent trend, for instance, is adding omega-3 fatty acids, known for their beneficial anti-inflammatory properties, to items like yogurt and bread. Reality check: omega-3s naturally occur in foods like fatty cold-water fish and some nuts, not in yogurt and bread! When synthetic nutrients are added to foods without their nutrient cofactors—the complementary nutrients that are needed for a nutrient to be properly absorbed and utilized—your body simply cannot use them appropriately.

If there is more packaging than product, it's probably not a great choice, so move on. If the packaging is trying hard to sell the product to you with claims like "Fat-Free!" "Low-Fat!" "Heart Healthy!" and "Whole Grain!" it is almost certainly not healthy. Real foods have no such labels and often have little to no packaging.

Buying anything labeled "low-fat," "nonfat," or "fat-free" is ill advised. Most dairy products found in grocery stores are produced from feedlot cows and are not real, whole foods. Fruity yogurts or yogurt drinks; sliced, string, or plastic-wrapped blocks of cheese; and milk that has been enriched or fortified with vitamins A and D are not in their whole, natural form, so avoid them. (For more on dairy and how to choose it, see page 29.)

Protein (Meat/Seafood/Eggs)

Before going to the grocery store, it is best to be prepared with a list of the meats and seafood you want in order of priority. Understanding the kinds of environments in which animals are raised and what kinds of feed they receive will help you choose the best quality. (See the guide to food quality on page 63 for details on what to look for.) Watch for sales of high-quality meats and seafood so that you can stock up. Consider investing in an extra freezer so you can buy in bulk at lower prices—it will pay for itself in no time.

Of course, a better way to save on meat is to find a local farm from which you can purchase a whole animal or a portion of one. They are typically butchered to your order, and if you don't want to buy an entire animal, look for someone to share the meat with you. Check out your local Weston A. Price Foundation chapter, CrossFit gym, Meetup.com group, or other communities centered around health and nutrition to find others looking for a "meat share."

Buy 100 percent grass-fed, pasture-raised meats whenever possible, and eat any cuts that appeal to you and are priced within your budget. Do not be concerned about the leanness of high-quality meat. If your budget dictates lower-quality meat, buy leaner cuts, as the fatty acid profile of conventional meats has a lower proportion of beneficial omega-3 fatty acids.

Meat from 100 percent pastured animals contains three to five times more conjugated linoleic acid (CLA) than meat from animals fed conventional diets. CLA is an important antioxidant that has been shown in many studies to combat cancer, heart disease, diabetes, and more. People often take CLA supplements when they want to lose weight, but it's better to consume it in whole foods.

Just like humans, animals store toxins in their fat, so if an animal has been exposed to poor quality or nonorganic food, pesticides, herbicides, fungicides, antibiotics, or exogenous hormones (hormones from an outside source), most of the residue from those toxins will be in the animal's fat. In the United States, meat is graded based on "marbling," the amount of fat swirling through the meat. While that fat is tasty, and I welcome it in my grass-fed meat (which is naturally leaner than grain-fed meat and never thickly marbled), stored toxins make fat the unhealthiest part of conventional meat. Conversely, whatever fat you can find on 100 percent grass-fed meat is healthy to eat because it does not contain toxins. Sadly, like humans, animals get fatter from the foods that are unnatural for them to eat, which is why conventionally raised meat has more marbling than grass-fed meat.

WHAT IF YOU'RE
A VEGETARIAN OR VEGAN?

Clearly, a book about eating Paleo is going to support the consumption of animal foods, and for good reason: our bodies are designed to digest animal proteins and to be fueled optimally by them. Amino acids are the building blocks of proteins, and there are certain essential amino acids that our bodies need and can't manufacture—we must eat them. Fortunately, animal foods contain all of these essential amino acids.

While it is possible to find all of the essential amino acids in combinations of certain plant foods (beans and rice, for example, or corn and peas), if it's nutrient-dense protein we're after, those combinations definitely don't deliver the greatest bang for our nutrition buck. Our digestive system, from our teeth to our stomach acid (which shouldn't be suppressed!) to our small and large intestines, was designed to process animal protein very well—we're physically *made* to eat meat. That's not a coincidence: animal foods contain far more nutrients than just protein, and these nutrients are often best absorbed by our bodies when we get them from animals. Plus, plant foods that contain protein have much more carbohydrate than protein, so if we're trying to get protein from plants, we often take in far more carbohydrate than we realize. (The chart on page 28 shows the nutritional breakdown of legumes compared to vegetables and animal protein—though they're often eaten for protein, legumes are much lower in protein than animal foods, are high in carbohydrates, and don't have as many vitamins and minerals as vegetables.)

While it's true that a very small percentage of people may thrive on a diet that's free of animal foods, the vast majority of us don't.

This doesn't mean that eating Paleo has to be an all-out meat-fest or carnivorous endeavor, of course. Humans are omnivores, and that presents a great wide-open door for us to eat a variety of both animal *and* plant foods!

If you've been struggling with low energy, inability to gain muscle (or weight in general), inability to lose body fat, weak hair or nails, or skin problems and you aren't currently eating animal foods (at least eggs and seafood if not red meat and poultry), then you may be deficient in some essential nutrients found in animal foods, and you'd be well served to consider adding them to your diet. And chances are, if you're curious about Paleo but haven't been eating animal foods, this is the perfect time to start.

I strongly recommend that you introduce animal foods into your diet very slowly. This is especially true if you have been following a vegan diet. If you have been eating dairy products as a vegetarian, you can introduce meat into your diet a bit faster. When you do not eat animal products, stomach acid production may be reduced because there is less demand for it. That doesn't mean your body won't bounce back to producing an adequate amount, but it's best to give your body some time to adjust to digesting these foods.

On the opposite page you'll find a week-by-week plan for gradually acclimating your body to meat over the course of one month. But if at any point you feel that your body isn't ready for the next step, just stay at your current step a little longer.

FROM PLANT-BASED TO PALEO

WEEK 1

Make bone broth (page 259) and sip it with meals (and any other time you like). You may use chicken bones at first, but try to work up to beef bones after a couple of days. If you'd rather try a soup made *with* the broth at first, my Butternut Sage Soup (page 394) is a delicious option.

WEEK 2

Put small bits of meat in the bone broth and chew them well as you drink it. You can also add other vegetables to the broth to make it a more complete soup. Eat this soup several times during the week.

WEEK 3

Make one of the slow cooker recipes in this book—Balsamic Braised Short Ribs (page 332), Orange Braised Beef (page 344), or Butternut Cocoa Chili (page 356)—and enjoy it several times over the course of the week.

WEEK 4

Make any of the meat recipes in this book and see how you feel. If you don't feel your body was ready for a full meal, just stay at the previous step for a longer period. You may also want to follow the helpful tips for increasing stomach acid on page 82.

Carbohydrates (Veggies/Fruit)

Buying produce that is in season in your area allows you to stick to locally grown items. You will also save money on these vegetables and fruits, since your grocer isn't paying high shipping costs. This is an environmentally conscious way to shop as well.

Vary the vegetables you eat to give your body a wider variety of nutrients. If you consistently reach for broccoli, try switching to Brussels sprouts. Instead of cabbage, try kale. Instead of potatoes, try sweet potatoes, beets, carrots, or turnips.

Do you always have to buy organic produce? Here are some rules of thumb:

- If you peel off a thick skin or outer layer of the produce before eating it, it's safe to choose nonorganic. This includes bananas, pineapples, kiwis, melons, onions, avocados, and citrus fruit (unless you are using the zest or peel).

- If you eat the item without peeling it or it has a very thin, porous skin, organic is better. This includes apples, berries, stone fruits (peaches, nectarines, plums, and cherries), bell peppers, and leafy greens.

- Choose organic vegetables and fruits from the Environmental Working Group's "The Dirty Dozen" list whenever possible. Nonorganic versions of these twelve vegetables and fruits have been shown in tests to contain the highest levels of pesticide, herbicide, and fungicide residue. Visit the Environmental Working Group's website (www.ewg.org) regularly, as the list may change from year to year. The website also hosts a more comprehensive list that ranks forty-eight fruits and vegetables according to their pesticide residue.

THERE IS A SEASON

To find out what produce is in season in your area, check out these websites, or simply search the web for "seasonal produce + [your state's name]."

www.simplesteps.org/eat-local

www.fieldtoplate.com/guide.php

Fats

A very important step in switching to a healthy Paleo lifestyle is making the highest-quality fats a top priority in your budget.

Fats comprise the most calorie-dense source of nutrition in your diet, and fatty acids are incorporated into your cells' phospholipid bilayer, a two-ply layer of molecules that forms cell membranes. While all macronutrients are incorporated into your cell tissues and contribute to the formation of new cells, fatty acids can take longer to change over during the natural progression of cell regeneration. For this reason, it is best to avoid poor-quality or oxidized oils (ones that have been damaged by light, heat, or air). Since battling cellular damage is one of your body's full-time jobs, the more you can make that job easier by avoiding poor-quality or damaged oils, the better.

Good Fats vs. Bad Fats

Saturated fats are more stable than unsaturated fats. Ever wonder why your high-quality olive oils are sold in dark green glass bottles? It's to keep light from damaging the oil. Ever wonder why coconut oil doesn't smell rancid after sitting on the counter without a lid but vegetable oil does? Air oxidizes vegetable oil and makes it rancid.

You can assume that most naturally occurring saturated fats are safe to cook with, while most unsaturated fats—called oils because they are liquid at ambient room temperature—are unsafe to cook with and are best for cold uses (if appropriate for consumption at all).

Remember that man-made trans fats are never healthy to eat. These include Crisco, Earth Balance—including the new version that claims to be a coconut product but actually contains soybean oil—Smart Balance, Benecol, margarine, Country Crock, and I Can't Believe It's Not Butter.

Seed oils are extremely high in monounsaturated fatty acids (MUFAs) and polyunsaturated fatty acids (PUFAs) at varying ratios, all of which are prone to oxidation, PUFAs most significantly. You wouldn't cook with fish oil, would you? Why would you want to cook with other oils that are very high in PUFAs? MUFAs, too—including olive oil—are pretty easy to damage with heat and air. Keep in mind that although many refined seed oils are marketed as ideal for cooking because they have a high smoke point, a high smoke point only matters if the fat or oil is fairly stable. (See the guide to cooking fats on page 65 for details on many popular cooking fats and oils.)

The process by which canola and other seed oils are made involves an expeller or screw press, high heat, and a wash with the chemical solvent (hexane). This produces a gray, foul-smelling oil that isn't smooth. It then has to be chemically bleached, deodorized, and dyed yellow before it becomes the oil you see in the bottle. That hardly sounds like a whole food, does it?

Cold-pressed fruit oils, such as olive, palm, and coconut oils, are not processed in this manner. As the name suggests, their processing stops after the fruits are pressed at low temperatures to extract the oil.

Shopping and Storage Tips

Eating good fats means never eating trans fats and avoiding highly processed vegetable oils and rancid oils. It also means only choosing fresh, high-quality nuts and seeds. If the nuts or seeds you buy smell off or rancid, toss them and buy new ones. The guide to fats and oils on page 64 will help you make intelligent choices.

There are only a handful of healthy fats and oils you need to buy at the grocery store. These are outlined in the next pages for both hot uses (cooking) and cold (salads and finishing).

Keep coconut oil and ghee in a cool, dark cupboard, and keep butter and bacon fat in the refrigerator. Do not refrigerate coconut oil, as it will become extremely hard and difficult to use without softening. If you are concerned about storing ghee in a cupboard, you can keep it in the refrigerator, but it should be shelf-stable for quite some time since it is pure fat, with no dairy proteins. Unsaturated oils like olive oil and cold-pressed sesame oil should be stored in dark containers or bottles and kept in either cool, dark places or the refrigerator.

If dairy products are a problem for you, grass-fed ghee is the best choice since, again, the dairy proteins have been removed, leaving only the butter oil behind.

DAMAGED PUFA?
You're doing well to avoid oxidized (damaged) omega-6 fatty acids by not cooking with or consuming refined seed oils. But what if the omega-3 supplement you are taking has been oxidized? Unless you're sure that it's safe, I recommend finding another way to increase your omega-3 intake: by eating it in whole foods.

EXTRA-VIRGIN
I highly recommend Kasandrinos Imports brand extra-virgin olive oil (www.kasandrinos. com) because it is has no additives or fillers and is pressed and bottled very quickly. Batches are immediately exported to the United States for sale, and it is the freshest, most delicious olive oil I have ever tasted.

"Can I still eat Paleo if I can't afford grass-fed and organic everything?"

Yes! It's important not to let perfect be the enemy of the good when it comes to making healthy choices. Making shifts away from refined foods and slowly starting to swap in better-quality ingredients not only is perfectly fine but will also get you feeling better right away. You don't need to be eating a "perfect Paleo diet" to benefit! Start by prioritizing healthy fats, then proteins, then produce. Using the guide to food quality on page 63, begin at the baseline and move up from there as your budget allows.

Over time, you may find you spend less on things like drugstore supplies (over-the-counter and even prescription medications), dining out, or even alcohol, allowing more wiggle room in your budget for better-quality food. And if that's never the case for you, it's still completely okay! The main goal is to get real, whole foods onto your plate and to remove the processed and refined foods—there's no need to stress yourself out worrying about perfection.

A Few Dollar-Stretching Tips

Contrary to what some people believe, you will save money on whole foods if you shop at local farmers' markets, where you can buy directly from the source. Each farm stand has its own prices, and these are often negotiable, especially if you are buying in larger quantities. The sellers are more likely to negotiate with you in the last hour before the market closes, when they want to empty their supplies. That's especially true on Sundays, since it's probably the last chance they have to sell their items for the week.

Another tip for staying within your budget is to buy produce and meat that's on sale in bulk, rather than shopping for particular meals.

You can also reduce your food budget by buying less-desirable cuts of meat. I know this is counterintuitive because most Americans are out there scarfing down boneless, skinless chicken breasts, even though bone-in, skin-on chicken legs are tastier and less expensive. But if you're shopping for poultry at a farmers' market or local farm (which is ideal), they will often only sell you a whole chicken. Great! Roast the whole thing (recipe on page 292), and after you've eaten it all, use the carcass to make broth (recipe on page 259). Organ meats from local farmers are often inexpensive because many people are turned off by them. Making chicken liver pâté (recipe on page 426) can be very inexpensive if your farmer doesn't have a high demand for chicken livers.

Stews, soups, and ground meats are excellent ways to eat healthy if you are budget-conscious. Most of the recipes in this book are not expensive to make, with the exception of those that call for wild salmon and other fish, scallops, or lamb chops. You can sometimes get great deals on lamb chops, however, if you buy directly from the farmer.

Guide to: Paleo Foods

Eat whole foods. Avoid foods that are modern, processed, and refined. Eat foods that are as close to their natural form as possible, and avoid foods that cause stress for the body (particularly by affecting blood sugar and digestion). Eat nutrient-dense foods to maintain energy levels. Enjoy your food, and hold positive thoughts while you consume it to keep the body in rest-and-digest mode (see page 77).

meat, seafood & eggs

INCLUDING BUT NOT LIMITED TO

Beef	Lamb	Carp	Salmon
Bison	Mutton	Clams	Sardines
Boar	Ostrich	Grouper	Scallops
Buffalo	Pork	Halibut	Shrimp
Chicken	Quail	Herring	Snails
Duck	Rabbit	Lobster	Snapper
Eggs	Squab	Mackerel	Swordfish
Game	Turkey	Mahi mahi	Trout
meats	Veal	Mussels	Tuna
Goat	Venison	Oysters	
Goose	Catfish	Prawns	

fats & oils

Avocado oil	Duck fat	Schmaltz
Bacon fat/lard	Ghee	Sesame oil (CP)
Butter	Macadamia oil	Suet
Coconut milk	Olive oil (CP)	Tallow
Coconut oil	Palm oil	Walnut oil

nuts & seeds

Almonds	Macadamia	Pumpkin seeds
Brazil nuts	nuts	Sesame seeds
Chestnuts	Pecans	Sunflower
Hazelnuts	Pine nuts	seeds
	Pistachios*	Walnuts

liquids

Almond milk,	Coconut water
homemade or store-	Herbal tea
bought**	Mineral water
Coconut milk	Water

superfoods

GRASS-FED DAIRY
Butter, ghee

ORGAN MEATS
Liver, kidneys, heart, etc.

SEA VEGETABLES
Dulse, kelp, seaweed

BONE BROTH
Homemade, not canned or boxed

FERMENTED FOODS
Sauerkraut, carrots, beets, high-quality yogurt, kefir, kombucha

NOTES

CP = cold-pressed
Bold = nightshades
Italics = goitrogenic
* = FODMAPs (page 149)
^ = buy organic

** = refer to the recommended products and brands guide

vegetables

INCLUDING BUT NOT LIMITED TO

Artichokes*	*Collard*	Lettuce^	Shallots*
Asparagus*	*greens^*	Lotus roots	Snap peas
Arugula	Cucumbers	Mushrooms*	*Spinach^*
Bamboo	Daikon	Mustard	Squash
shoots	Dandelion	greens*	Sugar snaps
Beets*	greens*	Okra*	Sunchokes*
Bok choy	**Eggplant***	Onions*	*Sweet*
*Broccoli**	Endive	Parsley	*potatoes*
Brussels	Fennel*	Parsnips	Taro
*sprouts**	Garlic*	**Peppers*^**	**Tomatillos**
*Cabbage**	Green beans	Purslane	**Tomatoes**
Carrots	Green onions*	Radicchio	Turnip greens
Cassava	Jicama*	*Radishes*	Turnips
*Cauliflower**	*Kale^*	Rapini	*Watercress*
Celery^	*Kohlrabi*	Rutabagas	Yams
Chard	Leeks*	Seaweed	Yuca

fruits

INCLUDING BUT NOT LIMITED TO

Apples*^	Grapefruit	Nectarines*^	Plums*
Apricots*	Grapes^	Oranges	Pomegranates
Avocados*	Guavas	Papayas	Raspberries
Bananas	Kiwis	Passionfruit	Rhubarb
Blackberries*	Lemons	*Peaches*^*	Star fruit
Blueberries^	Limes	*Pears**	*Strawberries^*
Cherries*	Lychees*	Persimmons*	Tangerines
Cranberries	Mangoes*	Pineapples	Watermelon*
Figs*	Melons	Plantains	

herbs & spices

INCLUDING BUT NOT LIMITED TO

Anise	Cumin	Mustard
Annatto	Curry	Oregano
Basil	Dill	**Paprika**
Bay leaf	Fennel*	Parsley
Caraway	Fenugreek	Pepper, black
Cardamom	Galangal	Peppermint
Carob	Garlic	Rosemary
Cayenne pepper	Ginger	Saffron
Celery seed	Horseradish*	Spearmint
Chervil	Juniper berry	Star anise
Chicory*	Kaffir lime leaves	Tarragon
Chili powder	Lavender	Thyme
Chipotle powder	Lemongrass	Turmeric
Chives	Lemon verbena	Vanilla
Cilantro	Licorice	*Wasabi**
Cinnamon	Mace	Za'atar
Clove	Marjoram	
Coriander	Mint	

Guide to: Stocking a Paleo Pantry

Shopping the perimeter of the grocery store, where you'll find produce and fresh meats, is ideal for the majority of your foods, but add spices and some pantry items to your arsenal for cooking up tasty dishes, and have some healthy pantry items on hand for when you need to make a meal in a pinch. Note that, although they're considered "pantry items," some of these foods need to be refrigerated.

herbs & spices

SOME HERBS CAN BE FOUND IN BOTH FRESH AND DRIED FORMS. INCLUDING BUT NOT LIMITED TO

Anise	Clove	Lemon verbena	Pumpkin pie spice
Annatto	Coriander	Licorice	Rosemary
Basil	Cumin	Mace	Saffron
Bay leaf	Curry	Marjoram	Sage
Caraway	Dill	Mint	Sea salt
Cardamom	Fennel	*Mustard*	Spearmint
Cayenne pepper	Fenugreek	Nutmeg	Star anise
Celery seed	Galangal	Onion powder*	Tarragon
Chervil	Garlic	Oregano	Thyme
Chicory*	Ginger	**Paprika**	Turmeric
Chili powder	*Horseradish*	Parsley	Vanilla
Chipotle	Juniper berry	Pepper, black	*Wasabi*
Chives	Kaffir lime leaves	Peppercorns, whole black	Za'atar
Cilantro	Lavender	Peppermint	
Cinnamon	Lemongrass		

canned & jarred

INCLUDING BUT NOT LIMITED TO

Anchovy paste	Fish roe	Salmon, wild	**Tomato sauce**
Applesauce*	Herring, wild	Sardines, wild	Tuna, wild
Capers	Olives	**Sun-dried tomatoes**	
Coconut milk*	Oysters	Sweet potato	
Coconut water/ juice*	Pickles	Tahini	
	Pumpkin	**Tomato paste**	

nuts, seeds & dried fruit

Almonds	Coconut,* shredded, flakes	Dried mango*	Sesame seeds
Almond butter	Dates	Dried pineapple	Sunflower seeds
Almond flour	Dried apples*	Dried raspberries	Walnuts
Banana chips (check ingredients)	Dried apricots*	Hazelnuts	
	Dried blueberries	Macadamia nuts	
Brazil nuts	Dried cranberries	Pecans	
Chestnuts	Dried currants	Pine nuts	
Coconut butter*	Dried figs*	Pistachios*	
		Pumpkin seeds	

add your own!

MAYBE YOU HAVE FAVORITE ITEMS NOT LISTED ABOVE THAT YOU KNOW ARE PALEO-FRIENDLY. WRITE THEM HERE AND USE THIS PAGE AS A SHOPPING LIST.

fats & oils

SEE THE GUIDE TO FATS & OILS (P. 64) FOR DETAILS

Avocado oil (CP)
Bacon fat
Coconut oil
Extra-virgin olive oil
Ghee
Macadamia oil (CP)
Palm oil
Palm shortening
Sesame oil (CP)
Walnut oil (CP)

sauces

Coconut aminos (soy replacement)
Fish sauce (Red Boat brand)
Hot sauce (gluten-free)
Mustard (gluten-free)
Vinegars: apple cider,* red wine, distilled, rice, and balsamic (avoid malt vinegar)

beverages

Green tea
Herbal tea
Mineral water
White tea
Organic coffee

treats & sweets

FOR OCCASIONAL USE

Carob powder
Cocoa powder
Dark chocolate
Honey
Maple syrup
Molasses

NOTES

CP = cold-pressed
bold = nightshades
italics = goitrogenic
* = FODMAPs (p. 149)

Buy organic as much as possible.

Guide to: Food Quality

Seek out real, whole food as much as possible. This includes foods without health claims on the packages or, better yet, not in packages at all. Think produce and butcher-counter meats and seafood. After you've mastered making proper food choices, it's important to begin looking at the quality of the items. While buying the best quality is ideal in a perfect world, don't let those "best" labels keep you from doing the best you can within your means.

meat, eggs & dairy

beef & lamb
Best! 100% grass-fed and finished, pasture-raised, local
Better: grass-fed, pasture-raised
Good: organic
Baseline: commercial (hormone- and antibiotic-free)

pork
Best! pasture-raised, local
Better: free-range, organic
Good: organic
Baseline: commercial

eggs & poultry
Best! pasture-raised, local
Better: free range, organic
Good: cage-free, organic
Baseline: commercial

dairy
ALWAYS BUY FULL-FAT
Best! grass-fed, raw/unpasteurized
Better: raw/unpasteurized
Good: grass-fed
Baseline: commercial or organic—*not recommended*

seafood

Best! wild
Better: wild-caught
Good: humanely harvested, non-grain-fed
Baseline: farm-raised—*not recommended*

WILD FISH / WILD-CAUGHT FISH
"Wild fish" were spawned, lived in, and were caught in the wild. "Wild-caught fish" may have been spawned or lived some part of their lives in a fish farm before being returned to the wild and eventually caught. The Monterey Bay Aquarium's Seafood Watch (www.seafoodwatch.org) continually updates a list of the most sustainable seafood choices.

what the labels on meat, eggs & dairy mean

pasture-raised
Animals can roam freely in their natural environment, where they are able to eat the nutritious grasses, plants, bugs, and grubs that are part of their natural diet. There is no specific pasture-raised certification, though certified organic meat must come from animals that have continuous access to pasture.

cage-free
Animals are uncaged inside barns or warehouses, but they generally do not have access to the outdoors. Beak cutting is permitted for chickens. There is no third-party auditing.

organic
Animals cannot receive hormones or antibiotics except in the case of illness. They consume organic feed and have outdoor access but do not necessarily use it. Animals might not be grass-fed. Certification is costly, and some reputable farms are forced to forgo it. Compliance is verified through third-party auditing.

natural
Meats are "minimally processed," but companies use this term deceptively. All cuts are, by definition, minimally processed and free of flavorings and chemicals.

free-range/roaming
Poultry has access to the outdoors at least 51 percent of the time, and ruminants are not in feedlots. There are no restrictions regarding what the birds can be fed. Beak cutting and forced molting through starvation are permitted. There is no third-party auditing.

naturally raised
This USDA-verified term generally means that the animals were raised without growth promoters or unnecessary antibiotics. It does not indicate anything about the animals' welfare or diet.

no added hormones
It is illegal to use hormones in raising poultry or pork; therefore, the use of this phrase on poultry or pork is a marketing ploy.

vegetarian-fed
The animals' feed is free of animal by-products but isn't federally inspected. Chickens are not vegetarians, so this label on chicken or eggs only serves to indicate that the chickens were not eating their natural diet.

produce

Best! local, organic, and seasonal
Better: local and organic
Good: organic or local
Baseline: conventional

WHEN TO BUY ORGANIC
Buy organic as often as possible, but if you need to prioritize, see the Environmental Working Group's "The Dirty Dozen" list of produce to buy organic (www.ewg.org).

PRODUCE SKUs
Starts with 9 = organic
Starts with 3 or 4 = conventionally grown
Starts with 8 = genetically modified (GMO) or irradiated—avoid

fats & oils

SEE THE GUIDE TO FATS & OILS (PAGE 64) FOR DETAILS
Best! organic, cold-pressed, and from well-raised animals
Better: organic, cold-pressed
Good: organic or conventional

nuts & seeds

KEEP COLD FOR FRESHNESS
Best! local, organic, kept cold
Better: local, organic
Good: organic
Baseline: conventional

Sources: www.humanesociety.org, www.ewg.org, www.sustainabletable.org

Guide to: Fats & Oils

Using the right fats and oils is essential to improving your health from the inside out, and keeping them stocked at home is the first step toward creating dishes from nutrient-dense, whole foods. Avoid overly processed and refined fats and oils. Opt for organic whenever possible. For more on the best fats and oils for hot and cold uses, see the guide to cooking fats on the opposite page.

eat these HEALTHY, NATURALLY OCCURRING, MINIMALLY PROCESSED FATS

saturated FOR HOT USES

BUY ORGANIC, UNREFINED FORMS

Coconut oil
Palm oil

IDEALLY FROM PASTURE-RAISED, GRASS-FED, ORGANIC SOURCES

Butter
Ghee, clarified butter
Lard, bacon grease (pork fat)
Tallow (beef fat)
Duck fat
Schmaltz (chicken fat)
Lamb fat
Full-fat dairy
Eggs, meat, and seafood

unsaturated FOR COLD USES

BUY ORGANIC, EXTRA-VIRGIN & COLD-PRESSED FORMS

Avocado oil
Flaxseed oil**
Macadamia nut oil
Olive oil
Sesame oil
Walnut oil
Nuts and seeds (including
 nut and seed butters)

NOTE: Unsaturated fats (typically liquid at room temperature) are easily damaged when heat is applied to them. Do not consume damaged fats.

**Cold-pressed flaxseed oil is okay for occasional use, but using it as a supplement or consuming 1 to 2 tablespoons daily is *not* recommended, as it's best to minimize your overall consumption of polyunsaturated fatty acids.

ditch these UNHEALTHY, MAN-MADE FATS & REFINED SEED OILS

Hydrogenated and partially hydrogenated oils, as well as man-made trans fats and "buttery spreads" like Earth Balance, Benecol, and I Can't Believe It's Not Butter, are not healthy. These oils are highly processed and oxidize easily with exposure to light, air, or heat.

Margarine/buttery spreads
Canola oil (also known as rapeseed oil)
Corn oil
Cottonseed oil
Grapeseed oil
Rice bran oil

Safflower oil
Soybean oil
Sunflower oil
Vegetable oil
Shortening made from one
 or more of the above oils

Guide to: Cooking Fats

Choose cooking fats and oils based on (1) how they're made—choose naturally occurring, minimally processed fats first; (2) their fatty acid composition—fats and oils with more saturated fats are more stable and less likely to be damaged or oxidized; and (3) their smoke point, which tells you how hot the fat can get before it's damaged, though this should be a secondary factor.

culinary whizzes, listen up: COOK WITH GOOD FATS!

ITEM NAME	% SFA	%MUFA	% PUFA	SMOKE POINT UNREFINED/REFINED
best bets for high-heat cooking—THE MOST STABLE FATS				
Coconut oil	86	6	2	350/450
Butter/ghee	63	26	.03	300/480
Cocoa butter	60	35	5	370
Tallow/suet (beef fat)	55	34	.03	400
Palm oil	54	42	.10	455
Lard/bacon fat (pork fat)	39	45	11	375
Duck fat	37	50	13	375
okay for moderate-heat cooking—MODERATELY STABLE FATS				
Avocado oil*	20	70	10	520
Macadamia nut oil*	16	80	4	410
Olive oil*	14	73	11	375
Peanut oil**	17	46	32	320/450
Rice bran oil**	25	38	37	415
not recommended for cooking—VERY UNSTABLE FATS				
Safflower oil**	8	76	13	225/510
Sesame seed oil*	14	40	46	450
Canola oil**	8	64	28	400
Sunflower oil**	10	45	40	225/440
Vegetable shortening**	34	11	52	330
Corn oil	15	30	55	445
Soybean oil	16	23	58	495
Walnut oil*	14	19	67	400
Grapeseed oil	12	17	71	420

SFA: saturated fatty acid   MUFA: monounsaturated fatty acid   PUFA: polyunsaturated fatty acid

* While not recommended for cooking, cold-pressed nut and seed oils that are stored in the refrigerator may be used after cooking for flavor.

** While the fatty acid profile of these oils may seem appropriate at first glance, the processing method they go through makes them unhealthy—they are not recommended for consumption, whether hot or cold.

Clearing Up Carb Confusion

These days there is a great deal of confusion about carbohydrates in the world of health and nutrition. Which are good and which are bad? How many carbohydrates should you eat and how often?

Let's get one thing straight first: not all carbs are bad. There are only three kinds of macronutrients that make up all foods: proteins, fats, and carbohydrates. So if a food isn't a protein or fat, it's a carbohydrate.

Good Carbs, Bad Carbs

But there are indeed "good" carbs and "bad" carbs. They probably aren't what you think, though. I'm not going to talk about complex carbs versus simple carbs. If I did, I'd be the same as the nutritionists who suggest you eat copious amounts of whole grains. We've been there and done that, and it certainly hasn't made us healthier.

Bad carbs:

- are void of nutrients needed to properly metabolize carbs
- may cause digestive distress
- are refined and/or man-made

Good carbs, however:

- contain easily digestible, bioavailable nutrients that make it possible to metabolize carbs at a cellular level
- are available in nature as whole foods

When I say "void of nutrients," what do I mean? Well, you've heard about "empty calories." To understand this concept, you need to get a picture of how carbohydrates are processed in your body.

Before the energy and nutrition from the food you eat can nourish your cells, it must be broken down into its various constituents. Your cells can't make use of a doughnut or strawberry! When you eat any kind of carbohydrate, your body uses micronutrients—specifically B vitamins (especially B5), phosphorus, magnesium, iron, copper, manganese, zinc, and chromium—to metabolize it. When you eat carbohydrates in refined forms, the food contains calories from the *macro*nutrients—the carbohydrate itself—but lacks the *micro*nutrient cofactors that help you put those calories to use at the cellular level. This is where the issue of good versus bad carbs makes a difference in your body, and it's why a diet rich in bad carbs makes you tired. Your cells are powered by both macro- and micronutrients, but they have to use stored micronutrients to break down bad carbs, instead of using the micronutrients in the food itself.

Just four teaspoons of table sugar (a bad carb) delivers a total of sixty calories in carbohydrate form. That's it. It doesn't give you anything else—no nutrients at all. One small sweet potato (a good carb), on the other hand, contains about sixty calories in

MACRO & MICRO
Protein, fat, and carbohydrates are macronutrients. They each carry calories with them to provide your body with energy. Vitamins and minerals are micronutrients. They do not carry calories, but they are necessary for the proper metabolism and assimilation of the fuel that macronutrients provide.

carbohydrate form but also gives you B vitamins, phosphorous, magnesium, iron, copper, manganese, zinc, and chromium. These are the exact micronutrients your body needs to metabolize carbohydrates. *This* is the difference between a whole, unrefined, nutrient-dense food and a refined, nutrient-poor food. (Incidentally, the sweet potato also gives you vitamin E, beta-carotene, vitamin C, calcium, potassium, zinc, and selenium.)

When you eat whole, nutrient-dense foods like sweet potatoes and other vegetables, fruits, roots, and tubers, you give your body everything it needs right in one package to effectively turn those calories into energy. In other words, eating whole, nutrient-dense foods allows you to make nutritional deposits into your body's energy bank account. Nutrient-poor foods like sugar ask your body for a withdrawal without making a deposit.

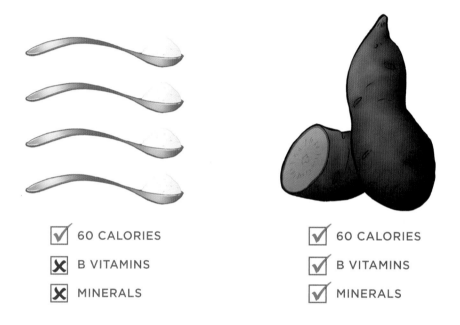

☑ 60 CALORIES ☑ 60 CALORIES
☒ B VITAMINS ☑ B VITAMINS
☒ MINERALS ☑ MINERALS

Are You Carb Loading for Your Desk Job?

Carbohydrates are a fast-acting fuel source and are broken down in your body into glucose (sugar) whether they begin as Pop-Tarts or fresh pineapple. If you become active shortly after eating, the glucose is used quickly. If not, the glucose is stored in your body as one of two things: glycogen (jargon for "stored glucose") or fat. *Yes, fat.*

Your body can only store glycogen in two places: your liver and your muscles. When you eat carbohydrates, your body checks to see how much is already stored in those two places before deciding how to handle what you've just eaten. If you have been active and used up some of the glycogen stores in your liver and muscles, your body will replenish it with glycogen from the new food.

While your body has only limited places to store glycogen, it has unlimited storage sites for fat. So what happens when there's no more room in your liver or muscles for glycogen, and you don't use the glucose you've eaten right away through activity? Your liver converts the extra glucose into one of two types of fat: triglycerides, which circulate in the blood, or adipose, which is stored on the body.

Carbohydrate storage that takes place after you exercise is the exception to this rule. Your muscles have first dibs on the carbs you eat in your post-workout meal (any meal eaten thirty minutes to two hours after exercise; just remember to go into rest-and-digest mode *before* eating). This allows your muscles to be replenished and restored for your next workout and is just one of the many benefits of exercise—you get carbohydrates right into your muscles rather than as fat on your bum, belly, or wherever else you don't want it.

Fat on your bum may be undesirable, but fat can also be stored closely around your organs. This is called visceral fat, and it's more dangerous than that extra junk in your trunk because it has the capacity to impede organ function.

Your genes have some say in how your body chooses where to store fat. You may know people, for example, who seem be able to eat lots of carbs, never work out, and remain thin. Their bodies are likely converting more of their excess carbohydrate intake into triglycerides and visceral fat than into visible body fat that would make their clothes tighter. They seem lucky because their clothing size remains the same, but they're actually in more trouble because visceral fat and high triglycerides are more dangerous than a little extra body fat. Unfortunately, the absence of any visible cue leaves people in the dark as to their inner state of health. Someone who isn't visibly overweight isn't necessarily healthy, particularly if they're eating more carbs than they are able to burn. But while genetics are factors in where you store fat, you can certainly improve your health by refusing to add to visceral fat and avoiding excess carbs.

Carb Here Often?

If you don't need to eat lots of carbs to fuel your daily life, what *do* you need to eat? That's easy—fat.

Fat is a perfect long-lasting fuel source for your body, but here's the catch: your body can't efficiently burn fat (from your food *or* from your fanny) if you are constantly eating a steady stream of carbohydrates.

In order to become "fat-adapted," meaning your body knows how to effectively use fat for fuel, you have to stop giving it carbs all day, every day. Sorry to be the bearer of bad news, but that's just how it works. Actually, this is great news because it means you don't have to eat every few hours to "fuel your metabolism." Quite the contrary! When you stop eating so many carbs and fearing natural, healthy fats (see page 33), your body burns not only the fat you eat but also body fat—the same fat you've been trying to burn off for years by cranking away on the elliptical machine.

So what's a good guide for balancing carbs, fat, and protein in your meals? Start with a breakfast that will keep you satiated until lunchtime: plan it around protein first and make sure you also add good fat, followed by carbs:

- **Protein:** Serve yourself a breakfast consisting of at least 20 grams of protein for women, 30 grams for men.

- **Fat:** Make sure there is adequate fat in the meal—anywhere from 15 to 50 grams, depending on the balance of calories you'll eat in carbs.

- **Carbs:** Any carbohydrate in the meal should be considered in terms of your activity levels during the day. Eat roughly 10 to 30 grams of carbs if you are less active and 30 to 60 grams if you are more active. If you're more active, you may do better if more of your calorie intake consists of carbs rather than extra fat.

Then balance the rest of your day's meals according to your activity level. You can use roughly the same ratio of protein to fat to carbs as for breakfast—about 30 percent protein, 50 percent fat, and 20 percent carbs if you're less active, or about 20 to 30 percent protein, 30 to 40 percent fat, and 30 to 40 percent carbs if you're more active. Just shift the amount of carbs slightly depending on when you exercise. For instance, if you exercise in the evening, you may want to consume fewer carbs at breakfast and lunch and more in your post-workout dinner to replenish what was depleted during exercise. Again, the meal plans to come (pages 156 to 243) will help you make smart choices based on the information you learn in this chapter.

SUFFICIENT CARBOHYDRATE INTAKE (FROM GOOD CARBS!)	GENERAL LIFESTYLE FACTORS ACTIVITY & STRESS LEVELS
VERY LOW CARB* 0–50 grams/day	Generally inactive or insulin-resistant and seeking to make drastic changes to sugar metabolism. Best for those interested in a ketogenic diet approach. **Not recommended for most people seeking general, optimal health.**
LOW CARB 50–75 grams/day	Not very active or participating in light to moderate cardiovascular activity that lasts less than 20 minutes per day. Also suitable for low-intensity/noncompetitive weight lifting and strength training. **This is a healthy range for many less-active people.**
MODERATE CARB 75–150 grams/day	Moderately active or completing low- to moderate-intensity cardiovascular activity that lasts between 20 and 60 minutes per day; generally active job or lifestyle; moderately stressful lifestyle. **This is a healthy range for most people.**
HIGHER CARB 150+ grams/day (up to around 300 grams)	Very active or completing intense cardiovascular or strength-building activity that lasts between 20 and 60 minutes per day; very active job with consistent movement; very stressful lifestyle that is mentally and physically demanding. **This is a healthy range for many people who are very active or have very stressful lives, including CrossFitters, strength athletes, and endurance athletes.**
HIGHER CARB 200+ grams/day	Pregnant or breastfeeding women. **This is a healthy range for women who are currently pregnant or who are breastfeeding.**

*A prolonged very low carb approach is not recommended for most people, as we may miss out on some of the beneficial micronutrients available in carbohydrate-rich foods. While nose-to-tail animal consumption, including all organ meats, would circumvent this issue, most people are not eating animals in this fashion today. Good carbs are also important for proper digestive function, as carbohydrates aid in balancing healthy gut flora.

Know this: Eat carbohydrates according to your average activity and stress levels to avoid extra body fat, keep triglyceride levels healthy, and prevent visceral fat around your organs.

When Low-Carb Is a Problem

While Paleo can be fairly low-carb by nature—after all, you're avoiding grains and legumes, the most carb-dense food sources—and a low-carb diet may be healthy and beneficial for lots of people, it certainly isn't *necessary* for everyone. You can reap the amazing anti-inflammatory benefits of a Paleo diet while eating healthy sources of carbs. Furthermore, it can be *un*healthy for some folks to eat low-carb, given their specific lifestyle, exercise patterns, and overall dietary needs.

What are some signs you've gone too low-carb for your needs?

- Fatigue and low energy; brain fog

- Inability to recover from exercise

- Waking from sleep once or more per night

- Feelings of anxiety, irritability, or depression

- Insatiable appetite, despite adding more protein and fat to your diet and eating sufficient calories

- Symptoms of low thyroid function without thyroid disease (diagnosed or subclinical): cold hands and feet, hair loss unrelated to stress or disease, constipation, dehydration

- After several months eating low-carb, you don't feel *better*

These symptoms may not necessarily be caused by a low-carb diet, but if you are experiencing them while eating low-carb, it's worth considering a shift.

While it's great to drop the fat phobia, it's important to remember that our bodies typically do very well with starchy carbs from healthy sources. Good carbs not only fuel us to handle different types of stressors, they also provide food for the beneficial bacteria in our large intestine! So the health of your gut microbiome, as well as your own energy and vitality, may depend on including healthy carbs in your diet.

If there's one gigantic pitfall I see folks falling into upon going Paleo, it's that they accidentally begin eating a low-carb diet. So how exactly does one *accidentally* eat low-carb?

Well, if you think about most of the foods included in a Paleo diet, they're naturally lower in carbs. Meat, eggs, seafood, vegetables, nuts and seeds—these are all part of a standard low-carb diet. Including fruit in that lineup bumps up carb intake somewhat, but lots of folks who go Paleo realize that one or two servings of fruit per day is plenty.

Additionally, we often forget to include starchy plant foods like potatoes, sweet potatoes, winter squash, beets, and plantains in our diet. These are all part of an overall very healthy and balanced Paleo diet, and there's no reason to avoid them. In fact, for many, the conscious inclusion of these foods is critical!

Looking for more sources of good carbs? Check out the guide to nutrient-dense carbs on page 75.

What I see happening most often is a lack of preparation: starchy plant foods require longer cooking times, while other vegetables can be ready to eat in just a few minutes. Forgetting to plan for the time to prepare starchy plant foods means that we avoid them, sometimes to our own detriment.

Here are some practical tips for making the inclusion of healthy carbs easier on a daily basis:

- Batch-bake potatoes and sweet potatoes. Instead of baking servings for one meal, bake lots of them at once every week so they're ready to go when you want them.

- Cook up a large batch of steamed sweet potatoes, puree, and freeze in silicone ice cube trays. Steaming gets the potatoes very soft and makes pureeing them easy, while freezing them in ice cube trays makes it easy to reheat a serving anytime. See the recipe on page 419.

- Take advantage of winter squash when it's in season or available, especially spaghetti squash, which provides many servings. (Spaghetti squash isn't the *most* carb-dense option, but for those who like a pasta replacement, it's more carb-dense than zucchini or other summer squash used to make noodles.)

- Use convenience items from the grocery store—canned sweet potato, pumpkin, and butternut squash are great, easy sources of carbs that are ready to go anytime. You can also find frozen butternut squash and sometimes potatoes that are easy to heat and eat. (Just watch out for junky oils and lots of additives/preservatives!)

- Make one-pot dishes like Butternut Cocoa Chili (page 356) to be sure you're getting good carbs in with your protein at each meal. Simply add a green vegetable or salad to either of those for a balanced plate.

When You Need More Carbs

If any of the below descriptions apply to you, you may do well eating more carbs on a regular basis:

- You work out/exercise/train at a level that's more intense than a walk or a light yoga class; your exercise frequently includes anaerobic bouts (you achieve a high heart rate), whether for short or long durations (high-intensity interval training, for example, or endurance athletics, where the intensity can vary from low to high).

- You're pregnant or breastfeeding; amenorrheic or dysmenorrheic; or a woman struggling with infertility.

- You're under intense physical, mental, or emotional stress—for instance, stress related to work, family or relationships, financial strain, training or exercise load, or the stress of healing from disease.

- You feel lethargic after a month of eating Paleo with the balance of foods falling outside of the starchy carbs category. (Note that this may be a problem of undereating in general or undereating carbs specifically.)

- You have a long and lean body type (often referred to as *ectomorph*) and find that gaining weight is a challenge.

In particular, athletes and those who are active often find that they're not eating enough carbs. If you have a moderately active lifestyle—particularly if you work in construction, physical education, personal training, or other jobs that require you stand on your feet all day—it can be helpful to consume more carbs. Carbs are mostly useful, however, in fueling high-intensity exercise that lasts for longer periods.

During high-intensity exercise, such as sprinting or a CrossFit-style workout, that lasts more than five minutes, your body relies on carbohydrates for fuel, but this doesn't mean you need to "carb-load" for a five-minute or even thirty-minute workout. Regular, moderate carb intake will provide you with sufficient fuel for these activities. However, if you regularly perform sixty minutes of high-intensity exercise, you may need to eat more carbs on those days. The chart on page 70 provides some guidelines for the amount of carbs needed for given activity levels and lifestyles.

If you're an athlete, you may find the Athletic Performance Meal Plan (page 168) to be helpful, not just for meal planning but also for lifestyle and supplement recommendations.

Simplifying Sweeteners

What about the different types of sweeteners? Eating less-refined sweeteners like raw honey, molasses, or maple syrup (and I mean 100 percent pure maple syrup, not Aunt Jemima's maple-flavored corn syrup) is not the same as eating sweet whole foods when it comes to micronutrients. These sweeteners carry *some* micronutrients, but they are still refined to a degree. Therefore, I don't recommend eating them regularly, but they are certainly better sweetener choices than white table sugar and agave nectar, which are more refined, or artificial noncaloric sweeteners.

Let's compare some sweetener choices.

	Calories	Carbohydrates	Other nutrients
MEDJOOL DATE	66	18 g	B vitamins, phosphorus, magnesium, iron, copper, manganese, zinc
MOLASSES, 1 tablespoon	58	15 g	B vitamins (especially B6), phosphorus, magnesium, iron, copper, manganese, zinc, chromium
MAPLE SYRUP, 1 tablespoon	52	13 g	Phosphorus, magnesium, iron, copper, manganese, zinc
TABLE SUGAR, 1 tablespoon	48	12 g	———————

Although dates, molasses, and maple syrup are less refined and do carry some nutrients and therefore are a better choice than table sugar, which has none, the best choice is really to stick to fruit and other naturally sweet whole foods.

HOW SWEET IT IS

Check out the guide to sweeteners on page 76 for more information.

Artificial noncaloric sweeteners are the least healthy choice of the bunch. I'm sure you realize by now that they're far from whole, real foods. If there are no calories, there are also no nutrients. Your body still uses nutrients to metabolize artificial sweeteners, even though it doesn't gain nutritional value from them. Again, this is one of those situations where you are withdrawing from your energy bank account without making a deposit, which can lead to low energy.

The biggest issue with artificial sweeteners, however, is that they are actually toxic. Yes, you read that correctly—they're *toxic*. They are processed by your liver and stored in your fat cells to keep them away from your bloodstream, where they can cause damage. Most people use noncaloric sweeteners to lower overall caloric intake in an effort to lose body fat, but they're actually filling their fat cells with toxins. This is one reason why detoxing from sugar and carbohydrate addiction can be painful. As the body burns fat for fuel instead of sugar, stored toxins are released from fat cells, often leading to headaches and fatigue.

Watch Out for Hidden Sugar

Sugar is hidden in nearly all packaged, bottled, and processed foods. This is an important lesson: whenever you buy groceries, turn every package of food around and read the ingredients. Even if it's a food you've bought many times before, the ingredients can change at any time. So read them again.

Even many dried fruits contain added sugar, which serves as a preservative and flavor enhancer. Does it make sense to you that fruit would need added sugar? It doesn't. Fruit is naturally sweet, so never buy any type of fruit or juice with sugar or any other sweetener on the ingredient list.

When you avoid consuming added sugar, you do yourself the additional favor of eliminating many packaged, factory-made, refined foods from your diet. You'll also eliminate many other harmful added ingredients, including synthetic chemicals.

Guide to: Nutrient-Dense Carbs

Removing grains, legumes, and refined foods from your diet doesn't mean that you need to avoid all carbohydrates! Check out this list of nutrient-dense starchy vegetables that are good sources of carbohydrates. (Keep in mind, though, that fruits and nuts are fairly high in carbohydrates, too.) These are some of your "good" carbs!

there *are* carbs beyond bread EAT UP

VEGETABLE	CARBS IN 100 G	FIBER IN 100 G	CARBS IN 1 CUP	MICRONUTRIENTS
Beets	10 g	2 g	17 g (sliced)	Folate, manganese
Butternut squash	10 g	—	22 g	Vitamin A (beta-carotene), vitamin C
Carrots	10 g	3 g	13 g (chopped)	Vitamin A (beta-carotene), vitamin K1
Cassava (raw)	38 g	2 g	78 g	Folate, potassium, manganese, thiamin, vitamin C
Jicama (raw)	9 g	5 g	12 g (sliced)	Vitamin C
Kohlrabi	7 g	1 g	11 g (sliced)	Copper, manganese, potassium, vitamin B6, vitamin C
Lotus root	16 g	3 g	19 g (sliced)	Copper, manganese, potassium, vitamin B6, vitamin C
Onions	10 g	1 g	21 g (chopped)	Potassium, vitamin C
Parsnips	17 g	4 g	27 g (sliced)	Manganese, vitamin C
Plantains	31 g	2 g	62 g (mashed)	Magnesium, potassium, vitamin A (beta-carotene), vitamin B6, vitamin C
Pumpkins	5 g	1 g	12 g (mashed)	Potassium, vitamin C, vitamin E
Rutabagas	9 g	2 g	21 g (mashed)	Manganese, potassium, vitamin C
Spaghetti squash	6 g	1 g	9 g	Trace
Sweet potatoes	21 g	3 g	58 g (mashed)	Iron, magnesium, manganese, potassium, vitamin A (beta-carotene), vitamin B6, vitamin C, vitamin E
Taro root	35 g	5 g	46 g (sliced)	Manganese, potassium, vitamin B6, vitamin E
Turnips	5 g	2 g	12 g (mashed)	Calcium, folate, manganese, potassium, vitamin B6, vitamin C
White potatoes	22 g	1 g	27 g (peeled)	Trace vitamin C
Winter squash	15 g	4 g	30 g (cubed)	Thiamin, vitamin B6, vitamin C
Yams	27 g	4 g	37 g (cubed)	Manganese, potassium, vitamin B6, vitamin C

Source: Nutritiondata.com

Guide to: Sweeteners

How many of these sweeteners do you use or find in your favorite packaged foods? Perhaps it's time for a change! Artificial sweeteners are never recommended, while the limited use of select natural sweeteners can be okay for treats and special occasions. But sweeteners should never be considered "food" or nourishment.

natural USE SPARINGLY

PREFERRED CHOICES ARE IN BOLD. USE ORGANIC FORMS WHENEVER POSSIBLE.

Brown sugar	Cane juice	**Maple syrup (dark)**
Dates (whole)	Cane juice crystals	**Molasses**
Date sugar	Coconut nectar	Palm sugar
Date syrup	Coconut sugar/crystals	**Stevia (green leaf or**
Cane sugar	**Fruit juice (real, fresh)**	**extract)**
Raw sugar	**Fruit juice concentrate**	
Turbinado sugar	**Honey (raw)**	

natural BUT NOT RECOMMENDED

Agave	Diastatic malt	Maltose
Agave nectar	Ethyl maltol	Malt syrup
Barley malt	Fructose	Mannitol
Beet sugar	Glucose	Muscovado
Brown rice syrup	Golden sugar	Refiner's syrup
Buttered syrup	Golden syrup	Sorbitol
Caramel	Grape sugar	Sorghum syrup
Carob syrup	High fructose corn syrup	Sucrose
Corn syrup	Invert sugar syrup	Treacle
Corn syrup solids	Lactose	Yellow sugar
Demerara sugar	Levulose	Xylitol and other sugar
Dextran	Light brown sugar	alcohols, which typically
Dextrose	Maltitol	end in "-ose"
Diastase	Maltodextrin	

artificial NEVER CONSUME

Acesulfame potassium (Sweet One)
Aspartame (Equal, NutraSweet)
Saccharin (Sweet'N Low)
Stevia, white/bleached (Truvia, Sun Crystals)
Sucralose (Splenda)
Tagatose

sugar is sugar BUT NOT REALLY

CONTRARY TO POPULAR BELIEF, NOT ALL SWEETENERS ARE THE SAME. WHILE ALL CALORIC SWEETENERS, BOTH ARTIFICIAL AND NATURAL, HAVE 16 CALORIES PER TEASPOON, THERE ARE OTHER FACTORS TO CONSIDER.

HOW IT'S MADE

The more highly refined a sweetener is, the worse it is for your body. For example, high fructose corn syrup (HFCS) and artificial sweeteners are modern, factory-made, highly refined products. Honey, maple syrup, green leaf stevia, and molasses are all much less processed and have been around for hundreds of years. Honey requires almost no processing, and as a result, I vote for raw, organic, local honey as the ideal natural sweetener.

WHERE IT'S USED

This is a reality check. When you read the ingredients label on packaged, processed foods, it becomes obvious that most of them use highly refined, low-quality sweeteners. Food manufacturers even hide sugar in foods that you didn't think were sweets! Many foods that have been made low-fat or nonfat have added sweeteners or artificial sweeteners—avoid these products!

HOW YOUR BODY PROCESSES IT

Here's where those HFCS commercials really got things wrong: your body actually does not metabolize all sugar the same way.

Interestingly enough, for quite some time sweeteners like HFCS and agave nectar were viewed as better options for diabetics because their high fructose content has to be processed by the liver before the sugar hits your bloodstream. This yielded a seemingly favorable result on blood sugar levels: they didn't skyrocket as quickly as they did with white sugar. However, it's now understood that isolated fructose metabolism is a complicated issue and that taxing the liver excessively with such sweeteners can be quite harmful to our health.

Fructose is the primary sugar in all fruit. When eating whole fruit, the micronutrients and fiber content of the fruit support proper metabolism and assimilation of the fructose. Whole foods for the win!

Healing Digestion

What happens in your gut is critical to your overall health. The food you eat can't nourish you properly if your digestive system isn't able to break it down into smaller molecules of nutrients that can be absorbed by the bloodstream and carried throughout the body to your cells.

This is how your body extracts energy from the foods you eat, and if this process is disrupted, the food that you eat isn't able to nourish you. This is especially important when you aren't feeling well or you know your digestion feels "off" somehow, because you need the nutrients from your food to be able to heal. So getting your digestion working smoothly is of utmost importance, not only for your digestive system itself but also for any other health challenges you're facing.

Digestion involves a series of steps that require several organs to work in concert with one another. Think of digestion as a top-to-bottom process. You may think it starts in your mouth and ends you-know-where, but digestion actually begins before the food enters your mouth. In fact, it begins in your brain.

The Brain

Remember when you were a kid, and your mother made you wait thirty minutes after lunch before swimming or running around to play?

There's a good reason to leave a window between eating and heightened activity: your body can't focus on digesting food when you ask it to perform other actions, like active play or exercise. Physical activity—or any activity that's stressful, including a dreaded work meeting or life event—occurs in a different physical *and* mental state (the "sympathetic-dominant" state, or "fight-or-flight mode") than what you need for digestion. In fact, your thoughts can impair or improve salivary response, stomach acid production, enzyme secretion, and the release of digestive hormones.

It's your brain's job to decide whether to divert attention to stress responses, such as when you exercise, or to nourishing functions, like resting and digesting. If you're in fight-or-flight mode because of a mental or physical stressor, your body diverts energy and blood flow away from the digestive process and toward other priorities, like managing and responding to the stressful stimuli.

If your brain senses that the body needs to be on alert or handling stressors, the natural cycle of "rest and digest" is switched off, which means that autonomic (automatic or subconscious) body functions are downregulated. Therefore, if you want to digest your food *optimally*, allow a mental break or "chill out" period when switching from a stressed state into a state where you are ready to rest and digest food (known as the "parasympathetic" state).

This goes against most things you've been told about post-workout nutrition, doesn't it? You have likely been told to make sure you eat within thirty minutes of working out, but you actually should wait until thirty minutes *after* your workout. What you've been taught is ideal for professional athletes and bodybuilders, but not for the average person.

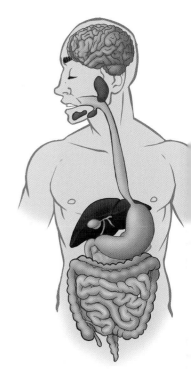

SYMPATHETIC VS. PARASYMPATHETIC

The sympathetic nervous system is dominant when you are in fight-or-flight mode, and the parasympathetic nervous system is dominant when you are in rest-and-digest mode. So in order to optimize all digestive functions, the parasympathetic nervous system needs to be dominant.

Unless you're extremely active and need extra calories as a result, as in the case of a coach who trains people all day or someone with a very active day job, the directive to eat within thirty minutes of a workout doesn't apply to you. (If your activity level is high and you want to eat immediately after a workout, liquid foods are easier to digest, as they don't require the same digestive function.)

The reason we have been told to eat within thirty minutes of working out is that we may gain a metabolic advantage from calories taken in during this window of time—because we've just depleted our nutrients somewhat during the workout, our bodies can utilize the carbohydrates and protein in food very quickly. The problem is that it's nearly impossible to gain this advantage from whole foods when your digestive system is still in fight-or-flight mode.

The average person who exercises regularly but does not train hard as a competitive athlete takes in sufficient food each day to replace the nutrients depleted by exercise. In fact, many of my clients have found that dropping their post-workout shake allows them to finally lose the fat they've been battling for months. Instead, they wait at least thirty minutes after a workout before eating solid, whole foods at their usual mealtime.

What Can Go Wrong?

If you don't relax into rest-and-digest mode before you eat, your digestive function won't work optimally, which means a decrease in stomach acid production as well as impaired (either too fast or too slow) overall digestion.

How to Fix It

Whether you're in fight-or-flight mode acutely from an intense workout or chronically from a stressful life, the fix is the same. Take a few moments—as many as you can—to relax and breathe when you sit down to eat. (Yes, I said sit down, and I don't mean in the car while driving!) Making a conscious effort to activate the rest-and-digest mode so that you can eat in a calm, mindful state will help your entire digestive process run smoothly—literally.

So relax, decompress, reset your mind, and take a few deep breaths before sitting down at the table to eat. Do your best not to eat on the run, in your car, or immediately before or after exercise.

The Mouth, Salivary Glands, and Esophagus

As you chew your food, three pairs of enzyme-releasing salivary glands begin the process of breaking it down. One enzyme, salivary amylase, starts breaking down carbohydrates, and another, lingual lipase, starts to break down fats. The next time you eat a starchy food, chew it for a while and you'll notice that it tastes sweeter as the complex carbohydrates are broken down into simple sugars. Saliva also helps to moisten your food before it is sent on its way down your esophagus and into your stomach.

While enzymes in saliva start the chemical breakdown of your food, the action of chewing begins the mechanical breakdown. Chewing also sends signals to your brain to initiate downstream digestive enzyme production, so that your entire system is primed for food. Ever feel a rumble in your stomach while chewing gum? That's because your body has been tricked into thinking you're about to send food down the pipe. Chewing gum can stimulate your appetite for this reason.

What Can Go Wrong?

If you don't chew properly, some of the symptoms you'll experience are bloating, belching, and undigested food particles in your stool, like corn or leafy greens. But these symptoms may also be a sign that you're eating foods your body doesn't tolerate.

How to Fix It

Chew your food well, of course! Beyond that, be sure to eat whole foods that your body tolerates well. Foods high in antinutrients, such as grains and legumes, have built-in defenses against digestive enzymes and the digestive process. Since these foods are primarily the seeds of plants, it's their job to survive that process so that they may go on to be planted and grow.

If you urgently run to the bathroom shortly after a meal, it's a surefire sign that your body has not tolerated something you have eaten. Corn, for example, is hard to chew completely due to its resilient outer coating. Anytime you see something in your stool that looks the same as it did on your plate, you have a problem. Your digestive tract is a place where food should be broken down completely into molecules that are only visible with a microscope. What you eliminate should be 80 percent bacteria, not mostly food.

A bowel transit time test (see page 91) uses whole sesame seeds to mark how long it takes for food to move through your system. This test perfectly illustrates that a grain or a seed of a plant may be hard for us to break down entirely. Even on a molecular level, some proteins may not be fully digested or assimilated by your body. Grains and legumes in particular fight your digestive system with antinutrients (more on that on page 96).

KIDS AND VEGGIES
Toddlers that have just begun to use their gums and teeth to chew foods typically have less amylase in their saliva to mix with carbohydrate-rich food. This is why your young one may like sweeter foods. Continue to offer less-sweet foods, because enzyme secretion will increase as the child's chewing and gumming of foods becomes more consistent.

What's wrong with legumes?

Well, you already know that beans are famous for causing gas. This is due to the presence of carbohydrates that our bodies can't properly break down. The bottom line is, if you're experiencing gas symptoms, you have eaten a food that you don't digest well.

It's possible to make beans more digestible by soaking, sprouting, and fermenting them, typically overnight. Many traditional food preparations take this approach, and often people trying traditional preparations find that the beans are easier to digest. To assume beans are a great protein source is misguided, however, as they are primarily a source of carbohydrates, not protein. So while soaking, sprouting, and fermenting may help you consume beans without digestive distress, I don't recommend it as a regular practice. More nutrient-dense foods are always a better choice!

The Stomach

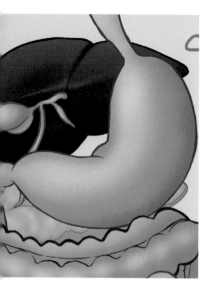

FUN FACT

While fat breakdown isn't a primary or significant action in the stomach of adults, it's a fairly active process in infants, who produce more lipase than adults because their ideal diet of breast milk is primarily composed of fats.

When you've eaten and feel full, your stomach usually holds about one to two liters of food and liquid, although because it can stretch, it can hold up to four liters. A healthy stomach has a thick mucosal lining and is an extremely acidic environment. Yes, you read that correctly! The acidic environment serves several important purposes. To begin with, it's your first line of defense against "bad bugs"—harmful bacteria and other pathogens that try to hitch a ride into your body by way of food. After you swallow, food passes through your esophagus and enters your stomach, where it's the job of stomach acid (hydrochloric acid, HCl) to kill any microscopic pathogenic material in your food before it passes through to the small intestine. You probably swallow more pathogens than you think, but we only hear about one of these pathogens when stomach acid fails to destroy it, leading to food poisoning or an infection.

The acidic environment of the stomach is also where the breakdown of proteins begins. An entire array of digestive reactions occur when food arrives in the stomach, as digestive-signaling hormones and enzymes "read" the contents of your stomach and begin to make secretions in response. The breakdown (or "denaturing") of food begins in the stomach by the actions of these enzymes.

Proteins are broken down by enzymes called proteases and peptidases, while fats are broken down by gastric lipase. While the majority of nutrients and other substances won't begin to be absorbed until they reach the small and large intestines, the absorption of water, some minerals, aspirin, and alcohol occurs in the stomach lining.

Last but not least, your stomach is responsible for the further mechanical digestion of food through "churning and burning," which breaks food down physically while mixing it with the gastric secretions. The resulting mix of denatured food and gastric secretions is called chyme.

What Can Go Wrong?

When your stomach's lining is sufficient and you have the right amount of stomach acid for the proper breakdown of food, you don't feel the high level of acidity in the stomach. When you have *low* stomach acid, you end up with—you guessed it—bad bugs. That leads, as you may suspect, to heartburn and acid reflux. Most people reach for an antacid when they feel heartburn or acid reflux, but the actual cause of the problem is usually too *little* stomach acid.

Acid reflux occurs as a result of increased pressure in the stomach, which in turn is caused by bacterial overgrowth and poor absorption of carbohydrates. Low or inadequate stomach acid is the root cause of both these factors because it allows bad bugs to thrive and doesn't fully break down certain foods. This causes pressure and allows acidic HCl to creep back up your esophagus, where it doesn't belong. The acid then causes a burning sensation in the sensitive lining of the esophagus.

So when you feel acid reflux or heartburn, you're actually feeling the effects of pressure and backup caused by poorly digested food and bacterial overgrowth—a result of too little stomach acid, not too much. The good news is, reducing bacteria growth and limiting carbohydrate intake can improve or even cure acid reflux.

Digestive enzymes decoded!

The first portion of the name of an enzyme tells you what type of molecule it will break down, while the second part, the "-ase," tells you it's an enzyme.

lipase = lipid (fat) breakdown enzyme

protease = protein breakdown enzyme

amylase = amylopectin (a carbohydrate) breakdown enzyme

Beyond simply breaking down foods, stomach acid is essential to the downstream signaling of appropriate enzyme secretions from other digestive organs, as well as the assimilation of minerals (like iron and calcium) and B vitamins (especially B12) into your cells. Many conditions that are the result of nutrient deficiencies—including anemia, depression, anxiety, fatigue from an iron or B12 deficiency, osteoporosis, and osteopenia—are rooted in low stomach acid. Other problems associated with low stomach acid include frequent bouts of food poisoning, gas, belching, or bloating after a meal despite chewing your food very well.

How to Fix It

Following the advice from the first two steps of the digestive process—getting into rest-and-digest mode and chewing foods well—will take you very far along the path to keeping your stomach acid at good levels. If, after taking those steps, you still experience symptoms of low stomach acid, you can take digestive bitters (a liquid tincture available at most health food stores) or a small amount of fresh lemon juice or apple cider vinegar. Taking these strong bitter or sour liquids in just a small shot of water about fifteen minutes before meals can help stimulate HCl production. If your symptoms are severe, you may find that supplementing with HCl directly is most effective.

If you experience symptoms of low stomach acid such as reflux, heartburn, or excessive fullness immediately after eating, even though you have eliminated grains, legumes, sugar, and refined foods from your diet, it could be that your body just needs more time to adjust before you see the results of your dietary changes. If you have been on acid-blocking drugs, proton-pump inhibitors (PPI), for an extended period of time, you will need to take further steps towards healing the lining of the stomach and small intestine to ensure you properly absorb and utilize nutrients from your food—see the suggestions in the box on page 82.

If symptoms of low stomach acid persist for longer than thirty days, there may be a more serious issue, such as a persistent gut pathogen. In this case, I recommend working with a practitioner who understands your desire to maintain a whole-foods diet and who will conduct a stool test to check for *H. pylori*, small intestine bacterial overgrowth (SIBO), and other problems. It is critical to resolve these issues in order to have full success with a nutrient-dense, whole-foods diet.

TRYING TO "SOAK UP" BOOZE WITH BREAD?
While this seems logical enough, it doesn't actually help slow the absorption of alcohol from your stomach to your bloodstream. A better approach would be to eat a meal or snack with some fat in it to lower the rate of gastric emptying.

FOR HEALTHY GUT FLORA

- Reduce your intake of carbohydrates, fiber, and sugar and sweeteners in all forms (including artificial), especially fructose. All of these may promote dysbiosis, imbalanced gut flora. This means you are feeding the bad bacteria in your digestive system and allowing them to increase in number. You may find that you are able to add low-fructose carbohydrate sources, such as sweet potato and melon, back to your diet after 1 to 2 months.

FOR BETTER STOMACH ACID PRODUCTION (USE JUST ONE AT A TIME!)

- Drink lemon juice or apple cider vinegar. Try about 1 tablespoon in 1 ounce of water 10 to 20 minutes before a meal to help promote natural stomach acid production.

- Take digestive bitters. You can find these in tincture form (liquid in a dropper) in many health food stores. Dosages vary, so follow the instructions on the bottle.

- Take HCl supplements. These can be found at any health food shop—usually as betaine HCl or as part of a combination of digestive enzyme support. I recommend only taking these supplements as part of a multipronged approach that includes eating in rest-and-digest mode and chewing well, both of which are critical. Start with a low dose of HCl per the instructions on the bottle and monitor your symptoms afterward. If you notice any heat or burning sensations in your upper gastric region, it means you have taken more than you need. If you take more HCl than you need but never feel a burning sensation, it may simply be a good sign of an intact stomach lining.

FOR HEALTHY STOMACH AND INTESTINAL LININGS

- Seek out supplements that support the linings of the stomach and small intestine. Chewable deglycerized licorice (sold as DGL in most places), marshmallow root, slippery elm, and peppermint herbal tea are helpful. (See the "Repair" step in the 4R Protocol on page 45 for more information.)

An important caution: Taking an HCl supplement is not advisable if you are taking any sort of anti-inflammatory medication, including aspirin, ibuprofen, and corticosteroids, all of which can damage the lining of the stomach and small intestine. Combining an HCl supplement with these drugs could further irritate the GI lining and increases your risk of gastric bleeding and ulcers.

The Liver and Gallbladder

The liver is a reddish-brown organ that weighs about three and a half pounds and sits in the upper right quadrant of the abdominal cavity, just below the diaphragm. The gallbladder is a much smaller (eight-by-four-centimeter) pouchlike organ that sits below the liver and connects to the duodenum (part of the small intestine) via the common bile duct. The common bile duct also connects the gallbladder and the pancreas.

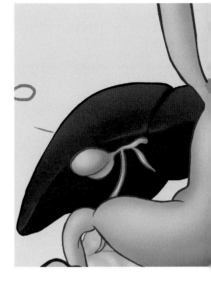

The liver is responsible for a lot of critical life functions, like detoxification and protein synthesis, but it also plays a very large role in the digestive process. It produces bile, a soaplike substance that emulsifies dietary fats such as butter, olive oil, and coconut oil—the way dish soap breaks up grease on a dirty pan—so you can digest them and assimilate them into your body's cells and tissues. The gallbladder stores bile and releases it based on signals from the brain that communicate how much bile is needed to properly break down dietary fats. You couldn't appropriately assimilate dietary fats, or fat-soluble vitamins A, D, E, and K, without your liver and gallbladder.

What Can Go Wrong?

The most common problem with the liver and gallbladder involves the signaling hormone cholecystokinin (CCK), which enables the brain to communicate with the gallbladder. If this process goes awry you may develop gallstones, which can cause pain or discomfort under your sternum or in the middle of your back after a fatty meal. This may indicate that there's a disruption in the normal flow of bile from your gallbladder or that gallstones have developed and are beginning to block the normal release of bile from the gallbladder. This blockage may occur within the gallbladder itself or in the common bile duct (the set of tubes that allow the liver, gallbladder, and pancreas to secrete into the small intestine).

Often, people attempt to eat a low-fat diet when these problems develop because they understand that the gallbladder is working in response to dietary fats. This approach only tends to make matters worse because, in an effort to eat less fat, they usually increase their intake of grains. The antinutrients in grains and the lower demand for bile secretion only disrupt the CCK hormone signals further. Then the gallbladder fails to secrete enough bile, which begins to back up.

Another—and possibly earlier—sign of a malfunctioning gallbladder or gallbladder-signaling problem is green, yellowish, or light-colored stool. This color pattern suggests that dietary fats have not been properly broken down before elimination, which may indicate that your bile production or secretion is impaired. If all is working smoothly, you won't feel any discomfort after a fatty meal, and your stool color will be normal. (Read more about identifying healthy stool on page 92.)

Bear in mind, too, that your liver serves many critical functions beyond digestion. It is also responsible for the uptake of fatty acids once they're broken down in the small intestine, and it screens all incoming toxins to determine the proper immune response against possible invaders. Poor liver function can mean you are less able to fight infections. So overwhelming your liver with antigens (compounds against which your body needs to launch an immune response), whether from environmental or dietary toxins, is not a good idea!

NO GALLBLADDER?

If your gallbladder has been removed, you may find that reducing your fat intake helps you feel better. Focus on fats that are easier for your body to break down without bile. Contrary to popular belief, saturated fats, such as butter and coconut oil, are easier to digest than unsaturated fats! This is because their chemical structure is much shorter than that of mono- or polyunsaturated fats, such as olive oil and walnut oil, so it's easier for our bodies to break them down.

How to Fix It

Eliminating all grain products from your diet is step one in supporting the digestive functions of your liver and gallbladder. This will help keep the signaling from your brain to your gallbladder working properly. Also, since your liver is taxed heavily by alcohol and excess fructose intake, I recommend limiting or even avoiding booze and fruit (especially juices).

Eat the majority of your dietary fats in the form of short- and medium-chain fatty acids (butter, ghee, and coconut oil) rather than longer-chain fats (olive oil or other nut oils), so your body can use the bile it secretes more efficiently.

You may also find that supplementing with bile salts, ox bile, or the digestive enzyme lipase helps your digestive process. This is particularly helpful if you have had your gallbladder removed.

The Pancreas

The pancreas is an organ that is part of your endocrine system, which means that it produces hormones. It sits with its "head" nestled adjacent the duodenum (part of your small intestine) and its "body" underneath your stomach. Your pancreas is responsible for the production and secretion of the hormones insulin and glucagon, as well as the digestive enzymes trypsin and chymotrypsin, which serve to break down peptide bonds in the proteins you eat. Remember that digestive enzymes were secreted in your stomach as well, so the pancreas is adding more into the mix now that food is moving toward your small intestine.

What do the pancreatic hormones do? Insulin, which is produced by the beta cells of the pancreas, signals your body to carry glucose (sugar) and other nutrients from the bloodstream to the liver, muscles, and brain. Insulin release is triggered primarily by the intake of dietary carbohydrates and secondarily by the intake of dietary protein.

Glucagon, produced by the alpha cells of the pancreas, is the counterregulatory hormone to insulin—whereas insulin lowers your blood sugar by moving it to the liver, muscles, and brain, glucagon signals your body to release glucose from storage in your liver in order to raise your blood sugar. Glucagon is released in response to the intake of dense sources of animal protein and in response to drops in blood glucose levels due to hunger or exercise.

What Can Go Wrong?

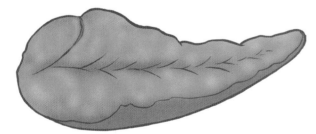

The river of hormones and enzymes should flow smoothly, but if you have a grain intolerance or very low intake of dietary fats, you can end up with an excess of bile, which then backs up. As a result, you might eventually develop gallbladder disease or gallstones, which can block the common bile duct. In some serious cases, this backup can lead to pancreatitis, which is inflammation of the pancreas.

Pancreatitis and gallbladder disease can cause a disruption in the pancreas's production and secretion of digestive enzymes and hormones. Any of these disorders may have serious negative effects on digestive function and overall health.

Diabetes is a disease of the pancreas as well. In the case of type 1 diabetes, your immune system destroys the beta cells of the pancreas, partly in an autoimmune response to the consumption of gluten-containing grain proteins (read more about this in the chapter on autoimmunity, page 93). This leaves the pancreas unable to produce adequate insulin, and in many cases, it stops producing insulin entirely. This is why a type 1 diabetic usually needs to inject insulin in order to properly assimilate nutrients.

Remember that insulin is involved in storing nutrients for your body to use later. For this reason, impaired pancreatic and insulin function can mean malnutrition and dangerous weight loss called wasting. These are common symptoms for a type 1 diabetic. Without the action of insulin, even if an individual eats plenty of food, the body can't pull the nutrients from the bloodstream and into the body's cells. Until insulin is injected and cellular nutrient storage occurs, a type 1 diabetic will continue to waste away. While most type 1 diabetics cannot regain any beta cell function, if the disease is detected early enough and a strictly grain-free diet is adopted, some may be able to reverse the condition.

While type 1 and type 2 diabetes both involve problems with nutrient storage, they're very different. A type 2 diabetic still has beta cell function, but insulin signaling is disrupted due to diet and lifestyle. Unfortunately, some type 2 diabetics may experience beta cell burnout or destruction, which means that not all beta cell function will be regained when they change their diet. Those people may need to inject insulin, although they usually need it to a lesser degree than people with type 1 diabetes.

How to Fix It

Pancreatic malfunction is often a downstream result of gallbladder malfunction, so address your gallbladder first (see page 83). If you have type 1 diabetes, it's critical that you completely eliminate gluten from your diet. This means looking for hidden gluten in foods and being diligent about your food choices and requests when dining out. (See page 107 for a guide to finding hidden gluten in foods.)

The Small Intestine

The small intestine is twenty feet of complex, hard-working, tubelike tissue that holds the key to much of your immune capability. There are three sections to the small intestine: the duodenum, which connects to the stomach; the jejunum, which comprises most of those twenty feet; and the ileum, which connects to the large intestine. Just on the other side of the cell walls that line your small intestine is a layer of gut-associated lymphoid tissue (GALT) and then your bloodstream.

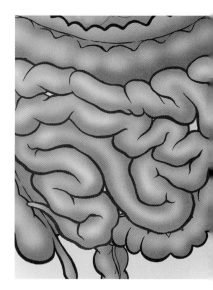

Your small intestine is where most of your food is broken into its end-usable forms of amino acids (from proteins), fatty acids (from fats), and glucose (from carbohydrates)—or not. If your food isn't completely broken down, what you get is digestive or stomach irritation, digestive malfunction, and nutrient malabsorption. As food particles, stomach acid, bile, digestive hormones, and enzymes move through the jejunum, they interact with its brush border lining. This is where your body decides if it recognizes food as particles it knows how to use (such as amino acids, fatty acids, glucose, vitamins, and minerals) or as an enemy. It's truly the make-or-break stage in the game of digestion and absorption.

Signs & symptoms of disrupted digestion

- Heartburn

- Frequent belching after meals

- Indigestion

- Feeling of fullness after meals

- Frequent stomach upset

- Gas or flatulence after meals

- Constipation

- Diarrhea

- Chronic intestinal infections: bacteria, yeast, parasites

- Chronic *Candida* infections (candidiasis), which can cause a host of symptoms, including skin rashes and vaginal yeast infections in women

- Undigested food in stool

- Known food sensitivities

What Can Go Wrong?

Before broken-down food particles are assimilated into your bloodstream, your immune system assesses whether they're safe or invading pathogens like bacteria or a virus. When the peace of your digestive tract is disturbed by food proteins that are hard to digest (mainly from grains or beans), an immune response is launched on the offending proteins because they're seen as invaders. You may feel this response in the form of digestive distress, or you may not feel any gastrointestinal upset at all. That's the kicker! Your body's reaction to a particular irritant may be *entirely* different from someone else's. One person's diarrhea is another's eczema, tendonitis, or migraine, for example. In fact, digestive irritation can lead to an inflammatory response *anywhere in your body*.

The problem starts upstream. Downregulated, low, or slow digestive-enzyme signaling or hormone signaling may cause inadequate release of digestive secretions from the liver, gallbladder, and pancreas. Low stomach acid (HCl) or disrupted cholecystokinin (CCK), for example—both "upstream" problems that occur before food reaches the small intestine— set the stage for these issues. If your upstream processes of digestion are broken, you run a greater risk of downstream malfunction as well.

Bacteria, which are found in smaller proportion in the stomach and most abundantly in the large intestine, can creep into the small intestine, promoting small intestinal bacterial overgrowth (SIBO). This can also cause an imbalance in the good and bad bacteria in the stomach that can lead to food intolerances and digestive upset.

The largest issue, however, is leaky gut, a condition that occurs within the small intestine and is 100 percent diet-related. For an explanation of leaky gut and how it contributes to autoimmune conditions, see page 93.

How to Fix It

You guessed it! Avoid foods that are hard to digest: grains and legumes. Also avoid foods that use up nutrients for their processing, yet leave few nutrients behind. These include refined foods, sugar, and alcohol. Your best bet is to follow the advice in the autoimmunity chapter (page 93), which addresses leaky gut.

SUSPECT SIBO?

For a more comprehensive look at SIBO, what it is, how to know if you have it, what to do about it, and how to talk to your doctor about it, check out my free e-book, Simplifying SIBO, *available at balancedbites.com/SIBO.*

The Large Intestine and Rectum

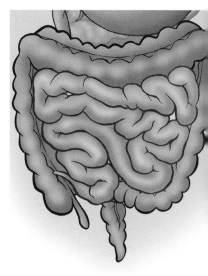

Stretching roughly five feet in length and comprising two parts, the cecum and the colon, your large intestine wraps around your small intestine and begins in the right lower portion of your abdomen, roughly at or below your belly button. It makes up about 20 percent of the entire length of your intestinal canal. Your rectum is the final portion of your large intestine and measures about four and a half to five inches in length.

The large intestine is the site of water absorption and the uptake of any nutrients—specifically micronutrients (vitamins and minerals)—remaining after the small intestine completes the bulk of the hard work. The large intestine's work takes place over roughly twelve to eighteen hours and concludes with the creation and compaction of fecal matter.

Proper gut flora is essential to good digestive function. The large intestine is where the majority of the gut flora (ideally beneficial bacteria, or "probiotics") live, and bacteria compose approximately 80 percent of the dry weight of stool.

What Can Go Wrong?

Inadequate or imbalanced gut flora is one of the primary issues behind poor large intestine function. If your eliminations are small, dense, difficult to pass, and foul-smelling, it can indicate extended transit time—your large intestine is taking too long to pass waste. Food can be in your large intestine for anywhere from ten hours, which is ideal, to three days, which is far too long.

How to Fix It

First of all, make sure that you drink enough water to be well hydrated. You need sufficient lubrication for your food to pass through your system. Don't overload on water, though. Contrary to popular belief, you can drink too much. This is because too much water can dilute your stomach acid if you drink it with meals. So enjoy your water between meals, and drink extra before and after exercise to replace what you lose in your sweat.

Next, add fermented foods to your diet:

- Raw sauerkraut (page 262) or kimchi (a Korean fermented cabbage dish that's similar to sauerkraut). Look for brands that don't contains preservatives and are sold cold.

- Fermented vegetables like shredded carrots (make with the sauerkraut recipe on page 262)

- Plain, full-fat yogurt made from raw, grass-fed milk (cow, goat, or sheep). Homemade, with a twenty-four-hour fermentation process, is best.

- Homemade kombucha (a fermented tea drink)

These fermented foods have moderate levels of probiotic content, which means that, when you eat varying amounts and types on a daily basis, they provide your digestive system with good bacteria. Making these items at home is a cost-effective way to balance the flora in your digestive system.

You can also take a supplement of probiotics in pill or powder form. There is no single brand or strain of probiotic bacteria that works best for everyone, so try one and see how

Is your appendix really useless?

Connected to your large intestine, your appendix was once believed to be a vestigial organ that doesn't have a function in the body and is expendable. But is that true? It is now believed that your appendix may enhance your immunity by holding a blueprint for your beneficial gut flora (intestinal bacteria).

Anytime you have to take antibiotics, for example, you wipe out all of your good intestinal bacteria. How does your body then restore the flora it needs? It initializes a recolonization of gut flora, and your appendix may play a part in this initialization, as well as determining the type of flora your body needs. With the proper balance of gut flora, your body is better able to fight off infections.

So what if your appendix has been removed? In that case, it's even more important to eat probiotic-rich foods and reinoculate with fermented foods and probiotic supplements.

you feel after taking it for a week. If your digestion improves, you have found a good one for you. If not, try another one with different bacterial strains or more potent quantities of bacteria. (Just compare the ingredients lists.)

Probiotic supplementation is also a good idea if you suffer from frequent diarrhea. When your digestive system rejects a food quickly, it often throws the baby out with the bathwater, so to speak, flushing the rest of the contents of your small and large intestines along with the irritant it decided was harmful. This may result in an imbalance in your gut flora that leaves your bowel movements feeling "off" for several days. Reinoculating with probiotics can help get your bathroom habits back on track.

Some probiotic supplements are sold in the refrigerated section of a health food or grocery store, while others are stored on the shelves. Which is better? It depends. While the refrigerated options are better protected and potentially fresher, some practitioners believe that if the probiotic needs to be refrigerated before you consume it, it stands little chance of remaining intact until it arrives where it's needed in your digestive system. But everyone is different, and I believe that finding the right probiotic for you is more a matter of trial and error. The proof is in the poop! And there's a good chance you won't need to try more than three, at most, to find a supplement that works for you.

Be sure to eat good sources of soluble fiber as well, including sweet potatoes, plantains, taro root, cassava, butternut squash, and any other vegetable, root, or tuber with starchy flesh. These feed the good bacteria and allow them to improve your digestion. Be sure to peel or remove any skin on these vegetables; it contains insoluble fiber, which is quite difficult to digest.

Diet isn't the only thing you need to address for optimal large intestine function. If you're stressed, your body isn't able to maintain its normal peristaltic (digestive muscle) motions, which move food particles through your digestive system. Stress can cause these muscle contractions to speed up or slow down. This happens frequently in travelers whose bodies are just "off" due to time changes, air pressure changes during airplane flights, or changes in the types of foods they eat.

Even changing your position during a bowel movement can help. Sitting on a toilet actually works against the way we were designed to defecate naturally because it causes the rectum to maintain a bent shape. On the other hand, squatting allows the rectum to achieve a straightened shape for easy stool passage.

Quick Tips for Optimizing Digestion

Brain: Your brain talks to your stomach and the rest of your digestive system. The best thing that you can do is sit down and relax before eating any food, whether it's a snack or a full meal. Take the time to decompress and get into the right state of mind for slow, mindful eating. Getting into rest-and-digest mode is the first step in digesting food properly.

Mouth, salivary glands, and esophagus: First, avoid foods high in antinutrients (grains and legumes), which resist digestive processing. Second, chew your food thoroughly, until it feels almost liquid in your mouth. Third, eliminate digestion-resistant insoluble fiber from your diet by avoiding whole grains, corn, and the skins of starchy tubers. If you experience gas, bloating, or undigested food in your stool, it is best to also limit leafy greens, cauliflower, apples, and pears, all of which are also sources of insoluble fiber.

Stomach: Remember that heartburn, acid reflux, belching, bloating after meals, and undigested food in your stool are all signs that your stomach acid is too low, not too high. Alter your diet, and take lemon juice, apple cider vinegar, or digestive bitters to increase your body's natural production of HCl and improve the integrity of your stomach's mucosal lining. This will help to ensure that you have adequate stomach acid to properly digest your food.

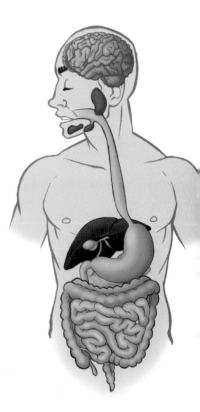

Liver and gallbladder: Pay close attention to how you feel after fatty meals, and check the color of your stools. Any pain or discomfort may indicate that you're not digesting fats well and that your liver and gallbladder need support. Be very strict about eliminating all grain products from your diet, and take supplemental digestive enzymes and ox bile if dietary changes don't bring enough improvement. Long-term damage can require more support and takes more time to heal, but eliminating grains and reducing overall stress are the critical first steps.

Pancreas: Remember that what happens early in the digestive process affects what happens downstream, and that adequate levels of stomach acid are critical for signaling the pancreas to secrete the appropriate amount of digestive enzymes. Your pancreas is smart, and it essentially "reads" the chyme from the stomach to determine its secretions before food moves on through your small intestine. If you have symptoms of poor digestion, or if you know that you have compromised pancreatic function, supplementing with digestive enzymes may be a good idea.

Small intestine: Any inflammatory condition is likely rooted in your ability to properly digest and absorb your food. If you struggle with acne, psoriasis, joint pain, or even an advanced autoimmune condition, you may be able to resolve the issue by healing your small intestine and getting it to function in a calm state rather than a chronic state of immune response.

Large intestine and rectum: If you're constipated, it should be your first order of business to get to the root of the problem and resolve it. If that means some short-term supplementation of probiotics until you can either buy or make your own fermented foods, that's what you should do. Constipation can be quite painful, as well as toxic. Food should move through your body in a timely fashion (about eighteen to twenty-four hours in total).

So, What's the Plan?

If, upon reading this chapter, you've discovered that healing your digestion needs to be your priority, then your best bet is to start following the Digestive Health 30-Day Meal Plan (page 192).

If you're trying to manage more than one health challenge, review the advice on selecting a meal plan (page 158) to dive deeper.

Guide to: Digestion

Since 60 to 80 percent of your immune system is in your gut, improving digestive function is the first step to calming systemic inflammation. When your digestion is working smoothly, without irritation, and your bowel transit time is healthy, your body's ability to maintain health is optimized and your immunity to infections improves.

improving digestive function

1. Relax and get yourself into rest-and-digest mode.

2. Chew your food slowly and completely to begin digestive signaling between your brain and your mouth and to prepare food for further breakdown in the stomach.

3. Minimize water intake with meals to maintain stomach acid concentration. Drink water in between meals when thirsty to promote healthy transit time and ensure food doesn't linger in the large intestine.

4. Avoid foods that are irritating to the system (primarily refined foods, grain products, legumes, and processed dairy) to allow for the best possible function of the small intestinal lining.

5. Avoid other dietary and lifestyle practices that promote leaky gut (as outlined on the guide to healing a leaky gut, page 106).

6. Eat probiotic foods regularly: sauerkraut, kimchi, other fermented vegetables, kombucha, and yogurt and kefir made from raw, grass-fed milk.

7. Use a box or platform to elevate your feet when eliminating. The more natural squatting position may help stool pass more easily.

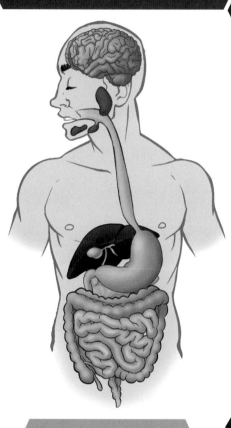

signs & symptoms of DISRUPTED DIGESTION

Belching
Bloating
Gas
Diarrhea
Gurgling

Problems with stool (see page 92)
Chronic inflammation

test your transit time

A healthy transit time is between 18 and 24 hours.

1. Swallow 2 tablespoons of white sesame seeds following a meal.

2. Note the time and date when the seeds are swallowed.

3. Watch your eliminations for the bulk of the seeds. While a few may be visible here or there, most of them will appear together. They will be intact.

4. Note the time and date when the seeds are eliminated.

too FAST?

Your diet may include foods that irritate your digestive system, and your body is attempting to move these foods through more quickly.

too SLOW?

Your diet may need more soluble fiber and good bacteria (probiotics). Additionally, be sure that you are drinking plenty of water in between meals and that you are finding enough time during the day to relax.

chronic inflammatory conditions CAN ALL BE RELATED TO POOR DIGESTIVE FUNCTION

Acne
Allergies
Alopecia
Alzheimer's disease
Amenorrhea
Anemia
Anxiety
Arthritis, rheumatoid arthritis
Asthma
Atherosclerosis
Attention deficit disorder (ADD)
Autoimmunity
Bloating

Bone diseases
Calcium deficiency
Cancer
Canker sores
Celiac disease
Chronic fatigue syndrome
Crohn's disease
Depression
Dermatitis
Diabetes (types 1 and 2)
Diverticulitis
Dyslexia
Eczema

Edema
Endometriosis
Epilepsy
Fatigue, lethargy
Fibromyalgia
Fibrosis
Gallbladder disease
Gastric ulcers
Heart disease
Hepatitis
Infertility
Inflammatory bowel disease
Irritable bowel syndrome

Joint pain and disease
Kidney disease
Lactose intolerance
Liver disease
Lupus
Migraines
Mood disorders
Multiple sclerosis
Nephritis
Pancreatitis
Parkinson's disease
Polycystic ovary syndrome, hormonal imbalances

Pre- and postnatal difficulties, including difficulty breast-feeding, infertility, and miscarriage
Psoriasis
Thyroid disorders
Ulcerative colitis
Vitamin and mineral deficiencies
Vitiligo
Weight gain
Weight loss

Guide to: Your Poop!

Understanding your eliminations will help you to figure out exactly what's going on with your digestive system. Track whether your toilet sees Ms. Ideal most often, or if some of her less-than-beautiful competitors are creeping onto the stage more than once in a while.

know your poop IT CAN TEACH YOU A LOT

FROM LEFT TO RIGHT, LET'S MEET OUR CONTESTANTS!

ms. ideal

Medium brown in color and solidly formed in the shape of an S or a C, passing easily and regularly one to two times per day.

ms. show off

Varying in color and generally solidly formed, she shows you pieces of foods you recently ate in their semi-whole, visibly identifiable form. She's what you'll see if you are not fully digesting your food and can indicate low stomach acid or a food intolerance.

ms. runny

Varying in color and generally unformed, she shows you pieces of foods you recently ate in their semi-whole, visibly identifiable form. She's what you'll see if you have eaten a food to which your body is reacting strongly and the "everybody out!" mechanism has been initiated. After a bout of diarrhea (multiple instances of loose stool over the course of one or more days), it is important to reinoculate your gut with probiotic content.

ms. rocky

Generally dark in color and formed into small balls or pellet shapes, she's what you'll see if you are experiencing a gut flora imbalance, dehydration, or stress, or if you're not eating enough soluble fiber. If she's in your toilet, your number-one priority is to get rid of her! Probiotic foods (or supplements, if you can't tolerate the foods), starchy vegetables, proper hydration, and meditative breathing will all help to get her moving on out.

ms. muscles

Generally medium to dark brown in color and with a shape that's a bit thicker and tougher to pass, she's what you'll see if you are eating a lot of processed forms of protein—shakes, bars, or even processed meats. If you see her, swap your processed forms of protein for whole forms like grass-fed steak, pasture-raised eggs, and wild-caught fish.

ms. swim team

Generally light, greenish, or even white in color, she's what you'll see if you have eaten refined, processed, or man-made fats, refined seed oils, or more natural fat than you can digest, or if your gallbladder isn't able to properly release bile in response to the fat you've eaten. Avoid bad fats, and consider having your gallbladder checked.

ms. toxic

Dark in color, strong in odor, and generally sinking to the bottom of the bowl, she's what you'll see if you have eaten too many processed or refined foods, you're eating a lot of nonorganic foods, or you're experiencing a general toxicity overload from your environment, personal care products, diet (particularly artificial sweeteners), habits (smoking), and use of plastics. Opt for organic, fresh, whole foods and plenty of water, and seek out ways to lower the toxin load in other areas of your life.

Illustration adapted with permission from *How to Eat, Move and Be Healthy!* by Paul Chek

Addressing Autoimmunity

An autoimmune disease develops when your immune system misidentifies your own body's cells as foreign and launches an attack upon them.

The kind of autoimmune disease you have, and therefore the symptoms you experience, depends on the kinds of cells that the body is attacking. For example, Hashimoto's thyroiditis is an autoimmune disease of the thyroid cells, while rheumatoid arthritis is an autoimmune disease of the joint tissue cells.

Leaky gut is often a major contributing factor to the initiation of autoimmune disease—in fact, it's at the root of almost every inflammatory condition—and it can also exacerbate the disease once it has begun. For this reason, both prevention and healing of leaky gut are critical. Our best defense against autoimmune diseases to which we may be genetically predisposed is to prevent or heal a leaky gut.

If you have already been diagnosed with an autoimmune condition, your best bet is to live in a way that consistently supports healing a leaky gut, since your gut is already weakened. This continuous care is important: about 25 percent of those with a single autoimmune disease go on to develop others.

What Is a Leaky Gut?

What happens in your small intestine doesn't always *stay* in your small intestine. Much of what goes on in the rest of your body begins with what happens in this organ, otherwise known as your gut. If you're dealing with an autoimmune condition, allergies, food intolerances, or other chronic inflammatory conditions, you're also dealing with a leaky gut.

small intestine lining: microvilli   **small intestine lining: villi**

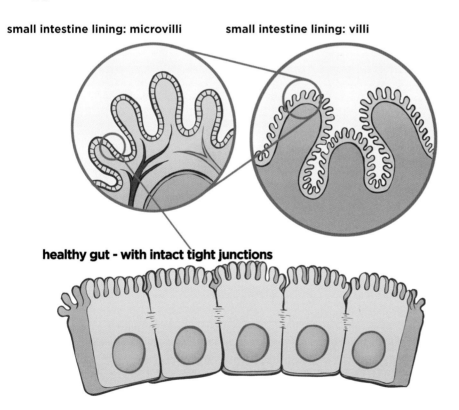

healthy gut - with intact tight junctions

So how does your gut become "leaky"? Clinically known as "increased intestinal permeability," leaky gut is a condition in which the cells that line your small intestine begin to lose their integrity. In a healthy gut, the lining of the small intestine allows nutrients to pass through while keeping bacteria, viruses, and other dangerous pathogens out of your bloodstream. For a myriad of reasons, this process can stop working properly. The normal tight junctions between the cells of the lining loosen, causing the entire defense system against invaders to become compromised. Rather than only allowing fully broken-down proteins in the form of single or short chains of amino acids to pass into your bloodstream, it allows larger, partially undigested chains of amino acids (proteins) to pass through. This is normal in infants, as their systems are not yet fully developed, but in adults, it leads to a myriad of health concerns and uncomfortable symptoms.

When food particles that are too large slip intact through the weakened and compromised lining of the small intestine, they interact with the layer of immune-system tissue on the other side of the brush border lining of your small intestine, which is known as gut-associated lymphoid tissue (GALT). At this layer, inflammatory molecules called cytokines respond to the intact food particles and tell your white blood cells to launch an attack.

This is the same type of immune response that happens when allergens or invaders like bacteria or viruses enter your body. In an effort to fix the problem, your body reads this scenario as disease and creates an inflammatory response.

LEAKY GUT—WITH *IMPAIRED* TIGHT JUNCTIONS

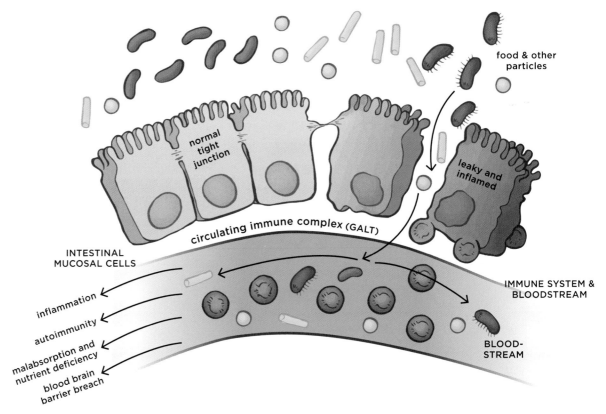

As you can see, your small intestine is an active part of your immune system, not just your digestive system. It's a barrier and a gatekeeper. And as Alessio Fasano, gastroenterologist and leading researcher in the field of celiac disease, autoimmunity, and intestinal permeability, put it, "increased permeability . . . can cause inflammation in a district distant from where the breach in intestinal barrier occurs." This is where systemic inflammation comes into the picture.

What Is Systemic Inflammation?

I have mentioned inflammation several times, but let's get clear on what it means inside your body. Inflammation is a biological response to infection, damaged cells, and other irritants. These all signal your immune system to initiate inflammation in the affected tissue to help treat the problem and send white blood cells to fix the problem. As your white blood cells do their work, they release free radicals, which are what can cause pain or discomfort—not the inflammation itself.

The inflammatory process in and of itself is not necessarily harmful. In fact, inflammation is necessary for survival. Acute inflammation is part of the healing process for a skin lesion like a cut, scrape, burn, or bruise, or when you have a trauma, like a golf ball hitting you in the head. It may also be a response to a tough workout or a minor sinus infection or cold. Our bodies are well equipped to deal with this type of inflammation, and, in an otherwise healthy person, the immune system can remain armed to handle this type of intermittent damage.

The problem occurs when, rather than being left to handle acute issues, your immune system is overworked by chronic irritation. When microscopic undigested food particles get into your bloodstream on a regular basis, your immune system is constantly responding to these invaders, creating chronic, systemic inflammation. It's like being in a constant state of low-grade infection. Your immune system never gets downtime between healing one problem and gearing up for another one, and an overworked immune system is less able to fight infections, cancer, diabetes, heart disease, and other diseases, and it's more likely to aggressively respond to environmental allergens like pollen, dust, and mold. Sixty to eighty percent of your immune system is located in your gut as GALT, and with that portion busy dealing with invading food particles, your body may only be able to use about 20 to 40 percent of your potential immune response to fight off that cold that's going around the office.

Know this: Food particles that pass through your gut lining without being broken down completely are seen as invaders, and your body responds in the same way it does to a virus or bacterial infection.

An even bigger problem is that a primed, overactive immune response may cascade into something even more serious: autoimmunity. All of our cells are made up of amino acids—the same amino acids that make up the protein we eat. In the case of a leaky gut, some of the undigested food particles that pass into your bloodstream contain amino acid chains that mimic body tissue proteins, or "self cells," and the resulting immune attack is launched indiscriminately. This means that your body attacks *both* the invading food-based amino acid chain *and* the similar or matching amino acid chains of the self cells.

ARE YOU INFLAMED?
Inflammation may rear its ugly head in a myriad of ways. To work on healing your digestive process as well as a leaky gut, check out the guides on pages 91 and 106.

MOLECULAR MIMICRY EXAMPLE:

AMINO ACIDS IN A GLUTEN PROTEIN   AMINO ACIDS IN A BODY (SELF) CELL

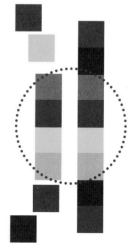

The cells under attack can be part of any body tissues, whether organs, hormones, or joint tissue. *This is what is called an autoimmune response—one in which the body attacks itself.* (Keep in mind, this isn't the same as an *immune response*, in which the body attacks foreign molecules.) For a list of some of the chronic inflammatory conditions related to poor digestive function, see page 91.

What Causes Leaky Gut?

The answer to what causes leaky gut is, in one sense, simple: stress! But there are many kinds of stressors, including environmental—which is usually what we think about stress and includes things like work, family, and lifestyle—and physical. Here, we'll focus first on a cause of physical stress: food. Food can cause stress on our system in multiple ways. Antinutrients in the foods we eat can cause immune flares or block the absorption of nutrients we need for energy and optimal functioning, and when we eat too many foods that are lacking in micronutrients, we aren't getting what our cells need to function properly.

Antinutrients

COULD

=

A LEAKY
GUT?

Let's look first at antinutrients. These are primarily plant-based defense mechanisms that are concentrated around the reproductive force in a seed or grain. Consider this: every living thing has a defense mechanism. Plants can't run away when they're under attack, so to ensure that they continue to thrive and grow, they have internal defenses to fight against predators. To the plant, and more specifically the seed or grain of a plant (its reproductive force), you are just such a predator. The plant's defense mechanisms— antinutrients—fight against your digestive system, blocking your ability to fully break the food down into harmless amino acids that are easily absorbed into your cells. In other words, antinutrients are elements within a food that either prevent or disrupt the proper digestion and absorption of the nutrients contained in that food.

Some believe that our bodies have simply not developed the digestive enzymes necessary to tolerate foods that contain antinutrients. It may also be that our modern upbringing has not supported the complete and healthy development of our digestive systems so that we might be able to tolerate these foods when eaten as a *small* part of our diet. So many of our modern habits contribute to weakened digestive function—a lifetime of eating refined foods, grain products, processed and pasteurized dairy products, and sugar, as well as round after round of antibiotics, stress, NSAID painkillers, and alcohol.

While your system is fully equipped to handle animal proteins, which don't carry antinutrients, eating large quantities of digestion-resistant foods—primarily grains—day after day can wreak havoc. Large quantities, in this case, can mean even just one slice of bread, one cracker, or a small serving of pasta. *Any portion of grain products can cause problems in your body.* Each time you eat one of these small portions, you consume hundreds or even thousands of tiny, antinutrient-bearing Trojan horses.

There are different kinds of antinutrients, and they affect your body in different ways. It's worth understanding a bit about how antinutrients work.

The following foods are richest in antinutrients:

- Whole grains, whole grain products, grain-like seeds, and legumes, including, but not limited to, wheat, barley, rye, oats, spelt, brown rice, corn, quinoa, lentils, red beans, black beans, pinto beans, and navy beans
- Refined grains and refined grain products, including white rice, flour, bread, cereal, crackers, cookies, and pasta

It's amazing, isn't it, that our culture's diet is centered around these antinutrient-rich foods? If I told you I had an omelet for breakfast, a slice of quiche for lunch, and an egg soufflé for dinner, you might say, "Isn't that a lot of eggs?" Yet if I had eaten cereal for breakfast, a sandwich for lunch, and pasta for dinner, it probably wouldn't occur to you to ask, "Isn't that a lot of grains?"

Most of the foods at stores and restaurants—pretty much everywhere, really—are at least partially grain-based. Even though our eating habits didn't center around grains for most of human history, we're so accustomed to grain-based foods today—both refined and so-called "whole" grains—that we seldom wonder if we're overdoing it. We have been taught that it's easy to digest grains. Not so! They're chock-full of difficult-to-digest antinutrients.

The methods of preparing grains and legumes that were used by traditional cultures helped neutralize antinutrients and made grains easier to digest. Even just a few decades ago, people knew that simply picking grains and legumes from plants and grinding them did not make them suitable for consumption, and that there are ways to make them more digestible by taking advantage of the way they work in nature. While the outer portion of grains and legumes forms a barrier when planted, the nutrients inside are there to fuel the seed on its mission to grow into a plant. Through soaking, sprouting, and fermenting, we can essentially trick grains and legumes (as well as seeds and nuts, for that matter) into thinking that they've been planted, allowing them to release some of their antinutrients and make their vitamins and minerals available and accessible.

Nevertheless, even if most people were willing to soak, sprout, and ferment their grains before eating them, these processes only help us digest grains and legumes slightly better. The reality is that meat, vegetables, and naturally occurring fats are all more nutrient-dense and less irritating to the gut than sprouted grains.

Phytates. Also known as phytic acid, phytates are indigestible, mineral-binding compounds found in the hulls of grains, legumes, nuts, and seeds. While ruminant animals like cows, sheep, and goats have adequate enzymes in their digestive systems to break down phytates, nonruminants, like humans, do not. Phytates bind to minerals within foods, including calcium, magnesium, iron, and zinc, and this process prevents their absorption in our bodies. This means that we're unable to actually use the minerals we consume when the food they're in also contains phytates.

Just how important are these minerals? Minerals play a role in every cellular function in your body. They are responsible for the proper formation and regeneration of structural tissues to prevent you from easily sustaining injuries such as fractures, broken bones, and torn ligaments. Minerals also serve as antioxidants to help you fight cancer, and they protect against heart disease by mediating the appropriate constriction and relaxation of blood vessels. Proper mineral reserves are also necessary to regulate hormones for fertility and stress management, among other things. There is no end to the number of body systems and tissues that require minerals for proper function. We simply need them for everything!

Mineral deficiencies can result in a myriad of symptoms, including suppressed immunity, fatigue, insomnia, irritability, heart palpitations, muscle cramps, restless leg syndrome, muscle spasms, asthma, migraines, constipation, and hormonal imbalances like premenstrual syndrome (PMS), polycystic ovary syndrome (PCOS), and infertility in both men and women.

We already know that soils today are depleted in mineral content, so the vegetables and fruits we eat are far less mineral-rich than those our ancestors ate. The high-stress, high-sugar, modern lifestyle also tends to deplete our systems of minerals, which means we need even more perhaps than our ancestors did when we go through life events like growth spurts, puberty, pregnancy, infection, intense exercise, illness, high stress, trauma, and surgery. All of these factors create a greater need for minerals and other nutrients. Therefore, we have to make sure not only that we get sufficient amounts in our diets but also that we're able to use the minerals we ingest. What's the point of eating a nutrient-rich food if your body can't actually access the nutrients?

Grains and legumes are not the only plants that contain phytates; nuts and seeds contain them, too. However, for most nuts and seeds, the hard outer shell is the first barrier to accessing the reproductive force of the plant, and once the shell is removed, most people tolerate them well in small quantities, though only as part of a balanced, mineral-rich Paleo diet. Phytates are the main reason why large quantities of nuts and seeds are not recommended. (You will notice that nuts and seeds are eliminated entirely in some of the meal plans in the book. This is to offer the best possible chance of healing for people with certain health conditions.)

Know this: You can absorb more of the minerals you consume in foods like leafy greens and bone broth by removing grains from your diet and limiting nuts and seeds. Remember that phytates keep minerals out of reach of your body's systems.

Lectins. These are sugar-binding proteins that are resistant to digestive enzymes and stomach acid. They are abundant in the seeds of plants and become less concentrated as the plant grows. They can stick to the cells in the lining of the small intestine, altering the texture of the cell walls and impairing digestive function.

Minerals are so important for our bodies—magnesium alone is required to complete over 300 enzymatic processes! Most of us don't obtain enough magnesium from our diets, so nutritionists frequently suggest that their clients take magnesium supplements.

We need the cells that line our small intestine to remain intact and ready to absorb nutrients. If they become sticky from overconsumption of lectin-rich foods, like grains and legumes, digestion becomes quite difficult. Grains and legumes are actually the seeds of plants, and when you eat a grain product, you're eating hundreds, if not thousands, of seeds. That's a lot of concentrated lectins!

Saponins. Bitter-tasting, soaplike molecules with the ability to puncture or create pores in cell membranes, saponins are often used as carriers for vaccines due to their ability to infiltrate cells. Saponins are the main antinutrient in quinoa. They also have the ability to stimulate an immune response from within your cells and can upregulate antibody production. When you create more antibodies, your body gets revved up to launch an immune response at the first sign of an undigested food particle in your bloodstream. This is what causes digestive distress after eating certain foods, but even if you don't experience digestive distress, it can lead to the more behind-the-scenes chronic inflammation. Remember, you don't want to eat foods that cause an immune response of any kind.

Gluten and Zonulin

You've probably seen the proliferation of gluten-free products in your supermarket in recent years. Gluten, which can cause health problems for so many people, is a protein found in wheat, barley, rye, and triticale. Gluten develops further when the proteins gliadin and glutenin within the grains are either manually or mechanically kneaded together along with a liquid. It is present in both sprouted and unsprouted whole grains, as well as in whole and refined grain flours.

In people with gluten sensitivity, the root of the problem is that gluten increases the body's levels of a molecule called zonulin. Simply put, zonulin, like antinutrients, loosens the tight junction between the cells in the lining of the small intestine. This can be an important part of the immune response—if you consume a dangerous bacteria, for instance, zonulin loosens those junctions to help flush out your system and get rid of the bacteria. But when there's no invader to respond to, keeping those junctions loose allows too-large intact food particles into the bloodstream, which is a factor in the development of inflammation, autoimmune diseases, and cancer.

Eggs contain antinutrients, too

As the reproductive force of the chicken (or other animal laying them), eggs contain built-in defense mechanisms that help them to resist predation, beyond the slight protection of their thin, easily cracked shells. When the mama bird gets up and walks away from her nest, antinutrients protect the eggs and help to warn other animals against their consumption. While most people are well adapted to eating eggs, some are sensitive to them for this reason.

Zonulin's action upon tight junctions is primarily triggered by the gliadin protein in gluten as well as exposure to bacteria. (Note that we're referring just to bacteria in the small intestine—gut bacteria that's helpful and necessary in the large intestine doesn't belong in the small intestine, and its presence there may be related to a condition known as small intestinal bacterial overgrowth, or SIBO.) When people with celiac disease—an autoimmune disease in which the consumption of gluten triggers the immune system to attack the lining of the small intestine—remove gluten from their diets, the autoimmune response shuts off as the level of zonulin decreases. According to Fasano, "Once gluten is removed from the diet, serum zonulin levels decrease, the intestine resumes its baseline barrier function, the autoantibody titers are normalized, the autoimmune process shuts off and, consequently, the intestinal damage (that represents the biological outcome of the autoimmune process) heals completely."

But it's not only those with celiac disease who experience trouble with gluten. Others who have a reaction to gluten are often referred to as having non-celiac gluten sensitivity (NCGS). There may be multiple reasons for the reaction: the presence of bacteria in the small intestine, for instance, or an intolerance to foods with high levels of FODMAPs (which, coincidentally, may also be related to the bacteria or SIBO—see page 149 for more on FODMAPs). There are so many intertwined reasons why someone may not tolerate gluten, and gluten intolerance can be temporary or lifelong. If you think you are experiencing a gluten intolerance but do not have celiac disease, working through the 4R Protocol (page 44) is your best bet for getting to the root of your discomfort and resolving it. For many with NCGS, consistently avoiding gluten may be required.

Other Stressors

There are many other stressors that are also related to leaky gut, including:

- physical or emotional trauma or stress (acute or chronic)
- anxiety
- overtraining/overexercising
- undereating
- NSAID painkillers
- antibiotics

Wheat as a source of protein?

Since the proteins in wheat are insoluble in water, the starch surrounding them can be washed away, and the isolated proteins can be added to foods to increase their protein levels. This is less common in the United States, but people in third-world countries often seek protein in gluten—although, because these lack some of the amino acids humans need, it's possible to be protein-deficient even while eating gluten-containing foods. In the United States, the isolated proteins are often added to flours to create high-gluten flour, which improves the texture of baked goods. They are also used to create wheat-based protein products that are often consumed by vegetarians or vegans in the form of seitan or meat-free "meats."

You'll find even more factors listed in the guide on page 106. If you're trying to heal a leaky gut, it's important to consider all these factors, not just the food you eat. In fact, many people who are eating and supplementing with everything "right" to heal a leaky gut (and following the 4R Protocol on page 44) find that one of these other stressors is at the root of their ongoing food intolerance and leaky gut symptoms. If you aren't experiencing the relief you expect once you've dialed in your nutrition, it's critical to pay attention to the holistic view of your health.

How Do You Know If You Have Leaky Gut?

The signs and symptoms of leaky gut include:

- multiple food allergies/intolerances
- difficulty digesting a wide variety of foods
- digestive upset (constipation or diarrhea)
- brain fog
- heightened seasonal or environmental allergies
- skin irritation (acne, eczema, psoriasis, rashes)
- autoimmunity (including autoimmune diseases such as rheumatoid arthritis, Hashimoto's thyroiditis, and psoriasis)
- nutrient deficiencies
- low energy

More symptoms are listed in the guide to healing a leaky gut (page 106).

Sound dismal? Don't sweat it! Leaky gut can usually be reversed by changing your diet and lifestyle. You can take an active role in improving the function of your gut barrier, which, in turn, will improve your immunity and ability to resist chronic diseases.

Figuring Out Your Food Intolerances

If you have trouble tolerating many foods, it's a strong sign that the real problem is a leaky gut. How do you know if your body can't tolerate a particular food? Most overt food allergies result in identifiable, immediate forms of discomfort. Someone with a tree nut or shellfish allergy knows immediately when they've eaten something they shouldn't: they often experience an itchy feeling in the mouth or a closed-up throat. Those who suffer from lactose intolerance can tell you how it feels shortly after they eat the offending dairy product—gas, bloating, or digestive discomfort. Those are all very obvious signs.

When it comes to grains, many—perhaps even most—people experience some kind of discomfort, whether acute or chronic, but not always the expected digestive discomfort. While some people have obvious allergies to protein constituents in grains (those diagnosed with celiac disease experience an autoimmune response to gluten proteins, for example), inflammation problems are usually caused by some level of *intolerance* to grains and legumes. If someone experiences symptoms after eating, they likely blame a food other than the grains, or they attribute the problem to something other than food. This is what makes grain intolerance so problematic. Many of the symptoms are not easily connected to diet, and delayed-onset reactions, including the chronic inflammatory conditions listed on page 91, are common.

You can experience food allergy or intolerance symptoms up to seventy-two hours after eating a meal. This means that even a food you ate *three days ago* can cause seemingly unrelated symptoms *today*. Those symptoms may be from one of the array of inflammatory conditions that go beyond digestive distress, or you may have a symptom that isn't on the list at all, all of which can make it difficult to figure out what food is causing the problem. Luckily, there's a method for determining the culprit.

When you experience a food intolerance reaction, your body is, in effect, under attack. You must allow your body to recover from the attack by avoiding the offending food(s) for at least two weeks (preferably three or four), which is how long it takes for the entire lining of your small intestine to heal. After that, you can gradually reintroduce the potentially offending foods to determine your intolerances—if you can't tolerate the food, you will have an identifiable response to it when you eat it again. This is what is called an "elimination/provocation diet" and it's the key to the 4R Protocol, which is explained in more detail on page 44. It works because your immune system gets a chance to rest and calm down before you try a potentially problematic food.

If you didn't have such a severe reaction when you were eating that problematic food more frequently, is it possible that you'd be able to acclimate your body to the food by eating a little of it every day? Unfortunately, it isn't that simple. This is where the chronic negative effects of a grain or other food intolerance really wreak havoc. The effects that you don't feel immediately are often far worse than the ones you do feel. This is the difference between an *acute* inflammatory response and a *chronic* inflammatory response. In the acute response, you feel the effects right away. Your body communicates, "This isn't good; don't eat it again!" The chronic response, however, leaves your body's systems overwhelmed with inflammation and stress due to an ongoing onslaught of the food. You don't have to be aware of the problem for it to become systemic and dangerous!

How Can You Prevent Leaky Gut?

If you currently feel healthy overall and don't experience any allergies, food intolerances, digestive issues, or other chronic inflammatory symptoms, then you may very well not have a leaky gut. If that's the case, give yourself a pat yourself on the back, because it's pretty rare to have an intact gut without having taken the steps I'm about to outline to heal it. Why? Well, most of us have been eating foods and make lifestyle choices day in and day out that promote leaky gut. And most of us have never taken the time to heal it.

So, to prevent leaky gut from happening, there are two great starting points: avoiding the factors that promote it and working to manage stress on a regular basis. However, for even better protection, I recommend that you regularly consume gut-healing foods like bone broth (or soups and stews that contain broth), anti-inflammatory foods like organic vegetables and fruits, and potent, antioxidant-rich herbs and spices like cilantro, turmeric, and cinnamon. More details on foods that support healthy digestion can be found in the Digestive Health 30-Day Meal Plan beginning on page 192.

"ALLERGIC" TO EVERYTHING?

If you've been tested for food allergies and the results showed that you're allergic to 50 foods, chances are you're not actually allergic to or even intolerant of all of those foods—you probably have a leaky gut! Once you heal your gut, it's likely that far fewer of those foods will cause any irritation.

When you're avoiding gluten and grains, finding flours to use can be tricky! While the flours listed below cannot be substituted 1:1 for wheat flour, many recipes for grain-free baked items detail how to blend them together.

NUT & SEED FLOURS	STARCHES & ROOT FLOURS
Almond flour/meal	Arrowroot starch/powder
Cashew flour (not strict Paleo, but grain-free)*	Cassava flour
Chestnut flour	Potato starch/flour
Coconut flour	Sweet potato flour/starch
Garbanzo flour (not strict Paleo, but grain-free)	Tapioca starch/flour
Hazelnut flour/meal*	
Peanut flour (not strict Paleo, but grain-free)	
Pecan flour/meal*	
Sunflower seed flour*	
Walnut flour/meal*	

*For recipes within this book, may be used interchangeably with almond flour or meal. Coconut flour absolutely cannot be used 1:1 for other types of nut flours—it's much higher in fiber and lower in protein and will not work the same way. If a recipe calls for 1 tablespoon of coconut flour as a thickener or to remove some moisture from a batter, for example, you can try 1 to 3 tablespoons of almond flour or another asterisked flour.

What Can You Do If You Think You Have a Leaky Gut?

Manage Stress

Managing stress is one of the best ways to start to improve leaky gut. This helps to reduce cortisol, your body's fight-or-flight hormone. Making cortisol places extreme demands on your body. In fact, my clients have consistently reported better digestive function on days of lower stress, like weekends and vacations. Incidentally, we could probably significantly reduce the need for several classes of medications, including antacids and NSAIDs, by reducing stress. Meditation, yoga, golf, walking, listening to relaxing music, and even fun activities with friends and family can all reduce stress.

Pay Attention to Your Diet

If you have an autoimmune condition, you may always have a leaky gut to some degree. This doesn't mean you should throw in the towel, however, and eat foods that you know contribute to the problem. If you have a known autoimmune condition, that's all the more reason to keep your diet and lifestyle ducks in a row. This gives your gut the best possible chance of properly digesting food and assimilating nutrients.

Most people who have one or more of the chronic inflammatory conditions listed on page 91 and change their diet report that their symptoms improve within anywhere from two weeks to six months. Even if you cannot control all the factors that caused your leaky gut, you may very well be able to take control of your health in ways you never thought possible and cross a few chronic conditions off your list.

Know this: If your health is not optimal, eliminate gut-irritating, antinutrient-rich foods—grains, legumes, processed dairy, and other refined foods—and you'll likely experience a dramatic improvement in your health. Oh, wait, that sounds an awful lot like a Paleo diet!

See a Health-Care Practitioner If You Like

You can see a health-care practitioner and have some diagnostic tests done if you want, but it's not critical—in most cases, the 4R Protocol (below) is truly the best approach. If you do want to have a test done, the lactulose-mannitol ratio test is the gold standard. For this test, you'll need to fast overnight, give an initial urine sample, and then consume a challenge drink containing lactulose and mannitol, two sugar molecules. After that, a second urine sample will show if your body was able to metabolize these two sugars or if they passed through your system undigested.

Based on the results of the test, your practitioner can determine the factors that are impacting your leaky gut most—whether it's a gluten sensitivity, a digestive infection, or any of the other contributing factors. While the exact cause is often difficult to pinpoint, this provides a starting point for the healing process, which always begins with the 4R Protocol.

Cyrex Labs also offers a test called the Intestinal Antigenic Permeability Screen that measures the immune response to undigested food particles.

Start the 4R Protocol

The most important step in healing a leaky gut is starting the 4R Protocol. It can be helpful for anyone dealing with any kind of digestive issue, but it's particularly beneficial in treating a leaky gut. The 4R Protocol is covered in more detail on page 44, but here are the basics.

Remove

ELIMINATE common dietary irritants: processed and refined foods, alcohol, grains, legumes, dairy, refined seed oils, and sugar.

AVOID anti-inflammatory medications, particularly NSAIDs.

Repair

EAT at least two to three 4-ounce servings of fatty cold-water fish (such as salmon, mackerel, and sardines) per week.

EAT at least 1 cup per day of starchy vegetables and fruits like sweet potatoes, butternut squash, and plantains.

EAT at least 1 cup per day of homemade bone broth, either in soups or stews or on its own.

DRINK 1 to 4 cups per day of herbal tea, such as peppermint and licorice root, and/or fresh aloe vera juice.

DRINK at least 32 ounces (4 cups) of water per day (in addition to the herbal tea recommended above).

SUPPLEMENT with 5 to 8 mg of L-glutamine per day to help repair the gut lining.

SUPPLEMENT with quercitin, a powerful antioxidant, to help with inflammation, and with deglycerized licorice (DGL), slippery elm, or marshmallow extract to promote the repair of the gut's mucosal lining.

Note: You may find a gut-healing supplement that includes many of these together in powder form.

Reinoculate

EAT probiotic foods like raw sauerkraut (page 262) or other fermented vegetables.

DRINK probiotic beverages like kombucha or water kefir.

SUPPLEMENT with probiotics in pill or powder form, if desired.

Reintroduce

EAT one of the eliminated foods at each of your meals and note any changes to your mood, energy, mental clarity, digestive function, and skin. Reintroduce one eliminated food every three days to discover which are causing problems and which are not.

Note: The reintroduction of gluten-containing grains is not recommended.

If Your Leaky Gut Is Still Unresolved...

If you've gone through the 4R Protocol but you're still having problems with a leaky gut, it's time to work one-on-one with a health-care practitioner.

So, What's the Plan?

If, upon reading this chapter, you've discovered that addressing your autoimmune condition needs to be your priority, then your best bet is to begin following one of these 30-Day Meal Plans:

- Autoimmune Conditions (page 174)
- Thyroid Health (page 238)
- Multiple Sclerosis, Fibromyalgia & Chronic Fatigue (page 222)

If you're unsure which plan is best to start with or you're managing more than one health challenge, review the advice on selecting a meal plan (page 158) to dive deeper.

Guide to: Healing a Leaky Gut

Leaky gut (also known as "intestinal permeability") occurs when your digestive system isn't functioning properly. Rather than allowing only fully broken-down proteins to pass into your bloodstream, it allows larger, partially undigested proteins to pass through. This leads to a myriad of health problems and uncomfortable symptoms.

signs & symptoms

gi distress

Constipation
Diarrhea
Pain
Bloating
Gas

nutrient malabsorption

Undesired weight loss or difficulty losing weight
Deficiencies in essential fatty acids, vitamins, and minerals

compromised immunity

Frequent colds or flus
Intense seasonal allergies
Inflammatory responses

HOW TO HEAL IT: THE 4R PROTOCOL

The most important step in healing leaky gut is following the 4R Protocol (see page 44 for details):

Remove damaging foods from your diet.

Repair the damage already done to the gut.

Reinoculate to restore healthy gut flora.

Reintroduce potentially problematic foods to see if they affect you.

how your gut gets leaky CONTRIBUTING FACTORS

START AT THE TOP FOR FACTORS THAT CAN BE CONTROLLED VIA DIET AND LIFESTYLE.

diet
Alcohol
Antinutrients
Dairy
Fast food
Grains (especially those containing gluten)
Legumes
Processed foods
Sugar
Trans fats and damaged fats

medications
Antacids
Antibiotics
Chemotherapy, radiation
Corticosteroids
NSAIDs
Xenobiotics, substances within the human body that are not made by or expected to be within the human body, such as bisphenol A (BPA), a known endocrine disruptor found in plastics

infections
H. pylori
Intestinal viruses
Parasitic infections
Small intestinal bacterial overgrowth (SIBO)
Yeast overgrowth

stress
Catecholamines (particularly adrenaline)
Cortisol (chronic or acute)
Low stomach acid

hormonal problems
Thyroid imbalances
Sex hormone imbalances
Cortisol (chronic stress)

immunological problems
AGEs (advanced glycation end products)*
Autoimmunity
Intestinal inflammation

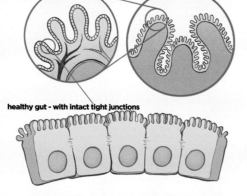

small intestine lining: microvilli   small intestine lining: villi

healthy gut - with intact tight junctions

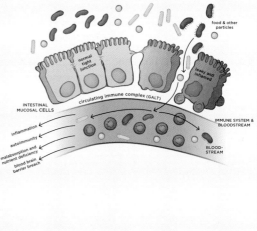

LEAKY GUT—WITH *IMPAIRED* TIGHT JUNCTIONS

*Advanced glycation end products (AGEs) are molecules that are formed when sugars react with proteins or fats in the body. They're a natural part of metabolism, but in high amounts, they contribute to aging and are linked to many chronic diseases, including diabetes, Alzheimer's disease, and heart disease.

Guide to: Gluten

Gluten is a protein found in wheat, rye, and barley that's associated with the development of leaky gut. Those with celiac disease *must* avoid gluten, but many people without celiac disease also find that their health improves when they eliminate gluten from their diet.

sources of gluten AND ITEMS THAT MAY CONTAIN HIDDEN GLUTEN

Ales	Communion	Imitation seafood	Orzo	Soy sauce	Vitamins
Barley	wafers	Khorasan wheat	Panko	Spelt	Wafers
Barley malt/	Couscous	(kamut)	Pasta	Spice blends	Wheat
extract	Croutons	Lipstick, lip gloss,	Roux	Stuffing	Wheat bran
Beer and lagers	Durum	and balms	Rye	Supplements	Wheat germ
Bran	Einkorn	Luncheon meats	Sauces	Thickeners	Wheat starch
Breading	Emmer	Malt	Seitan	Triticale	
Broth	Farina	Marinades	Self-basting	Udon	
Brown rice syrup	Farro	Matzo meal	poultry	Vinegar (malt	
Bulgur	Graham flour	Meat, sausages	Semolina	only)	
Candy coating	Herb blends	Medications	Soup base	Vital wheat gluten	

gluten-free (BUT STILL NOT RECOMMENDED)

Nearly all processed foods and grains carry some risk of cross-contamination with gluten. For the safest approach to a strict gluten-free diet, eat only whole, unprocessed foods.

Amaranth	Flax	Potato starch	Seed flour
Arrowroot	Millet	Quinoa	Sorghum
Bean flour	Montina	Rice	Soy
Buckwheat	Nut flour	Rice bran	Tapioca
Corn	Potato flour	Sago	Teff

most common sources of HIDDEN GLUTEN

Alcohol
Beer, malt beverages, grain alcohols

Cosmetics
Makeup, shampoo, and other personal-care items

Dressings
Thickened with flour or packaged with gluten-containing additives

Fried foods
Cross-contaminated with breaded items in fryers

Medications, vitamins, and supplements

Processed / packaged foods
Include gluten-containing additives

Sauces, soups, and stews
Thickened with flour

Soy, teriyaki, and hoisin sauces
Fermented with wheat

Vinegar
Malt varieties

SIGNS OF GLUTEN INTOLERANCE

Abdominal bloating
Fatigue
Skin problems or rashes
Diarrhea or constipation
Irritability, moodiness
Change in energy levels
Unexpected weight loss, mouth ulcers, depression, and even Crohn's disease are all more severe gluten allergy symptoms that you may experience.

Consult with your nutritionist or physician if you experience symptoms of gluten exposure that result in prolonged discomfort.

gluten-free BOOZE*

Bourbon	Sake
Champagne	Scotch
Cognac	Sherry
Gin	Tequila
Gluten-free	Vermouth
beers	Vodka
Grappa	Whiskey
Hard cider	Wine
Mead	
Rum	

i am allergic TO GLUTEN

I have a severe allergy and have to follow a STRICT gluten-free diet.

I may become very ill if I eat food containing flours or grains of wheat, barley, rye, or oats.

Does this food contain flour or grains of wheat, barley, rye, or oats? If you, the chef, or kitchen staff are uncertain about what the food contains, please tell me.

I CAN eat food containing rice, maize, potatoes, vegetables, fruit, eggs, cheese, milk, meat, and fish—as long as they are NOT cooked with wheat flour, batter, breadcrumbs, or sauce containing any of those ingredients.

Thank you for your help!

For more gluten-guides, visit: www.celiactravel.com

for more information ON GLUTEN

These sites are not necessarily about the Paleo diet, but they provide ample information on following a 100 percent gluten-free diet.

celiac.com	celiaclife.com	elanaspantry.com
celiac.org	celiacsolution.com	glutenfreegirl.com
celiaccentral.org	celiactravel.com	surefoodsliving.com

*Although distillation should remove gluten from alcohol, for someone with overt celiac disease or a severe gluten intolerance, it's best to avoid alcohols made from wheat, barley, and rye.

Balancing Blood Sugar

Getting your blood sugar levels regulated is one of the most important steps you can take in improving your health.

When food sends your blood sugar on a roller coaster ride, it can affect how you feel all day, and blood sugar that's frequently too high can lead to problems like insulin resistance, obesity, and type 2 diabetes. While the way the body handles blood sugar can seem complicated, keeping your blood sugar stable is often as simple as making some changes to the food you eat. In short, keeping your blood sugar stable by eating real, whole foods—including good carbs, not bad carbs (see page 67)—will set your body up for success.

Insulin Is Like Your Mom: It Constantly Wants to Put Stuff Away

Insulin is a storage hormone, and your pancreas releases it primarily in response to dietary carbohydrates. It is insulin's job to take nutrients from your bloodstream, where they land after you digest your food, and deliver them into your cells, which use them for energy. So, just like your mom picks up stuff lying around the house and puts it in its rightful place, insulin finds nutrients in your bloodstream and tries to put them in their rightful place—your cells. This is why people with type 1 diabetes can experience wasting. Without insulin injections, they do not have enough of the hormone to get nutrients to their cells.

Insulin does its job over a period of one to two hours after you eat a meal, so it "cleans up the mess" pretty quickly. Bad carbs make a bigger mess that sends insulin into overdrive to put it all away and bring your blood sugar level back to normal—a critical function, since high blood sugar is toxic. Normal blood sugar is about 4 grams, the equivalent of just 1 teaspoon of sugar. An hour or two after eating, if insulin has been able to do its job, your blood sugar levels should return to this normal level.

However, if your blood sugar levels are consistently elevated after meals because you're eating a lot of carbs, causing large amounts of insulin to be released into your bloodstream every time you eat, over time you can become what is called "insulin-resistant." Just as you can stop noticing a messy room after a while, your body begins to lose its ability to sense the insulin that your pancreas has released. The insulin in your bloodstream becomes like your nagging mother. It sends signals to "pick up your room," but your body ignores those signals, just like a teenager who tunes out her mom, and your cells can no longer "hear" the message that there is sugar in your bloodstream. As a result, the sugar can't get into your cells and be converted into energy.

Does this mean that eating more than 4 grams of carbohydrates at a time is toxic? Of course not! Your body's insulin response to carbohydrates depends largely on the types and amounts of carbs you eat, as well as how often you eat them. When you eat a lot of carbs, your body needs to release a lot of insulin to bring your blood sugar back down to nontoxic levels. When you eat a lot of carbs *frequently*, you release a lot of insulin on a consistent basis. All of these are normal responses, but it means insulin is constantly moving sugar into cells, and if you're consuming more carbs than your body can use or store as glycogen, it ends up being stored as fat. And when you're constantly adding to your fat stores, you're not using the fat you already have for fuel. Here it is in a nutshell:

> High blood sugar = high insulin response
> High insulin = storage mode
> Storage mode = not burning fat for fuel

Glucagon Is Like a Kid: It Wants to Take All the Toys Out of Storage

To understand "releasing" mode, we need to understand how the hormone glucagon works. Glucagon is also produced by your pancreas, but unlike insulin, glucagon wants to use her stuff rather than put it away.

Insulin and glucagon are counterregulatory hormones. While insulin's job is to keep putting nutrients away, glucagon's job is to pull nutrients from their storage sites in your body when they're needed for fuel. When glucagon is the dominant hormone in your bloodstream, it signals both glucose and fat to move from storage into your blood for use as fuel. When insulin is dominant, it's impossible for glucagon to work. In other words, the dominant hormone dictates whether nutrients are stored or released for use. This is the difference between storage mode and release mode.

> *Know this: You can't have your bread and burn fat, too! In order to access and use stored body fat for energy, you need to be in release mode, not storage mode.*

You want glucagon to be dominant because it allows you to burn stored nutrients for fuel rather than store them away. How do you create glucagon dominance? You habitually eat a diet and live a lifestyle that promotes a strong glucagon response.

Eat dense sources of protein. A dense source of protein is one that comes from an animal source and is not buried in insulin-demanding carbohydrates. Steak, for example, contains a large amount of protein and no carbohydrates at all. While protein elicits an insulin response just as carbs do (because insulin is needed to take amino acids into muscle cells), it elicits an even stronger glucagon response. That's because in the absence of carbohydrates, there's more insulin in the bloodstream than needed, and without glucagon releasing glucose from storage, your blood sugar levels would drop too low. By contrast, it's hard to get a strong glucagon response from beans because insulin responds to their carbohydrates, overpowering glucagon's efforts. This is why many people who seek protein from strictly vegetarian sources have trouble losing body fat: they eat carb-dense protein sources that prompt the release of insulin, so glucagon never becomes dominant.

Exercise. When you exercise, your body looks for available fuel sources to power your muscles. The very first, most easily accessible fuel comes directly from your bloodstream. But you can't perform work for very long on the 4 grams of sugar circulating in your bloodstream, especially if it has been a while since you've eaten and insulin has cleared those nutrients away. Glucagon then goes to work to raise your blood sugar levels by burning stored body fat. Glucagon also works with cortisol, your fight-or-flight hormone, to signal to your body, "Hey! Work's happening here! Let's deliver some fuel to where it's needed!" This process goes smoothly and comfortably when your body is accustomed to burning fat for energy. But what if you're used to eating a lot of carbohydrates, especially in small meals every few hours, as so many nutritionists and TV doctors have recommended? Well, that's when insulin becomes the dominant hormone in your bloodstream *all the time,* and glucagon can't do its job properly. Let's say you're hungry an hour before you plan to exercise, and you know that within another hour, you'll be starving. So in response to this hunger, you have a snack, right? Then you go to the gym, hoping to burn off body fat during your workout, but that doesn't happen. The nutrients from the snack are still up for grabs in your body because they haven't been pulled from your bloodstream into storage, and they'll be used *before* anything that is stored away. Eating too close to a workout means you're using the nutrients from that food, *not* stored body fat. Rather than forcing your body to access what is stored, you've given it new fuel to use.

Your body always prefers to use glucose (the basic unit of carbs) from your bloodstream because it's easier and quicker to access than stored body fat. But if glucose isn't around, your body will burn fat for energy, and if your body is well adapted to burning fat for fuel—which is what happens when you stop eating too many carbs—you won't feel the need for that pre-workout snack.

If losing body fat is your goal, you're best served by avoiding carbs and eating more fats and proteins to become fat-adapted. Eating extra food before and after a workout is generally not a good idea. Remember: that extra food is what gets burned during your workout, not stored body fat. Extra food before and after a workout is a good idea only if you want to maintain your weight and muscle mass, not if you want to lose weight.

How do you know if you're primarily burning sugar or fat for fuel? Ask yourself if you can make it through a workout without a snack right beforehand if it has been a couple of hours since you've eaten. Don't get me wrong; I'm not suggesting you challenge yourself to avoid eating if you're starving before a workout or feeling lightheaded, especially if you have passed out during a workout before. However, it is important to realize that you're probably burning sugar for fuel, and your body is not releasing enough glucagon to allow you to access stored nutrients. You are a sugar-burner and will only feel balanced if you add more sugar to the tank . . . unless and until you become fat-adapted. To get out of this cycle, reduce your overall carb intake (using the chart on page 70 as a guide) and allow your body to realize that it can and should use the fat you eat and the fat in your body's reserves. Glucagon will send signals to help your body burn body fat, but it can't do that if insulin is always at work responding to carbs.

Let yourself get hungry before you eat again. When you get hungry, it's because your blood sugar levels have dropped. It is then glucagon's job to find stored sugar and bring it into your bloodstream to keep that blood sugar level at the healthy 4 grams. I've already mentioned that high blood sugar is toxic, but so is low blood sugar. It's all about balance! Why is it that after twelve hours without food, you haven't passed out from

FASTING GLUCOSE

Have you ever wondered why your blood sugar levels stay constant even after a 12-hour fast before you have blood drawn for testing? This is because of glucagon—it keeps your blood sugar normal in the absence of food to keep you alive and conscious.

hypoglycemia (blood sugar below 4 grams)? Glucagon senses any drop in blood sugar and brings sugar into your bloodstream to prevent you from passing out. Pretty cool, huh?

Eating well-balanced meals of nutrient-dense foods, including good carbs, allows your body to easily move from a state of low blood sugar to balanced, even blood sugar without a negative impact. Imbalanced blood sugar, for any reason, creates a stress response in your body. Eating too many bad carbs on a regular basis sends your body into a constant state of battle, fighting to keep the sugar in your bloodstream normal, which triggers the release of the stress hormone, cortisol.

Blood Sugar and Cortisol

Blood sugar that's too high or too low, for any reason, creates a stress response in your body. It sends your body into a constant state of battle, fighting to keep the sugar in your bloodstream normal, and that triggers the release of the stress hormone cortisol.

Emotional stressors are probably already causing an excess of cortisol production in your body. Like our ancestors, we are wired to handle acute stressors—moments that demand an instantaneous fight-or-flight response—followed by periods of rest and recovery. Unfortunately, the lifestyles we lead today tend to come with everyday emotional stress, which causes our bodies to produce marathon-like levels of stress hormones and places us at a constant systemic stress level of 4 or 5 out of 10. While we can handle a level of 7, 8, 9, or even 10, as long as it is brief and followed by a period of very low levels of stress, a constant level of 4 or 5 without a rest period wears us down.

Add the physical stress of your body's response to carb overload to that everyday emotional stress, and you have chronically elevated cortisol. Furthermore, since the different elements of the endocrine system are interdependent and stress hormones "talk" to sex hormones and every other hormone in your body, elevated cortisol can lead to other endocrine problems, including inhibited adrenal or thyroid function, low testosterone, and even infertility.

Dysglycemia—high or low blood sugar—is one of the biggest contributors to overproduction of cortisol. Since you may not always be able to control your emotional stress levels, it makes sense to reduce your cortisol levels by controlling blood sugar through better diet and lifestyle choices.

Cortisol is released from your adrenal glands, two triangle-shaped glands that sit right on top of your kidneys. High stress elicits a cortisol response, which in turn tells the body to stop storing nutrients—in effect, to ignore insulin—and instead pull nutrients from storage.

Now, on an *acute* basis, as in during exercise, this stress response allows us to complete our workout (we're in "fight-or-flight" mode), then the body calms back down and nutrient storage functions resume. But when the body is in a high stress state on a *chronic* basis, this becomes problematic. Constantly asking the body to ignore insulin can lead to insulin resistance, further metabolic complications, or even type 2 diabetes.

The causes of high stress in the body are nearly endless, and chronically high blood sugar is just one of them. So what if you're stressed out all the time but want to keep your insulin levels in check? Lowering your carb intake to match your activity levels will take you far, but it won't get you the entire way. Your hormones need to play nicely together to create this equation: burning fat = moderate insulin release + higher glucagon release + healthy cortisol release.

DYSGLYCEMIA

Dysglycemia is a constant state of high or low blood sugar. It contributes to countless hormonal and systemic issues, as well as many chronic inflammatory conditions.

When Sugar Takes Its Toll

Both high and low blood sugar can have profound effects on your ability to think clearly and maintain a positive mood. When your blood sugar levels are high, you feel foggy-headed or sleepy. People often refer to this as a "food coma." How do you feel after a lunch of a few slices of pizza, a bowl of pasta, or even rice and beans? If you're like most people, you feel tired, uncomfortably full, and not quite sharp. You may sit at your desk wishing you could take a nap rather than work on the report that's due.

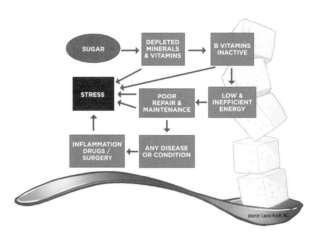

You know that post-Thanksgiving-dinner sleepy feeling that people attribute to the tryptophan in the turkey? It is probably not due to tryptophan at all but rather to the piles of mashed potatoes, rolls, and pumpkin pie that we eat before sitting on the couch to watch football. Too many carbohydrates can easily lead to this feeling of brain fog and fatigue. Now, if you had *played* football for a couple of hours before dinner, your response to that amount of carbohydrates would be totally different because your body would have needed to be replenished with more carbs.

A high refined-carbohydrate meal, or even snack, often results in such a strong insulin response that it can drop your blood sugar back to normal pretty quickly (if your pancreas is working as it should) and subsequently finish its job by leaving you with *low* blood sugar. Without the proper nutrients accompanying the carbohydrates, the complex mechanisms of satiety and blood sugar regulation may fail to achieve the delicate balance necessary to feel normal. This is best exemplified by the all-too-common need for a mid-morning snack after a breakfast of a bagel, pastry, or even a bowl of oatmeal (I used to call this "second breakfast").

When your blood sugar levels are too low, you feel irritable and ready to snap if anyone gets between you and your next meal. When extreme hunger sets in, it's hard to think clearly. Chances are, you can only think about one thing: food. This is how low blood sugar affects your brain.

Blood Sugar and Your Immune System

The stress that bad carbs put on your body can affect more than just your endocrine system. Those foods take nutrients but don't give any back, and the constant withdrawals from your "energy bank account" can eventually leave you broke—just as if you kept withdrawing all of your money from the bank without making any deposits. If you have no money in the bank, there is nothing to withdraw from your account, and your body is similar. You need to deposit nutrients before trying to withdraw them.

Eating refined foods depletes vitamins and minerals and leads to low energy. While you feel the lack of energy, that depletion is also happening at a cellular level. Not only are your cells unable to make energy for you, but they also can't do their job of repair and maintenance as sugar depletes the nutrients—especially B vitamins and vitamin C—that your immune system needs.

Know this: Much as inflammation in your gut can lead to any chronic inflammatory condition, nutrient depletion can also lead to many illnesses because it weakens your immunity.

Get Off the Blood Sugar Roller Coaster

Roller coasters are fun, but not when it comes to blood sugar. And your blood sugar roller coaster can start with breakfast. This is because breakfast really *is* the most important meal of the day for people with blood sugar imbalances. But what do most people eat for breakfast? A big helping of sugar, of course.

When you sit down to breakfast, do you eat a bowl of high fiber, whole grain cereal with skim or low-fat milk? Perhaps it's a bowl of steel-cut or old-fashioned oatmeal with a banana, walnuts, brown sugar, or raisins. Maybe it's a whole wheat bagel with peanut butter and an apple or a cup of nonfat yogurt with granola and berries on top. All of these breakfasts are commonly viewed as ideal in today's health-oriented populations. According to conventional wisdom, these foods support heart health and even fat loss, but this couldn't be further from the truth.

Starting your day with these kinds of grain-heavy foods is one of the reasons you feel the need to eat five or six times a day. You've heard from countless sources that you should eat small meals this often, but do you *enjoy* eating that way? Every single client I've coached who was following this type of meal plan has reported to me that they don't enjoy having to eat so often and feel stressed about choosing what to eat several times a day.

To better illustrate how the blood sugar roller coaster works, let's compare three different breakfasts and how they act within the body. Two of these meals probably look pretty familiar to you, though Meal #3 may not be what you're used to seeing for breakfast. If you're a veteran of the Paleo lifestyle, Meal #1 probably looks like a common morning in your past, while Meal #2 or Meal #3 should look like a more recent morning.

Meal #1:
conventional wisdom,
low fat

Meal #2:
real foods,
lower carb / higher fat

Meal #3:
real foods, higher
protein / higher carb

- 1/2 cup dry oats (yields
  1 cup cooked)
  + 2 tablespoons raisins
  + 2 teaspoons brown sugar
- 12 ounces orange juice
- 16 ounces coffee
  + 2 ounces skim milk
  + 2 teaspoons sugar

Calories: 438
Total fat: 4 g
   Saturated fat: 1 g
Cholesterol: 1 mg
Total carbohydrates: 94 g
   Dietary fiber: 5 g
   Sugars: 24 g
Protein: 12 g
Vitamin A: 13%*
Vitamin C: 266%*
Calcium: 16%*
Iron: 16%*

- 2 whole eggs
- 1 cup cooked broccoli
- 1/2 avocado
- 2 large tomato slices
- 16 ounces coffee
  + 1 ounce coconut milk

Calories: 440
Total fat: 31 g
   Saturated fat: 9 g
Cholesterol: 429 mg
Total carbohydrates: 24 g
   Dietary fiber: 10 g
   Sugars: 7 g
Protein: 10 g
Vitamin A: 72%*
Vitamin C: 191%*
Calcium: 18%*
Iron: 18%*

- 2 whole eggs
- 1/2 cup cooked kale
- 1/2 cup blueberries
- 1 large sweet potato
  (180 grams)
- 2 ounces turkey
- 16 ounces coffee, black

Calories: 440
Total fat: 13 g
   Saturated fat: 3 g
Cholesterol: 455 mg
Total carbohydrates: 57 g
   Dietary fiber: 9 g
   Sugars: 23 g
Protein: 26 g
Vitamin A: 72%*
Vitamin C: 125%*
Calcium: 18%*
Iron: 25%*

Meal #1: Conventional Wisdom, Low Fat

Meal #1 is what we'd consider a healthy breakfast if we were following conventional wisdom, which assures us that eating a low-fat meal rich in whole grains will provide lasting energy and nutrition to power us through the morning. Since conventional wisdom also tells us that saturated fat and cholesterol are unhealthy, we're left with few options for breakfast—if we're not eating eggs, what else is there for breakfast besides grains and fruit? Perhaps processed dairy like nonfat or low-fat yogurt? (For a truly healthy egg-free breakfast plan, see page 178.)

If you've made yourself Meal #1, congratulations—you've just created a lovely bowl of sugar, topped with sugar, and finished off with sugar, with a glass of sugar and some coffee with sugar and sugar added. Was that what you intended to do this morning? Sit down to a gigantic breakfast of sugar?

How do you feel after that breakfast? Pretty good, right? I'll bet you feel amped up and powered for the morning . . . until about an hour later, maybe two or three hours at the most. Then what happens? If you're like many of my clients, you'll say, "I'm hungry again." And all from your purportedly healthy low-fat, high-carb oatmeal breakfast.

How's that working for you? It certainly hasn't worked for the thousands of people I've counseled over the years. Many are more than just hungry after a few hours; they're shaky and even irrational, desperate to find something to eat.

When you crash from eating that oatmeal breakfast, you probably reach for whatever is around, which is usually more carbs, such as a granola bar or crackers, to get you through until lunch. Then noon hits and it's lunchtime. You munch on your whole wheat turkey sandwich with chips and an iced tea. That's healthy, right?

Then, at about 3:00 p.m., you need an afternoon pick-me-up. Maybe you reach for a skim milk latte and a pastry from Starbucks. Come on, who doesn't love their Starbucks fix? Plus, it's an excuse to get out of the office.

The end of the workday arrives, and you're feeling pretty hungry again, unsure how to make it through either your 6:00 workout or the commute home in traffic before you can get to a plate of pasta for dinner. So you grab a handful of nuts on your way out of the office (finally, some fat!).

Your entire day has been a roller coaster ride, climbing up the steepest of hills and rushing back down. The flat parts of the ride are when your body can relax and burn fat for energy. When you eat your oatmeal (or other high-carb, low-fat breakfast), however, your blood sugar levels climb way up high until you head down the other side of that steep hill about an hour later, when the crash of low blood sugar comes. Not as much fun as a real roller coaster ride, is it? To your body, each part of the ride is a negative stressor.

When it comes to blood sugar regulation, the flat part of the ride before and after the hills is where your body wants to stay. But if you continue to eat meals that are high in carbs and low in fat, you'll take that roller coaster car right back up another hill. Luckily, getting off the roller coaster is easy.

Simply put, your body needs fat and protein to feel full for a long period of time. This feeling of fullness isn't about filling your stomach, though! Don't be fooled by the silly notion that "bulk and fiber" are what fill you up. It's nutrients that make you feel satisfied, and protein and fat pack the most powerful, nutrient-rich punch. And nutrients, in turn, allow your body to have a healthy hormonal response to your food that ultimately lets you feel full an hour, two hours, three hours, and even longer after a meal.

Meal #2: Real Foods, Lower Carb / Higher Fat

Let's take a look at how your morning goes if you eat Meal #2, the real-food Paleo meal that's lower in carbs and higher in fats. You eat this breakfast of eggs, veggies, and coffee at about 7:00 a.m., and two hours later, you feel fine. Three hours pass, and you're still fine. Four hours approach, and you may start to notice some hunger.

Noon rolls around, and you have a container of leftovers from last night's dinner ready to go. This includes some roasted chicken (recipe on page 292), perhaps on some leafy greens with carrots, avocado, and homemade dressing made with extra-virgin olive oil and lemon juice. Easy!

The end of your workday comes, and you head to the gym or drive home, feeling like you could eat but won't pass out if you don't. Whether you work out or simply drive home, you never feel shaky or disoriented from low blood sugar.

This is the difference between fueling your body primarily with sugar and carbs and fueling it primarily with proteins and fats. Remember, this doesn't mean you should never eat carbs! It simply means that you should eat good carbs in an amount that's

appropriate for your lifestyle. When you are fat-adapted, your body can access stored body fat for energy when you haven't eaten. If you never give your body a break from burning carbohydrates as a primary fuel source, it never has the opportunity to burn fat for fuel.

Meal #3: Real Foods, Higher Protein / Higher Carb

Now, to really throw a curveball into the mix, let's look at Meal #3, the real-food Paleo meal that's lower in fat but higher in both carbs and protein than Meal #2. This breakfast of eggs, fruit, turkey, a mix of leafy *and* starchy veggies, and coffee may not look like what you're accustomed to seeing on a breakfast plate, but it shows a completely normal and healthy way of putting breakfast together—with real foods that don't need to be considered "breakfast" foods. Three hours after eating this meal, you may want a bit of a snack, but you're not feeling famished or as if your blood sugar is crashing. At the four-hour mark after breakfast, you're getting ready for a healthy lunch.

The rest of the day pans out similar to the way it would if you ate Meal #2. Even though this meal is lower in fat and higher in carbs than Meal #2, it contains good carbs and a more substantial amount of protein than the other two meals. The combination of more protein (from the turkey) and carbs (from the sweet potato and blueberries) and less fat can provide as much satiety as Meal #2 does. The difference here is that this balance of fat, carbohydrates, and protein is ideal for someone who is physically active, works out, or is an athlete.

The Takeaway

Most people try low-fat diets because they want to burn stored body fat. But these diets don't typically give your body a chance to learn how to use fat for energy. Your system simply becomes accustomed to fueling on nutrient-poor carbs. When you get hungry, which happens quickly because you're not eating much protein and bad carbs are swiftly cleared from your bloodstream, your body is not in a hormonal state to allow stored body fat to easily be accessed for energy. This is a fantastic way to live and eat only if you want to keep big food companies in business by buying their cereal, granola bars, breads, crackers, cookies, and pastas. But choosing a breakfast that looks more like Meal #2 or #3 will set you up for better satiety and fat-burning all day.

Maintaining even blood sugar levels is the key to not only satiety but also mental clarity, positive moods, fat loss, hormonal balance, and reduced inflammation. Whether your goal is fat loss or good health, regulating your blood sugar is absolutely necessary.

So, What's the Plan?

If, upon reading this chapter, you've discovered that balancing your blood sugar needs to be your priority, then your best bet is to begin following one of these 30-Day Meal Plans:

- Blood Sugar Regulation (page 180)
- Adrenal Health (page 162)
- Healthy Hormones (page 204)
- Neurological Health (page 228)

If you're unsure which plan is best to start with or you're managing more than one health challenge, review the advice on selecting a meal plan (page 158) to dive deeper.

Managing Stress

As much as we'd like to believe our mind—our thoughts, feelings, and emotions—and our body—the physical, physiological, visible part of who we are—operate independently, it's simply not the case. Our thoughts, beliefs, emotions, and feelings shape what we become physically.

If your mindset is cemented in negativity, your actions won't follow a positive path towards growth and change. For example, if you believe that you will not heal from your health challenge, then it's extremely unlikely that you'll take the positive actions that are needed for healing, and so it becomes a self-fulfilling prophecy.

On the other hand, if you believe that you can heal, that belief and positive mindset lead to actions that align with a healing path. You'll work on getting quality sleep, eating foods that are healthy for you, and adjusting other elements of your lifestyle in order to help yourself.

You are not a victim of your body or your disease.

Life doesn't happen *to* us unless we let it. We have the power to be an active participant, making choices for ourselves each day, or we can allow others to make choices for us. The pervasiveness of indecision that we face on a daily basis often leads to a situation where we feel like we aren't in control.

Take Control of Your Life

Managing stress to avoid its myriad psychological and physical effects may require changes to your lifestyle. In my life, I certainly had to do more than just change my diet.

When I decided to pursue nutrition coaching as a full-time career, it wasn't without great reflection. I was living in a nice, top-floor apartment in San Francisco with parking, laundry, a view, and a dishwasher. It was an enviable lifestyle in many ways, but keeping that fancy roof with all the trimmings over my head meant I had to work at a job that didn't feed my soul. I dreaded waking up every single morning.

Are you in a similar situation, constantly complaining about your job? Your body? Your significant other? Your friends? Your life? Would you consider yourself happy with your everyday life? Do you live for the weekends? Are there days you dread waking up?

These questions get to the heart of the choices you make every day, and they help you to identify whether you're living a life of your own choosing. Brian Tracy, one of my favorite motivational speakers, says in his *The Psychology of Achievement* series of talks, "We feel good about ourselves to the exact degree to which we feel we are in control of our own lives."

Do you feel you're driving your life, or do you feel everything in your life is driving you? If you feel that having a family and the responsibility to provide financially for their needs prevents you from making a career or life change, look closely at your expenses. Do you need that fancy car? Do you need that big house or extra garage? Freeing up the money you need to make the change you want may even be as simple as forgoing your daily latte, which can easily add up to a $1,000-a-year habit.

When we feel out of control in our lives, we experience great stress. In *The Paleo Solution*, Robb Wolf puts it well: "A stunning amount of . . . stress is self-induced. . . . If you have weight or health issues, work yourself to death, have a closet full of clothes you never wear, and a house full of crap you never use, then maybe you need to do some thinking about how you approach your life."

If stress is a problem in your life, it's time to make some new choices about how to handle it and learn stress management techniques. You now know better than ever how big an effect stress has on both your psychological and physical health.

Practicing gratitude is the first step in being in control of your own thoughts and actions. If you have a positive mental attitude, full of thankfulness for what is instead of anger or disdain for what isn't, your sense of power and direction completely shifts.

Practice an Attitude of Gratitude

Several years ago, I came across an online article that helped change how I think about positivity and gratitude. On health educator Charles Poliquin's website (www. charlespoliquin.com), weight loss coach Jonny Bowden published a post entitled, "The Nine Habits of Highly Healthy People." One of those habits was creating a "gratitude list." He wrote: "By making a list of things you're grateful for, you focus the brain on positive energy. Gratitude is incompatible with anger and stress. Practice using your underutilized 'right brain' and spread some love. Focusing on what you're grateful for—even for five minutes a day—has the added benefit of being one of the best stress-reduction techniques on the planet."

Some people think a gratitude list is hippy-dippy Pollyanna nonsense, but if you are in a constant state of stress that is negatively impacting your health, it's worth a try, isn't it? After all, most of us tend to focus on the negatives and never stop to think about all the positives in our lives.

It's most effective to create a gratitude list every day, but at the very least, stop and make such a list whenever it crosses your mind or when you are in a particularly stressful state of mind. Simply pause and remember what's most important to you.

You can share your list with your friends or loved ones or keep it to yourself. It doesn't matter if no one ever sees it but you, but that said, I find that telling people in your life that you are grateful for their presence always yields positive results.

How much would it lower your stress level if someone told you today that they appreciate you? (I thought so!) It might even help in your quest toward healing a leaky gut. You can download a blank gratitude list from the book resources page on my website, balancedbites.com/practicalpaleo.

Stress and Adrenal Problems

Although stress plays a major role in overall health, it can also be the primary cause of an altered adrenal profile—when the level of cortisol, a stress hormone produced by the adrenal glands, is out of balance with your system.

An altered adrenal profile, typically a result of HPA axis dysregulation—a disruption in the feedback loop among the hypothalmus, pituitary, and adrenal glands, which are constantly communicating about stress and stress hormones—is often referred to as adrenal fatigue. While "adrenal fatigue" is an easy term to use, it's not technically accurate, as it indicates that the adrenal glands themselves can become worn out. The true root

cause of low or high cortisol output from the adrenal glands is a dysregulation in the signaling sent from the brain to the adrenal glands. The adrenal glands themselves do not determine how much cortisol to produce; that's entirely governed by the hypothalamus and pituitary gland.

THE HYPOTHALAMIC–PITUITARY–ADRENAL AXIS

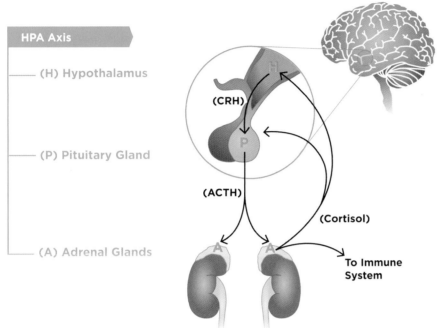

HPA Axis

— (H) Hypothalamus

— (P) Pituitary Gland

— (A) Adrenal Glands

(CRH)

(ACTH)

(Cortisol)

To Immune System

The single biggest contributing factor to an altered adrenal profile is stress. It sounds simple enough, but stress comes in so many varieties and forms that it's impossible to avoid all together. What we must do is identify stressors in our lives and reduce them as much as possible, and then help our bodies manage unavoidable stressors by making diet and lifestyle modifications that lower the stress load on our systems.

Contributors to the stress that leads to adrenal fatigue can be lifestyle stressors such as: lack of sleep, poor food choices, use of stimulants, pulling "all-nighters" or "pushing through" a day despite being tired, perfectionism, staying in no-win situations for too long, overtraining, and lack of fun or stress-relieving practices. People who have lifestyles that make them more prone to adrenal fatigue include students, medical professionals, workaholics, and single parents, as well as those who: are unhappily married, are unhappy or unsatisfied at work, are self-employed or starting a new business, abuse drugs or alcohol, or have alternating shift schedules.

Furthermore, life events that can lead to adrenal fatigue include: unrelieved pressure or stress at work, any crisis or severe emotional trauma, the death of a loved one, major surgery, extended or chronic illness, sudden change in life situations (such as loss of a job or moving to a location without friend or family support) and repeated or extended chemical exposure. The problem of stress might not be such an issue if we weren't compounding many stressors over the course of days, weeks, months, and years without much downtime for our systems. So, while an altered adrenal profile can come on suddenly, triggered by a traumatic life event, most commonly it is experienced after a gradual, cumulative effect of multiple stressors.

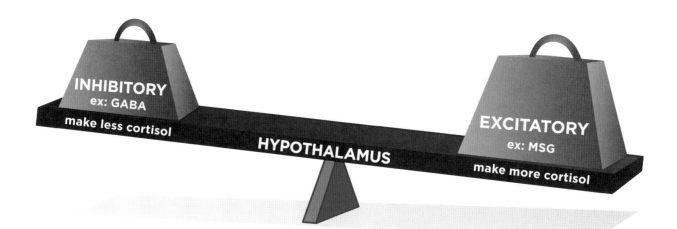

If you are curious about your own adrenal health status, contact a naturopath, chiropractor, certified nutrition consultant, or other practitioner in your area to find out if they can run an adrenal salivary index test for you. You may also find the Adrenal Health 30-Day Meal Plan (page 162) to be helpful.

So, What's the Plan?

If, upon reading this chapter, you suspect that stress may be at the root of your health challenges, then your best bet is to begin following the Adrenal Health 30-Day Meal Plan (page 162).

If you are experiencing hormonal balance issues as a result of poor stress management, start with one of the following plans:

- Healthy Hormones (page 204)
- Thyroid Health (page 238)

You can also review the advice on selecting a meal plan (page 158) to dive deeper if you discover that more than one health challenge is present.

Still wondering which meal plan is right for you?

If your health goal or challenge hasn't been specifically addressed by the content in the previous four chapters (Healing Digestion, Addressing Autoimmunity, Balancing Blood Sugar, and Managing Stress), then your best bet is to review the advice on selecting a meal plan on page 158.

Many of the meal plans address specific health concerns and goals, including:

- Cancer Recovery (page 186)
- Multiple Sclerosis, Fibromyalgia & Chronic Fatigue (page 222)
- Heart Health (page 210)
- Athletic Performance (page 168)

Living a Paleo Lifestyle

You've committed to eating a Paleo diet. You've cut out processed and refined foods and learned how to eat real, whole foods at every meal and snack. You've done the 4R Protocol and found out what foods you can tolerate well and what foods will send your system into a tailspin. You're feeling great—energized, strong, and healthy. Now there's just one problem: dealing with the rest of the world.

There's no doubt that eating a Paleo-style diet is not the norm in our society. By and large, Americans still like easy, processed, refined foods, and when we make the decision to try something different that works better for us, we often encounter difficulties. Friends and family don't understand or even disapprove of our choices, our kids don't want to try the new way of eating, and dining out and traveling require more forethought and planning.

The good news is, navigating these pitfalls becomes much easier with time and practice, and your better health is absolutely worth it.

Inviting Friends and Family to Try Paleo

When you've found something that really works and makes you feel so much better, it's natural to want your loved ones to try it, too. I'm often asked, "How can I get my friends and family to go Paleo with me?" Unfortunately, the short answer is, you can't. I know that's not what most people want to hear, but it's the truth. People need to come to the decision to make a lifestyle change completely on their own—when they're ready, and in a way that they feel will work for them.

That said, there are ways you *can* encourage and support change in others. The approach that will work best for a particular friend or family member depends primarily on two things: (1) their current objections to eating Paleo, and (2) their own personal way of making changes that stick for them—because we don't all do this in the same way! Some people do great going cold turkey and changing their plan overnight to tackle a 30-day challenge, for example, while others like a slow roll. (For more on going all-in or making gradual changes, see page 40.)

Here are my best tips to supporting those around you in making positive changes, whether in their diet or other areas of their life:

1. ***Be the change.*** If there's one thing that motivates people around you, it's watching you live what you believe in, day in and day out. Talking means nothing without action, and when you let people see you put changes into place and maintain them, it sends a powerful message. You show them not only that change is possible but exactly how to make it happen, and how to *maintain* it.

   One of the biggest objections to Paleo is that it's hard, so when you show people how easy it can be (after some transition and practice, of course), they'll be far more willing to give it a whirl. And, along the same lines, when you're around folks you're trying to support in their change, don't complain about it being difficult, a struggle, or a challenge. Keep a positive attitude and look at the amazing results you're seeing, rather than dwelling on any limitations or moments of stress.

2. **Don't preach!** The most annoying thing anyone can do is to proselytize and shout from the rooftops about their new way of eating (or exercising, or anything else, for that matter), as if they've found the great panacea to all the ails of the world. The truth is that while Paleo is an *amazing* way to eat and live, it isn't the only way to be healthy. People can improve their health greatly by putting the first few steps of the changeover into action, while perhaps still eating some foods that you avoid.

   We're all different, and your constitution—the combination of your particular genes and the epigenetic expression of your DNA (that is, how your genes interact with your environment)—is not the same as anyone else's, even if you're twins! So the way specific foods impact you isn't necessarily going to be the same for anyone else.

3. **Avoid paralyzing others with "Paleo perfectionism."** If someone is interested in making the change to a Paleo-style diet, don't overwhelm or paralyze them with the minutiae of eating *only* organic, grass-fed, "perfectly Paleo" food. That may be your own goal, but simply changing basic food choices is the foundational step; from there, people will naturally begin to seek better sources if it's important to them. Be available to help provide information when the time comes, but don't shove every local farm's phone number or CSA signup form in their faces. Give them the time and space to figure things out, and they'll know they can ask for more information as they want it.

4. **Make it easier on them!** Get your friend a copy of this book and bookmark your favorite recipes. Maybe help stock their pantry with a gift of some popular Paleo swaps—like coconut aminos, ghee, organic spice blends, and a grain-free flour or two—or offer to go with them to the grocery store to help them find foods that will work for them. And send them to my website, balancedbites.com, where they can connect with me and my team via the blog, by signing up for my weekly e-mails, or by leaving comments/questions on posts. I'm also on social media outlets like Facebook, Instagram, and Twitter—all linked directly from my website. I'm always happy to answer questions and offer tips to help people who are just starting out with Paleo!

Remember that changing the way we eat is a big decision. Your family and friends may not be ready or willing to try Paleo quite yet, and it's so important to remember that you weren't always thinking this way, either. Cut people some slack and remember that there are some encouraging ways to go about this, as well as ways that will unnecessarily create pushback and resistance from those around you—and you want to avoid that if at all possible!

Eating Paleo with Kids

When we start making the transition to Paleo, it's common to encounter resistance from kids—after all, they're probably perfectly happy with eating the way they're used to. But the truth is, it's *your* responsibility to help your children eat better, especially when they're too young to go to the store and buy junk food. (By the way, I'm sure I was doing this at a *very* young age—taking two dollars to my corner 7-Eleven to buy five- and ten-cent candies—so I understand that keeping your older kids from doing this may be harder than it sounds.) For young children, the changeover may be difficult if they've been raised on anything and everything, or even just a bit more "junk" than you'd like to admit. But change *is* possible for them. It will simply take tenacity, creativity, and dedication.

Your best bet in creating change in kids ages three or four and up is to get them involved. Sure, they may reject some of your new, healthy ideas at first, but when kids are able to participate hands-on with the process of selecting and cooking the food they eat (and growing it, too, if you can start a garden!), they're far more receptive to trying new things *and* admitting to liking them.

These three steps are simple, easy ways to help kids get involved in the kitchen, from planning a meal to cooking it:

1. **Let them choose recipes from cookbooks.** Open this book up to the recipe section and let them select something to make that week. If they gravitate towards only treats or baked goodies, have them also choose something more robust, like a main dish or veggie side, to go alongside it.

2. **Get them involved at the grocery store.** Ask them to find a specific ingredient (that you know they can reach!) in the produce section, or have them pick a vegetable or fruit—perhaps something new they haven't tried before—to bring at home and use in a recipe, or to prepare in a new way. Searching online is a great way to find new methods of preparation for fruits and veggies.

3. **Give them kid-friendly tasks in the kitchen.** If they're very young, they can help wash veggies or tear large lettuce leaves for a salad. As they get a bit older, they can measure ingredients with you, mix salad dressings or sauces, and eventually learn to chop some things up and work with heat to cook their foods.

What you'll be teaching your children through these steps is far more important than even the changes in their food each day. It's all about empowerment and a skill set that will help them take care of themselves as they grow up! So many kids today never learn these basic life skills, and by getting your kids involved in the kitchen, especially when they're young, you'll get their excited engagement to transform how they look at food. Instead of just fighting a battle whenever they want to eat junk food, you can empower them to get creative in the kitchen—cooking is a lot like a fun art project that you get to eat when it's done. They'll build kitchen confidence that'll translate into broader abilities for a lifetime, and it'll take the pressure off of you as you work to keep things as healthy as possible in the kitchen.

Dealing with Unsupportive Friends and Family

Not everyone will support your decision to eat a Paleo diet, and the lack of support can turn supposedly fun occasions, from holiday get-togethers to office parties, into stressful events. When you're faced with a critical friend or family member, it's important to consider the reason behind their lack of support. Whether it's a well-meaning grandmother, a curious but skeptical coworker, a disappointed parent, a vegan or vegetarian uncle, a doctor cousin, or even your best buddy who's been with you since your pizza-and-wings days, there's always an underlying, more *complete* meaning to the way they express their lack of support. Once you identify the reason behind their disapproval, you can plan how to handle your interactions with this person going forward. Here are some common criticisms and what they often really mean:

What they say: "I'm concerned about your health"; "The Paleo diet is really unhealthy with all that fat/meat"

What it means: "This way of eating flies in the face of everything I know about good nutrition, and I don't understand how it could be healthy for you."

How to handle it: Assure your loved one that you've done your homework on this way of eating. You know that it sounds a bit out there compared to what we've been taught for a long time, but you're focused on eating real, whole foods, and there is no reason to worry. You can also let them know that you're eating plenty of vegetables and fresh foods, and that if you are feeling anything short of amazing, you'll definitely reconsider your approach.

What they say: "What do you mean you don't want a piece of [insert your old favorite homemade food here]? I made it just for you!"

What it means: "I'm upset or confused because I made this and you aren't eating it, and it makes me feel like you don't love/need me or value my effort."

How to handle it: If the food isn't one you can have without ill effects, this situation is best handled preemptively. If you know ahead of time that your grandmother plans to make her famous coconut layer cake for Easter, perhaps you can have a chat with her about why you wouldn't be able to eat it and talk about alternatives you can eat. Of course, not everyone is receptive to the request, but you can show her an alternative grain-free recipe that she could tweak to make her own. Clearly her famous recipe isn't going to be quite the same if it's altered to be grain-free, but this approach shows her that you know she loves to make your favorite cake and that you want to enjoy it, but the original recipe isn't something you can eat anymore. If she's not open to changing her recipe, then simply let her know that you have always loved her cake but you're doing something for your health right now, and ask her to respect that you'll decline to have some this year.

If you're looking for some healthier alternatives to treats, the flourless brownies on page 458 are an excellent swap for their flour-filled counterpart. And for more amazing grain-free baked goods, I recommend the books *Make it Paleo*, *Make it Paleo II*, and *Gather*, all by Haley Mason and Bill Staley, and *Every Last Crumb*, by Brittany Angell.

What they say: "Why aren't you eating the bread? It's so good, and it's always been your favorite!" [Usually said as they eat the food you've just turned down.]

What it means: "I don't understand why you've changed"; "Your choices make me feel uncomfortable and insecure about my own choices"

How to handle it: First, know that often when people comment on *our* choices, it's more of a reflection of how they feel about *their own* choices than anything else. Sure, friends may raise a curious eyebrow when you turn down your old favorite food at a party, for example. But a good friend will recognize that growth is a part of life and respect that you have made a change for yourself, whether for now or for the long term, and leave it at that. If you feel the need to explain yourself, have a simple sentence or two in mind as a response. Here are some ideas (of course, use your own experiences in terms of which food you've excluded and what relief or benefit you've experienced):

"I've been avoiding gluten lately as a test, and I've noticed I don't get those crazy headaches anymore."

"I decided to try avoiding sugar for a while and have been feeling really good—my energy has been so much better—so I'm going to stick with it."

"Remember that acne that I used to struggle with? Well, since eliminating grains, I've had much clearer skin and it's made me feel a lot better."

What they say: "Eating Paleo/gluten-free is a fad—most people aren't actually allergic to gluten, and it's silly to eliminate it unless you have celiac disease."

What it means: "I think that what you're doing seems pointless or overly/ unnecessarily rigid"; "That sounds hard and I don't think I could do it, so instead, I'm going to criticize what you're doing"

How to handle it: Focus on how you're feeling and let them know that what the way of eating is called (Paleo, gluten-free, whatever it is) is less important to you than how much better you feel now that you've made some changes to the way you eat.

In general, remember that difficult situations happen to everyone, and we need to be prepared. We can handle them in whatever way works best for us, and one of those ways may to be avoid certain people whenever possible. Of course, with family, this isn't always easy! So stand up for yourself without becoming defensive, be calm and confident in your own choices, and keep the focus on how you feel rather than any dogmatic views about nutrition. While it's easy for people to debate topics of nutrition, regardless of whether or not their arguments are sound, it's impossible for someone to tell you that you don't feel better eating the way you do.

Avoid being argumentative yourself and calmly shift the conversation to other topics whenever things seem to be getting sticky and out of hand. Pick your battles, make some concessions, try not to be a Paleo perfectionist at a party or event, and generally avoid certain hot-button topics. And if a friend or family member is honestly interested in what you're doing but has questions that you aren't prepared to answer in the moment, point them to this book. The easiest way to support someone else is to share resources that they can refer to again and again.

Coming to Terms with Baked Goods

If there's one hot topic in Paleo books and the blogosphere, it's "Paleo-fied" baked goods! A lot of the typical American diet centers around grain-based baked goods—think bread, pizza crust, hamburger and hot dog buns, sandwiches, and of course treats like cookies and cake. It can be tough to give all these up when you switch to Paleo, so many people look for grain-free, Paleo-friendly alternatives that look and taste as close to the real thing as possible.

There are absolutely pros and cons to Paleo baked goods, both homemade and prepared, and their prevalence on social media, in books, and on blogs. Real, whole foods should be the bulk and the focus of what we're eating, and while grain-free Paleo treats can have a place within our diet, they may also be a major distraction from the whole point of the dietary change.

It's important to recognize that for many people, going Paleo means giving up literally *everything* they are eating day in and day out. This can be extremely daunting, and even the idea of it can keep people from considering the switch. A huge number people find comfort in re-creating their favorite foods in grain-free versions when they first go Paleo. But this can be both a great thing and a slippery slope. For some, eating baked goods that look like old favorites can prevent them from adjusting their mindset to focus on real, whole foods.

Ultimately, the decision about how (or if) you include Paleo baked treats needs to be yours. To help you decide, here's my list of pros and cons about these treats. But how you move forward from here is up to you!

PROS

- They're great for allergen-free birthdays and other celebrations and help (mostly) children to not feel excluded, especially in school.

- Making them at home can help you keep the culture, tradition, and joy that exist around the traditional versions. For instance, with grain-free flours, you don't have to give up making Christmas cookies during the holidays.

- When you make Paleo treats at home, the time involved can help you appreciate them more and also allow you to eat less of them. You'll also source quality ingredients, so you know that what's in them is safe for you to eat.

- They provide a more nutrient-dense version of a treat that might otherwise include some of the poorest-quality fats and carb sources (vegetable oils and refined grain flours). This is certainly not a reason to eat more of them, but it's a reason why they're a better choice than their commercially made counterparts.

Can't seem to escape Paleo treats?

If you don't like seeing recipes for treats in the Paleo community . . . don't like or share them on your social media feeds! The community's response to these recipes is what perpetuates their creation and sharing. When a blogger or author creates a healthy meat-and-veggies recipe and a baked treat recipe to share and sees the community clamor over the baked treat recipe, it's clear which one people want to have more of. While each author, blogger, and recipe creator needs to own their part in that process, it's also your personal decision to either feed into it or not.

CONS

- They can stall your progress toward weight loss and better health or even keep it from ever beginning. The calorie density of a Paleo brownie or cookie, for example, is likely no different from that of the conventional version, and these treats may crowd out better-quality food choices.

- Since they combine sugar and fat or salt, sugar, and fat and are hyperpalatable, they can fuel emotional eating (eating when you want comfort, rather than listening to your body and eating when you are hungry).

- If you're eating a lot of treats, you may not be changing your eating habits the way you want to—they can distract you from focusing on whole foods.

Ultimately, whether or not these treats are problematic comes down to the individual. We are all different in the ways in which these types of foods impact us. Some of us aren't overly tempted by them, but many of us are, and when we make a tray of grain-free brownies and proceed to eat all of them instead of perhaps just one, it's clearly not good for our health.

Remember, no one has ever said that treats will help anyone lose weight or heal from disease. They exist to make you feel better—emotionally and socially. And that's a lot of power to give a cookie, don't you think?

Paleo in Public: Dining Out

As a nutritionist, I have heard every reason under the sun why people can't keep their eating habits in check when they're away from the comforts of their coconut oil–stocked kitchens. I promise that you can still be social while maintaining a Paleo lifestyle.

Know Before You Go

When you are planning to eat at a restaurant, preview the menu to determine what will work for you. (If there are truly no healthy options, choose a different restaurant!) Most restaurants post their menus on their websites, and choosing what you'll order before you arrive not only lets you pick the healthiest option, it also gives you more time to visit with your meal companions. Bear in mind, too, that many restaurants will accommodate changes to a particular meal if you give them advance notice. Call the restaurant before you go to inquire about a gluten-free menu option, for example, or simply ask how the dishes that sound good to you are prepared.

With a growing number of diners requesting gluten-free dishes, a lot of chain restaurants, such as Legal Sea Foods, P.F. Chang's, Outback Steakhouse, and Bonefish Grill, now offer separate gluten-free menus. This doesn't mean that your dining experience will necessarily be perfectly Paleo, but making gluten-free choices will help you avoid digestive upset for the most part.

When you make reservations, use that opportunity to let the restaurant know about your special needs. If you are using an online reservation system, use the comments or notes section to share this information. If you prefer to be discreet about your dietary requirements, both of these quiet methods can help you avoid discomfort at the table while ordering.

Then, before you go, eat a small snack of soy-free jerky, nuts, nut butter, a few bites of avocado, or leftover meat. If you aren't starving when you sit at the table, you will be much more likely to stay on track.

Navigating the Menu

Once you are seated at the restaurant, pass on the breadbasket. It can be hard to resist bread if it's right in front of you. Don't test yourself! If everyone in your party is agreeable, simply ask the server not to bring bread to the table and request olives, celery sticks, carrots, or cucumber slices, if they're available.

Finger foods are often breaded, fried, or made with grains, dairy products, and seed oils, but healthier options made from simple, clean ingredients are easy to find. Look for grilled, broiled, or baked meat dishes, which are less likely to be breaded. Or simply skip the appetizers, or opt for a salad starter.

If a meal comes with french fries, bread, or pasta, ask that these are left off of your plate or substitute vegetables instead. Look at the menu for vegetables that might be available. If you see grilled squash as a side with another dish, chances are that you can ask for it with your entrée. Be an aware diner, however. Don't ask for mashed sweet potatoes if they aren't listed anywhere on the menu.

Some restaurants charge a bit extra for vegetables if you order them separately but will make a swap without blinking. You may even end up with a huge pile of veggies for no extra charge simply because the restaurant isn't accustomed to making substitutions and wants to accommodate you.

Of course, when making special requests, always be polite to your server. Nine times out of ten, he or she is trying to meet your needs as much as possible, and these days many kitchen and wait staff members are more educated about food allergies. Just make sure you phrase your request as a serious question ("If there's any soy sauce in it, can you leave it out?"), not an off-putting demand ("You have to make it without soy sauce!"). If you have been diagnosed with celiac disease or have an extreme gluten sensitivity or food allergy, carry a detailed information card containing your dining requirements (a cutout card is included in the guide to gluten on page 107). This will help the server understand that you are not trying to be difficult.

SONO CELIACO

Celiac disease is actually very common in Italy, where wheat pasta was born. As a result, most restaurants there cater to gluten-free diners, making it easy to navigate an Italian vacation and still avoid wheat products. Carry a dining information card (see page 107) in Italian, or simply say, "Sono celiaco," which means "I have celiac disease."

Ask the Right Questions

Even if your sensitivity is not severe, you can be firm in your requests while also remaining polite. Don't make assumptions about the contents of the dishes.

Ask the server for details; they're used to it. It's the only way to feel confident that the meal you'll be served will leave you feeling full and satisfied, not sick and disappointed. Some of the most important questions to ask include:

- "Is any part of what I'm ordering breaded or dusted with flour of any kind?" Often meat and seafood dishes are breaded or even lightly dusted with flour before sautéing, baking, broiling, or roasting. At higher-end restaurants, this step can usually be left out when the chef prepares your meal.

- "I'm allergic to gluten. Can you find out if there is gluten or flour in the sauce or any other part of this dish?" Be sure to let your server know that if there is any uncertainty, you'd be happy to order something else that the server knows is safe.

- "What kind of frying oil do you use?" Most restaurants use vegetable oil for frying, so fried foods are usually not a good option when dining out. That includes sweet potato fries. It's the oil that is the problem, not the potatoes. Plus, sweet potato fries are typically dusted or coated in flour before frying!

The Best Choices for Different Cuisines

Italian food

Don't skimp on protein. Choose broiled, baked, or grilled chicken, fish, shrimp, or red meat. You can even order meatballs with red sauce, but be sure to ask if they contain flour or breadcrumbs, as some do. Order vegetables or salad on the side. Obviously, avoid bread, pasta, and breaded meats, such as Parmesan and francese dishes. At Italian restaurants, protein sources are often dusted with flour before cooking even if they're not breaded and fried, so be sure to ask about this, as most of these dishes can be prepared without the flour. Other healthy options include the antipasto platter with meat and vegetables and grilled vegetables with olive oil and balsamic vinegar.

If you are dying for pasta, the restaurant may have a gluten-free option. While I don't recommend this as a regular practice, ordering gluten-free pasta in a restaurant is better than buying this refined product to prepare at home—that way, you can enjoy it as an occasional treat rather than make it part of your everyday meals, which should have more vegetables and other nutrient-dense foods. Pay attention to how you feel afterward, however. Many people are as sensitive to gluten-free pastas as to those containing gluten. All refined grain products can leave you feeling lethargic and tired after a meal, which is not a sign that you have eaten healthful food. At home, you can make noodles from zucchini (recipe on page 403) as a nutritious substitute.

Mexican food

Choose primarily meat, salsa, and guacamole at a Mexican restaurant. If you're having an appetizer, ask the server for jicama, cucumbers, raw celery, or carrots to dip into guacamole. If it's an upscale Mexican restaurant, ask about a side of vegetables to add to your entrée. Skip tortillas and chips, which contain both corn and wheat flour, as well as beans and rice. Ask if there is flour in any sauces and opt for grilled meats. At some casual restaurants, like Chipotle, you can find meat that is not cooked in vegetable or soybean oil.

Japanese food and sushi

Sashimi is an easy option, or you can simply ask that the sushi rolls you order be made without rice. I do this every time I eat sushi. Most sushi chefs will roll them any way you order them, even if the server thinks at first that it may not be possible. Ask for extra daikon radish (the white shredded stuff you thought was just a garnish), and eat that as filler along with your sashimi or rolls. Avoid fried and tempura rolls as well as rolls that add tempura flakes for crunch, or simply ask that the flakes be omitted. While some sushi restaurants don't allow modifications, most will gladly accommodate your requests if you ask politely.

If you order rolls that come with sauces, be sure to let your server know that you cannot have anything with soy in it. In addition to soy sauce, this includes eel sauce and ponzu. If you are sure you are not sensitive to soy, bring your own wheat-free organic tamari (available in natural food stores or online). Commercially prepared soy sauces are made with wheat, and the vast majority of people find that avoiding even trace amounts of wheat helps them feel better.

If, like me, you're sensitive to both gluten *and* soy, try coconut aminos in place of soy sauce. This fermented coconut product has a taste and texture that's almost identical to soy sauce. You can dip your sushi in it as well as use it in recipes that call for soy sauce. It is one of the best substitutes I have found in years, and I now actually prefer its taste to that of soy sauce.

Avoid teriyaki dishes, gyoza (dumplings), edamame, and most other appetizers. As much as I love seaweed salad and think that sea vegetables are an excellent food choice, they are typically prepared commercially (not on location at the restaurant) and are loaded with soy sauce and, often, monosodium glutamate (MSG), which is a neurotoxic food additive.

Indian food

At an Indian restaurant, tandoori meats and grilled or roasted vegetables that are not drowning in sauces are best. Skip the naan and the rice, of course. If you would like to enjoy a curry dish, ask your server whether flour is used in the sauce. Traditionally, Indian food was cooked in ghee, but most modern Indian restaurants have moved on to less-expensive vegetable oils. Request that ghee is used if it is available.

Thai food

Opt for a curry dish or other coconut milk–based dish without the rice. Ask the server if the dish includes soy sauce, as this is often a problem with many Thai dishes. Many Thai restaurants now list gluten-free dishes on the menu, so choosing one of those options is one of the easiest ways to avoid grains while enjoying Thai food. But most Thai food is naturally gluten-free, and the main grain used is rice. While I don't recommend rice consumption as a regular practice for most people, if you feel that you can tolerate a small amount of white rice or rice noodles without digestive upset, you can indulge while dining out on Thai food, as long as it is a rare occurrence. This means once a month at most. Again, pay attention to how you feel after eating rice. Many people experience lethargy or bloating after meals containing rice.

Pizza

There is simply no great way to enjoy a healthy version of pizza while dining out. If you want pizza, make one at home instead using almond or coconut flour. If you search online for "meatza recipe" or "Paleo pizza crust recipe," you will find instructions. After you have followed the Paleo dietary guidelines for a while, you may discover that you can handle gluten-free restaurant items on occasion. Then, you may be safe to order a gluten-free pizza. Keep in mind, however, that the cheese used is usually the lowest quality possible, as restaurants often source ingredients based on price.

Chinese food

If you have a favorite local Chinese restaurant, it may be worth developing a relationship with them and finding out if they can omit the soy sauce from some of their dishes and substitute coconut aminos that you provide or, if you are not sensitive to soy but are sensitive to gluten, an organic, gluten-free tamari. Beyond that, unless you know that the restaurant is willing to cater to special requests for no MSG and sauces without added sugar or soy sauce, I recommend avoiding Chinese food when dining out. If you're in a pinch, steamed dishes are generally safe, but it's better to cook Chinese food at home, such as a stir-fry using coconut oil and coconut aminos. If you are sensitive to coconut, you can cook with ghee or another animal fat and use a sauce made from tahini (see page 432) as a finisher.

Paleo Party Prowess

If you're headed to a party, ask the host or hostess what they plan to serve so that you know what to expect. Of course, don't make a fuss about your dietary needs unless they're open and friendly about accommodating you. If you do feel comfortable explaining your way of eating to them, let them know that grilled, baked, or roasted meats and vegetables with herbs and spices are all perfectly fine. Be sure to explain that some sauces can be problematic, so if it's possible, leaving them on the side is ideal.

Assuming there will be food you can eat at a party is a surefire way to be disappointed and hungry. After all, most people use parties as an excuse to indulge in treats or unhealthy food. So consider bringing a dish or two that you know will satisfy your hunger. The host or hostess will be happy to have the contribution, and you'll be relieved to know that you won't be hungry all night or suffering later. There are plenty of party-friendly recipes in this book that will surely please a crowd!

Paleo on the Go

I know firsthand how tricky it can be to find good food while traveling away from home, but it's certainly not impossible with just a little bit of forethought and planning.

Before You Hit the Road (or Air, or Water...)

About one to two weeks ahead, think about any special travel foods you may want to order online, like jerky, bars, or dried fruits. Some brands we love are Steve's PaleoGoods (jerky and dried fruit), Sophia's Survival Food (jerky), and EPIC (jerky bars).

Take advantage of travel review sites like Trip Advisor and Yelp. Reading restaurant reviews ahead of time and searching for popular terms like *gluten-free, organic, grass-fed*, and even *farm-to-table* can help take the stress out of deciding where to eat while you're on the road.

At hotels and resorts and on cruise ships, don't be afraid to ask questions and make requests to customize your experience. The staff is there to make your stay enjoyable and will be happy to accommodate you. Of course, calling ahead to communicate any special needs also helps, but on-the-spot requests for gluten-free meals, for example, can typically be catered to pretty easily.

Request a mini fridge in your hotel room. If necessary, explain that you have food allergies. Every hotel has them for medical purposes, so calling or making the request ahead of time is your best bet. Alternatively, book a room in a suites/extended-stay venue that has a kitchenette. These are becoming more and more popular and are not necessarily more expensive than other types of hotels.

Find a grocery store. Prior to your departure date, search online to locate a grocery store like Whole Foods, Trader Joe's, or other organic grocers or natural food co-ops at your destination and stock up when you arrive.

Pack more food than you think you'll need. You'll never be sorry that you carried some extra snacks, but a delay on the tarmac or an unexpected, extended time without food handy can leave you hungry and scavenging for less-healthy choices. Err on the side of packing a bit more to keep yourself well prepared.

Carry These Items with You

- A small can opener
- A small but sharp knife (only in your checked bag, not your carry-on, or the TSA will confiscate it)
- Small empty food storage containers and sealable plastic bags for leftovers or ice
- Disposable plastic utensils or a set of reusable utensils
- A few paper or lightweight reusable plates
- A small salt shaker (Redmond Real Salt makes one)
- Travel-sized jars of spices and herbs, such as black pepper, cinnamon, garlic powder, rosemary, and oregano
- A small sponge and dish soap (if you have reusable items). This is especially helpful during a road trip.

Foods to Take with You

When you travel, you may need to pack foods with you or make a stop at a local grocery store upon arrival in order to stay on track. Here is a list of protein, carbohydrate, and fat options that travel well or that can be kept in a hotel room with a mini fridge.

Easy Protein

- Clean-ingredient deli meats (avoid any with added sugar or sweeteners, natural flavors, carrageenan, BHA, BHT, or other additives besides salt and seasonings)
- Canned wild salmon, tuna, and sardines. Vital Choice (available online), Wild Planet, Whole Foods, and Trader Joe's are good brands.
- Wild smoked salmon or precooked wild shrimp
- Imported meats like prosciutto and chorizo, which often only contain pork, spices, and salt as ingredients
- Whole roasted chicken (plain or with just salt and pepper, or with only ingredients you recognize, as most contain undesirable ingredients)
- Jerky or kits from companies like Steve's Original, Sophia's Survival Food, or US Wellness Meats. Avoid brands with soy or additives you don't recognize.
- Hard-boiled eggs
- Nuts (though more fat than protein)

Easy Fats

- Extra-virgin olive oil in a portable, spillproof container
- Coconut oil sold in packets (Artisana brand) or packed in a spillproof container
- Packets of nut butter or coconut butter (Artisana brand), or a jar packed in your checked suitcase
- Macadamia nuts, walnuts, hazelnuts
- Coconut flakes

- Guacamole
- Dark chocolate (80 percent cacao or higher) that's good-quality and low in sugar

Easy Carbohydrates

- Vegetables that travel well, like carrots, celery, and bell peppers
- Salads, "naked" and with lots of veggies
- Romaine lettuce hearts (perfect for wrapping proteins)
- Canned sweet potato or butternut squash (don't forget the can opener!)
- Fruits that travel well, like apples, oranges, other citrus fruits, grapes, and bananas. Berries are easy if you have a cooler bag. Fruit salad is easy to find in most places, even at the airport.
- Fruit/nut bars (Lärabar is a good brand) or trail mix without additives

Tips for the Trip

Use a cooler bag with a leakproof ice pack to keep foods fresh in your hotel room. Pack your ice pack in your checked luggage wrapped in zip-top bags so that it doesn't leak.

Pack foods in tall/narrow containers that stay upright and won't spill. Rinse and reuse containers you bring and any food containers you purchase along the way.

Use lots of small and large zip-top bags. Not only do they hold food and prevent spills, they can also hold ice from an ice machine or messy trash from your travels.

Keep extra protein and fat sources, like jerky, nuts, or nut butter packets, on hand in case of a flight delay. They're lightweight, so it's easy to pack extra. Sophia's Survival Foods is one of my favorite brands.

In a pinch, very dark chocolate, nuts, and/or trail mix can work as healthy snacks and are often a healthier choice than protein bars or other available snacks.

Bunless burgers can often be made to order even if they're not on the menu—which they usually aren't.

Bring sea salt and organic black pepper in small containers to season bland travel food. I like Redmond Real Salt, and I refill their salt shakers with pepper for my trips.

Air Travel Tips

Use small, 2- to 3-ounce spillproof containers for liquids. If possible, make sure the volume size of the container is stamped on it so that the TSA can see it easily, though tiny bottles up to 4 ounces are usually fine. I highly recommend carrying extra-virgin olive oil this way for use on salads. (Note: Clear bottles are fine for small amounts of EVOO since you'll consume them before they are rancid.)

Use clear containers for semi-solid items like guacamole, so that they can be viewed easily.

Dry foods are perfectly acceptable in carry-on bags, so don't hesitate to bring food with you. This even means leftovers from dinner, a salad, and other homemade items. Only liquids and semi-liquids are ever in question.

Take advantage of frequent flyer benefits such as "club rooms," which may offer healthy snacks. For example, the United Club often stocks fruit like apples and bananas as well as organic tea bags that can be used in-flight. The options for Paleo aren't amazing, but they exist and are free, so if you have access to these benefits, use them!

Bring a refillable water bottle. While you can certainly buy bottled water once you're through security, you can easily refill a bottle in any airport. They all have water fountains, and many even offer filtered water.

You can usually find salads with meat at airport food vendors. Simply remove any unwanted ingredients and ask for lemons to use for dressing with the olive oil you have brought with you.

Cruise Ship Travel Tips

You likely won't have a mini fridge on the ship; instead, you'll have a "beverage cooler." This means that foods stored in it won't be chilled to 40°F or below, as is recommended for food safety. While some foods will be okay in these coolers overnight or for a short time, most won't.

You may bring large bottles of liquids onto a cruise ship. (Keep in mind that you'll need to store them in checked luggage during air travel or purchase them after your flight.) There are typically limitations on how much water and alcohol you can bring aboard, so check with your cruise line in advance.

Many ships will offer a gluten-free menu, but they require advance notice (several weeks to a couple of months). Check your booking information and be sure to call or e-mail the cruise line if you need to make this request. While most ships can accommodate gluten-free diets easily when they're a dietary preference, if you have celiac disease and need to be even more diligent, contacting the cruise line ahead of time can make all the difference.

Guide to: Dining Out
Tips & tricks for navigating menus and making healthy choices

AMERICAN FOOD

AVOID: Fried foods, anything breaded, sandwiches, wraps, and premixed dressings. Ask about flour used in sauces, soups, and stews—you may need to avoid many of those as well.

ENJOY: Bunless or lettuce-wrapped burgers and salads with lemon or vinegar and olive oil. Grilled foods are a good option.

CHINESE FOOD

AVOID: Dishes in sauces, fried foods, dumplings, noodles, and rice. Unless you know the restaurant well enough to make special requests for no MSG and sugar-free sauces, it's best to avoid Chinese food. Many of the sauces contain hidden sweeteners.

ENJOY: If you have a trusted restaurant or find yourself without another option, ask for steamed chicken, shrimp, or beef with vegetables. Avoid sauces and keep it simple. When you're eating Paleo, homemade Chinese food is best.

INDIAN FOOD

AVOID: Naan, rice, and paneer (a cheese). Ask about flour/gluten in sauces and spice rubs.

ENJOY: Meats and veggies that are grilled or roasted and are not drowning in sauces. Tandoori meats are often marinated in yogurt, so they are a grey-area food.*

ITALIAN FOOD & PIZZA

AVOID: Bread, pasta, and breaded meats. Ask about sauces and preparation (meatballs often contain breadcrumbs). There is simply no great way to enjoy a healthy version of pizza while dining out.

ENJOY: Broiled chicken, fish, shrimp, or other protein with red sauce and veggies or salad on the side. If you're craving pizza, make "meatza" or pizza with a Paleo-friendly crust at home.

JAPANESE FOOD & SUSHI

AVOID: Rice, anything fried or tempura-battered, and imitation crab. Avoid soy sauce, eel sauce, ponzu, and spicy sauces, as they often contain monosodium glutamate (MSG).

ENJOY: Sashimi or broiled fish.

MEDITERRANEAN FOOD

AVOID: Pasta, pita, couscous, tabbouleh, falafel, faro, orzo, rice, and other grains; cheeses; sauces that use yogurt.

ENJOY: Grilled meats, kebobs (but ask if flour is added; it shouldn't be), vegetables, eggplant and other vegetable dips.

MEXICAN FOOD

AVOID: Tortillas and chips (both corn and flour), beans, and anything fried.

ENJOY: Meat, veggies, salsa, and guacamole—often you can ask for these ingredients to be placed over a salad. Ask for celery, carrots, or cucumber to dip into guacamole or salsa. Ask for a side of vegetables instead of beans and rice.

THAI FOOD

AVOID: Sauces that contain soy and peanuts,* noodles, and desserts.

ENJOY: A curry dish or other coconut milk-based dish without rice, soups, and proteins with vegetables (but ask about flour and soy in sauces).

Two amazing resources for easy Paleo-friendly recipes are *Gather: The Art of Paleo Entertaining,* by Hayley Mason and Bill Staley, which provides an entire at-home takeout-fakeout feast; and *Paleo Takeout: Restaurant Favorites Without the Junk,* by Russ Crandall, which includes recipes for dishes from various cuisines.

tips & tricks for smart dining

Don't arrive starving. Eat a small snack of some nuts or nut butter, or even a few bites of avocado or leftover meat, before you head out the door.

Preview the restaurant's menu online before you go.

Check out reviews from other diners on a site like Yelp.com or TripAdvisor.com (especially when traveling).

Pass on the bread basket—it'll keep temptation away! Ask for sliced veggies or olives instead.

Skip the appetizers or opt for a salad starter.

Entrées are easy. While finger food is often breaded, fried, or otherwise carb-loaded, entrées that are made of simpler ingredients can be easy to find.

Look for grilled, broiled, or baked options, which are usually safer bets for Paleo dining. But ask the server for details on how things are prepared; they're used to questions! Be polite, but get the answers you need.

Make substitutions. If a meal comes with french fries, bread, or pasta, ask that the kitchen leave it off of the plate or substitute some vegetables instead.

AT PARTIES

Ask the host what they plan on serving so you know what to expect. Bring a dish or two that you know you can enjoy and that will satisfy your hunger.

---

*While I recommend strictly eliminating grey-area foods during your Paleo elimination and reintroduction period (see page 44), after that, you may find that you can enjoy them now and then when dining out, in the overall context of a healthy, balanced, nutrient-dense diet. Grey-area foods include high-quality dairy, gluten-free grains (including rice), peanuts, and cashews. See page 46 for more on when, why, and how to possibly reintroduce these foods.

Guide to: Travel

Highlights of tips & tricks for keeping things healthy while you travel. For the full details, see pages 136 to 137.

before you hit the road (or air, or water . . .)

· About 1–2 weeks ahead, order online any special travel foods, like jerky, bars, or dried fruits.

· Look up healthy restaurants on sites like TripAdvisor and Yelp.

· At hotels and resorts and on cruise ships, don't be afraid to ask questions in advance and make requests to customize your experience.

· Request a mini fridge in your hotel room.

· Find a grocery store at your destination so you can stock up when you arrive.

· Pack more food than you think you'll need.

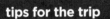

tips for the trip

• Use a cooler bag with a leakproof ice pack to keep foods fresh in your hotel room.

• Pack foods in tall/narrow containers that stay upright and won't spill.

• Use lots of small and large zip-top bags to hold food, ice, and trash.

• Keep extra protein and fat sources, like jerky, nuts, or nut butter packets, on hand in case of a flight delay.

• In a pinch, very dark chocolate, nuts, and/or trail mix can work as healthy snacks.

• Bunless burgers can often be made to order.

• Bring sea salt and organic black pepper in small containers to season bland travel food.

air travel tips

• Use small, 2- to 3-ounce spillproof containers for liquids.

• Use clear containers for semi-solid items like guacamole, so that they can be viewed easily.

• Dry foods are perfectly acceptable in carry-on bags, so don't hesitate to bring food with you.

• Take advantage of frequent flyer benefits such as "club rooms," which may offer healthy snacks.

• Bring a refillable water bottle.

• You can usually find salads with meat at airport food vendors.

cruise ship travel tips

• While some foods will be okay overnight in the cabin's "beverage cooler," most won't.

• You may bring large bottles of liquids onto a cruise ship.

• Many ships will offer a gluten-free menu, but they require advance notice (several weeks to a couple of months).

Frequently Asked Questions

Still curious about a few things? You're not alone! Here are some of the most popular questions I'm asked.

General

Should I be counting calories?

For most general health goals, I do not recommend counting calories. Here's why:

- When you eat a Paleo diet, restricting calories means restricting nutrients. This is because counting calories limits your intake of whole, nutrient-dense foods, thereby limiting your intake of the vitamins and minerals you need for your cells to function well.

- Most people feel satisfied when they eat real, whole foods in reasonable portions. (See page 52 for basic portion size recommendations.) These foods balance the hormone signals that respond to dense sources of protein, naturally occurring fats, and vegetables and ensure steady, even blood sugar levels, which promotes long-term satiety. Translation: you aren't likely to overeat whole foods.

- Counting calories adds stress to your life. You have to weigh and measure all of your food, log it into some kind of calculator, and worry over the minutiae of what you eat. Adding stress to your life is not a good idea. You're stressed enough already, aren't you?

That said, calories do count at some point. For those who are struggling with fat loss, want to gain weight, or need to maintain athletic performance, counting calories can be a useful tool. And the awareness that comes from logging your food intake can, of course, be a tremendous eye-opener. Often people believe they are eating too much when they're actually not eating enough to sustain their metabolism. This means that their daily activities require more calories than they realize to keep their bodies well fueled. Eating too few or too many calories can be problematic, and a numerical assessment of your overall intake is a good starting point for figuring out whether eating more or less will be beneficial.

For example, for most women, 1200 calories is the minimum amount necessary for simply waking up and being alive for a day. For men, the number is likely around 1600 calories. Our bodies use calories to perform basic life functions like breathing and thinking. If you restrict calories below these numbers, you fail to supply adequate nutrients for these functions, so trying to exercise on top of that nutrient deficiency can cause your body to hold on to fat as a protective mechanism instead of using it for fuel.

Therefore, people who want to lose body fat often actually need to eat more. If you undereat, you don't give your body the chance to complete metabolic processes. It's like asking your car to run without enough gas in the tank.

If you have a metabolic issue that prevents you from feeling hunger signals, keeping track of calories can help you to make appropriate adjustments and make sure you're eating enough. If you are indeed eating too much, it's easy to figure out what you're adding that isn't necessary to feel satisfied. It may be a few extra ounces of protein or an extra tablespoon of coconut oil or nut butter. Just 2 to 3 extra ounces of protein at each meal can add up to an entire extra serving over the course of the day.

If you're unsure how to proceed with your own fat loss goals and, after tracking your intake for a few days, find that you may be undereating or overeating, I recommend working one on one with a coach or nutritionist. Seek out someone who specializes in macronutrient breakdowns for fat loss and who will also create a sample meal plan for you that focuses on real food—not calorie-free sweeteners or other non-food ingredients.

If I can't afford to buy everything grass-fed, wild-caught, organic, and perfectly sourced, will I still reap the health benefits of this way of eating?

Yes! Many of the health benefits you'll experience come from simply the elimination of modern refined foods. Once you've gotten those foods out of your diet, you can work little by little to improve the quality of the foods you eat, as your budget allows. (Check out my tips for eating Paleo on a budget on page 60.)

What can I eat for breakfast?

Real food! What other animal on the planet eats "breakfast foods"? You can eat anything for breakfast as long as you stick to the Paleo way of eating. You may just need an extra ten minutes to cook some meat or eggs. (For meals without any eggs at all, see the Autoimmune Conditions 30-Day Meal Plan on page 174.)

A strict Paleo diet isn't giving me the relief I thought it would. Should I follow the Autoimmune Protocol (AIP)?

If your health status isn't improving after two to three months on a strict Paleo diet, you may find that eliminating grains, legumes, dairy, and sweeteners simply isn't enough to get to the root of what ails you. To take it further, you may want to try eliminating eggs, nuts, seeds, and nightshade vegetables—the basic framework of AIP.

For many, eliminating these additional foods can be effective. However, if your *lifestyle* is not supporting healing, or if you've only completed step 1 of the 4R Protocol (page 44), you will need to take a more complete approach to your healing process. The Autoimmune Conditions 30-Day Meal Plan (page 174) includes recommendations outside of removing more foods from your diet. Put these into action first and see if you can feel better without avoiding eggs, nightshades, nuts, and seeds.

Eliminating more and more foods can create stress, which can itself have inflammatory effects on the body. Additionally, if you have any history of developing an overly restrictive or disordered eating pattern, or you feel that you could be prone to this, I would not recommend this approach.

Eliminating more foods from your diet is a very personal decision, and one that shouldn't be taken lightly or with the assumption that it is always the best answer.

Are "superfoods" real? Do I need to be eating them?

It's fair to say that some foods are superior to other foods when it comes to their impact on our bodies. But let's clarify what "superfood" truly means—it's about potent nutrient density, not about magical superpowers. Many foods could be considered superfoods with this definition, but they're not likely the ones you're thinking of: acai berries, goji berries, even blueberries. While all of those may be perfectly healthy and delicious, they're not superpowered.

Some of nature's most powerful superfoods are liver, egg yolks, grass-fed and pastured beef, and wild fatty cold-water fish, like salmon. Calorie for calorie, these foods contain more essential vitamins and minerals that are critical for optimal human health—and difficult to find in other places—than other foods. We're talking about nutrients like choline, vitamin A, B vitamins, conjugated linoleic acid (CLA), and omega-3 fatty acids in the form of EPA and DHA, which our bodies need (versus ALA, alpha linolenic acid, which is the form of omega-3 available in foods like walnuts and chia seeds; it can be converted to EPA and DHA, but not very efficiently).

Vitamins and Supplements

Should I take supplements for general health?

It's easy to get caught up in a lot of hype about supplements, but your priority for at least the first three months should be to adjust your diet and lifestyle. For this reason, you'll notice that the Squeaky Clean Paleo 30-Day Meal Plan (page 234) does not include any supplements. Once you've made significant diet and lifestyle changes, I recommend getting your vitamin D levels tested by a doctor, holistic nutritionist, or naturopath. This is one of the most common deficiencies today, and vitamin D performs a large number of functions in the body. Beyond that, proper vitamin and mineral intake can be achieved largely from a well-balanced Paleo diet, as long as you're digesting and absorbing food properly. If you sense that you're deficient in something, find a practitioner who can help you determine if your digestion is working properly and if you need to make any adjustments regarding your diet and supplementation. There are a wide array of diagnostic tests that can be done, including an Organix Profile, available at a lab called Metametrix (only accessible to health-care practitioners), which may help you discover underlying micronutrient imbalances or impairment in your body's metabolic processes.

Should I take supplements if I have a medical condition?

The 30-Day Meal Plans in this book include supportive nutrients found in foods, as well as supplements to consider. I have not included dosages or prescriptive quantities because these vary based on each person's individual needs. However, the plans provide a great jumping-off point for you to create an approach that will work for you, including making smart choices regarding supplementation. If you feel that you need more assistance after about a month on a plan you have created for yourself, I recommend working with a holistic or Paleo-oriented practitioner. Ultimately, supplements should be taken just as the name suggests, on a supplemental basis—as an addition to food, not a replacement for it.

Should I take a fish oil supplement?

Fish oil (or any other isolated omega-3 fatty acid supplement) is geared toward balancing the ratio of omega-3s to omega-6s in your body. If you're eating the Standard American Diet, that ratio is likely 1:10 to 1:20. Ideally, it should be under 1:4, if possible.

But I don't generally recommend isolated fish oil supplementation for a few reasons. First, nutrients in food are much more bioavailable than supplements. Instead of supplementation, I recommend that you eat fish (a whole food) to increase your intake of omega-3.

It's also difficult to know and trust the source of isolated omega-3 supplements. Additionally, omega-3 is a polyunsaturated fatty acid (PUFA), and PUFAs are highly susceptible to damage (oxidation from heat, light, and air) if not handled carefully and appropriately. I don't trust that the delicate polyunsaturated fats in most omega-3 supplements were not damaged in the processing and extraction of the oil. Consuming damaged isolated omega-3 supplements is likely far worse than consuming none at all, so I don't recommend them.

When it comes to balancing your ratio of omega-3s to omega-6s, I always recommend reducing omega-6 intake drastically (as you will do when you eliminate vegetable oils, grains, and legumes) before adding any supplementation of omega-3 fatty acids. If you're concerned about systemic inflammation, you may even want to watch your intake of omega-6-rich items other than oils. Nuts high in omega-6 fatty acids include almonds, pecans, pine nuts, pistachios, and hazelnuts.

Why have you stopped recommending fermented cod liver oil?

While a large number of people, including many who followed meal plans in this book, have reported extremely positive results with fermented cod liver oil (FCLO), there has been controversy regarding several aspects of its healthfulness and nutritional efficacy in recent years. There's no consensus one way or the other, but to err on the side of caution, I've decided to go back to basics and remove the recommendation from my plans. This doesn't mean that I believe that FCLO is harmful or lacks the nutritional benefits it claims to deliver: if you currently take FCLO and feel you've received benefits from doing so, this isn't cause for alarm or a recommendation that you stop.

I will not be recommending a substitute for FCLO (though some have suggested replacing it with extra-virgin cod liver oil) because of concerns about consuming a refined source of isolated PUFA—see the answer to the question above on fish oil supplements for more information. That answer also provides advice for increasing omega-3s in your diet.

To increase your intake of vitamin A and K2, which were also purported to be found in FCLO, you can eat more liver from pastured animals (my Chicken Liver Pâté, page 426, and Bacon & Superfood Meatloaf, page 330, are excellent ways to do so) as well as eat more foods rich in vitamin K2: salami or other fermented meats, Gouda cheese, and natto, a fermented soy product. Many sources of vitamin K2 are not considered to be "Paleo," so this should be done at your own discretion and following the 4R Protocol outlined on pages 44 to 47.

How is vitamin K2 different from vitamin K1? Don't leafy greens contain vitamin K1?

Yes, leafy greens contain vitamin K1 (phylloquinone), which is largely responsible for supporting blood clotting and other body functions. This is why people who take blood-thinning medications are cautioned against eating too many leafy greens. Vitamin K2 (menaquinone) is still being heavily researched for its role in human health, but we already know it plays an important role in directing the placement and proper integration of calcium throughout the body. If you want to optimize your bone and heart health, make sure you get enough vitamin K2 from foods or concentrated food supplements. K2 is found primarily in animal foods, particularly those that many people today do not include in their diets, such as hard and soft cheeses from *grass-fed* milk, egg yolks, butter from *grass-fed* cows, and liver. Dairy products from animals that are not grass-fed are not sources of vitamin K2.

Specific Foods and Swaps

Is _____ Paleo?

If you often find yourself wondering if specific foods are allowed on a Paleo diet, please read pages 47 to 49, which have important information on this topic and the thought process surrounding it. Then refer to the list below for answers on some commonly questioned foods.

- Wheat and other gluten-containing foods: No

- Legumes (beans and lentils): No

- Green beans, peas, snow peas, and sugar snap peas: Yes

- Chocolate (isn't it a bean?!): Yes, it's Paleo-friendly, especially when very dark (little to no sugar added) and soy-free. Look for brands without soy lecithin, like Taza and Theo.

- Coffee (also a bean, right?): Yes. I recommend that you seek out organic coffee because it can otherwise have high amounts of pesticide residue.

- Bacon: Yes. I recommend using the highest-quality you can find; refer to the guide to food quality on page 63. Strictly avoid brands containing the additives BHA and BHT, which may be carcinogenic.

- Kombucha: Yes, the majority of sugar that is added to make this fermented tea beverage is "eaten" by the bacteria in the fermentation process. If you find a kombucha with more than about 15 grams of carbohydrates per serving, generally from fruit added for flavor, sugar may have been added after the initial fermentation, so it's not the best choice.

- Quinoa: No. Though often folks refer to it as a seed, its grainlike qualities typically put it in the "not Paleo" category.

- Chia seeds: Yes

- Peanuts and cashews: Technically, no. But it may be worth testing elimination and reintroduction of these, especially if you're allergic to other "Paleo" nuts, like almonds and walnuts and are looking for possible substitutes.

- Unrefined natural sweeteners (honey, maple syrup, molasses, coconut sugar): In strict Paleo terms, sweeteners are *not* part of the plan, with the exception perhaps of honey or date paste. But most people consider unrefined sweeteners such as these to be acceptable after the initial stages of cleaning up your diet, as long as they are used in small amounts. You'll find that there are fewer recipes for treats in this book compared to most Paleo cookbooks, and I use fairly low amounts of sweeteners in those recipes for this reason.

I see a lot of Paleo people eating white rice, but isn't it a grain? Is it allowed on Paleo?

Technically, no, rice is not Paleo, whether white, brown, or wild. Rice is a grain and grains are not considered part of a strict Paleo diet.

That said, lots of people who once ate strict Paleo or who still eat *mostly* Paleo include white rice in their diets. There are a couple of reasons for this.

First, one of the key problems with grains is their digestibility (or lack thereof). But when rice is polished, the brown exterior that contains potentially tougher-to-digest components is removed. The white rice that remains—which is mostly just starch—tends to be easier to digest, and you'll often hear it referred to as a "safe starch" for this reason. During the reintroduction phase of the 4R Protocol (page 46), many people find that they tolerate white rice (and possibly some other gluten-free grains) well.

Second, many athletes and very active people find that it's difficult to get enough carbohydrates by relying solely on starchy vegetables, or they want more options for easy, unrefined starch when away from home, and they may not want to add fruit for various reasons. Adding white rice, if you tolerate it well, can be a great way to get more carbohydrates without consuming refined flour-based foods. Furthermore, in the context of a diet rich in vegetables, meat, and healthy fats, the inclusion of white rice isn't likely to crowd out more nutrient-dense options.

What about white potatoes?

I've never considered white potatoes to not be Paleo. Though they can be problematic for those who are sensitive to nightshade vegetables (tomatoes, potatoes, peppers, and eggplants), most people tolerate white potatoes just fine. If you find that you don't feel great after eating white potatoes, try peeling them first so you aren't consuming the antinutrients in the peel. If you still find that they don't work well for you, you can of course enjoy sweet potatoes exclusively—they are not part of the nightshade family, and they are lower in starch (which is hard to digest for some people).

Why should I incorporate more organ meats into my diet? And how?!

Many people find it daunting to think about eating offal such as liver, heart, tongue, oxtail, and even kidneys. But our ancestors (and even our grandparents and many of our parents!) grew up eating these regularly. It's only in a modern, processed, and manufactured food landscape—one where we are no longer raising our own animals for consumption—that we turn up our noses at these foods. Organ meats are some of the most nutrient-dense foods available, and those who came before us knew that we shouldn't waste these parts of the animal. If we want to be respectful to the animals we eat, we eat nose-to-tail as much as possible, consuming as many parts as we can and using the bones for broth. Plus, finding a way to incorporate organ meats into our diet can help us save money.

The easiest way to eat these foods is to try recipes that include them with other great flavors. Some recipes use smaller amounts of organ meats, while others feature them as the main source of protein. I recommend starting slowly, with my Chicken Liver Pâté recipe on page 426 or the Bacon & Superfood Meatloaf on page 330. From there, branch out and try recipes in other books, like *Mediterranean Paleo Cooking,* which I coauthored with Caitlin Weeks and Nabil Boumrar and which features several recipes for beef heart and liver, as well as a delicious oxtail recipe.

Do I really need to stop eating bread, pasta, and cereal forever?

It can take some time to create new habits, and it can be difficult at first. But it's worth completely eliminating these foods from your diet for at least one month so that you can closely examine how you feel when you reintroduce them. You will then know just how much they affect your overall health. (The 4R Protocol outlined on pages 44 to 47 is a good guide to eliminating grains and other problematic foods.)

You are likely to feel significantly different after eliminating these foods. It can be pretty profound! It may make you never want to touch them again.

The most important goal, of course, is to eliminate processed foods, but remember that gluten has specific properties that are detrimental to your health beyond what you feel on the surface. Gluten has the ability to activate the enzyme zonulin, which contributes to leaky gut (see page 99 for more information). This is why many longtime Paleo eaters may splurge on some grains from time to time but tend to keep the splurges to gluten-free options.

When people strive to change their diet and eliminate grain products, they sometimes forget to follow these steps, which make it easier:

- Consider all of your options for food throughout the day ahead of time. Preparation is key!

- Pack a meal to take with you when you know there might not be anything appropriate for you to eat during the course of your day.

- Review menu choices before going to a restaurant, and ask the wait staff how meals are prepared to avoid hidden gluten.

If wiping out all of your favorite foods feels suffocating, make use of the recipes in this book for items like squash noodles (page 403), muffins made with coconut flour (pages 276 to 279), and pancakes made with canned pumpkin (page 284), as well as other resources that have recipes for grain-free breads, pizzas, and more (see page 126 for some suggestions). These can help you make the transition away from grains and factory-made packaged foods.

Is it safe to bake with nut flours?

If you've decided to include some grain-free treats in your life (see page 128 for more on making that decision), you may realize that you're now baking with flours made from nuts loaded with polyunsaturated fatty acids (PUFAs). And, if you've reviewed the guide to cooking fats on page 65, you know that cooking with these delicate fats isn't recommended because their quality degrades once they're heated to a certain point.

While baking with nut flours *does* heat them, the baked item itself doesn't likely reach the temperature that the oven is set to. So, for example, baking a loaf of almond flour–based banana bread in a 350°F oven won't raise the temperature of the bread itself that high. Additionally, when you are cooking with a whole food rather than an isolated oil or fat, the components of the food itself (protein, fiber, vitamins, minerals, polyphenols, and so on) protect the delicate oils from damage. This is true of whole fish as well—we can still get healthy omega-3 fatty acids from cooked salmon, for example. And while nuts and seeds can certainly become rancid (if a jar of whole nuts or a bag of nut flour smells off, don't eat or use it), they're much more stable than the isolated oils. (Note: It's a good idea to store raw nuts, seeds, and their flours in the refrigerator or freezer to extend their shelf life.)

A more important concern about baking with nut or seed flours is relative portion sizes. If you were to eat a handful of almonds, for example, you'd be eating roughly ten to twenty almonds, whereas eating a single portion of an item baked with almond flour would mean consuming anywhere from twenty to fifty almonds. The same concern applies to nut and seed butters as well. Overdoing it with nuts or seeds can result in digestive distress, acne, hormonal imbalances, or overconsumption of calories, leading to an inability to lose body fat (we often don't realize exactly how many calories we are eating with nut butters or flours since the portions are so calorie-dense).

Where will I get carbs if I don't eat grains?

There are plenty of carbohydrate sources aside from refined foods and grain products. The chart of nutrient-dense sources of carbs on page 75 lists nineteen of them! Sweet potatoes are fast and easy to cook in the oven, and cooking one large butternut squash will give you several servings. Here are a few of my favorite carb-dense go-to dishes: Smoky Grilled Squash & Pineapple (page 408), Acorn Squash with Cinnamon & Coconut Butter (page 406), and Sweet & Savory Potatoes (page 421).

Are coconut, almond, and soy milks healthy to drink?

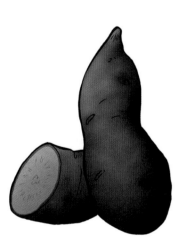

If you aren't eating cereal, you probably won't need milk except perhaps for coffee or an occasional recipe. In that case, I recommend organic, full-fat coconut milk without added texturizers (such as guar gum or xanthan gum). If you can't find a brand that meets all three of these criteria, choose a full-fat, organic coconut milk. Thai Kitchen, Natural Value, and Whole Foods brands fall into this category. Be aware, however, that guar and xanthan gums are derived from legumes, and while most people feel fine after consuming these small amounts of legume-derived ingredients, others react with digestive distress. If you find that you're using coconut milk daily and experiencing symptoms of inflammation, try making your own coconut milk—you can easily find instructions online. If that works, it was likely the additives that irritated your system. If that doesn't work, you may have an intolerance to coconut. Stop using coconut milk and see how you feel after two weeks.

If you know you don't tolerate coconut milk, or if you don't like it, you can also make your own fresh almond milk or other nut milks. Again, a simple web search will yield many recipes for homemade nut milks. Avoid prepackaged almond milk, since it's usually loaded with additives—as is soy milk, which also has a number of other problems.

I recommend that everyone avoid soy milk. The first problem, of course, is that it isn't a whole food—it's refined and processed. Soy also carries compounds called "trypsin inhibitors," which can interfere with your ability to properly digest proteins. Additionally, soy has been shown to disrupt normal endocrine function and to promote estrogen-like hormonal activity. Today's environment is already loaded with many other xenoestrogens (compounds that mimic natural estrogen hormones), including BPA in plastics and aluminum cans, BHA and BHT (food preservatives), parabens found in lotions and skin care items, and the insecticides, fungicides, and herbicides used to treat nonorganic foods—so it's best to avoid adding more to your system through soy. (For more on soy, check out *The Whole Soy Story* by Kaayla T. Daniel.)

What are FODMAPs? Who should avoid them?

FODMAPs is an acronym that stands for "fermentable oligo-di-monosaccharides and polyols." These are types of carbohydrates that can be difficult for some people to digest, resulting in symptoms that range from gas and bloating to IBS-like responses of diarrhea, constipation, or a combination/alternation of the two. Unlike other foods that aren't tolerated as a result of incomplete digestion within the small intestine, FODMAP foods become irritating to people for different reasons:

- Overgrowth of the wrong type of bacteria in the system (dysbiosis)
- Overgrowth of bacteria in the wrong part of the digestive system, usually the small intestine, where bacteria don't normally live (this condition is known as "small intestinal bacterial overgrowth," or SIBO)
- Low stomach acid production or secretion, which also contributes to the previous two bacterial issues
- A gut pathogen or infection, often obtained during travel abroad

Within the complete list of Paleo foods on page 61, FODMAP foods have been identified with an asterisk (*). If you find that you react to these foods, I recommend working with a naturopath, chiropractor, or other practitioner who can submit stool tests to labs for analysis in order to determine the root cause of the intolerance.

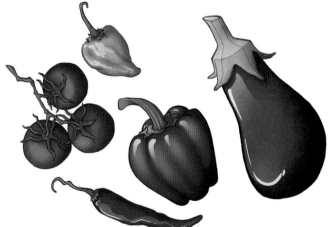

What are nightshades? Who should avoid them?

Nightshades are a family of plants that contain certain alkaloid compounds that can be irritating to those suffering from joint pain and inflammation. Tomatoes, white potatoes, peppers (all kinds, bell and hot), and eggplants are the most commonly consumed nightshades. Black pepper and sweet potatoes are *not* nightshades, however. Paprika is derived from peppers and should therefore be avoided—and if a packaged food contains "spices" without listing which are included, paprika is probably one of them.

Some other, less frequently consumed nightshades include tomatillos, tobacco, goji berries, cape gooseberries (also known as ground cherries—but regular gooseberries, Bing cherries, and Rainier cherries are not nightshades), garden huckleberries (not blueberries), and ashwagandha (an herb).

If you suffer from joint pain, joint inflammation, arthritis, cracking, or any other joint-related issues, eliminate nightshades from your diet for at least thirty days. (See the meal plan on page 178 for nightshade-free options.) The recipes in this book include nightshade-free variations wherever possible.

Won't my cholesterol be too high if I eat lots of eggs?

According to Uffe Ravnskov, a leading researcher and expert on cholesterol, the direct effect of a lower dietary cholesterol intake on serum (blood) cholesterol measures about 0.5 percent. Yes, you read that correctly. That's it!

Cholesterol is a precursor molecule for all of our hormones. We need it, and it isn't healthy to have a cholesterol level that is too low. It helps repair damaged tissues, and our bodies make as much as we need to function properly and fix oxidative damage.

High cholesterol doesn't run in your family unless there is a genetic predisposition for the rare condition called "familial hypercholesterolemia," which is the inability to process lipoprotein molecules properly and keeps blood cholesterol levels extremely high. Most people with a family history of high cholesterol have a family history of poor diet and lifestyle, not an actual genetic disorder.

Typically, your cholesterol numbers will improve by medical standards when you're on a Paleo diet as a result of the reduced stress and lowered inflammation in your system, which in turn results from avoiding sugar, grains, legumes, processed dairy products, and refined foods.

High cholesterol is generally a sign that something else is wrong, and the body is responding by producing more cholesterol in an attempt to repair it. Does high cholesterol mean you are less healthy or more prone to heart disease or death? I don't think so. In one report, Ravnskov even shows that cholesterol can protect us against heart disease. In short, the alarm about cholesterol is unfounded. Enjoy your eggs, yolks included.

Do I need to stop drinking alcohol?

Avoid alcohol entirely if you want to see the best possible results in the shortest possible time. This may mean that you abstain for thirty to sixty days, or it may mean you need to abstain for three to six months. For general health, one to two drinks per week of gluten-free alcoholic beverages (see page 107 for a list) should not be problematic. If you are dealing with a health condition, however, eliminating alcohol is highly recommended.

Do I need to stop drinking coffee?

It's a healthy goal to decrease your caffeine consumption to two cups (total of 16 ounces) or fewer per day, and don't drink it after noon if you want to get a good night's sleep. One cup of regular coffee contains roughly 150 milligrams of caffeine, and one shot of espresso contains about 50 to 75 milligrams of caffeine.

If you are propping yourself up on multiple cups of coffee or other caffeinated drinks (such as energy drinks or sodas) throughout the day, it's a sign that your system is running on fumes. First, try to get better and more sleep if at all possible. If you're simply staying up late or riding a blood sugar roller coaster, address your diet and lifestyle habits. Focus on sleep first, and then caffeine intake should be easier to limit.

If you feel you have a healthy relationship with caffeine and you can enjoy just one cup in the morning, go ahead and drink it. Just don't lie to yourself about it. Be honest and assess your use (or abuse) of caffeine.

What should I drink if I'm tired of plain water?

Adding freshly cut and squeezed lemon, lime, or orange wedges is a great way to give your water a kick. You can also try a "spa water" approach by adding cucumber slices with fresh mint leaves and other fruits or berries (just a couple of slices or pieces are plenty) to make it more interesting. Bubbly mineral water is also a good choice, either plain or with some citrus or other whole-food flavors added. You can also sip on warm broth (see the recipe on page 259) when the weather is cooler.

Getting Fit and Losing Weight

What's the best way to gain muscle mass but not body fat?

First of all, get adequate sleep! If you aren't sleeping well, you're at a disadvantage hormonally, and body composition is all about hormone balance. More sleep means more release of growth hormones, which is beneficial to building muscle as well as burning fat.

Next, make sure you are absorbing the nutrients from what you eat. Adding calories to your intake is pointless if your digestion is shot, so work on improving your digestion. If you have a leaky gut, review the steps on pages 103 to 105 to heal it first. Don't eat foods that irritate your system.

Once you're getting enough sleep and have healed your leaky gut—the two most important steps and what you absolutely must address first—follow these tips:

- Eat more protein (food, not powder), and chew your food well. (Read more about protein powder on page 152 and more about why chewing matters on page 78.)

- Reduce stress.

- Lift heavy things. I'm not a strength coach, so turn to a well-trained expert for help there.

- If you tolerate dairy products, add some raw, grass-fed dairy in the form of whole milk, cream, and/or kefir to your food intake.

- Go for calorie density first and appetite drivers thereafter. In other words, eat fats like coconut milk, dried coconut, avocado, macadamia nuts, and walnuts, and add extra-virgin olive oil on salads. Then you could try eating a few more starchy and carb-rich foods to help increase your appetite. You can also drink smoothies. Make one with full-fat coconut milk and some fruit or even sweet potato and cinnamon.

If you are doing everything right and not adding muscle mass, get your hormone levels tested and work with a practitioner to balance your levels.

What about protein powders?

They aren't food. Okay, I'll bend just a little: if you're looking to gain muscle mass or you're a hard-charging athlete who needs extra fuel beyond real meals to maintain your current level of muscle mass and performance, protein powders can be useful. But before you turn to them, refer to my answer to the last question if you want to add muscle mass. If your sleep and digestion are a problem, protein shakes are not the solution.

If you're on a mass-gain mission and are chowing down as much food as you can but still need to get some more calories and protein in your system, some powdered food might be okay for you. The best types of protein powder are either purely egg white or non-denatured whey protein from a grass-fed source. When you mix it into your shakes, add it at the very end and pulse it just a few times in the blender so that you don't denature the protein. That said, these are isolated nutrients and should be viewed as supplements, not a replacement for food. If you are capable of eating food, you should eat food.

For most people, powdered nutrition is not essential, and I find that it should be reserved for those with diminished capacity to chew and swallow, like the elderly and those suffering from dysphagia (inability to swallow).

What's the best approach to losing body fat?

Reducing body fat overall is about achieving a hormonal balance. Therefore, the first step is to reduce systemic inflammation by getting your digestive function and blood sugar in check. Additionally, adequate sleep is critical, as cortisol levels are regulated during restful sleep. Cortisol is going to drive your hormonal boat in either a favorable or unfavorable direction, so keep it in check.

If you are getting great sleep, your digestion is good, and your blood sugar is well balanced throughout the day, here are a few more tips:

- Monitor your carbohydrate intake relative to your activity level. This doesn't mean that everyone needs to be on a low-carb or zero-carb diet to lose body fat. It does mean, however, that if you are a very sedentary person, your carbohydrate intake should be limited to roughly 50 to 75 grams per day or fewer for at least one to three months to see how your body responds. If you are active daily, you may be able to take in about 75 to 100 grams of carbohydrates per day, and more if you are *very* active daily (for example, if your job requires constant standing or walking or involves manual labor). Reducing carbohydrate intake relative to your activity levels will allow your body to make better use of your own stored body fat as a fuel source in between meals. See page 70 for more on appropriate carbohydrate intake levels.

- If you are hungry, eat more protein, which will help you to feel satiated.

- Reduce your stress levels and prioritize sleep, as stress and lack of sleep can undo everything you do right nutritionally. Don't let your hard work of eating well be for nothing!

I'm doing everything right, but I'm not losing weight. Why?

If you've been following a Paleo diet strictly for at least three months without weight loss (if you needed to lose weight), there may be other factors at play. For many people, changes in diet and lifestyle go a long way toward rebalancing their body's systems. If you're not seeing the progress you'd like to see, your problems may be a result of hormonal imbalances, heavy metal or environmental toxicity, stress, overtraining, or lack of sleep. Bear in mind, too, that some people simply require longer periods (up to a year) of sustained intake of healthy foods before they see noticeable change. As daunting as that may sound, think about how long you have spent making poor food choices. When you think in those terms, a year isn't so long for your body to readjust. Changing your diet is not a magic bullet, though it can certainly work amazingly well in a very short period of time for a lot of people.

PART 2
MEAL PLANS

Selecting and Using a 30-Day Meal Plan

The meal plans that follow are designed to support your individual needs, whether you're managing a diagnosed condition or suspected health challenge or you're working toward a particular health goal.

A Brief Overview of the Meal Plans

Adrenal Health (page 162)

For those with general fatigue or adrenal concerns, such as adrenal fatigue, HPA axis dysregulation, or an otherwise altered adrenal profile. In addition, if you've been experiencing high levels of stress or think that your current ability to handle physical and/or emotional stress is impaired, this is the plan for you.

Athletic Performance (page 168)

For those who want to maintain or improve their performance as an athlete or sustain moderate to high training volume. While many assume that fat loss is their goal, if you're training four or more times per week with moderate to high intensity (CrossFit or training for competitive endurance events, for example), then focusing on supporting your performance is a good idea. Supporting your performance means supporting your metabolism and physical activity needs, and that often leads to desired fat loss.

Autoimmune Conditions (page 174)

For those with chronic illnesses in which the immune system attacks the body's own cells, such as Addison's disease, celiac disease, Crohn's disease, Hashimoto's thyroiditis, rheumatoid arthritis, and type 1 diabetes, among others.

Blood Sugar Regulation (page 180)

For those who have any unwanted variation in blood sugar levels, including dysglycemia (unbalanced blood sugar), hypoglycemia (low blood sugar), type 1 diabetes, and type 2 diabetes.

Cancer Recovery (page 186)

For those recovering from any type of cancer.

Digestive Health (page 192)

For those with problems in the large and small bowel, such as leaky gut, irritable bowel syndrome, inflammatory bowel disease (including Crohn's disease and colitis), and celiac disease.

Fat Loss (page 198)

For those interested in losing body fat who are otherwise in good health. However, for most people, fat loss doesn't need to be the focus: supporting your body's needs naturally supports fat loss. If your instinct is to select this plan first, I recommend that you dig a bit deeper and ask yourself what your real goal is, and look at the other plans available to see what might better support your health.

Healthy Hormones (page 204)

For men with low testosterone and women who have hormone-related problems of the reproductive system, including PMS, amenorrhea, PCOS, endometriosis, uterine fibroids, or infertility.

Heart Health (page 210)

For those with concerns about cholesterol levels or high blood pressure.

Liver Detox Support (page 216)

For anyone who wants to support the liver and its work in removing toxins from the bloodstream, as well as for those who still have unresolved concerns after trying other 30-Day Meal Plans.

Multiple Sclerosis, Fibromyalgia & Chronic Fatigue (page 222)

For those with these conditions, which can cause, among other symptoms, fatigue, muscle pain, and weakness.

Neurological Health (page 228)

For those with conditions affecting the brain and nervous system, such as Parkinson's disease and Alzheimer's disease.

Squeaky Clean Paleo (page 234)

For anyone who wants to try a strict Paleo diet that incorporates only whole foods and doesn't allow for grain-free "treats."

Thyroid Health (page 238)

For those with thyroid conditions, including both hypothyroidism (such as Hashimoto's thyroiditis) and hyperthyroidism.

Selecting a Meal Plan

After you read the descriptions of the meal plans on pages 156 to 157, you may know immediately which you want to try. But if you haven't eaten Paleo before, I recommend starting with the Squeaky Clean Paleo 30-Day Meal Plan (page 234). Once you've tried the Squeaky Clean plan for thirty days, you may find that you want to switch to another plan that's more specifically designed to address your needs. And as you know, making swaps within the food choices for each plan is certainly an option.

I've created the flow chart of sorts below to show you one way of moving through various meal plans, in order from most generally helpful to most specific and restrictive. This isn't meant to be prescriptive—you can always do whatever works best for you!—but starting at the top and proceeding through the following levels it may help you achieve better health with fewer rules or restrictions.

Let's consider one possible example. If you're new to Paleo and your goal is to improve your athletic performance, you'll want to start—just like everyone!—with the Squeaky Clean Paleo plan. After thirty days, you can try the Blood Sugar Regulation plan, which has fewer restrictions than the Athletic Performance plan, or you can go straight to the Athletic Performance plan.

Here's another example: if you want to address your hormone health and you're new to Paleo, you can start with Squeaky Clean Paleo and then try Blood Sugar Regulation; if you're not seeing enough improvement on that plan, you can try the Adrenal Health plan, and if you're still not seeing the improvement you want, you can try the Healthy Hormones plan. Or you can go straight from Squeaky Clean Paleo to Healthy Hormones. But keep in mind that the higher level plans have fewer restrictions, and you may find that following one of these is enough to resolve your health concerns.

If members of your family are experiencing different health challenges, I recommend cooking according to the most restrictive plan and then adding back in off-limits foods for those who can tolerate them. It may not be easy at first, but once you get the hang of it, this is the best way to meet everyone's needs.

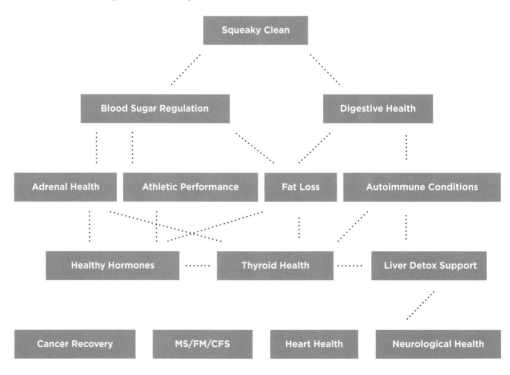

Foundational Plan

Squeaky Clean (page 234)

This plan is the best place to start if:

- you're new to Paleo (even if you have specific health challenges or goals). Simply transitioning away from processed and refined foods and over to a whole-foods-based approach will get your health back on track and create a solid foundation on which to build.
- you're completing a Paleo challenge at your gym
- you're looking for a nutritional reboot and the other plans don't seem to suit your needs
- you're looking to bust sugar cravings but want a plan that's longer than the 21-Day Sugar Detox (my three-week plan detailed in a separate book and online program—visit www.21DSD.com for details)

Healing Plans

Blood Sugar Regulation (page 180)

If you've already been eating Paleo for at least a month, or you've already followed the Squeaky Clean plan, and you're experiencing cravings, energy imbalances, or other signs of blood sugar dysregulation (see page 180), or if you have a related diagnosed condition, then this plan is your next best option.

Digestive Health (page 192)

If you've already been eating Paleo for at least a month, or you've already followed the Squeaky Clean plan, and you're experiencing digestive distress, irregular eliminations, or signs of digestive upset (constipation, diarrhea, undigested food in stool, loose stools, or other problems with elimination), or you have a related diagnosed condition, then this plan is your next best option.

Targeted Plans

Adrenal Health (page 162)   **Autoimmune Conditions (page 174)**
Athletic Performance (page 168)   **Fat Loss (page 198)**

Once you've followed Squeaky Clean Paleo and either Blood Sugar Regulation or Digestive Health, or if you've been eating Paleo for more than three months and don't struggle with blood sugar imbalances or digestive distress, then you can move ahead to focus on plans targeted to supporting more granular goals.

Select one of these plans depending on your goals or current health challenges—see pages 156 to 157 for descriptions.

A note on autoimmune conditions: Many people who are struggling with autoimmune conditions jump immediately to the Autoimmune Conditions plan. However, that's the most restrictive plan, and most people will experience great relief and benefit from plans that are less strict. In addition, if the system affected by your condition is addressed in another plan, you may want to look to that plan for other nuances to the diet, lifestyle, and supplement recommendations. For example, if you have Hashimoto's thyroiditis, the Autoimmune Conditions plan is a great place to start, but recommendations in the Thyroid Health plan will also be relevant.

Condition-Specific Plans

Once you've followed the initial three levels of plans, or if you've been eating Paleo for more than three months and you've been diagnosed with a specific condition that fits one of these plans, then you can move ahead to focus on plans targeted to supporting these more granular goals. Alternatively, you can begin with Squeaky Clean Paleo and then go straight to these plans if they suit your needs best.

See pages 156 to 157 for descriptions of these plans.

Using a Meal Plan

Diet & Lifestyle Recommendations

The most important part of these plans are the diet and lifestyle recommendations— while the recipe suggestions are meant to make your life easier and help you plan meals, the diet and lifestyle recommendations matter even more when it comes to addressing your particular health concerns.

Read the add and avoid lists at the beginning of the meal plan you want to follow before diving into it. Some of the recipes in the 30-day calendar might need to be slightly altered depending on which meal plan you are following. The overarching add and avoid lists should serve as a compass for navigating the meal plan and any other interesting recipes you find in this book, other books, or on the Web.

Nutritional Supplements & Herbs to Consider

ADDITIONAL RESOURCES

Disease Prevention and Treatment, 5th ed. Life Extension Media.

Alternative Medicine: The Definitive Guide, 2nd ed. Ed. Larry Trivieri Jr. and John W. Anderson.

Encyclopedia of Nutritional Supplements: The Essential Guide for Improving Your Health Naturally. By Michael Murray.

The recommended supplements and herbs are general guidelines and are intended to point you in a direction rather than serve as a prescription. Many of you will be working one-on-one with a practitioner who will recommend these supplements to you, and the notes in the plan can serve as a reference for their utility and purpose in your overall health plan. If you are operating on your own, you may choose to conduct further research on the recommendations in order to tailor them to your specific needs. The resources listed at left will provide a wealth of additional information on all of the conditions for which the meal plans have been created.

Supportive Nutrients & Foods That Contain Them / Quick List

As a complement to the information on supplements and herbs, this section highlights foods that have high amounts of the nutrients that are particularly beneficial on the selected plan. The Quick List is designed to be an easy reference for foods that are ideal for your nutrient needs on a particular plan, so this is a good place to look first for recommendations and ideas for swaps if you don't want to follow the recipes in the plan exactly.

30 Days of Meals

A basic Paleo diet is the foundation of all of the meal plans, and roughly 80 percent of the food choices in each thirty-day menu are the same or similar across the plans. (Remember, one of the great things about Paleo is that eating real, whole foods and avoiding processed, refined foods is always better for your health, no matter what challenges you're facing.) The variations from plan to plan are nuanced—for instance, there are fewer leafy greens, which can be difficult to digest for those with digestive health problems, in the meal plans for those issues; since those struggling with neurological conditions often do better on a low-carb or ketogenic diet, there are fewer carbs in those plans; there's less red meat for those in cancer recovery (not because I believe that population should avoid red meat but because they've likely been advised by a doctor to avoid it); and those looking to optimize their athletic performance will find more carbohydrate-rich foods in that plan.

If you find that the food choices in a particular 30-Day Meal Plan don't suit your tastes, or your family members have varying needs while you want to follow a targeted plan, it's perfectly fine to make variations to the meals you prepare. You can easily swap out entire recipes or, more specifically, swap out proteins, veggies, or other items for foods you prefer. However, if the diet and lifestyle recommendations suggest adding or avoiding certain foods, be sure to make that a priority—any other swaps are up to you.

Read the entire meal plan before you get started. If you see that a meal or parts of a meal repeat, you can save yourself a lot of cooking time by preparing extra so that you have the appropriate amount of leftovers.

Many of the recipes can be made with interchangeable protein sources. For example, ground turkey can sometimes be used in place of beef, and in some cases chicken can be used instead of pork.

Snacks have not been planned, as the meals should provide plenty of food to satisfy your appetite. If you find you need more food, try eating additional small servings of the foods in your meal plan.

30-DAY MEAL PLANS

Adrenal Health

adrenal fatigue

hypothalamic pituitary adrenal (hpa) axis dysregulation

altered adrenal profile

general fatigue

follow this plan if:

» You're experiencing fatigue or brain fog, you're slow to get started in the mornings, or you have difficulty recovering from exercise (post-workout fatigue lasts longer than 20 to 30 minutes).

» You get headaches with physical or mental stress or experience afternoon headaches, or you have blurred vision.

» You have depression, anxiety, or unstable behavior.

» You become shaky or light-headed if meals are missed or delayed.

» You have hemorrhoids or varicose veins.

» You get dizzy when moving from sitting or lying to standing, or you have transient dizzy spells.

» You have a weak immune system, allergies, or asthma.

» You have gastric ulcers or feel full/bloated after meals.

» You crave sweets, caffeine, or cigarettes.

» You have difficulty falling asleep or staying asleep.

Note: Having one or two of these symptoms is not likely to indicate an altered adrenal profile, but having several of them may. If you have many of these symptoms and have not yet been tested for hypothyroidism, it's a good idea to get tested.

DISCLAIMER:

The information in this book is not intended to be a replacement for professional medical diagnosis or treatment for a medical condition. It consists solely of nutritional and lifestyle recommendations to support a healthier body.

diet & lifestyle recommendations

add [+]

OMEGA-3-RICH FOODS
Omega-3 fatty acids help manage the inflammatory effects that may result from chronically elevated cortisol levels.

HIMALAYAN SEA SALT
Add a pinch to meals for more trace minerals.

POSITIVE MINDSET
Cultivate a positive mental outlook by creating a gratitude list regularly (see page 120). A positive mental outlook is often a result of feeling that we have control over our own lives, and it can yield calmer thoughts overall.

STRESS MANAGEMENT
Develop a guided meditation or slow-breathing practice, or begin to practice qigong.

LOW-INTENSITY MOVEMENT
For movement without systemic stress, take walks outside, swim (not for speed!), or practice gentle yoga. Weight train with moderate weight (not to exceed 50% to 70% of your capability) and keep your stress/adrenaline response low while training.

SLEEP
Establish a regular bedtime routine and sleep hours (ideally 10 p.m. to 6 a.m.) and avoid sleeping pills. Use mild, calming herbs when needed for relaxation at bedtime.

SUNSHINE
Whenever possible, get sun exposure during waking hours to help regulate your circadian rhythm.

LAUGHTER & PLAY
Find games or activities you enjoy doing, connect with others while doing them, and find something that brings you joy and laughter.

avoid [–]

ALCOHOL, CAFFEINE & NUTRIENT-POOR FOODS
These can be taxing to your system, and it's best to avoid them while healing. If you currently drink coffee, titrate your consumption down slowly and eventually work to either an organic, Swiss Water Process decaf or green tea, then to herbal teas exclusively.

HIGH-INTENSITY EXERCISE
Overly intense exercise (high-intensity interval training or similar workouts) and chronic cardiovascular exercise (30–60+ minutes at a steady state of intensity, like jogging or biking) can provoke a stress response in the body.

EXPOSURE TO BLUE & BRIGHT LIGHT
Install apps like f.lux or Night Shift on your computer or phone, use amber goggles, and keep overhead lights to a minimum after sundown.

TOXIC RELATIONSHIPS/PEOPLE & NEGATIVE EMOTIONS
Reduce emotional stress by learning to say no, practicing mindfulness, and meditating. The Headspace app may be helpful for guided meditations.

HARSH CLEANING & HYGIENE PRODUCTS
Opt for gentle, natural alternatives, such as soap nuts for laundry, vinegar and water for cleaning countertops, and baking soda and peroxide for cleaning and whitening surfaces, laundry, teeth, and more. Consider skipping shampoo and going "no-poo" instead. Safe makeup recommendations may be found at skindeep.org.

I highly recommend the Dr. Lam website (www.drlam.com) for additional and extensive information on adrenal fatigue.

nutritional supplements & herbs to consider

Low and elevated cortisol can have similar symptoms, so the only way to be sure which supplements listed below will work best for you is to have your saliva tested by a healthcare practitioner. Some of the supplements may be contraindicated for you and could make matters worse. If you haven't been tested, follow the recommendations for general support.

These recommendations are made as a starting point. Do your own research and determine which supplements may serve you best. Remember that supplements should be used for a short period of time, one to six months, and that it's best to get as many of your nutrients from food as possible. See page 165 for specific food-based nutrients on which to focus. The items below are listed in no particular order.

FOR ALL TYPES OF ALTERED ADRENAL PROFILES & GENERAL SUPPORT

» **ADAPTOGENIC HERBS** such as ashwagandha, holy basil, American ginseng, Panax ginseng, Siberian ginseng (eleuthero), schisandra, and ginger root help to modulate cortisol levels and normalize blood pressure and heart rate. They also increase metabolic rate by stimulating the production of digestive enzymes for protein and fat.

» **MAGNESIUM** is required for more than 300 enzymatic processes in the body, and most people are deficient in it. It is also useful in blood sugar regulation. Look for magnesium glycinate or magnesium malate forms.

» **B VITAMINS** are critical in assisting neurotransmitters and therefore are important for brain health and the proper functioning of nerves and muscles. Vitamin B5 is needed for the manufacture of adrenal hormones and red blood cells, which makes it beneficial for energy. Note that B6 is contraindicated in those taking levodopa for Parkinson's disease.

» **VITAMIN C** is a potent antioxidant that is critical for cortisol production. Note that in some rare, severe cases of fatigue, vitamin C may make symptoms worse (the body has a harder time metabolizing it, which puts further stress on the body).

» **ADRENAL GLANDULAR** supplements in the desiccated form (dried, ground, and encapsulated) can support the normal function of the adrenal glands.

» **N-ACETYL L-TYROSINE** is the precursor amino acid from which the body makes dopamine, which is then converted to norepinephrine and then to epinephrine.

» **GINKGO BILOBA** is a powerful antioxidant that helps to calm and balance the neurotransmitters that tell the brain how to physically respond to stress.

» **DIGESTIVE ENZYMES** help to break down food when stress is high and digestive function is impaired. Look for a blend of enzymes.

FOR ELEVATED CORTISOL

» **CHAMOMILE and PASSION-FLOWER** are calming herbs that can be consumed as supplements or in teas.

» **PHOSPHATIDYLSERINE** supports a healthy endocrine response to stress and is helpful for that tired-but-wired feeling when taken a few hours before bed.

» **L-THEANINE** is a calming amino acid that works by increasing GABA (an inhibitory neurotransmitter) and creates a sense of calm and well-being in the brain. GABA may also be supplemented directly if you don't have a noticeable response to L-theanine.

FOR LOW CORTISOL

» **ACETYLCHOLINE** supports circadian rhythm function to improve sleep and supports brain and neurotransmitter function.

» **LICORICE ROOT** is an herb that may naturally help to extend the half-life of cortisol in the bloodstream. To help sustain energy levels through the afternoon, try drinking licorice root tea in place of caffeinated drinks or other stimulants, or take licorice root extract. It's best to consume licorice root no later than about 3 p.m., as it may have slightly stimulating effects (less severe than coffee).

supportive nutrients & foods that contain them

B VITAMINS

Critical in assisting neurotransmitters and therefore important for brain health and for the proper functioning of nerves and muscles

» Liver, bison, lamb
» Flounder, haddock, salmon, trout, tuna
» Brewer's yeast (Lewis Labs brand only)
» Mushrooms
» Hazelnuts, walnuts
» Trace amounts: pecans, sun-flower seeds, broccoli, Brussels sprouts, other dark leafy greens

VITAMIN C

A potent antioxidant with anti-inflammatory properties

» Beets, bell peppers, broccoli, Brussels sprouts, cauliflower, collard greens, daikon radishes, garlic, kale, mustard greens, parsley, spinach
» Cantaloupes, kiwis, lemons, oranges, papayas, pineapples, strawberries

VITAMIN E

An antioxidant that benefits neurological function, smooth-muscle growth, and cel-lular communication

» Broccoli, Brussels sprouts, spinach
» Extra-virgin olive oil
» Pecans

MAGNESIUM

Critical for cellular energy production, which helps battle fatigue, and for proper calcium metabolism, which is necessary for vascular health

» Beets, kale, other green leafy vegetables
» Pumpkin seeds (pepitas)

OMEGA-3 FATS

An anti-inflammatory essential fatty acid

» Cold-water fish, such as salmon, herring, and mackerel
» Pecans, walnuts

ZINC

A potent antioxidant often low in people with inflammatory conditions; aids in vitamin A metabolism

» Oysters, shellfish
» Lamb, red meat
» Pumpkin seeds (pepitas)

quick LIST

proteins

Beef
Bison
Eel
Eggs
Lamb
Mackerel
Oysters
Salmon
Shellfish

fats

Coconut oil
Extra-virgin olive oil
Grass-fed butter/ghee
Pumpkin seeds (pepitas)
Walnuts

vegetables

Beets
Bell peppers
Broccoli
Brussels sprouts
Butternut squash
Cauliflower
Daikon radishes
Okra
Spinach
Sweet potatoes

fruits

Grapefruit
Lemons
Oranges
Peaches
Pineapple

superfoods

Bone broth
Liver
Sauerkraut

spices

Basil
Cilantro
Cinnamon
Cumin
Garlic
Ginger
Oregano
Parsley
Turmeric

DAY	BREAKFAST	LUNCH	DINNER
1	Swirly Crustless Quiche (270), Perfectly Baked Bacon (260), [NR] sweet potato**	[MA] Mustard-Glazed Chicken Thighs (317), green salad* with Balsamic Vinaigrette (434)	Grilled Garlic Flank Steak with Peppers & Onions (334), [NR] baked potato** with ghee (261)
2	*leftover* Swirly Crustless Quiche, *leftover* Grilled Garlic Flank Steak with Peppers & Onions	[NR] canned wild salmon with olives, avocado, lemon juice, tomato, EVOO over green salad*	Bacon Jalapeño Burgers (360), Sweet Potato Pancakes (285), [NR] steamed spinach*
3	*leftover* Sweet Potato Pancakes, *leftover* Mustard-Glazed Chicken Thighs	*leftover* Bacon Jalapeño Burgers, *leftover* Sweet Potato Pancakes, [NR] steamed spinach*	[MA] Lemony Lamb Dolmas (368), Cilantro Cauli-Rice (412), banana
4	Pesto Scrambled Eggs (286), *leftover* Cilantro Cauli-Rice, [MA] Raw Sauerkraut (262)	*leftover* Lemony Lamb Dolmas, green salad* with EVOO, berries	Citrus Macadamia Nut Sole (378), Whipped Sweet Potatoes** (419)
5	*leftover* Citrus Macadamia Nut Sole, [NR] plantains cooked in CO**	Nori Salmon Handroll (388), banana with almond butter	Beef & Veggie Stir-Fry (348), [NR] winter squash**
6	Pumpkin Pancakes (284), breakfast sausage made with Italian Blend (256) & ground meat	*leftover* Beef & Veggie Stir-Fry, [NR] sweet potato**	Lamb Lettuce Boats with Avoziki Sauce (370), Smashed Potatoes with Garlic & Onions (411)
7	[NR] eggs any style, Perfectly Baked Bacon (260), [MA] Crispy Sweet Potato Coins (410)	green salad* with canned wild salmon, asparagus*, lemon juice with EVOO, *leftover* Smashed Potatoes	Citrus & Herb Whole Roasted Chicken (292), [NR] baked potato**, Simple Baked Kale Chips* (425)
8	Carrot Gingerbread Muffins (278), *leftover* breakfast sausage, berries	Dairy-Free Caesar Salad (396), *leftover* Citrus & Herb Whole Roasted Chicken, apple	Restaurant-Style Lettuce Cups (312), roasted parsnips**
9	Swirly Crustless Quiche (270), bacon, [NR] sweet potato**, [MA] Raw Sauerkraut (262)	Indian Spiced Burgers with Smashed Roasted Garlic (342), broccoli*, berries	Spinach Artichoke Stuffed Chicken (310), [NR] baked potato**
10	omelet or Pesto Scrambled Eggs (286), avocado, banana with almond butter	*leftover* Spinach Artichoke Stuffed Chicken, [NR] baked potato**	Coffee BBQ Rubbed Pork with Seared Pineapple (318), Mashed Faux-Tatoes (418)
11	[MA] Home Fries & Sausage Skillet (268), apple	*leftover* Coffee BBQ Rubbed Pork with Seared Pineapple, green salad* with EVOO	Balsamic Braised Short Ribs (332), Candied Carrots (415), green salad* with EVOO
12	*leftover* Home Fries & Sausage Skillet	*leftover* Balsamic Braised Short Ribs, *leftover* Candied Carrots, green salad* with EVOO	Mediterranean Baked Chicken with Cauliflower (294), [NR] baked potato**
13	[MA] Fluffy Banana Pancakes (282), Perfectly Baked Bacon (260), [MA] Raw Sauerkraut (262)	*leftover* Mediterranean Baked Chicken with Cauliflower, berries	Lemon Rosemary Broiled Salmon (375), Asparagus with Lemon & Olives (409), [NR] sweet potato**
14	*leftover* Lemon Rosemary Broiled Salmon, *leftover* Asparagus with Lemon & Olives, berries	[MA] Buffalo Chicken Lettuce Wraps (299), banana with almond butter	Grilled Tuna Over Fresh Noodle Salad (384), avocado, berries
15	[NR] scrambled eggs with olives, spinach*, avocado, apple with almond butter	*leftover* Grilled Tuna Over Fresh Noodle Salad, avocado	Italian-Style Stuffed Peppers (358), green salad* with Balsamic Vinaigrette (434), [NR] baked potato**
16	Peach Blueberry Smoothie (289), [MA] Blueberry Maple Sausage (273)	*leftover* Italian-Style Stuffed Peppers, green salad* with Balsamic Vinaigrette (434)	Bacon-Wrapped Smoky Chicken Thighs (298), Sweet & Savory Potatoes (421), [NR] spinach*

Adrenal Health

DAY	BREAKFAST	LUNCH	DINNER
17	[MA] Bacon & Egg Salad (287), avocado, spinach or kale*, [MA] Raw Sauerkraut (262)	*leftover* Bacon-Wrapped Smoky Chicken Thighs, *leftover* Sweet & Savory Potatoes, spinach*	Spaghetti Squash Bolognese (338), Simple Baked Kale Chips* (425), berries
18	[MA] Pumpkin Pancakes (284), *leftover* Blueberry Maple Sausage	*leftover* Spaghetti Squash Bolognese, apple with almond butter	Thanksgiving Stuffing Meatballs (326), Simple Cranberry Sauce (436), Mashed Faux-Tatoes (418)
19	*leftover* Bacon & Egg Salad, avocado, spinach or kale*, [MA] Raw Sauerkraut (262), apple	*leftover* Thanksgiving Stuffing Meatballs, *leftover* Cranberry Sauce, *leftover* Mashed Faux-Tatoes	Lemon & Bacon Scallops with Roasted Potatoes (376), Lemon Roasted Romanesco* (417)
20	Paleo Avocado "Toast" (264), [NR] eggs any style, berries	*leftover* Lemon & Bacon Scallops, *leftover* Lemon Roasted Romanesco*	Orange & Olive Braised Chicken (306), Yellow Cauli-Rice (413), Baked Potato Chips (430)
21	[MA] breakfast sausage made with Italian Blend (256) & ground meat, [NR] eggs any style, Raw Sauerkraut (262)	[MA] Six-Minute Salmon Bowls (382), mango	Souvlaki Kebabs (290), Greek Salad with Avoziki Dressing (402), Baked Potato Chips (430)
22	[MA] Breakfast Fried "Rice" (266), apple with almond butter	*leftover* Souvlaki Kebabs, *leftover* Greek Salad with Avoziki Dressing, berries	Orange Braised Beef (344), Butternut Sage Soup** (394), berries
23	*leftover* Breakfast Fried "Rice," banana with almond butter	*leftover* Orange Braised Beef, *leftover* Butternut Sage Soup**	Hayley's Skirt Steak Tacos (346), choice of salsa (433), Smoky Grilled Squash & Pineapple (408)
24	[MA] Sweet Potato Pancakes (285), bacon, apple with almond butter	[MA] Tangy Taco Salad (350), *leftover* salsa, *leftover* Smoky Grilled Squash & Pineapple	Bacon & Superfood Meatloaf (330), Mashed Faux-Tatoes (418), green salad* with EVOO
25	[NR] eggs any style, avocado, spinach or kale*, [MA] Raw Sauerkraut (262)	[MA] Quick & Easy Salmon Cakes (374), green salad* with EVOO, avocado, olives	Seared Scallops with Orange Glaze (386), Cilantro Cauli-Rice (412), [NR] steamed bok choy*
26	[MA] Acorn Squash with Coconut Butter (406), Apple Sage Sausage (272)	[MA] Italiano Salad (398), Honey Mustard Dressing (434)	Grandma Barbara's Stuffed Mushrooms (324), *leftover* Italiano Salad, berries
27	[MA] Pumpkin Cranberry Muffins (277), *leftover* Apple Sage Sausage	*leftover* Grandma Barbara's Stuffed Mushrooms, green salad* with EVOO, berries	Orange Sesame Meatballs (328), Whipped Sweet Potatoes (419)
28	[MA] Apple Cinnamon Egg Muffins (280), bacon, berries	*leftover* Orange Sesame Meatballs, *leftover* Whipped Sweet Potatoes	Lemon & Artichoke Chicken (296), Broc-Cauli Chowder with Bacon (392), apple
29	*leftover* Apple Cinnamon Egg Muffins, bacon, berries	*leftover* Lemon & Artichoke Chicken, *leftover* Broc-Cauli Chowder with Bacon	The Easiest Tacos (362), Crispy Plantain Chips (431), choice of salsa (433)
30	[MA] Fluffy Banana Pancakes (282), [MA] Blueberry Maple Sausage (273)	*leftover* The Easiest Tacos, *leftover* Crispy Plantain Chips, *leftover* salsa	Mini Mediterranean Kebabs (352), Sautéed Spinach with Pine Nuts & Currants* (423)

» *A complete shopping list for this meal plan can be found on balancedbites.com*

NOTES

*****: or other green vegetable; green salad is any lettuce and/or non-starchy vegetables
********: or other starchy vegetable (refer to page 75)
EVOO: Extra-virgin olive oil, or use any dressing from pages 434–435 on salads
CO: Coconut oil
MA: Make-Ahead all or part of the recipe
NR: No Recipe (use any simple prep)

If no page number is listed, simply prepare the items as noted or any way you like. For additional protein, vegetable, and fat recommendations, refer to the QUICK LIST that is associated with your meal plan!

Athletic Performance

30-DAY MEAL PLANS

While fueling needs can vary greatly from athlete to athlete, there are basic guidelines that will get you started in the right direction. This plan provides an overall higher carbohydrate intake and a focus on nutrient-dense foods and superfoods. The best way to figure out how well this or any other meal plan works for your performance needs and goals is to keep records of your diet and activities on a daily basis so you can analyze your results and assess where changes may need to be made. Detailed records will also be helpful when approaching a health-care practitioner for assistance on modifying your approach in any way. Information is king.

Refer to the book resources page on balancedbites.com for a handy nutrition and performance tracking form to download.

DISCLAIMER:

The information in this book is not intended to be a replacement for professional medical diagnosis or treatment for a medical condition. It consists solely of nutritional and lifestyle recommendations to support a healthier body.

diet & lifestyle recommendations

add [+]

SUPERFOODS & PROBIOTICS

Eat superfoods as often as possible (see page 61). Consume 1/4 cup raw sauerkraut (page 262) or other fermented vegetables daily, especially with breakfast.

PROTEIN

Add protein to satisfy appetite for longer periods of time (meals focused on both fat and protein will help).

NUTRIENT-DENSE FOODS

Replenish nutrient stores that have been depleted by excess refined foods.

STARCHY CARBOHYDRATES

Eat approximately 50–75 g or more of carbohydrates before and after your workout, depending on the length of the workout. (See page 75 for nutrient-dense carb sources.) Track how you feel and add or subtract carbs if you are not making progress or don't feel well-fueled for your training.

SMART TRAINING

Listen to your body and take rest and recovery days when necessary.

SLEEP

Sleep at least eight hours every night in a dark room in order to recover from exercise and have a healthy hormonal balance.

MASSAGE

Be sure you are taking care of your body with regular sports massage, chiropractic care, and/or Active Release Techniques (ART).

avoid [–]

GLUTEN

100% of the time. See the guide to gluten on page 107.

OVERTRAINING

Be smart and rest when you are in pain. Allowing an inflammatory process in your body to do its job will bring you back to training much stronger than if you push through pain (from injury, not just from a hard workout).

EXCESSIVE SUPPLEMENTATION

Eat real food to obtain nutrients: your body knows how to use real, whole foods better than any supplement. Try some of the recommended supplements in this plan, but you certainly don't need to be obtaining all the nutrients listed in supplement form.

LOW-QUALITY PROTEIN POWDERS

Using a protein shake for post-workout recovery can be useful and effective, but beware low-quality shakes or powders with too many additives. Seek out a grass-fed whey source or egg white protein if you tolerate them. Monitor your digestion and signs of chronic inflammation carefully and eliminate powders at any sign of intolerance.

Athletic Performance

nutritional supplements & herbs to consider

These recommendations are made as a starting point. Do your own research and determine which supplements may serve you best. Remember that supplements should be used for a short period of time, one to six months, and that it's best to get as many of your nutrients from food as possible. See page 171 for specific food-based nutrients on which to focus. The items below are listed in no particular order.

» **VITAMIN A (retinol)** helps to maintain the integrity of the gut lining. It also helps maintain immunity when balanced with vitamin D, and it is necessary for the assimilation of dietary minerals. It is depleted by stress and strenuous physical exercise.

» **B VITAMINS (especially B1, B7, B12)** are critical in assisting neurotransmitters and therefore are important for brain health and the proper functioning of nerves and muscles.

» **VITAMIN B1 (thiamin)** is beneficial for nerve and muscle activity. Magnesium is required to activate thiamin.

» **VITAMIN B7 (biotin)** is a coenzyme required for the metabolism of glucose, amino acids, and lipids.

» **VITAMIN B12 (cobalamin)** supports homocysteine metabolism, energy metabolism, and immune and nerve function.

» **VITAMIN C** is a potent antioxidant with anti-inflammatory properties. It also helps to regenerate vitamin E and improves iron absorption.

» **COENZYME Q10** (CoQ10, ubiquinone) enhances cellular energy production, and it can help alleviate fatigue as well as muscle and joint pain. Statin drugs are known to deplete CoQ10.

» **VITAMIN E** is an antioxidant that benefits neurological function, smooth-muscle growth, and cellular communication.

» **L-GLUTAMINE** helps heal the cells that line the small intestine and aids in general cellular repair and recovery.

» **LIPOIC ACID (alpha-lipoic acid)** has antioxidant properties and may increase glucose uptake from the bloodstream by promoting the conversion of carbohydrates into energy.

» **MAGNESIUM** is required for more than 300 enzymatic processes in the body, and most people are deficient in it. It is also useful in blood sugar regulation. Look for magnesium glycinate or magnesium malate forms.

» **CARNITINE/L-CARNITINE** can improve insulin sensitivity and glucose storage, and it optimizes fat and carbohydrate metabolism. It may also improve the utilization of fat as an energy source. Cofactors include iron, vitamin C, vitamin B3 (niacin), and vitamin B6

» **OMEGA-3 FATS** are anti-inflammatory essential fatty acids.

» **ZINC** is a potent antioxidant that aids in vitamin A metabolism. May be taken as ZMA (zinc and magnesium).

supportive nutrients & foods that contain them

VITAMIN A (RETINOL)
Helps maintain the lining of the gut
» Liver, eel
» Grass-fed butter, clarified butter, or ghee

VITAMIN B1
» Brewer's yeast (Lewis Labs brand only)
» Trace amounts: sunflower seeds, Brazil nuts, hazelnuts, walnuts, garlic, almonds

VITAMIN B7
Required for the metabolism of glucose, amino acids, and lipids
» Liver
» Brewer's yeast (Lewis Labs brand only)
» Trace amounts: Swiss chard, walnuts, pecans, almonds

VITAMIN B12
Supports energy metabolism and immune function
» Liver, kidneys
» Flounder, halibut, salmon, sardines, trout, tuna
» Clams, oysters, scallops
» Eggs, beef, lamb
» Cheese (raw/grass-fed)

VITAMIN C
A potent antioxidant with anti-inflammatory properties
» Beets, bell peppers, broccoli, Brussels sprouts, cauliflower, collard greens, garlic, kale, mustard greens, parsley, spinach
» Lemons, strawberries

CARNITINE
Essential for fat metabolism
» Red meat (darker meat has more)

CONJUGATED LINOLEIC ACID (CLA)
A potent antioxidant that supports fat loss
» Grass-fed beef and lamb

VITAMIN D
A potent immune system modulator that is best obtained from sun exposure
» Cold-water fish (salmon, herring, mackerel)
» Grass-fed butter or ghee

VITAMIN E
An antioxidant that benefits neurological function, smooth-muscle growth, and cellular communication
» Broccoli, Brussels sprouts, spinach
» Extra-virgin olive oil
» Pecans

IRON
Essential for properly transporting oxygen in the blood from the lungs to body tissues
» Beef, bison, lamb
» Liver

LIPOIC ACID (ALA)
May improve cellular energy production and has antioxidant properties
» Red meat, organ meats
» Trace amounts: spinach

OMEGA-3 FATS
An anti-inflammatory essential fatty acid
» Cold-water fish, such as salmon, herring, and mackerel
» Pecans, walnuts

ZINC
A potent antioxidant often low in people with inflammatory conditions; aids in vitamin A metabolism
» Oysters, shellfish
» Lamb, red meat
» Pumpkin seeds (pepitas)

quick LIST

proteins
Beef
Bison
Chicken
Eel
Lamb
Liver
Salmon
Scallops
Swordfish

fats
Coconut oil
Extra-virgin olive oil
Grass-fed butter/ghee
Red palm oil

vegetables
Beets
Broccoli
Brussels sprouts
Butternut squash
Cauliflower
Daikon radishes
Kale
Okra
Squash
Sweet potatoes

fruits
Berries
Citrus
Melons
Tropical fruits

superfoods
Bone broth
Liver

spices
Basil
Cilantro
Cinnamon
Cumin
Garlic
Ginger
Oregano
Parsley
Turmeric

DAY	BREAKFAST	LUNCH	DINNER
1	Swirly Crustless Quiche (270), Perfectly Baked Bacon (260), [NR] sweet potato**	[MA] Mustard-Glazed Chicken Thighs (317), green salad* with Balsamic Vinaigrette (434)	Grilled Garlic Flank Steak with Peppers & Onions (334), [NR] baked potato** with ghee (261)
2	*leftover* Swirly Crustless Quiche, *leftover* Grilled Garlic Flank Steak with Peppers & Onions	[NR] canned wild salmon with olives, avocado, lemon juice, tomato, EVOO over green salad*	Bacon Jalapeño Burgers (360), Sweet Potato Pancakes (285), [NR] steamed spinach*
3	*leftover* Sweet Potato Pancakes, *leftover* Mustard-Glazed Chicken Thighs	*leftover* Bacon Jalapeño Burgers, *leftover* Sweet Potato Pancakes, [NR] steamed spinach*	[MA] Lemony Lamb Dolmas (368), Cilantro Cauli-Rice (412), banana
4	Pesto Scrambled Eggs (286), *leftover* Cilantro Cauli-Rice, [MA] Raw Sauerkraut (262)	*leftover* Lemony Lamb Dolmas, green salad* with EVOO, berries	Citrus Macadamia Nut Sole (378), Whipped Sweet Potatoes** (419)
5	*leftover* Citrus Macadamia Nut Sole, [NR] plantains cooked in CO**	Nori Salmon Handroll (388), banana with almond butter	Beef & Veggie Stir-Fry (348), [NR] winter squash**
6	Pumpkin Pancakes (284), breakfast sausage made with Italian Blend (256) & ground meat	*leftover* Beef & Veggie Stir-Fry, [NR] sweet potato**	Lamb Lettuce Boats with Avoziki Sauce (370), Smashed Potatoes with Garlic & Onions (411)
7	[NR] eggs any style, Perfectly Baked Bacon (260), [MA] Crispy Sweet Potato Coins (410)	green salad* with canned wild salmon, asparagus*, lemon juice with EVOO, *leftover* Smashed Potatoes	Citrus & Herb Whole Roasted Chicken (292), [NR] baked potato**, Simple Baked Kale Chips* (425)
8	Carrot Gingerbread Muffins (278), *leftover* breakfast sausage, berries	Dairy-Free Caesar Salad (396), *leftover* Citrus & Herb Whole Roasted Chicken, apple	Restaurant-Style Lettuce Cups (312), roasted parsnips**
9	Swirly Crustless Quiche (270), bacon, [NR] sweet potato**, [MA] Raw Sauerkraut (262)	Indian Spiced Burgers with Smashed Roasted Garlic (342), broccoli*, berries	Spinach Artichoke Stuffed Chicken (310), [NR] baked potato**
10	omelet or Pesto Scrambled Eggs (286), avocado, banana with almond butter	*leftover* Spinach Artichoke Stuffed Chicken, [NR] baked potato**	Coffee BBQ Rubbed Pork with Seared Pineapple (318), Mashed Faux-Tatoes (418)
11	[MA] Home Fries & Sausage Skillet (268), apple	*leftover* Coffee BBQ Rubbed Pork with Seared Pineapple, green salad* with EVOO	Balsamic Braised Short Ribs (332), Candied Carrots (415), green salad* with EVOO
12	*leftover* Home Fries & Sausage Skillet	*leftover* Balsamic Braised Short Ribs, *leftover* Candied Carrots, green salad* with EVOO	Mediterranean Baked Chicken with Cauliflower (294), [NR] baked potato**
13	[MA] Fluffy Banana Pancakes (282), Perfectly Baked Bacon (260), [MA] Raw Sauerkraut (262)	*leftover* Mediterranean Baked Chicken with Cauliflower, berries	Lemon Rosemary Broiled Salmon (375), Asparagus with Lemon & Olives (409), [NR] sweet potato**
14	*leftover* Lemon Rosemary Broiled Salmon, *leftover* Asparagus with Lemon & Olives, berries	[MA] Buffalo Chicken Lettuce Wraps (299), banana with almond butter	Grilled Tuna Over Fresh Noodle Salad (384), avocado, berries
15	[NR] scrambled eggs with olives, spinach*, avocado, apple with almond butter	*leftover* Grilled Tuna Over Fresh Noodle Salad, avocado	Italian-Style Stuffed Peppers (358), green salad* with Balsamic Vinaigrette (434), [NR] baked potato**
16	Peach Blueberry Smoothie (289), [MA] Blueberry Maple Sausage (273)	*leftover* Italian-Style Stuffed Peppers, green salad* with Balsamic Vinaigrette (434)	Bacon-Wrapped Smoky Chicken Thighs (298), Sweet & Savory Potatoes (421), spinach*

Athletic Performance

DAY	BREAKFAST	LUNCH	DINNER
17	[MA] Bacon & Egg Salad (287), avocado, spinach or kale*, [MA] Raw Sauerkraut (262)	*leftover* Bacon-Wrapped Smoky Chicken Thighs, *leftover* Sweet & Savory Potatoes, spinach*	Spaghetti Squash Bolognese (338), Simple Baked Kale Chips* (425), berries
18	[MA] Pumpkin Pancakes (284), *leftover* Blueberry Maple Sausage	*leftover* Spaghetti Squash Bolognese, apple with almond butter	Thanksgiving Stuffing Meatballs (326), Simple Cranberry Sauce (436), Mashed Faux-Tatoes (418)
19	*leftover* Bacon & Egg Salad, avocado, spinach or kale*, [MA] Raw Sauerkraut (262), apple	*leftover* Thanksgiving Stuffing Meatballs, *leftover* Cranberry Sauce, *leftover* Mashed Faux-Tatoes	Lemon & Bacon Scallops with Roasted Potatoes (376), Lemon Roasted Romanesco* (417)
20	Paleo Avocado "Toast" (264), [NR] eggs any style, berries	*leftover* Lemon & Bacon Scallops, *leftover* Lemon Roasted Romanesco*	Orange & Olive Braised Chicken (306), Yellow Cauli-Rice (413), Baked Potato Chips (430)
21	[MA] breakfast sausage made with Italian Blend (256) & ground meat, [NR] eggs any style, Raw Sauerkraut (262)	[MA] Six-Minute Salmon Bowls (382), mango	Souvlaki Kebabs (290), Greek Salad with Avoziki Dressing (402), Baked Potato Chips (430)
22	[MA] Breakfast Fried "Rice" (266), apple with almond butter	*leftover* Souvlaki Kebabs, *leftover* Greek Salad with Avoziki Dressing, berries	Orange Braised Beef (344), Butternut Sage Soup** (394), berries
23	*leftover* Breakfast Fried "Rice," banana with almond butter	*leftover* Orange Braised Beef, *leftover* Butternut Sage Soup**	Hayley's Skirt Steak Tacos (346), choice of salsa (433), Smoky Grilled Squash & Pineapple (408)
24	[MA] Sweet Potato Pancakes (285), bacon, apple with almond butter	[MA] Tangy Taco Salad (350), *leftover* salsa, *leftover* Smoky Grilled Squash & Pineapple	Bacon & Superfood Meatloaf (330), Mashed Faux-Tatoes (418), green salad* with EVOO
25	[NR] eggs any style, avocado, spinach or kale*, [MA] Raw Sauerkraut (262)	[MA] Quick & Easy Salmon Cakes (374), green salad* with EVOO, avocado, olives	Seared Scallops with Orange Glaze (386), Cilantro Cauli-Rice (412), [NR] steamed bok choy*
26	[MA] Acorn Squash with Coconut Butter (406), Apple Sage Sausage (272)	[MA] Italiano Salad (398), Honey Mustard Dressing (434)	Grandma Barbara's Stuffed Mushrooms (324), *leftover* Italiano Salad, berries
27	[MA] Pumpkin Cranberry Muffins (277), *leftover* Apple Sage Sausage	*leftover* Grandma Barbara's Stuffed Mushrooms, green salad* with EVOO, berries	Orange Sesame Meatballs (328), Whipped Sweet Potatoes (419)
28	[MA] Apple Cinnamon Egg Muffins (280), bacon, berries	*leftover* Orange Sesame Meatballs, *leftover* Whipped Sweet Potatoes	Lemon & Artichoke Chicken (296), Broc-Cauli Chowder with Bacon (392), apple
29	*leftover* Apple Cinnamon Egg Muffins, bacon, berries	*leftover* Lemon & Artichoke Chicken, *leftover* Broc-Cauli Chowder with Bacon	The Easiest Tacos (362), Crispy Plantain Chips (431), choice of salsa (433)
30	[MA] Fluffy Banana Pancakes (282), [MA] Blueberry Maple Sausage (273)	*leftover* The Easiest Tacos, *leftover* Crispy Plantain Chips, *leftover* salsa	Mini Mediterranean Kebabs (352), Sautéed Spinach with Pine Nuts & Currants* (423)

» *A complete shopping list for this meal plan can be found on balancedbites.com*

NOTES

*: or other green vegetable; green salad is any lettuce and/or non-starchy vegetables
**: or other starchy vegetable (refer to page 75)
EVOO: Extra-virgin olive oil, or use any dressing from pages 434–435 on salads
CO: Coconut oil
MA: Make-Ahead all or part of the recipe
NR: No Recipe (use any simple prep)

If no page number is listed, simply prepare the items as noted or any way you like. For additional protein, vegetable, and fat recommendations, refer to the QUICK LIST that is associated with your meal plan!

Autoimmune Conditions

30-DAY MEAL PLANS

While their root causes and resulting symptoms may vary slightly, autoimmune conditions share underpinnings in digestive distress and, specifically, increased intestinal permeability (leaky gut; see page 93). This meal plan is similar to the one for digestive health, but it is designed to be a more specific protocol for those diagnosed with an autoimmune condition. After completing this plan, you may find that additional therapeutic interventions for your condition will help further put your symptoms into remission. However, you may also discover that a basic Paleo approach works well for you without further limitations or omissions.

autoimmune conditions include but are not limited to:

- » Addison's disease
- » Alzheimer's disease
- » Asthma
- » Celiac disease
- » Chronic fatigue syndrome
- » Crohn's disease
- » Eczema
- » Graves' disease
- » Hashimoto's thyroiditis
- » Lupus
- » Multiple sclerosis
- » Parkinson's disease
- » Pernicious anemia
- » Psoriasis
- » Raynaud's disease
- » Rheumatoid arthritis
- » Scleroderma
- » Type 1 diabetes
- » Vitiligo

All of the above conditions, as well as any chronic inflammatory condition (see page 91), can be helped by following an autoimmune protocol for at least thirty days and a basic Paleo diet template thereafter, with varying levels of detail based on your main concerns and symptoms. Several of the above conditions also have specific meal plans later in this section.

DISCLAIMER:

The information in this book is not intended to be a replacement for professional medical diagnosis or treatment for a medical condition. It consists solely of nutritional and lifestyle recommendations to support a healthier body.

diet & lifestyle recommendations

add [+]

WELL-COOKED FOODS
Meals such as braised meats, stews, soups, and slow-cooked foods are easier to digest.

NUTRIENT-DENSE FOODS
Replenish nutrient stores that have been depleted by excess refined foods.

SUPERFOODS
Make bone broth (page 259) and drink it or cook with it regularly.

STRESS MANAGEMENT
Develop a guided meditation practice or slow breathing practice, or begin to practice qigong.

MOVEMENT
For movement without systemic stress, take walks outside, swim (not for speed!), or practice gentle yoga.

Slowly begin weight training with moderate to heavy weight, not excessively demanding in terms of stress response or cortisol output.

avoid [–]

GUT IRRITANTS
Foods that are known to cause immunological responses, including **grains, legumes, dairy (even grass-fed), eggs, nuts, seeds, and nightshades;** also large quantities of vegetables and fruits that are high in insoluble fiber, such as leafy greens, raspberries, and strawberries. **All recipes have notes for substitutions where possible. Please follow these!**

GLUTEN
100% of the time. See the guide to gluten on page 107.

ALCOHOL, CAFFEINE, CHOCOLATE
These can all promote leaky gut.

STRESS
Make lifestyle changes to avoid stressful situations.

PAIN MEDICATIONS
Including aspirin, acetaminophen, ibuprofen, and corticosteroids. These can promote leaky gut.

HARSH CLEANING & HYGIENE PRODUCTS
Opt for gentle, natural alternatives, such as soap nuts for laundry, vinegar and water for cleaning countertops, and baking soda and peroxide for cleaning and whitening surfaces, laundry, teeth, and more. Consider skipping shampoo and going "no-poo" instead. Safe makeup recommendations may be found at skindeep.org.

HIGH-INTENSITY EXERCISE
Overly intense exercise (high-intensity interval training or similar workouts) and chronic cardiovascular exercise (30–60+ minutes at a steady state of intensity, like jogging or biking) can provoke a stress response in the body.

nutritional supplements & herbs to consider

These recommendations are made as a starting point. Do your own research and determine which supplements may serve you best. Remember that supplements should be used for a short period of time, one to six months, and that it's best to get as many of your nutrients from food as possible. See page 177 for specific food-based nutrients on which to focus. The items below are listed in no particular order.

» **VITAMIN A (retinol)** helps to maintain the integrity of the mucosal lining of the gut. It also helps maintain immunity when balanced with vitamin D, and it is necessary for the assimilation of dietary minerals.

» **COENZYME Q10** (CoQ10, ubiquinone) enhances cellular energy production, and it can help alleviate fatigue as well as muscle and joint pain. Statin drugs are known to deplete CoQ10.

» **DIGESTIVE ENZYMES** help to break down food for absorption while your gut is healing. Look for a blend of enzymes.

» **L-GLUTAMINE** aids in the healing of the cells that line the small intestine.

» **HERBAL TEAS** that are calming to your digestive system include peppermint, ginger, kudzu, marshmallow root, and slippery elm.

» **LICORICE ROOT** is an herb that aids in repairing the mucosal lining of the gut and stomach. Look for licorice root tea, an extract of the herb, or a chewable tablet called DGL.

» **ALOE VERA JUICE** (unless it promotes loose stool)

» **MAGNESIUM** is required for more than 300 enzymatic processes in the body, and most people are deficient. It is also useful in blood sugar regulation. Look for magnesium glycinate or magnesium malate forms.

» **PHOSPHATIDYLCHOLINE** enhances the integrity of the GI tract, repairs the mucosal lining of the gut, and aids in fatty acid digestion. This supplement is especially important if you are avoiding eggs.

» **PROBIOTIC SUPPLEMENTS** for better digestion. Try different brands to find one that works best for you. Start slowly, with small dosages. Brands available from health-care practitioners are often more potent than commercial brands.

» **QUERCITIN** is a potent antioxidant that promotes better immunity.

» **SELENIUM & ZINC** are antioxidants that protect against free-radical damage. Supplements may be necessary because it's difficult to obtain adequate amounts from food.

» **ZINC CARNOSINE** may improve gut mucosa and gut lining integrity.

FOR MORE RELIEF

If you continue to suffer from the symptoms below, consider eliminating these foods on a continued basis or as part of the 4R Protocol, outlined on page 44.

Joint pain, mobility issues: Eliminate nightshade vegetables, eggs, nuts, and seeds.

Skin conditions: Eliminate eggs, nuts, seeds, and all forms of dairy (even grass-fed).

supportive nutrients & foods that contain them

VITAMIN A (RETINOL)

Helps maintain the lining of the gut

» Liver, eel
» Grass-fed butter, clarified butter, or ghee (reintroduce only after 30 days without them)

BUTYRIC ACID

Helps to decrease intestinal permeability

» Grass-fed butter, clarified butter, or ghee (reintroduce only after 30 days without them)

VITAMIN C

A potent antioxidant with anti-inflammatory properties

» Beets, broccoli, Brussels sprouts, cauliflower, daikon radishes, garlic
» Lemon juice

VITAMIN D

A potent immune-system modulator best obtained from sun exposure

» Cold-water fish (salmon, herring, mackerel)
» Grass-fed butter or ghee (reintroduce only after 30 days without them)

GLYCINE

Helps repair the gut lining and increases stomach acid production

» Bone broth (page 259)
» Gelatin

OMEGA-3 FATS

An anti-inflammatory essential fatty acid

» Cold-water fish, such as salmon, herring, and mackerel
» Pecans, walnuts

PROBIOTICS

Promote healthy gut flora, which is critical for proper digestion and elimination

» Fermented vegetables: cabbage (sauerkraut/kimchi), carrots, beets
» Kombucha (fermented tea)

SELENIUM

An antioxidant that protects against free-radical damage

» Eggs
» Garlic, red Swiss chard, turnips

SOLUBLE FIBER

Feeds the beneficial bacteria in the gut

» Butternut squash, sweet potatoes
» Bananas, plantains

ZINC

A potent antioxidant often low in people with inflammatory conditions

» Oysters, shellfish
» Lamb, red meat

quick LIST

proteins

Beef
Bison
Cold-water fish (salmon, herring, mackerel)
Eel
Lamb
Liver
Oysters
Shellfish

fats

Animal fats
Coconut oil
Extra-virgin olive oil
Red palm oil

vegetables

Beets
Broccoli
Brussels sprouts
Butternut squash
Cauliflower
Daikon radishes
Garlic
Okra
Sweet potatoes
Swiss chard

fruits

Bananas
Blueberries
Lemon juice
Plantains

superfoods

Bone broth
Fermented vegetables
Liver

spices

Basil
Cilantro
Cinnamon
Cumin
Garlic
Ginger
Oregano
Parsley
Turmeric

DAY	BREAKFAST	LUNCH	DINNER
1	[MA] Breakfast Fried "Rice" ⇆ (266), [MA] Raw Sauerkraut (262)	Mustard-Glazed Chicken Thighs (317), green salad* with EVOO	Grilled Garlic Flank Steak with Peppers & Onions ⇆ (334), [NR] baked sweet potato**
2	*leftover* Breakfast Fried "Rice," [MA] Raw Sauerkraut (262)	*leftover* Grilled Garlic Flank Steak with Peppers & Onions, avocado, lemon juice, EVOO over green salad*	Mediterranean Baked Chicken with Cauliflower ⇆ (294)
3	Peach Blueberry Smoothie (289), [MA] Blueberry Maple Sausage (273)	*leftover* Mediterranean Baked Chicken with Cauliflower	[MA] Lemony Lamb Dolmas (368), Cilantro Cauli-Rice (412)
4	Peach Blueberry Smoothie (289), *leftover* Blueberry Maple Sausage	*leftover* Lemony Lamb Dolmas, *leftover* Cilantro Cauli-Rice	Seared Scallops with Orange Glaze (386), [NR] butternut squash**
5	Paleo Avocado "Toast" ⇆ (264)	Nori Salmon Handroll (388)	Beef & Veggie Stir-Fry ⇆ (348), Yellow Cauli-Rice (413)
6	*leftover* Paleo Avocado "Toast"	*leftover* Beef & Veggie Stir-Fry	Lamb Lettuce Boats with Avoziki Sauce ⇆ (370)
7	Cherry Vanilla Smoothie (289), [MA] breakfast sausage made with Italian Blend (256) & ground meat	[NR] canned wild salmon, asparagus*, avocado, lemon juice, EVOO	Citrus & Herb Whole Roasted Chicken (292), Baked Beets with Fennel (420)
8	Cherry Vanilla Smoothie (289), *leftover* breakfast sausage	Dairy-Free Caesar Salad (396), *leftover* Citrus & Herb Whole Roasted Chicken	Restaurant-Style Lettuce Cups ⇆ (312)
9	*leftover* Restaurant-Style Lettuce Cups, blueberries	Indian Spiced Burgers with Smashed Roasted Garlic (342), [NR] steamed broccoli*	Pesto Fettuccine with Shrimp ⇆ (380)
10	[NR] smoked salmon, sliced avocado, blueberries	Simple Shrimp Ceviche ⇆ (389), green salad* with EVOO	Cumin-Spiced Pork Tenderloin (320), [NR] sweet potatoes**
11	[MA] Breakfast Fried "Rice" ⇆ (266), [MA] Raw Sauerkraut (262)	*leftover* Cumin-Spiced Pork Tenderloin, [NR] sweet potatoes**	Orange Braised Beef (344), Candied Carrots (415), spinach*
12	*leftover* Breakfast Fried "Rice," [MA] Raw Sauerkraut (262)	*leftover* Orange Braised Beef, *leftover* Candied Carrots, spinach*	Savory Baked Chicken Legs ⇆ (316), [NR] baked sweet potato**
13	[NR] smoked salmon, spinach*, [MA] Raw Sauerkraut (262)	*leftover* Savory Baked Chicken Legs, [NR] baked sweet potato**	Lemon Rosemary Broiled Salmon (375), Asparagus with Lemon & Olives (409), [NR] sweet potato**
14	*leftover* Lemon Rosemary Broiled Salmon, *leftover* Asparagus with Lemon & Olives*	[MA] Chicken Liver Pâté (426), [MA] Crispy Plantain Chips (431) or cucumber and carrot slices	Grilled Tuna Over Fresh Noodle Salad (384)
15	Paleo Avocado "Toast" ⇆ (264)	*leftover* Chicken Liver Pâté, cucumber and carrot slices, banana	Italian-Style Stuffed Peppers ⇆ (358), Mashed Faux-Tatoes (418)
16	*leftover* Paleo Avocado "Toast"	*leftover* Italian-Style Stuffed Peppers, *leftover* Mashed Faux-Tatoes	Bacon-Wrapped Smoky Chicken Thighs ⇆ (298), Whipped Sweet Potatoes (419), green salad*

Autoimmune Conditions

DAY	BREAKFAST	LUNCH	DINNER
17	Cherry Vanilla Smoothie (289), [MA] Apple Sage Sausage (272)	*leftover* Bacon-Wrapped Smoky Chicken Thighs, green salad* with EVOO	Spaghetti Squash Bolognese ⇆ (338)
18	Cherry Vanilla Smoothie (289), *leftover* Apple Sage Sausage	*leftover* Spaghetti Squash Bolognese	Thanksgiving Stuffing Meatballs (326), Simple Cranberry Sauce (436), Mashed Faux-Tatoes (418)
19	*leftover* Thanksgiving Stuffing Meatballs, blueberries	[NR] canned wild salmon, asparagus*, avocado, lemon juice, EVOO	Lemon & Bacon Scallops ⇆ (376), Lemon Roasted Romanesco* (417)
20	Home Fries & Sausage Skillet ⇆ (268)	*leftover* Lemon & Bacon Scallops, *leftover* Lemon Roasted Romanesco*	Orange & Olive Braised Chicken (306), Yellow Cauli-Rice (413), green salad* with EVOO
21	*leftover* Orange & Olive Braised Chicken, *leftover* Yellow Cauli-Rice	[MA] Six-Minute Salmon Bowls (382)	Souvlaki Kebabs (290), Greek Salad with Avoziki Dressing ⇆ (402)
22	[MA] Breakfast Fried "Rice" ⇆ (266)	*leftover* Souvlaki Kebabs, *leftover* Greek Salad with Avoziki Dressing	Orange Braised Beef (344), Butternut Sage Soup** (394)
23	*leftover* Breakfast Fried "Rice"	*leftover* Orange Braised Beef, *leftover* Butternut Sage Soup**	Hayley's Skirt Steak Tacos ⇆ (346), choice of salsa ⇆ (433), fresh pineapple or mango
24	Peach Blueberry Smoothie (289), [MA] Blueberry Maple Sausage (273)	[MA] Tangy Taco Salad ⇆ (350), *leftover* salsa	Bacon & Superfood Meatloaf ⇆ (330), Mashed Faux-Tatoes (418), green salad* with EVOO
25	Peach Blueberry Smoothie (289), *leftover* Blueberry Maple Sausage	[NR] canned wild salmon, green salad* with EVOO, avocado, olives, blueberries	Seared Scallops with Orange Glaze (386), Yellow Cauli-Rice (413), [NR] steamed bok choy*
26	Home Fries & Sausage Skillet ⇆ (268)	[MA] Italiano Salad ⇆ (398), Honey Mustard Dressing (434)	Grandma Barbara's Stuffed Mushrooms ⇆ (324), *leftover* Italiano Salad
27	*leftover* Home Fries & Sausage Skillet ⇆	*leftover* Grandma Barbara's Stuffed Mushrooms, green salad* with EVOO	Orange Sesame Meatballs ⇆ (328), Yellow Cauli-Rice (413)
28	Cherry Vanilla Smoothie (289), [MA] Apple Sage Sausage (272)	*leftover* Orange Sesame Meatballs, *leftover* Yellow Cauli-Rice	Lemon & Artichoke Chicken (296), Broc-Cauli Chowder with Bacon (392)
29	Cherry Vanilla Smoothie (289), *leftover* Apple Sage Sausage	*leftover* Lemon & Artichoke Chicken, *leftover* Broc-Cauli Chowder with Bacon	The Easiest Tacos (362), Crispy Plantain Chips (431), choice of salsa ⇆ (433)
30	[NR] smoked salmon, sliced avocado, blueberries	*leftover* The Easiest Tacos, *leftover* Crispy Plantain Chips, *leftover* salsa	Prosciutto & Caramelized Onion Burger ⇆ (343), Green Beans with Shallots (406)

» *A complete shopping list for this meal plan can be found on balancedbites.com*

NOTES

⇆ Follow notes on recipe for EGG-FREE, NUT & SEED-FREE & NIGHTSHADE-FREE

*: or other green vegetable; green salad is any lettuce and/or non-starchy vegetables

**: or other starchy vegetable (refer to page 75)

EVOO: Extra-virgin olive oil, or use any dressing from pages 434–435 on salads

CO: Coconut oil

MA: Make-Ahead all or part of the recipe

NR: No Recipe (use any simple prep)

If no page number is listed, simply prepare the items as noted or any way you like. For additional protein, vegetable, and fat recommendations, refer to the QUICK LIST that is associated with your meal plan!

Blood Sugar Regulation

If you have been diagnosed with type 1 diabetes and have not previously used the Autoimmune Condition 30-Day Meal Plan, use the 30-day menu from that plan and follow the lifestyle, supplement, and nutrient recommendations from this plan.

blood sugar imbalances (dysglycemia)

symptoms include:

» Blood sugar levels that are high or low, or high then low
» Energy highs and lows throughout the day

low blood sugar (hypoglycemia)

symptoms include:

» General fatigue
» Inability to focus
» Low blood pressure
» Headaches
» Incoherent speech
» Weakness in legs
» Weight gain
» Carbohydrate cravings
» Mood imbalances, such as irritability, negativity, crying spells, mood swings, antisocial behavior, depression, anxiety
» Constant hunger, compulsive eating
» Loss of appetite
» Loss of sex drive
» Rapid heartbeat

type 1 diabetes (hyperglycemia, autoimmune)

In type 1 diabetes, the body's immune system attacks the pancreatic beta cells and destroys them, so they are incapable of producing insulin. Many of those with type 1 diabetes have undiagnosed celiac disease and may go on to develop Hashimoto's thyroiditis.

symptoms include:

» Weight loss and malabsorption
» Excessive thirst
» Often correlates with celiac disease and related symptoms
» Generally diagnosed in children following infections that trigger autoimmunity

type 2 diabetes (hyperglycemia)

symptoms include:

» Abdominal adiposity (belly fat)
» Difficulty losing weight
» Fatigue, especially after meals
» High blood glucose
» Loss of lean muscle mass
» Carbohydrate cravings
» Symptoms of hypoglycemia
» Secondary symptoms include: metabolic syndrome, irregular periods, PCOS, cardiovascular disease

You may also benefit from this meal plan if you've been diagnosed with:

» Gestational diabetes
» Metabolic syndrome
» Hormonal imbalances (such as PCOS or infertility)

You may also use this meal plan as a first step intervention for the conditions below before using the Neurological Health 30-Day Meal Plan (page 228), depending on how advanced the disease is:

» Alzheimer's disease
» Parkinson's disease

DISCLAIMER:
The information in this book is not intended to be a replacement for professional medical diagnosis or treatment for a medical condition. It consists solely of nutritional and lifestyle recommendations to support a healthier body.

diet & lifestyle recommendations

add [+]

FAT
Many people experiencing dysglycemia patterns are unnecessarily avoiding fats and overeating carbohydrates, which contributes further to these conditions.

PROTEIN
Protein helps satisfy appetite for longer periods of time. Focusing meals on both fat and protein will help.

NUTRIENT-DENSE FOODS
Replenish nutrient stores that have been depleted by excess refined foods.

SUPERFOODS
Eat superfoods as often as possible (see page 61). Make bone broth (page 259) and drink it or cook with it regularly. Consume 1/4 cup raw sauerkraut (page 262) daily, especially with breakfast.

STRESS MANAGEMENT
Develop a guided meditation or slow-breathing practice, or begin to practice qigong.

MOVEMENT
For movement without systemic stress, take walks outside, swim (not for speed!), or practice gentle yoga.

Slowly begin weight training with moderate to heavy weight, not excessively demanding in terms of stress response or cortisol output.

Ensure activity is fueled appropriately and in advance: do not exercise if you are experiencing symptoms of low blood sugar, and eat a small protein/fat/carbohydrate snack 60–90 minutes before exercise to maintain blood sugar levels.

avoid [–]

GLUTEN
100% of the time. See the guide to gluten on page 107.

REFINED FOODS & SWEETENERS
These can provoke blood sugar fluctuations.

ALCOHOL, CAFFEINE & CHOCOLATE
These can promote hypoglycemic events.

STRESS
Make lifestyle changes to avoid stressful situations.

FASTING
Don't go for more than 4–5 hours without food. Once your blood sugar has become consistently stable, you may allow more hours to pass between meals.

CHRONIC CARDIOVASCULAR EXERCISE
30–60+ minutes of cardiovascular exercise at a steady state of intensity, like jogging or biking, can lead to episodes of low blood sugar, as well as provoke a stress response.

nutritional supplements & herbs to consider

These recommendations are made as a starting point. Do your own research and determine which supplements may serve you best. Remember that supplements should be used for a short period of time, one to six months, and that it's best to get as many of your nutrients from food as possible. See page 183 for specific food-based nutrients on which to focus. The items below are listed in no particular order.

» **VITAMIN B3 (niacin)** supports blood sugar regulation and may lower cholesterol levels. The niacinamide form may be useful in healing early-onset type 1 diabetes.

» **VITAMIN B5 (pantothenic acid & pantethine)** may help lower cholesterol and triglycerides. Look for a B-complex for a balanced dose.

» **VITAMIN B7 (biotin)** is a coenzyme required for the metabolism of glucose, amino acids, and lipids.

» **VITAMIN C** is a potent antioxidant with anti-inflammatory properties. It helps regenerate vitamin E and is particularly beneficial for diabetics.

» **CHROMIUM (chromium picolinate, polynicotinate, chelavite)** may improve insulin sensitivity and reduce appetite.

» **CARNITINE/L-CARNITINE** can improve insulin sensitivity and glucose storage, and it optimizes fat and carbohydrate metabolism. It may also improve the utilization of fat as an energy source. Cofactors include iron, vitamin C, vitamin B3 (niacin), and vitamin B6.

» **HERBS AND TEAS:** Blood-sugar-regulating and adaptogenic herbs, teas, and spices; digestive bitters; schizandra, ginseng; peppermint, ginger, cinnamon

» **COENZYME Q10** (CoQ10, ubiquinone) enhances cellular energy production, and it can help alleviate fatigue as well as muscle and joint pain. Statin drugs are known to deplete CoQ10.

» **VITAMIN E** may reduce oxidative stress-induced insulin resistance.

» **L-GLUTAMINE** helps to calm cravings for sugar and carbohydrates.

» **LIPOIC ACID (alpha-lipoic acid)** has antioxidant properties and may increase glucose uptake from the bloodstream by promoting the conversion of carbohydrates into energy.

» **MAGNESIUM** is required for more than 300 enzymatic processes in the body, and most people are deficient in it. It is also useful in blood sugar regulation. Look for magnesium glycinate or magnesium malate forms.

» **N-ACETYL CYSTEINE (NAC)** may reduce the glycation processes that lead to cataract formation.

» **SELENIUM & ZINC** are antioxidants that protect against free-radical damage. Supplements may be necessary because it's difficult to obtain adequate amounts from food.

supportive nutrients & foods that contain them

VITAMIN A (RETINOL)

Helps maintain the lining of the gut

» Liver, eel
» Grass-fed butter, clarified butter, or ghee

VITAMIN B5

Essential for the manufacture of adrenal hormones and red blood cells

» Brewer's yeast
  (Lewis Labs brand only)

BUTYRIC ACID

Helps to decrease intestinal permeability

» Grass-fed butter, clarified butter, or ghee

VITAMIN C

A potent antioxidant with anti-inflammatory properties

» Beets, broccoli, Brussels sprouts, cauliflower, daikon radishes, garlic
» Lemon juice

VITAMIN D

A potent immune system modulator that is best obtained from sun exposure

» Cold-water fish (salmon, herring, mackerel)
» Grass-fed butter or ghee

GLYCINE

Helps repair the gut lining and increases stomach acid production

» Bone broth (page 259)
» Gelatin

OMEGA-3 FATS

An anti-inflammatory essential fatty acid

» Cold-water fish, such as salmon, herring, and mackerel
» Pecans, walnuts

PROBIOTICS

Promote healthy gut flora, which is critical for proper digestion and elimination

» Fermented vegetables: cabbage (sauerkraut/kimchi), carrots, beets
» Kombucha (fermented tea)

SELENIUM

An antioxidant that protects against free-radical damage

» Eggs
» Garlic, red Swiss chard, turnips

SOLUBLE FIBER

Feeds beneficial bacteria in the gut. Eat in small amounts if your digestion needs support.

» Butternut squash, sweet potatoes
» Plantains

ZINC

A potent antioxidant often low in people with inflammatory conditions; aids in vitamin A metabolism

» Oysters, shellfish
» Lamb, red meat

quick LIST

proteins

Beef
Chicken
Eggs
Grass-fed dairy
Lamb
Pork
Salmon
Shellfish
Tuna

fats

Coconut oil
Extra-virgin olive oil
Grass-fed butter/ghee
Walnuts

vegetables

Beets
Bell pepper
Broccoli
Brussels sprouts
Cabbage
Cauliflower
Mushrooms
Parsnips
Swiss chard
Turnip greens

fruits

Berries
Lemon juice
Lime juice

superfoods

Bone broth
Liver
Sauerkraut

spices

Basil
Black pepper
Chili powder
Cilantro
Cinnamon
Cloves
Garlic
Thyme
Turmeric

DAY	BREAKFAST	LUNCH	DINNER
1	Swirly Crustless Quiche (270), Perfectly Baked Bacon (260), [MA] Raw Sauerkraut (262)	[MA] Mustard-Glazed Chicken Thighs (317), green salad* with Balsamic Vinaigrette (434)	Grilled Garlic Flank Steak with Peppers & Onions (334), broccoli*, berries
2	*leftover* Swirly Crustless Quiche, *leftover* Grilled Garlic Flank Steak with Peppers & Onions	[NR] canned wild salmon with olives, avocado, lemon juice, tomato, EVOO over green salad*	Bacon Jalapeño Burgers (360), Sweet Potato Pancakes (285), Swiss chard*
3	*leftover* Sweet Potato Pancakes, *leftover* Mustard-Glazed Chicken Thighs	*leftover* Bacon Jalapeño Burgers, [NR] steamed spinach*	[MA] Lemony Lamb Dolmas (368), Cilantro Cauli-Rice (412)
4	Pesto Scrambled Eggs (286), *leftover* Cilantro Cauli-Rice, [MA] Raw Sauerkraut (262)	*leftover* Lemony Lamb Dolmas, green salad* with EVOO	Citrus Macadamia Nut Sole (378), Baked Beets with Fennel (420)
5	*leftover* Citrus Macadamia Nut Sole, *leftover* Baked Beets with Fennel	Nori Salmon Handroll (388), berries	Beef & Veggie Stir-Fry (348), berries
6	[NR] eggs any style, breakfast sausage made with Italian Blend (256) & ground meat, Brussels sprouts*	*leftover* Beef & Veggie Stir-Fry, berries	Lamb Lettuce Boats with Avoziki Sauce (370), berries
7	[NR] eggs any style, Perfectly Baked Bacon (260), kale*, [MA] Raw Sauerkraut (262)	green salad* with canned wild salmon, asparagus*, Basil Shallot Vinaigrette (434)	Citrus & Herb Whole Roasted Chicken (292), Simple Baked Kale Chips* (425), cauliflower*
8	Swirly Crustless Quiche (270), berries, [NR] eggs hard-boiled or any style	Dairy-Free Caesar Salad (396), *leftover* Citrus & Herb Whole Roasted Chicken	Restaurant-Style Lettuce Cups (312)
9	*leftover* Swirly Crustless Quiche (270), [NR] steamed broccoli*, [MA] Raw Sauerkraut (262)	Indian Spiced Burgers with Smashed Roasted Garlic (342), [NR] steamed broccoli*	Pesto Fettuccine with Shrimp (380)
10	Pesto Scrambled Eggs (286), *leftover* Pesto Fettuccine with Shrimp, sliced avocado	[MA] Buffalo Chicken Lettuce Wraps (299)	Coffee BBQ Rubbed Pork with Seared Pineapple (318), green salad* with EVOO
11	[MA] Home Fries & Sausage Skillet (268)	*leftover* Coffee BBQ Rubbed Pork with Seared Pineapple, green salad* with EVOO	Balsamic Braised Short Ribs (332), Mashed Faux-Tatoes (418), green salad* with EVOO
12	*leftover* Home Fries & Sausage Skillet	*leftover* Balsamic Braised Short Ribs, *leftover* Mashed Faux-Tatoes, green salad* with EVOO	Mediterranean Baked Chicken with Cauliflower (294), berries*
13	[MA] Zucchini Pancakes (271), Perfectly Baked Bacon (260), [MA] Raw Sauerkraut (262)	*leftover* Mediterranean Baked Chicken with Cauliflower	Lemon Rosemary Broiled Salmon (375), Asparagus with Lemon & Olives (409), [NR] sweet potato**
14	*leftover* Lemon Rosemary Broiled Salmon, *leftover* Asparagus with Lemon & Olives*	Simple Shrimp Ceviche (389), green salad* with EVOO & lemon juice	Grilled Tuna Over Fresh Noodle Salad (384), berries
15	[NR] scrambled eggs with mushrooms, olives, [NR] steamed spinach*, avocado	*leftover* Grilled Tuna Over Fresh Noodle Salad, berries	Italian-Style Stuffed Peppers (358), green salad* with Balsamic Vinaigrette (434)
16	[MA] Blueberry Maple Sausage (273), [NR] eggs any style, Brussels sprouts*	*leftover* Italian-Style Stuffed Peppers, green salad* with Basil Shallot Vinaigrette (434)	Bacon-Wrapped Smoky Chicken Thighs (298), green salad* with EVOO

Blood Sugar Regulation

DAY	BREAKFAST	LUNCH	DINNER
17	[MA] Bacon & Egg Salad (287) in a Swiss chard wrap*, avocado, [MA] Raw Sauerkraut (262)	*leftover* Bacon-Wrapped Smoky Chicken Thighs, green salad* with EVOO	Spaghetti Squash Bolognese (338), Simple Baked Kale Chips* (425), berries
18	[MA] Zucchini Pancakes (271), *leftover* Blueberry Maple Sausage	*leftover* Spaghetti Squash Bolognese, green salad* with Basil Shallot Vinaigrette (434)	Thanksgiving Stuffing Meatballs (326), Simple Cranberry Sauce (436), Mashed Faux-Tatoes (418)
19	*leftover* Bacon & Egg Salad in a Swiss chard* wrap, avocado, [MA] Raw Sauerkraut (262)	*leftover* Thanksgiving Stuffing Meatballs, *leftover* Cranberry Sauce, *leftover* Mashed Faux-Tatoes	Lemon & Bacon Scallops with Roasted Potatoes (376), Lemon Roasted Romanesco* (417)
20	Paleo Avocado "Toast" (264), [NR] eggs any style, berries	*leftover* Lemon & Bacon Scallops, *leftover* Lemon Roasted Romanesco*	Orange & Olive Braised Chicken (306), Yellow Cauli-Rice (413), green salad* with EVOO
21	[MA] breakfast sausage made with Italian Blend (256) & ground meat, [NR] eggs any style, Raw Sauerkraut (262)	[MA] Six-Minute Salmon Bowls (382)	Souvlaki Kebabs (290), Greek Salad with Avoziki Dressing (402), berries
22	[MA] Breakfast Fried "Rice" (266), berries	*leftover* Souvlaki Kebabs, *leftover* Greek Salad with Avoziki Dressing, berries	Orange Braised Beef (344), Butternut Sage Soup** (394)
23	*leftover* Breakfast Fried "Rice," berries	*leftover* Orange Braised Beef, *leftover* Butternut Sage Soup**	Hayley's Skirt Steak Tacos (346), choice of salsa (433), Smoky Grilled Squash & Pineapple (408)
24	[NR] eggs any style, bacon, *leftover* Smoky Grilled Squash & Pineapple	[MA] Tangy Taco Salad (350), *leftover* salsa	Bacon & Superfood Meatloaf (330), Mashed Faux-Tatoes (418), green salad* with EVOO
25	[NR] eggs any style, mushrooms, spinach or kale*, avocado, [MA] Raw Sauerkraut (262)	[MA] Quick & Easy Salmon Cakes (374), green salad* with EVOO, avocado, olives	Seared Scallops with Orange Glaze (386), Cilantro Cauli-Rice (412), [NR] steamed bok choy*
26	[MA] Zucchini Pancakes (271), [MA] Apple Sage Sausage (272), berries	[MA] Italiano Salad (398), Basil Shallot Vinaigrette (434)	Grandma Barbara's Stuffed Mushrooms (324), *leftover* Italiano Salad
27	*leftover* Zucchini Pancakes, *leftover* Apple Sage Sausage, berries	*leftover* Grandma Barbara's Stuffed Mushrooms, green salad* with Basil Shallot Vinaigrette (434)	Orange Sesame Meatballs (328), Cilantro Cauli-Rice (412), berries
28	[NR] eggs any style, Perfectly Baked Bacon (260), Brussels sprouts*	*leftover* Orange Sesame Meatballs, *leftover* Cilantro Cauli-Rice	Lemon & Artichoke Chicken (296), Broc-Cauli Chowder with Bacon (392)
29	[MA] Apple Cinnamon Egg Muffins (280), bacon or sausage	*leftover* Lemon & Artichoke Chicken, *leftover* Broc-Cauli Chowder with Bacon	The Easiest Tacos (362), Cilantro Cauli-Rice (412), choice of salsa (433)
30	*leftover* Apple Cinnamon Egg Muffins, bacon or sausage	*leftover* The Easiest Tacos, *leftover* Cilantro Cauli-Rice, *leftover* salsa	Mini Mediterranean Kebabs (352), Sautéed Spinach with Pine Nuts & Currants* (423)

» *A complete shopping list for this meal plan can be found on balancedbites.com*

NOTES

*: or other green vegetable; green salad is any lettuce and/or non-starchy vegetables
**: or other starchy vegetable (refer to page 75)
EVOO: Extra-virgin olive oil, or use any dressing from pages 434–435 on salads
CO: Coconut oil
MA: Make-Ahead all or part of the recipe
NR: No Recipe (use any simple prep)

If no page number is listed, simply prepare the items as noted or any way you like. For additional protein, vegetable, and fat recommendations, refer to the QUICK LIST that is associated with your meal plan!

Cancer Recovery

30-DAY MEAL PLANS

While an anti-inflammatory diet and healthy lifestyle are the cornerstones of preventing cancer, we can't always control every aspect of what may cause our bodies to fall ill. That said, there are many ways to give yourself the best possible chance for recovery. Many people find transitioning to a new way of eating while dealing with illness to be overwhelming, but it can provide your body with what it needs to heal. Along with an intensely strong positive mental outlook, food provides the raw materials for your cells to rebuild anew.

You'll notice that there's less red meat included in the meals in this plan than in all of the other plans in this book. This is not because I believe that if you're recovering from cancer, you should avoid red meat completely, but rather because you've likely been advised by your doctor to avoid it. I don't want to present a plan that you feel unsure about following, and it's certainly possible to get most of the nutrients you need from foods other than red meat. But if you have any concerns about your iron intake, talk to your doctor.

If you are interested in a ketogenic diet approach to cancer recovery, you may also want to consider incorporating aspects of the diet and lifestyle recommendations from the Neurological Health 30-Day Meal Plan (page 228), specifically regarding minimal carbohydrate intake from starchy vegetables and fruits and increased dietary fats.

DISCLAIMER:
The information in this book is not intended to be a replacement for professional medical diagnosis or treatment for a medical condition. It consists solely of nutritional and lifestyle recommendations to support a healthier body.

diet & lifestyle recommendations

add [+]

NUTRIENT-DENSE FOODS
Replenish nutrient stores that have been depleted by excess refined foods.

SUPERFOODS
Eat superfoods as often as possible (see page 61). Make bone broth (page 259) and drink it or cook with it regularly. Make liver regularly. Consume 1/4 cup raw sauerkraut (page 262) daily, especially with breakfast.

PROTEIN
Protein helps to heal the lining of the gut.

MEDICINAL MUSHROOMS
Reishi, shiitake, maitake, and other mushrooms, in food or extract form, counter the side effects of chemotherapy and radiation.

ANTIOXIDANT-RICH FOODS
Eat deeply colored foods, such as leafy greens, berries, and sweet potatoes.

STRESS MANAGEMENT
Develop a guided meditation or slow-breathing practice, or begin to practice qigong. Practice biofeedback, tai chi, and/or guided imagery for deep relaxation.

SLEEP
Melatonin, a potent antioxidant necessary to recharge and power your immune system, is produced during overnight sleep in a dark room.

MOVEMENT
For movement without systemic stress, take walks outside, swim (not for speed!), or practice gentle yoga.

avoid [–]

GLUTEN & DAIRY
100% of the time. See the guide to gluten on page 107. Avoid dairy for its potential growth-promotion effects. (Butter and ghee are okay.)

RESTAURANTS / DINING OUT
Avoid the damaged and man-made fats most often used in restaurant foods.

REFINED FOODS, SWEETENERS, CAFFEINE
Cancer cells feed on sugar; they have about eight times the receptors for sugar as normal cells. Eat only nutrient-dense carbohydrates (see page 75).

ALCOHOL, TOBACCO, NICOTINE & MSG
These require detoxification and/or may have some neurotoxic effects.

PROCESSED MEATS
Avoid those with synthetic chemical preservatives such as BHA and/or BHT. Read ingredient lists carefully for these items.

CHARRED FOODS

NONORGANIC FOODS & COMMERCIALLY RAISED MEATS
Use the Dirty Dozen and Clean Thirteen lists from the Environmental Working Group (EWG) to identify the best produce to purchase organic and what has few toxins when purchased conventionally grown. Avoid meats with added hormones, artificial colors, and other food additives.

HARSH CLEANING & HYGIENE PRODUCTS
Opt for gentle, natural alternatives, such as soap nuts for laundry, vinegar and water for cleaning countertops, and baking soda and peroxide for cleaning and whitening surfaces, laundry, teeth, and more. Consider skipping shampoo and going "no-poo" instead. Safe makeup recommendations may be found at skindeep.org.

nutritional supplements & herbs to consider

These recommendations are made as a starting point. Do your own research and determine which supplements may serve you best. Remember that supplements should be used for a short period of time, one to six months, and that it's best to get as many of your nutrients from food as possible. See page 189 for specific food-based nutrients on which to focus. The items below are listed in no particular order.

» **VITAMIN A (retinol)** helps to maintain the integrity of the mucosal lining of the gut. It also helps maintain immunity when balanced with vitamin D, and it is necessary for the assimilation of dietary minerals.

» **B VITAMINS** are critical in assisting neurotransmitters and therefore are important for brain health and the proper functioning of nerves and muscles. Look for a B-complex supplement with B12.

» **VITAMIN C** is a potent antioxidant with anti-inflammatory properties.

» **CURCUMIN** is a potent antioxidant that supports immune health.

» **COENZYME Q10** (CoQ10, ubiquinone) enhances cellular energy production, and it can help alleviate fatigue as well as muscle and joint pain. Statin drugs are known to deplete CoQ10.

» **DIINDOYLMETHANE (DIM)** may inhibit tumor formation and help to induce cancer cell death in breast, colon, prostate, and lung cancers.

» **VITAMIN E** is an antioxidant that benefits neurological function, smooth-muscle growth, and cellular communication. It may also reduce oxidative stress-induced insulin resistance.

» **EPIGALLOCATECHIN GALLATE (EGCG / green tea extract)** is a potent antioxidant that promotes angiogenesis. It may be best to wait three weeks after chemo to consume.

» **GLUTATHIONE** is an antioxidant that aids in liver detox processes and the regeneration of vitamins A, C, and E.

» **HERBS AND TEAS:** green tea (for EGCG), ginger

» **L-GLUTAMINE** aids in the healing of the cells that line the small intestine.

» **LIPOIC ACID (alpha-lipoic acid)** has antioxidant properties and may increase glucose uptake from the bloodstream by promoting the conversion of carbohydrates into energy.

» **MAGNESIUM** is required for more than 300 enzymatic processes in the body, and most people are deficient in it. It is also useful in blood sugar regulation. Look for magnesium glycinate or magnesium malate forms.

» **N-ACETYL CYSTEINE (NAC)** supports liver function.

» **OMEGA-3 FATS** are anti-inflammatory essential fatty acids.

» **PROTEOLYTIC ENZYMES** are anti-inflammatory.

» **SELENIUM & ZINC** are antioxidants that protect against free-radical damage. Supplements may be necessary because it's difficult to obtain adequate amounts from food.

supportive nutrients & foods that contain them

VITAMIN A (RETINOL)

Helps maintain the lining of the gut

» Liver, eel

» Grass-fed butter, clarified butter, or ghee

VITAMIN C

A potent antioxidant with anti-inflammatory properties

» Beets, bell peppers, broccoli, Brussels sprouts, cauliflower, collard greens, garlic, kale, mustard greens, parsley, spinach

» Lemons, strawberries

CAROTENOIDS

» Alpha-carotene: pumpkin, carrots

» Cryptoxanthin: citrus, peaches, apricots

» Lycopene: tomato, guava, watermelon, pink grapefruit

» Lutein: kale, spinach, collard greens, beet greens

» Zeaxanthin: green vegetables, citrus

» Beta carotene: kale, broccoli, sweet potatoes, carrots, red pepper, mango, apricots, peaches, persimmons, cantaloupe

CURCUMIN

» Turmeric: dried or fresh

DIINDOLYLMETHANE (DIM)

» Broccoli, Brussels sprouts, cauliflower, kale, chard, collards

VITAMIN D

A potent immune system modulator that is best obtained from sun exposure

» Cold-water fish (salmon, herring, mackerel)

» Grass-fed butter or ghee

VITAMIN E

An antioxidant that benefits neurological function, smooth-muscle growth, and cellular communication

» Broccoli, Brussels sprouts, spinach (cooked)

» Extra-virgin olive oil

» Pecans

FLAVONOIDS

May promote apotosis (programmed cell death) in cancer cells while sparing normal cells

» Green tea

LIMONENE

May have antiangiogenic effects

» Citrus

MAGNESIUM

Critical for cellular energy production, which helps battle fatigue, and for proper calcium metabolism, which is necessary for vascular health

» Beets, kale, other green leafy vegetables

» Pumpkin seeds (pepitas)

OMEGA-3 FATS

An anti-inflammatory essential fatty acid

» Cold-water fish, such as salmon, herring, and mackerel

» Pecans, walnuts

POLYPHENOLS

May help to inhibit the growth of oral, colon, and prostate cancer cells

» Blueberries, cherries, pomegranates, strawberries

PROTEOLYTIC ENZYMES

May be supportive in combating adverse effects of chemotherapy and radiation

» Papayas, pineapples

quick LIST

proteins

Chicken
Herring
Liver
Mackerel
Oysters
Salmon
Shellfish
Tuna
Turkey

fats

Coconut oil
Red palm oil
Pecans
Walnuts

vegetables

Beets
Broccoli
Brussels sprouts
Butternut squash
Cauliflower
Daikon radish
Okra
Squash
Sweet potatoes
Swiss chard

fruits

Berries
Citrus
Melons
Tropical fruit

superfoods

Bone broth
Sauerkraut

spices

Basil
Cilantro
Cinnamon
Cumin
Garlic
Ginger
Oregano
Parsley
Turmeric

DAY	BREAKFAST	LUNCH	DINNER
1	Swirly Crustless Quiche (270), Perfectly Baked Bacon (260), [MA] Raw Sauerkraut (262)	[MA] Mustard-Glazed Chicken Thighs (317), green salad* with Balsamic Vinaigrette (434)	Simple Shrimp Ceviche (389), Lemon Roasted Romanesco (417)
2	leftover Swirly Crustless Quiche, leftover Lemon Roasted Romanesco	[NR] canned wild salmon with olives, avocado, lemon juice, tomato, EVOO over green salad*	Winter Kale Salad (396), [NR] chicken or salmon
3	[MA] Sweet Potato Pancakes (285), leftover Mustard-Glazed Chicken Thighs	leftover Winter Kale Salad, leftover chicken or salmon	Lemon Rosemary Broiled Salmon (375), Asparagus with Lemon & Olives (409), [NR] sweet potato**
4	Pesto Scrambled Eggs (286), leftover Asparagus with Lemon & Olives, [MA] Raw Sauerkraut (262)	leftover Lemon Rosemary Broiled Salmon, green salad* with EVOO	Citrus Macadamia Nut Sole (378), [NR] butternut squash**
5	leftover Citrus Macadamia Nut Sole, leftover butternut squash**	Nori Salmon Handroll (388), berries	Savory Baked Chicken Legs (316), Baked Beets with Fennel (420)
6	Pumpkin Pancakes (284), breakfast sausage made with Italian Blend (256) & ground turkey	leftover Savory Baked Chicken Legs, leftover Baked Beets with Fennel	Lamb Lettuce Boats (made with turkey) with Avoziki Sauce (370), berries
7	[NR] eggs any style, mushrooms, spinach*, [MA] Raw Sauerkraut (262)	green salad* with canned wild salmon, asparagus*, lemon juice with EVOO	Citrus & Herb Whole Roasted Chicken (292), Simple Baked Kale Chips* (425), [NR] baked sweet potato**
8	[MA] N'Oatmeal (288), berries, [NR] eggs any style	Dairy-Free Caesar Salad (396), leftover Citrus & Herb Whole Roasted Chicken	Restaurant-Style Lettuce Cups with ground turkey (312)
9	Swirly Crustless Quiche (270), [NR] steamed broccoli*, [MA] Raw Sauerkraut (262)	Indian Spiced Burgers (made with turkey) with Smashed Roasted Garlic (342), [NR] steamed broccoli*	Pesto Fettuccine with Shrimp (380), berries
10	Pesto Scrambled Eggs (286), leftover Pesto Fettuccine with Shrimp, sliced avocado	Simple Shrimp Ceviche (389), green salad* with EVOO	Coffee BBQ Rubbed Pork with Seared Pineapple (318), green salad* with EVOO
11	[MA] Home Fries & Sausage Skillet (268), berries	leftover Coffee BBQ Rubbed Pork with Seared Pineapple, green salad* with EVOO	Seared Scallops with Orange Glaze (386), Cilantro Cauli-Rice (412) green salad* with EVOO
12	leftover Home Fries & Sausage Skillet, berries	leftover Seared Scallops with Orange Glaze, green salad* with EVOO	Mediterranean Baked Chicken with Cauliflower (294), [NR] baked potato**
13	[MA] Zucchini Pancakes (271), [MA] Raw Sauerkraut (262), berries	leftover Mediterranean Baked Chicken with Cauliflower	Lemon Rosemary Broiled Salmon (375), Asparagus with Lemon & Olives (409), [NR] sweet potato**
14	leftover Lemon Rosemary Broiled Salmon, leftover Asparagus with Lemon & Olives*	[MA] Buffalo Chicken Lettuce Wraps (299), berries	Grilled Tuna Over Fresh Noodle Salad (384)
15	[NR] scrambled eggs with mushrooms, olives, spinach*, avocado	leftover Grilled Tuna Over Fresh Noodle Salad	Italian-Style Stuffed Peppers made with turkey (358), green salad* with Balsamic Vinaigrette (434)
16	Peach Blueberry Smoothie (289), [MA] Blueberry Maple Sausage (273)	leftover Italian-Style Stuffed Peppers, green salad* with EVOO	Mustard-Glazed Chicken Thighs (317), green salad* with EVOO

Cancer Recovery

DAY	BREAKFAST	LUNCH	DINNER
17	Peach Blueberry Smoothie (289), *leftover* Blueberry Maple Sausage	*leftover* Mustard-Glazed Chicken Thighs, green salad* with EVOO	Spaghetti Squash Bolognese made with ground turkey (338), Simple Baked Kale Chips* (425)
18	[MA] Pumpkin Pancakes (284), breakfast sausage made with Italian Blend (256) & ground turkey	*leftover* Spaghetti Squash Bolognese, green salad* with EVOO	Thanksgiving Stuffing Meatballs (326), Simple Cranberry Sauce (436), Mashed Faux-Tatoes (418)
19	*leftover* Pumpkin Pancakes, *leftover* breakfast sausage	*leftover* Thanksgiving Stuffing Meatballs, *leftover* Cranberry Sauce, *leftover* Mashed Faux-Tatoes	Lemon & Bacon Scallops with Roasted Potatoes (376), Lemon Roasted Romanesco* (417)
20	Paleo Avocado "Toast" (264), [NR] eggs any style, [MA] Raw Sauerkraut (262)	*leftover* Lemon & Bacon Scallops, *leftover* Lemon Roasted Romanesco*	Orange & Olive Braised Chicken (306), Yellow Cauli-Rice (413), green salad* with EVOO
21	*leftover* Paleo Avocado "Toast," [NR] eggs any style, *leftover* Raw Sauerkraut	[MA] Six-Minute Salmon Bowls (382)	Souvlaki Kebabs (290), Greek Salad with Avoziki Dressing (402), berries
22	[MA] Breakfast Fried "Rice" without bacon (266), apple	*leftover* Souvlaki Kebabs, *leftover* Greek Salad with Avoziki Dressing	[MA] Slow-Cooked Salsa Verde Chicken (302), Mexican Chicken & Avocado Soup (390)
23	*leftover* Breakfast Fried "Rice," apple	*leftover* Slow-Cooked Salsa Verde Chicken, *leftover* Mexican Chicken & Avocado Soup	Buffalo Chicken Lettuce Wraps (299), choice of salsa (433), Smoky Grilled Squash & Pineapple (408)
24	[NR] eggs any style, mushrooms, avocado, *leftover* Smoky Grilled Squash & Pineapple	[MA] Tangy Taco Salad made with ground turkey (350), *leftover* salsa	Citrus Macadamia Nut Sole (378), [NR] butternut squash**
25	[NR] eggs any style, mushrooms, spinach*, [NR] butternut squash**, avocado, [MA] Raw Sauerkraut (262)	[MA] Quick & Easy Salmon Cakes (374), green salad* with EVOO, avocado, olives	Seared Scallops with Orange Glaze (386), Cilantro Cauli-Rice (412), [NR] steamed bok choy*
26	[MA] Zucchini Pancakes (271), *leftover* Seared Scallops with Orange Glaze, berries	[MA] Italiano Salad (398), Honey Mustard Dressing (434)	Grandma Barbara's Stuffed Mushrooms (324), *leftover* Italiano Salad
27	[MA] N'Oatmeal (288), Apple Sage Sausage (272)	*leftover* Grandma Barbara's Stuffed Mushrooms, green salad* with EVOO	Orange Sesame Meatballs with ground pork and turkey (328), Cilantro Cauli-Rice (412), berries
28	*leftover* N'Oatmeal, *leftover* Apple Sage Sausage	*leftover* Orange Sesame Meatballs, *leftover* Cilantro Cauli-Rice, berries	Lemon & Artichoke Chicken (296), Broc-Cauli Chowder with Bacon (392), berries
29	[MA] Apple Cinnamon Egg Muffins (280), breakfast sausage made with Italian Blend (256) & ground turkey	*leftover* Lemon & Artichoke Chicken, *leftover* Broc-Cauli Chowder with Bacon, berries	The Easiest Tacos with ground turkey (362), Crispy Plantain Chips (431), choice of salsa (433), berries
30	*leftover* Apple Cinnamon Egg Muffins, *leftover* breakfast sausage	*leftover* The Easiest Tacos, *leftover* Crispy Plantain Chips, *leftover* salsa	Restaurant-Style Lettuce Cups with ground turkey (312), berries

» *A complete shopping list for this meal plan can be found on balancedbites.com*

NOTES

*: or other green vegetable; green salad is any lettuce and/or non-starchy vegetables

**: or other starchy vegetable (refer to page 75)

EVOO: Extra-virgin olive oil, or use any dressing from pages 434–435 on salads

CO: Coconut oil

MA: Make-Ahead all or part of the recipe

NR: No Recipe (use any simple prep)

If no page number is listed, simply prepare the items as noted or any way you like. For additional protein, vegetable, and fat recommendations, refer to the QUICK LIST that is associated with your meal plan!

Digestive Health

If your symptoms are very severe, use the lifestyle, supplement, and nutrient recommendations from this plan and the monthly menu from the Autoimmune Conditions 30-Day Meal Plan (page 174).

leaky gut
symptoms include:

» Undesired weight loss or difficulty losing weight
» Digestive distress
» Food allergies or intolerances to a wide variety of seemingly unrelated foods; "allergic to everything" types of reactions; or food allergy tests that show an extremely high number of allergenic foods
» Chronic inflammatory and autoimmune conditions (see page 91)

irritable bowel syndrome (IBS)
symptoms include:

» Abdominal pain with change in bowel habits that may alternate between IBS-C (constipation) and IBS-D (diarrhea) and/or gas and bloating that is relieved by defecation
» Altered elimination frequency, form, and ease of passage
» Mucus in stools
» Feeling that there is more stool left in the body after defecation
» Leaky gut symptoms, especially food allergies/ intolerances

inflammatory bowel disease (IBD)
symptoms include:

» Aching all over (often occurs after an infection or trauma)
» Similar symptoms to IBS but more severe and chronic
» Encompasses Crohn's disease, colitis, and ulcerative colitis

crohn's disease
symptoms include:

» Inflammation or swelling anywhere along the GI tract but typically in the ileum (part of the small intestine); may affect all layers of the gut lining
» Inflammatory patches can become strictures
» Experience of extreme bouts of diarrhea (10–20 times per day)
» Pain and tenderness in the lower right part of abdomen
» Serious symptoms of malnutrition and fatigue

colitis and ulcerative colitis
symptoms include:

» Symptoms similar to Crohn's, but the problem is located in the colon and/or rectum; inflammation is limited to the top layer of gut lining
» Symptoms may be intermittent, with periods of remission

celiac disease
symptoms include:

» A severe intolerance to gluten
» Fatigue
» Bone or joint pain
» Anemia
» Weight loss
» Digestive problems, including diarrhea and constipation
» Numbness and tingling in the hands and feet
» A latent, silent, or "non-classical" celiac disease sufferer may experience symptoms that mimic those of any of the previously listed digestive conditions or any chronic inflammatory or autoimmune condition

DISCLAIMER:

The information in this book is not intended to be a replacement for professional medical diagnosis or treatment for a medical condition. It consists solely of nutritional and lifestyle recommendations to support a healthier body.

diet & lifestyle recommendations

add [+]

WELL-COOKED FOODS
Meals such as braised meats, stews, soups, and slow-cooked foods are easier to digest.

NUTRIENT-DENSE FOODS
Replenish nutrient stores that have been depleted by excess refined foods.

SUPERFOODS
Make bone broth (page 259) and drink it or cook with it regularly.

SOLUBLE FIBER
Eat starchy vegetables, such as sweet potatoes, butternut squash, carrots, and cassava, to feed the beneficial bacteria in your gut and promote proper stool motility.

STRESS MANAGEMENT
Develop a guided meditation or slow-breathing practice, or begin to practice qigong.

MOVEMENT
For movement without systemic stress, take walks outside, swim (not for speed!), or practice gentle yoga.

Slowly begin weight training with moderate to heavy weight, not excessively demanding in terms of stress response or cortisol output.

avoid [–]

GLUTEN
100% of the time. See the guide to gluten on page 107.

GUT IRRITANTS
Foods that are known to cause immunological responses, including **grains, legumes, dairy (even grass-fed), nuts, and seeds;** also large quantities of **foods that are high in insoluble fiber,** such as leafy greens, raspberries, and strawberries. Avoiding eggs is optional; if you do, refer to the breakfast items in the Autoimmune Conditions 30-Day Meal Plan (page 174).

Optional: You may find that avoiding FODMAP foods (see page 149) helps for a period of time. See page 61 for a list of FODMAPs; they're also noted in each recipe. The 30-day menu for this plan includes FODMAP foods because most people tolerate them well, but remove them if you need to.

ALCOHOL, CAFFEINE & CHOCOLATE
These can all promote leaky gut.

PAIN MEDICATIONS
Including aspirin, acetaminophen, ibuprofen, naproxen, and corticosteroids.

HARSH CLEANING & HYGIENE PRODUCTS
Opt for gentle, natural alternatives, such as soap nuts for laundry, vinegar and water for cleaning countertops, and baking soda and peroxide for cleaning and whitening surfaces, laundry, teeth, and more. Consider skipping shampoo and going "no-poo" instead. Safe makeup recommendations may be found at skindeep.org.

HIGH-INTENSITY EXERCISE
Overly intense exercise (high-intensity interval training or similar workouts) and chronic cardiovascular exercise (30–60+ minutes at a steady state of intensity, like jogging or biking) can provoke a stress response in the body.

nutritional supplements & herbs to consider

These recommendations are made as a starting point. Do your own research and determine which supplements may serve you best. Remember that supplements should be used for a short period of time, one to six months, and that it's best to get as many of your nutrients from food as possible. See page 195 for specific food-based nutrients on which to focus. The items below are listed in no particular order.

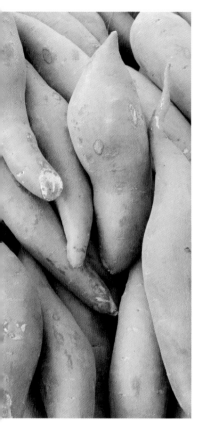

» **VITAMIN A (retinol)** helps to maintain the integrity of the mucosal lining of the gut. It also helps maintain immunity when balanced with vitamin D, and it is necessary for the assimilation of dietary minerals.

» **ARTICHOKE LEAF EXTRACT** has antioxidant properties and supports the liver; it also heals the chronic inflammatory state of digestive distress and aids in the digestion of fats. If you are avoiding FODMAPs, this supplement may not be ideal for you.

» **DIGESTIVE ENZYMES** help to break down food for absorption while your gut is healing. Look for a blend of enzymes.

» **L-GLUTAMINE** aids in the healing of the cells that line the small intestine.

» **HERBAL TEAS** that are calming to your digestive system include peppermint, ginger, kudzu, marshmallow root, and slippery elm.

» **LICORICE ROOT** is an herb that aids in repairing the mucosal lining of the gut and stomach. Look for licorice root tea, an extract of the herb, or a chewable tablet called DGL.

» **ALOE VERA JUICE** (unless it promotes loose stool)

» **MAGNESIUM** is required for more than 300 enzymatic processes in the body, and most people are deficient in it. It is also useful in blood sugar regulation. Look for magnesium glycinate or magnesium malate forms.

» **OX BILE / BILE SALTS** help the body to emulsify dietary fats, especially unsaturated fats, so they're particularly helpful for those without a gallbladder.

» **PHOSPHATIDYLCHOLINE** enhances the integrity of the GI tract, repairs the mucosal lining of the gut, and aids in fatty acid digestion. This supplement is especially important if you are avoiding eggs.

» **QUERCETIN** is a potent antioxidant that promotes better immunity.

» **SELENIUM & ZINC** are antioxidants that protect against free-radical damage. Supplements may be necessary because it's difficult to obtain adequate amounts from food.

» **ZINC CARNOSINE** may improve gut mucosa and gut lining integrity.

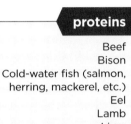

supportive nutrients & foods that contain them

VITAMIN A (RETINOL)

Helps maintain the lining of the gut

» Liver, eel
» Grass-fed butter, clarified butter, or ghee

BROMELAIN

An enzyme with anti-inflammatory properties

» Pineapple

BUTYRIC ACID

Helps to decrease intestinal permeability

» Grass-fed butter, clarified butter, or ghee

VITAMIN C

A potent antioxidant with anti-inflammatory properties

» Beets, broccoli, Brussels sprouts, cauliflower, daikon radishes, garlic
» Lemon juice

VITAMIN D

A potent immune system modulator that is best obtained from sun exposure

» Cold-water fish (salmon, herring, mackerel)
» Grass-fed butter or ghee

GLYCINE

Helps repair the gut lining and increases stomach acid production

» Bone broth (page 259)
» Gelatin

OMEGA-3 FATS

An anti-inflammatory essential fatty acid

» Cold-water fish, such as salmon, herring, and mackerel
» Pecans, walnuts

PROBIOTICS

Promote healthy gut flora, which is critical for proper digestion and elimination

» Fermented vegetables: cabbage (sauerkraut/kimchi), carrots, beets
» Kombucha (fermented tea)

SELENIUM

An antioxidant that protects against free-radical damage

» Eggs
» Garlic, red Swiss chard, turnips

SOLUBLE FIBER

Feeds beneficial bacteria in the gut

» Butternut squash, sweet potatoes
» Bananas, plantains

ZINC

A potent antioxidant often low in people with inflammatory conditions; aids in vitamin A metabolism

» Oysters, shellfish
» Lamb, red meat

quick LIST

proteins

Beef
Bison
Cold-water fish (salmon, herring, mackerel, etc.)
Eel
Lamb
Liver
Oysters
Shellfish

fats

Coconut oil
Extra-virgin olive oil
Grass-fed butter/ghee

vegetables

Beets
Broccoli (cooked)
Brussels sprouts
Butternut squash
Cauliflower (cooked)
Daikon radish
Okra
Spinach
Squash (all kinds)
Sweet potatoes

fruits

Bananas
Blueberries
Lemon juice
Plantains

superfoods

Bone broth
Liver
Sauerkraut

spices

Basil
Cilantro
Cinnamon
Cumin
Garlic
Ginger
Oregano
Parsley
Turmeric

Digestive Health

DAY	BREAKFAST	LUNCH	DINNER
1	Swirly Crustless Quiche (270), Perfectly Baked Bacon (260), [MA] Raw Sauerkraut (262)	[MA] Mustard-Glazed Chicken Thighs (317), [MA] Baked Beets with Fennel (420)	Grilled Garlic Flank Steak with Peppers & Onions (334), [NR] baked potato** with ghee (261)
2	*leftover* Swirly Crustless Quiche, *leftover* Grilled Garlic Flank Steak with Peppers & Onions	*leftover* Mustard-Glazed Chicken Thighs, *leftover* Baked Beets with Fennel	Bacon Jalapeño Burgers (360), Sweet Potato Pancakes (285), [NR] steamed spinach*
3	*leftover* Sweet Potato Pancakes, *leftover* Mustard-Glazed Chicken Thighs	*leftover* Bacon Jalapeño Burgers, green salad* with Balsamic Vinaigrette (434)	[MA] Lemony Lamb Dolmas (368), Cilantro Cauli-Rice (412)
4	Pesto Scrambled Eggs (286), *leftover* Cilantro Cauli-Rice, [MA] Raw Sauerkraut (262)	*leftover* Lemony Lamb Dolmas, green salad* with EVOO	Savory Baked Chicken Legs (316), [NR] butternut squash**
5	*leftover* Savory Baked Chicken Legs, *leftover* butternut squash**	Nori Salmon Handroll (388)	Beef & Veggie Stir-Fry (348), banana
6	Pumpkin Pancakes (284), breakfast sausage made with Italian Blend (256) & ground meat	*leftover* Beef & Veggie Stir-Fry	Lamb Lettuce Boats with Avoziki Sauce (370)
7	[NR] eggs any style, Perfectly Baked Bacon (260), [MA] Raw Sauerkraut (262)	[NR] canned wild salmon, asparagus*, lemon juice with EVOO	Citrus & Herb Whole Roasted Chicken (292), Whipped Sweet Potatoes (419)
8	[NR] eggs any style, Perfectly Baked Bacon (260), [MA] Raw Sauerkraut (262)	[MA] Butternut Sage Soup (394), *leftover* Citrus & Herb Whole Roasted Chicken	Restaurant-Style Lettuce Cups (312), banana
9	Swirly Crustless Quiche (270), [NR] steamed broccoli*, [MA] Raw Sauerkraut (262)	Indian Spiced Burgers with Smashed Roasted Garlic (342), *leftover* Whipped Sweet Potatoes	Pesto Fettuccine with Shrimp ⇆ nut-free (380), banana
10	Pesto Scrambled Eggs (286), *leftover* Pesto Fettuccine with Shrimp, sliced avocado	Simple Shrimp Ceviche (389), green salad* with EVOO	Coffee BBQ Rubbed Pork with Seared Pineapple (318), Mashed Faux-Tatoes (418)
11	[MA] Bacon & Egg Salad (287), avocado, [MA] Raw Sauerkraut (262)	*leftover* Coffee BBQ Rubbed Pork with Seared Pineapple, *leftover* Mashed Faux-Tatoes	Balsamic Braised Short Ribs (332), Candied Carrots (415), [NR] spaghetti squash**
12	*leftover* Bacon & Egg Salad, avocado, [MA] Raw Sauerkraut (262)	*leftover* Balsamic Braised Short Ribs, *leftover* Candied Carrots, spaghetti squash**	Mediterranean Baked Chicken with Cauliflower (294), [NR] baked potato**
13	[MA] Zucchini Pancakes (271), Perfectly Baked Bacon (260), [MA] Raw Sauerkraut (262)	*leftover* Mediterranean Baked Chicken with Cauliflower	Lemon Rosemary Broiled Salmon (375), Asparagus with Lemon & Olives (409), [NR] sweet potato**
14	*leftover* Lemon Rosemary Broiled Salmon, *leftover* Asparagus with Lemon & Olives*	[MA] Buffalo Chicken Lettuce Wraps (299)	Grilled Tuna Over Fresh Noodle Salad (384)
15	[NR] scrambled eggs with olives, [NR] steamed spinach*, avocado	*leftover* Grilled Tuna Over Fresh Noodle Salad	Italian-Style Stuffed Peppers (358), Mashed Faux-Tatoes (418)
16	Peach Blueberry Smoothie (289), [MA] Blueberry Maple Sausage (273)	*leftover* Italian-Style Stuffed Peppers, *leftover* Mashed Faux-Tatoes	Bacon-Wrapped Smoky Chicken Thighs (298), Whipped Sweet Potatoes (419)

Digestive Health

DAY	BREAKFAST	LUNCH	DINNER
17	[MA] Bacon & Egg Salad (287), avocado, [MA] Raw Sauerkraut (262)	*leftover* Bacon-Wrapped Smoky Chicken Thighs, *leftover* Whipped Sweet Potatoes	Spaghetti Squash Bolognese (338), banana
18	[MA] Pumpkin Pancakes (284), *leftover* Blueberry Maple Sausage	*leftover* Spaghetti Squash Bolognese, banana	Thanksgiving Stuffing Meatballs (326), Simple Cranberry Sauce (436), Mashed Faux-Tatoes (418)
19	*leftover* Bacon & Egg Salad, avocado, [MA] Raw Sauerkraut (262)	*leftover* Thanksgiving Stuffing Meatballs, *leftover* Cranberry Sauce, *leftover* Mashed Faux-Tatoes	Lemon & Bacon Scallops with Roasted Potatoes (376), Lemon Roasted Romanesco* (417)
20	Paleo Avocado "Toast" (264), [NR] eggs any style	*leftover* Lemon & Bacon Scallops, *leftover* Lemon Roasted Romanesco*	Orange & Olive Braised Chicken (306), Yellow Cauli-Rice (413), green salad* with EVOO
21	[MA] breakfast sausage made with Italian Blend (256) & ground meat, [NR] eggs any style, Raw Sauerkraut (262)	[MA] Six-Minute Salmon Bowls (382), banana	Souvlaki Kebabs (290), *leftover* Yellow Cauli-Rice
22	[MA] Breakfast Fried "Rice" (266)	*leftover* Souvlaki Kebabs, [NR] baked sweet potato	Orange Braised Beef (344), Butternut Sage Soup** (394)
23	*leftover* Breakfast Fried "Rice"	*leftover* Orange Braised Beef, *leftover* Butternut Sage Soup**	Hayley's Skirt Steak Tacos (346), choice of salsa (433), Smoky Grilled Squash & Pineapple (408)
24	[NR] eggs any style, bacon, *leftover* Smoky Grilled Squash & Pineapple	[MA] Mexican Chicken & Avocado Soup (390), [MA] Crispy Plantain Chips (431)	Bacon & Superfood Meatloaf (330), Mashed Faux-Tatoes (418)
25	[NR] eggs any style, avocado, [MA] Raw Sauerkraut (262)	*leftover* Mexican Chicken & Avocado Soup, banana	Seared Scallops with Orange Glaze (386), Cilantro Cauli-Rice (412), [NR] steamed bok choy*
26	[MA] Zucchini Pancakes (271), Perfectly Baked Bacon (260)	[MA] Quick & Easy Salmon Cakes (374), *leftover* Mashed Faux-Tatoes	Grandma Barbara's Stuffed Mushrooms (324), Whipped Sweet Potatoes (419)
27	Apple Sage Sausage (272), [NR] eggs any style, apple	*leftover* Grandma Barbara's Stuffed Mushrooms, *leftover* Whipped Sweet Potatoes	Orange Sesame Meatballs ⇆ (328), Cilantro Cauli-Rice (412)
28	*leftover* Apple Sage Sausage, [NR] eggs any style, apple	*leftover* Orange Sesame Meatballs, *leftover* Cilantro Cauli-Rice	Lemon & Artichoke Chicken (296), Broc-Cauli Chowder with Bacon (392)
29	[MA] Apple Cinnamon Egg Muffins (280), bacon or sausage	*leftover* Lemon & Artichoke Chicken, *leftover* Broc-Cauli Chowder with Bacon	The Easiest Tacos (362), Crispy Plantain Chips (431), choice of salsa (433)
30	*leftover* Apple Cinnamon Egg Muffins, bacon or sausage	*leftover* The Easiest Tacos, *leftover* Crispy Plantain Chips, *leftover* salsa	Mini Mediterranean Kebabs (352), Yellow Cauli-Rice (413)

» *A complete shopping list for this meal plan can be found on balancedbites.com*

NOTES

⇆ Follow notes on recipe for EGG-FREE, NUT & SEED-FREE & NIGHTSHADE-FREE

*: or other green vegetable; green salad is any lettuce and/or non-starchy vegetables

**: or other starchy vegetable (refer to page 75)

EVOO: Extra-virgin olive oil, or use any dressing from pages 434–435 on salads

CO: Coconut oil

MA: Make-Ahead all or part of the recipe

NR: No Recipe (use any simple prep)

If no page number is listed, simply prepare the items as noted or any way you like. For additional protein, vegetable, and fat recommendations, refer to the QUICK LIST that is associated with your meal plan!

Fat Loss

30-DAY MEAL PLANS

While the root causes of weight gain and weight-loss resistance vary greatly from person to person, there are basic dietary guidelines that will get you started in the right direction. This plan keeps your overall carbohydrate intake lower than it may have been before while still fueling your body appropriately for exercise.

If you are completely new to the Paleo way of eating, you may want to try the Squeaky Clean Paleo 30-Day Meal Plan (page 234) or the Blood Sugar Regulation 30-Day Meal Plan (page 180) first. Those plans are somewhat less strict, and you may still lose a sufficient amount of weight with those plans.

Other populations who may benefit from this meal plan include:

» People who experience sugar and carbohydrate cravings
» People who have trouble digesting fruit or suspect bacterial or fungal overgrowth

diet & lifestyle recommendations

add [+]

SUPERFOODS & PROBIOTICS
Eat superfoods as often as possible (see page 61). Consume 1/4 cup raw sauerkraut (page 262) or other fermented vegetables daily, especially with breakfast.

PROTEIN
Eat protein to satisfy the appetite for longer periods (meals focused on both fat and protein will help).

NUTRIENT-DENSE FOODS
Replenish nutrient stores that have been depleted by excess refined foods.

STARCHY CARBOHYDRATES
Eat approximately 30–75 g of carbohydrates after (not before) a workout (see page 75 for nutrient-dense carb sources). The exact amount will depend on the length of the workout. Track how you feel and add or subtract carbs if you are not making progress or don't feel well-fueled for exercise the next day.

STRESS MANAGEMENT
Develop a guided meditation or slow-breathing practice, or begin to practice qigong.

SLEEP
Sleep at least eight hours every night in a dark room in order to wake up refreshed and without cravings during the day.

MOVEMENT
For movement without systemic stress, take walks outside, swim (not for speed!), or practice gentle yoga.

Slowly introduce weight training with moderate to heavy loads, not excessively demanding in terms of stress response or cortisol output. If you are not fatigued, try high-intensity exercise for 5–25 minutes a few times per week (not more than four).

avoid [–]

GLUTEN & DAIRY
Gluten 100% of the time. See the guide to gluten on page 107. Avoid dairy for its potential growth-promotion effects. (Butter and ghee are okay.)

EXCESS DIETARY FAT
Avoid adding a lot of extra fat when cooking. However, there's no need to avoid naturally occurring fat in foods such as meat, seafood, eggs, and avocado.

FRUIT
The sweet taste may trigger the desire for more sweet foods. Eat fruit only in small amounts as a dessert.

REFINED FOODS, SWEETENERS & ALCOHOL
These impair the liver's ability to detoxify and lose fat.

EXCESS CAFFEINE
Caffeine can be a stressor and may increase cortisol response and promote weight-loss resistance.

ENVIRONMENTAL TOXINS
Toxins and exogenous hormones that imitate estrogen (xenoestrogens) can disrupt hormonal balance and may be introduced through commercially raised meats, pesticides in nonorganic foods, and the excessive use of plastics. As much as possible, avoid using plastic and purchasing items packaged in plastic. Buy in bulk when you can, use reusable fabric bags instead of plastic shopping bags, and use stainless steel water bottles instead of plastic bottles.

CHRONIC CARDIOVASCULAR EXERCISE
30–60+ minutes of cardiovascular exercise at a steady state of intensity, like jogging or biking, can lead to episodes of low blood sugar, as well as provoke a stress response.

nutritional supplements & herbs to consider

These recommendations are made as a starting point. Do your own research and determine which supplements may serve you best. Remember that supplements should be used for a short period of time, one to six months, and that it's best to get as many of your nutrients from food as possible. See page 201 for specific food-based nutrients on which to focus. The items below are listed in no particular order.

» **VITAMIN A (retinol)** helps to maintain the integrity of the mucosal lining of the gut. It also helps maintain immunity when balanced with vitamin D, and it is necessary for the assimilation of dietary minerals. Vitamin A is depleted by stress, strenuous physical exercise, pregnancy, lactation, and infection.

» **CARNITINE/L-CARNITINE** can improve insulin sensitivity and glucose storage, and it optimizes fat and carbohydrate metabolism. It may also improve the utilization of fat as an energy source. Cofactors include iron, vitamin C, vitamin B3 (niacin), and vitamin B6.

» **CHROMIUM** may improve insulin sensitivity and reduce appetite. Look for chromium picolinate, polynicotinate, or chelavite.

» **L-GLUTAMINE** aids in the healing of the cells that line the small intestine.

» **LIPOIC ACID (alpha-lipoic acid)** has antioxidant properties and may increase glucose uptake from the bloodstream by promoting the conversion of carbohydrates into energy.

» **MAGNESIUM** is required for more than 300 enzymatic processes in the body, and most people are deficient in it. It is also useful in blood sugar regulation. Look for magnesium glycinate or magnesium malate forms.

» **OMEGA-3 FATS** are anti-inflammatory essential fatty acids.

» **PROBIOTICS** promote healthy gut flora, which is critical for proper digestion and elimination.

» **MANGANESE** is beneficial for energy metabolism and thyroid hormone function. Intake should be balanced with magnesium, calcium, iron, copper, and zinc. Antacids may inhibit manganese absorption.

supportive nutrients & foods that contain them

VITAMIN A (RETINOL)

Helps maintain the lining of the gut

» Liver, eel

» Grass-fed butter, clarified butter, or ghee

VITAMIN B3

Supports blood sugar regulation and may lower cholesterol levels

» Liver, chicken, lamb

» Salmon, tuna

» Brewer's yeast (Lewis Labs brand only)

» Trace amounts: sesame seeds, sunflower seeds, almonds, mushrooms

VITAMIN B7

Required for the metabolism of glucose, amino acids, and lipids

» Liver

» Brewer's yeast (Lewis Labs brand only)

» Trace amounts: Swiss chard, walnuts, pecans, almonds

VITAMIN C

A potent antioxidant with anti-inflammatory properties

» Beets, bell peppers, broccoli, Brussels sprouts, cauliflower, collard greens, garlic, kale, mustard greens, parsley, spinach

» Lemons, strawberries

CHROMIUM

May improve insulin sensitivity and reduce appetite

» Liver

» Cheese (raw/grass-fed)

» Brewer's yeast (Lewis Labs brand only)

» Trace amounts: apples, carrots, green peppers, parsnips, spinach

CARNITINE

Essential for fat metabolism

» Red meat (darker meat has more)

CONJUGATED LINOLEIC ACID (CLA)

A potent antioxidant that supports fat loss

» Grass-fed beef and lamb

VITAMIN D

A potent immune system modulator that is best obtained from sun exposure

» Cold-water fish (salmon, herring, mackerel)

» Grass-fed butter or ghee

MAGNESIUM

Critical for cellular energy production, which helps battle fatigue, and for proper calcium metabolism, which is necessary for vascular health

» Beets, kale, other green leafy vegetables

» Pumpkin seeds (pepitas)

MANGANESE

Beneficial for blood sugar regulation, energy metabolism, and thyroid hormone function

» Beet greens, rhubarb, turnip greens

» Pecans, walnuts

» Cinnamon, cloves, thyme, turmeric

OMEGA-3 FATS

An anti-inflammatory essential fatty acid

» Cold-water fish, such as salmon, herring, and mackerel

» Pecans, walnuts

PROBIOTICS

Promote healthy gut flora, which is critical for proper digestion and elimination

» Fermented vegetables: cabbage (sauerkraut/kimchi), carrots, beets

» Kombucha (fermented tea)

quick LIST

proteins

Beef
Chicken
Eggs
Lamb
Oysters
Salmon
Sardines
Shellfish
Tuna

fats

Coconut oil
Eggs
Extra-virgin olive oil
Grass-fed butter/ghee

vegetables

Beets
Broccoli
Brussels sprouts
Cabbage
Carrots
Cauliflower
Daikon radishes
Green bell pepper
Parsnips
Swiss chard

fruits

Green apples
Lemons
Limes

superfoods

Bone broth
Liver

spices

Basil
Cilantro
Cinnamon
Cumin
Garlic
Ginger
Oregano
Parsley
Turmeric

DAY	BREAKFAST	LUNCH	DINNER
1	Swirly Crustless Quiche (270), Perfectly Baked Bacon (260), [MA] Raw Sauerkraut (262)	[MA] Mustard-Glazed Chicken Thighs (317), green salad* with Balsamic Vinaigrette (434)	Grilled Garlic Flank Steak with Peppers & Onions (334), green salad* with EVOO
2	*leftover* Swirly Crustless Quiche, *leftover* Grilled Garlic Flank Steak with Peppers & Onions	[NR] canned wild salmon with olives, avocado, lemon juice, tomato, EVOO over green salad*	[MA] Slow-Cooked Salsa Verde Chicken (302), green salad* with Spicy Lime Dressing (434)
3	[MA] Zucchini Pancakes (271), *leftover* Mustard-Glazed Chicken Thighs	*leftover* Slow-Cooked Salsa Verde Chicken, green salad* with Spicy Lime Dressing (434)	[MA] Lemony Lamb Dolmas (368), Cilantro Cauli-Rice (412)
4	*leftover* Zucchini Pancakes, Perfectly Baked Bacon (260) [MA] Raw Sauerkraut (262)	*leftover* Lemony Lamb Dolmas, green salad* with EVOO	Citrus Macadamia Nut Sole (378), Green Beans with Shallots (406)
5	*leftover* Citrus Macadamia Nut Sole, *leftover* Green Beans with Shallots	Nori Salmon Handroll (388)	Beef & Veggie Stir-Fry (348)
6	Pumpkin Pancakes (284), breakfast sausage made with Italian Blend (256) & ground meat	*leftover* Beef & Veggie Stir-Fry	Lamb Lettuce Boats with Avoziki Sauce (370)
7	[NR] eggs any style, Perfectly Baked Bacon (260), kale*, [MA] Raw Sauerkraut (262)	[NR] canned wild salmon over green salad, asparagus*, lemon juice with EVOO	Citrus & Herb Whole Roasted Chicken (292), Simple Baked Kale Chips* (425), broccoli*
8	[NR] eggs hard-boiled or any style, [NR] steamed spinach* with ghee (261), berries	Winter Kale Salad (396), *leftover* Citrus & Herb Whole Roasted Chicken	Restaurant-Style Lettuce Cups (312)
9	Swirly Crustless Quiche (270), [NR] steamed broccoli* with ghee (261), [MA] Raw Sauerkraut (262)	[MA] Indian Spiced Burgers with Smashed Roasted Garlic (342), *leftover* Winter Kale Salad	Simple Shrimp Ceviche (389), green salad* with EVOO
10	*leftover* Swirly Crustless Quiche, sliced avocado	*leftover* Simple Shrimp Ceviche, green salad* with EVOO, berries	Coffee BBQ Rubbed Pork with Seared Pineapple (318), green salad* with EVOO
11	[MA] Home Fries & Sausage Skillet (268)	*leftover* Coffee BBQ Rubbed Pork with Seared Pineapple, green salad* with EVOO	Balsamic Braised Short Ribs (332), [NR] spaghetti squash**, green salad* with EVOO
12	*leftover* Home Fries & Sausage Skillet	*leftover* Balsamic Braised Short Ribs, *leftover* spaghetti squash, green salad* with EVOO	Mediterranean Baked Chicken with Cauliflower (294)
13	[MA] Zucchini Pancakes (271), Perfectly Baked Bacon (260), [MA] Raw Sauerkraut (262)	*leftover* Mediterranean Baked Chicken with Cauliflower	Lemon Rosemary Broiled Salmon (375), Asparagus with Lemon & Olives (409)
14	*leftover* Zucchini Pancakes, Perfectly Baked Bacon (260), [MA] Raw Sauerkraut (262)	*leftover* Lemon Rosemary Broiled Salmon, *leftover* Asparagus with Lemon & Olives	Grilled Tuna Over Fresh Noodle Salad (384)
15	[NR] scrambled eggs with olives, [NR] steamed spinach*, avocado	*leftover* Grilled Tuna Over Fresh Noodle Salad	Italian-Style Stuffed Peppers (358), green salad* with Balsamic Vinaigrette (434)
16	[MA] Blueberry Maple Sausage (273), [NR] eggs any style, spinach*	*leftover* Italian-Style Stuffed Peppers, green salad* with EVOO	Chicken Satay Sandwiches with Blistered Peppers (314), green salad* with EVOO

Fat Loss

DAY	BREAKFAST	LUNCH	DINNER
17	[MA] Bacon & Egg Salad (287), avocado, spinach or kale*, [MA] Raw Sauerkraut (262)	*leftover* Chicken Satay Sandwiches with Blistered Peppers, green salad* with EVOO	Spaghetti Squash Bolognese (338), Simple Baked Kale Chips* (425)
18	*leftover* Bacon & Egg Salad, avocado, spinach or kale*, [MA] Raw Sauerkraut (262)	*leftover* Spaghetti Squash Bolognese, green salad* with EVOO	Thanksgiving Stuffing Meatballs (326), Simple Cranberry Sauce (436), Mashed Faux-Tatoes (418)
19	Swirly Crustless Quiche (270), Perfectly Baked Bacon (260), [MA] Raw Sauerkraut (262)	*leftover* Thanksgiving Stuffing Meatballs, *leftover* Cranberry Sauce, *leftover* Mashed Faux-Tatoes	Lemon & Bacon Scallops with Roasted Potatoes (376), Lemon Roasted Romanesco* (417)
20	Paleo Avocado "Toast" (264), [NR] eggs any style or other protein of choice	*leftover* Lemon & Bacon Scallops, *leftover* Lemon Roasted Romanesco*	Orange & Olive Braised Chicken (306), Yellow Cauli-Rice (413)
21	[MA] breakfast sausage made with Italian Blend (256) & ground meat, [NR] eggs any style, Raw Sauerkraut (262)	[MA] Six-Minute Salmon Bowls (382)	Souvlaki Kebabs (290), Greek Salad with Avoziki Dressing (402)
22	[MA] Breakfast Fried "Rice" (266)	*leftover* Souvlaki Kebabs, *leftover* Greek Salad with Avoziki Dressing	Orange Braised Beef (344), [NR] roasted cauliflower*
23	*leftover* Breakfast Fried "Rice"	*leftover* Orange Braised Beef, *leftover* roasted cauliflower*	Hayley's Skirt Steak Tacos (346), choice of salsa (433), Smoky Grilled Squash & Pineapple (408)
24	[NR] eggs any style, bacon, *leftover* Smoky Grilled Squash & Pineapple	[MA] Tangy Taco Salad (350), *leftover* salsa	Bacon & Superfood Meatloaf (330), Mashed Faux-Tatoes (418), green salad* with EVOO
25	[NR] eggs any style, avocado, kale*, [MA] Raw Sauerkraut (262)	[MA] Quick & Easy Salmon Cakes (374), green salad* with EVOO, avocado, olives	Seared Scallops with Orange Glaze (386), Cilantro Cauli-Rice (412), [NR] steamed bok choy*
26	[MA] Zucchini Pancakes (271), Perfectly Baked Bacon (260)	[MA] Italiano Salad (398) with Honey Mustard Dressing (434)	Grandma Barbara's Stuffed Mushrooms (324), *leftover* Italiano Salad
27	[MA] Apple Sage Sausage (272), spinach*, berries	*leftover* Grandma Barbara's Stuffed Mushrooms, green salad* with EVOO	Orange Sesame Meatballs (328), Cilantro Cauli-Rice (412)
28	*leftover* Apple Sage Sausage, spinach*, avocado	*leftover* Orange Sesame Meatballs, *leftover* Cilantro Cauli-Rice	Lemon & Artichoke Chicken (296), Broc-Cauli Chowder with Bacon (392)
29	[MA] Apple Cinnamon Egg Muffins (280), bacon or sausage	*leftover* Lemon & Artichoke Chicken, *leftover* Broc-Cauli Chowder with Bacon	The Easiest Tacos (362), choice of salsa (433), [NR] roasted broccoli*, berries
30	*leftover* Apple Cinnamon Egg Muffins, bacon or sausage	*leftover* The Easiest Tacos, *leftover* salsa, berries	Mini Mediterranean Kebabs (352), Sautéed Spinach with Pine Nuts & Currants* (423)

» *A complete shopping list for this meal plan can be found on balancedbites.com*

NOTES

*****: or other green vegetable; green salad is any lettuce and/or non-starchy vegetables

******: or other starchy vegetable (refer to page 75)

EVOO: Extra-virgin olive oil, or use any dressing from pages 434–435 on salads

CO: Coconut oil

MA: Make-Ahead all or part of the recipe

NR: No Recipe (use any simple prep)

If no page number is listed, simply prepare the items as noted or any way you like. For additional protein, vegetable, and fat recommendations, refer to the QUICK LIST that is associated with your meal plan!

Healthy Hormones

Maintaining a healthy hormone balance begins with two things: stress management and blood sugar regulation. Once stress and blood sugar are in check, focusing on supporting your body's digestion and detoxification systems become critical.

If you have a hormonal imbalance, addressing any underlying issues is the best first step. For that reason, I recommend trying any of the applicable plans below (listed in order of importance) before turning to this plan:

» Adrenal Health (page 162)
» Digestive Health, Leaky Gut Protocol (page 192)
» Liver Detox Support (page 216)
» Thyroid Health (page 238)

The Blood Sugar Regulation 30-Day Meal Plan (page 180) may also be helpful for healthy hormones.

follow this plan if:

» You've already followed the adrenal health plan for at least three months and you're still experiencing hormonal imbalance problems.
» You have painful or irregular periods (dysmenorrhea).
» You are amenorrheic (have no monthly period).
» You've been diagnosed with fibrocystic breast disease, uterine fibroids, or cervical dysplasia.
» You've been diagnosed with PCOS or endometriosis, or you struggle with infertility.

» You experience premenstrual syndrome (PMS), characterized by any of the following just before your monthly period: tension, depression, anxiety, panic attacks, mood swings or irritability, substance abuse, migraines, headaches, faintness or dizziness, acne, hives, backache, joint pain, edema, sinusitis, sore throat, hoarseness, breast tenderness or swelling.
» You experience low libido.
» You are a man with low testosterone.

Note: Unless otherwise specified, the recommendations in the plan will work for both men and women.

DISCLAIMER:

The information in this book is not intended to be a replacement for professional medical diagnosis or treatment for a medical condition. It consists solely of nutritional and lifestyle recommendations to support a healthier body.

diet & lifestyle recommendations

add [+]

PROBIOTIC-RICH FOODS
Eat about 1/4 cup of raw sauerkraut (page 262) or other fermented vegetables daily, preferably with breakfast.

PROTEIN
Add protein to keep you feeling full longer, and make sure there's some fat in your meals as well.

CHOLESTEROL, NATURALLY SATURATED FATS & OMEGA-3-RICH FOODS
Healthy hormone production relies upon these nutrients. (See pages 31 to 34 for more on cholesterol and saturated fats.) Omega-3 fatty acids help manage the inflammatory effects that may result from chronically elevated cortisol levels.

NUTRIENT-DENSE FOODS
Replenish nutrient stores that have been depleted by excess refined foods.

STRESS MANAGEMENT
Develop a guided meditation or slow-breathing practice, or begin to practice qigong.

POSITIVE MINDSET
Cultivate a positive mental outlook by creating a gratitude list regularly (see page 120). A positive mental outlook is often a result of feeling that we have control over our own lives, and it can yield calmer thoughts overall.

SLEEP
Establish a regular bedtime routine and sleep hours (ideally 10 p.m. to 6 a.m.) and avoid sleeping pills. Use mild, calming herbs when needed for relaxation at bedtime. Melatonin, which is produced during quality sleep, may help reduce estrogen production.

SUNSHINE
Whenever possible, get sun exposure during waking hours to help regulate your circadian rhythm.

LAUGHTER & PLAY
Find games or activities you enjoy doing, connect with others while doing them, and find something that brings you joy and laughter.

avoid [−]

OXIDIZED, OMEGA-6-RICH FATS
Seed and vegetable oils, which most restaurants use regularly, are high in omega-6 fats, tend to be oxidized (damaged), and should be avoided. (See page 64 for a list of these kinds of fats.) Some nuts and seeds are also high in omega-6 fats and should also be avoided: Brazil nuts, sunflower seeds, and almonds.

CAFFEINE, SWEETENERS & REFINED FOODS
All of these can provoke blood sugar fluctuations. If you currently drink coffee, titrate your consumption down slowly and eventually work to either an organic, Swiss Water Process decaf or green tea, then to herbal teas exclusively.

ALCOHOL, ILLEGAL DRUGS & MEDICATIONS
The liver prioritizes clearing the blood of alcohol and other chemical substances, so clearing other substances (including hormones) and managing blood sugar take lower priority when they're present. Avoid alcohol, drugs, and medications, including liver-taxing OTC painkillers such as aspirin, acetaminophen, ibuprofen, naproxen, and corticosteroids. If you become ill, use natural remedies, and talk to your doctor about options for eliminating noncritical prescription medications. This is not a recommendation to cease taking any medications, simply a recommendation to seek alternatives that support healthy hormones. Never stop or change medications without first talking to your doctor.

HORMONAL BIRTH CONTROL
Seek birth control methods that do not introduce exogenous hormones to your body. This is not a recommendation to cease taking any medications, simply a recommendation to seek alternatives that support healthy hormones. Talk to your health-care practitioner about the birth control options that will work best for you, and never stop taking any medication without consulting him or her first.

EXPOSURE TO BLUE & BRIGHT LIGHT
Install apps like f.lux or Night Shift on your computer or phone, use amber goggles, and keep overhead lights to a minimum after sundown.

TOXIC RELATIONSHIPS/PEOPLE & NEGATIVE EMOTIONS
Reduce emotional stress by learning to say no, practicing mindfulness, and meditating. The Headspace app may be helpful for guided meditations.

HARSH CLEANING & HYGIENE PRODUCTS
Opt for gentle, natural alternatives, such as soap nuts for laundry, vinegar and water for cleaning countertops, and baking soda and peroxide for cleaning and whitening surfaces, laundry, teeth, and more. Consider skipping shampoo and going "no-poo" instead. Safe makeup recommendations may be found at skindeep.org.

ENVIRONMENTAL TOXINS
Toxins and exogenous hormones that imitate estrogen (xenoestrogens) can disrupt hormonal balance and may be introduced through commercially raised meats, pesticides in nonorganic foods, and the excessive use of plastics. Avoid using plastic and purchasing items packaged in plastic. Buy in bulk when you can, use reusable fabric bags instead of plastic shopping bags, and use stainless steel water bottles instead of plastic bottles.

NONORGANIC FOODS & COMMERCIALLY RAISED MEATS
Use the Dirty Dozen and Clean Thirteen lists from the Environmental Working Group (EWG) to identify what should be purchased organic and what can be purchased conventionally grown. Avoid meats with added hormones, artificial colors, and other food additives.

DENTAL AMALGAMS (SILVER FILLINGS)
Consider holistic or biological dentistry to replace existing amalgams.

I recommend The Hormone Cure *by Dr. Sara Gottfried for additional and extensive information on healthy female hormone balance.*

nutritional supplements & herbs to consider

These recommendations are made as a starting point. Do your own research and determine which supplements may serve you best. Remember that supplements should be used for a short period of time, one to six months, and that it's best to get as many of your nutrients from food as possible. See page 207 for specific food-based nutrients on which to focus. The items below are listed in no particular order.

FOR GENERAL HORMONE SUPPORT (WOMEN & MEN)

» **MAGNESIUM** is required for more than 300 enzymatic processes in the body, and most people are deficient in it. It is also useful in blood sugar regulation. Look for magnesium glycinate or magnesium malate forms.

» **B VITAMINS** are critical in assisting neurotransmitters and therefore are important for brain health and for the proper functioning of nerves and muscle. Look for a B-complex supplement with B12 to support fertility.

» **VITAMIN C** is a potent antioxidant that is critical for cortisol production. Note that in some rare, severe cases of fatigue, vitamin C may make symptoms worse (the body has a harder time metabolizing it, which puts further stress on the body).

» **VITAMIN E** is an antioxidant that benefits cellular communication and may reduce oxidative stress-induced insulin resistance.

» **DIINDOLYLMETHANE (DIM) & CALCIUM D-GLUCARATE** support estrogen metabolism and help clear it from the body, which may be helpful for both men and women experiencing estrogen dominance or levels of estrogen that are higher than desired.

» **PHOSPHATIDYLSERINE** supports a healthy endocrine response to stress and is helpful for that tired-but-wired feeling when taken a few hours before bed.

» **MACA ROOT** may contribute to an overall healthy and balanced mood as well as a healthy libido. In men, maca may support healthy sperm count.

» **SELENIUM** is an antioxidant that is important in the production of thyroid hormones. Absorption may be decreased by high zinc intake, so it must be balanced with zinc.

» **ZINC** is a potent antioxidant that aids in vitamin A metabolism. People with inflammatory conditions are often deficient in zinc.

FOR FEMALE HORMONE SUPPORT

» **GAMMA LINOLENIC ACID (GLA)** is an anti-inflammatory fatty acid that can be taken in the form of borage or evening primrose oil. It may be helpful in combating painful periods or acne caused by hormonal imbalances.

FOR MALE HORMONE SUPPORT (ESPECIALLY LOW TESTOSTERONE)

» **CARNITINE/L-CARNITINE** can improve insulin sensitivity and glucose storage, and it optimizes fat and carbohydrate metabolism. It may also improve the utilization of fat as an energy source. Cofactors include iron, vitamin C, vitamin B3 (niacin), and vitamin B6.

» **COENZYME Q10** (CoQ10, ubiquinone) enhances cellular energy production, and it can help alleviate fatigue as well as muscle and joint pain. It is also a potent antioxidant and may support healthy sperm levels. Statin drugs are known to deplete CoQ10.

supportive nutrients & foods that contain them

B VITAMINS

Critical in assisting neurotransmitters and therefore important for brain health and for the proper functioning of nerves and muscles

» Liver, bison, lamb
» Flounder, haddock, salmon, trout, tuna
» Brewer's yeast (Lewis Labs brand only)
» Mushrooms
» Hazelnuts, walnuts
» Trace amounts: pecans, sunflower seeds, broccoli, Brussels sprouts, other dark leafy greens

VITAMIN C

A potent antioxidant with anti-inflammatory properties

» Beets, bell peppers, broccoli, Brussels sprouts, cauliflower, collard greens, daikon radishes, garlic, kale, mustard greens, parsley, spinach
» Cantaloupes, kiwis, lemons, oranges, papayas, pineapples, strawberries

VITAMIN E

An antioxidant that benefits neurological function, smooth-muscle growth, and cellular communication

» Broccoli, Brussels sprouts, spinach
» Extra-virgin olive oil
» Pecans

MAGNESIUM

Critical for cellular energy production, which helps to battle fatigue, and for proper calcium metabolism, which is necessary for vascular health

» Beets, kale, other green leafy vegetables
» Pumpkin seeds (pepitas)

OMEGA-3 FATS

An anti-inflammatory essential fatty acid

» Cold-water fish, such as salmon, herring, and mackerel
» Pecans, walnuts

SATURATED FATS

Support healthy cholesterol levels and hormone production (when from healthy sources)

» Coconut oil, grass-fed butter or ghee
» Eggs (with the yolks)
» Grass-fed/pastured red meats

ZINC

A potent antioxidant often low in people with inflammatory conditions; aids in vitamin A metabolism

» Oysters, shellfish
» Lamb, red meat
» Pumpkin seeds (pepitas)

quick LIST

proteins

Beef
Bison
Eel
Eggs
Lamb
Mackerel
Oysters
Salmon
Shellfish

fats

Coconut oil
Extra-virgin olive oil
Grass-fed butter/ghee
Pumpkin seeds
Walnuts

vegetables

Beets
Bell peppers
Broccoli
Brussels sprouts
Butternut squash
Cauliflower
Daikon radishes
Seaweed
Spinach
Squash

fruits

Cherries
Citrus
Melons
Raspberries
Peaches

superfoods

Bone broth
Green tea
Liver
Sauerkraut

spices

Basil
Cilantro
Cinnamon
Cumin
Garlic
Ginger
Oregano
Parsley
Turmeric

Healthy Hormones

DAY	BREAKFAST	LUNCH	DINNER
1	Swirly Crustless Quiche (270), Perfectly Baked Bacon (260), [MA] Raw Sauerkraut (262)	[MA] Mustard-Glazed Chicken Thighs (317), green salad* with Balsamic Vinaigrette (434)	Grilled Garlic Flank Steak with Peppers & Onions (334), broccoli*, berries
2	leftover Swirly Crustless Quiche, leftover Grilled Garlic Flank Steak with Peppers & Onions	[NR] canned wild salmon with olives, avocado, lemon juice, tomato, EVOO over green salad*	Bacon Jalapeño Burgers (360), Sweet Potato Pancakes (285), Swiss chard*
3	leftover Sweet Potato Pancakes, leftover Mustard-Glazed Chicken Thighs	leftover Bacon Jalapeño Burgers, green salad* with Balsamic Vinaigrette (434), [NR] steamed spinach*	[MA] Lemony Lamb Dolmas (368), Cilantro Cauli-Rice (412)
4	Pesto Scrambled Eggs (286), leftover Cilantro Cauli-Rice, [MA] Raw Sauerkraut (262)	leftover Lemony Lamb Dolmas, green salad* with EVOO	Citrus Macadamia Nut Sole (378), Baked Beets with Fennel (420)
5	leftover Citrus Macadamia Nut Sole, leftover Baked Beets with Fennel	Nori Salmon Handroll (388), berries	Beef & Veggie Stir-Fry (348), berries
6	[NR] eggs any style, breakfast sausage made with Italian Blend (256) & ground meat, Brussels sprouts*	leftover Beef & Veggie Stir-Fry, berries	Lamb Lettuce Boats with Avoziki Sauce (370), berries
7	[NR] eggs any style, Perfectly Baked Bacon (260), kale*, [MA] Raw Sauerkraut (262)	green salad* with canned wild salmon, asparagus*, Basil Shallot Vinaigrette (434)	Citrus & Herb Whole Roasted Chicken (292), Simple Baked Kale Chips* (425), cauliflower*
8	Swirly Crustless Quiche (270), bacon or sausage, berries	Dairy-Free Caesar Salad (396), leftover Citrus & Herb Whole Roasted Chicken	Restaurant-Style Lettuce Cups (312)
9	leftover Swirly Crustless Quiche (270), [NR] steamed broccoli*, [MA] Raw Sauerkraut (262)	Indian Spiced Burgers with Smashed Roasted Garlic (342), [NR] steamed broccoli*	Pesto Fettuccine with Shrimp (380)
10	Pesto Scrambled Eggs (286), leftover Pesto Fettuccine with Shrimp, sliced avocado	[MA] Buffalo Chicken Lettuce Wraps (299)	Coffee BBQ Rubbed Pork with Seared Pineapple (318), green salad* with EVOO
11	[MA] Home Fries & Sausage Skillet (268)	leftover Coffee BBQ Rubbed Pork with Seared Pineapple, green salad* with EVOO	Balsamic Braised Short Ribs (332), Mashed Faux-Tatoes (418), green salad* with EVOO
12	leftover Home Fries & Sausage Skillet	leftover Balsamic Braised Short Ribs, leftover Mashed Faux-Tatoes, green salad* with EVOO	Mediterranean Baked Chicken with Cauliflower (294), berries*
13	[MA] Zucchini Pancakes (271), Perfectly Baked Bacon (260), [MA] Raw Sauerkraut (262)	leftover Mediterranean Baked Chicken with Cauliflower	Lemon Rosemary Broiled Salmon (375), Asparagus with Lemon & Olives (409), [NR] sweet potato**
14	leftover Lemon Rosemary Broiled Salmon, leftover Asparagus with Lemon & Olives*	Simple Shrimp Ceviche (389), green salad* with EVOO & lemon juice	Grilled Tuna Over Fresh Noodle Salad (384), berries
15	[NR] scrambled eggs with mushrooms, olives, [NR] steamed spinach*, avocado	leftover Grilled Tuna Over Fresh Noodle Salad, berries	Italian-Style Stuffed Peppers (358), green salad* with Balsamic Vinaigrette (434)
16	[MA] Blueberry Maple Sausage (27), [NR] eggs any style, Brussels sprouts*	leftover Italian-Style Stuffed Peppers, green salad* with Basil Shallot Vinaigrette (434)	Bacon-Wrapped Smoky Chicken Thighs (298), green salad* with EVOO

Healthy Hormones

DAY	BREAKFAST	LUNCH	DINNER
17	[MA] Bacon & Egg Salad (287) in a Swiss chard wrap*, avocado, [MA] Raw Sauerkraut (262)	leftover Bacon-Wrapped Smoky Chicken Thighs, green salad* with EVOO	Spaghetti Squash Bolognese (338), Simple Baked Kale Chips* (425), berries
18	[MA] Zucchini Pancakes (271), leftover Blueberry Maple Sausage	leftover Spaghetti Squash Bolognese, green salad* with Basil Shallot Vinaigrette (434)	Thanksgiving Stuffing Meatballs (326), Simple Cranberry Sauce (436), Mashed Faux-Tatoes (418)
19	leftover Bacon & Egg Salad in a Swiss chard* wrap, avocado, [MA] Raw Sauerkraut (262)	leftover Thanksgiving Stuffing Meatballs, leftover Cranberry Sauce, leftover Mashed Faux-Tatoes	Lemon & Bacon Scallops with Roasted Potatoes (376), Lemon Roasted Romanesco* (417)
20	Paleo Avocado "Toast" (264), [NR] eggs any style, berries	leftover Lemon & Bacon Scallops, leftover Lemon Roasted Romanesco*	Orange & Olive Braised Chicken (306), Yellow Cauli-Rice (413), green salad* with EVOO
21	[MA] breakfast sausage made with Italian Blend (256) & ground meat, [NR] eggs any style, Raw Sauerkraut (262)	[MA] Six-Minute Salmon Bowls (382)	Souvlaki Kebabs (290), Greek Salad with Avoziki Dressing (402), berries
22	[MA] Breakfast Fried "Rice" (266), berries	leftover Souvlaki Kebabs, leftover Greek Salad with Avoziki Dressing, berries	Orange Braised Beef (344), Butternut Sage Soup** (394)
23	leftover Breakfast Fried "Rice," berries	leftover Orange Braised Beef, leftover Butternut Sage Soup**	Hayley's Skirt Steak Tacos (346), choice of salsa (433), Smoky Grilled Squash & Pineapple (408)
24	[NR] eggs any style, bacon, leftover Smoky Grilled Squash & Pineapple	[MA] Tangy Taco Salad (350), leftover salsa	Bacon & Superfood Meatloaf (330), Mashed Faux-Tatoes (418), green salad* with EVOO
25	[NR] eggs any style, mushrooms, spinach or kale*, avocado, [MA] Raw Sauerkraut (262)	[MA] Quick & Easy Salmon Cakes (374), green salad* with EVOO, avocado, olives	Seared Scallops with Orange Glaze (386), Cilantro Cauli-Rice (412), [NR] steamed bok choy*
26	[MA] Zucchini Pancakes (271), Apple Sage Sausage (272), berries	[MA] Italiano Salad (398), Basil Shallot Vinaigrette (434)	Grandma Barbara's Stuffed Mushrooms (324), leftover Italiano Salad
27	leftover Zucchini Pancakes, leftover Apple Sage Sausage, berries	leftover Grandma Barbara's Stuffed Mushrooms, green salad* with Basil Shallot Vinaigrette (434)	Orange Sesame Meatballs (328), Cilantro Cauli-Rice (412), berries
28	[NR] eggs any style, Perfectly Baked Bacon (260), Brussels sprouts*	leftover Orange Sesame Meatballs, leftover Cilantro Cauli-Rice	Lemon & Artichoke Chicken (296), Broc-Cauli Chowder with Bacon (392)
29	[MA] Apple Cinnamon Egg Muffins (280), bacon or sausage	leftover Lemon & Artichoke Chicken, leftover Broc-Cauli Chowder with Bacon	The Easiest Tacos (362), Cilantro Cauli-Rice (412), choice of salsa (433)
30	leftover Apple Cinnamon Egg Muffins, bacon or sausage	leftover The Easiest Tacos, leftover Cilantro Cauli-Rice, leftover salsa	Mini Mediterranean Kebabs (352), Sautéed Spinach with Pine Nuts & Currants* (423)

» *A complete shopping list for this meal plan can be found on balancedbites.com*

NOTES

*: or other green vegetable; green salad is any lettuce and/or non-starchy vegetables

**: or other starchy vegetable (refer to page 75)

EVOO: Extra-virgin olive oil, or use any dressing from pages 434–435 on salads

CO: Coconut oil

MA: Make-Ahead all or part of the recipe

NR: No Recipe (use any simple prep)

If no page number is listed, simply prepare the items as noted or any way you like. For additional protein, vegetable, and fat recommendations, refer to the QUICK LIST that is associated with your meal plan!

Heart Health

30-DAY MEAL PLANS

Before trying the menu for this slightly more limited plan, you may want to follow the lifestyle, supplement, and nutrient recommendations from this plan and the monthly menu from the Squeaky Clean Paleo 30-Day Meal Plan (page 234).

cholesterol concerns

may cause one or more of the following:

» Low blood markers for high-density lipoproteins (HDL)
» High blood markers for low-density lipoproteins (LDL)
» High triglycerides (circulating blood lipids)
» Total cholesterol:HDL ratio outside of an ideal range between 3 and 4 (divide your total cholesterol by your HDL marker to find this number)
» High blood markers of oxidized LDL (if you have access to such tests)

blood pressure concerns

may cause one or more of the following:

» General fatigue
» Energy changes throughout the day
» Waking up tired
» Insomnia
» Inability to focus, brain fog, mental disturbances, mental confusion
» Blurred vision
» Low blood pressure
» Headaches
» Trembling
» Incoherent speech
» Weakness in legs
» Dry mouth

» Weight gain
» Mood imbalances, such as irritability, negativity, sense of gloom, crying spells, mood swings, erratic behavior, antisocial behavior, depression, anxiety, hypersensitivity
» Cravings for sugar and carbohydrates
» Constant hunger
» Compulsive eating
» Loss of appetite
» Loss of sex drive
» Rapid heartbeat, fluttering in chest

DISCLAIMER:

The information in this book is not intended to be a replacement for professional medical diagnosis or treatment for a medical condition. It consists solely of nutritional and lifestyle recommendations to support a healthier body.

diet & lifestyle recommendations

add [+]

NUTRIENT-DENSE FOODS
Replenish nutrient stores that have been depleted by excess refined foods.

STRESS MANAGEMENT
Develop a guided meditation or slow-breathing practice, or begin to practice qigong. Practice biofeedback, tai chi, and/or guided imagery for deep relaxation.

MOVEMENT
For movement without systemic stress, take walks outside, swim (not for speed!), or practice gentle yoga.

Slowly begin weight training with moderate to heavy weight, not excessively demanding in terms of stress response or cortisol output.

avoid [–]

GLUTEN
100% of the time. See the guide to gluten on page 107.

RESTAURANTS / DINING OUT
Avoid the damaged and man-made fats most often used in restaurant foods.

REFINED FOODS, BAD CARBS, SWEETENERS, CAFFEINE, ALCOHOL & MSG
These can all provoke blood sugar fluctuations and systemic stress. Also avoid packaged foods with excess sodium.

ALCOHOL, TOBACCO, NICOTINE
These all require detoxification and may impair liver function and promote systemic inflammation.

STRESS
Make lifestyle changes to avoid stressful situations.

CHRONIC CARDIOVASCULAR EXERCISE
30–60+ minutes of cardiovascular exercise at a steady state of intensity, like jogging or biking, can provoke a stress response.

nutritional supplements & herbs to consider

These recommendations are made as a starting point. Do your own research and determine which supplements may serve you best. Remember that supplements should be used for a short period of time, one to six months, and that it's best to get as many of your nutrients from food as possible. See page 213 for specific food-based nutrients on which to focus. The items below are listed in no particular order.

» **VITAMIN A (retinol)** helps to maintain the integrity of the mucosal lining of the gut. It also helps maintain immunity when balanced with vitamin D, and it is necessary for the assimilation of dietary minerals.

» **VITAMIN B3 (niacin)** supports blood sugar regulation and may lower cholesterol levels.

» **VITAMIN B5 (pantothenic acid & pantethine)** may lower cholesterol and triglycerides in the pantethine form, especially in diabetics.

» **VITAMIN B7 (biotin)** is a coenzyme required for the metabolism of glucose, amino acids, and lipids.

» **VITAMIN B9 (folate)** supports healthy red blood cells, boosts growth, and reduces risks of birth defects. Look for a B-complex supplement for a balanced dose.

» **VITAMIN C** is a potent antioxidant with anti-inflammatory properties that supports immune function. It promotes collagen production and supports carnitine synthesis. It also helps to regenerate vitamin E and improves iron absorption.

» **COENZYME Q10** (CoQ10, ubiquinone) enhances cellular energy production, and it can help alleviate fatigue as well as muscle and joint pain. Statin drugs are known to deplete CoQ10.

» **VITAMIN E** is an antioxidant that protects against free-radical damage.

» **LIPOIC ACID (alpha-lipoic acid)** has antioxidant properties and may improve cellular energy production and support liver function. It may also be helpful to cardiac patients.

» **MAGNESIUM** is required for more than 300 enzymatic processes in the body, and most people are deficient in it. It is also useful in blood sugar regulation. Look for magnesium glycinate or magnesium malate forms.

» **OMEGA-3 FATS** are anti-inflammatory essential fatty acids.

» **SELENIUM & ZINC** are antioxidants that protect against free-radical damage. Supplements may be necessary because it's difficult to obtain adequate amounts from food.

Heart Health

supportive nutrients & foods that contain them

B VITAMINS (especially B3, B6, B9)
Critical in assisting neurotransmitters and therefore important for brain health and for the proper functioning of nerves and muscles
» Liver, lamb, chicken
» Egg yolks
» Salmon, sardines, tuna
» Grass-fed dairy
» Brewer's yeast (Lewis Labs brand only)
» Mushrooms
» Walnuts
» Trace amounts: pecans, sunflower seeds, romain lettuce, cauliflower

VITAMIN C
A potent antioxidant with anti-inflammatory properties
» Beets, bell peppers, broccoli, Brussels sprouts, cauliflower, collard greens, daikon radishes, garlic, kale, mustard greens, parsley, spinach
» Lemons, strawberries

CALCIUM
Plays a key role in cell signaling, nerve function, and muscle contraction. Be sure to also consume grass-fed butter to assimilate calcium properly.
» Dark leafy greens

CHOLESTEROL
Does not affect blood cholesterol levels. Necessary for converting sunlight into vitamin D, for proper brain function, and for hormone production.
» Egg yolks
» Seafood/shellfish
» Beef, lamb

VITAMIN D
A potent immune system modulator that is best obtained from sun exposure
» Cold-water fish (salmon, herring, mackerel)
» Grass-fed butter or ghee

LIPOIC ACID (ALA)
May improve cellular energy production and has antioxidant properties
» Red meat, organ meats

MAGNESIUM
Critical for cellular energy production, which helps battle fatigue, and for proper calcium metabolism, which is necessary for vascular health
» Beets, kale, other green leafy vegetables
» Pumpkin seeds (pepitas)

OMEGA-3 FATS
An anti-inflammatory essential fatty acid
» Cold-water fish, such as salmon, herring, and mackerel
» Pecans, walnuts

POTASSIUM
Known to support kidney function as well as vasodilation (widening of the blood vessels)
» Asparagus, spinach, Swiss chard, yams
» Avocados, bananas, cantaloupe, grapefruit, honeydew, nectarines, oranges, papayas

PROBIOTICS
Promote healthy gut flora, which is critical for proper digestion and elimination
» Fermented vegetables: cabbage (sauerkraut/kimchi), carrots, beets
» Kombucha (fermented tea)

SELENIUM
An antioxidant that protects against free-radical damage
» Eggs
» Garlic, red Swiss chard, turnips

SODIUM
Use unrefined, mineral-rich sea salt (Celtic or Real Salt brand)

ZINC
A potent antioxidant often low in people with inflammatory conditions; aids in vitamin A metabolism
» Oysters, shellfish
» Lamb, red meat
» Pumpkin seeds (pepitas)

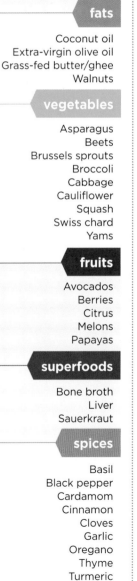

quick LIST

proteins
Chicken
Eggs
Herring
Mackerel
Oysters
Pork
Salmon
Shellfish
Tuna

fats
Coconut oil
Extra-virgin olive oil
Grass-fed butter/ghee
Walnuts

vegetables
Asparagus
Beets
Brussels sprouts
Broccoli
Cabbage
Cauliflower
Squash
Swiss chard
Yams

fruits
Avocados
Berries
Citrus
Melons
Papayas

superfoods
Bone broth
Liver
Sauerkraut

spices
Basil
Black pepper
Cardamom
Cinnamon
Cloves
Garlic
Oregano
Thyme
Turmeric

DAY	BREAKFAST	LUNCH	DINNER
1	Swirly Crustless Quiche (270), [MA] Raw Sauerkraut (262), melon	[MA] Mustard-Glazed Chicken Thighs (317), green salad* with Balsamic Vinaigrette (434)	Grilled Garlic Flank Steak with Peppers & Onions (334), [NR] sweet potato**
2	*leftover* Swirly Crustless Quiche, *leftover* Grilled Garlic Flank Steak with Peppers & Onions	[NR] canned wild salmon with olives, avocado, lemon juice, tomato, EVOO over green salad*	Bacon Jalapeño Burgers (360), Sweet Potato Pancakes (285), [NR] steamed spinach*
3	*leftover* Sweet Potato Pancakes, *leftover* Mustard-Glazed Chicken Thighs	*leftover* Bacon Jalapeño Burgers, green salad* with Balsamic Vinaigrette (434)	[MA] Lemony Lamb Dolmas (368), Cilantro Cauli-Rice (412)
4	Pesto Scrambled Eggs (286), *leftover* Cilantro Cauli-Rice, [MA] Raw Sauerkraut (262)	*leftover* Lemony Lamb Dolmas, green salad* with EVOO	Citrus Macadamia Nut Sole (378), [NR] butternut squash**
5	*leftover* Citrus Macadamia Nut Sole, *leftover* butternut squash**	Nori Salmon Handroll (388), melon	Beef & Veggie Stir-Fry (348)
6	Pumpkin Pancakes (284), breakfast sausage made with Italian Blend (256) & ground meat	*leftover* Beef & Veggie Stir-Fry, melon	Lamb Lettuce Boats with Avoziki Sauce (370)
7	[NR] eggs any style, Brussels sprouts*, [MA] Raw Sauerkraut (262)	green salad* with canned wild salmon, asparagus*, lemon juice with EVOO	Citrus & Herb Whole Roasted Chicken (292), Simple Baked Kale Chips* (425)
8	N'Oatmeal (288), berries, [NR] eggs hard-boiled or any style	Dairy-Free Caesar Salad (396), *leftover* Citrus & Herb Whole Roasted Chicken	Chicken Liver Pâté (426), cucumber and carrot slices, broccoli*, berries
9	Swirly Crustless Quiche (270), [NR] steamed broccoli*, [MA] Raw Sauerkraut (262)	*leftover* Chicken Liver Pâté (426), cucumber and carrot slices, berries, broccoli*	Pesto Fettuccine with Shrimp (380)
10	Pesto Scrambled Eggs (286), *leftover* Pesto Fettuccine with Shrimp, sliced avocado	Simple Shrimp Ceviche (389), green salad* with EVOO	Coffee BBQ Rubbed Pork with Seared Pineapple (318), green salad* with EVOO
11	[MA] Home Fries & Sausage Skillet (268)	*leftover* Coffee BBQ Rubbed Pork with Seared Pineapple, green salad* with EVOO	Balsamic Braised Short Ribs (332), Candied Carrots (415), green salad* with EVOO
12	*leftover* Home Fries & Sausage Skillet	*leftover* Balsamic Braised Short Ribs, *leftover* Candied Carrots, green salad* with EVOO	Mediterranean Baked Chicken with Cauliflower (294), [NR] baked potato**
13	[MA] Zucchini Pancakes (271), Perfectly Baked Bacon (260), [MA] Raw Sauerkraut (262)	*leftover* Mediterranean Baked Chicken with Cauliflower	Lemon Rosemary Broiled Salmon (375), Asparagus with Lemon & Olives (409), [NR] sweet potato**
14	*leftover* Lemon Rosemary Broiled Salmon, *leftover* Asparagus with Lemon & Olives*	[MA] Buffalo Chicken Lettuce Wraps (299)	Grilled Tuna Over Fresh Noodle Salad (384)
15	[NR] scrambled eggs with olives, [NR] steamed spinach*, avocado	*leftover* Grilled Tuna Over Fresh Noodle Salad	Italian-Style Stuffed Peppers (358), green salad* with Balsamic Vinaigrette (434)
16	Peach Blueberry Smoothie (289), [MA] Blueberry Maple Sausage (273)	*leftover* Italian-Style Stuffed Peppers, green salad* with EVOO	Mustard-Glazed Chicken Thighs (317), green salad* with EVOO

Heart Health

DAY	BREAKFAST	LUNCH	DINNER
17	[NR] eggs any style, avocado, kale*, [MA] Raw Sauerkraut (262), berries	*leftover* Mustard-Glazed Chicken Thighs, green salad* with EVOO	Spaghetti Squash Bolognese (338), Simple Baked Kale Chips* (425)
18	[MA] Pumpkin Pancakes (284), *leftover* Blueberry Maple Sausage	*leftover* Spaghetti Squash Bolognese, green salad* with EVOO	Thanksgiving Stuffing Meatballs (326), Simple Cranberry Sauce (436), Mashed Faux-Tatoes (418)
19	[NR] eggs any style, avocado, kale*, [MA] Raw Sauerkraut (262), berries	*leftover* Thanksgiving Stuffing Meatballs, *leftover* Cranberry Sauce, *leftover* Mashed Faux-Tatoes	Lemon & Bacon Scallops with Roasted Potatoes (376), Lemon Roasted Romanesco* (417)
20	Paleo Avocado "Toast" (264), [NR] eggs any style	*leftover* Lemon & Bacon Scallops, *leftover* Lemon Roasted Romanesco*	Orange & Olive Braised Chicken (306), Yellow Cauli-Rice (413), green salad* with EVOO
21	[MA] breakfast sausage made with Italian Blend (256) & ground meat, [NR] eggs any style, Raw Sauerkraut (262)	[MA] Six-Minute Salmon Bowls (382)	Souvlaki Kebabs (290), Greek Salad with Avoziki Dressing (402)
22	[MA] Breakfast Fried "Rice" (266), melon	*leftover* Souvlaki Kebabs, *leftover* Greek Salad with Avoziki Dressing	Orange Braised Beef (344), Butternut Sage Soup** (394)
23	*leftover* Breakfast Fried "Rice," melon	*leftover* Orange Braised Beef, *leftover* Butternut Sage Soup**	Hayley's Skirt Steak Tacos (346), choice of salsa (433), Smoky Grilled Squash & Pineapple (408)
24	[NR] eggs any style, avocado, *leftover* Smoky Grilled Squash & Pineapple	[MA] Tangy Taco Salad (350), *leftover* salsa	Bacon & Superfood Meatloaf (330), Mashed Faux-Tatoes (418), green salad* with EVOO
25	[NR] eggs any style, avocado, spinach or kale*, [MA] Raw Sauerkraut (262)	[MA] Quick & Easy Salmon Cakes (374), green salad* with EVOO, avocado, olives	Seared Scallops with Orange Glaze (386), Cilantro Cauli-Rice (412), [NR] steamed bok choy*
26	[MA] Zucchini Pancakes (271), Perfectly Baked Bacon (260)	[MA] Italiano Salad (398) with Honey Mustard Dressing (434)	Grandma Barbara's Stuffed Mushrooms (324), *leftover* Italiano Salad
27	[MA] N'Oatmeal (288), Apple Sage Sausage (272)	*leftover* Grandma Barbara's Stuffed Mushrooms, green salad* with EVOO	Orange Sesame Meatballs (328), Cilantro Cauli-Rice (412)
28	*leftover* N'Oatmeal, *leftover* Apple Sage Sausage	*leftover* Orange Sesame Meatballs, *leftover* Cilantro Cauli-Rice	Lemon & Artichoke Chicken (296), Broc-Cauli Chowder with Bacon (392)
29	[MA] Apple Cinnamon Egg Muffins (280), avocado, apple	*leftover* Lemon & Artichoke Chicken, *leftover* Broc-Cauli Chowder with Bacon	The Easiest Tacos (362), Crispy Plantain Chips (431), choice of salsa (433)
30	*leftover* Apple Cinnamon Egg Muffins, avocado, apple	*leftover* The Easiest Tacos, *leftover* Crispy Plantain Chips, *leftover* salsa	Mini Mediterranean Kebabs (352), Sautéed Spinach with Pine Nuts & Currants* (423)

» *A complete shopping list for this meal plan can be found on balancedbites.com*

NOTES

*: or other green vegetable; green salad is any lettuce and/or non-starchy vegetables

**: or other starchy vegetable (refer to page 75)

EVOO: Extra-virgin olive oil, or use any dressing from pages 434–435 on salads

CO: Coconut oil

MA: Make-Ahead all or part of the recipe

NR: No Recipe (use any simple prep)

If no page number is listed, simply prepare the items as noted or any way you like. For additional protein, vegetable, and fat recommendations, refer to the QUICK LIST that is associated with your meal plan!

Liver Detox Support

30-DAY MEAL PLANS

Supporting liver detox—the process by which the liver removes toxins from the bloodstream—can be useful for a variety of symptoms, health challenges, and conditions.

follow this plan if:

» You're unable to lose body fat despite "doing everything right."
» You're experiencing skin irritation (rashes, acne, eczema).
» You have digestive issues that remain unresolved after following the Digestive Health 30-Day Meal Plan (page 192) and completing the 4R Protocol (page 44). These issues may include poor fat digestion and/or poor gallbladder function (see page 83 for details), leaky gut (see page 93), and other IBS/IBD issues.
» You have blood sugar regulation issues that remain unresolved after following the Blood Sugar Regulation 30-Day Meal Plan (page 180).

The liver filters both endogenous toxins—those originating within the body, such as used hormones, neurotransmitters, and lipopolysaccharides from the GI tract—and exogenous toxins—those introduced from outside the body, such as alcohol, medications, food additives, heavy metals, synthetic hormones, cleaning products and cosmetics, herbicides, and pesticides. The liver's detox process is ongoing twenty-four/seven, and it occurs in two phases.

In phase 1, toxins are transformed into chemicals that can then be metabolized in phase 2. When toxins move through phase 1, they aren't yet ready to be removed from the body—they must first be processed in phase 2.

In phase 2, toxins are attached to water-soluble molecules for transport out of the body, primarily via urine or stool. This involves multiple processes that each serve to detoxify different substances from the body: methylation, sulfation, glucuronidation, glutathione conjugation, acetylation, and amino acid conjugation. Methylation in particular has been receiving a lot of attention lately. In methylation, a methyl donor (part of a molecule) gets attached to enzymes that need to be carried out of the body. Methylation specifically detoxifies estrogens, catecholamines (a kind of neurotransmitter), histamine, some heavy metals, and some medications.

In addition, during methylation, folic acid and folate are converted into forms the body can use. However, in people with a genetic variation called the MTHFR mutation, that process can be less efficient, which can increase the risk of heart disease, stroke, and other health problems. It also can lead to deficiency in folate (also known as vitamin B9).

Some toxins, like nicotine and estrogens, have to be removed through more than one process. However, it isn't critical to understand the details of how each detox pathway functions and what toxins it works to clear in order to support your liver in its work. And when you realize exactly how much work the liver is doing constantly, it becomes clear how important supporting liver detox can be for your overall health.

Is a 21-Day Sugar Detox (21DSD) the same as liver detox support? Not exactly. While the 21DSD will absolutely support liver detox, the additional supplements and lifestyle factors involved with supporting liver detox create an entirely different protocol. The 21DSD isn't the same type of therapeutic plan offered here, which addresses health challenges outside of sugar and carb cravings, low energy, and poor sleep quality—three of the main reasons folks begin a 21DSD.

DISCLAIMER:
The information in this book is not intended to be a replacement for professional medical diagnosis or treatment for a medical condition. It consists solely of nutritional and lifestyle recommendations to support a healthier body.

diet & lifestyle recommendations

add [+]

SULFUR-RICH FOODS
Add egg yolks, alliums (such as onions and garlic), and cruciferous vegetables (such as cauliflower, broccoli, cabbage, and kale) to support the liver's detox functions.

FILTERED WATER
Remove toxins and unwanted chemicals from your drinking water and water you use to make broth and soups. The Berkey filtration system is a good option.

GREEN JUICE
Make green juice fresh at home for the best nutrient value, using primarily vegetables—a mix of dark leafy greens (such as kale and Swiss chard) and water-rich foods (such as cucumbers and celery)—and minimal fruit (for example, 1/2 green apple or less per serving). Add freshly squeezed lemon or lime as well. Eight ounces a day is a good amount to aim for. In most cases, eating vegetables is better than juicing them, but to support liver detox, getting the nutrients without the excess fiber may be beneficial.

TIME OUTSIDE
Make time for walks, hikes, or even simply sitting outside in green space. If you can spend at least a few hours per week away from the toxic burdens of everyday life while enjoying nature, your overall health will benefit.

REST & DIGEST
Resting puts your body into a parasympathetic-dominant nervous system mode that encourages the entire digestive process to happen much more smoothly and encourages optimal liver function.

MOVEMENT
For movement without systemic stress, take walks outside, swim (not for speed!), or practice gentle yoga. If you're not also struggling with fatigue or an autoimmune condition, you can add high-intensity movement as well.

DRY SKIN BRUSHING
This helps exfoliate the skin to improve detox through pores. Dry brushing can also stimulate the lymphatic system and increase circulation.

avoid [–]

ALCOHOL
When you consume alcohol, the liver makes processing it its top priority and makes clearing other toxins and managing metabolic functions a lower priority.

HIGH-INTENSITY EXERCISE
Overly intense exercise (high-intensity interval training or similar workouts) and chronic cardiovascular exercise (30–60+ minutes at a steady state of intensity, like jogging or biking) can provoke a stress response in the body.

NONORGANIC FOODS & COMMERCIALLY RAISED MEATS
Use the Dirty Dozen and Clean Thirteen lists from the Environmental Working Group (EWG) to identify what should be purchased organic and what can be purchased conventionally grown. Avoid meats with added hormones, artificial colors, and other food additives.

RESTAURANTS / DINING OUT
Avoid damaged and man-made fats, which may tax the liver. Seek out organic and farm-to-table restaurants and avoid fried foods.

HARSH CLEANING & HYGIENE PRODUCTS
Opt for gentle, natural alternatives, such as soap nuts for laundry, vinegar and water for cleaning countertops, and baking soda and peroxide for cleaning and whitening surfaces, laundry, teeth, and more. Consider skipping shampoo and going "no-poo" instead. Safe makeup recommendations may be found at skindeep.org.

OVER-THE-COUNTER (OTC) & PRESCRIPTION MEDICATIONS & HORMONAL BIRTH CONTROL
Avoid liver-taxing OTC painkillers, including aspirin, acetaminophen, ibuprofen, naproxen, and corticosteroids. If you become ill, use natural remedies instead of OTC medications. Talk to your doctor about options for eliminating noncritical prescription medications, and seek birth control methods that do not introduce exogenous hormones to your body. This is not a recommendation to cease taking any medications, simply a recommendation to seek alternatives that support a healthy liver. Never stop or change medications without first talking to your doctor.

CAFFEINE
If you notice that you can drink caffeinated beverages close to bedtime and still fall asleep easily, your liver may be overactive in phase 1.

DENTAL AMALGAMS (SILVER FILLINGS)
Consider holistic or biological dentistry to replace existing amalgams.

Liver Detox Support

nutritional supplements & herbs to consider

These recommendations are made as a starting point. Do your own research and determine which supplements may serve you best. Remember that supplements should be used for a short period of time, one to six months, and that it's best to get as many of your nutrients from food as possible. See page 219 for specific food-based nutrients on which to focus. The items below are listed in no particular order.

» **B VITAMINS** are critical in the function of the liver for metabolic processes. If you have a diagnosed liver condition, avoid B3 (niacin) as it may disrupt normal function in those cases.

» **VITAMIN C** is a potent antioxidant with anti-inflammatory properties that supports immune function.

» **VITAMIN E** is an antioxidant that protects against free-radical damage.

» **MAGNESIUM** is required for more than 300 enzymatic processes in the body, and most people are deficient in it. It is also useful in blood sugar regulation. Look for magnesium glycinate or magnesium malate forms.

» **MILK THISTLE (SILYMARIN)** supports liver detox and is available in herbal tea, tincture, or capsule form.

» **OX BILE / BILE SALTS** help the body to emulsify dietary fats, especially unsaturated fats, so they're particularly helpful for those without a gallbladder.

» **PHOSPHATIDYLCHOLINE** is one of the most important substances for liver protection and liver-cell integrity. This supplement is especially important if you are avoiding or are allergic to eggs.

» **SELENIUM & ZINC** are antioxidants that are antagonistic to heavy metals like lead, mercury, cadmium, and aluminum. Selenium supports cancer recovery, immune function, cardiac health, inflammatory conditions, vision, and proper fetal growth. Absorption may be decreased by high zinc intake, so these minerals should be balanced.

» **FOLIC ACID** facilitates methylation, one of the detoxification process that happens in phase 2. 5-MTHF is a natural form that is readily bioavailable. Note that if you have an MTHFR or DHFR gene mutation, supplementation with folic acid may be contraindicated and the 5-MTHF form may be a better option.

» **CALCIUM D-GLUCARATE** may help to inhibit toxins produced by gut bacteria.

» **N-ACETYL CYSTEINE (NAC)** supports liver function and the production of glutathione, an important nutrient for both phases of liver detox.

» **GLYCINE** supports phase 2 liver detox.

» **ACETYL L-CARNITINE** may help preserve glutathione levels in the body. Glutathione is an important nutrient for both phases of liver detox.

» **SAM-e** may help prevent oxidative damage and is critical to phase 2 liver detox. SAM-e is not recommended for those with Parkinson's disease or bipolar disorder and should not be taken for two weeks prior to surgery.

supportive nutrients & foods that contain them

B VITAMINS

Critical in assisting neurotransmitters and therefore important for brain health and for the proper functioning of nerves and muscles

- » Liver, bison, lamb
- » Flounder, haddock, salmon, trout, tuna
- » Brewer's yeast (Lewis Labs brand only)
- » Mushrooms
- » Hazelnuts, walnuts
- » Trace amounts: pecans, sunflower seeds, broccoli, Brussels sprouts

VITAMIN C

A potent antioxidant with anti-inflammatory properties

- » Beets, bell peppers, broccoli, Brussels sprouts, cauliflower, collard greens, daikon radishes, garlic, kale, mustard greens, parsley, spinach
- » Cantaloupes, kiwis, lemons, oranges, papayas, pineapples, strawberries

CHOLINE

Important for cell membrane integrity, nerve-muscle communication, and liver function

- » Eggs
- » Organ meat: liver, heart, kidneys
- » Fish roe (eggs), caviar, cod
- » Cauliflower (cooked)

VITAMIN E

An antioxidant that benefits neurological function, smooth-muscle growth, and cellular communication

- » Broccoli, Brussels sprouts, spinach
- » Extra-virgin olive oil
- » Pecans

GLUTATHIONE

An antioxidant that aids in liver detox processes

- » Asparagus, broccoli, garlic
- » Avocado
- » Cumin, ginger, turmeric

GLYCINE

An amino acid that is often depleted by toxins and is necessary for optimal glucose metabolism

- » Bone broth (page 259)
- » Collagen peptides
- » Gelatin

MAGNESIUM

Critical for cellular energy production, which helps battle fatigue, and for proper calcium metabolism, which is necessary for vascular health

- » Beets, kale, other green leafy vegetables
- » Pumpkin seeds (pepitas)

SUPEROXIDE DISMUTASE (SOD)

Known to support the detoxification of free radicals generated in phase 1 liver detox

- » Cantaloupe

SELENIUM

An antioxidant that protects against free-radical damage

- » Eggs
- » Garlic, red Swiss chard, turnips

ZINC

A potent antioxidant often low in people with inflammatory conditions; aids in vitamin A metabolism

- » Oysters, shellfish
- » Lamb, red meat
- » Pumpkin seeds (pepitas)

quick LIST

proteins

Beef
Bison
Collagen peptides
Eggs
Gelatin
Lamb
Liver
Oysters
Shellfish

fats

Avocados
Extra-virgin olive oil
Grass-fed butter/ghee
Pumpkin seeds
Pecans

vegetables

Asparagus
Beets
Broccoli
Brussels sprouts
Butternut squash
Cauliflower
Daikon radishes
Kale
Red Swiss chard
Turnips

fruits

Cantaloupes
Kiwis
Lemons
Pineapples

superfoods

Bone broth
Liver
Sauerkraut
Spices

spices

Basil
Cilantro
Cinnamon
Cumin
Garlic
Ginger
Oregano
Parsley
Turmeric

Liver Detox Support

DAY	BREAKFAST	LUNCH	DINNER
1	Swirly Crustless Quiche (270), avocado, [MA] Raw Sauerkraut (262)	[MA] Mustard-Glazed Chicken Thighs (317), green salad* with Balsamic Vinaigrette (434)	Grilled Garlic Flank Steak with Peppers & Onions (334), [NR] baked potato with ghee (261)**
2	*leftover* Swirly Crustless Quiche, *leftover* Grilled Garlic Flank Steak with Peppers & Onions	[NR] canned wild salmon with olives, avocado, lemon juice, tomato, EVOO over green salad*	Bacon Jalapeño Burgers (360), Sweet Potato Pancakes (285), [NR] steamed spinach*
3	*leftover* Sweet Potato Pancakes, *leftover* Mustard-Glazed Chicken Thighs	*leftover* Bacon Jalapeño Burgers, green salad* with Balsamic Vinaigrette (434)	[MA] Lemony Lamb Dolmas (368), Cilantro Cauli-Rice (412)
4	Pesto Scrambled Eggs (286), *leftover* Cilantro Cauli-Rice, [MA] Raw Sauerkraut (262)	*leftover* Lemony Lamb Dolmas, green salad* with EVOO	Citrus Macadamia Nut Sole (378), Baked Beets with Fennel (420)
5	*leftover* Citrus Macadamia Nut Sole, *leftover* Baked Beets with Fennel	Nori Salmon Handroll (388)	Beef & Veggie Stir-Fry (348)
6	Pumpkin Pancakes (284), breakfast sausage made with Italian Blend (256) & ground meat	*leftover* Beef & Veggie Stir-Fry, cantaloupe	Lamb Lettuce Boats with Avoziki Sauce (370), cantaloupe
7	[NR] eggs any style, mushrooms, chard*, avocado, [MA] Raw Sauerkraut (262)	green salad* with canned wild salmon, asparagus*, lemon juice with EVOO, cantaloupe	Citrus & Herb Whole Roasted Chicken (292), Simple Baked Kale Chips* (425), [NR] beets
8	N'Oatmeal (288), [NR] eggs any style, berries	Dairy-Free Caesar Salad (396), *leftover* Citrus & Herb Whole Roasted Chicken	Restaurant-Style Lettuce Cups (312)
9	Swirly Crustless Quiche (270), [NR] steamed broccoli*, [MA] Raw Sauerkraut (262)	[MA] Chicken Liver Pâté (426), cucumber and carrot slices, broccoli*, berries	Pesto Fettuccine with Shrimp (380), pineapple
10	Pesto Scrambled Eggs (286), *leftover* Pesto Fettuccine with Shrimp, sliced avocado	*leftover* Chicken Liver Pâté, cucumber and carrot slices, broccoli*, berries	Cumin-Spiced Pork Tenderloin (320), green salad* with EVOO
11	[MA] Home Fries & Sausage Skillet (268)	*leftover* Cumin-Spiced Pork Tenderloin, green salad* with EVOO	Balsamic Braised Short Ribs (332), Candied Carrots (415), green salad* with EVOO
12	*leftover* Home Fries & Sausage Skillet	*leftover* Balsamic Braised Short Ribs, *leftover* Candied Carrots, green salad* with EVOO	Mediterranean Baked Chicken with Cauliflower (294), cantaloupe
13	[MA] Zucchini Pancakes (271), avocado, [MA] Raw Sauerkraut (262)	*leftover* Mediterranean Baked Chicken with Cauliflower, cantaloupe	Lemon Rosemary Broiled Salmon (375), Asparagus with Lemon & Olives (409), [NR] sweet potato**
14	*leftover* Lemon Rosemary Broiled Salmon, *leftover* Asparagus with Lemon & Olives*	[MA] Buffalo Chicken Lettuce Wraps (299), pineapple	Bacon & Superfood Meatloaf (330), Mashed Faux-Tatoes (418), green salad* with EVOO
15	[NR] scrambled eggs with mushrooms, [NR] steamed chard*, avocado	*leftover* Bacon & Superfood Meatloaf, *leftover* Mashed Faux-Tatoes, green salad* with EVOO	Italian-Style Stuffed Peppers (358), green salad* with Balsamic Vinaigrette (434)
16	Peach Blueberry Smoothie (289), [MA] Blueberry Maple Sausage (273)	*leftover* Italian-Style Stuffed Peppers, green salad* with EVOO	Bacon-Wrapped Smoky Chicken Thighs (298), green salad* with EVOO, pineapple

Liver Detox Support

DAY	BREAKFAST	LUNCH	DINNER
17	[MA] Bacon & Egg Salad (287), avocado, chard or kale*, [MA] Raw Sauerkraut (262)	*leftover* Bacon-Wrapped Smoky Chicken Thighs, green salad* with EVOO	Spaghetti Squash Bolognese (338), Simple Baked Kale Chips* (425), pineapple
18	[MA] Pumpkin Pancakes (284), *leftover* Blueberry Maple Sausage	*leftover* Spaghetti Squash Bolognese, green salad* with EVOO, pineapple	Thanksgiving Stuffing Meatballs (326), Simple Cranberry Sauce (436), Mashed Faux-Tatoes (418)
19	*leftover* Bacon & Egg Salad, avocado, kale*, [MA] Raw Sauerkraut (262), cantaloupe	*leftover* Thanksgiving Stuffing Meatballs, *leftover* Cranberry Sauce, *leftover* Mashed Faux-Tatoes	Lemon & Bacon Scallops with Roasted Potatoes (376), Lemon Roasted Romanesco* (417)
20	Paleo Avocado "Toast" (264), [NR] eggs any style	*leftover* Lemon & Bacon Scallops, *leftover* Lemon Roasted Romanesco*	Orange & Olive Braised Chicken (306), Yellow Cauli-Rice (413), green salad* with EVOO
21	[MA] breakfast sausage made with Italian Blend (256) & ground meat, [NR] eggs any style, Raw Sauerkraut (262)	[MA] Six-Minute Salmon Bowls (382)	Souvlaki Kebabs (290), Greek Salad with Avoziki Dressing (402), pineapple
22	[MA] Breakfast Fried "Rice" (266)	*leftover* Souvlaki Kebabs, *leftover* Greek Salad with Avoziki Dressing, pineapple	Orange Braised Beef (344), Baked Beets with Fennel (420)
23	*leftover* Breakfast Fried "Rice"	*leftover* Orange Braised Beef, *leftover* Baked Beets with Fennel	Hayley's Skirt Steak Tacos (346), choice of salsa (433), Smoky Grilled Squash & Pineapple (408)
24	[NR] eggs any style, mushrooms, avocado, *leftover* Smoky Grilled Squash & Pineapple	[MA] Chicken Liver Pâté (426), cucumber and carrot slices, broccoli*, berries	Bacon & Superfood Meatloaf (330), Mashed Faux-Tatoes (418), green salad* with EVOO
25	[NR] eggs any style, mushrooms, spinach*, avocado, [MA] Raw Sauerkraut (262), cantaloupe	*leftover* Chicken Liver Pâté, cucumber and carrot slices, broccoli*, berries	Seared Scallops with Orange Glaze (386), Cilantro Cauli-Rice (412), [NR] steamed bok choy*
26	[MA] Zucchini Pancakes (271), avocado, cantaloupe	[MA] Italiano Salad (398), Honey Mustard Dressing (434)	Grandma Barbara's Stuffed Mushrooms (324), *leftover* Italiano Salad
27	[MA] N'Oatmeal (288), Apple Sage Sausage (272)	*leftover* Grandma Barbara's Stuffed Mushrooms, green salad* with EVOO, pineapple	Orange Sesame Meatballs (328), Cilantro Cauli-Rice (412)
28	*leftover* N'Oatmeal, *leftover* Apple Sage Sausage	*leftover* Orange Sesame Meatballs, *leftover* Cilantro Cauli-Rice, pineapple	Lemon & Artichoke Chicken (296), Baked Beets with Fennel (420)
29	[MA] Apple Cinnamon Egg Muffins (280), bacon or sausage	*leftover* Lemon & Artichoke Chicken, *leftover* Baked Beets with Fennel	The Easiest Tacos (362), Crispy Plantain Chips (431), Pineapple Salsa (433)
30	*leftover* Apple Cinnamon Egg Muffins, bacon or sausage	*leftover* The Easiest Tacos, *leftover* Crispy Plantain Chips, *leftover* Pineapple Salsa	Mini Mediterranean Kebabs (352), Sautéed Spinach with Pine Nuts & Currants* (423)

» *A complete shopping list for this meal plan can be found on balancedbites.com*

NOTES

*****: or other green vegetable; green salad is any lettuce and/or non-starchy vegetables

******: or other starchy vegetable (refer to page 75)

EVOO: Extra-virgin olive oil, or use any dressing from pages 434–435 on salads

CO: Coconut oil

MA: Make-Ahead all or part of the recipe

NR: No Recipe (use any simple prep)

If no page number is listed, simply prepare the items as noted or any way you like. For additional protein, vegetable, and fat recommendations, refer to the QUICK LIST that is associated with your meal plan!

Multiple Sclerosis, Fibromyalgia & Chronic Fatigue

30-DAY MEAL PLANS

Before trying the menu for this slightly more limited plan, you may want to follow the lifestyle, supplement, and nutrient recommendations from this plan and the monthly menu from the Autoimmune Conditions 30-Day Meal Plan (page 174).

multiple sclerosis
symptoms include:

» Muscle wasting
» Weakness
» Dysphagia (difficulty swallowing)
» Jerking
» Spastic movements
» Loss of balance
» Twitches
» Tics
» Tingling sensation (pins & needles)
» Sensitivity to heat and cold
» Loss of sensation and electric shock sensations
» Loss of muscle and speech coordination and paralysis (complete or partial)

» Blurred or double vision
» Eye pain
» Blindness
» Urinary urgency
» Incontinence, hesitancy, or retention
» Cognitive dysfunction, such as memory problems (short or long term)
» Depression
» May lead to complete incapacitation (a bedridden state)

For more information on a dietary approach for MS, I recommend checking out Dr. Terry Wahls's website, www.terrywahls.com.

fibromyalgia
symptoms include:

» Tightening and thickening of myofascia (connective tissue)
» Aching all over (often occurs after an infection or trauma)

chronic fatigue syndrome
symptoms include:

» Unexplained fatigue that is not a result of exertion, is not resolved by bed rest, and is severe enough to reduce previously maintained daily activity levels

For at least six months:

» Unexplained or new headaches
» Short-term memory or concentration impairment
» Muscle pain
» Pain/redness/swelling in multiple joints

» Unrestful sleep
» Post-exertion malaise lasting for more than 24 hours
» Sore throat
» Tender lymph nodes in the neck or armpits

Other populations who may benefit from this meal plan include those diagnosed with:

» Scleroderma
» Arthritis, osteoarthritis, or rheumatoid arthritis

DISCLAIMER:
The information in this book is not intended to be a replacement for professional medical diagnosis or treatment for a medical condition. It consists solely of nutritional and lifestyle recommendations to support a healthier body.

diet & lifestyle recommendations

add [+]

NUTRIENT-DENSE FOODS
Replenish nutrient stores that have been depleted by excess refined foods.

SUPERFOODS
Eat superfoods as often as possible (see page 61). Make bone broth (page 259) and drink it or cook with it regularly. Make liver regularly. Consume 1/4 cup raw sauerkraut (page 262) daily, especially with breakfast.

ORGANIC FOODS
Eat as often as possible to avoid toxins.

POSITIVE MINDSET
Cultivate a positive mental outlook by creating a gratitude list regularly (see page 120). A positive mental outlook is often a result of feeling that we have control over our own lives, and it can yield calmer thoughts overall.

STRESS MANAGEMENT
Develop a guided meditation or slow-breathing practice, or begin to practice qigong. Practice biofeedback, tai chi, and/or guided imagery for deep relaxation.

MOVEMENT
For movement without systemic stress, take walks outside, swim (not for speed!), or practice gentle yoga.

MASSAGE
Get gentle massages. Look into the Feldenkrais method and find a practitioner.

avoid [–]

NIGHTSHADE FOODS
If you experience pain in your joints, avoid nightshades: tomatoes, potatoes, peppers, and eggplants. See page 61 for a list of Paleo nightshade foods. In recipes that contain nightshades, use the substitutions and modifications.

RESTAURANTS / DINING OUT
Avoid the damaged and man-made fats most often used in restaurant foods.

REFINED FOODS, SWEETENERS, CAFFEINE & ALCOHOL
These can all provoke blood sugar fluctuations and systemic stress.

HARSH CLEANING & HYGIENE PRODUCTS
Opt for gentle, natural alternatives, such as soap nuts for laundry, vinegar and water for cleaning countertops, and baking soda and peroxide for cleaning and whitening surfaces, laundry, teeth, and more. Consider skipping shampoo and going "no-poo" instead. Safe makeup recommendations may be found at skindeep.org.

HEATING PADS, CHLORINATED WATER & FLUORIDE

DENTAL AMALGAMS (SILVER FILLINGS)
Consider holistic or biological dentistry to replace existing amalgams.

HIGH-INTENSITY EXERCISE
Overly intense exercise (high-intensity interval training or similar workouts) and chronic cardiovascular exercise (30–60+ minutes at a steady state of intensity, like jogging or biking) can lead to low-blood-sugar episodes and provoke a stress response in the body.

nutritional supplements & herbs to consider

These recommendations are made as a starting point. Do your own research and determine which supplements may serve you best. Remember that supplements should be used for a short period of time, one to six months, and that it's best to get as many of your nutrients from food as possible. See page 225 for specific food-based nutrients on which to focus. The items below are listed in no particular order.

» **ACETYL L-CARNITINE** may help to preserve glutathione levels in the body. Glutathione is an important neuro-protective nutrient.

» **VITAMIN C** is a potent antioxidant with anti-inflammatory properties that supports immune function. It promotes collagen production and supports carnitine synthesis. It also helps to regenerate vitamin E and improves iron absorption.

» **COENZYME Q10** (CoQ10, ubiquinone) enhances cellular energy production, and it can help alleviate fatigue as well as muscle and joint pain. Statin drugs are known to deplete CoQ10.

» **CURCUMIN** is a potent antioxidant.

» **VITAMIN D** is a potent immune system modulator that is best obtained from sun exposure. Proper balance with vitamin A is important.

» **DIGESTIVE ENZYMES** help to break down food for absorption while your gut is healing. Look for a blend of enzymes.

» **GABA** is a calming neurotransmitter that can be helpful if you have trouble sleeping.

» **GINKGO BILOBA** is a potent antioxidant herb.

» **5-HTP** can help to increase dopamine and possibly alleviate pain.

» **MAGNESIUM** is required for more than 300 enzymatic processes in the body, and most people are deficient in it. It is also useful in blood sugar regulation. Look for magnesium glycinate or magnesium malate forms.

» **MILK THISTLE** supports liver detox and is available in herbal tea, tincture, or capsule form.

» **N-ACETYL CYSTEINE (NAC)** supports liver function.

» **OMEGA-3 FATS** are anti-inflammatory essential fatty acids.

» **PROBIOTICS** promote healthy gut flora, which is critical for proper digestion and elimination.

» **SAM-e** may help to prevent oxidative damage, maintain cognitive function, and improve mental outlook.

supportive nutrients & foods that contain them

B VITAMINS

Critical in assisting neurotransmitters and therefore important for brain health and for the proper functioning of nerves and muscles

» Liver, bison
» Brewer's yeast (Lewis Labs brand only)
» Mushrooms
» Trace amounts: pecans, sunflower seeds, broccoli, Brussels sprouts

BROMELAIN

An enzyme with anti-inflammatory properties

» Pineapple

VITAMIN C

A potent antioxidant with anti-inflammatory properties

» Beets, bell peppers, broccoli, Brussels sprouts, cauliflower, collard greens, daikon radishes, garlic, kale
» Cantaloupe, kiwi, lemons, oranges, papaya, pineapple

VITAMIN D

A potent immune system modulator that is best obtained from sun exposure

» Cold-water fish (salmon, herring, mackerel)
» Grass-fed butter or ghee

CARNITINE

Essential for fat metabolism

» Red meat

CHOLINE

Important for cell membrane integrity, nerve-muscle communication, and liver function

» Eggs
» Organ meat: liver, heart, kidneys
» Fish roe (eggs), caviar, cod
» Cauliflower (cooked)

VITAMIN E

An antioxidant that benefits neurological function, smooth-muscle growth, and cellular communication

» Broccoli, Brussels sprouts, spinach (cooked)
» Extra-virgin olive oil
» Pecans

GLUTATHIONE

An antioxidant that aids in liver detox processes

» Asparagus, broccoli, garlic
» Avocado
» Cumin, ginger, turmeric

MAGNESIUM

Critical for cellular energy production, which helps battle fatigue, and for proper calcium metabolism, which is necessary for vascular health

» Beets, kale, other green leafy vegetables
» Pumpkin seeds (pepitas)

OMEGA-3 FATS

An anti-inflammatory essential fatty acid

» Cold-water fish, such as salmon, herring, and mackerel
» Pecans, walnuts

PROBIOTICS

Promote healthy gut flora, which is critical for proper digestion and elimination

» Fermented vegetables: cabbage (sauerkraut/kimchi), carrots, beets
» Kombucha (fermented tea)

ZINC

A potent antioxidant often low in people with inflammatory conditions; aids in vitamin A metabolism

» Oysters, shellfish
» Lamb, red meat
» Pumpkin seeds (pepitas)

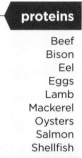

quick LIST

proteins

Beef
Bison
Eel
Eggs
Lamb
Mackerel
Oysters
Salmon
Shellfish

fats

Coconut oil
Extra-virgin olive oil
Grass-fed butter/ghee
Pumpkin seeds

vegetables

Beets
Broccoli
Brussels sprouts
Butternut squash
Carrots
Cauliflower
Daikon radish
Okra
Spinach
Sweet potato

fruits

Bananas
Blueberries
Lemon
Pineapple

superfoods

Bone broth
Liver
Sauerkraut

spices

Basil
Cilantro
Cinnamon
Cumin
Garlic
Ginger
Oregano
Parsley
Turmeric

Multiple Sclerosis, Fibromyalgia & Chronic Fatigue

DAY	BREAKFAST	LUNCH	DINNER
1	Swirly Crustless Quiche (270), avocado, [MA] Raw Sauerkraut (262)	[MA] Mustard-Glazed Chicken Thighs (317), green salad* with Balsamic Vinaigrette (434)	Grilled Garlic Flank Steak with Peppers & Onions (334), [NR] baked potato with ghee (261)**
2	*leftover* Swirly Crustless Quiche, *leftover* Grilled Garlic Flank Steak with Peppers & Onions	[NR] canned wild salmon with olives, avocado, lemon juice, tomato, EVOO over green salad*	Bacon Jalapeño Burgers (360), Sweet Potato Pancakes (285), [NR] steamed spinach*
3	*leftover* Sweet Potato Pancakes, *leftover* Mustard-Glazed Chicken Thighs	*leftover* Bacon Jalapeño Burgers, green salad* with Balsamic Vinaigrette (434)	[MA] Lemony Lamb Dolmas (368), Cilantro Cauli-Rice (412)
4	Pesto Scrambled Eggs (286), *leftover* Cilantro Cauli-Rice, [MA] Raw Sauerkraut (262)	*leftover* Lemony Lamb Dolmas, green salad* with EVOO	Citrus Macadamia Nut Sole (378), Baked Beets with Fennel (420)
5	*leftover* Citrus Macadamia Nut Sole, *leftover* Baked Beets with Fennel	Nori Salmon Handroll (388)	Beef & Veggie Stir-Fry (348)
6	Pumpkin Pancakes (284), breakfast sausage made with Italian Blend (256) & ground meat	*leftover* Beef & Veggie Stir-Fry, cantaloupe	Lamb Lettuce Boats with Avoziki Sauce (370), cantaloupe
7	[NR] eggs any style, mushrooms, chard*, avocado, [MA] Raw Sauerkraut (262)	green salad* with canned wild salmon, asparagus*, lemon juice with EVOO, cantaloupe	Citrus & Herb Whole Roasted Chicken (292), Simple Baked Kale Chips* (425), [NR] beets
8	N'Oatmeal (288), [NR] eggs any style, berries	Dairy-Free Caesar Salad (396), *leftover* Citrus & Herb Whole Roasted Chicken	Restaurant-Style Lettuce Cups (312)
9	Swirly Crustless Quiche (270), [NR] steamed broccoli*, [MA] Raw Sauerkraut (262)	[MA] Chicken Liver Pâté (426), cucumber and carrot slices, broccoli*, berries	Pesto Fettuccine with Shrimp (380), pineapple
10	Pesto Scrambled Eggs (286), *leftover* Pesto Fettuccine with Shrimp, sliced avocado	*leftover* Chicken Liver Pâté, cucumber and carrot slices, broccoli*, berries	Cumin-Spiced Pork Tenderloin (320), green salad* with EVOO
11	[MA] Home Fries & Sausage Skillet (268)	*leftover* Cumin-Spiced Pork Tenderloin, green salad* with EVOO	Balsamic Braised Short Ribs (332), Candied Carrots (415), green salad* with EVOO
12	*leftover* Home Fries & Sausage Skillet	*leftover* Balsamic Braised Short Ribs, *leftover* Candied Carrots, green salad* with EVOO	Mediterranean Baked Chicken with Cauliflower (294), cantaloupe
13	[MA] Zucchini Pancakes (271), avocado, [MA] Raw Sauerkraut (262)	*leftover* Mediterranean Baked Chicken with Cauliflower, cantaloupe	Lemon Rosemary Broiled Salmon (375), Asparagus with Lemon & Olives (409), [NR] sweet potato**
14	*leftover* Lemon Rosemary Broiled Salmon, *leftover* Asparagus with Lemon & Olives*	[MA] Buffalo Chicken Lettuce Wraps (299), pineapple	Bacon & Superfood Meatloaf (330), Mashed Faux-Tatoes (418), green salad* with EVOO
15	[NR] scrambled eggs with mushrooms, [NR] steamed chard*, avocado	*leftover* Bacon & Superfood Meatloaf, *leftover* Mashed Faux-Tatoes, green salad* with EVOO	Italian-Style Stuffed Peppers (358), green salad* with Balsamic Vinaigrette (434)
16	Peach Blueberry Smoothie (289), [MA] Blueberry Maple Sausage (273)	*leftover* Italian-Style Stuffed Peppers, green salad* with EVOO	Bacon-Wrapped Smoky Chicken Thighs (298), green salad* with EVOO, pineapple

Multiple Sclerosis, Fibromyalgia & Chronic Fatigue

DAY	BREAKFAST	LUNCH	DINNER
17	[MA] Bacon & Egg Salad (287), avocado, chard or kale*, [MA] Raw Sauerkraut (262)	*leftover* Bacon-Wrapped Smoky Chicken Thighs, green salad* with EVOO	Spaghetti Squash Bolognese (338), Simple Baked Kale Chips* (425), pineapple
18	[MA] Pumpkin Pancakes (284), *leftover* Blueberry Maple Sausage	*leftover* Spaghetti Squash Bolognese, green salad* with EVOO, pineapple	Thanksgiving Stuffing Meatballs (326), Simple Cranberry Sauce (436), Mashed Faux-Tatoes (418)
19	*leftover* Bacon & Egg Salad, avocado, kale*, [MA] Raw Sauerkraut (262), cantaloupe	*leftover* Thanksgiving Stuffing Meatballs, *leftover* Cranberry Sauce, *leftover* Mashed Faux-Tatoes	Lemon & Bacon Scallops with Roasted Potatoes (376), Lemon Roasted Romanesco* (417)
20	Paleo Avocado "Toast" (264), [NR] eggs any style	*leftover* Lemon & Bacon Scallops, *leftover* Lemon Roasted Romanesco*	Orange & Olive Braised Chicken (306), Yellow Cauli-Rice (413), green salad* with EVOO
21	[MA] breakfast sausage made with Italian Blend (256) & ground meat, [NR] eggs any style, Raw Sauerkraut (262)	[MA] Six-Minute Salmon Bowls (382)	Souvlaki Kebabs (290), Greek Salad with Avoziki Dressing (402), pineapple
22	[MA] Breakfast Fried "Rice" (266)	*leftover* Souvlaki Kebabs, *leftover* Greek Salad with Avoziki Dressing, pineapple	Orange Braised Beef (344), Baked Beets with Fennel (420)
23	*leftover* Breakfast Fried "Rice"	*leftover* Orange Braised Beef, *leftover* Baked Beets with Fennel	Hayley's Skirt Steak Tacos (346), choice of salsa (433), Smoky Grilled Squash & Pineapple (408)
24	[NR] eggs any style, mushrooms, avocado, *leftover* Smoky Grilled Squash & Pineapple	[MA] Chicken Liver Pâté (426), cucumber and carrot slices, broccoli*, berries	Bacon & Superfood Meatloaf (330), Mashed Faux-Tatoes (418), green salad* with EVOO
25	[NR] eggs any style, mushrooms, spinach*, avocado, [MA] Raw Sauerkraut (262), cantaloupe	*leftover* Chicken Liver Pâté, cucumber and carrot slices, broccoli*, berries	Seared Scallops with Orange Glaze (386), Cilantro Cauli-Rice (412), [NR] steamed bok choy*
26	[MA] Zucchini Pancakes (271), avocado, cantaloupe	[MA] Italiano Salad (398), Honey Mustard Dressing (434)	Grandma Barbara's Stuffed Mushrooms (324), *leftover* Italiano Salad
27	[MA] N'Oatmeal (288), Apple Sage Sausage (272)	*leftover* Grandma Barbara's Stuffed Mushrooms, green salad* with EVOO, pineapple	Orange Sesame Meatballs (328), Cilantro Cauli-Rice (412)
28	*leftover* N'Oatmeal, *leftover* Apple Sage Sausage	*leftover* Orange Sesame Meatballs, *leftover* Cilantro Cauli-Rice, pineapple	Lemon & Artichoke Chicken (296), Baked Beets with Fennel (420)
29	[MA] Apple Cinnamon Egg Muffins (280), bacon or sausage	*leftover* Lemon & Artichoke Chicken, *leftover* Baked Beets with Fennel	The Easiest Tacos (362), Crispy Plantain Chips (431), Pineapple Salsa (433)
30	*leftover* Apple Cinnamon Egg Muffins, bacon or sausage	*leftover* The Easiest Tacos, *leftover* Crispy Plantain Chips, *leftover* Pineapple Salsa	Mini Mediterranean Kebabs (352), Sautéed Spinach with Pine Nuts & Currants* (423)

» *A complete shopping list for this meal plan can be found on balancedbites.com*

NOTES

*: or other green vegetable; green salad is any lettuce and/or non-starchy vegetables
**: or other starchy vegetable (refer to page 75)
EVOO: Extra-virgin olive oil, or use any dressing from pages 434–435 on salads
CO: Coconut oil
MA: Make-Ahead all or part of the recipe
NR: No Recipe (use any simple prep)

If no page number is listed, simply prepare the items as noted or any way you like. For additional protein, vegetable, and fat recommendations, refer to the QUICK LIST that is associated with your meal plan!

Neurological Health

30-DAY MEAL PLANS

Before trying the menu for this slightly more limited plan, you may want to follow the lifestyle, supplement, and nutrient recommendations from this plan and the monthly menu from the Blood Sugar Regulation 30-Day Meal Plan (page 180).

parkinson's disease
symptoms include:

» Slowed movement
» Muscular rigidity and tightness
» Resting tremor that improves with movement
» Postural instability (using a shuffle or tiny steps to maintain balance)

alzheimer's disease
symptoms include:

» Memory loss, progressive short- and long-term impairment that is more severe than is typically associated with age
» Repetitive questioning
» Decline in vocabulary (word loss)
» Forgetting of familiar names
» Difficulty with numbers, spatial relations, and time

Other populations who may benefit from this meal plan include:

» Epileptics
» Type 2 diabetics
» Anyone seeking a ketogenic diet approach

DISCLAIMER:
The information in this book is not intended to be a replacement for professional medical diagnosis or treatment for a medical condition. It consists solely of nutritional and lifestyle recommendations to support a healthier body.

diet & lifestyle recommendations

add [+]

FATS
Eat more fats in order to fuel the brain with ketones rather than glucose (see the guide to fats and oils on page 64). Coconut oil is especially therapeutic.

ANTIOXIDANT-RICH FOODS
Eat deeply colored foods such as leafy greens, berries, and carrots.

ORGANIC
Eat organic as often as possible to avoid toxins.

POSITIVE MINDSET
Cultivate a positive mental outlook by creating a gratitude list regularly (see page 120). A positive mental outlook is often a result of feeling that we have control over our own lives, and it can yield calmer thoughts overall.

STRESS MANAGEMENT
Develop a guided meditation or slow-breathing practice, or begin to practice qigong. Practice biofeedback, tai chi, and/or guided imagery for deep relaxation.

DETOX
Consider detoxification methods for heavy metals (particularly mercury).

MENTAL EXERCISES
Practice mental exercises to keep the brain active and engaged, such as reading, puzzles, games, and anything else that is mentally stimulating and enjoyable.

HYDROTHERAPY
Try hydrotherapy, a water-based pain relief physiotherapy treatment.

MASSAGE
For Parkinson's disease, get gentle massages. Look into the Feldenkrais method and find a practitioner.

avoid [–]

GLUTEN & DAIRY
100% of the time. See the guide to gluten on page 107. Avoid dairy because of a potential morphine-like effect. (Butter and ghee are okay.)

STARCHY CARBOHYDRATES
Consume 50 g of carbs per day. Create a food journal if necessary to keep track.

RESTAURANTS / DINING OUT
Avoid the damaged and man-made fats most often used in restaurant foods.

SWEETENERS, CAFFEINE
These can provoke blood sugar fluctuations and systemic stress.

ALCOHOL, TOBACCO, NICOTINE & MSG
These are products that require detoxification and/or may have some neurotoxic effects.

HARSH CLEANING & HYGIENE PRODUCTS
Opt for gentle, natural alternatives, such as soap nuts for laundry, vinegar and water for cleaning countertops, and baking soda and peroxide for cleaning and whitening surfaces, laundry, teeth, and more. Consider skipping shampoo and going "no-poo" instead. Safe makeup recommendations may be found at skindeep.org.

FERMENTED FOODS
If you are prone to migraines, avoid the tyramines found in fermented foods.

DENTAL AMALGAMS (SILVER FILLINGS)
Consider holistic or biological dentistry to replace existing amalgams.

HIGH-INTENSITY EXERCISE
Overly intense exercise (high-intensity interval training or similar workouts) and chronic cardiovascular exercise (30–60+ minutes at a steady state of intensity, like jogging or biking) can provoke a stress response in the body.

nutritional supplements & herbs to consider

These recommendations are made as a starting point. Do your own research and determine which supplements may serve you best. Remember that supplements should be used for a short period of time, one to six months, and that it's best to get as many of your nutrients from food as possible. See page 231 for specific food-based nutrients on which to focus. The items below are listed in no particular order.

» **LIPOIC ACID (alpha-lipoic acid)** has antioxidant properties and may improve cellular energy production and support liver function.

» **ACETYL L-CARNITINE** may help to preserve glutathione levels in the body. Glutathione is an important neuro-protective nutrient.

» **VITAMIN C** is a potent antioxidant with anti-inflammatory properties that supports immune function. It promotes collagen production and supports carnitine synthesis. It also helps to regenerate vitamin E and improves iron absorption.

» **COENZYME Q10** (CoQ10, ubiquinone) enhances cellular energy production, and it can help alleviate fatigue as well as muscle and joint pain. Statin drugs are known to deplete CoQ10.

» **VITAMIN D** is a potent immune system modulator that is best obtained from sun exposure. Proper balance with vitamin A is important.

» **GABA** is a calming neurotransmitter that can be helpful if you have trouble sleeping.

» **GINKGO BILOBA** is a potent antioxidant herb.

» **5-HTP** can help to increase dopamine and possibly alleviate pain.

» **MAGNESIUM** is required for more than 300 enzymatic processes in the body, and most people are deficient in it. It is also useful in blood sugar regulation. Look for magnesium glycinate or magnesium malate forms.

» **MILK THISTLE** supports liver detox and is available in herbal tea, tincture, or capsule form.

» **N-ACETYL CYSTEINE (NAC)** supports liver function.

» **OMEGA-3 FATS** are anti-inflammatory essential fatty acids.

» **PASSIONFLOWER** may help to reduce tremors in Parkinson's disease.

» **PHOSPHATIDYLCHOLINE** enhances the integrity of the GI tract, repairs the mucosal lining of the gut, and aids in fatty acid digestion. This supplement is especially important if you are avoiding eggs.

» **PHOSPHATIDYLSERINE** supports cell membrane integrity and may improve memory and cognition. It has been shown to blunt the release of cortisol in response to stress.

» **PROBIOTICS** promote healthy gut flora, which is critical for proper digestion and elimination.

» **SAM-e** may help to prevent oxidative damage, maintain cognitive function, and improve mental outlook.

» **SELENIUM** is an antioxidant that is antagonistic to heavy metals like lead, mercury, cadmium, and aluminum. It supports cancer recovery, immune function, cardiac health, inflammatory conditions, vision, and proper fetal growth. Absorption may be decreased by high zinc intake, so these minerals should be balanced.

» **SUPER OXIDE DISMUTASE (SOD)** is an anti-inflammatory that prevents free-radical damage.

» **DIGESTIVE ENZYMES** help to break down food for absorption while your gut is healing. Look for a blend of enzymes.

» **ZINC** is a potent antioxidant that aids in vitamin A metabolism. People with inflammatory conditions are often deficient in zinc. It should be balanced with selenium.

supportive nutrients & foods that contain them

B VITAMINS
Critical in assisting neurotransmitters and therefore important for brain health and for the proper functioning of nerves and muscles
» Liver, bison, lamb
» Flounder, haddock, salmon, trout, tuna
» Brewer's yeast (Lewis Labs brand only)
» Mushrooms
» Hazelnuts, walnuts
» Trace amounts: pecans, sunflower seeds, broccoli, Brussels sprouts, other dark leafy greens

VITAMIN C
A potent antioxidant with anti-inflammatory properties
» Beets, bell peppers, broccoli, Brussels sprouts, cauliflower, collard greens, daikon radishes, garlic, kale, mustard greens, parsley, spinach
» Lemons, strawberries

VITAMIN D
A potent immune system modulator that is best obtained from sun exposure
» Cold-water fish (salmon, herring, mackerel)
» Grass-fed butter or ghee

CHOLINE
Important for cell membrane integrity, nerve-muscle communication, and liver function
» Eggs
» Organ meat: liver, heart, kidneys
» Fish roe (eggs), caviar, cod
» Cauliflower (cooked)

VITAMIN E
An antioxidant that benefits neurological function, smooth-muscle growth, and cellular communication
» Broccoli, Brussels sprouts, spinach (cooked)
» Extra-virgin olive oil
» Pecans

GLUTATHIONE
An antioxidant that aids in liver detox processes
» Asparagus, broccoli, garlic
» Avocado
» Cumin, ginger, turmeric

LIPOIC ACID (ALA)
May improve cellular energy production and has antioxidant properties
» Red meat, organ meats

MAGNESIUM
Critical for cellular energy production, which helps battle fatigue, and for proper calcium metabolism, which is necessary for vascular health
» Beets, kale, other green leafy vegetables
» Pumpkin seeds (pepitas)

OMEGA-3 FATS
An anti-inflammatory essential fatty acid
» Cold-water fish, such as salmon, herring, and mackerel
» Pecans, walnuts

POTASSIUM
Supports nerve function and smooth muscle contractions
» Avocado
» Spinach, Swiss chard

PROBIOTICS
Promote healthy gut flora, which is critical for proper digestion and elimination, Limit or avoid these foods if you are prone to migraines.
» Fermented vegetables: cabbage (sauerkraut/kimchi), carrots, beets
» Kombucha (fermented tea)

SELENIUM
An antioxidant that protects against free-radical damage
» Eggs
» Garlic, red Swiss chard, turnips

ZINC
A potent antioxidant often low in people with inflammatory conditions; aids in vitamin A metabolism
» Oysters, shellfish
» Lamb, red meat
» Pumpkin seeds (pepitas)

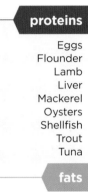

quick LIST

proteins
Eggs
Flounder
Lamb
Liver
Mackerel
Oysters
Shellfish
Trout
Tuna

fats
Coconut oil
Extra-virgin olive oil
Grass-fed butter/ghee
Walnuts

vegetables
Beets
Broccoli
Brussels sprouts
Butternut squash
Cauliflower
Daikon radish
Leafy greens
Okra
Spinach
Sweet potatoes

fruits
Blueberries
Lemons
Oranges
Strawberries

superfoods
Bone broth
Liver

spices
Basil
Cilantro
Cinnamon
Cumin
Garlic
Ginger
Oregano
Parsley
Turmeric

DAY	BREAKFAST	LUNCH	DINNER
1	Swirly Crustless Quiche (270), Perfectly Baked Bacon (260), [MA] Raw Sauerkraut (262)	[MA] Mustard-Glazed Chicken Thighs (317), green salad* with Balsamic Vinaigrette (434)	Grilled Garlic Flank Steak with Peppers & Onions (334), [NR] spinach* with ghee (261)
2	*leftover* Swirly Crustless Quiche, *leftover* Grilled Garlic Flank Steak with Peppers & Onions	[NR] canned wild salmon with olives, avocado, lemon juice, tomato, EVOO over green salad*	Bacon Jalapeño Burgers (360), [NR] roasted broccoli* with ghee (261)
3	*leftover* Mustard-Glazed Chicken Thighs, *leftover* roasted broccoli*	*leftover* Bacon Jalapeño Burgers, green salad* with Balsamic Vinaigrette (434)	[MA] Lemony Lamb Dolmas (368), Cilantro Cauli-Rice (412)
4	Pesto Scrambled Eggs (286), *leftover* Cilantro Cauli-Rice, [MA] Raw Sauerkraut (262)	*leftover* Lemony Lamb Dolmas, green salad* with EVOO	Citrus Macadamia Nut Sole (378), [NR] roasted cauliflower* with ghee (261)
5	*leftover* Citrus Macadamia Nut Sole, [NR] butternut squash**	Nori Salmon Handroll (388)	Beef & Veggie Stir-Fry (348), berries
6	breakfast sausage made with Italian Blend (256) & ground meat, [NR] kale* cooked in CO	*leftover* Beef & Veggie Stir-Fry, berries	Lamb Lettuce Boats with Avoziki Sauce (370)
7	[NR] eggs any style, Perfectly Baked Bacon (260), kale*, [MA] Raw Sauerkraut (262)	green salad* with canned wild salmon, asparagus*, lemon juice with EVOO	Citrus & Herb Whole Roasted Chicken (292), Simple Baked Kale Chips* (425), cauliflower*
8	[NR] eggs any style, Perfectly Baked Bacon (260), kale*, [MA] Raw Sauerkraut (262)	Dairy-Free Caesar Salad without the potatoes (396), *leftover* Citrus & Herb Whole Roasted Chicken	Restaurant-Style Lettuce Cups (312), berries
9	Swirly Crustless Quiche (270), [NR] steamed broccoli*, [MA] Raw Sauerkraut (262)	Indian Spiced Burgers with Smashed Roasted Garlic (342), [NR] steamed broccoli*	Pesto Fettuccine with Shrimp (380), berries
10	Pesto Scrambled Eggs (286), *leftover* Pesto Fettuccine with Shrimp, sliced avocado	Simple Shrimp Ceviche (389), green salad* with EVOO	Cumin-Spiced Pork Tenderloin (320), green salad* with EVOO, cauliflower*
11	[MA] Home Fries & Sausage Skillet made with parsnips instead of potatoes (268), berries	*leftover* Cumin-Spiced Pork Tenderloin, green salad* with EVOO, cauliflower*	Balsamic Braised Short Ribs (332), Mashed Faux-Tatoes (418), green salad* with EVOO
12	*leftover* Home Fries & Sausage Skillet, berries	*leftover* Balsamic Braised Short Ribs, *leftover* Mashed Faux-Tatoes, green salad* with EVOO	Mediterranean Baked Chicken with Cauliflower (294), spinach*
13	[MA] Zucchini Pancakes (271), Perfectly Baked Bacon (260), [MA] Raw Sauerkraut (262)	*leftover* Mediterranean Baked Chicken with Cauliflower, spinach*	Lemon Rosemary Broiled Salmon (375), Asparagus with Lemon & Olives (409), kale*
14	*leftover* Lemon Rosemary Broiled Salmon, *leftover* Asparagus with Lemon & Olives*	[MA] Buffalo Chicken Lettuce Wraps (299), berries	Grilled Tuna Over Fresh Noodle Salad (384), berries
15	[NR] scrambled eggs with olives, [NR] steamed spinach*, avocado, [MA] Raw Sauerkraut (262)	*leftover* Grilled Tuna Over Fresh Noodle Salad	Italian-Style Stuffed Peppers (358), green salad* with Balsamic Vinaigrette (434)
16	[NR] scrambled eggs with olives, [NR] steamed spinach*, avocado, [MA] Raw Sauerkraut (262)	*leftover* Italian-Style Stuffed Peppers, green salad* with EVOO, berries	Bacon-Wrapped Smoky Chicken Thighs (298), green salad* with EVOO, berries

Neurological Health

DAY	BREAKFAST	LUNCH	DINNER
17	[MA] Bacon & Egg Salad (287), avocado, spinach or kale*, [MA] Raw Sauerkraut (262)	*leftover* Bacon-Wrapped Smoky Chicken Thighs, green salad* with EVOO	Spaghetti Squash Bolognese (338), Simple Baked Kale Chips* (425)
18	*leftover* Bacon & Egg Salad, avocado, spinach or kale*, [MA] Raw Sauerkraut (262)	*leftover* Spaghetti Squash Bolognese, green salad* with EVOO	Thanksgiving Stuffing Meatballs (326), Mashed Faux-Tatoes (418), broccoli*
19	[MA] Home Fries & Sausage Skillet with parsnips instead of potatoes (268), berries	*leftover* Thanksgiving Stuffing Meatballs, *leftover* Mashed Faux-Tatoes, broccoli*	Lemon & Bacon Scallops made without roasted potatoes (376), Lemon Roasted Romanesco* (417)
20	*leftover* Home Fries & Sausage Skillet, berries	*leftover* Lemon & Bacon Scallops, *leftover* Lemon Roasted Romanesco*	Orange & Olive Braised Chicken (306), Yellow Cauli-Rice (413), green salad* with EVOO
21	[MA] breakfast sausage made with Italian Blend (256) & ground meat, [NR] eggs any style, Raw Sauerkraut (262)	[MA] Six-Minute Salmon Bowls (382)	Souvlaki Kebabs (290), Greek Salad with Avoziki Dressing (402), berries
22	[MA] Breakfast Fried "Rice" (266), avocado, berries	*leftover* Souvlaki Kebabs, *leftover* Greek Salad with Avoziki Dressing, berries	Orange Braised Beef (344), Roasted Brussels Sprouts (416)
23	*leftover* Breakfast Fried "Rice," avocado, berries	*leftover* Orange Braised Beef, *leftover* Roasted Brussels Sprouts	Hayley's Skirt Steak Tacos (346), choice of salsa (433)
24	[NR] eggs any style, Perfectly Baked Bacon (260), [NR] kale* cooked in CO, [MA] Raw Sauerkraut (262)	[MA] Tangy Taco Salad (350), *leftover* salsa	Bacon & Superfood Meatloaf (330), Mashed Faux-Tatoes (418), green salad* with EVOO
25	[NR] eggs any style, Perfectly Baked Bacon (260), avocado, kale*, [MA] Raw Sauerkraut (262)	[MA] Quick & Easy Salmon Cakes (374), green salad* with EVOO, avocado, olives	Seared Scallops with Orange Glaze (386), Cilantro Cauli-Rice (412), [NR] steamed bok choy*
26	[MA] Zucchini Pancakes (271), Perfectly Baked Bacon (260), avocado	[MA] Italiano Salad (398), Basil Shallot Vinaigrette (434)	Grandma Barbara's Stuffed Mushrooms (324), *leftover* Italiano Salad
27	Swirly Crustless Quiche (270), Perfectly Baked Bacon (260), [MA] Raw Sauerkraut (262)	*leftover* Grandma Barbara's Stuffed Mushrooms, green salad* with EVOO	Orange Sesame Meatballs (328), Cilantro Cauli-Rice (412)
28	*leftover* Swirly Crustless Quiche, breakfast sausage made with Italian Blend (256) & ground meat	*leftover* Orange Sesame Meatballs, *leftover* Cilantro Cauli-Rice	Lemon & Artichoke Chicken (296), Broc-Cauli Chowder with Bacon (392)
29	[MA] Apple Cinnamon Egg Muffins (280), Perfectly Baked Bacon (260) or sausage	*leftover* Lemon & Artichoke Chicken, *leftover* Broc-Cauli Chowder with Bacon	The Easiest Tacos (362), choice of salsa (433), avocado, berries
30	*leftover* Apple Cinnamon Egg Muffins, Perfectly Baked Bacon (260) or sausage	*leftover* The Easiest Tacos, *leftover* salsa, avocado, berries	Mini Mediterranean Kebabs (352), Sautéed Spinach with Pine Nuts & Currants* (423)

» *A complete shopping list for this meal plan can be found on balancedbites.com*

NOTES

*: or other green vegetable; green salad is any lettuce and/or non-starchy vegetable

**: or other starchy vegetable (refer to page 75)

EVOO: Extra-virgin olive oil, or use any dressing from pages 434–435 on salads

CO: Coconut oil

MA: Make-Ahead all or part of the recipe

NR: No Recipe (use any simple prep)

For Parkinson's disease: If you take levodopa, do not eat foods rich in vitamin B6 (like bananas, liver, and fish) while taking the medication. Stick to smaller protein portions before doses and a larger portion of protein in the evening after your final dose.

If no page number is listed, simply prepare the items as noted or any way you like. For additional protein, vegetable, and fat recommendations, refer to the QUICK LIST that is associated with your meal plan!

Squeaky Clean Paleo

30-DAY MEAL PLANS

If you are not looking for help with a specific condition or goal but would rather simply take on what is known as a strict or "clean" Paleo diet, this is the plan for you. You'll be eating only whole foods, without any grain-free treats. This approach requires that you read labels especially closely to catch additives that can sneak into your foods, especially hidden sugar and gluten.

There are no specific nutrient or supplement recommendations for this plan. If you have particular health goals, please refer to the other 30-Day Meal Plans and use those recommendations for this plan.

DISCLAIMER:

The information in this book is not intended to be a replacement for professional medical diagnosis or treatment for a medical condition. It consists solely of nutritional and lifestyle recommendations to support a healthier body.

diet & lifestyle recommendations

add [+]

SUPERFOODS & PROBIOTICS

Eat superfoods as often as possible (see page 61). Consume 1/4 cup raw sauerkraut (page 262) or other fermented vegetables daily, especially with breakfast.

PROTEIN

Eat protein to satisfy the appetite for longer periods (meals focused on both fat and protein will help).

NUTRIENT-DENSE FOODS

Replenish nutrient stores that have been depleted by excess refined foods.

STARCHY CARBOHYDRATES AFTER EXERCISE

Eat approximately 30–75 g of carbohydrates before and after a workout (see page 75 for nutrient-dense carb sources). The exact amount will depend on the length of the workout. Track how you feel and add or subtract carbs if you are not making progress or don't feel well-fueled for exercise the next day.

SMART TRAINING

Listen to your body and take rest and recovery days when necessary.

STRESS MANAGEMENT

Develop a guided meditation or slow-breathing practice, or begin to practice qigong. Practice biofeedback, tai chi, and/or guided imagery for deep relaxation.

SLEEP

Sleep at least eight hours every night in a dark room in order to wake up refreshed and without cravings during the day.

avoid [–]

GLUTEN & DAIRY

Gluten 100% of the time. See the guide to gluten on page 107. Avoid dairy for its potentially gut-irritating or allergenic effects. (Butter and ghee are okay.)

REFINED FOODS & SWEETENERS

Artificial sweeteners and caffeine can provoke blood sugar fluctuations.

EXCESS CAFFEINE

Caffeine can be a stressor and may increase cortisol response and promote weight-loss resistance.

ALCOHOL

DAY	BREAKFAST	LUNCH	DINNER
1	Swirly Crustless Quiche (270), Perfectly Baked Bacon (260), [MA] Raw Sauerkraut (262)	[MA] Mustard-Glazed Chicken Thighs (317), green salad* with Balsamic Vinaigrette (434)	Grilled Garlic Flank Steak with Peppers & Onions (334), [NR] baked potato** with ghee (261)
2	leftover Swirly Crustless Quiche, leftover Grilled Garlic Flank Steak with Peppers & Onions	[NR] canned wild salmon with olives, avocado, lemon juice, tomato, EVOO over green salad*	Bacon Jalapeño Burgers (360), Sweet Potato Pancakes (285), [NR] steamed spinach*
3	leftover Sweet Potato Pancakes, leftover Mustard-Glazed Chicken Thighs	leftover Bacon Jalapeño Burgers, green salad* with Balsamic Vinaigrette (434)	[MA] Lemony Lamb Dolmas (368), Cilantro Cauli-Rice (412)
4	Pesto Scrambled Eggs (286), leftover Cilantro Cauli-Rice, [MA] Raw Sauerkraut (262)	leftover Lemony Lamb Dolmas, green salad* with EVOO	Citrus Macadamia Nut Sole (378), [NR] butternut squash**
5	leftover Citrus Macadamia Nut Sole, leftover butternut squash**	Nori Salmon Handroll (388)	Beef & Veggie Stir-Fry (348)
6	Pumpkin Pancakes (284), breakfast sausage made with Italian Blend (256) & ground meat	leftover Beef & Veggie Stir-Fry	Lamb Lettuce Boats with Avoziki Sauce (370)
7	[NR] eggs any style, Perfectly Baked Bacon (260), kale*, [MA] Raw Sauerkraut (262)	green salad* with canned wild salmon, asparagus*, lemon juice with EVOO	Citrus & Herb Whole Roasted Chicken (292), Simple Baked Kale Chips* (425), [NR] sweet potato**
8	N'Oatmeal (288), berries, [NR] eggs any style	Dairy-Free Caesar Salad (396), leftover Citrus & Herb Whole Roasted Chicken	Restaurant-Style Lettuce Cups (312)
9	Swirly Crustless Quiche (270), [NR] steamed broccoli*, [MA] Raw Sauerkraut (262)	Indian Spiced Burgers with Smashed Roasted Garlic (342), [NR] steamed broccoli*	Pesto Fettuccine with Shrimp (380)
10	Pesto Scrambled Eggs (286), leftover Pesto Fettuccine with Shrimp, sliced avocado	Simple Shrimp Ceviche (389), green salad* with EVOO	Coffee BBQ Rubbed Pork with Seared Pineapple (318), green salad* with EVOO
11	[MA] Home Fries & Sausage Skillet (268)	leftover Coffee BBQ Rubbed Pork with Seared Pineapple, green salad* with EVOO	Balsamic Braised Short Ribs (332), Candied Carrots (415), green salad* with EVOO
12	leftover Home Fries & Sausage Skillet	leftover Balsamic Braised Short Ribs, leftover Candied Carrots, green salad* with EVOO	Mediterranean Baked Chicken with Cauliflower (294), [NR] baked potato**
13	[MA] Zucchini Pancakes (271), Perfectly Baked Bacon (260), [MA] Raw Sauerkraut (262)	leftover Mediterranean Baked Chicken with Cauliflower	Lemon Rosemary Broiled Salmon (375), Asparagus with Lemon & Olives (409), [NR] sweet potato**
14	leftover Lemon Rosemary Broiled Salmon, leftover Asparagus with Lemon & Olives	[MA] Buffalo Chicken Lettuce Wraps (299)	Grilled Tuna Over Fresh Noodle Salad (384)
15	[NR] scrambled eggs with olives, [NR] steamed spinach*, avocado	leftover Grilled Tuna Over Fresh Noodle Salad	Italian-Style Stuffed Peppers (358), green salad* with Balsamic Vinaigrette (434)
16	Peach Blueberry Smoothie (289), [MA] Blueberry Maple Sausage (273)	leftover Italian-Style Stuffed Peppers, green salad* with EVOO	Bacon-Wrapped Smoky Chicken Thighs (298), green salad* with EVOO

Squeaky Clean Paleo

DAY	BREAKFAST	LUNCH	DINNER
17	[MA] Bacon & Egg Salad (287), avocado, spinach or kale*, [MA] Raw Sauerkraut (262)	*leftover* Bacon-Wrapped Smoky Chicken Thighs, green salad* with EVOO	Spaghetti Squash Bolognese (338), Simple Baked Kale Chips* (425)
18	[MA] Pumpkin Pancakes (284), *leftover* Blueberry Maple Sausage	*leftover* Spaghetti Squash Bolognese, green salad* with EVOO	Thanksgiving Stuffing Meatballs (326), Simple Cranberry Sauce (436), Mashed Faux-Tatoes (418)
19	*leftover* Bacon & Egg Salad, avocado, spinach or kale*, [MA] Raw Sauerkraut (262)	*leftover* Thanksgiving Stuffing Meatballs, *leftover* Cranberry Sauce, *leftover* Mashed Faux-Tatoes	Lemon & Bacon Scallops with Roasted Potatoes (376), Lemon Roasted Romanesco* (417)
20	Paleo Avocado "Toast" (264), [NR] eggs any style	*leftover* Lemon & Bacon Scallops, *leftover* Lemon Roasted Romanesco*	Orange & Olive Braised Chicken (306), Yellow Cauli-Rice (413), green salad* with EVOO
21	[MA] breakfast sausage made with Italian Blend (256) & ground meat, [NR] eggs any style, Raw Sauerkraut (262)	[MA] Six-Minute Salmon Bowls (382)	Souvlaki Kebabs (290), Greek Salad with Avoziki Dressing (402)
22	[MA] Breakfast Fried "Rice" (266)	*leftover* Souvlaki Kebabs, *leftover* Greek Salad with Avoziki Dressing	Orange Braised Beef (344), Butternut Sage Soup** (394)
23	*leftover* Breakfast Fried "Rice"	*leftover* Orange Braised Beef, *leftover* Butternut Sage Soup**	Hayley's Skirt Steak Tacos (346), choice of salsa (433), Smoky Grilled Squash & Pineapple (408)
24	[NR] eggs any style, bacon, *leftover* Smoky Grilled Squash & Pineapple	[MA] Tangy Taco Salad (350), *leftover* salsa	Bacon & Superfood Meatloaf (330), Mashed Faux-Tatoes (418), green salad* with EVOO
25	[NR] eggs any style, avocado, spinach or kale*, [MA] Raw Sauerkraut (262)	[MA] Quick & Easy Salmon Cakes (374), green salad* with EVOO, avocado, olives	Seared Scallops with Orange Glaze (386), Cilantro Cauli-Rice (412), [NR] steamed bok choy*
26	[MA] Zucchini Pancakes (271), Perfectly Baked Bacon (260)	[MA] Italiano Salad (398), Honey Mustard Dressing (434)	Grandma Barbara's Stuffed Mushrooms (324), *leftover* Italiano Salad
27	[MA] N'Oatmeal (288), Apple Sage Sausage (272)	*leftover* Grandma Barbara's Stuffed Mushrooms, green salad* with EVOO	Orange Sesame Meatballs (328), Cilantro Cauli-Rice (412)
28	*leftover* N'Oatmeal, *leftover* Apple Sage Sausage	*leftover* Orange Sesame Meatballs, *leftover* Cilantro Cauli-Rice	Lemon & Artichoke Chicken (296), Broc-Cauli Chowder with Bacon (392)
29	[MA] Apple Cinnamon Egg Muffins (280), bacon or sausage	*leftover* Lemon & Artichoke Chicken, *leftover* Broc-Cauli Chowder with Bacon	The Easiest Tacos (362), Crispy Plantain Chips (431), choice of salsa (433)
30	*leftover* Apple Cinnamon Egg Muffins, bacon or sausage	*leftover* The Easiest Tacos, *leftover* Crispy Plantain Chips, *leftover* salsa	Mini Mediterranean Kebabs (352), Sautéed Spinach with Pine Nuts & Currants* (423)

» *A complete shopping list for this meal plan can be found on balancedbites.com*

NOTES

*****: or other green vegetable; green salad is any lettuce and/or non-starchy vegetables
******: or other starchy vegetable (refer to page 75)
EVOO: Extra-virgin olive oil, or use any dressing from pages 434–435 on salads
CO: Coconut oil
MA: Make-Ahead all or part of the recipe
NR: No Recipe (use any simple prep)

If no page number is listed, simply prepare the items as noted or any way you like. For additional protein, vegetable, and fat recommendations, refer to the QUICK LIST that is associated with your meal plan!

Thyroid Health

30-DAY MEAL PLANS

Thyroid disorders can be very delicate to balance, so I strongly recommend that you work closely with a trusted health-care practitioner in making dietary, lifestyle, and nutritional supplement changes.

If you have been recently diagnosed with a thyroid condition or are new to the Paleo way of eating, use the lifestyle, supplement, and nutrient recommendations from this plan and the monthly menu from the Autoimmune Conditions 30-Day Meal Plan (page 174).

hypothyroidism (autoimmune Hashimoto's or otherwise)
symptoms include:

» Difficulty losing weight
» Sudden weight gain
» Constipation
» Fatigue
» Lethargy

» Low energy
» Irregular menstrual cycles, female hormonal imbalances
» Low body temperature

hyperthyroidism
symptoms include:

» Enlarged thyroid
» Bulging eyes
» Rash on lower legs
» Rapid heartbeat

» Weight loss
» Fatigue
» Anxiety
» Diarrhea

Note: Hyperthyroidism is less common than hypothyroidism.

DISCLAIMER:
The information in this book is not intended to be a replacement for professional medical diagnosis or treatment for a medical condition. It consists solely of nutritional and lifestyle recommendations to support a healthier body.

diet & lifestyle recommendations

add [+]

PROTEIN

Add protein to satisfy appetite for longer periods of time (meals focused on both fat and protein will help).

NUTRIENT-DENSE FOODS

Replenish nutrient stores that have been depleted by excess refined foods.

SUPERFOODS

Eat superfoods as often as possible (see page 61). Make bone broth (page 259) and drink it or cook with it regularly. Make liver regularly. Use the sauerkraut recipe on page 262 to make fermented carrots or beets and consume 1/4 cup daily, especially with breakfast.

SAFE SUN EXPOSURE

Ten minutes of sun exposure each day when the sun is at its peak, or longer when the sun is not as strong, promotes vitamin D production. Do not burn.

STRESS MANAGEMENT

Develop a guided meditation or slow-breathing practice, or begin to practice qigong.

MOVEMENT

For movement without systemic stress, take walks outside, swim (not for speed!), or practice gentle yoga.

avoid [–]

GLUTEN

100% of the time. See the guide to gluten on page 107.

EXCESS GOITROGENIC FOODS

Eat only cooked goitrogenic (potentially thyroid-inhibiting) foods and avoid raw and fermented goitrogenic vegetables (like cabbage) as fermentation increases goitrogen levels. See page 61 for a list of Paleo foods with goitrogens.

REFINED FOODS, SWEETENERS & CAFFEINE

These can all provoke blood sugar fluctuations and systemic stress, which inhibit thyroid function.

ALCOHOL

It can induce hypoglycemic events, which inhibit thyroid function.

STRESS

Make lifestyle changes to avoid stressful situations.

CHRONIC CARDIOVASCULAR EXERCISE

30–60+ minutes of cardiovascular exercise at a steady state of intensity, like jogging or biking, can lead to episodes of low blood sugar, as well as provoke a stress response.

nutritional supplements & herbs to consider

These recommendations are made as a starting point. Do your own research and determine which supplements may serve you best. Remember that supplements should be used for a short period of time, one to six months, and that it's best to get as many of your nutrients from food as possible. See page 241 for specific food-based nutrients on which to focus. The items below are listed in no particular order.

» **VITAMIN A (retinol)** helps to maintain the integrity of the mucosal lining of the gut. It also helps maintain immunity when balanced with vitamin D, and it is necessary for the assimilation of dietary minerals.

» **ADAPTOGENIC HERBS** help modulate energy up or down as your body requires. Rotate among ashwagandha, holy basil, and rhodiola

» **VITAMIN B5 (pantothenic acid & pantethine)** is needed for the manufacture of adrenal hormones and red blood cells, which makes it beneficial for energy.

» **VITAMIN B7 (biotin)** is a coenzyme required for the metabolism of glucose, amino acids, and lipids.

» **VITAMIN B12 (cobalamin)** supports energy metabolism and immune function, and it may help regulate circadian rhythms by improving melatonin secretion. (In other words, it may help you sleep better.)

» **VITAMIN C** is a potent antioxidant with anti-inflammatory properties that supports immune function.

» **CHROMIUM (chromium picolinate, polynicotinate, chelavite)** may improve insulin sensitivity and reduce appetite.

» **VITAMIN D** is a potent immune system modulator that is best obtained from sun exposure. Proper balance with vitamin A is important.

» **VITAMIN E** is an antioxidant that benefits cellular communication and may reduce oxidative stress-induced insulin resistance.

» **IODINE** may support healing of hyperthyroidism and non-autoimmune thyroiditis. However, it may exacerbate problems in those with Hashimoto's/autoimmune thyroiditis. If you have Hashimoto's or are unsure of the type of hypothyroidism you have, do not supplement with iodine. Consult a health-care practitioner before supplementing with iodine.

» **MAGNESIUM** is required for more than 300 enzymatic processes in the body, and most people are deficient in it. It is also useful in blood sugar regulation. Look for magnesium glycinate or magnesium malate forms.

» **OMEGA-3 FATS** are anti-inflammatory essential fatty acids.

» **PROBIOTICS** promote healthy gut flora, which is critical for proper digestion and elimination. Hypothyroidism is commonly associated with constipation.

» **SELENIUM** is an antioxidant that is important in the production of thyroid hormone. It is antagonistic to heavy metals like lead, mercury, cadmium, and aluminum. Absorption may be decreased by high zinc intake, so it must be balanced with zinc.

» **THYROID GLANDULAR** helps with hypothyroidism—work with your health-care practitioner to determine if this is right for you.

» **ZINC** is a potent antioxidant that aids in vitamin A metabolism. People with inflammatory conditions are often deficient in zinc.

» **MANGANESE** is beneficial for energy metabolism and thyroid hormone function. Intake should be balanced with magnesium, calcium, iron, copper, and zinc. Antacids may inhibit manganese absorption.

supportive nutrients & foods that contain them

Thyroid Health

VITAMIN A (RETINOL)
Helps maintain the lining of the gut
» Liver, eel
» Grass-fed butter, clarified butter, or ghee

VITAMIN B5
Essential for the manufacture of adrenal hormones and red blood cells
» Liver
» Brewer's yeast (Lewis Labs brand only)
» Mushrooms
» Trace amounts: pecans, sunflower seeds

VITAMIN B7
Required for the metabolism of glucose, amino acids, and lipids
» Liver
» Brewer's yeast (Lewis Labs brand only)
» Trace amounts: Swiss chard, walnuts, pecans, almonds

VITAMIN B12
Supports energy metabolism and immune function
» Liver, kidneys
» Flounder, halibut, salmon, sardines, trout, tuna
» Clams, oysters, scallops
» Eggs, beef, lamb
» Cheese (raw/grass-fed)

VITAMIN C
A potent antioxidant with anti-inflammatory properties
» Beets, bell peppers, broccoli, Brussels sprouts, cauliflower, collard greens, daikon radishes, garlic
» Cantaloupes, kiwis, lemons, oranges, papayas, pineapple

CHOLINE
Essential for cell membrane integrity, nerve-muscle communication, and liver function
» Eggs
» Organ meat: liver, heart, kidneys
» Fish roe (eggs), caviar, cod
» Cauliflower (cooked)

CHROMIUM
May improve insulin sensitivity and reduce appetite
» Liver
» Cheese (raw/grass-fed)
» Brewer's yeast (Lewis Labs brand only)
» Trace amounts: apples, carrots, green peppers, parsnips, spinach

VITAMIN E
Benefits cellular communication and may reduce oxidative stress-induced insulin resistance
» Broccoli, Brussels sprouts, spinach
» Extra-virgin olive oil
» Pecans

IODINE
May support healing of hyperthyroidism and non-autoimmune thyroiditis
» Wild fish
» Seaweed, kelp, dulse

LIPOIC ACID (ALA)
May improve cellular energy production and has antioxidant properties
» Red meat, organ meats

MANGANESE
Beneficial for blood sugar regulation, energy metabolism, and thyroid hormone function
» Beet greens, rhubarb, turnip greens
» Pecans, walnuts
» Cinnamon, cloves, thyme, turmeric

OMEGA-3 FATS
An anti-inflammatory essential fatty acid
» Cold-water fish, such as salmon, herring, and mackerel
» Pecans, walnuts

PROBIOTICS
Promote healthy gut flora, which is critical for proper digestion and elimination
» Fermented vegetables: cabbage (sauerkraut/kimchi), carrots, beets
» Kombucha (fermented tea)

SELENIUM
An antioxidant that protects against free-radical damage
» Eggs
» Garlic, red Swiss chard, turnips

ZINC
A potent antioxidant often low in people with inflammatory conditions; aids in vitamin A metabolism
» Oysters, shellfish
» Lamb, red meat
» Pumpkin seeds (pepitas)

quick LIST

proteins

Beef
Herring
Lamb
Mackerel
Oysters
Salmon
Sardines
Shellfish
Tuna

fats

Animal fats
Coconut oil
Extra-virgin olive oil
Grass-fed butter/ghee

vegetables

Beets
Carrots
Fennel
Green beans
Green bell pepper
Lettuce
Mushrooms
Parsnips
Squash
Swiss chard

fruits

Cantaloupes
Citrus
Strawberries
Tropical fruits

superfoods

Bone broth
Fermented carrots
Liver

spices

Basil
Black pepper
Chili powder
Cilantro
Cinnamon
Cloves
Garlic
Thyme
Turmeric

DAY	BREAKFAST	LUNCH	DINNER
1	Swirly Crustless Quiche (270), Perfectly Baked Bacon (260)	[MA] Mustard-Glazed Chicken Thighs (317), green salad* with Balsamic Vinaigrette (434)	Grilled Garlic Flank Steak with Peppers & Onions (334), [NR] baked potato** with ghee (261)
2	leftover Swirly Crustless Quiche, leftover Grilled Garlic Flank Steak with Peppers & Onions	[NR] canned wild salmon with olives, avocado, lemon juice, tomato, EVOO over green salad*	Bacon Jalapeño Burgers (360), Sweet Potato Pancakes (285), [NR] steamed spinach*
3	leftover Sweet Potato Pancakes, leftover Mustard-Glazed Chicken Thighs	leftover Bacon Jalapeño Burgers, green salad* with Balsamic Vinaigrette (434)	[MA] Lemony Lamb Dolmas (368), Cilantro Cauli-Rice (412), berries
4	Pesto Scrambled Eggs (286), leftover Cilantro Cauli-Rice	leftover Lemony Lamb Dolmas, green salad* with EVOO, berries	Citrus Macadamia Nut Sole (378), [NR] butternut squash**
5	leftover Citrus Macadamia Nut Sole, leftover butternut squash**	Nori Salmon Handroll (388), mango	Beef & Veggie Stir-Fry (348), mango
6	Pumpkin Pancakes (284), breakfast sausage made with Italian Blend (256) & ground meat	leftover Beef & Veggie Stir-Fry, mango	Lamb Lettuce Boats with Avoziki Sauce (370), strawberries
7	[NR] eggs any style, Perfectly Baked Bacon (260), [NR] chard*	green salad* with canned wild salmon, asparagus*, lemon juice with EVOO	Citrus & Herb Whole Roasted Chicken (292), Simple Baked Kale Chips* (425), [NR] sweet potato**
8	N'Oatmeal (288), berries, [NR] eggs hard-boiled or any style	Dairy-Free Caesar Salad (396), leftover Citrus & Herb Whole Roasted Chicken	Restaurant-Style Lettuce Cups (312)
9	Swirly Crustless Quiche (270), [NR] steamed broccoli*, fermented carrots (262)	Indian Spiced Burgers with Smashed Roasted Garlic (342), [NR] steamed broccoli*	Pesto Fettuccine with Shrimp (380), strawberries
10	Pesto Scrambled Eggs (286), leftover Pesto Fettuccine with Shrimp, sliced avocado	Simple Shrimp Ceviche (389), green salad* with EVOO, strawberries	Coffee BBQ Rubbed Pork with Seared Pineapple (318), green salad* with EVOO
11	[MA] Home Fries & Sausage Skillet (268), strawberries	leftover Coffee BBQ Rubbed Pork with Seared Pineapple, green salad* with EVOO	Balsamic Braised Short Ribs (332), Candied Carrots (415), green salad* with EVOO
12	leftover Home Fries & Sausage Skillet, strawberries	leftover Balsamic Braised Short Ribs, leftover Candied Carrots, green salad* with EVOO	Mediterranean Baked Chicken with Cauliflower (294), [NR] baked potato**
13	[MA] Zucchini Pancakes (271), Perfectly Baked Bacon (260), fermented carrots (262)	leftover Mediterranean Baked Chicken with Cauliflower	Lemon Rosemary Broiled Salmon (375), Asparagus with Lemon & Olives (409), [NR] sweet potato**
14	leftover Lemon Rosemary Broiled Salmon, leftover Asparagus with Lemon & Olives	[MA] Chicken Liver Pâté (426), cucumber and carrot slices, berries	Grilled Tuna Over Fresh Noodle Salad (384)
15	[NR] scrambled eggs with olives, spinach*, avocado, fermented carrots (262)	leftover Chicken Liver Pâté, cucumber and carrot slices, berries	Italian-Style Stuffed Peppers (358), green salad* with Balsamic Vinaigrette (434)
16	Peach Blueberry Smoothie (289), [MA] Blueberry Maple Sausage (273)	leftover Italian-Style Stuffed Peppers, green salad* with EVOO	Bacon-Wrapped Smoky Chicken Thighs (298), green salad* with EVOO

Thyroid Health

DAY	BREAKFAST	LUNCH	DINNER
17	[MA] Bacon & Egg Salad (287), avocado, spinach or chard*, fermented carrots (262)	*leftover* Bacon-Wrapped Smoky Chicken Thighs, green salad* with EVOO	Spaghetti Squash Bolognese (338), Simple Baked Kale Chips* (425)
18	[MA] Pumpkin Pancakes (284), *leftover* Blueberry Maple Sausage	*leftover* Spaghetti Squash Bolognese, green salad* with EVOO	Thanksgiving Stuffing Meatballs (326), Simple Cranberry Sauce (436), [NR] baked sweet potato**
19	*leftover* Bacon & Egg Salad, avocado, spinach or chard*, fermented carrots (262)	*leftover* Thanksgiving Stuffing Meatballs, *leftover* Cranberry Sauce, *leftover* baked sweet potato**	Lemon & Bacon Scallops with Roasted Potatoes (376), Lemon Roasted Romanesco* (417)
20	Paleo Avocado "Toast" (264), [NR] eggs any style	*leftover* Lemon & Bacon Scallops, *leftover* Lemon Roasted Romanesco*, mango	Orange & Olive Braised Chicken (306), [NR] baked potato**, green salad* with EVOO
21	[MA] breakfast sausage made with Italian Blend (256) & ground meat, [NR] eggs any style, fermented carrots (262)	[MA] Six-Minute Salmon Bowls (382), berries	Souvlaki Kebabs (290), Greek Salad with Avoziki Dressing (402), mango
22	[MA] Breakfast Fried "Rice" (266), berries	*leftover* Souvlaki Kebabs, *leftover* Greek Salad with Avoziki Dressing, mango	Orange Braised Beef (344), Butternut Sage Soup** (394)
23	*leftover* Breakfast Fried "Rice," berries	*leftover* Orange Braised Beef, *leftover* Butternut Sage Soup**	Hayley's Skirt Steak Tacos (346), choice of salsa (433), Smoky Grilled Squash & Pineapple (408)
24	[NR] eggs any style, bacon, *leftover* Smoky Grilled Squash & Pineapple	[MA] Tangy Taco Salad (350), *leftover* salsa	Bacon & Superfood Meatloaf (330), Mashed Faux-Tatoes (418), green salad* with EVOO
25	[NR] eggs any style, avocado, spinach or chard*, fermented carrots (262)	[MA] Quick & Easy Salmon Cakes (374), green salad* with EVOO, avocado, olives	Seared Scallops with Orange Glaze (386), Cilantro Cauli-Rice (412), [NR] steamed bok choy*
26	[MA] Zucchini Pancakes (271), Perfectly Baked Bacon (260), berries	[MA] Italiano Salad (398), Honey Mustard Dressing (434)	Grandma Barbara's Stuffed Mushrooms (324), *leftover* Italiano Salad
27	[MA] N'Oatmeal (288), Apple Sage Sausage (272)	*leftover* Grandma Barbara's Stuffed Mushrooms, green salad* with EVOO	Orange Sesame Meatballs (328), Cilantro Cauli-Rice (412), berries
28	*leftover* N'Oatmeal, *leftover* Apple Sage Sausage	*leftover* Orange Sesame Meatballs, *leftover* Cilantro Cauli-Rice, berries	Lemon & Artichoke Chicken (296), Broc-Cauli Chowder with Bacon (392)
29	[MA] Apple Cinnamon Egg Muffins (280), bacon or sausage	*leftover* Lemon & Artichoke Chicken, *leftover* Broc-Cauli Chowder with Bacon	The Easiest Tacos (362), Crispy Plantain Chips (431), choice of salsa (433)
30	*leftover* Apple Cinnamon Egg Muffins, bacon or sausage	*leftover* The Easiest Tacos, *leftover* Crispy Plantain Chips, *leftover* salsa	Mini Mediterranean Kebabs (352), Sautéed Spinach with Pine Nuts & Currants* (423)

» *A complete shopping list for this meal plan can be found on balancedbites.com*

NOTES

*: or other green vegetable; green salad is any lettuce and/or non-starchy vegetables
**: or other starchy vegetable (refer to page 75)
EVOO: Extra-virgin olive oil, or use any dressing from pages 434–435 on salads
CO: Coconut oil
MA: Make-Ahead all or part of the recipe
NR: No Recipe (use any simple prep)

If no page number is listed, simply prepare the items as noted or any way you like. For additional protein, vegetable, and fat recommendations, refer to the QUICK LIST that is associated with your meal plan!

PART 3
RECIPES

Using the Recipes in This Book

Each recipe includes standard information:

① Recipe category indicating the type of dish. Note that some recipes include sides as well as main dishes.

② Recipe name, prep time, cooking time, and yield or servings the recipe makes

③ Allergens contained in the recipe as written. If an ingredient is optional or an alternative is noted in the ingredient list and the change will not affect the essence of the dish, its icon will not be included. (For a complete list of recipes and allergens, see the chart on pages 465 to 467.) For food allergy purposes, coconut is not considered a nut, so if it is present in a recipe, the "Nuts & Seeds" icon will not be included. For details on nightshades and FODMAPs, see page 149. This section also highlights special recipe categories. See below for details on the icons.

④ Introductory text either explaining the inspiration for the dish or providing serving suggestions

⑤ Tips for ingredient swaps or variations and other helpful info

⑥ Ingredients list

⑦ Preparation instructions

GET THE FACTS

To access the complete nutrition facts (including per-serving calories, fat, protein, carbs, and more) for each recipe, go to balancedbites.com/ practicalpaleo

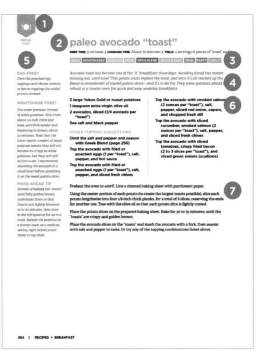

Recipe Icons Key

NUTS & SEEDS Contains nuts or seeds. Seed-based spices are *not* called out with this icon.

EGGS Contains eggs

NIGHTSHADES Contains tomatoes, potatoes, peppers, or eggplant or spices with these ingredients

FODMAPS Contains foods or spices high in FODMAPs

Notes on how to make the dish without the allergen will be listed in the side margin when applicable.

21DSD Is compliant with the 21-Day Sugar Detox or can be made compliant with a noted modification

SPICE BLEND Uses a spice blend in the book or can be made with a blend from the book instead of the spices listed

Notes on how to make the dish compliant with the 21DSD program or how to use a spice blend if it isn't called for the ingredients list will be listed in the side margin.

QUICK & EASY Has a short ingredient list or is quick and easy to make

MEAL Is a complete meal; additional sides are not necessary. (But adding more veggie sides is always okay!)

LOW & SLOW Cooks at a low temperature for many hours and can be made in an electric slow cooker

PARTY Perfect for serving at parties

FAMILY Particularly family-friendly

ONE POT Uses only one pot or pan to cook everything

FREEZE ME Freezes and defrosts/reheats well

Of course, some of these notes are subjective—just because a recipe doesn't have a PARTY icon, for example, certainly doesn't mean you can't take that dish to a party or gathering, and your family may enjoy dishes not marked FAMILY. Don't allow the icons to limit you—they are merely guides.

To purchase ready-made Practical Paleo Spice Blends, visit: **www.practicalpaleospices.com**

A Few Notes on Ingredients

HIGH-QUALITY INGREDIENTS, SUCH AS GRASS-FED & ORGANIC

I recommend that you source the best possible ingredients you can given your budget (see the guide to food quality on page 63). I also recommend using *only* organic spices (this is not specified in the ingredients lists, but it applies to all recipes). In each recipe, I'll note if there is an ingredient other than a spice that I think is particularly important to purchase organic, usually because non-organic versions may have a high pesticide count (coffee is one example).

SPICE BLENDS & OTHER RECIPE COMPONENTS

Some recipes call for the use of spice blends or other recipes in this book, and I recommend preparing those ahead of time. The preparation time for making those subrecipes (or recipe components) is not included in the main recipe's prep time. An icon on the recipe page indicates when a premade Practical Paleo Spice Blend is available (or will soon be available) for purchase, to save you time and effort. **Spice blends from the book can be purchased online at www.practicalpaleospices.com.**

PROTEINS & COOKING FATS

Often recipes have multiple options for proteins, such as ground beef, pork, or turkey, or for cooking fats, such as coconut oil, ghee, or butter. When listed in this way, the first item listed is the one I recommend for the recipe, but others may be used when the first item isn't available or isn't a food you can or want to eat, or when you want to try something different. For example, the Butternut Cocoa Chili on page 356 lists "ground beef or bison"; even though beef is listed first, if you want to try bison, go for it! If a slow-cooker recipe calls for beef, for example, you can use any tougher cut you like. You can ask your butcher for a recommendation or Google a cut you have on hand to see what type of cooking methods work best for it. In other words, don't feel limited by the type or cut of protein listed, or by the cooking fat listed. You can make changes to make a recipe work for you. You'll find a complete list of recommended fats for cooking on page 65.

GRATED OR MINCED GARLIC

I often call for garlic to be grated or minced. I highly recommend using a microplane grater/zester "stick" (Oxo Good Grips is my favorite brand) for this task, as it makes life much easier. This tool is multipurpose and is great for zesting citrus as well, so purchasing one is worthwhile if you don't own one already.

Common Ingredient Swaps & Options

PROTEINS

In most dishes, the main protein can easily be swapped for what you have on hand, what is available locally, and/or what is most affordable.

Note that cooking preparation and times may vary slightly (always use the doneness indicator in the recipe or your previous knowledge about the cooking methods for your selected protein to guide your process), but the recipes will work flavorwise with these various protein options:

- chicken thighs – chicken leg quarters – chicken drumsticks – chicken breast (chicken breast will dry out faster than any dark meat cut, and bone-in meat will take longer to cook)
- ground turkey or chicken (dark meat works best for flavor) – ground beef – ground bison – ground pork
- beef stew meat – bison stew meat – lamb stew meat – pork stew meat (shoulder or butt cut into cubes)
- flank steak – skirt steak – tri-tip
- shrimp – chicken – tuna

FATS

Cooking fats are interchangeable, as are fats used for cold preparations. In some baked goods that call for solid fats, using solid fats instead of liquid or melted forms may make a difference in the recipe.

- ghee/clarified butter – butter – coconut oil – lard – tallow
- extra-virgin olive oil – avocado oil – macadamia nut oil

VEGETABLES

Swapping vegetables or vegetable-based products may not be as obvious in some recipes as it is in others. Here are some ideas for simple swaps:

- tomato paste – canned pumpkin puree – canned butternut squash puree
- zucchini noodles – carrot noodles – parsnip noodles
- carrots – parsnips – turnips
- sweet potatoes – potatoes – turnips

NUTS & SEEDS

You can substitute nearly any nut or seed for any other in a recipe, with the exception of coconut. Coconut is much higher in fiber and lower in protein than typical nuts and seeds, so it won't work the same way.

how to: dice an onion

1. Pinch the base of the knife blade between your thumb and forefinger.

2. Extend your remaining fingers around the handle.

3. Grip the handle with your middle, ring, and little fingers. Leave your thumb and forefinger pinching the knife blade.

4. Practice: Using a wood or composite-surface cutting board, place the tip of the knife on the board and then rock the blade back and down, cutting your imaginary item. You can also place the back of the knife on the board and rock the blade forward and through the imaginary item.

5. Place the fingers of your free hand on the onion, making sure to curl your fingers slightly in to keep them safe. Place the blade of your knife on the onion.

6. Using the rocking motion previously practiced, cut off the bottom of the onion. Notice how this gives the onion a flat bottom.

7. Turn the onion over so that it is resting on the flat bottom you just created. Slice the onion in half, leaving part of the root intact on each side.

8. Separate the onion and work with one half at a time.

9. Peel the outer skin and the first layer of the onion if necessary/desired.

10. Inserting the tip of your knife near the root, slice down in 1/4- to 1/2-inch sections across, leaving the root end of the onion intact.

11. Turn the onion 45 degrees and slice across the previous cuts in 1/4- to 1/2-inch increments.

12. Continue to chop until you near the end of the onion.

13. Make the last chop about 1 inch from the end of the onion.

14. Turn the onion so that the root is pointing upward.

15. Make one or two additional slices closer to the end.

16. Flip the onion back over one final time.

17. Finish chopping the remaining part.

18. Drop all of the diced pieces into a bowl.

NO MORE TEARS

If you struggle with tears when chopping onions, here are two tips that can help: 1) use a sharp knife to cut them, and 2) store your onions in the refrigerator rather than on the countertop, as chopping chilled onions tends to prevent tears.

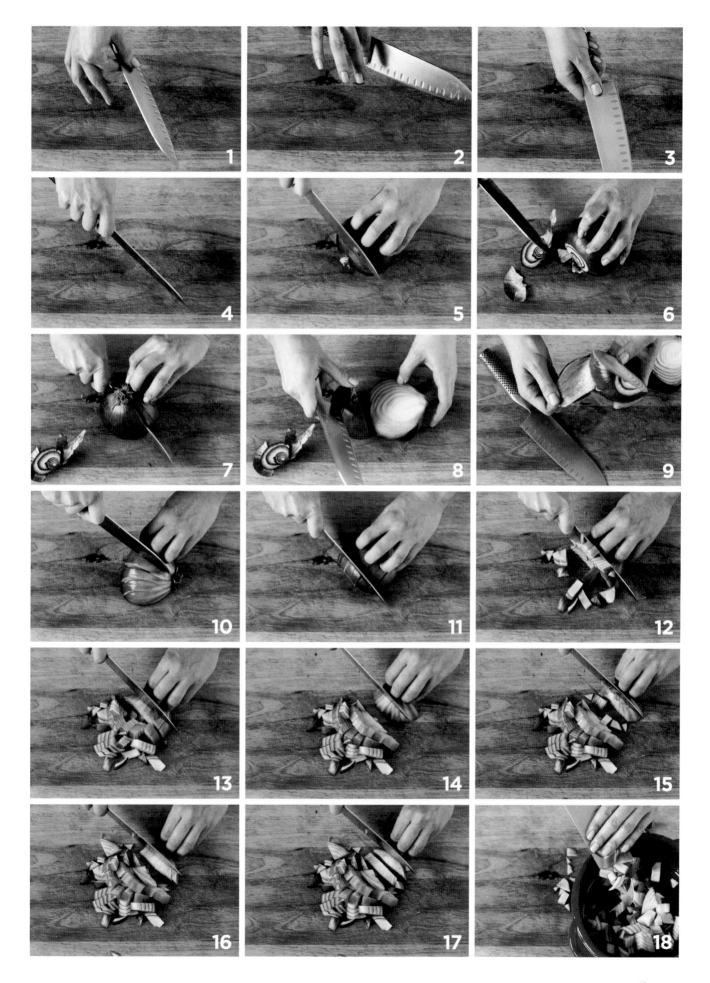

how to: dice a pepper

1. Pinch the base of the knife blade between your thumb and forefinger.

2. Extend your remaining fingers around the handle.

3. Grip the handle with your middle, ring, and little fingers. Leave your thumb and forefinger pinching the knife blade.

4. Practice: Using a wood or composite-surface cutting board, place the tip of the knife on the board and then rock the blade back and down, cutting your imaginary item. You can also place the back of the knife on the board and rock the blade forward and through the imaginary item.

5. Remove the stem from the pepper and place the pepper on the cutting board, bottom facing up. Place the fingers of your free hand on the pepper, making sure to curl your fingers slightly in to keep them safe. Finally, place the blade of your knife across the center of the bottom of the pepper and slice in half using the rocking motion previously practiced.

6 and 7. Remove the white center and stem.

8. Chop the remaining pepper into sections along the ribs (white parts).

9. Place the side of your knife into a pepper section, press down, and slide the blade sideways to begin removing the ribs.

10. To finish removing the ribs, pinch the opposite side of the pepper and continue to move the knife away from your hand.

11. Clean the remaining white ribs and seeds away from the pepper sections.

12 to 14. Slice the sections into 1/4-inch sticks.

15 to 17. Slice across the sticks evenly to create 1/4-inch dice.

18. Drop all of the diced pieces into a bowl.

HEY, HOT STUFF!

When working with hot peppers, remember that the heat is in the ribs (the white center parts) and the seeds. Clear those away to reduce the overall heat of the pepper, then remember to wash your hands before touching your face!

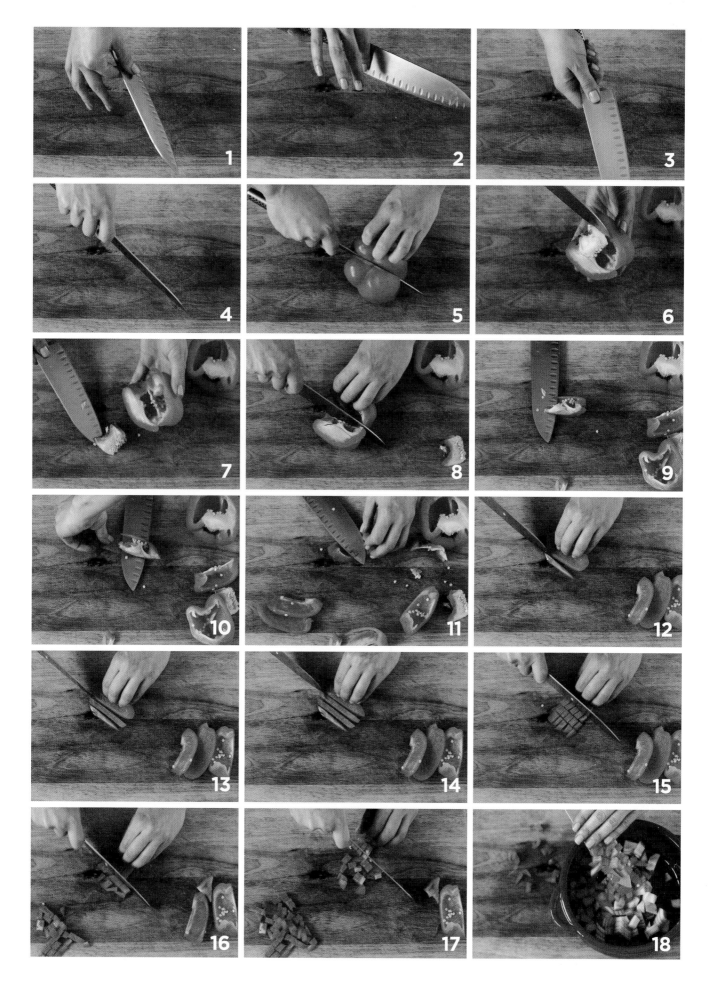

how to: chop anything

Follow instructions on the previous pages regarding how to hold the knife and your guide hand.

All food can be chopped using the same principles.

You always create one of three "shapes" when chopping:

1) slices

2) sticks

3) dice or cubes

Slices: The first, basic cut made before a food can be cut into sticks. The garlic below left is being sliced very thinly.

Sticks: Slices cut into even portions that are often longer than they are wide. The sweet potato on the top left of the opposite page is being cut into sticks.

Julienne: Slices that are cut into matchstick-sized pieces—about 1/8 inch wide and anywhere from 1 to 3 inches long. The red bell pepper on the bottom left of the opposite page is being julienned. You will julienne an item before you finely dice it.

Diced: Sticks that are cut into evenly sized pieces, typically from 1/4 to 3/4 inch in size, but as small as 1/8 inch. The sweet potato on the top right of the opposite page is being diced.

Finely diced: Cut evenly into about 1/8- to 1/4-inch pieces. The red bell pepper on the bottom right of the opposite page and in the bowl of ingredients below right are examples of finely diced items.

Cubed: Cut into evenly sized pieces, typically from 3/4 to 1 inch in size.

Minced: Chopped into pieces smaller than 1/4 inch that may not be entirely even in size. Recipes often call for garlic to be minced.

Shredded: Cut into short, thin pieces using a box grater or the shredding disc on a food processor. Foods like carrots and zucchini are often shredded.

Grated: Very finely minced using a fine box grater or Microplane. Grating makes an ingredient's structure nearly indistinguishable in a recipe. Foods like raw garlic can easily be grated into recipes.

HELPFUL TIP

It's useful to peel roots and tubers before chopping them. Do this with a vegetable peeler.

This also applies to mangoes, as I find that they're easier to chop all at once if they're peeled first. However, they can be a bit slippery to hold for this part of the process.

how to: season while cooking

When no specific measurement is provided, all food can be seasoned using these basic principles:

A pinch: Use your thumb and first three fingers to grab the salt, pepper, or other spice or spice blend to add to your food. Many people mistakenly believe that a pinch of seasoning would be taken between the thumb and index finger, but this will leave you with very little flavor. The only time this smaller, two-finger pinch may be applicable is in baking, and in that case the recipe instructions may call for a scant pinch or small pinch. In most cases, though, including the recipes in this book, the three-finger pinch is what is meant.

A few pinches: Use your thumb and first three fingers to grab the salt, pepper, or other spice or spice blend to add to your food, then repeat at least three times.

Season lightly: Either use the pinching method (pictured) or shake from a seasoning bottle with a shaker top to give your food a light dusting of salt and/or spice or spice blend.

Season generously: Either use the pinching method (pictured) or shake from a seasoning bottle with a shaker top to give your food a substantial coating of the salt and/or spice or spice blend.

how to: butterfly and grill a chicken breast

Because of the naturally uneven shape of a chicken breast, it's easy to either undercook or overcook it when it's left whole. Splitting it into a flat piece, called butterflying, allows for quicker, more even cooking, yielding a much juicier result.

1. To butterfly the chicken, place a boneless chicken breast on a cutting board with the thickest side facing your knife blade.

2 to 4. Set your non-cutting hand on top of the chicken and, while pressing down slightly on the chicken with your palm to keep it from moving (keeping your fingers out straight), begin cutting down the length of the side of the breast, keeping your knife parallel to the cutting board. Carefully slide the knife through the center so that the thickness is cut in half.

5. Continue to slice almost completely through the chicken breast, leaving it connected in the center so that it flattens out to a "butterfly" or heart shape. The chicken should now be 1/4 to 1/2 inch thick.

6 to 8. Flip the chicken breast over and, if present, remove the tender by slicing against the edge of the breast just far enough to remove it without separating the butterflied breast.

9. To grill the chicken, preheat a grill or grill pan to medium heat. Season the chicken according to the recipe you're using, or season generously as pictured here. Brush the hot grill or grill pan with melted coconut oil or ghee, then cook the chicken for 4 to 5 minutes per side, depending on the thickness. When you notice that the chicken has turned white up around the sides and toward the middle, it's time to flip it. Take the chicken off the grill and allow to sit for at least 5 minutes before slicing to eat.

SEASON LIGHTLY

SEASON GENEROUSLY

1

2

3

4

5

6

7

8

9

signature spice blends

YIELD: About 1/2 cup (8 tablespoons) per recipe, unless otherwise noted

FOR ALL SPICE BLENDS:

Combine all of the ingredients in a bowl. Store in a small, airtight container in a cool, dark place. Use these blends as they appear in recipes throughout the book—or anytime! To order online, visit practicalpaleospices.com.

* EVERYTHING BLEND

2 tablespoons dried oregano leaves
1 1/2 tablespoons garlic powder
1 1/2 tablespoons onion powder
1 tablespoon dried ground rosemary
1 tablespoon turmeric powder
1 1/2 teaspoons sea salt
1 teaspoon black pepper

ITALIAN BLEND

2 1/2 tablespoons dried parsley
1 1/2 tablespoons granulated garlic
1 1/2 tablespoons granulated onion
1 tablespoon fennel seeds, ground
1 tablespoon dried ground sage
1 teaspoon sea salt
1 teaspoon black pepper or 1/4 teaspoon white pepper

Note: *Use 2 tablespoons per pound of meat to make sausage.*

GREEK BLEND *

3 tablespoons dried lemon peel
3 tablespoons dried oregano leaves
2 tablespoons granulated garlic
1 tablespoon sea salt
2 teaspoons black pepper

SMOKY BLEND

2 tablespoons smoked paprika
2 tablespoons granulated onion
1 tablespoon chipotle powder
1 tablespoon sea salt
1 tablespoon sweet paprika
1 1/2 teaspoons ground cinnamon
1 1/2 teaspoons black pepper

*
STARRED BLENDS ARE AIP-FRIENDLY WITHOUT CHANGES

CHORIZO BLEND

2 tablespoons chipotle powder
2 tablespoons smoked paprika
1 1/2 tablespoons granulated onion
1 1/2 tablespoons granulated garlic
1 1/2 teaspoons sea salt
1 teaspoon black pepper

Note: *When adding this blend to meat, combine 1 1/2 teaspoons of apple cider vinegar with each tablespoon of spice mix. Use 2 tablespoons of Chorizo Blend per pound of meat.*

DINER BLEND

2 tablespoons dried oregano leaves
2 tablespoons paprika
1 1/2 tablespoons granulated onion
1 1/2 tablespoons granulated garlic
1 1/2 teaspoons sea salt
1 1/2 teaspoons black pepper
1 teaspoon dried ground rosemary

COOLING BLEND

2 tablespoons dried oregano leaves
2 tablespoons turmeric powder
1 tablespoon ground cinnamon
1 tablespoon ground cumin
1 tablespoon granulated onion
1 tablespoon granulated garlic
1 teaspoon black pepper

COFFEE BBQ RUB

2 tablespoons ground coffee

3 tablespoons palm, turbinado, maple, or other large granulated sugar (optional)

1 tablespoon smoked paprika

2 teaspoons coarse sea salt

2 teaspoons granulated garlic

2 teaspoons dried onion flakes (minced onions) or 3/4 teaspoon granulated onion

2 teaspoons sweet paprika

1 teaspoon dried granulated orange peel or 2 teaspoons minced fresh orange peel

YIELD: 9 tablespoons

CHANGE IT UP

Use decaf coffee if you're sensitive to caffeine.

If using fresh peel, try clementine instead of orange.

BREAKFAST SAUSAGE BLEND ✳

2 tablespoons granulated onion

2 tablespoons granulated garlic

1 tablespoon dried parsley

2 teaspoons ground cinnamon

1 teaspoon dried ground sage

1 1/2 teaspoons sea salt

1 1/2 teaspoons black pepper

Note: *Use 2 tablespoons per pound of meat to make sausage.*

NIGHTSHADE-FREE TACO & FAJITA BLEND

1 1/2 tablespoons turmeric powder

1 1/2 tablespoons granulated garlic

1 1/2 tablespoons granulated onion

1 tablespoon ground coriander

1 tablespoon sea salt

2 teaspoons black pepper

2 teaspoons ground cumin

INDIAN BLEND

3 tablespoons granulated onion

2 tablespoons garam masala

2 tablespoons ground coriander

1 teaspoon sea salt

1 teaspoon black pepper

1 teaspoon ground cinnamon

1 teaspoon red pepper flakes

TACO & FAJITA BLEND

2 tablespoons chili powder

1 1/2 tablespoons granulated garlic

1 1/2 tablespoons granulated onion

1 tablespoon ground coriander

2 teaspoons ground cumin

2 teaspoons smoked paprika

1 teaspoon sea salt

1 teaspoon black pepper

SAVORY BLEND

1 tablespoon granulated garlic

1 tablespoon granulated onion

1 tablespoon rosemary leaves

1 1/2 teaspoons dried ground sage

1 1/2 teaspoons paprika

1 1/2 teaspoons sea salt

1 teaspoon black pepper

YIELD: 5 tablespoons

MEGA MEDITERRANEAN BLEND

1 tablespoon dried parsley

1 tablespoon dried oregano leaves

1 tablespoon dried thyme leaves

1 tablespoon paprika

1 tablespoon toasted sesame seeds

1 1/2 teaspoons ground coriander

1 1/2 teaspoons ground cumin

1 1/2 teaspoons dried orange peel

1/2 teaspoon black pepper

1/2 teaspoon granulated garlic

1/2 teaspoon granulated onion

1/2 teaspoon sea salt

1/4 teaspoon ground allspice

1/4 teaspoon ground cinnamon

NIGHTSHADE-FREE?

Do not make spice blends containing paprika, chili powder, chipotle powder, or red pepper flakes.

FODMAP-FREE?

Eliminate the onion and garlic.

lemon & herb salt blends

PREP TIME: 20 minutes | **COOKING TIME:** 4 hours | **YIELD:** 1/2 cup

`21DSD` `SPICE BLEND` `FAMILY`

NOTES

If a recipe calls for one of these salt blends and you do not have it prepared, simply use a 1:1 ratio of crushed dried herb leaves or grated lemon zest to coarse sea salt.

I highly recommend that you make both a rosemary and a sage salt blend to keep on hand for use on their own as well as in the recipes in this book!

You can dehydrate your herbs overnight in a heated oven that's been turned off or let them dry out for several hours on the lowest setting—just keep an eye on them so they don't burn. To fill your house with herbal aromas, allow the process to take longer at a lower temperature.

Creating a blend of your favorite herbs with sea salt is an easy way to keep big flavor on hand to add to any dish in a pinch (literally!). Use a coarse, unrefined, mineral-rich salt (either white or gray). You can often find these salts in bulk at a grocery co-op, online, or even at your local grocery store.

1 cup fresh herbs (such as rosemary, sage, or thyme leaves, or equal parts sage and rosemary leaves) or grated lemon zest

1/2 cup coarse sea salt

Preheat the oven to 250°F or the lowest setting (a "warm" setting will work, too).

If making an herb salt blend, spread out each type of herb on its own rimmed baking sheet and dry in the oven until the leaves break apart when handled between your fingers. This takes roughly 4 hours.

If making lemon salt, preheat the oven to 200°F, spread out the grated lemon zest on a rimmed baking sheet, and dry in the oven until it's crispy. This takes about 3 hours. It's ideal to check on it roughly every 30 minutes to make sure it doesn't burn.

Using a food processor or a mortar and pestle, grind the dried herbs or zest with the salt to your desired consistency. Re-dry the salt blend in the oven if any moisture remains.

Store the salt blend in a glass jar in a cool, dry place.

mineral-rich bone broth

PREP TIME: 5 minutes | **COOKING TIME:** 8 to 24 hours | **YIELD:** 2 quarts (64 ounces) broth

FODMAPS 21DSD **LOW & SLOW** **FAMILY** **ONE POT**

There is nothing easier than making broth. It's as simple as boiling water, and making your own allows you to avoid food additives. With this recipe, you'll never buy boxed or canned broth/stock again.

4 quarts filtered water

1 1/2 to 2 pounds bones (beef knuckle bones, marrow bones, meaty bones, chicken or turkey necks, chicken or turkey carcass bones, or any bones you have around)

2 tablespoons apple cider vinegar

2 teaspoons sea salt, or to taste (optional)

Cloves from 1 whole head of garlic, peeled and smashed with the side of a knife (optional)

Place all of the ingredients in a slow cooker. Set the heat to high and bring to a boil, then reduce the heat setting to low. Allow the broth to cook for a minimum of 8 hours and up to 24 hours—the longer it cooks, the better.

Turn off the slow cooker and allow the broth to cool. Strain the broth through a fine-mesh strainer or cheesecloth. Pour the cooled broth into glass jars and store in the refrigerator for up to a few days or freeze for later use.

Before using the broth, chip away at the top and discard any fat that has solidified. You can drink the broth, use it as a base for soups and stews, or use it in any recipe that calls for broth or stock.

FODMAP-FREE?
Make your broth without the garlic.

CHANGE IT UP
To make vegetable broth, replace the bones with 4 carrots, 2 stalks of celery, and 1 onion, all chopped into 1/2-inch pieces, and 4 cloves of garlic, smashed with the side of a knife. After bringing everything to a boil, simmer on low heat for 6 hours. Do not overcook vegetable broth, as it may become bitter.

NOTE
If you don't have a slow cooker, you can use an enameled cast-iron pot in a 300°F oven or simmer the broth in a pot on the stovetop on the lowest possible heat setting that allows tiny bubbles to consistently appear in the broth after you have brought it to a boil.

KITCHEN BASICS

perfectly baked bacon

PREP TIME: 5 minutes | **COOKING TIME:** 20 to 30 minutes | **YIELD:** 1 pound bacon

`21DSD` `QUICK & EASY` `PARTY` `FAMILY`

CHANGE IT UP

Use beef or lamb bacon if you prefer. Turkey "bacon" is not bacon.

You can also make this recipe in a toaster oven with a baking rack and tray if you're cooking a smaller portion.

QUALITY MATTERS

Try to buy bacon from a local farmer who pasture-raises pigs. Ask what the animals are being fed, and visit the farm if you can to see their living conditions. Bacon is not inherently unhealthy, but copious amounts of feedlot pork are not good for you. See page 63 for more information on choosing quality meats.

You may be surprised by the sparse appearance of bacon in the recipes in this book. I generally only bake it and serve it with sunny-side-up eggs and raw sauerkraut in the morning. It's worth the wait.

1 pound pastured bacon

Preheat the oven to 350°F. Place slices of bacon evenly on a wire baking rack positioned over a rimmed baking sheet (see photo). Bake until the bacon is cooked to your liking, 20 to 30 minutes depending on thickness.

If you are baking pastured pork bacon, it's a good idea to save the fat. Allow it to cool slightly, then pour it into a glass or ceramic container and store in the refrigerator for later use in recipes and as a cooking fat.

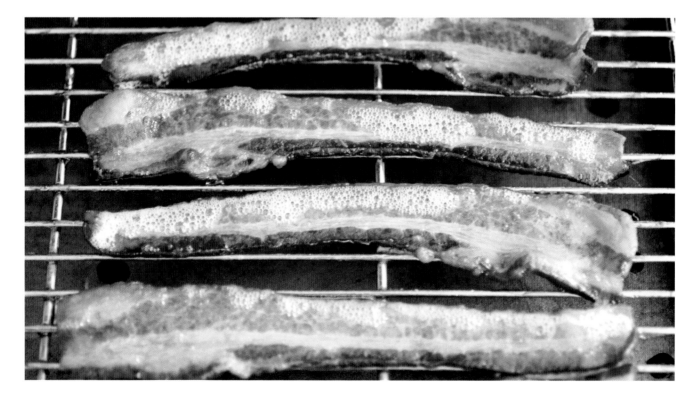

clarified butter & ghee

PREP TIME: — | **COOKING TIME:** 20 to 30 minutes | **YIELD:** 2 pounds clarified butter or ghee

`21DSD` `FAMILY` `ONE POT`

Butter is an extremely nutrient-dense food that is loaded with vitamin A, vitamin D, and even vitamin K2. Still, many people cannot tolerate lactose, so clarifying grass-fed butter is a fantastic way to retain the nutrients while skimming away the potentially irritating milk sugars and proteins. Clarified butter, the first step in making ghee, is made by cooking the butter until all of the milk solids can be skimmed off the top; ghee is made when the clarified butter is cooked a bit longer and the milk solids are allowed to brown and fall to the bottom of the pot, creating a nuttier, richer flavor.

BETTER BUTTER

Grass-fed butter is available in most grocery stores. Kerrygold and Organic Valley are two brands that are pretty easy to find.

2 pounds grass-fed/pastured butter

Slowly melt the butter in a medium-sized heavyweight saucepan over low heat.

To make clarified butter: Allow the butter to come to a simmer; eventually the milk solids will begin to float and become foamy at the top of the oil. Skim these milk solids off and remove the butter from the heat. It is now clarified butter. Pour it through a cheesecloth to strain out any remaining milk solids and store it in a glass jar.

To make ghee: If you'd like to turn the clarified butter into ghee, instead of skimming the milk solids, allow them to continue to cook slowly until they become browned and sink to the bottom. When there is no longer any material waiting to brown and sink to the bottom of the oil, the ghee is finished. Pour it through a cheesecloth to strain out the browned milk solids and store it in a glass jar.

You can keep clarified butter or ghee on the countertop if the ambient temperature in your home isn't too warm and you're confident that you've removed all of the milk proteins, since it is purely a fat at this point. If you notice any mold, then the clarified butter/ghee has spoiled. Alternatively, you may store it in the refrigerator for several months or longer.

raw probiotic sauerkraut (classic or roasted jalapeño & garlic)

PREP TIME: 30 minutes | **FERMENTING TIME:** 1 to 2 weeks | **YIELD:** About two 32-ounce jars

`NIGHTSHADES` `FODMAPS` `21DSD` `QUICK & EASY` `FAMILY`

NIGHTSHADE-FREE?
Omit the jalapeños.

FODMAP-FREE?
Omit the cabbage and use shredded carrots only.

CHANGE IT UP
Add ginger to the jalapeño and garlic version.

Fermented foods are a must-have probiotic addition to your daily diet. These instructions are detailed and may seem complicated, but the process is actually quite simple. Once you make this recipe, repeating it with your own twist will be a cinch! You'll need two 32-ounce glass mason jars for the finished product.

1 large head green cabbage, sliced into thin strips (set the large outer leaves aside)

3 tablespoons sea salt, divided

2 large carrots, shredded

CLASSIC

1 tablespoon caraway seeds

ROASTED JALAPEÑO & GARLIC

2 large or 4 small cloves garlic, thinly sliced

1 to 2 jalapeño peppers, roasted and sliced (see page 360)

1/2 to 1 teaspoon black pepper (optional)

Place one-third of the sliced cabbage in a large bowl and sprinkle 1 tablespoon of the salt over it. Using your hands, squeeze the cabbage until water begins to come out of it.

Repeat this process, adding the remaining cabbage and salt to the bowl one-third at a time. This will take time and elbow grease, so be ready to get your hands involved.

Add the carrots and the ingredient(s) for the flavor of your choice to the mixture and combine with your hands.

Fill two 32-ounce mason jars evenly, pressing the mixture down so that water releases and rises above the line of the vegetables with 2 inches of space remaining at the top.

Wedge the reserved large outer leaves into the tops of the jars so that the mixture is pressed below and the water level rises above the leaves. A shot glass or ceramic or glass pinch bowl serves nicely as additional weight to hold the mixture down securely.

Set the filled jars aside in a rimmed pan or dish so that any spillover will be contained.

Store the jars in a secure, cool, darkish place where they will not be disturbed.

Check on your sauerkraut every day or two to make sure that the water level remains above the vegetables and that no vegetables are coming into contact with air. The fermentation process happens underwater, so if you see anything touching the surface, use a clean spoon to remove it. You may also see some growth or mold form around the top of the liquid—this is normal, but it's best to remove it when you see it. If you need to, add some fresh water to make sure that everything is below the water line. The weights should help a lot with this.

Allow the sauerkraut to sit for at least 7 days and up to 2 weeks, tasting it daily after 7 days.

Once the sauerkraut tastes the way you like it, place the lids on the jars and store them in the refrigerator. The sauerkraut will last indefinitely while refrigerated and will not continue to ferment.

paleo avocado "toast"

PREP TIME: 5 minutes | **COOKING TIME:** About 35 minutes | **YIELD:** 4 servings (2 pieces of "toast" each)

EGGS | NIGHTSHADES | FODMAPS | 21DSD | SPICE BLEND | QUICK & EASY | MEAL | PARTY | FAMILY

EGG-FREE?

Omit the poached egg toppings and choose salmon or bacon toppings for added protein instead.

NIGHTSHADE-FREE?

Use sweet potatoes instead of white potatoes. Slice them about 1/4 inch thick and bake until fork-tender and beginning to brown, about 30 minutes. Note that the lower starch content of sweet potatoes means they will not become as crispy as white potatoes, but they will still be fun to eat. I recommend smashing the avocado in a small bowl before spreading it on the sweet potato slices.

MAKE-AHEAD TIP

Instead of baking the "toasts" until fully golden brown, underbake them so that they're just lightly browned, 25 to 30 minutes, then store in the refrigerator for up to a week. Reheat the potatoes in a toaster oven on a medium setting right before you're ready to top them.

Avocado toast has become one of the "it" breakfasts these days. Avoiding bread has meant missing out, until now! Thin potato slices replace the toast, and once it's all stacked up the flavor is reminiscent of loaded potato skins—and it's to die for. Prep some potatoes ahead to reheat in a toaster oven for quick and easy weekday breakfasts.

2 large Yukon Gold or russet potatoes

1 teaspoon extra-virgin olive oil

2 avocados, sliced (1/4 avocado per "toast")

Sea salt and black pepper

OTHER TOPPING SUGGESTIONS

Omit the salt and pepper and season with Greek Blend (page 256)

Top the avocado with fried or poached eggs (1 per "toast"), salt, pepper, and hot sauce

Top the avocado with fried or poached eggs (1 per "toast"), salt, pepper, and sliced fresh chives

Top the avocado with smoked salmon (2 ounces per "toast"), salt, pepper, sliced red onion, capers, and chopped fresh dill

Top the avocado with sliced cucumber, smoked salmon (2 ounces per "toast"), salt, pepper, and sliced fresh chives

Top the avocado with sliced tomatoes, crispy fried bacon (2 to 3 slices per "toast"), and sliced green onions (scallions)

Preheat the oven to 400°F. Line a rimmed baking sheet with parchment paper.

Using the center portion of each potato (to create the largest toasts possible), slice each potato lengthwise into four 1/8-inch-thick planks, for a total of 8 slices, reserving the ends for another use. Toss with the olive oil so that each potato slice is lightly coated.

Place the potato slices on the prepared baking sheet. Bake for 30 to 35 minutes, until the "toasts" are crispy and golden brown.

Place the avocado slices on the "toasts" and mash the avocado with a fork, then season with salt and pepper to taste. Or try any of the topping combinations listed above.

breakfast fried "rice"

PREP TIME: 20 minutes | **COOKING TIME:** 30 minutes | **YIELD:** 4 servings

NUTS & SEEDS | EGGS | NIGHTSHADES | FODMAPS | 21DSD | MEAL | FAMILY | ONE POT

SEED-FREE?
Omit the sesame seeds.

NIGHTSHADE-FREE?
Omit the red bell pepper.

EGG-FREE?
Omit the egg and add extra protein of your choice.

This is a great breakfast option if you're looking for something satisfying that delivers a meat-and-veggie punch all at once. If you need to eat egg-free, you can easily up the protein content of the meal by adding a bit more meat of your choice instead of the eggs. Make it ahead and simply reheat it to eat to save time on busy mornings!

4 slices bacon, chopped

2 sausage links, casings removed, or 1/4 pound ground pork mixed with 2 teaspoons Breakfast Sausage Blend (page 257)

1/2 cup diced red onions

1/2 cup diced carrots

1/2 cup diced red bell peppers

4 cloves garlic, smashed with the side of a knife

4 cups shredded cauliflower florets (about 1 head cauliflower)

1/4 cup coconut aminos

2 to 3 dashes of fish sauce

2 tablespoons ghee (page 261)

4 large eggs

FOR GARNISH

Sliced green onions (scallions)

Chopped fresh cilantro

Sesame seeds

Cook the bacon in a large skillet over medium heat for about 5 minutes, until done to your liking. Remove the bacon from the skillet and set aside; leave the grease in the pan.

Crumble the sausage meat into the pan and cook for 9 to 10 minutes, until the sausage is cooked through. Set aside on the plate with the bacon.

Add the onions, carrots, and bell peppers to the skillet. Cook for 8 to 10 minutes, until the onions start to turn translucent and the peppers and carrots start to lose their crunch. Add the garlic and cook for 1 to 2 minutes longer, until the garlic starts to turn golden brown.

Add the sausage and bacon back to the skillet, then add the shredded cauliflower, coconut aminos, and fish sauce and stir to combine. Cook for 3 to 4 minutes, until the cauliflower is soft but not mushy.

Create a well in the middle of the mixture and add the ghee. Once the ghee has melted, crack the eggs into the well and use a wooden spoon to lightly scramble the eggs for 1 to 2 minutes. Gently fold the eggs into the fried "rice."

Serve garnished with sliced green onions, chopped cilantro, and sesame seeds.

home fries & sausage skillet

PREP TIME: 5 minutes | **COOKING TIME:** 12 to 16 minutes | **YIELD:** 4 servings

`NIGHTSHADES` `FODMAPS` `21DSD` `SPICE BLEND` `QUICK & EASY` `MEAL` `FAMILY` `ONE POT`

NIGHTSHADE-FREE?

Omit the garnish of red pepper flakes and use sweet potatoes, parsnips, or turnips instead of white potatoes.

FODMAP-FREE?

Omit the onion and garlic from the spice blends.

INGREDIENT TIP

When using potatoes in a breakfast recipe, your best bet is to precook them ahead of time (at least the night before) by boiling them until fork-tender. Keep the cooked potatoes stored in the refrigerator until you're ready to cut and brown them.

A morning without eggs can seem challenging at first, but it's quite simple when you break it down and realize that tons of breakfast-friendly foods work great together in a quick skillet like this one! Whether you simply want to change things up or you have an egg allergy or sensitivity, give this skillet breakfast a try—it's hearty and satisfying.

1 pound ground pork

1 tablespoon Italian Blend (page 256)

2 cups chopped kale

1 tablespoon ghee (page 261), bacon fat, or butter

2 large Yukon Gold potatoes, parboiled and diced

2 tablespoons Diner Blend (page 256)

FOR GARNISH (OPTIONAL)

Red pepper flakes

Coarse sea salt

Chopped fresh chives

Heat a large skillet over medium heat. Add the pork, season with the Italian Blend, and stir to incorporate. Cook the meat for 5 minutes, stirring to break it up with a spatula as it cooks, then add the kale. Continue cooking for another 5 to 7 minutes, until the kale begins to wilt and the meat is cooked through. Remove the pork and kale from the skillet and set aside.

Melt the ghee in the skillet, still over medium heat, then add the potatoes and Diner Blend, gently stirring to coat the potatoes with the fat and spices. Spread the potatoes into an even layer and cook for 2 to 4 minutes, until they start to brown. Stir midway through cooking so they don't stick. If they do start to stick, add a little more ghee to the pan.

Return the meat and kale to the pan, then garnish with red pepper flakes, coarse sea salt, and chives, if desired.

swirly crustless quiche

PREP TIME: 20 minutes | **COOKING TIME:** 45 minutes | **YIELD:** 6 servings

EGGS 21DSD **SPICE BLEND** FAMILY FREEZE ME

CHANGE IT UP

Athletes can try adding shredded sweet potato to this recipe for an added kick of good carbs.

This is a great go-to recipe that you can freeze and reheat in a toaster oven. Try using different types of vegetables and spices to change the flavors each time you make it. If you have ground meat on hand, turn it into Italian sausage by mixing it with the Italian Blend on page 256 and add it to this recipe.

1 tablespoon butter, bacon fat, or coconut oil

1 large zucchini, shredded or grated

2 large carrots, shredded or grated

12 large eggs, beaten

2 teaspoons Herb Salt Blend made with equal parts rosemary and sage (page 258) or spice blend of choice

Preheat the oven to 375°F. Grease a 9 by 13-inch baking dish with the butter.

Strain the zucchini with a cheesecloth or strainer bag, pressing to release the excess water. (This step isn't absolutely necessary but will give your quiche a better consistency.)

In a large bowl, mix together the zucchini, carrots, eggs, and rosemary-sage salt (if using).

Pour the egg mixture into the greased baking dish. For a swirled effect, use a fork to create a circular pattern before baking.

Bake for about 45 minutes, until the edges are brown. The quiche will puff up while baking and then deflate when removed from the oven.

BREAK
FAST

zucchini pancakes

PREP TIME: 10 minutes | **COOKING TIME:** 20 minutes | **YIELD:** About 8 small pancakes (2 servings)

EGGS FODMAPS 21DSD **SPICE BLEND** QUICK & EASY FAMILY FREEZE ME

Looking for a pancake recipe that's savory instead of sweet? Look no further! Make extras to reheat anytime, or eat them cold the next day.

3 large eggs
1 tablespoon coconut flour
1/4 teaspoon sea salt
1/4 teaspoon black pepper

2 cups shredded zucchini
Coconut oil or bacon fat, for pan-frying

In a medium-sized mixing bowl, beat the eggs with the coconut flour, salt, and pepper.

Strain the zucchini with a cheesecloth or strainer bag, pressing to release the excess water. (This step isn't absolutely necessary but will give your pancakes a better consistency.) Add the shredded zucchini to the bowl with the egg mixture and mix until well combined.

Heat about 1/8 inch of coconut oil in a large skillet over medium heat. Spoon the mixture into the skillet to make "cakes" that are 4 to 6 inches in diameter. Cook for 3 to 4 minutes on the first side and 2 to 3 minutes on the second side, until they hold together, flipping once as you would standard pancakes.

Serve warm or at room temperature.

SPICE BLEND SWAP

Instead of using only salt and pepper, try adding 1 teaspoon of Greek or Italian Blend (page 256).

NOTE

A food processor fitted with a shredding disc makes shredding the zucchini super quick and easy, but you can also shred the zucchini by hand.

apple sage sausage

PREP TIME: 10 minutes | **COOKING TIME:** 6 to 10 minutes | **YIELD:** 4 servings

FODMAPS | 21DSD | **SPICE BLEND** | QUICK & EASY | FAMILY | FREEZE ME

MAKE IT 21DSD

Use a green apple (Granny Smith) in this recipe.

These quick and easy sausage patties can be made ahead in a large batch (double or even triple this recipe) and frozen for later use.

1 pound ground pork

1 medium apple, shredded, with the juice squeezed out (about 1/4 cup)

1/4 cup minced onions

2 tablespoons Breakfast Sausage Blend (page 257)

1 to 2 fresh sage leaves, minced, plus additional whole leaves for garnish (optional)

2 teaspoons ghee (page 261), for the pan

In a mixing bowl, combine the pork, apple, onions, spice blend, and chopped sage and mix with your hands until everything is evenly incorporated. Form the mixture into 8 evenly sized patties.

Heat the ghee in a large skillet over medium heat. When hot, place the patties in the pan and cook for 3 to 5 minutes per side, or until cooked through and browned.

If desired, fry some sage leaves (about 1 per patty) in the pork fat left in the pan until crispy to garnish the sausage patties.

blueberry maple sausage

PREP TIME: 10 minutes | **COOKING TIME:** 6 to 10 minutes | **YIELD:** 4 servings

`FODMAPS` `21DSD` `SPICE BLEND` `QUICK & EASY` `FAMILY` `FREEZE ME`

As with the Apple Sage Sausage (opposite), this easy recipe can be made ahead in a large batch (doubled or even tripled) and frozen for later use. You can make this sausage without the sweetener, but the tiny bit used here really gives these patties a great flavor.

FODMAP-FREE?
Omit the granulated onion and garlic from the Breakfast Sausage Blend.

1 pound ground pork

2 tablespoons Breakfast Sausage Blend (page 257)

2 to 3 teaspoons pure maple syrup

1/2 cup fresh blueberries

2 teaspoons ghee (page 261), for the pan

In a mixing bowl, combine the pork, spice blend, and maple syrup and mix with your hands until everything is evenly incorporated. Gently fold in the blueberries and form the mixture into 8 evenly sized patties.

Heat the ghee in a large skillet over medium heat. When hot, place the patties in the pan and cook for 3 to 5 minutes per side, or until cooked through and browned.

charlie's big fat italian frittata

PREP TIME: 15 minutes | **COOKING TIME:** 1 hour

YIELD: 8 servings (or more if you're serving it for a party in smaller portions)

EGGS | NIGHTSHADES | FODMAPS | 21DSD | SPICE BLEND | MEAL | PARTY | FAMILY | ONE POT

NOTE

To save time making the potato crust, you can use parboiled potatoes. If you do, I recommend using Yukon Gold potatoes and slicing them 1/4 inch thick. Alternatively, you can make this recipe without a crust by skipping those steps entirely and loading the egg mixture into a greased baking dish to cook it as you would a typical frittata.

My dad is a New Year's Day baby, so when I was growing up, the first day of the year in our household was even more special. To celebrate now, my parents almost always host a big brunch for their friends and prepare tons of food for everyone to enjoy. Along with an antipasto platter, fruit salad, and more, my dad always cooks up a big frittata with a potato crust like this one for the event. Mangia!

1/2 pound russet potatoes

2 tablespoons ghee (page 261), melted, divided

Sea salt and black pepper

4 ounces pepperoni slices, divided

1/2 cup artichoke hearts, chopped, plus more for garnish

1/2 cup sun-dried tomatoes, chopped

1 dozen large eggs, beaten

1 tablespoon Italian Blend (page 256)

2 cups loosely packed spinach, chopped

3 tablespoons full-fat coconut milk

Preheat the oven to 375°F.

Use the slicing blade of a food processor to slice the potatoes about 1/8 inch thick. If you do not own a food processor, use a sharp knife to slice them.

Brush a large oven-safe skillet or large baking dish with half of the ghee, then line it with the potato slices, allowing them to overlap slightly. Brush the potatoes with more of the ghee, then season lightly with salt and pepper. Bake for 30 minutes, until the potatoes are cooked through and fork-tender.

Chop two-thirds of the sliced pepperoni, reserving the remaining third for a topping. Heat a medium-sized skillet over medium heat. Add the artichokes, sun-dried tomatoes, and the chopped pepperoni and season with a few pinches each of salt and pepper. Cook for 3 to 4 minutes, until the pepperoni starts to brown and the flavors combine. Turn off the heat.

In a bowl, combine the eggs, spice blend, spinach, and coconut milk.

Spread the sun-dried tomato mixture evenly over the potatoes, then pour the egg mixture over top. Place the remaining pepperoni slices on top. Bake for 25 minutes, or until the eggs puff up and the edges are browned. Garnish with additional chopped artichoke hearts.

lemon blueberry muffins

PREP TIME: 15 minutes | **COOKING TIME:** 35 to 40 minutes | **YIELD:** 1 dozen muffins

`EGGS` `FODMAPS` `QUICK & EASY` `PARTY` `FAMILY`

CHANGE IT UP

For standard blueberry muffins, replace the lemon juice with 1 teaspoon of apple cider vinegar and omit the lemon zest.

KITCHEN TIP

Parchment paper muffin liners are the key to grain-free/Paleo baking that won't stick! Don't use standard papers here—trust me, nothing sticks to the parchment liners, and you'll be thrilled with the results.

If you love blueberries, these are the treat for you—they're packed with a fresh burst of the blue gems!

6 large eggs
1/2 cup butter or coconut oil, melted
1/4 cup pure maple syrup
1 teaspoon pure vanilla extract
Grated zest and juice of 1 lemon
1/2 cup coconut flour

1/4 cup tapioca flour or arrowroot starch
1/2 teaspoon sea salt
1/2 teaspoon baking soda
1 cup fresh blueberries

Preheat the oven to 350°F. Line a 12-well muffin tin with parchment paper liners.

In a large mixing bowl, whisk together the eggs, butter, maple syrup, vanilla extract, lemon zest, and lemon juice. Sift the coconut flour, tapioca flour, salt, and baking soda into the wet ingredients and stir until well combined. Gently fold in the blueberries.

Fill the lined muffin cups evenly with the batter and bake for 35 to 40 minutes, until a toothpick inserted into the center of a muffin comes out clean.

Store the muffins on the countertop for 1 day or in the refrigerator for up to 5 days.

pumpkin cranberry muffins

PREP TIME: 15 minutes | **COOKING TIME:** 35 to 40 minutes | **YIELD:** 1 dozen muffins

EGGS FODMAPS QUICK & EASY **PARTY** FAMILY

This recipe is sure to be a fall favorite in your house, and it's a great way to use up canned pumpkin. For an extra pop of cranberry flavor, spread some Simple Cranberry Sauce (page 436) on top.

6 large eggs

1/2 cup butter or coconut oil, melted

1/4 cup canned pumpkin

1/4 cup pure maple syrup

1 teaspoon pure vanilla extract

1/2 cup coconut flour

1/4 cup tapioca flour or arrowroot starch

1 tablespoon pumpkin pie spice

1/2 teaspoon sea salt

1/2 teaspoon baking soda

1/2 cup fresh cranberries

Preheat the oven to 350°F. Line a 12-well muffin tin with parchment paper liners.

In a large mixing bowl, whisk together the eggs, butter, pumpkin, maple syrup, and vanilla extract. Sift the coconut flour, tapioca flour, pumpkin pie spice, salt, and baking soda into the wet ingredients and stir until well combined. Gently fold in the cranberries.

Fill the lined muffin cups evenly with the batter and bake for 35 to 40 minutes, until a toothpick inserted into the center of a muffin comes out clean.

Store the muffins on the countertop for 1 day or in the refrigerator for up to 5 days.

CHANGE IT UP

If fresh cranberries aren't in season, use dried cranberries. Add chopped walnuts for some crunch.

KITCHEN TIP

Parchment paper muffin liners are the key to grain-free/Paleo baking that won't stick! Don't use standard papers here—trust me, nothing sticks to the parchment liners, and you'll be thrilled with the results.

carrot gingerbread muffins

PREP TIME: 20 minutes | **COOKING TIME:** 35 to 40 minutes | **YIELD:** 1 dozen muffins

`EGGS` `FODMAPS` `PARTY` `FAMILY`

CHANGE IT UP

The frosting works with other muffins as well. Top the Pumpkin Cranberry Muffins on page 277 with it, or use lemon zest instead of orange and use it to frost the Blueberry Lemon Muffins on page 276.

KITCHEN TIP

Parchment paper muffin liners are the key to grain-free/Paleo baking that won't stick! Don't use standard papers here—trust me, nothing sticks to the parchment liners, and you'll be thrilled with the results.

These muffins are a fantastic way to sneak some veggies into a treat. Each one contains about 1/4 cup of carrots, while the spiciness of the gingerbread is an indulgence.

6 large eggs
1/2 cup melted butter, ghee (page 261), or coconut oil
1/2 cup pure maple syrup
1/4 cup blackstrap molasses
1 teaspoon pure vanilla extract
1/2 teaspoon lemon juice
1/2 cup coconut flour
3 tablespoons tapioca flour or arrowroot starch
1 teaspoon ground cinnamon
1 teaspoon ginger powder
1/2 teaspoon ground cloves
1/2 teaspoon sea salt
1/2 teaspoon baking soda
3 cups shredded carrots
1/2 cup raisins (optional)

FROSTING (OPTIONAL)

1/4 cup coconut butter, softened
1/4 cup coconut oil
1/4 teaspoon grated fresh ginger
1 tablespoon grated orange zest
1 tablespoon unsweetened shredded coconut
1 tablespoon pure maple syrup

Preheat the oven to 350°F. Line a 12-well muffin tin with parchment paper liners.

In a large mixing bowl, whisk together the eggs, butter, maple syrup, molasses, vanilla extract, and lemon juice. Sift the coconut flour, tapioca flour, cinnamon, ginger powder, cloves, salt, and baking soda into the wet ingredients. Add the carrots and raisins (if using) and stir together. Allow the batter to sit for 10 minutes to thicken.

Fill the lined muffin cups evenly with the batter and bake for 35 to 40 minutes, until a toothpick inserted into the center of a muffin comes out clean.

While the muffins are baking, combine all of the frosting ingredients until smooth.

Remove the muffins from the pan and allow them to cool before frosting. Store on the countertop for 1 day or in the refrigerator for up to 5 days.

apple cinnamon egg muffins

PREP TIME: 15 minutes | **COOKING TIME:** About 40 minutes | **YIELD:** 1 dozen muffins

`EGGS` `FODMAPS` `21DSD` `FAMILY`

FODMAP-FREE?
Make this recipe with 2 chopped bananas instead of apples.

MAKE IT 21DSD
Do not add the maple syrup.

NOTE
For more sweetness, add a couple of chopped dried Medjool dates to the apples as they cook.

KITCHEN TIP
Parchment paper muffin liners are the key to grain-free/Paleo baking that won't stick! Don't use standard papers here—trust me, nothing sticks to parchment liners, and you'll be thrilled with the results.

CHANGE IT UP
Substitute lightly cooked pears or bananas for the apples.

Add 1/4 cup chopped nuts or unsweetened shredded coconut for texture and healthy fats.

I wanted a breakfast made from only whole ingredients that would still seem like a treat. The result was these Apple Cinnamon Egg Muffins. You can easily make a savory version by using the ingredients for my Swirly Crustless Quiche (page 270) and baking them as described here. Keep in mind that these are egg muffins, so the result will not be like a pastry but more like a slightly sweet egg dish.

3 large green apples, chopped into 1/2-inch pieces (about 2 cups)

3 tablespoons warm water

2 teaspoons ground cinnamon, divided

9 large eggs

3 tablespoons full-fat coconut milk

1 1/2 tablespoons butter, ghee (page 261), or coconut oil, melted

1 tablespoon pure maple syrup (optional)

1 1/2 tablespoons coconut flour

1/4 teaspoon baking soda

Pinch of sea salt

Preheat the oven to 350°F. Line a 12-well muffin tin with parchment paper liners.

In a medium-sized skillet over medium heat, sauté the apples, water, and 1 1/2 teaspoons of the cinnamon until the apples are the consistency of chunky applesauce or apple pie filling. Set aside to cool.

In a medium-sized mixing bowl, whisk the eggs, coconut milk, melted butter, maple syrup (if using), coconut flour, remaining 1/2 teaspoon of cinnamon, baking soda, and salt until well combined. Add the cooled apples, reserving 1/4 cup for garnish.

Spoon 1/4 cup of the batter into each lined muffin cup. Gently spoon about 1 teaspoon of the remaining apple mixture onto the top of each muffin.

Bake for 35 to 40 minutes, until puffed up and cooked through. Enjoy the muffins with some extra butter on top, if desired.

fluffy banana pancakes

PREP TIME: 10 minutes, plus time for the batter to set up | **COOKING TIME:** 20 minutes
YIELD: About 1 dozen 3-inch pancakes (2 servings)

EGGS QUICK & EASY FAMILY FREEZE ME

I've been working on a fluffy pancake recipe for years now, ever since the thinner, more delicate Pumpkin Pancakes (page 284) became a reader favorite. While the pumpkin version is lower in carbs and perfect for everyone, this version packs more carbs for those who need them, and it has a fluffier texture that's much closer to the grain-based pancakes you've left behind. These reheat beautifully, so go ahead and make a double batch!

2 ripe bananas, mashed

4 large eggs

1 teaspoon lemon juice

1 teaspoon pure vanilla extract

1 tablespoon melted ghee (page 261),
     butter, or coconut oil, plus extra
     for the pan

3 tablespoons coconut flour

2 tablespoons tapioca flour or
     arrowroot starch

1/2 teaspoon baking soda

Pinch of sea salt

FOR SERVING

Butter or ghee

Banana slices

Pure maple syrup

Fresh berries

Whisk the bananas, eggs, lemon juice, vanilla, and melted ghee together. Sift the coconut flour, tapioca flour, baking soda, and salt into the wet ingredients. Allow the batter to rest on the countertop for 5 to 10 minutes to thicken slightly.

Heat a large skillet over medium-low heat. Grease the skillet and spoon the batter into the skillet to make pancakes of your desired size. When a few bubbles appear, after about 2 minutes, flip the pancakes once to finish cooking. Repeat until you've used up all of the batter.

Serve with butter or ghee, sliced bananas, maple syrup, and fresh berries.

pumpkin pancakes

PREP TIME: 10 minutes | **COOKING TIME:** 20 minutes | **YIELD:** About 8 small pancakes (2 servings)

EGGS FODMAPS 21DSD QUICK & EASY FAMILY FREEZE ME

NUT-FREE?

Use coconut flour, or try using 1 to 2 tablespoons of arrowroot starch or tapioca flour and allowing the batter to sit for 5 to 10 minutes to see how it sets up before adding more.

MAKE IT 21DSD

Omit the maple syrup from the batter, and top the pancakes with compliant fruit (if using) or other condiments.

CHANGE IT UP

Instead of using maple syrup to sweeten the batter, try adding a mashed ripe banana. If you add a banana, the yield will increase.

When fall rolls around, it seems only natural to want to make as many recipes as possible that use pumpkin! This is a quick and easy way to take an inexpensive ingredient (canned pumpkin) and turn it into something delicious.

4 large eggs

1/2 cup canned pumpkin

2 tablespoons pure maple syrup

1 teaspoon pure vanilla extract

1 teaspoon ground cinnamon

1 teaspoon pumpkin pie spice

1/2 teaspoon baking soda

Pinch sea salt

2 tablespoons coconut flour or 3 tablespoons almond flour (optional; use if your batter is very runny)

1 tablespoon butter, ghee (page 261), or coconut oil, plus extra for the pan and for serving

Ground cinnamon or sliced bananas, for serving

In a large mixing bowl, whisk together the eggs, pumpkin, maple syrup (if using), and vanilla extract. Sift the cinnamon, pumpkin pie spice, baking soda, and salt into the wet ingredients and stir together until smooth. If the batter seems runny, sift in the optional flour, stir well to combine, then allow the batter to sit for 10 minutes to thicken. Note that these pancakes have a slightly thinner texture than others you may make that contain more starch.

Melt the butter in a large skillet over medium-low heat. Pour the melted butter into the batter and stir to combine.

Grease the skillet and return it to the heat. Spoon the batter into the skillet to make pancakes of your desired size. When a few bubbles appear on top, flip the pancakes once to finish cooking. Repeat with the remaining batter, regreasing the skillet between batches.

Serve with butter and a dusting of cinnamon or some sliced bananas.

sweet potato pancakes (burger buns)

PREP TIME: 15 minutes | **COOKING TIME:** 20 minutes | **YIELD:** 4 or 5 large pancakes (2 servings)

EGGS FODMAPS 21DSD QUICK & EASY FAMILY FREEZE ME

Enjoy these pancakes for breakfast or use them as buns for any burger! They can be made a few days ahead and reheated. For a lower-carb option, make them with shredded carrots instead of sweet potatoes.

3 large eggs

2 teaspoons coconut flour

1/2 teaspoon ground cinnamon

1/4 teaspoon ginger powder

1/4 teaspoon sea salt

2 cups shredded sweet potatoes

Coconut oil, for pan-frying

In a medium-sized mixing bowl, beat the eggs with the coconut flour, cinnamon, ginger powder, and salt. Mix in the shredded sweet potatoes until well combined.

Heat about 1/8 inch of coconut oil in a large skillet over medium heat. Spoon the mixture into the skillet to make "cakes" that are 4 to 6 inches in diameter (if using as burger "buns," make the pancakes about 4 to 5 inches in diameter). Cook for 2 to 3 minutes per side, until they hold together, flipping once as you would a regular pancake.

EGG-FREE?
Omit the eggs and coconut flour, then sauté the ingredients in a pan with 2 tablespoons of ghee or coconut oil to create a delicious hash. Or use white potatoes without the coconut flour or eggs.

FODMAP-FREE?
Omit the coconut flour and use 1/4 cup of any nut or seed flour.

NOTE
A food processor fitted with a shredding disc makes shredding the sweet potatoes super quick and easy, but you can also shred them by hand.

CHANGE IT UP
Replace the cinnamon and ginger with 1/4 teaspoon of dried rosemary leaves.

pesto scrambled eggs

PREP TIME: 5 minutes (not including pesto) | **COOKING TIME:** 3 minutes | **YIELD:** 2 servings

NUTS & SEEDS | EGGS | FODMAPS | 21DSD | QUICK & EASY | FAMILY

NOTE

You can also top fried or hard-boiled eggs with pesto—yum!

In this recipe, basic scrambled eggs are spruced up with some pesto. These eggs go great with a side of Perfectly Baked Bacon (page 260).

1 tablespoon butter, ghee (page 261), or coconut oil

4 large eggs

1 to 2 tablespoons Dairy-Free Pesto (page 380), plus extra for serving

Melt the butter in a skillet over medium heat.

Crack the eggs directly into the pan, then scramble them slowly—combining the yolks and whites loosely so that the color variation is still visible between the two. I recommend a heat-resistant silicone spatula for this task.

About 1 minute into cooking, add the pesto and continue to scramble the eggs, mixing the pesto in gently.

Once the eggs are no longer runny, they are done.

Serve with extra pesto.

bacon & egg salad

PREP TIME: 10 minutes (not including mayo or bacon) | **COOKING TIME:** 10 minutes
YIELD: 4 servings

EGGS 21DSD QUICK & EASY FAMILY

Egg salad is an old favorite of mine, but commercial mayonnaise is out of the question when you're avoiding refined seed oils. This take on a classic uses Paleo Mayonnaise and gets that bacon-y taste right into the dish.

SERVE IT UP
*Serve with sliced cucumber
or celery sticks.*

12 large eggs

1/4 cup Paleo Mayonnaise (page 438) made with bacon fat, or purchase an avocado oil variety

12 slices Perfectly Baked Bacon (page 260), chopped

2 tablespoons chopped fresh chives (optional)

Sea salt and black pepper

Take the eggs out of the refrigerator and allow them to come to room temperature. Fill a large pot with 8 cups of water and bring to a boil.

Place the eggs in the boiling water for 10 minutes. Transfer the eggs to a large bowl of ice water for 10 minutes. This will keep them from turning green around the yolks.

Peel the eggs, place them in a bowl, and mash them with a potato masher or large fork. Mix in the mayonnaise, bacon, and chives (if using). Season with salt and pepper to taste.

n'oatmeal

PREP TIME: 10 minutes | **COOKING TIME:** 10 minutes | **YIELD:** 1 large serving

NUTS & SEEDS | FODMAPS | 21DSD | QUICK & EASY | FAMILY

NUT-FREE?
Make the Pumpkin Tahini version, or replace the almond butter in the Coco-Nutty version with tahini or sunflower seed butter.

MAKE IT 21DSD
Omit the optional sweetener and dried fruit. Use only program-approved fruits to sweeten and enhance these.

CHANGE IT UP
Play with combining different types of nut butter!

SERVE IT UP
Top with berries, nuts, or seeds of your choice. Pictured here are raspberries, almonds, blueberries, and pumpkin seeds.

If you miss having a warm bowl of cereal in the morning, try these alternatives.

COCO-NUTTY

6 tablespoons warm water or full-fat coconut milk

1/4 cup unsweetened shredded coconut

2 tablespoons almond butter

1 teaspoon honey or pure maple syrup (optional)

1/2 teaspoon ground cinnamon

1/4 teaspoon pure vanilla extract

PUMPKIN TAHINI (NUT-FREE)

1/2 cup canned pumpkin

1/4 cup warm water

1 tablespoon tahini (sesame paste), raw or roasted

1 tablespoon unsweetened shredded coconut

1 tablespoon raisins

1 teaspoon honey or pure maple syrup (optional)

1/4 teaspoon pure vanilla extract

1/4 teaspoon ground cinnamon

Combine all of the ingredients for the flavor of your choice in a small mixing bowl.

Transfer the porridge to a saucepan and warm over low heat until it reaches your desired temperature.

quick breakfast smoothies

PREP TIME: 5 minutes | **COOKING TIME:** – | **YIELD:** 1 serving each

FODMAPS QUICK & EASY FAMILY

These easy smoothies can be made quickly right before blending, or you can portion out the frozen fruit in a to-go blender cup the night before and stash it in the freezer to save even more time in the morning. Simply scale up for more than one serving. I whip this up after I work out, but it also makes a great afternoon snack, after-dinner treat, or breakfast-on-the-go when paired with hard-boiled eggs or sausage!

CHERRY VANILLA

3/4 cup frozen, pitted cherries

1/2 cup ice

1/4 cup frozen blueberries

1/4 cup water

1/4 cup full-fat coconut or almond milk

1 teaspoon pure maple syrup or 1/8 teaspoon green stevia (optional)

1/8 teaspoon pure vanilla extract

3 scoops grass-fed collagen peptides

PEACH BLUEBERRY

3/4 cup frozen sliced peaches (6 to 8 slices)

1/2 cup ice

1/4 cup frozen blueberries

1/4 cup water

1/4 cup full-fat coconut or almond milk

1 teaspoon pure maple syrup or 1/8 teaspoon green stevia (optional)

1/8 teaspoon pure vanilla extract

3 scoops grass-fed collagen peptides

CHARGED CHOCOLATE BANANA

1 frozen sliced banana

4 ounces cold brew or chilled strong-brewed coffee, or 2 shots of espresso, chilled

1/2 cup ice

1/4 cup full-fat coconut or almond milk

1 heaping tablespoon unsweetened cocoa powder

1 teaspoon pure maple syrup or 1/8 teaspoon green stevia (optional)

1/8 teaspoon pure vanilla extract

3 scoops collagen peptides

The preparation of all of the smoothies is the same. Place the ingredients for the smoothie of your choice in a blender and blend until smooth. If you prefer a thinner smoothie, add more water or milk to your liking.

souvlaki kebabs

PREP TIME: 10 minutes, plus time to marinate the chicken

COOKING TIME: 20 minutes | **YIELD:** 4 to 6 servings

NIGHTSHADES · FODMAPS · 21DSD · SPICE BLEND · QUICK & EASY · PARTY · FAMILY

SPECIAL EQUIPMENT

Skewers (if using wood skewers, soak them in water for 30 minutes before using)

NIGHTSHADE-FREE?

Omit the tomatoes from the salad and double the amount of cucumber.

FODMAP-FREE?

Omit the onion and garlic.

SPICE BLEND SWAP

Replace the oregano, turmeric, salt, and pepper in the marinade with 2 teaspoons of Greek Blend (page 256).

CHANGE IT UP

Use another boneless lean protein, such as pork tenderloin or lamb leg meat, instead of chicken.

Greek flavors are some of my absolute favorites! Lemon, oregano, and a rich-tasting extra-virgin olive oil are magic together, and they take me back to our trip to Greece to see where the olives for Kasandrinos brand oil are grown. I've added some turmeric to what would otherwise be a more traditional souvlaki marinade to up the nutritional value and the visual impact of these skewers. They're perfect for a cookout or even a weeknight meal.

GREEK MARINADE

1/4 cup extra-virgin olive oil

Grated zest and juice of 2 lemons

1 small red onion, thinly sliced

2 large cloves garlic, minced

1 tablespoon minced fresh oregano

1/2 teaspoon turmeric powder

1/2 teaspoon sea salt

1/2 teaspoon black pepper

2 pounds boneless, skinless chicken breasts

1 small red onion

FOR GARNISH

Coarse sea salt

Minced fresh oregano

TOMATO AND CUCUMBER SALAD (OPTIONAL)

1 pint grape tomatoes, halved or quartered

1/4 cup Kalamata olives, pitted

1 large cucumber, sliced into half-moons

Juice of 1 lemon

2 tablespoons extra-virgin olive oil

1/2 teaspoon minced fresh oregano (optional)

Sea salt and black pepper

Make the marinade: Combine the ingredients for the marinade in a mixing bowl.

Marinate the chicken: Cut the chicken breast into 1 1/2-inch chunks. Add the chicken to the marinade and refrigerate for at least 20 minutes or up to overnight.

When you're ready to grill the chicken, preheat a grill or grill pan to medium-high heat and remove the chicken from the marinade (discard any remaining marinade). Cut the red onion into 1 1/2-inch chunks, then arrange the marinated chicken pieces on skewers, alternating them with the onion pieces.

Grill the skewers for 3 to 5 minutes on each side, until the chicken is seared but not burned and the internal temperature registers 165°F, 16 to 20 minutes total.

Make the salad (optional): Toss the tomatoes, olives, and cucumber with the lemon juice, olive oil, and oregano (if using). Season to taste with salt and pepper.

Garnish the kebabs with a sprinkling of coarse sea salt and fresh oregano leaves, and serve with the salad, if desired.

citrus & herb
whole roasted chicken

PREP TIME: 10 minutes | **COOKING TIME:** 1 to 2 hours | **YIELD:** 4 to 6 servings

FODMAPS | 21DSD | SPICE BLEND | QUICK & EASY | FAMILY | ONE POT

FODMAP-FREE?

Leave out the garlic and onion.

SPICE BLEND SWAP

Instead of the Herb Salt Blend and pepper, try sprinkling the chicken with the Greek, Mega Mediterranean, or Diner Blend (pages 256 to 257) to make it a totally new kind of bird.

One of the easiest ways to save money on protein is to buy whole animals, and chickens are no exception. Several people can eat a whole chicken for dinner, and the carcass can be used to make bone broth.

1/4 cup butter, ghee (page 261), coconut oil, bacon fat, or duck fat, melted

1 whole chicken

1 onion, cut into large chunks

4 to 6 cloves garlic, peeled and smashed with the side of a knife

1 orange or lemon, cut into 6 pieces

6 to 8 large carrots, cut into large chunks

1 tablespoon Herb Salt Blend of choice (page 258)

Black pepper

Preheat the oven to 375°F.

Brush the bottom of a large roasting pan with some of the melted butter.

Remove any gizzards or organs (sometimes found in a paper or plastic wrapping) from the inside of the chicken. Stuff the chicken with the onion, garlic, and some of the citrus. Place the carrots and the remaining citrus wedges around the chicken in the roasting pan. Brush the chicken with the remaining melted butter and sprinkle it with the herb salt blend and 3 or 4 generous pinches of black pepper.

Roast until the chicken reaches 165°F when a thermometer is placed between the leg and breast and the juices run clear when the meat is sliced. The exact cooking time depends on the size of the bird but is about 20 minutes per pound.

mediterranean baked chicken with cauliflower

PREP TIME: 10 minutes | **COOKING TIME:** 40 minutes | **YIELD:** 4 servings

`NIGHTSHADES` `FODMAPS` `21DSD` `SPICE BLEND` `QUICK & EASY` `FAMILY` `ONE POT`

NIGHTSHADE-FREE?

Omit the pepperoncini.

TURN DOWN THE HEAT

If your family doesn't like hot peppers, leave out the pepperoncini or replace them with roasted bell peppers.

I'm always looking for ways to simplify prep work in the kitchen for easy weeknight meals, and this is the perfect solution. One pan with meat, veggies, and seasonings—boom! What could be better? If your family enjoys the Lemon & Artichoke Chicken on page 296, this is another great dish to try.

1 head cauliflower

2 tablespoons extra-virgin olive oil or melted ghee (page 261), plus extra for the chicken

1/4 cup sliced pepperoncini, plus extra for garnish

1/3 cup capers

2 ounces pancetta, diced (about 1/4 cup)

2 large cloves garlic, thinly sliced

2 tablespoons Mega Mediterranean Blend (page 257), divided

3 pounds bone-in, skin-on chicken thighs

Sea salt and black pepper

Lemon wedges, for garnish

Preheat the oven to 400°F.

Cut the cauliflower into florets and place in a large glass or ceramic baking dish. Toss the cauliflower together with the olive oil, pepperoncini, capers, pancetta, and garlic, then season with 2 teaspoons of the spice blend. Toss again to evenly distribute the seasoning.

Place the chicken thighs on top of the cauliflower, then brush them with some olive oil and season with the remaining 1 tablespoon plus 1 teaspoon of spice blend and a few pinches each of salt and pepper. Top with the extra pepperoncini slices and bake for about 40 minutes, until the internal temperature of the chicken reaches 165°F.

Garnish with lemon wedges.

lemon & artichoke chicken

PREP TIME: 10 minutes | **COOKING TIME:** 50 minutes | **YIELD:** 4 servings

FODMAPS 21DSD SPICE BLEND QUICK & EASY FAMILY ONE POT

FODMAP-FREE?

Omit the shallots/onion and replace the artichoke hearts with thinly sliced carrots or parsnips.

SPICE BLEND SWAP

Instead of just salt and pepper, season the chicken with the Greek Blend (page 256).

CHANGE IT UP

You can make this recipe with whole chicken legs; bone-in, skin-on chicken breasts; or a whole chicken.

This is a twist on a classic chicken piccata using whole, bone-in, skin-on cuts, and it carries all of the flavor with none of the flour! This is sure to be a weeknight-dinner go-to favorite for your family.

4 tablespoons butter, ghee (page 261), or coconut oil, divided

2 shallots or 1/4 onion, sliced

2 cups artichoke hearts, thawed and/or drained and rinsed

1/4 cup capers, drained

Juice of 2 lemons

Sea salt and black pepper

2 pounds bone-in, skin-on chicken pieces

Preheat the oven to 375°F.

In a large, oven-safe skillet over medium heat, melt 2 tablespoons of the butter. Add the shallots and sauté until translucent. Add the artichoke hearts, capers, and lemon juice and season generously with salt and pepper. Stir to combine.

Place the chicken pieces in the skillet, season generously with salt and pepper, and top each piece with a small pat of the remaining 2 tablespoons of butter. Place the skillet in the oven and bake for 45 minutes, or until the chicken reaches an internal temperature of 165°F.

bacon-wrapped
smoky chicken thighs

PREP TIME: 10 minutes | **COOKING TIME:** 40 minutes | **YIELD:** 2 servings

NIGHTSHADES FODMAPS 21DSD SPICE BLEND QUICK & EASY PARTY FAMILY

NIGHTSHADE-FREE?
Instead of the Smoky Blend, try the Savory Blend.

CHANGE IT UP
Try this recipe with pork tenderloin instead of chicken thighs. Follow the same instructions but bake the tenderloin until it reaches an internal temperature of 145°F (30 to 40 minutes).

What do you do when you get home with a pack of bone-in chicken thighs only to discover that you accidentally bought the skinless ones? Wrap them in bacon! Add my Smoky Blend and you have a delicious dish.

4 skinless chicken thighs (bone-in or boneless)

2 teaspoons Smoky Blend (page 256), divided

8 slices bacon

Preheat the oven to 375°F.

Sprinkle the chicken thighs with 1 teaspoon of the spice blend. Wrap each thigh in 2 slices of bacon. Sprinkle the chicken with the remaining 1 teaspoon of spice blend and bake for about 40 minutes, until the internal temperature reaches 165°F.

INGREDIENT TIP
You can certainly make this recipe with chicken breasts instead of thighs if you prefer. Also, note that this recipe was developed for skinless chicken, since the bacon helps keep the meat moist during cooking and adds flavor (and besides, wrapping the bacon around the chicken skin will not allow the skin to crisp). If you buy chicken with the skin on, I recommend removing the skin and baking it in a separate pan, dusted with some Smoky Blend, until it is crispy to enjoy as a snack or to chop up and use as a salad topper.

buffalo chicken lettuce wraps

PREP TIME: 10 minutes | **COOKING TIME:** 5 to 10 minutes | **YIELD:** 2 large or 4 small servings

NIGHTSHADES FODMAPS 21DSD QUICK & EASY PARTY FAMILY

Lettuce wraps are one of my favorite ways to take whatever random protein I have in the refrigerator and turn it into something delicious and handheld. The crunch and freshness of lettuce wrapped around this spicy chicken is a fun change of pace from Buffalo wings.

1 pound boneless, skinless chicken thighs

2 teaspoons chipotle powder

1/2 teaspoon garlic powder

1/2 teaspoon onion powder

Sea salt and black pepper

2 tablespoons coconut oil

1 head butter lettuce or other lettuce of choice, leaves separated

1 avocado, sliced

1/2 cup cherry or grape tomatoes, halved

2 tablespoons chopped green onions (scallions)

NIGHTSHADE-FREE?
Omit the chipotle powder and tomatoes.

FODMAP-FREE?
Omit the garlic powder, onion powder, avocado, and green onions; top with cilantro instead.

CHANGE IT UP
Have a favorite hot sauce? Use 1 tablespoon in place of the chipotle powder, garlic powder, and onion powder.

Slice the chicken thighs into 1/4-inch strips. In a mixing bowl, toss the chicken with the chipotle powder, garlic powder, and onion powder and season generously with salt and pepper.

In a skillet over medium heat, melt the coconut oil, then place the chicken thighs in the skillet. Cook for 5 to 10 minutes, turning occasionally, until the chicken is white all the way through.

Serve in lettuce cups topped with avocado slices, halved cherry or grape tomatoes, and chopped green onions.

POULTRY

one-pot sausage & chicken spaghetti squash bake

PREP TIME: 15 minutes | **COOKING TIME:** About 1 hour | **YIELD:** 4 servings

EGGS NIGHTSHADES FODMAPS 21DSD SPICE BLEND MEAL FAMILY ONE POT FREEZE ME

EGG-FREE?
Omit the egg.

NOTE
If you are using chicken breast, add 1 tablespoon of ghee or other cooking fat to the pot before adding the chicken.

Spaghetti squash is a classic Paleo pasta replacement, and this dish brings it together with protein and bold flavors to create a complete meal your whole family will love. If your family enjoys more traditional sauce-covered pasta dishes, check out the Spaghetti Squash Bolognese on page 338.

1 medium spaghetti squash, about 5 pounds

2 tablespoons extra-virgin olive oil, divided

1/2 pound ground pork, beef, or turkey

1 tablespoon Italian Blend, divided (page 256)

1 small yellow onion, sliced

1 red bell pepper, sliced

1 clove garlic, grated or minced

Sea salt and black pepper

1/2 pound boneless, skinless chicken thighs or breast, cut into 1-inch pieces (see Note)

2 cups loosely packed spinach, chopped

2 tablespoons chopped fresh basil

1 large egg, beaten

1/2 cup pizza sauce (use a no-sugar-added variety)

FOR GARNISH
Chopped fresh basil

Coarse sea salt

Red pepper flakes

Make the spaghetti squash noodles: Preheat the oven to 375°F and follow the instructions in the recipe for Spaghetti Squash Bolognese on page 338. After you remove the squash from the oven, lower the oven temperature to 350°F.

While the squash is roasting, prepare the rest of the ingredients: Heat a large oven-safe pot, such as an enameled cast-iron skillet, over medium-high heat and add the ground meat. Season with 1 1/2 teaspoons of the spice blend. Cook for 6 to 7 minutes, until the meat is browned, breaking the meat up with a spatula as it cooks. Remove the meat using a slotted spoon, leaving about 1 tablespoon of oil behind.

Lower the heat to medium and add the onion, bell pepper, and garlic and season with a few pinches each of salt and pepper. Cook for 4 to 5 minutes, until the onion is translucent and starting to brown. If there are too many brown bits on the bottom of the pan and things are beginning to burn, add a couple tablespoons of water and use a wooden spoon to loosen the bits. Remove the vegetables from the pot and set aside. If you added water to the pan during cooking, add a teaspoon of ghee or other cooking fat to the pan before adding the chicken.

Add the chicken to the pot, season with the remaining 1 1/2 teaspoons of spice blend, and cook for 6 to 8 minutes, until cooked through.

Return the sausage and vegetables to the pot, then add the cooked spaghetti squash noodles, spinach, basil, and egg and stir everything thoroughly to combine. Taste and add more salt and pepper, if needed (keeping in mind you will be garnishing the dish with coarse sea salt).

Dollop spoonfuls of the pizza sauce over the top and bake for 15 to 20 minutes, until the egg is cooked and everything is warmed through together.

Garnish with fresh basil, coarse salt, and red pepper flakes before serving.

slow-cooked salsa verde chicken

PREP TIME: 10 minutes (not including broth or plantain chips)
COOKING TIME: 3 1/2 to 4 hours | **YIELD:** 9 to 12 servings

`NIGHTSHADES` `FODMAPS` `21DSD` `SPICE BLEND` `LOW & SLOW` `PARTY` `FAMILY` `ONE POT`

SLOW-COOK IT

Place all of the ingredients in a slow cooker and cook, covered, on low for 4 to 6 hours, until the chicken is fork-tender and pulls apart easily.

This chicken is super versatile! Whether you use it in soups (page 390), in lettuce-wrapped tacos, or atop a taco salad (page 350) or cilantro and lime–infused cauli-rice (page 412), you'll find yourself reaching for it over and over as a quick, ready-to-go protein source. You can make this in a Dutch oven or a slow cooker; I personally prefer the texture of the chicken when it's cooked in a Dutch oven.

3 pounds boneless, skinless chicken breasts or thighs

1 large onion, sliced

4 to 6 cloves garlic, smashed with the side of a knife

1 (24-ounce) jar salsa verde

1/3 cup chicken Bone Broth (page 259) (optional)

1/4 cup tomato paste

2 tablespoons extra-virgin olive oil

1 tablespoon paprika

2 teaspoons ground cumin

2 teaspoons ground coriander

2 teaspoons sea salt

2 teaspoons black pepper

2 bay leaves

FOR SERVING (OPTIONAL)

1 recipe Crispy Plantain Chips (page 431)

Sliced avocado

Fresh cilantro

Lime wedges

Preheat the oven to 325°F.

Place all of the ingredients in an enameled Dutch oven or other large, heavy, oven-safe pot and stir to combine, coating the chicken with the sauce.

Cover and place into the oven for 3 hours, or until the chicken is fork-tender and pulls apart easily. After 3 hours, adjust the lid so that it's off-center and return the pot to the oven for an additional 30 minutes to 1 hour to allow the liquid to reduce to a thick sauce.

Remove the chicken from the Dutch oven (reserve the sauce) and allow it to cool slightly before shredding with two forks or a fork and spoon. Toss the shredded meat in the reserved sauce.

If desired, serve with plantain chips, garnished with avocado slices, cilantro, and a squeeze of lime.

PRACTICAL PALEO | 303

dairy-free pepperoni chicken parm

PREP TIME: 25 minutes | **COOKING TIME:** About 25 minutes | **YIELD:** 4 servings

`NUTS & SEEDS` `EGGS` `NIGHTSHADES` `FODMAPS` `21DSD` `SPICE BLEND` `FAMILY` `FREEZE ME`

SPICE BLEND SWAP

Replace the dried herbs, spices, and salt in the breading with 1 tablespoon of Italian Blend (page 256).

FREEZE ME

Freeze the "breaded" chicken pieces after they've been cooked and cooled but without any other toppings on them.

SERVE IT UP

Serve over zucchini noodles (page 380) or spaghetti squash (page 338) and drizzle with extra-virgin olive oil for added flavor and richness.

Does chicken parm really need an introduction? This is serious comfort food right here, and your family will love this dairy-free version. If you've learned that you can enjoy dairy without issues, feel free to use some high-quality fresh mozzarella in place of the béchamel. You can also make this recipe with eggplant or veal cutlets instead of chicken for a change of pace.

1 1/2 pounds boneless, skinless chicken thighs

Sea salt and black pepper

1/4 cup duck fat, bacon fat, lard, or coconut oil

BREADING

1 cup almond flour or other raw nut or seed meal or flour

2 tablespoons tapioca flour or arrowroot starch

1 teaspoon dried oregano leaves

1/2 teaspoon garlic powder

1/2 teaspoon paprika

1/2 teaspoon sea salt

1/2 teaspoon black pepper

1 large egg

BÉCHAMEL SAUCE

1/2 cup full-fat coconut milk

2 tablespoons tapioca flour or arrowroot starch

1/2 teaspoon sea salt

1/2 teaspoon black pepper

1 clove garlic, smashed with the side of a knife

1/4 pound thinly sliced clean-ingredient pepperoni or other spicy cured meat of choice (optional)

1/2 cup spaghetti sauce (use a no-sugar-added variety)

Fresh basil leaves, for garnish

Preheat the oven to 350°F. Line a rimmed baking sheet with parchment paper.

Tear two large sheets of plastic wrap from a roll and place one sheet on a large cutting board. Next, set one chicken thigh onto the plastic wrap, then cover the chicken with the other sheet of plastic wrap. Using a kitchen mallet, evenly pound the chicken out until it's roughly 1/4-inch in thickness. Repeat this process for all pieces of chicken. Season the chicken on both sides with a few pinches each of salt and pepper.

Place a large, heavy-bottomed, high-sided skillet or sauté pan over medium-high heat. Melt the duck fat in the pan and allow it to become hot, about 5 minutes. While the fat is heating up, bread the chicken.

Create a "breading" station for the chicken: In a large, shallow bowl or dish, whisk the almond flour, tapioca flour, oregano, garlic powder, paprika, salt, and pepper until well combined. In a second large, shallow bowl or dish, whisk the egg until well beaten. Dunk the chicken into the egg mixture to coat it completely, allowing excess egg to drip off. Next, place the chicken into the flour mixture to coat it completely, gently shaking off any excess. Repeat this process for all pieces of chicken.

Place the chicken into the hot pan and cook for 3 to 4 minutes on each side, until the breading has turned golden brown. Place the browned chicken on the prepared baking sheet. Once all of the chicken has been browned, place the pan in the oven and bake for 10 minutes or until the internal temperature of the chicken reaches 165°F.

Meanwhile, make the béchamel sauce: Combine the ingredients in a small saucepan and heat over medium-low heat, whisking often, until it thickens, then remove the pan from the heat. You will know the mixture is ready when you can run your finger down the back of a wooden spoon coated with the sauce and the sauce does not spread. Remove the smashed garlic before serving.

When the chicken is done, remove the pan from the oven and cover each piece of chicken with a single, thin layer of pepperoni, then a spoonful of spaghetti sauce, and then the béchamel sauce. Repeat this process for all pieces of chicken. Keep any remaining sauce aside for a final drizzle over the chicken before baking.

Place an oven rack in the top position and preheat the oven to a high broil setting. Place the chicken back into the oven on the top rack for 2 minutes or until the béchamel is lightly browned. If your oven doesn't have a broil setting, you can simply place the chicken back into a 350°F oven for 5 additional minutes.

Garnish with fresh basil before serving.

POULTRY

orange & olive braised chicken

PREP TIME: 10 minutes (not including broth) | **COOKING TIME:** 1 hour | **YIELD:** 4 servings

FODMAPS 21DSD MEAL LOW & SLOW PARTY FAMILY ONE POT

MAKE IT 21DSD

Use lemon juice and zest instead of orange.

When I ran a meal delivery business (Balanced Bites) back in 2008, this was a favorite meal of my clients. They loved the contrasting flavors of the salty olives and sweet orange, and how tender the chicken becomes. You'll love this served with Cilantro or Yellow Cauli-Rice (pages 412 to 413). If this dish becomes one of your favorites, don't miss the recipes in the cookbook Mediterranean Paleo Cooking, *which feature many of these same ingredients!*

2 tablespoons ghee (page 261)

2 yellow onions, sliced

4 large cloves garlic, grated or minced

4 bone-in, skin-on chicken legs (about 2 pounds)

Sea salt and black pepper

1 teaspoon dried oregano leaves

1 (6-ounce) can pitted Calvestrano or green olives (about 1 cup), drained

Grated zest and juice of 1 orange (reserve the zest for garnish)

1/4 cup chicken Bone Broth (page 259)

FOR GARNISH

Grated orange zest (from above)

Chopped fresh cilantro or parsley

Preheat the oven to 350°F.

Melt the ghee in an enameled Dutch oven or other large oven-safe pan over medium heat. Add the onions and cook for 5 to 7 minutes, until the onions become translucent and begin to brown. Add the garlic and cook for 1 to 2 more minutes, until the garlic starts to turn golden brown.

Season both sides of the chicken with a few pinches each of salt and pepper and the oregano. Make a well in the middle of the onion and garlic mixture and add the chicken legs skin side down. Cook for 5 to 6 minutes, until the chicken skin starts to crisp up. Flip the chicken and add the olives, orange juice, and chicken broth to the skillet, filling in the space around the chicken legs.

Bake for 45 minutes or until the chicken reaches an internal temperature of 165°F.

Garnish with the orange zest and fresh herbs.

smoky buffalo wings

PREP TIME: 10 minutes | **COOKING TIME:** About 35 minutes | **YIELD:** 4 servings

NIGHTSHADES FODMAPS 21DSD SPICE BLEND QUICK & EASY PARTY FAMILY

MAKE IT 21DSD

Omit the honey.

2 dozen chicken wings

3 tablespoons Smoky Blend (page 256)

1/4 cup melted coconut oil, ghee (page 261), or butter

2 to 3 tablespoons hot sauce (depending on heat preference)

1 teaspoon honey (optional)

Preheat the oven to 375°F and place a wire baking rack on a rimmed baking sheet.

Place the wings in a large mixing bowl. Sprinkle about half of the spice blend over the wings, then toss to coat; repeat with the other half of the spice blend. Place the wings smooth skin side up on the baking rack, not touching. Sprinkle any spice blend left in the bowl over the wings.

Bake for 30 to 40 minutes, until the chicken reaches an internal temperature of 165°F and is cooked through (no pink remains) and the skin is crispy. If you want to crisp the skin further, turn the oven to a low broil setting and broil for about 5 minutes.

In a large bowl, whisk together the melted oil, hot sauce, and honey (if using), starting with 2 tablespoons of hot sauce. Taste and add more hot sauce, 1 teaspoon at a time, as desired. If you accidentally add too much, add a bit more oil or honey to the sauce. Toss the wings in the sauce right when they come out of the oven.

honey garlic teriyaki wings

PREP TIME: 5 minutes, plus time to marinate | **COOKING TIME:** 30 minutes | **YIELD:** 4 servings

NUTS & SEEDS FODMAPS QUICK & EASY PARTY FAMILY

SEED-FREE?

Omit the sesame oil and seeds and use olive oil in the marinade.

FODMAP-FREE?

Omit the garlic and green onion garnish.

MARINADE

1/3 cup coconut aminos

1 tablespoon cold-pressed sesame oil

2 to 3 teaspoons honey, or to taste

1 teaspoon fish sauce

1 teaspoon white sesame seeds or a combination of black and white

1 teaspoon granulated garlic

1/2 teaspoon apple cider vinegar

1/2 teaspoon sea salt

1/2 teaspoon black pepper

1/4 teaspoon ginger powder

Hot sauce, to taste

2 dozen chicken wings

FOR GARNISH

White and/or black sesame seeds

Sliced green onions (scallions) (optional)

In a large mixing bowl, mix together the marinade ingredients. Taste the mixture and make any adjustments necessary (salt, hot sauce, honey).

Toss the chicken wings in the marinade and place in the refrigerator for at least 1 hour or up to overnight.

Preheat the oven to 375°F and place a wire baking rack on a rimmed baking sheet.

Spread the chicken wings evenly on the baking rack and bake for about 30 minutes, until the chicken reaches an internal temperature of 165°F and is cooked through.

For crispy skin, turn the oven to a low broil setting and broil for about 5 minutes.

Garnish with sesame seeds and green onions, if desired.

spinach artichoke stuffed chicken

PREP TIME: 20 minutes (not including dip or broth) **|** **COOKING TIME:** 35 minutes
YIELD: 4 servings

NUTS & SEEDS | NIGHTSHADES | FODMAPS | 21DSD | SPICE BLEND | PARTY | FAMILY | ONE POT

NUT-FREE?

Use the nut-free variation for the Spinach Artichoke Dip filling.

NIGHTSHADE-FREE?

Season the chicken with a mixture of salt, pepper, and granulated garlic instead of the Diner Blend (which contains paprika).

NOTE

You can substitute bacon for the prosciutto, using 2 slices per roll—you'll need 4 to 8 slices. Sear the bacon-wrapped chicken rolls in the pan for 1 to 2 minutes per side, until the bacon starts to crisp up and turn slightly brown, before placing in the oven to bake. If you use bacon, you will not need to brush the rolls with additional fat before baking.

Trust me when I tell you that the effort you will put into making the stuffing for this recipe will be well worth it. Plus, you'll have plenty of it to enjoy as a stand-alone dip or for a second batch of this chicken. This is hands-down my favorite chicken recipe in this book! I couldn't stop eating this one when it came out of the oven, and I know your family will love it. This dish pairs perfectly with the Mashed Faux-Tatoes on page 418 or the Yellow Cauli-Rice on page 413.

1 pound boneless, skinless chicken breast, butterflied (see page 254), pounded thin, and cut into 4 pieces

2 teaspoons Diner Blend (page 256)

1 cup Dairy-Free Spinach Artichoke Dip (page 429)

4 ounces sliced prosciutto

1 tablespoon ghee (page 261)

1/4 cup chicken Bone Broth (page 259), plus extra if needed

8 cups loosely packed baby spinach (about 12 ounces)

Sea salt and black pepper

Preheat the oven to 350°F.

Lightly season both sides of the chicken with the Diner Blend.

Place about 2 to 3 tablespoons of the dip on the smaller end of each piece of chicken, then roll up the chicken beginning on the filled side. Next, wrap each piece with prosciutto so the chicken is fully covered. Depending on the size of your chicken, you may need 1 to 2 slices of prosciutto per chicken breast. Tie each chicken breast with kitchen string, so the prosciutto and dip stays secure.

In a large oven-safe skillet, melt the ghee over medium heat. Add the chicken rolls and brush a little of the melted ghee over the top of each piece. Pour the chicken broth around the chicken and place in the oven for 30 minutes or until a meat thermometer inserted into the center of the dip inside the roll reads 165°F.

Remove the chicken from the pan. The pan should be coated with a layer of liquid; if not, add 2 to 3 tablespoons of chicken broth.

Place the pan on the stovetop over medium heat and add the spinach. Season lightly with salt and pepper and cook for 2 to 3 minutes, until the spinach has wilted.

Divide the spinach among 4 plates and top each portion with a chicken roll.

restaurant-style lettuce cups with sesame sauce

PREP TIME: 20 minutes | **COOKING TIME:** 15 minutes | **YIELD:** 3 to 4 servings

NUTS & SEEDS NIGHTSHADES FODMAPS 21DSD QUICK & EASY MEAL PARTY FAMILY FREEZE ME

NIGHTSHADE-FREE?

Omit the bell peppers from the toppings.

FODMAP-FREE?

Omit the bell peppers and red cabbage from the toppings.

FREEZE ME

Freeze the cooked and seasoned meat and defrost it to enjoy with fresh vegetables when you're ready.

Asian flavors used to be tough to replicate without soy, but the deep, rich flavor that was once found only in soy sauce is brought out by a fermented coconut product called coconut aminos. You can find coconut aminos in most health food stores as well as from online retailers. As with soy sauce, a little bit goes a long way!

2 tablespoons coconut oil or sustainably sourced red palm oil

1 pound ground turkey

2 tablespoons coconut aminos

1 1/2 tablespoons Chinese 5-spice

Sea salt and black pepper

1 tablespoon sesame seeds, for garnish

1 head butter or Bibb lettuce, leaves separated

SAUCE

2 teaspoons raw or roasted tahini (sesame paste), almond butter, or sunflower seed butter

2 tablespoons coconut aminos

1 tablespoon cold-pressed sesame oil

1 teaspoon sesame seeds, for garnish

TOPPINGS

1 large carrot, shredded (about 1/2 cup)

1/4 cup chopped fresh cilantro

1/2 cup sliced bell peppers, assorted colors

1/2 cup chopped cucumber

1/4 cup shredded red cabbage

1 lime, cut into wedges

In a large skillet over medium heat, melt the oil. Add the ground turkey, coconut aminos, Chinese 5-spice, and several pinches each of salt and pepper. With a wooden spoon or heat-resistant spatula, break up the meat and spread the spices around. Cook until browned.

Make the sauce: Combine all of the ingredients except for the sesame seeds in a small mixing bowl.

Garnish the meat and sauce with the sesame seeds.

Use as many or as few of the toppings as you like and serve in lettuce cups.

chicken satay sandwiches with blistered peppers

PREP TIME: 30 minutes, plus time to marinate the chicken

COOKING TIME: 10 minutes | **YIELD:** 4 servings

`NUTS & SEEDS` `NIGHTSHADES` `FODMAPS` `21DSD` `MEAL` `PARTY` `FAMILY`

NIGHTSHADE-FREE?

Omit the red pepper flakes from the sauce, the Blistered Shishito Peppers, and red bell pepper garnish.

HOW TO MAKE BLISTERED SHISHITO PEPPERS:

Toss 12 ounces of shishito peppers (or other small peppers) in a large skillet that's been preheated over high heat with about 2 teaspoons of the cooking fat of your choice and a few pinches of fine sea salt. Sauté until charred, and finish with coarse sea salt before serving.

PARTY TIME!

Cut chicken breast into strips or use tenders and place the pieces on skewers before marinating to grill up as single-serving bites with the sauce at a party—fun!

At first glance, this recipe uses a lot of ingredients, but most of them are spices you likely have on hand or that are easily found in any grocery store. Stocking your pantry and fridge with a few special Paleo staples like coconut aminos and fish sauce will make cooking Asian-inspired recipes a cinch!

MARINADE

1/2 cup full-fat coconut milk

1 teaspoon grated or minced fresh garlic

1 teaspoon grated or minced fresh ginger

1 teaspoon turmeric powder

1/2 teaspoon ground coriander

1/2 teaspoon sea salt

1/2 teaspoon black pepper

1 small onion, thinly sliced, or 1 tablespoon onion powder

1 1/2 pounds boneless, skinless chicken breast, butterflied (see page 254)

SLAW

Juice of 1 lime

2 tablespoons extra-virgin olive oil

Sea salt and black pepper

1 cup thinly sliced or shredded cabbage, red or green or a combination

1/4 cup shredded carrots

SATAY SAUCE

1/2 cup almond butter, sunflower seed butter, or tahini (sesame paste), raw or roasted

1/2 cup coconut aminos

1/4 cup organic rice vinegar

A few dashes of fish sauce

1/4 teaspoon ground black pepper

1/4 teaspoon sea salt

1/4 teaspoon red pepper flakes

1/2 teaspoon toasted sesame seeds

FOR SERVING

1 head butter lettuce, separated into leaves

1 recipe Blistered Shishito Peppers (recipe at left) (optional)

FOR GARNISH (OPTIONAL)

Sliced red bell pepper

Chopped fresh cilantro

Lime wedges

In a mixing bowl, combine the ingredients for the marinade. Note that it will be a thick, more pastelike marinade rather than a more liquid-y marinade. Place the chicken in the bowl and massage the marinade into it. Refrigerate for at least 20 minutes or up to overnight.

While the chicken marinates, prepare the slaw and satay sauce. To make the slaw, whisk together the lime juice, olive oil, and a few pinches each of salt and pepper in a mixing bowl, then toss the cabbage and carrots in the dressing and set aside. In a separate mixing bowl, whisk together the sauce ingredients until combined and set aside.

Preheat a grill or grill pan to medium-high heat. Grill the chicken for 4 to 5 minutes per side, depending on the thickness of the chicken, until it's white all the way through. When you notice that the chicken has turned white up around the sides and toward the middle, it's time to flip it.

To serve, place a piece of chicken on top of a lettuce leaf and top with the slaw and optional garnishes. Serve with the satay sauce and Blistered Shishito Peppers, if desired.

savory baked chicken legs

PREP TIME: 5 minutes | **COOKING TIME:** 45 minutes to 1 hour | **YIELD:** 3 to 6 servings

`NUTS & SEEDS` `NIGHTSHADES` `FODMAPS` `21DSD` `SPICE BLEND` `QUICK & EASY` `FAMILY`

NIGHTSHADE-FREE?

Use a nightshade-free spice blend.

FODMAP-FREE?

Use a FODMAP-free spice blend.

MAKE IT 21DSD

Use any spice blend except the Coffee BBQ Rub, which contains sugar.

CHANGE IT UP

Substitute bone-in, skin-on chicken breasts for the legs.

SERVE IT UP

With a simple green salad or Roasted Brussels Sprouts (page 416).

I love the ease and versatility of baked chicken. Because you can switch up the cooking fat and whatever spices you like, the possibilities are endless. To simplify things even further, I recommend that you top the chicken legs with one of my spice blends.

6 chicken legs

1 to 2 tablespoons butter, ghee (page 261), bacon fat, or coconut oil, melted

2 tablespoons spice blend of choice (pages 256 to 257)

Preheat the oven to 375°F.

Place the chicken legs on a rimmed baking sheet or in a baking dish and brush them with the melted butter. Sprinkle the spice blend evenly over the chicken legs.

Bake for 45 minutes to 1 hour, until a thermometer reads 165°F when inserted into the center of a chicken leg.

Pictured: Greek Blend and Mega Mediterranean Blend

mustard-glazed chicken thighs

PREP TIME: 5 minutes | **COOKING TIME:** 45 minutes | **YIELD:** 4 to 6 servings

`21DSD` `SPICE BLEND` `QUICK & EASY` `PARTY` `FAMILY`

Honey mustard is easy to re-create without any sweetener when it's made with a healthy fat like butter, ghee, or coconut oil. Use whichever you like best, or try mixing them.

1/4 cup butter, ghee (page 261), or coconut oil, melted

2 tablespoons gluten-free mustard

1 teaspoon Herb Salt Blend made with sage (page 258) or 1/2 teaspoon sea salt plus 1/2 teaspoon dried ground sage

A few pinches of black pepper

12 bone-in, skin-on chicken thighs

Preheat the oven to 425°F.

In a small mixing bowl, combine the melted butter, mustard, sage salt, and pepper. Place the chicken thighs on a rimmed baking sheet or in a baking dish and brush the butter mixture evenly over each one.

Bake for 45 minutes, or until a thermometer reads 165°F when inserted into the center of a chicken thigh.

NOTE

These are fantastic reheated in the oven or toaster oven, and they make a delicious mild breakfast as well.

CHANGE IT UP

Use bone-in, skin-on chicken breasts if you don't have chicken thighs.

SERVE IT UP

With Mashed Faux-Tatoes (page 418).

coffee BBQ rubbed pork with seared pineapple

PREP TIME: 10 minutes, plus time to marinate the pork (not including broth)
COOKING TIME: 40 minutes | **YIELD:** 6 servings

`NIGHTSHADES` `FODMAPS` `SPICE BLEND` `PARTY` `FAMILY` `ONE POT`

NIGHTSHADE-FREE?
Use the Cumin-Spiced Pork Tenderloin spice mixture on page 320 in place of the Coffee BBQ Rub.

MAKE IT EASIER
Purchase precut pineapple spears or wedges instead of cutting the pineapple yourself.

We absolutely love cooked pineapple in our house. Whether it's grilled or sautéed, it's a favorite to pair with lots of different proteins. Here I've combined the tropical fruit with pork tenderloin that is infused with a smoky coffee spice rub. When paired with a green salad and cauliflower rice or baked white or sweet potatoes, it creates the perfect Hawaiian-inspired weeknight meal.

2 boneless pork tenderloins (about 2 pounds)

1/4 cup Coffee BBQ Rub (page 257)

1 teaspoon bacon fat, coconut oil, ghee (page 261), or butter

1/4 cup beef or chicken Bone Broth (page 259) or water

1/2 fresh pineapple, peeled and cut into 1/4-inch-thick spears

Sliced green onions (scallions), for garnish (optional)

Marinate the pork: Place the pork tenderloins in a shallow dish and pat dry with a paper towel. Season all sides of the meat evenly with the spice rub. Cover the dish and let the pork marinate, refrigerated, for at least 1 hour or up to overnight. The longer the pork marinates, the more crustlike the spice rub will become.

When you're ready to cook the pork, preheat the oven to 375°F.

Heat a large oven-safe pan over medium-high heat. Add the cooking fat and let it melt completely to coat the pan. Sear the meat all over until lightly browned, 2 to 3 minutes per side. Place the pan in the oven and roast the pork for 20 to 25 minutes for medium-rare, or until the internal temperature registers 145°F.

Remove the pork from the pan and let it rest for 5 to 10 minutes. Place the pan over high heat and pour the broth into the pan to deglaze it. Use a wooden spoon to loosen all the brown bits stuck to the bottom (this will give the dish lots of extra flavor). Reduce the liquid over high heat for 2 to 3 minutes, stirring often, until it thickens slightly.

Add the pineapple spears to the pan and cook for 5 minutes, turning the spears so they're evenly coated in the glaze.

Once the pork has rested, slice on the bias and serve with the pineapple spears. Garnish with sliced green onions, if desired.

PORK

cumin-spiced pork tenderloin with root vegetables

PREP TIME: 20 minutes | **COOKING TIME:** 45 minutes to 1 hour | **YIELD:** 4 to 6 servings

FODMAPS 21DSD PARTY FAMILY

FODMAP-FREE?

Omit the onion and garlic and substitute carrots for the parsnips.

SERVE IT UP

This dish pairs nicely with Roasted Brussels Sprouts (page 416).

This dish was inspired by a cooking class that I took in San Francisco called "Food of Spain." The combination of cumin and garlic complements the pork nicely. Served over roasted root vegetables, this dish is simple enough for a weeknight meal but creates an elegant enough presentation to serve to dinner guests.

SPICE BLEND

1 tablespoon ground cumin

1 tablespoon ground coriander

1 tablespoon granulated garlic or garlic powder

1 teaspoon sea salt

1 teaspoon black pepper

2 pork tenderloins (about 2 pounds)

2 tablespoons bacon fat or other cooking fat of choice

2 onions, chopped into large pieces

4 parsnips, peeled and chopped

2 cloves garlic, peeled and smashed with the side of a knife

Seeds of 1 pomegranate (about 1/2 cup) (optional)

2 to 3 sprigs fresh rosemary

Preheat the oven to 375°F.

In a small mixing bowl, combine the cumin, coriander, granulated garlic, salt, and pepper.

Using paper towels, pat the pork tenderloins dry. Apply the spice blend to the meat generously to create a crust.

Melt the bacon fat in a large skillet over medium-high heat. Place the pork tenderloins in the hot skillet and sear on all sides, about 2 minutes per side.

Place the onions, parsnips, garlic cloves, and pomegranate seeds (if using) in a large roasting dish, topped by the seared pork tenderloins. Place the rosemary sprigs on top of the pork, then roast for 30 to 40 minutes, until the internal temperature of the pork reaches 145°F. If you need to continue to roast the vegetables until they are soft, simply remove the pork and set it aside on a cutting board to rest while the vegetables finish roasting for another 10 to 15 minutes.

Slice the tenderloins on the bias (diagonally) and serve over the vegetables.

PORK

chorizo meatballs

PREP TIME: 10 minutes | **COOKING TIME:** 30 minutes | **YIELD:** 1 dozen meatballs

NIGHTSHADES FODMAPS 21DSD SPICE BLEND QUICK & EASY PARTY FAMILY FREEZE ME

CHANGE IT UP
Substitute beef or a combination of ground pork and ground chicken.

FREEZE ME
Double or triple the recipe and make extras for leftovers or to freeze for later use.

This recipe makes a simple, quick weeknight dinner if you make the Chorizo Blend ahead of time and keep it on hand. These meatballs are also great as an appetizer at a party or as a meal served over Mashed Faux-Tatoes (page 418), as pictured.

1 pound ground pork

2 tablespoons Chorizo Blend (page 256)

1 tablespoon apple cider vinegar

1 clove garlic, grated or minced

1 small onion, finely diced

1/4 cup chopped fresh cilantro, for garnish

Preheat the oven to 375°F.

In a medium-sized mixing bowl, combine the ground pork, spice blend, vinegar, garlic, and onion with your hands until the spice mixture looks evenly dispersed.

Form the meat into twelve 1 1/3-ounce meatballs, about the size of golf balls, and place in a baking dish or on a rimmed baking sheet. Bake for 30 minutes or until cooked through.

Garnish with cilantro before serving.

PORK

grandma barbara's stuffed mushrooms

PREP TIME: 20 minutes | **COOKING TIME:** 30 minutes
YIELD: 1 dozen stuffed mushrooms (3 to 4 meal-sized portions)

NIGHTSHADES | FODMAPS | 21DSD | SPICE BLEND | QUICK & EASY | PARTY | FAMILY

NIGHTSHADE-FREE?

Leave out the bell peppers.

MAKE IT EASIER

To save time, mince the bell peppers and onions in a food processor before sautéing them, then use the food processor to chop the spinach.

CHANGE IT UP

Substitute ground turkey for the pork.

Stuff 4 large portobello caps instead of 12 baby mushrooms.

My grandma used to make a big spread of appetizers every holiday, and I always requested her stuffed mushrooms. The original recipe calls for breadcrumbs, so this is an adaptation, but don't worry—the tops of these get crispy even without the grains.

1 dozen baby portobello mushroom caps, cleaned

1 tablespoon bacon fat or other cooking fat of choice

1/4 cup minced red bell peppers

1/4 cup minced yellow onions

1 pound Italian sausage, casings removed, or 1 pound ground pork combined with 2 tablespoons Italian Blend (page 256)

2 cups spinach, minced

1 clove garlic, grated or minced

Preheat the oven to 350°F.

Place the mushrooms on a rimmed baking sheet with the "cup" sides facing down and bake for 10 minutes, or just enough to release some of the moisture. Do this before or while you prepare the filling mixture.

Make the filling: In a large skillet over medium heat, melt the bacon fat, then add the bell peppers and yellow onions and sauté until the onions are translucent and soft. Add the sausage and cook it until little or no pink remains (about 5 minutes), stirring occasionally to break up any large chunks of meat. Add the spinach and garlic to the pan and stir to combine.

Turn the mushrooms "cup" side up and fill them with the sausage mixture. Place them back in the oven and bake for about 20 minutes, until golden brown on top.

thanksgiving stuffing meatballs

PREP TIME: 20 minutes | **COOKING TIME:** 40 minutes | **YIELD:** 2 dozen meatballs

NUTS & SEEDS | FODMAPS | 21DSD | QUICK & EASY | PARTY | FAMILY | FREEZE ME

NUT-FREE?

Omit the chestnuts.

MAKE IT 21DSD

Serve the meatballs without the cranberry sauce.

NOTES

Use precooked and peeled chestnuts, readily available at most grocery stores during the winter holiday season, or substitute walnuts or pecans if chestnuts are not available.

CHANGE IT UP

Want to use ground turkey instead? Go ahead! I recommend using 1 pound of ground turkey and 1 pound of ground pork for the best flavor and texture.

FREEZE ME

Make these into patties instead of meatballs to freeze and save for quick and easy breakfasts!

If you've ever wished you could eat something that tastes like Thanksgiving any time of the year without cooking a whole feast, here's your chance! These tiny pork meatballs pack all the flavor of the season and are perfect with Simple Cranberry Sauce (page 436) for dipping.

2 pounds ground pork

2 tablespoons Italian Blend (page 256)

2 teaspoons butter, bacon fat, or coconut oil

1/4 cup minced onions

1/4 cup minced celery

1/4 cup grated or shredded carrots

1/4 cup minced chestnuts (see Notes)

Preheat the oven to 375°F.

In a medium-sized mixing bowl, combine the pork and spice blend until the spices are evenly incorporated throughout the meat.

In a large skillet over medium heat, melt the butter. Place the onions, celery, and carrots in the pan and sauté until the onions and celery are translucent. Add the chestnuts and continue to cook for another 2 minutes.

Set the chestnut mixture aside to cool until you can touch it comfortably. Then combine the mixture with the meat and form into twenty-four 1 1/2-ounce meatballs.

Place the meatballs in a baking dish or on a rimmed baking sheet and bake for 30 minutes, or until cooked all the way through.

orange sesame meatballs

PREP TIME: 15 minutes | **COOKING TIME:** 30 minutes | **YIELD:** 3 dozen meatballs

`NUTS & SEEDS` `NIGHTSHADES` `FODMAPS` `PARTY` `FAMILY` `FREEZE ME`

SEED-FREE?

Omit the sesame seeds.

NIGHTSHADE-FREE?

Omit the red pepper flakes.

If you're missing dumplings and other Asian favorites while eating Paleo, these should definitely get into your weeknight rotation. Your whole family will love these flavor-packed meatballs and the sweet and tangy glaze!

1 tablespoon coconut aminos

2 to 3 dashes of fish sauce

1/4 cup minced green onions (scallions)

1/4 cup minced fresh cilantro

1 teaspoon grated or minced fresh ginger (about 1/2-inch piece)

1 teaspoon grated or minced garlic (about 2 cloves)

2 teaspoons toasted sesame seeds

1 teaspoon sea salt

1 teaspoon black pepper

1 pound ground pork

1 pound ground chicken or turkey, preferably dark meat for the best flavor

SAUCE

3/4 cup coconut aminos

Grated zest and juice of 1 orange (about 1/4 cup juice; reserve zest for garnish)

1/2 teaspoon granulated garlic

1/4 teaspoon granulated onion

2 to 3 dashes of fish sauce

2 pinches of ginger powder

FOR GARNISH

Sliced green onions (scallions)

Red pepper flakes (optional)

Orange zest (from above)

Toasted black and/or white sesame seeds

Preheat the oven to 375°F. Line a rimmed baking sheet with foil and set a wire baking rack on the baking sheet.

In a large mixing bowl, combine the coconut aminos, fish sauce, green onions, cilantro, ginger, garlic, sesame seeds, salt, and pepper. Add the meat to the bowl and mix to thoroughly combine with the seasonings. Form the meat into thirty-six 3/4-ounce meatballs and place on the baking rack.

Bake for 30 minutes, or until cooked through.

In a small saucepan, whisk together the ingredients for the sauce. Bring the sauce to a simmer over medium-low heat, then continue to simmer until the sauce reduces by half, 5 to 7 minutes. Tilt the pan frequently to prevent the sauce from burning.

Remove the meatballs from the oven and toss them in the sauce while they are still warm.

Garnish with green onions, red pepper flakes (if using), orange zest, and sesame seeds.

bacon & superfood meatloaf

PREP TIME: 15 minutes (not including caramelized onions) **| COOKING TIME:** About 1 1/2 hours
YIELD: 10 servings

NUTS & SEEDS | EGGS | NIGHTSHADES | FODMAPS | 21DSD | SPICE BLEND | FAMILY | FREEZE ME

NUT-FREE?

Use coconut flour.

EGG-FREE?

Omit the eggs.

NIGHTSHADE-FREE?

*Use the Nightshade-Free
Ketchup on page 437 instead
of tomato-based ketchup and
omit the paprika.*

MAKE IT 21DSD

*Use the Sweetener-Free
Ketchup recipe that's in your
21DSD guide book.*

EQUIPMENT TIP

*If you are making this dish
without a loaf pan, form
the meat into a loaf shape,
place it on a parchment- or
foil-lined rimmed baking
sheet, and bake for 1 hour 15
minutes.*

MAKE IT EASIER

*I recommend pulsing the
chicken livers in a food
processor to get them minced
very finely. Not only is doing
this task in a food processor
faster than doing it by hand
with a knife, but the resulting
texture will be finer, which
helps the liver "disappear"
in the meatloaf. And
"disappearing" liver is what
you want if you are sensitive
to the taste or texture of liver!*

*One of the most common questions I get is about how to incorporate liver into everyday
cooking for the whole family. Well, folks, this kid-tested and family-approved meatloaf is
your answer! It's also amazing as leftovers, reheated by the slice in a skillet with a little
bacon fat.*

1 tablespoon ghee (page 261), bacon
    fat, butter, or coconut oil

1 small onion, finely diced

1 stalk celery, finely diced

1 carrot, finely diced

2 cloves garlic, grated or minced

1 1/2 pounds ground beef

1 1/2 pounds ground pork

1/2 pound chicken livers, minced

2 large eggs

2 tablespoons organic ketchup

1 teaspoon ground cumin

1 teaspoon granulated onion

1 teaspoon granulated garlic

1 teaspoon paprika

1 teaspoon black pepper

1 teaspoon sea salt

2 tablespoons coconut flour or
    3 tablespoons almond flour

OPTIONAL TOPPINGS

5 tablespoons organic ketchup

1 large onion, diced and caramelized
    (see page 343)

4 slices bacon, cut in half

Preheat the oven to 350°F.

Line an 8 1/2 by 4 1/2-inch loaf pan with parchment paper and place it in a rimmed baking
sheet to catch any drips while baking.

In a large skillet over medium-high heat, melt the ghee. Add the onion, celery, carrot, and
fresh garlic and cook for 3 to 5 minutes, until the carrot is slightly tender and the onion is
translucent. Remove the vegetables from the pan and set aside to cool slightly before adding them to the meat mixture.

In a large mixing bowl, mix together the beef, pork, chicken livers, eggs, 2 tablespoons of
ketchup, spices, salt, and coconut flour. Add the cooked vegetables and combine thoroughly before transferring to the prepared loaf pan.

If using the optional toppings, brush the top of the meatloaf with 5 tablespoons of
ketchup. Spread a layer of caramelized onions on top of the ketchup, then top it all off with
slices of bacon.

Bake the meatloaf for 1 1/2 hours, or until a meat thermometer inserted in the center reads
160°F. If the top looks like it is burning before the inside is fully cooked, cover with foil and
continue to bake.

balsamic braised short ribs

PREP TIME: 5 minutes | **COOKING TIME:** 4 to 6 hours | **YIELD:** 6 to 8 servings

`NIGHTSHADES` `FODMAPS` `21DSD` `SPICE BLEND` `LOW & SLOW` `PARTY` `FAMILY` `ONE POT` `FREEZE ME`

NIGHTSHADE-FREE?

Replace the tomato sauce with 1/2 cup canned pumpkin and 1/2 cup beef Bone Broth (page 259).

MAKE IT 21DSD

Omit the dates.

SLOW-COOK IT

Don't have a Dutch oven? Cook everything in a slow cooker for 4 to 6 hours, or until the meat easily pulls apart from the bone.

I had a handful of favorite meals back in the day when I ran an organic meal delivery business, and braised balsamic beef was at the top of the list. I've updated that recipe to include dates instead of brown sugar as the sweetener, and the result is a rich flavor that your family will love. Try serving it with Candied Carrots (page 415). This is also a fantastic dish to make for a potluck or Super Bowl party.

2 tablespoons Savory Blend (page 257)

2 to 3 pounds bone-in beef short ribs

1 tablespoon coconut oil

1 (15-ounce) can plain tomato sauce

1/2 cup balsamic vinegar

6 cloves garlic, peeled and smashed with the side of a knife

4 Medjool dates, pitted

Sliced green onions (scallions), for garnish

Rub the spice blend into the short ribs.

Melt the coconut oil in a large skillet over medium-high heat. Sear the short ribs for 1 to 2 minutes per side, until they are slightly browned.

Preheat the oven to 300°F.

Place the short ribs, tomato sauce, balsamic vinegar, garlic, and dates in a large enameled cast-iron Dutch oven. Cover, place in the oven, and cook for 4 to 6 hours, until the meat is tender enough to be pulled apart from the bones with a fork.

Shred the meat and serve. Garnish with green onions, if desired.

grilled garlic flank steak with peppers & onions

PREP TIME: 20 minutes | **COOKING TIME:** 15 minutes | **YIELD:** 3 to 4 servings

NIGHTSHADES FODMAPS 21DSD QUICK & EASY PARTY FAMILY

NIGHTSHADE-FREE?

Omit the bell pepper and serve over grilled squash and carrots.

FODMAP-FREE?

Season only with sea salt and black pepper and serve over grilled carrots instead of the peppers and onions.

CHANGE IT UP

Serve this steak over any grilled or sautéed vegetables.

This is one of those go-to recipes for a weeknight meal or a cookout. Use the leftover steak to top a salad or to pair with eggs for breakfast the next morning.

3 cloves garlic, grated or finely minced

1 1/2 to 2 pounds flank steak

Sea salt and black pepper

1 tablespoon bacon fat, butter, ghee (page 261), or coconut oil

1 onion, cut into 1/2-inch dice

1 bell pepper (any color), cut into 1/2-inch dice

Fresh cilantro, for garnish (optional)

Preheat a grill to medium-high heat. Massage the garlic into the steak and season liberally with salt and pepper.

Grill for about 5 minutes per side, turning the steak one quarter-turn halfway through cooking to achieve crosshatch grill marks. Set the cooked steak aside to rest.

In a large skillet over medium-high heat, melt the bacon fat. Add the onion and bell pepper and sauté until soft and slightly browned on the edges.

Slice the steak on a slight angle against the grain. Serve over the onion and pepper, garnished with cilantro, if desired.

green sauce marinated steak & plantain bowl

PREP TIME: 25 minutes, plus time to marinate the steak (not including green sauce, cauli-rice, or pico de gallo) | **COOKING TIME:** 25 to 30 minutes | **YIELD:** 4 to 6 servings

`NIGHTSHADES` `FODMAPS` `21DSD` `SPICE BLEND` `MEAL`

SPICE BLEND SWAP

Replace the salt and spices in the marinade with 1 tablespoon of Taco & Fajita Blend (page 257).

LOVE PLANTAINS?

The sweet, ripe plantains pair perfectly with the savory spices in this dish. You can also serve these sautéed plantains with eggs and bacon or sausage for breakfast!

This preparation will quickly become your favorite way to enjoy steak. It's bold and flavorful and can be used to top salads or enjoyed on its own, as in this recipe.

GREEN SAUCE MARINADE

2 tablespoons Diane's Magic Green Sauce (page 439)

1 tablespoon extra-virgin olive oil

Juice of 2 limes

1/2 teaspoon sea salt

1/2 teaspoon black pepper

1/2 teaspoon chili powder

1/2 teaspoon ground coriander

1/2 teaspoon ground cumin

1/2 teaspoon paprika

2 pounds flank steak

2 red bell peppers, sliced

SAUTÉED SWEET PLANTAINS

1/2 teaspoon ground cinnamon

1/2 teaspoon paprika

1/2 teaspoon sea salt

1/4 teaspoon coconut sugar (optional)

2 black (very ripe) plantains

1/4 cup coconut oil, ghee (page 261), or butter, or more as needed

FOR SERVING

1 recipe Cilantro Cauli-Rice (page 412) (optional)

2 avocados, sliced

Fresh pico de gallo, store-bought or homemade (page 433) (optional)

FOR GARNISH (OPTIONAL)

Chopped fresh cilantro

Lime wedges

Make the marinade: In a large glass baking dish, whisk together the green sauce, olive oil, lime juice, salt, and spices.

Marinate the steak: Place the steak in the baking dish with the marinade and massage the seasonings into it. Place in the refrigerator to marinate for at least 20 minutes or up to overnight.

When ready to grill the steak, preheat a grill or grill pan to high heat. Cook the steak for 3 to 5 minutes per side, depending on the thickness and desired level of doneness. Set the cooked steak aside to rest for 10 minutes. While the steak is resting, grill the sliced bell peppers until they are soft and have grill marks, about 5 minutes, turning as needed to prevent burning.

Make the plantains: In a small bowl, combine the cinnamon, paprika, salt, and sugar (if using); set aside. Cut the plantains on the bias into 1/4-inch-thick slices.

Heat the coconut oil in a sauté pan over medium heat. Use enough oil to completely cover the bottom of the pan and come at least halfway up the sides of the plantain slices. Add the plantains in a single layer, working in batches so as not to overcrowd the pan, and cook for 3 to 4 minutes per side, until lightly browned and cooked through. The plantains are ready to flip when they release from the bottom of the pan with little resistance. Place the sautéed plantains on a paper towel–lined plate and season immediately with the spice mixture.

To serve, slice the steak against the grain into thin strips. Place the steak over the cauli-rice (if using) and add the grilled bell pepper strips, sautéed plantains, and sliced avocado. If desired, garnish with cilantro and a squeeze of fresh lime juice and enjoy with fresh pico de gallo.

spaghetti squash bolognese

PREP TIME: 15 minutes | **COOKING TIME:** 45 minutes | **YIELD:** 3 to 4 servings

NIGHTSHADES FODMAPS 21DSD QUICK & EASY MEAL FAMILY ONE POT FREEZE ME

NIGHTSHADE-FREE?
Use canned pumpkin instead of tomato paste.

MAKE IT 21DSD
Omit the white wine.

CHANGE IT UP
Serve this sauce over zucchini noodles (page 380).

A traditional meat sauce, Bolognese is usually made with heavy cream and a variety of meats. To keep this version dairy-free, I use coconut milk instead of cream.

1 spaghetti squash
Sea salt and black pepper

BOLOGNESE SAUCE
2 tablespoons bacon fat or butter
1 onion, finely diced
1 carrot, finely diced
1 stalk celery, finely diced
1 clove garlic, minced or grated
1/2 pound ground veal or beef

1/2 pound ground pork
4 slices bacon, chopped
1/2 cup full-fat coconut milk
1/2 cup dry white wine (optional)
3 ounces (1/2 small can) tomato paste
Sea salt and black pepper

Thinly sliced fresh basil, for garnish (optional)

Preheat the oven to 375°F.

Slice the spaghetti squash in half crosswise. Scoop out the seeds, then sprinkle the cut sides with salt and pepper. Place both halves facedown on a rimmed baking sheet and roast for 35 to 45 minutes, until the flesh of the squash is translucent and the skin begins to soften and easily separates from the "noodles" inside.

Allow the squash to cool enough that you can handle it, then scoop out the "noodles" into a large serving bowl. Set aside.

While the squash is roasting, make the sauce: In a large skillet over medium-high heat, melt the bacon fat. Add the onion, carrot, and celery and sauté until the onion and celery are translucent. Add the garlic and cook for an additional minute, until fragrant.

Add the veal, pork, and bacon and cook until browned through. Once the meat is done, add the coconut milk, white wine (if using), and tomato paste and simmer over medium-low heat for 20 to 30 minutes, until the sauce is well combined and any alcohol is cooked out.

Add salt and pepper to taste before removing the sauce from the heat. Serve over the roasted spaghetti squash noodles, garnished with thinly sliced fresh basil, if desired.

meatball sandwich burgers with marinara

PREP TIME: 10 minutes | **COOKING TIME:** 20 minutes (not including portobello "buns")
YIELD: 4 burgers

NUTS & SEEDS | EGGS | NIGHTSHADES | FODMAPS | 21DSD | SPICE BLEND | PARTY | FAMILY

NUT-FREE?
Omit the almond flour.

EGG-FREE?
Omit the egg.

FODMAP-FREE?
Omit the granulated garlic and onion.

SPICE BLEND SWAP
Replace the dried seasonings used for the meat with 1 tablespoon of Italian Blend (page 256).

HOW TO MAKE PORTOBELLO "BUNS":
On a grill or grill pan preheated to medium-high heat, grill 8 stemmed mushroom caps, "cup" side down, for about 10 minutes, until they begin to soften. You can also bake them on a rimmed baking sheet in a preheated 350°F oven for about 10 minutes.

Growing up in an Italian New Jersey family meant eating meatball and eggplant sandwiches pretty often! This burger is a twist on those classics. It can easily be made without the eggplant if you want to simplify it, or you can make it more like a meatball parm sandwich by topping it with the béchamel sauce on page 304.

GRILLED EGGPLANT
1 medium eggplant, cut into 8 (1/2-inch) slices
1 tablespoon extra-virgin olive oil
Sea salt

BURGERS
3/4 pound ground beef
3/4 pound ground pork
1/2 cup chopped fresh basil
1/4 cup chopped fresh parsley
1 teaspoon dried oregano leaves
1 teaspoon black pepper
1/2 teaspoon granulated garlic
1/2 teaspoon granulated onion
1 teaspoon sea salt
1 tablespoon almond flour
1 large egg

FOR SERVING
8 Portobello "Buns" (instructions at left) or 8 large lettuce leaves for wrapping
8 large fresh basil leaves
1 cup pizza sauce or marinara (use a no-sugar-added variety), warmed
1 red onion, sliced

Preheat a grill or grill pan to medium-high heat. Brush the eggplant slices with the olive oil and sprinkle with a few pinches of salt. Grill for 5 to 6 minutes, until softened and browned with grill marks, turning as needed to prevent burning.

Prepare the portobello "buns," if using them to serve the burgers.

Make the burgers: In a large mixing bowl, combine the meat, herbs, spices, salt, almond flour, and egg; using your hands, mix everything together until well integrated. Form the meat into four 6-ounce patties, adding a thumbprint dimple in the center of each one to allow for even cooking.

Grill the burgers over medium-high heat for 5 minutes per side or until cooked to 145°F in the center.

To serve, place 2 slices of grilled eggplant in a portobello "bun" or lettuce leaf, then add a burger patty, a couple of basil leaves, 1/4 cup of the pizza sauce, and a couple of slices of onion. Top with another mushroom cap or lettuce leaf.

indian spiced burgers with smashed roasted garlic

PREP TIME: 15 minutes (not including caramelized onions, portobello "buns," or mayo)
COOKING TIME: 45 minutes | **YIELD:** 4 burgers

`EGGS` `NIGHTSHADES` `FODMAPS` `21DSD` `SPICE BLEND` `PARTY` `FAMILY`

EGG-FREE?

Omit the Paleo Mayonnaise.

NIGHTSHADE-FREE?

Don't top the burgers with tomato slices.

CARB IT UP

Serve on a Sweet Potato Pancake bun (page 285) for a satisfying post-workout meal.

Any of the spice blends in this book (see pages 256 to 257) are fantastic for kicking up a plain old burger. These burgers are seasoned with the Indian Blend and cilantro and, like the Meatball Sandwich Burgers, are served between portobello "buns" or lettuce wraps. Pair them with a salad, Baked Potato Chips (page 430), or roasted veggies for a simple supper.

ROASTED GARLIC

1 head garlic

2 tablespoons ghee (page 261) or extra-virgin olive oil

1 large yellow onion, diced and caramelized (see page 343)

BURGERS

1 1/2 pounds ground beef, pork, or turkey

1/3 cup chopped fresh cilantro

1 1/2 tablespoons Indian Blend (page 257)

FOR SERVING

8 Portobello "Buns" (see page 340) or 8 large lettuce leaves for wrapping

1/4 cup Paleo Mayonnaise (page 438), or purchase an avocado oil variety

Lettuce leaves (omit if using lettuce for wrapping instead of "buns")

Tomato slices

Roasted garlic (from above)

Preheat the oven to 350°F.

Roast the garlic: Slice the tips off of the head of garlic, then place it, cut side up, on a large square of foil. Top with the 2 tablespoons of ghee, wrap the foil around the garlic, and roast for about 45 minutes, until the cloves are golden brown and soft. When the garlic is done and cool enough to handle, gently squeeze each clove out of the skin and spread on your burgers like you would a thick sauce.

While the garlic roasts, caramelize the onion, following the method on page 343.

When the onion is caramelized, preheat a grill or grill pan to medium-high heat.

In a large mixing bowl, combine the meat, cilantro, and spice blend and mix with your hands until well combined. Form the meat into four 6-ounce patties, adding a thumbprint dimple in the center of each one to allow for even cooking.

Place the burgers on the grill and cook as follows: for beef burgers, grill for 4 to 5 minutes per side or to your desired level of doneness; for pork or turkey burgers, grill for 5 to 6 minutes per side or until they are cooked through with no remaining pink and have reached an internal temperature of 160°F (for pork) or 165°F (for turkey).

To serve, mix the cooled caramelized onions with the mayonnaise, then place each patty on a portobello "bun" or lettuce leaf. Top with lettuce (if using "buns"), a tomato slice, some roasted garlic, and a spoonful of the onion mayonnaise, and finish with another mushroom cap or lettuce leaf.

prosciutto & caramelized onion burgers with roasted garlic aioli

PREP TIME: 15 minutes (not including mayo or "buns") | **COOKING TIME:** 45 minutes
YIELD: 4 burgers

EGGS FODMAPS 21DSD QUICK & EASY **PARTY** FAMILY

ROASTED GARLIC AIOLI

1 head garlic

2 tablespoons ghee (page 261) or extra-virgin olive oil

1/4 cup Paleo Mayonnaise (page 438), or purchase an avocado oil variety

CARAMELIZED ONIONS

1 teaspoon ghee (page 261), coconut oil, or butter

1 large yellow onion, diced

Sea salt

8 slices prosciutto

BURGERS

1 1/2 pounds ground beef

1 cup packed fresh spinach, chopped, plus a few whole leaves for topping

1 teaspoon sea salt

1 teaspoon black pepper

FOR SERVING

8 Portobello "Buns" (see page 340) or 8 large lettuce leaves for wrapping

EGG-FREE?
Omit the mayonnaise.

CARB IT UP
Serve on a Sweet Potato Pancake bun (page 285) for a satisfying post-workout meal.

Have two oven racks evenly spaced in the oven and preheat the oven to 350°F.

Roast the garlic: Slice the tips off of the head of garlic, then place it, cut side up, on a large square of foil. Top it with the 2 tablespoons of ghee, wrap the foil around the garlic, and roast for about 45 minutes, until the cloves are golden brown and soft. When the garlic is done and cool enough to handle, gently squeeze each clove out of the skin and mash with a fork into a paste; set aside.

Caramelize the onion: Melt the teaspoon of ghee in a medium skillet over medium-low heat. Add the onion, season with a few pinches of salt, and slowly cook the onion until caramelized and golden brown, 20 to 25 minutes, adding water and scraping the browned bits off of the bottom of the pan as needed to prevent burning. Remove from the heat and let cool to room temperature.

While the garlic is roasting and the onion is caramelizing, prepare the prosciutto: Take each prosciutto slice and twirl into a roselike shape. Place on a rimmed baking sheet and bake for 15 minutes or until slightly crispy.

When the onion is caramelized, preheat a grill or grill pan to medium-high heat.

In a large mixing bowl, combine the beef, spinach, salt, and pepper and mix with your hands until well combined. Form the beef into four 6-ounce patties, adding a thumbprint dimple in the center of each one to allow for even cooking.

Grill the burgers for 4 to 5 minutes per side or to your desired level of doneness.

Make the roasted garlic aioli: Mix the roasted garlic (from above) with the mayonnaise.

Place each burger patty on a portobello "bun" or lettuce leaf, top with some spinach leaves, 2 prosciutto roses, a spoonful of the aioli, and some caramelized onions, and finish with another mushroom cap or lettuce leaf.

orange braised beef

PREP TIME: 10 minutes (not including broth) | **COOKING TIME:** 4 to 6 hours | **YIELD:** 4 servings

`NUTS & SEEDS` `NIGHTSHADES` `FODMAPS` `LOW & SLOW` `FAMILY` `ONE POT` `FREEZE ME`

FODMAP-FREE?

Leave out the garlic.

SLOW-COOK IT

Skip searing the meat, place all of the ingredients in a slow cooker, and cook on low for 6 to 8 hours, until the meat pulls apart easily.

Beef shanks are an underutilized cut of meat, but they're often one of the most affordable, especially when you buy grass-fed. An enameled cast-iron Dutch oven or slow cooker does a good job of making this tougher cut of meat tender and melt-in-your-mouth delicious.

2 large beef shanks (about 2 1/2 pounds) or 1 1/2 to 2 pounds beef stew meat

Sea salt and black pepper

1 tablespoon butter, ghee (page 261), or coconut oil

2 teaspoons fennel seeds

1 teaspoon black peppercorns

2 oranges

2 cups beef Bone Broth (page 259)

4 cloves garlic, peeled and smashed with the side of a knife

1 teaspoon ground cumin

2 large sweet potatoes, peeled and cut into 2-inch chunks

Preheat the oven to 325°F.

Season both sides of the beef shanks liberally with salt and pepper. Melt the butter in a large enameled cast-iron Dutch oven over medium-high heat, then sear the shanks for 2 to 3 minutes per side, until golden brown.

Place the fennel seeds and peppercorns in a tea ball infuser or tie them up in a small piece of cheesecloth. Juice one of the oranges. Combine the broth, orange juice, garlic, and cumin in a bowl.

Put the sweet potatoes, spice ball (or bag), and 1 cup of the broth mixture in the pot. Add more of the broth mixture as needed until the liquid comes about halfway up the sides of the meat. If you want to garnish the finished dish with orange zest, grate the zest of the remaining orange and set the zest aside. Cut half of the orange into slices and place in the pot, setting the remaining half aside. Place in the oven and cook for 4 to 6 hours, until the meat is tender enough to be pulled apart with a fork.

Gently pull the meat off the bones. Serve the meat with the sweet potatoes, squeezing the remaining orange half over each plate for a pop of brightness. Sprinkle some of the reserved orange zest (if using) over each serving.

hayley's skirt steak tacos

PREP TIME: 20 minutes | **COOKING TIME:** About 10 minutes | **YIELD:** 4 servings

NIGHTSHADES FODMAPS 21DSD QUICK & EASY FAMILY

NIGHTSHADE-FREE?

Omit the chili powder and tomatoes and top the tacos with a nightshade-free salsa—try mango, pineapple, or cucumber (see page 433).

FODMAP-FREE?

Omit the garlic and avocado.

CHANGE IT UP

Top these simple steak tacos with anything you like, such as thinly sliced red onions, guacamole, or any of the Five Kinds of Salsa (page 433).

Lettuce tacos are one of my favorite weeknight meals. I wrap nearly any kind of protein in lettuce and top it with avocado. This recipe is named after Hayley Mason, co-author of Make it Paleo, who originated it.

1 head butter lettuce or romaine lettuce
Grated zest and juice of 1 lime
2 cloves garlic, grated or minced
1/2 teaspoon chili powder
Sea salt and black pepper
1 1/2 to 2 pounds skirt steak

TACO TOPPERS

24 cherry tomatoes, quartered, or 1 large tomato, chopped into 1-inch pieces
1 avocado, thinly sliced
1/4 cup chopped fresh cilantro
1 lime, cut into wedges

Gently separate the leaves of lettuce and rinse them off. Set aside to dry.

In a large mixing bowl, whisk together the lime zest, lime juice, garlic, chili powder, and several pinches each of salt and pepper. Place the skirt steak in the bowl and massage the seasonings into it.

Preheat a grill or grill pan to medium-high heat.

Grill the steak for about 3 minutes per side for medium doneness. Set the cooked steak aside to rest for 10 minutes, then slice it against the grain into thin strips. You may want to cut the steak into two or three sections before slicing, as skirt steaks are typically very long.

Serve the steak, tomatoes, avocado slices, and chopped cilantro in the lettuce leaves with lime wedges on the side.

BEEF
& BISON

beef & veggie stir-fry

PREP TIME: 15 minutes | **COOKING TIME:** 10 minutes | **YIELD:** 4 servings

NUTS & SEEDS | NIGHTSHADES | FODMAPS | 21DSD | QUICK & EASY | MEAL | FAMILY | ONE POT

SEED-FREE?

Omit the sesame seeds.

NIGHTSHADE-FREE?

Omit the bell peppers and use sugar snap peas or snow peas instead.

FODMAP-FREE?

Use only vegetables from the Paleo foods list that are not marked as FODMAPs (see page 61) and omit the red onions and garlic.

CHANGE IT UP

Substitute chicken or pork for the beef.

Use any vegetables you like.

CHOP, CHOP!

Learn how to chop veggies on pages 252 to 253.

After a long week of cooking and using up almost all of the veggies you bought for the week, a stir-fry is the perfect answer to the "I don't feel like cooking" blues. Chop up whatever you have (aiming for a total of 4 cups), add a few key ingredients, like coconut aminos, water chestnuts, and sesame seeds, and you're all set.

1 1/2 to 2 pounds skirt steak

2 tablespoons coconut oil

1 cup julienned red onions

1 cup chopped broccoli

1 cup string beans, ends trimmed

1 cup julienned bell peppers (any color)

STIR-FRY SAUCE

2 tablespoons coconut aminos

2 to 3 drops of fish sauce (optional)

2 tablespoons warm water

2 cloves garlic, minced or grated

1/4 to 1/2 teaspoon minced or grated fresh ginger

FOR SERVING

1/4 cup sliced water chestnuts

2 tablespoons chopped green onions (scallions)

1 tablespoon sesame seeds, raw or toasted

Spread the skirt steak across a large cutting board and cut it into sections about 4 inches long, cutting with the grain of the meat. Then cut against the grain to slice each section into 1/4-inch-thick strips.

Place a large skillet over medium-high heat. When it's hot, melt the coconut oil in the skillet. Add the steak and allow it to brown on both sides, 1 to 2 minutes per side. Remove the steak from the skillet and set aside.

Place the onions, broccoli, string beans, and bell peppers in the pan. Cook for about 5 minutes, until fork-tender.

While the vegetables cook, combine the sauce ingredients and mix well.

Add the meat back to the pan, followed by the sauce, and heat through for about 2 minutes.

Plate the stir-fry and top with the water chestnuts, green onions, and sesame seeds.

tangy taco salad

PREP TIME: 20 minutes | **COOKING TIME:** 10 minutes | **YIELD:** 4 meal-sized salads

NIGHTSHADES | FODMAPS | 21DSD | SPICE BLEND | QUICK & EASY | MEAL | PARTY | FAMILY | FREEZE ME

NIGHTSHADE-FREE?

Use the Nightshade-Free Taco & Fajita Blend on page 257 and omit the bell pepper and tomatoes. Use cucumber or fruit salsa and add shredded carrots for color.

FODMAP-FREE?

Omit the granulated garlic and onion from the spice blend, the fresh garlic, and the avocado.

FREEZE ME

Freeze the cooked and seasoned meat and defrost it to enjoy with fresh salad vegetables and toppings when you're ready.

CHANGE IT UP

Try substituting ground bison, turkey, or chicken in place of the beef.

Use Spicy Lime Dressing (page 434) instead of lime juice as the dressing.

You can also serve this dish as tacos with lettuce-leaf "shells."

Ground beef gets kicked up to a whole new place when you make it into taco meat and pair it with some fun toppings. Cook up a batch of Crispy Plantain Chips (page 431) to enjoy alongside the salad.

1 pound ground beef

2 tablespoons Taco & Fajita Blend (page 257)

2 cloves garlic, grated or minced

8 cups chopped romaine lettuce

1 bell pepper (any color), sliced

1 cup sliced or chopped tomatoes

1 cup salsa, any kind (recipes on page 433)

1 avocado, sliced, or 1 cup guacamole

Chopped fresh cilantro, for garnish

2 limes, quartered, for serving

In a large skillet over medium-high heat, cook the meat until thoroughly browned and cooked through, adding the spice blend and garlic when the meat is about halfway done.

While the meat is cooking, arrange the lettuce and bell pepper slices on a large serving platter or in four individual serving bowls. Top with the browned meat, tomatoes, salsa, and avocado slices.

Garnish with cilantro and squeeze lime juice over the salad as dressing.

mini mediterranean kebabs (kofta)

PREP TIME: 15 minutes (not including tzatziki) | **COOKING TIME:** 30 minutes
YIELD: 18 mini kebabs (6 servings)

`NIGHTSHADES` `FODMAPS` `21DSD` `SPICE BLEND` `PARTY` `FAMILY` `FREEZE ME`

SPECIAL EQUIPMENT
18 extra-large wooden cocktail sticks or small skewers (if using wood skewers, soak them in water for 30 minutes before using)

NIGHTSHADE-FREE?
Omit the paprika.

SPICE BLEND SWAP
Replace the spices and salt with 2 1/2 tablespoons of Mega Mediterranean Blend (page 257).

FREEZE ME
Freeze the cooked and seasoned meat and defrost it to enjoy when you're ready.

The bold flavors of Mediterranean food are amazing when paired with a cooling sauce like tzatziki. In this recipe, the savory spices contrast nicely with the bright, creamy sauce—it's an amazing combination. This recipe is perfect to bring to a party or can be made without the cocktail sticks for an easy weeknight dinner.

1 tablespoon chopped fresh basil

1 tablespoon chopped fresh cilantro

1 tablespoon chopped fresh mint

1 teaspoon black pepper

1 teaspoon ground coriander

1 teaspoon ground cumin

1 teaspoon granulated garlic

1 teaspoon granulated onion

1 teaspoon paprika

1/2 teaspoon ground cinnamon

1/4 teaspoon ground allspice

1 teaspoon sea salt

Grated zest of 2 lemons

1 small yellow onion, minced (about 1/2 cup)

2 pounds ground beef, lamb, or turkey

1 tablespoon extra-virgin olive oil (if using lean meat)

SAUCE
1 recipe Dairy-Free Tzatziki (Avoziki) (page 370)

Juice of 1/2 lemon

1 teaspoon chopped fresh dill

1 teaspoon chopped fresh mint

1/4 to 1/2 cup full-fat coconut milk

FOR GARNISH
Torn fresh basil leaves

Torn fresh cilantro leaves

Torn fresh mint leaves

Lemon wedges

Preheat the oven to 375°F. Line a rimmed baking sheet with foil, then place a wire baking rack on top of it.

Make the kofta: In a large mixing bowl, combine the herbs, spices, salt, lemon zest, and onion. Add the meat and mix to thoroughly combine it with the seasonings. If you are using a leaner cut of meat (such as lean ground beef or ground turkey breast), add the tablespoon of olive oil to the mixture at this point. Form the meat into 18 kofta (oblong) shapes, about 1 1/2 ounces each, and insert an extra-large wooden cocktail stick into each one. Alternatively, make smaller meatballs for use with toothpicks or without sticks entirely to save a step.

Place the kofta on the prepared baking sheet and bake for 30 minutes, until cooked through.

While the kofta are baking, combine the ingredients for the sauce, adding enough coconut milk to make a thick dipping sauce.

Garnish the kofta with fresh herbs and a squeeze of lemon juice. Serve with the dipping sauce.

mom's stuffed cabbage rolls with tomato cranberry sauce

PREP TIME: 30 minutes (not including cranberry sauce) | **COOKING TIME:** 45 minutes
YIELD: 12 to 15 cabbage rolls (4 to 6 servings)

`NIGHTSHADES` `FODMAPS` `MEAL` `FAMILY` `ONE POT` `FREEZE ME`

NIGHTSHADE-FREE?

Replace the tomatoes with 16 ounces of canned pumpkin and 16 ounces of Bone Broth, any type (page 259).

MAKE-AHEAD NOTE

It's a good idea to make the cranberry sauce ahead of time.

INGREDIENT TIPS

Savoy cabbage is different from regular green cabbage, as it is softer and has curly edges. If you can't find it, regular green cabbage will work fine.

You may need to steam the cabbage leaves in batches since they're very large. Allow time for this process.

My mom has made this dish for as long as I can remember. Her recipe calls for canned cranberry sauce, but this is a healthier alternative. Make a double batch and freeze the rolls for later.

1 head savoy cabbage, leaves carefully separated to remain intact

1 cup grated or shredded cauliflower

1 teaspoon butter, ghee (page 261), or coconut oil

Sea salt and black pepper

1 pound ground beef

1 to 2 cloves garlic, grated or minced

1/2 onion, finely diced

1 teaspoon dried rosemary leaves

1 (32-ounce) can crushed or diced tomatoes

1 cup Simple Cranberry Sauce (page 436)

Preheat the oven to 350°F.

Fill a large pot with 2 inches of water (use a steamer basket if you have one) and steam the cabbage leaves until they are soft. Set aside to cool.

While the cabbage is steaming, sauté the cauliflower in the butter in a large skillet over medium heat for just a few minutes, until it is slightly softened. Add salt and pepper to taste. Remove the cauliflower from the heat and set aside.

In a large mixing bowl, combine the cooked cauliflower, ground beef, garlic, onion, rosemary, and several generous pinches each of salt and pepper until well incorporated.

Place 1/4 to 1/3 cup of the meat mixture on the end of a cabbage leaf and roll it like a burrito, rolling the bottom up, followed by the sides, and then tucking the end underneath. Repeat with the remaining meat mixture and cabbage leaves. Lay the cabbage rolls tucked side down in a deep oven-safe pot or baking dish.

Combine the tomatoes and cranberry sauce in the skillet that you used to cook the cauliflower. Pour the sauce over the cabbage rolls.

Place the pot in the oven and cover with foil or a lid. Bake for about 45 minutes, until the meat is cooked all the way through.

butternut cocoa chili

PREP TIME: 20 minutes | **COOKING TIME:** 4 to 6 hours | **YIELD:** 4 to 6 servings

NIGHTSHADES FODMAPS 21DSD MEAL LOW & SLOW PARTY FAMILY ONE POT FREEZE ME

FODMAP-FREE?

Leave out the garlic and onion. Add 3 to 4 peeled and chopped parsnips or carrots to make a bulkier dish.

SLOW-COOK IT

Place all of the ingredients in a slow cooker, break up the meat with a large spoon, and cook on low for 6 to 8 hours.

FAMILY-FRIENDLY TIP

If you're using a brand-new package of chipotle powder and you're unsure of how much heat your family will like, leave it out. If you find that you would have liked the kick, add the chipotle powder next time!

CHANGE IT UP

This recipe can be made with beef or bison stew meat or ground turkey or chicken instead of red meat if you prefer.

Before I went Paleo, my traditional chili recipe was a standard part of my cooking arsenal, but once I eliminated beans from my diet, chili was off the menu for a long time. That changed with the creation of this fantastic recipe, which uses butternut squash and smoky flavors to satisfy my chili cravings.

3 or 4 cloves garlic, peeled and smashed with the side of a knife

2 tablespoons chili powder

2 tablespoons unsweetened cocoa powder

1 tablespoon ground cinnamon

1 tablespoon smoked paprika

1 teaspoon chipotle powder (omit for a milder chili)

1 teaspoon ground cumin

2 teaspoons sea salt

2 teaspoons black pepper

1 (28-ounce) can crushed tomatoes or 4 cups diced fresh tomatoes

2 tablespoons melted ghee (page 261), coconut oil, or other cooking fat of choice

2 pounds ground beef or bison

2 cups peeled and cubed butternut squash

2 bell peppers (any color), diced

1 large onion, diced

Preheat the oven to 325°F.

In a bowl, mix the garlic, chili powder, cocoa powder, cinnamon, smoked paprika, chipotle powder, cumin, salt, and pepper with the tomatoes.

Place the ghee, meat, squash, bell peppers, onion, and seasoned tomato mixture in a large enameled cast-iron Dutch oven. Break up the meat with a large spoon and stir to distribute the ingredients. Cover, place in the oven, and cook for 4 to 6 hours, until the chili is cooked through.

italian-style stuffed peppers

PREP TIME: 20 minutes | **COOKING TIME:** 10 to 35 minutes | **YIELD:** 4 servings

NIGHTSHADES FODMAPS 21DSD SPICE BLEND MEAL FAMILY FREEZE ME

NIGHTSHADE-FREE?

Stuff hollowed-out summer squash instead of peppers and omit the tomatoes. To use winter squash, precook the squash until they're mostly soft, then bake for 15 to 20 minutes once stuffed.

FODMAP-FREE?

Omit the onion, garlic, and Italian Blend; use 1 teaspoon of Rosemary Salt Blend (page 258); and stuff the mixture into squash instead of peppers.

SPICE BLEND SWAP

Instead of the Italian Blend, try the Greek or Mega Mediterranean Blend (pages 256 to 257) for a twist on this classic dish.

CHANGE IT UP

Add 2 cups of minced baby spinach to the meat.

COOKING TIP

It's best not to use acidic ingredients (like tomatoes or vinegar) in cast-iron cookware since the acid will interact with the iron. This is a good time to use an enameled cast-iron or stainless-steel skillet.

One of the easiest ways to turn ground meat into a special meal is to stuff it into an elegant "package." Use any color of bell peppers, or even another type of vegetable, like a summer or winter squash, to make this all-in-one meal.

2 bell peppers (any color), halved and cleaned

1 tablespoon bacon fat or coconut oil

1/2 large onion, diced

Sea salt and black pepper

1/2 cup diced tomatoes, fresh or canned

4 cloves garlic, grated or minced

1 pound ground beef, bison, turkey, or chicken

1 tablespoon Italian Blend (page 256)

6 fresh basil leaves, minced, plus extra leaves for garnish

Preheat the oven to 375°F.

Place the bell pepper halves facedown in a roasting dish and roast for 10 to 15 minutes, until just a bit softened. (You can skip this step if you want to keep the peppers more firm/raw.)

While the peppers are roasting, heat the bacon fat in a large skillet over medium-high heat. Add the onion and a few pinches each of salt and pepper and sauté until the onion is translucent and slightly browned on the edges. Add the tomatoes and garlic to the pan and simmer for about 2 minutes.

Add the meat and spice blend and cook until fully done. Taste the mixture and adjust the seasoning to your liking (more salt, more pepper, etc.). Mix in the minced basil.

Remove the peppers from the oven and flip them over. Spoon some of the stuffing mixture into each pepper. You can go ahead and eat them at this point or put them back in the oven for 15 to 20 minutes to allow the flavors of the bell pepper and meat mixture to blend together. Serve garnished with fresh basil leaves.

You can refrigerate or freeze and reheat the stuffed peppers later.

bacon jalapeño burgers

PREP TIME: 10 minutes (not including bacon or pancake buns)

COOKING TIME: 15 minutes | **YIELD:** 4 burgers

`NIGHTSHADES` `FODMAPS` `21DSD` `SPICE BLEND` `QUICK & EASY` `PARTY` `FAMILY`

SPICE BLEND SWAP

Use 1 1/2 tablespoons of Diner Blend (page 256) in place of the spices and salt used to season the meat.

FAMILY-FRIENDLY TIP

Use a roasted green bell pepper if your family doesn't enjoy the kick of jalapeño.

CHANGE IT UP

Use ground beef or lamb instead of bison.

Top the burgers with bacon and Roasted Garlic Aioli (page 343) for added depth of flavor.

SERVE IT UP

Serve with a green salad or grilled vegetables to round out your plate.

The sweetness of a Sweet Potato Pancake "bun" complements the spiciness of this burger nicely.

1 jalapeño pepper

1 1/2 pounds ground bison

1 1/2 teaspoons onion powder

1 1/2 teaspoons smoked paprika

1/2 teaspoon black pepper

1/2 teaspoon sea salt

FOR SERVING

4 slices Perfectly Baked Bacon (page 260)

8 Sweet Potato Pancakes (page 285), for buns

Organic ketchup

Whole-grain or spicy brown mustard

Pickles

Roast the jalapeño pepper: Place the jalapeño pepper over an open flame or on a very hot grill until the skin is blackened all over. Remove from the heat and peel the skin off of the pepper under cool running water. Remove the seeds and membranes if you don't like heat, or leave them in if you do. Chop the pepper.

In a large mixing bowl, combine the ground bison, jalapeño pepper, spices, and salt with your hands until well integrated. Form the mixture into four equal-sized patties, adding a thumbprint dimple in the center of each one to allow for even cooking.

Grill the burgers for 4 to 5 minutes per side for medium-rare doneness, or to your preferred level of doneness. Top with the bacon and serve between Sweet Potato Pancakes as the buns (as pictured), with ketchup, mustard, and pickles or your favorite burger toppings.

PRACTICAL PALEO | 361

the easiest tacos (nightshade-free)

PREP TIME: 15 minutes | **COOKING TIME:** About 10 minutes | **YIELD:** 4 servings

FODMAPS | 21DSD | SPICE BLEND | QUICK & EASY | MEAL | PARTY | FAMILY | FREEZE ME

SPICE BLEND SWAP

Use the regular Taco & Fajita Blend (page 257) if you can eat nightshades.

TOP IT OFF

Serve the tacos topped with any of the Five Kinds of Salsa on page 433, but avoid the tomato and bell pepper versions if you need to remain nightshade-free.

Lettuce-wrapped tacos are a dish that everyone can make, and they are a perfect dinner for those times when there's "nothing to eat." We almost always have ground meat on hand, as well as a few of the other staple ingredients in this dish, like the spice blends, cilantro, and limes. As long as you have some fresh lettuce, you're good to go!

1 tablespoon ghee (page 261), butter, or extra-virgin olive oil

1 pound ground beef, turkey, or chicken

2 tablespoons Nightshade-Free Taco & Fajita Blend (page 257)

2 teaspoons apple cider vinegar

FOR SERVING

1 head iceberg lettuce or butter lettuce, leaves separated

1/2 cup sliced purple cabbage

1/4 cup diced red onion

1 avocado, sliced

1/4 cup fresh cilantro leaves

1 lime, cut into wedges

Melt the ghee in a large skillet over medium heat. Add the ground meat and spice blend and cook for about 5 minutes, until the meat is cooked about halfway through, using a wooden spoon to break up the meat as it cooks.

Add the apple cider vinegar to the skillet, reduce the heat to low, and continue to cook until the meat is fully cooked through, another 5 to 6 minutes.

To serve, spoon some of the meat mixture into a lettuce leaf and top with cabbage, red onion, avocado, cilantro, and a squeeze of lime juice.

LAMB

slow-cooked mediterranean stew

PREP TIME: 10 minutes | **COOKING TIME:** 6 hours | **YIELD:** 6 to 8 servings

NIGHTSHADES | 21DSD | SPICE BLEND | LOW & SLOW | FAMILY | ONE POT | FREEZE ME

NIGHTSHADE-FREE?

Leave out the tomatoes, use 3 cups of Bone Broth (page 259) as your braising liquid, and omit the paprika from the Mega Mediterranean Blend.

NOTE

I like Kalamata olives for this recipe, but you can also use green olives if you have them on hand, or use a combination of both, as pictured.

SLOW-COOK IT

Place all of the ingredients in a slow cooker and cook on low for a minimum of 6 hours or overnight, until the lamb is very tender.

When your days are busy and filled with activity, slow-cooked recipes make life much easier. You simply put everything in a pot and let the oven (or slow cooker) do the work. The end result is an amazingly flavorful meal—with little effort on your part!

1 (4-pound) lamb roast

2 onions, cut into quarters

4 large carrots, chopped into 1-inch pieces

6 to 8 cloves garlic, peeled and smashed with the side of a knife

1/4 cup pitted Kalamata olives

1/4 cup brine from olives

1/4 cup pitted Calvestrano olives

1 (28-ounce) can whole peeled plum tomatoes with juice

1 tablespoon Mega Mediterranean Blend (page 257)

FOR SERVING (OPTIONAL)

1 recipe Cilantro Cauli-Rice (page 412)

Preheat the oven to 275°F.

Place all of the ingredients in an enameled cast-iron Dutch oven and braise in the oven for 6 hours, until the lamb is very tender. Alternatively, braise the ingredients in a 200°F oven overnight.

Serve the stew over cauli-rice or on its own.

LAMB

lamb chops with olive tapenade

PREP TIME: 10 minutes | **COOKING TIME:** 5 to 10 minutes | **YIELD:** 4 servings

FODMAPS   21DSD   SPICE BLEND   QUICK & EASY   PARTY   FAMILY

SERVE IT UP

Enjoy these chops with a green salad or Sautéed Spinach with Pine Nuts & Currants (page 423).

Lamb and olives are a perfect combination. Enjoy these simple chops with the salty and delicious olive spread.

OLIVE TAPENADE

1/2 cup pitted Kalamata olives

2 tablespoons extra-virgin olive oil

1 tablespoon capers

1/2 teaspoon anchovy paste

1/2 teaspoon dried oregano leaves

Juice of 1/2 lemon

LAMB CHOPS

2 tablespoons bacon fat or coconut oil

2 pounds lamb chops

1 tablespoon Greek Blend (page 256)

Make the olive tapenade: Combine the olives, olive oil, capers, anchovy paste, oregano, and lemon juice in a food processor and process until fairly smooth, but with some texture remaining.

Preheat the oven to 400°F.

In a large oven-safe skillet over medium heat, melt the bacon fat. While the pan heats, sprinkle both sides of the lamb chops with the Greek Blend. Sear the chops for 2 minutes on each side, then place the entire pan in the hot oven for 2 minutes. Remove the chops from the oven.

To serve, top each lamb chop with a dollop of the tapenade.

LAMB

lemony lamb dolmas (stuffed grape leaves)

PREP TIME: 40 minutes | **COOKING TIME:** 50 minutes | **YIELD:** 20 to 24 dolmas (serves 4 as an entree)

FODMAPS 21DSD **SPICE BLEND** **PARTY** **FAMILY**

FODMAP-FREE?
Omit the onion and cauliflower.

SPICE BLEND SWAP
Replace the salt and spices with 1 1/2 tablespoons of Mega Mediterranean Blend (page 257).

INGREDIENT TIP
Grape leaves are typically found in grocery stores near the olives, capers, and other Greek-inspired food items. They come in a tall jar filled with brine. If you can't find grape leaves, steamed cabbage leaves work great in this recipe. Check out the method for preparing cabbage to roll with a filling on page 354!

This dish pairs well with the following recipes: Olive Tapenade (page 366), Dairy-Free Tzatziki (Avoziki) (page 370), and Roasted Garlic Tahini Sauce (page 432).

1 tablespoon coconut oil or ghee (page 261)

1 small onion, finely diced

1 pound ground lamb

2 tablespoons currants or raisins

1 teaspoon ground cumin

1 teaspoon ground nutmeg

1 teaspoon dried oregano leaves

1/2 teaspoon ground cinnamon

1 cup shredded or grated cauliflower

Juice of 1 lime

Sea salt and black pepper

20 grape leaves (about 1 [16-ounce] jar)

1 lemon

1/4 cup water

2 to 3 bay leaves

2 tablespoons sliced almonds

Preheat the oven to 350°F.

In a large skillet over medium heat, melt the coconut oil. Add the onion and sauté until translucent. Add the lamb, currants, cumin, nutmeg, oregano, and cinnamon and cook until the lamb is still just slightly pink inside.

Add the shredded cauliflower to the skillet, stir to combine, and cook for an additional 2 to 3 minutes. Pour the lime juice over the meat mixture, season generously with salt and pepper, and stir to combine. Set the meat and cauliflower mixture aside to cool slightly.

Gently separate and unroll the grape leaves, as they are somewhat delicate. Spoon a small amount of the lamb mixture onto the center, bottom portion of a leaf (pictured) and roll the bottom of the leaf up. Fold the sides over and continue to roll until the end is tucked underneath. Place the dolmas seam side down in a baking dish. Repeat with the rest of the grape leaves and filling.

Thinly slice half of the lemon, then place the lemon slices on top of the dolmas. Squeeze the other half of the lemon over the dolmas, then pour the water over the dolmas. Top with the bay leaves and almonds.

Cover with foil and bake for 30 to 45 minutes, until the leaves darken and the water evaporates. Remove the bay leaves before eating.

LAMB

lamb lettuce boats
with avoziki sauce

PREP TIME: 20 minutes | **COOKING TIME:** 10 minutes | **YIELD:** 4 servings

`NIGHTSHADES` `FODMAPS` `21DSD` `SPICE BLEND` `QUICK & EASY` `MEAL` `FAMILY`

NIGHTSHADE-FREE?
Omit the tomatoes.

FODMAP-FREE?
Leave off the tzatziki.

SPICE BLEND SWAP
Replace the oregano, salt, and pepper used to season the lamb with 1 tablespoon of Greek Blend (page 256).

NOTE
These are fantastic with the Olive Tapenade on page 366 (pictured at bottom)!

I've been known to wrap pretty much anything in lettuce—and lamb is no exception! This fresh and tasty combination has bold flavors. It's an unexpected and fun way to present lamb.

1 1/2 to 2 pounds boneless lamb kebab/stew meat

1 1/2 teaspoons dried oregano leaves

Sea salt and black pepper

2 tablespoons ghee (page 261) or coconut oil

DAIRY-FREE TZATZIKI (AVOZIKI)

1 ripe avocado

1/4 cup peeled and grated cucumber

2 tablespoons extra-virgin olive oil

1 teaspoon minced fresh dill

1 small clove garlic, grated

Juice of 1 lemon

Sea salt and black pepper to taste

FOR SERVING

8 large romaine lettuce leaves

1 1/2 cups cherry tomatoes, halved, or 1 regular tomato, diced

1 medium cucumber, finely diced

2 lemons, cut in half

In a mixing bowl, season the lamb with the oregano and a generous amount of salt and pepper.

In a skillet over medium-high heat, melt the ghee. Add the lamb pieces and cook for 2 to 3 minutes, until browned on one side, then flip to brown the other side for another 2 minutes or so.

Make the tzatziki: Combine all of the ingredients in a small food processor or with a hand blender.

Once the meat is cooked, chop it into 1/2-inch pieces.

Place the romaine lettuce leaves on serving plates and top with the chopped lamb, tomatoes, and cucumber. Squeeze the lemon halves over the lettuce boats, then top with the tzatziki.

spiced lamb meatballs with balsamic-fig compote

PREP TIME: 20 minutes | **COOKING TIME:** 30 minutes
YIELD: Sixteen meatballs (2 meal-sized servings)

FODMAPS | SPICE BLEND | QUICK & EASY | LOW & SLOW | PARTY | FAMILY | FREEZE ME

FODMAP-FREE?

Omit the onion powder from the meatballs and enjoy them with Olive Tapenade (page 366) instead of the fig compote.

SPICE BLEND SWAP

Replace the salt and spices with 1 tablespoon of Mega Mediterranean Blend (page 257).

NOTE

This recipe is a simple way to take dried fruit to a new level. You can use fresh figs if you have them, which require less water and less cooking time. I love the sweet and tangy combination of figs and vinegar.

These spiced meatballs are delicious with my Balsamic-Fig Compote, but if pairing them with a fruit sauce isn't your thing, have no fear! They're also fantastic with Roasted Garlic Tahini Sauce (page 432) or Olive Tapenade (page 366).

1 pound ground lamb
3/4 teaspoon sea salt
1 teaspoon ground cumin
1 teaspoon onion powder
1/2 teaspoon ground cinnamon
1/4 teaspoon ground allspice
1/4 teaspoon black pepper

BALSAMIC-FIG COMPOTE
1/2 cup water
1/2 cup balsamic vinegar
4 dried figs, sliced
1 sprig fresh rosemary

Preheat the oven to 375°F.

In a mixing bowl, use your hands to combine the lamb with the salt and spices. Form into about 16 small meatballs (1 1/2 inches in diameter, 1 ounce each) and place in a large baking dish. Bake for 30 minutes, until cooked through.

While the meatballs are baking, make the compote: In a small saucepan, combine the water, vinegar, figs, and rosemary. Simmer until the mixture becomes thick. Add more vinegar if it tastes too sweet, and reduce the sauce further if it tastes too tart. Discard the rosemary sprig.

Serve the meatballs warm from the oven with the compote.

quick & easy salmon cakes

PREP TIME: 10 minutes | **COOKING TIME:** 20 minutes | **YIELD:** 4 patties

EGGS   FODMAPS   21DSD   SPICE BLEND   QUICK & EASY   FAMILY

FODMAP-FREE?

Leave out the shallots, garlic, and green onions—season with extra fresh herbs.

Do not use coconut flour or coconut oil.

CHANGE IT UP

Vary the seasonings for a new taste experience—try the Greek Blend (page 256) instead of the Savory.

If you're looking to dress up the canned wild salmon that you've been buying, this is the recipe for you! It's quick and easy, and it can be made mostly from ingredients you are likely to have on hand.

- 2 (6-ounce) cans wild salmon, drained
- 2 large eggs, beaten
- 3 tablespoons minced shallots
- 1 to 2 cloves garlic, minced or grated
- 2 tablespoons minced green onions (scallions)
- 2 teaspoons gluten-free mustard (optional)
- 1 teaspoon Savory Blend (page 257)
- 1 to 2 teaspoons coconut flour, if needed
- 1/4 to 1/2 cup coconut oil, ghee (page 261), or butter, for the pan

Combine the salmon, eggs, shallots, garlic, green onions, mustard (if using), and spice blend in a small mixing bowl. If the consistency is runny, sift the coconut flour over the mixture, starting with 1 teaspoon, and combine well.

In a large skillet over medium heat, melt enough coconut oil to create a layer about 1/4 inch deep. Form the salmon mixture into four equal-sized patties and place them in the pan, all at once or two at a time, depending on the size of your pan. Cook the patties on one side for 4 to 5 minutes, until browned, then flip and continue frying until cooked all the way through, another 3 to 5 minutes.

Serve warm or cold as leftovers.

lemon rosemary broiled salmon

PREP TIME: 5 minutes | **COOKING TIME:** 15 minutes | **YIELD:** 3 to 4 servings

`21DSD` `SPICE BLEND` `QUICK & EASY` `FAMILY` `ONE POT`

Homemade rosemary salt (page 258) has been a go-to in my kitchen for a long time. This recipe was a happy accident—I never would have thought to pair rosemary with fish—but I tried it and it was delicious!

1 lemon

2 tablespoons butter, ghee (page 261), or coconut oil, divided

1 (1-pound) wild salmon fillet, either 1 large piece or cut into 3 or 4 portions

1 teaspoon Herb Salt Blend made with rosemary (page 258)

NOTE

If you don't have a broiler or if your oven doesn't have a broil setting, you can bake the salmon at 350°F for 10 to 15 minutes.

CHANGE IT UP

These seasonings also work beautifully with chicken.

Place an oven rack in the top position and preheat the oven to a low broil setting.

Cut the lemon in half and thinly slice one of the halves into half-moons. If using butter, slice it into thin pats. Place half of the butter pats in a baking dish, or spread 1 tablespoon of the ghee or coconut oil over the bottom of the dish. Place the salmon in the dish and sprinkle with the rosemary salt. Place the remaining half of the butter (or ghee or coconut oil) on top of the salmon and top with slices of lemon.

Broil on low for 10 to 12 minutes, until the salmon is cooked to your liking. Squeeze the reserved lemon half over the top of the fish before serving.

SEAFOOD

lemon & bacon scallops with roasted potatoes

PREP TIME: 15 minutes (not including broth) | **COOKING TIME:** 30 minutes | **YIELD:** 4 servings

NIGHTSHADES FODMAPS 21DSD **SPICE BLEND** **QUICK & EASY** **MEAL** **FAMILY**

NIGHTSHADE-FREE?
Replace the white potatoes with sweet potatoes, parsnips, or turnips.

FODMAP-FREE?
Omit the granulated garlic.

SPICE BLEND SWAP
Replace the dried herbs, spices, and salt used to season the potatoes with 2 1/2 tablespoons of Everything Blend (page 256) or Savory Blend (page 257).

Season the scallops with 1 tablespoon of Everything Blend instead of the salt and spices listed.

COOKING TIP
Because cast iron conducts and holds heat better than any other type of cookware, it's my go-to choice for almost all of my cooking. For this recipe, though, I recommend using a stainless-steel skillet. Cast iron's wonderful ability to retain heat makes it very easy to overcook your scallops.

Scallops make for a quick weeknight meal that seems fancy, but they are simple to prepare. The bacon and lemon add a great balance of smokiness and brightness that you'll absolutely love. Served with roasted potatoes atop a bed of tender lettuce, this meal-in-one will quickly become a go-to for family dinners.

ROASTED POTATOES
2 pounds Yukon Gold or red potatoes

1 tablespoon extra-virgin olive oil

2 teaspoons dried rosemary leaves

2 teaspoons granulated garlic

1 teaspoon sea salt

1 teaspoon black pepper

LEMON & BACON SCALLOPS
2 pounds large wild sea scallops

2 teaspoons sea salt

2 teaspoons black pepper

1/2 teaspoon granulated garlic

1/2 teaspoon turmeric powder

8 slices bacon, diced

2 teaspoons ghee (page 261) or butter

Juice of 4 lemons

2/3 cup chicken Bone Broth (page 259)

2 heads butter lettuce, leaves separated, for serving

1/4 cup chopped fresh chives, for garnish

Preheat the oven to 375°F.

Rinse the potatoes and cut them into 1-inch pieces. Toss the potatoes with the olive oil, rosemary, garlic, salt, and pepper. Spread out on two rimmed baking sheets and bake for 30 minutes, or until fork-tender and browned on the edges, stirring halfway through cooking.

While the potatoes roast, prepare the scallops: Lay the scallops on a paper or cloth towel and pat dry on each side. In a small bowl, combine the salt and spices for the scallops, then lightly season both sides of the scallops with the spice mixture.

Cook the bacon in a large skillet over medium heat until crispy, 5 to 7 minutes. Remove the bacon from the skillet and set aside.

Remove all but 2 to 3 tablespoons of the bacon fat and add the ghee. Return the skillet to medium heat and place the scallops in the hot pan, with at least 1 inch of space between them. (Don't crowd the pan or the scallops won't sear.) Sear the scallops for 2 to 3 minutes on each side, until lightly browned and no longer translucent. (The total cooking time will vary according to the thickness of the scallops, the size of the pan, and the number of batches required to cook the scallops to avoid overcrowding.)

Once all the scallops are seared, remove them from the pan. Turn the heat under the skillet to high and pour in the lemon juice and chicken broth to deglaze the pan. Use a wooden spoon to release the seared bits from the bottom of the pan to flavor the sauce. Reduce the remaining liquid over high heat for 2 to 3 minutes, stirring often, until the sauce is thick enough to lightly coat the back of a spoon.

Serve the scallops and roasted potatoes over lettuce leaves. Spoon the sauce over the scallops and garnish with bacon and chives.

SEAFOOD

citrus macadamia nut sole

PREP TIME: 10 minutes | **COOKING TIME:** 15 minutes | **YIELD:** 3 to 4 servings

NUTS & SEEDS | FODMAPS | 21DSD | QUICK & EASY | FAMILY

CHANGE IT UP

Use pecans, walnuts, or almonds if you prefer.

Substitute lemon or lime zest for the orange.

Try this recipe with flounder or halibut.

While I was growing up, my mom used to make nut-topped fish nearly every week. Her recipe would change from time to time, but it always included butter and some kind of light or white fish.

1/4 cup chopped macadamia nuts

Grated zest of 1 orange

1 pound lemon sole or other whitefish fillets

2 tablespoons melted ghee (page 261), butter, or coconut oil

Sea salt and black pepper

Strips of orange zest, for garnish (optional)

Place an oven rack in the top position and preheat the oven to a low broil setting.

In a small mixing bowl, combine the nuts and grated orange zest, reserving some of the zest for garnish, if desired (or use strips of zest from an additional orange for garnish). Set aside.

Place the sole on a rimmed baking sheet, brush evenly with the melted ghee, then season with several pinches each of salt and pepper. Top with the nut-zest mixture.

Broil the fish for about 10 minutes, until opaque all the way through. Garnish with the reserved grated orange zest or strips of orange zest.

pesto fettuccine with shrimp

PREP TIME: 30 minutes | **COOKING TIME:** 25 minutes
YIELD: 2 meal-sized portions or 4 side dish–sized servings

NUTS & SEEDS | FODMAPS | 21DSD | QUICK & EASY | MEAL | FAMILY

NUT-FREE?

Try substituting unsweetened shredded coconut or sunflower seeds for the nuts, or simply leave the nuts out of the pesto.

FODMAP-FREE?

Omit the garlic.

NOTE

If you have precooked shrimp to use, be sure to warm them before tossing them with the sauce and noodles.

EQUIPMENT TIP

Use a spiral slicer to make spaghetti-shaped noodles instead of flat fettuccine shapes.

INGREDIENT TIP

Nutritional yeast is often added to dairy-free recipes to impart a "cheesy" flavor. It's not essential here, but it's worth trying if you haven't before. If you have an MTHFR genetic mutation, note that many nutritional yeasts have synthetic folic acid added to them, and you may need to avoid them for this reason.

If you miss pasta, zucchini noodles are a fantastic replacement. They're more flavorful and nutrient-dense and can carry a sauce just like traditional noodles. Use a julienne or regular vegetable peeler to make them, depending on the shape of noodles you want.

DAIRY-FREE PESTO

1/2 cup macadamia nuts or pine nuts

1/2 cup extra-virgin olive oil or macadamia nut oil

2 loosely packed cups fresh basil or cilantro leaves

2 tablespoons nutritional yeast (optional)

1 clove garlic

Sea salt and black pepper

2 dozen large shrimp

ZUCCHINI NOODLES

4 zucchini or yellow squash

Sea salt and black pepper

Make the pesto: Place the nuts, oil, herbs, nutritional yeast (if using), garlic, and a generous pinch each of salt and pepper in a food processor and blend until smooth. Taste and add more seasoning if desired.

Peel and devein the shrimp, pulling the tail off first, then the rest of the shell.

Make the zucchini noodles: Place a steamer basket in a large pot and boil about an inch of water. While the water is heating, run a julienne or regular vegetable peeler along each of the zucchini until you reach the center, seedy part. Steam the zucchini noodles for 3 to 5 minutes. Set the steamed noodles aside in a colander or on paper towels to allow the excess water to drain.

Steam the shrimp for about 3 minutes, until they're pink all the way through.

Place the steamed zucchini noodles in a mixing bowl with the pesto and toss until well combined. Top the noodles with the shrimp and season to taste with salt and pepper. Serve warm.

SEAFOOD

six-minute salmon bowls

PREP TIME: 5 minutes (not including rice) | **COOKING TIME:** 6 to 8 minutes | **YIELD:** 4 servings

`NUTS & SEEDS` `FODMAPS` `21DSD` `SPICE BLEND` `QUICK & EASY` `MEAL`

SEED-FREE?

Omit the seaweed salad and sesame seeds.

FODMAP-FREE?

Omit the Everything Blend and season the salmon simply with a few pinches of salt and pepper. Leave out the cauli-rice, avocado, and mango and serve the salmon over arugula with other low-FODMAP accompaniments of your choosing.

MAKE IT 21DSD

Don't use the mango, and avoid seaweed salad if it contains added sugar.

INGREDIENT TIP

Seaweed salad without added dyes or other junky ingredients can be tricky to find. It should not be fluorescent green! If you don't have access to a clean-ingredient option, simply add some crumbled dried seaweed snacks that have been roasted with olive oil instead.

Salmon is my absolute favorite fish, and I've enjoyed this preparation for every meal of the day—yes, even breakfast! The entire dish comes together very quickly.

4 (6-ounce) wild salmon fillets

Sea salt and black pepper

1 tablespoon Everything Blend (page 256)

4 cups arugula

1 recipe Cilantro Cauli-Rice (page 412)

1 lemon, halved

FOR SERVING

2 tablespoons coconut aminos

1 avocado, sliced (optional)

1/2 mango, sliced (optional)

1 cup seaweed salad (optional; see Ingredient Tip)

2 teaspoons sesame seeds (optional)

Heat a large oven-safe skillet, preferably cast-iron, over high heat.

Place an oven rack in the top position. Turn on the oven to the broil setting.

Use a paper towel to pat the salmon dry on both sides. Lightly season the skin side of the salmon with salt and pepper and season the other side generously with the spice blend.

Place the salmon skin side down in the preheated dry skillet and sear for 2 minutes. Then place the skillet under the broiler for 4 minutes, until the salmon is opaque in the center or cooked to your liking.

Serve the salmon over a bed of arugula and cauli-rice. Squeeze some fresh lemon juice over the fish.

Dress the bowls with coconut aminos and top with the avocado slices, mango slices, seaweed salad, and sesame seeds, if using,

SEAFOOD

grilled tuna over fresh noodle salad

PREP TIME: 20 minutes | **COOKING TIME:** 10 minutes | **YIELD:** 4 servings

`21DSD` `QUICK & EASY` `MEAL`

EQUIPMENT TIP

You can find a julienne peeler online as well as in most kitchen gadget shops.

CHANGE IT UP

Don't like or can't find daikon radishes? You can make the noodles for the salad out of zucchini or yellow squash (see page 380)—or use all carrots.

Grilled tuna is a fantastic treat, especially in the summertime. This cold daikon noodle salad is a fresh and tasty way to complement the grilled fish. If you don't have an outdoor grill, a grill pan will do the trick!

1 tablespoon sustainably sourced red palm oil or ghee (page 261), melted

1 pound wild tuna steaks

1/2 teaspoon Lemon Salt Blend (page 258), or 1/4 teaspoon salt plus the grated zest of 1/2 lemon

1/4 teaspoon ground coriander

A few pinches of black pepper

FRESH NOODLE SALAD

2 to 3 large daikon radishes (about 3 pounds)

1 large carrot

2 tablespoons chopped fresh cilantro

2 tablespoons extra-virgin olive oil or cold-pressed sesame oil

Juice of 1 lemon

Sea salt and black pepper to taste

FOR FINISHING

1 to 2 lemon wedges

1 tablespoon extra-virgin olive oil

Preheat a grill or grill pan to medium-high heat.

Brush the red palm oil over both sides of the tuna. Combine the lemon salt, coriander, and pepper in a small bowl and sprinkle the mixture evenly over both sides of the tuna.

Grill the tuna for 2 to 3 minutes per side for medium-rare (fairly pink throughout) or until done to your liking. If you are enjoying wild, sashimi-grade tuna, you can leave it nearly rare. If you are eating a wild but lower-grade tuna, cook until it is just pink in the very center, 4 to 5 minutes per inch of fish.

Make the salad: Rinse and peel the outer skins of the daikon radishes with a standard vegetable peeler. Using a julienne peeler (or continue with the standard peeler if you don't have a julienne peeler), continue to "peel" the radishes into noodle-shaped pieces. Repeat this process with the carrot.

In a large mixing bowl, toss the radish and carrot "noodles" with the chopped cilantro, olive oil, lemon juice, salt, and pepper. Serve immediately to retain the crunch, as the daikon will become soggy if it sits too long.

To serve, plate the tuna over the noodle salad. Squeeze the lemon wedge(s) over the top and drizzle with the olive oil.

SEAFOOD

seared scallops with orange glaze

PREP TIME: 5 minutes | **COOKING TIME:** 15 minutes | **YIELD:** 2 large or 3 to 4 small servings

`NUTS & SEEDS` `FODMAPS` `21DSD` `QUICK & EASY` `FAMILY`

Scallops are simple to cook, but they require your undivided attention, as overcooking them will yield a rubbery result. Fresh scallops are ideal for this recipe; previously frozen scallops are not recommended here because they tend to give off a lot of water and are difficult to sear.

1 pound large wild scallops

Sea salt and black pepper

1/2 teaspoon garlic powder

2 tablespoons butter, ghee (page 261), or coconut oil

DEGLAZING LIQUID

1/4 cup coconut aminos

1/4 cup fresh orange juice (about 1 juicy orange)

1 tablespoon butter, ghee (page 261), or coconut oil

FOR GARNISH

Grated zest of 1 orange

1 teaspoon sesame seeds

Lay the scallops on a paper or cloth towel and pat them on each side to remove the excess moisture. Sprinkle both sides lightly with salt, pepper, and garlic powder.

Melt the butter in a stainless-steel skillet or well-seasoned cast-iron skillet over medium-high heat. Place the scallops in the hot pan, leaving at least 1 inch of space between them. Sear for 2 to 3 minutes, until the scallops are browned on the bottom and white at least a third of the way through and release easily from the pan. Flip the scallops to sear the other side for another 1 to 2 minutes, until the second side is browned and releases easily from the pan. The cooking time will vary depending on the thickness of the scallops. Take care not to overcook them. The scallops should be just white almost all the way through, but with a bit of translucent color remaining at the very center to allow for carryover cooking. (By the time you plate them, they should be perfectly cooked through.)

While the scallops are cooking, combine the deglazing liquid ingredients in a small bowl.

After removing the scallops from the pan, turn up the heat to high and pour in the deglazing liquid. Use a whisk to remove the seared bits from the bottom of the pan to flavor the sauce. Let the sauce cook and reduce over high heat for 4 to 5 minutes, until it becomes thick and sticky.

To serve, spoon about 1/2 teaspoon of the sauce over each scallop. Garnish with orange zest and sesame seeds.

SEED-FREE?

Omit the sesame seed garnish.

FODMAP-FREE?

Leave out the garlic powder. If you are extremely sensitive to coconut, the coconut aminos may be problematic for you, but if you aren't sure, you may want to try it before you assume that you can't have it in this form.

MAKE IT 21DSD

Use lemon juice instead of orange.

HOW TO DEGLAZE A PAN:

Pour your liquid of choice into a very hot pan that has flavor-filled bits seared into the bottom of it. Whisk the liquid to remove the bits from the bottom of the pan and help flavor the sauce. Then allow the remaining liquid to simmer rapidly over high heat for a few minutes before straining the sauce to serve.

CHANGE IT UP

This sauce would work nicely with any other type of seafood or with chicken or pork. Try it with bone-in pork chops for a gourmet weeknight treat!

SEAFOOD

nori salmon handroll

PREP TIME: 5 minutes | **COOKING TIME:** – | **YIELD:** 1 snack-sized handroll

FODMAPS | 21DSD | QUICK & EASY | MEAL | PARTY

CHANGE IT UP
Use canned wild salmon if you don't have or don't care for lox or smoked salmon.

For a super-fast snack or lunch option, roll your favorite fish—or even leftover chicken or turkey—into a seaweed wrapper and off you go!

1 sheet toasted nori (dried seaweed)

1/4 avocado, mashed or sliced

2 ounces wild brined salmon (lox) or smoked salmon

2 slices cucumber

1 green onion (scallion), minced

1 very thin slice of lemon (optional)

Place the nori on a cutting board and layer the avocado, smoked salmon, cucumber, green onion, and lemon slice (if using) on top.

Wrap the nori around the ingredients and enjoy.

simple shrimp ceviche

PREP TIME: 15 minutes, plus at least 30 minutes to chill | **COOKING TIME:** – | **YIELD:** 4 servings

NIGHTSHADES FODMAPS 21DSD SPICE BLEND QUICK & EASY PARTY

This recipe is always a hit at parties, and it's fantastic for an outdoor barbecue. For the best flavor, prepare the ceviche a couple of hours ahead and let it marinate in the citrus juice.

NIGHTSHADE-FREE?
Omit the bell peppers.

- 1 pound shrimp, peeled, deveined, cooked until opaque, and cooled
- 1/2 jalapeño pepper (seeds and white ribs removed), finely diced
- 1/4 red bell pepper, finely diced
- 1/4 orange or yellow bell pepper, finely diced
- 1/4 cup peeled and diced jicama
- 1/4 cup diced cucumber (skin on)
- 2 tablespoons extra-virgin olive oil
- 2 tablespoons chopped fresh cilantro
- 1 tablespoon finely diced shallots
- Juice of 1 lime
- Juice of 1 lemon
- 1 ripe avocado, diced
- 2 cups sliced cucumbers, for dipping

Chop the cooked, cooled shrimp into 1/4- to 1/2-inch pieces. In a large mixing bowl, combine the shrimp with the jalapeño, bell peppers, jicama, cucumber, olive oil, cilantro, shallots, and citrus juices.

Chill the mixture in the refrigerator for at least 30 minutes (2 hours is best). Before serving, gently stir in the avocado and serve with the cucumber slices.

mexican chicken & avocado soup

PREP TIME: 10 minutes (not including broth) | **COOKING TIME:** 25 minutes | **YIELD:** 8 servings

FODMAPS · 21DSD · SPICE BLEND · QUICK & EASY · MEAL · PARTY · FAMILY · ONE POT · FREEZE ME

FODMAP-FREE?
Omit the onion and garlic and the avocado garnish.

SPICE BLEND SWAP
Use 2 to 3 tablespoons of either of the Taco & Fajita Blends on page 257 (with or without nightshades).

FREEZE ME
Freeze the soup without the avocado added.

COOKING TIP
I highly recommend that you use homemade chicken broth for this recipe. Not only will it provide more nutrition than the store-bought variety, but it will also impart maximum flavor. Be sure to adjust the amount of salt that you add according to how salty your broth is and taste the soup often to adjust.

CHANGE IT UP
If you can tolerate nightshades, add 1 teaspoon each of paprika and chili powder.

Soup is a comfort food that we enjoy year-round in San Francisco. You never know when you'll be faced with a foggy, chilly day, whether summer or fall! This soup is a perfect answer to the chill and comes together very quickly using chicken you've already cooked. You can use my Slow-Cooked Salsa Verde Chicken or any other appropriately seasoned, shredded cooked chicken you have on hand.

1 tablespoon ghee (page 261), butter, coconut oil, or bacon fat

4 stalks celery, finely diced

1 large yellow onion, finely diced

4 carrots, finely diced

2 cloves garlic, grated or minced

1 tablespoon ground coriander

1 tablespoon ground cumin

1 teaspoon sea salt

1 teaspoon black pepper

2 quarts (64 ounces) chicken Bone Broth (page 259)

1 cup canned pumpkin (for nightshade-free, pictured) or 1/2 cup tomato paste

1 1/2 pounds shredded, cooked chicken or 8 servings Slow-Cooked Salsa Verde Chicken (page 302)

FOR GARNISH

2 avocados, sliced

Chopped fresh cilantro

Lime wedges

Coarse sea salt and coarsely cracked black pepper

Melt the ghee in a large pot over medium heat. Add the celery, onion, and carrots and cook for 4 to 5 minutes, until tender. Add the garlic and cook for 1 minute more. Add the coriander, cumin, salt, pepper, broth, and pumpkin and stir to combine. Bring to a boil, then lower the heat and let the soup simmer for 10 minutes.

Add the shredded chicken to the pot and stir to combine. Heat briefly, just to warm the chicken, then taste for seasoning, adding more salt and pepper if needed.

Ladle the soup into bowls and garnish each serving with avocado slices, cilantro, a squeeze of lime juice, and some coarse salt and cracked pepper.

broc-cauli chowder with bacon

PREP TIME: 20 minutes (not including broth, roasted garlic, or bacon)
COOKING TIME: 20 minutes | **YIELD:** 8 servings

FODMAPS   21DSD   FAMILY   FREEZE ME

CHANGE IT UP

You can make this soup with just broccoli or just cauliflower.

If you're looking for an easy way to eat your veggies, this chowder is it! In every bowl of this creamy soup, you get a heaping helping of both broccoli and cauliflower.

4 cups chopped broccoli, steamed

2 to 3 cups chicken or beef Bone Broth (page 259), divided

4 cups chopped cauliflower, steamed

4 to 6 cloves roasted garlic (see page 342) (optional)

Sea salt and black pepper

4 slices Perfectly Baked Bacon (page 260), chopped, for garnish

Using a blender, liquefy the broccoli with 1 cup of the broth until smooth. Repeat the process with the cauliflower and another cup of broth. Add the roasted garlic, if using, to either of the batches before blending again.

Combine the veggie purees in a large pot over medium heat. Add salt and pepper to taste, keeping in mind that the bacon garnish will add some saltiness. Simmer for 10 minutes, stirring to combine the two purees. Add up to another cup of broth, 1/4 cup at a time, if the soup is too thick.

Garnish with the chopped bacon and serve.

butternut sage soup

PREP TIME: 30 minutes (not including broth) | **COOKING TIME:** 45 minutes

YIELD: 4 to 6 servings

`FODMAPS` `21DSD` `SPICE BLEND` `PARTY` `FAMILY` `FREEZE ME`

This soup is so rich and creamy, you won't miss the dairy!

1 butternut squash (2 1/2 to 3 pounds)

4 tablespoons bacon fat, coconut oil, or ghee (page 261), divided

1 yellow onion, diced

4 cloves garlic, peeled and smashed with the side of a knife

1 teaspoon Herb Salt Blend made with sage (page 258) or a few pinches each of dried ground sage and sea salt

Black pepper

2 cups Bone Broth, ideally chicken (page 259)

2 tablespoons full-fat coconut milk (optional)

2 tablespoons water, or more if needed

Juice of 1 orange

FRIED SAGE LEAVES

1 to 2 tablespoons butter or ghee (page 261)

8 to 12 fresh sage leaves

Preheat the oven to 400°F.

Remove the skin from the butternut squash with a vegetable peeler, then slice the squash in half lengthwise and remove the seeds. Cut the squash into 1-inch cubes and place them in a roasting pan. Melt 1 tablespoon of the bacon fat and toss with the squash cubes. Place the pan in the oven and roast for about 40 minutes, until the squash is fork-tender.

While the squash roasts, sauté the onion with the remaining 3 tablespoons of bacon fat in a large pot over medium heat. When the onion begins to brown on the edges, add the garlic, followed by the sage salt blend and a few pinches of pepper. Cook for about 2 minutes to take the edge off the raw garlic. Add the broth, coconut milk (if using), and water and bring to a simmer.

Add the roasted squash to the soup and stir. Add the orange juice just before turning off the heat.

After the soup has cooled a bit, pour it into a blender and blend until smooth. Be careful not to fill the blender more than about halfway because the steam will cause the liquid to expand. Blend the soup in 2 or 3 batches if necessary. Add a touch more water if the soup is too thick. Divide the soup among 4 to 6 serving bowls.

Make the fried sage leaves: Melt the butter in a small saucepan or cast-iron skillet over medium heat, then fry the sage leaves in the butter until they begin to bubble up and become crispy and slightly darker.

Garnish each bowl of soup with a couple of fried sage leaves.

dairy-free caesar salad

PREP TIME: 10 minutes (not including dressing or bacon)
COOKING TIME: 30 to 40 minutes | **YIELD:** 4 servings

NIGHTSHADES FODMAPS 21DSD MEAL PARTY FAMILY

NIGHTSHADE-FREE?

Use sweet potatoes instead of white potatoes for the "croutons."

CHANGE IT UP

Add grilled steak, fish, or shrimp instead of chicken.

I'm a huge fan of creamy Caesar salad, so eliminating dairy has meant missing out on this classic—until now! This salad is so hearty that it eats like a complete meal—no need for additional sides.

"CROUTONS"

4 small russet potatoes

1 teaspoon melted ghee (page 261)

Sea salt

3 romaine lettuce hearts, separated into leaves

2 boneless, skinless chicken breast halves, butterflied and grilled (see page 254), then sliced

1/2 cup Dairy-Free Caesar Dressing (page 434)

4 slices Perfectly Baked Bacon (page 260), roughly chopped

2 tablespoons capers

Preheat the oven to 375°F.

Make the "croutons": Use the slicing blade of a food processor to slice the potatoes cross-wise, about 1/8 inch thick. If you don't own a food processor, use a sharp knife to slice them.

Toss the potatoes with the melted ghee and sprinkle them lightly with salt. Spread out on a rimmed baking sheet and bake for 30 to 40 minutes, until they start to turn golden brown. After about 25 minutes, check the potatoes to make sure that they are not burning and turn them once.

Divide the lettuce, "croutons," and chicken among four plates, then drizzle on the dressing. Top with the bacon and capers before serving.

winter kale salad

PREP TIME: 10 minutes (not including dressing) | **COOKING TIME:** – | **YIELD:** 4 servings

NUTS & SEEDS FODMAPS 21DSD QUICK & EASY PARTY

NUT-FREE?

Omit the pistachios.

FODMAP-FREE?

Omit the pomegranate seeds and beets; add strawberries instead.

MAKE IT 21DSD

Omit the oranges and pomegranate seeds and add sliced green apple instead.

CHANGE IT UP

Add grilled chicken, steak, fish, or shrimp.

6 cups chopped kale

1/2 cup Spicy Lime Dressing (page 434)

2 oranges, segmented

1 fennel bulb, sliced

1 cup diced roasted beets

1/2 cup shelled pistachios

1/2 cup pomegranate seeds (1 small pomegranate)

Place the kale in a large bowl and massage it gently with your hands, squeezing it to begin to bruise it—this makes it easier to digest. Pour in the dressing and toss to coat the kale evenly. Arrange the kale on a serving platter or in individual serving bowls and top with the oranges, fennel, beets, pistachios, and pomegranate seeds.

italiano salad

PREP TIME: 15 minutes (not including dressing) | **COOKING TIME:** 45 minutes to 1 hour
YIELD: 4 servings

NUTS & SEEDS NIGHTSHADES FODMAPS 21DSD MEAL PARTY FAMILY

NUT-FREE?

Omit the pine nuts.

NIGHTSHADE-FREE?

Omit the sun-dried tomatoes
from the salad and the
red pepper flakes from the
dressing.

FODMAP-FREE?

Omit the artichokes and
onion. Limit the sun-
dried tomatoes or use
fresh tomatoes instead.
Use Balsamic Vinaigrette
(page 434) or Basil Shallot
Vinaigrette (page 434)
without the honey.

MAKE IT 21DSD

Omit the honey from the
dressing, or use Balsamic
or Basil Shallot Vinaigrette
(without honey) instead.

*My husband, Scott, and I often have lunch dates at a local spot here in San Francisco where
they serve a salad very similar to this, and it's always my favorite. I've re-created it here for
you, but if you're ever in town, stop by the Blue Barn to try the inspiration for this one!*

1 large red onion, sliced

1 teaspoon extra-virgin olive oil

1 tablespoon balsamic vinegar

Sea salt

4 small russet potatoes, diced

1 teaspoon melted ghee (page 261)

8 cups arugula or other dark leafy
 lettuce mix

2 whole boneless, skinless chicken
 breasts, butterflied and grilled
 (see page 254), then cubed

1 cup halved artichoke hearts

1 cup sun-dried tomatoes, roughly
 chopped

1/2 cup toasted pine nuts (pignoli)

1/2 cup Honey Mustard Dressing
 (page 434)

Have two oven racks evenly spaced in the oven and preheat the oven to 375°F. Line two
rimmed baking sheet with parchment paper.

Toss the onion slices with the olive oil and balsamic vinegar until evenly coated. Season
with a few pinches of salt and spread out on one of the prepared baking sheets. Bake for
45 minutes to 1 hour, until the onions are translucent and browned, turning once halfway
through. When done, remove from the oven and set aside.

After the onions have been in the oven for about 15 minutes, toss the potatoes with the
ghee and season with a few pinches of salt. Spread the potatoes out on the other prepared
baking sheet and bake for 30 to 40 minutes, until they start to turn golden brown. After
about 25 minutes, check the potatoes to make sure that they are not burning and turn
them once. Set aside.

To serve, arrange the arugula in a large serving bowl and top with the potatoes, chicken,
artichoke hearts, sun-dried tomatoes, pine nuts, and roasted onions. Toss or top with the
dressing before serving.

flank steak salad with fruit & balsamic vinaigrette

PREP TIME: 10 minutes (not including dressing) | **COOKING TIME:** – | **YIELD:** 1 meal-sized salad

NUTS & SEEDS | FODMAPS | 21DSD | QUICK & EASY | MEAL | PARTY | FAMILY

Flank steak is a fantastic protein to grill up and have on hand to use in a variety of ways. Prepare the steak by following the recipe on page 334, then use the leftovers to make this salad for lunch the next day.

2 cups baby spinach or mixed greens

4 to 6 ounces leftover sliced grilled flank steak (page 334)

1/4 cup sliced Granny Smith apples

2 white button or baby bella mushrooms, sliced

2 tablespoons fresh raspberries

1 tablespoon sliced almonds

2 tablespoons Balsamic Vinaigrette (page 434)

NUT-FREE?
Omit the almonds.

FODMAP-FREE?
Omit the apple and mushrooms; add grated carrots instead.

MAKE IT 21DSD
Omit the berries.

CHANGE IT UP
Use walnuts or pecans instead of almonds. Use any seasonal fruit.

Plate the spinach and top with the grilled steak, apple slices, mushrooms, raspberries, and almonds. Drizzle on the vinaigrette.

mixed greens salad with persimmons, asparagus & fennel

PREP TIME: 10 minutes (not including dressing) | **COOKING TIME:** – | **YIELD:** 2 servings

`FODMAPS` `QUICK & EASY` `PARTY` `FAMILY`

NOTE

Top this salad with grilled chicken or fish for a complete meal.

Persimmons are one of my favorite fall and winter fruits. Seasonally available for only a short time, their flavor is worth the wait. Replace persimmons with apples at other times of the year.

4 cups mixed greens

8 thin asparagus spears, trimmed and cut into 1- to 2-inch lengths

1 persimmon, thinly sliced into half-moons

1/4 cup thinly sliced fennel bulb (reserve the fronds for garnish if desired)

Orange zest (grated or strips), for garnish (optional)

1/4 cup Orange Vinaigrette (page 434)

Divide the mixed greens between two individual serving plates. Top the greens with the asparagus, persimmon, and fennel bulb. Garnish with the reserved fennel fronds and orange zest, if desired, then dress with the vinaigrette.

prosciutto & berries salad

PREP TIME: 5 minutes (not including dressing) | **COOKING TIME:** – | **YIELD:** 4 servings

FODMAPS | QUICK & EASY | MEAL | PARTY | FAMILY

8 cups baby arugula

1/2 cup fresh blueberries

1/2 cup pomegranate seeds
(1 small pomegranate)

8 ounces prosciutto, pulled apart into
pieces

1 avocado, sliced

1/2 cup Basil Shallot Vinaigrette
(page 434)

Arrange the arugula on a large platter, then top it with the berries, pomegranate seeds, and prosciutto. Place the avocado slices on top of the salad and dress with the vinaigrette.

greek salad
with avoziki dressing

PREP TIME: 15 minutes (not including tzatziki) | **COOKING TIME:** — | **YIELD:** 2 servings

NIGHTSHADES FODMAPS 21DSD SPICE BLEND QUICK & EASY PARTY FAMILY

NIGHTSHADE-FREE?

Omit the tomatoes and add chopped cooked beets for color instead.

SERVE IT UP

Pair this salad with the lamb chops on page 366.

The most traditional Greek salads don't include any lettuce, but this is my twist on the classic.

4 cups chopped romaine lettuce

1/2 cup cucumber slices

1/2 cup halved cherry tomatoes

1/4 cup pitted and halved Kalamata olives

2 tablespoons capers

AVOZIKI DRESSING

1/4 cup Dairy-Free Tzatziki (Avoziki) (page 370)

2 tablespoons extra-virgin olive oil

1/2 teaspoon Greek Blend (page 256)

Plate the romaine lettuce and top it with the cucumbers, cherry tomatoes, olives, and capers.

In a small mixing bowl, combine the tzatziki and olive oil.

Top the salad with the dressing and sprinkle with the spice blend.

summer squash
caprese noodle salad

PREP TIME: 30 minutes | **COOKING TIME:** – | **YIELD:** 4 to 6 servings

NIGHTSHADES · FODMAPS · 21DSD · QUICK & EASY · PARTY · FAMILY

If Caprese salad is one of your favorites at Italian restaurants, you'll love this recipe. It's especially great at a summertime cookout.

4 to 6 medium zucchini or yellow squash

1 cup cherry tomatoes, quartered

1/4 cup fresh basil leaves, thinly sliced

1/4 cup extra-virgin olive oil

1 clove garlic, grated or minced

Sea salt and black pepper

Chop the ends off the zucchini and use a julienne peeler or spiral slicer to make fettuccine-like noodles, peeling down to the center seedy section. You should have 5 cups of noodles. (You can use a standard peeler if you don't have a julienne peeler.) Discard the seedy centers.

In a medium-sized mixing bowl, combine the cherry tomatoes, basil, olive oil, garlic, and salt and pepper to taste.

Toss the squash with the tomato mixture and serve on plates or in bowls.

NIGHTSHADE-FREE?
Leave out the tomatoes—add shredded carrots for color instead.

CHANGE IT UP
For a warm dish, steam the squash noodles for about 2 minutes. Remove the noodles from the steamer pot and allow them to sit in the basket over a plate to drain for 10 minutes before combining the noodles with the tomato mixture.

rainbow red cabbage salad

PREP TIME: 30 minutes | **COOKING TIME:** – | **YIELD:** 4 to 6 servings

NUTS & SEEDS FODMAPS 21DSD QUICK & EASY PARTY FAMILY

MAKE IT 21DSD

Omit the mango.

CHANGE IT UP

If mango isn't in season, fresh apple chunks work nicely.

If you don't have macadamia nut oil, try extra-virgin olive oil.

Bring this bright, crisp salad to a party or barbecue to make a colorful impression! It pairs nicely with Citrus Macadamia Nut Sole (page 378).

1 cup thinly sliced or shredded red cabbage

1/2 cup shredded carrots

1/2 cup shredded broccoli stems

1/2 mango, finely diced

Juice of 1 to 2 limes

2 tablespoons macadamia nut oil

Sea salt and black pepper

2 tablespoons chopped macadamia nuts, for garnish

In a large mixing bowl, combine the cabbage, carrots, broccoli stems, and mango.

Top the vegetable mixture with the lime juice, macadamia nut oil, and salt and pepper to taste. Toss to coat the mixture well with the dressing.

Transfer to a serving dish and garnish with the chopped macadamia nuts.

sautéed red cabbage with onions & apples

PREP TIME: 15 minutes | **COOKING TIME:** 20 to 30 minutes | **YIELD:** 4 servings

`FODMAPS` `21DSD` `FAMILY`

This sweet and savory dish is great when paired with any type of roasted or grilled meat, and it also works well as a side dish to eggs in the morning.

1 large yellow onion, thinly sliced
1 tablespoon bacon fat or coconut oil
1/2 head red cabbage, thinly sliced
2 to 4 tablespoons apple cider vinegar

1 tablespoon Herb Salt Blend made with rosemary (page 258)
1 green apple, sliced into matchsticks

In a large enameled or stainless-steel pot over medium heat, sauté the onion in the bacon fat. When the onion is mostly translucent, add the cabbage and cook until it begins to soften, 4 to 5 minutes.

Add 2 tablespoons of the vinegar and rosemary salt blend and allow the cabbage and onion to cook, uncovered, until the cabbage is softened and fork-tender, about 10 minutes. Add some water to the pot if it becomes dry while the cabbage is cooking.

Add the apple and cook until soft, 2 to 3 minutes. Taste and add more vinegar, if desired, to make the dish more sour/acidic.

NOTE

I don't recommend a cast-iron skillet for this dish since it includes vinegar, which is very acidic and may react with cast iron.

CHANGE IT UP

Instead of using plain bacon fat, chop and render 2 to 3 slices of bacon for the cooking fat and add the cooked bacon meat to the cabbage mixture when plating.

For a slightly sweeter version, add 2 to 4 tablespoons chopped dried cranberries (find a no-sugar-added brand or dry some yourself).

acorn squash with cinnamon & coconut butter

PREP TIME: 5 minutes | **COOKING TIME:** 35 to 45 minutes | **YIELD:** 2 to 4 servings

`NUTS & SEEDS` `FODMAPS` `21DSD` `QUICK & EASY` `FAMILY`

NUT-FREE?

Use seeds for crunch, or use toasted coconut to keep it both nut-free and seed-free.

MAKE IT 21DSD

Don't use the dried fruit topping.

CHANGE IT UP

Try making this recipe with sweet potatoes, yams, or any other kind of winter squash.

Roasting winter squash is a soul-warming experience. The aroma that comes from the oven as the squash roasts and nears doneness is amazing. This dish is almost a dessert, but without any added sweeteners.

1 acorn squash

1/4 cup coconut butter (also called coconut manna or coconut cream concentrate)

3 pinches of ground cinnamon

Pinch of sea salt

2 tablespoons raisins or currants (optional)

2 tablespoons sliced almonds or chopped walnuts (optional)

Preheat the oven to 375°F.

Slice the squash lengthwise down the middle and remove the seeds. Place it cut side down in a baking dish and bake for 35 to 45 minutes, until the squash is fork-tender and the edges are beginning to brown.

When the squash is cooked, remove it from the oven and turn the halves cut side up. While it's still warm, fill the centers with equal amounts of the coconut butter and dust with the cinnamon and salt. Top with the dried fruit and nuts, if using. Serve warm.

green beans with shallots

PREP TIME: 5 minutes | **COOKING TIME:** 15 minutes | **YIELD:** 4 servings

`FODMAPS` `21DSD` `QUICK & EASY` `PARTY` `FAMILY`

FODMAP-FREE?

Leave out the shallots and season the green beans with lemon zest instead.

Although it has "bean" in its name, the green bean is mostly pod, not bean, so green beans are a perfectly healthy green vegetable to enjoy.

1 pound green beans, ends trimmed

2 tablespoons butter, ghee (page 261), or coconut oil, divided

2 shallots, sliced

Sea salt and black pepper

Set a steamer basket over 1 inch of boiling water. Place the green beans in the steamer basket and cook for about 8 minutes, until they turn a brighter shade of green.

While the green beans are steaming, melt 1 tablespoon of the butter in a medium-sized skillet over medium heat. Sauté the shallots in the melted butter until they are translucent and the edges are golden brown. Season with a few pinches each of salt and pepper.

Remove the green beans from the steamer basket and place them in a serving bowl. Top with the remaining 1 tablespoon of butter and toss to combine.

Place the cooked shallots on top of the green beans and serve.

smoky grilled squash & pineapple

PREP TIME: 15 minutes | **COOKING TIME:** 45 minutes | **YIELD:** 8 servings

`NIGHTSHADES` `SPICE BLEND` `PARTY` `FAMILY`

EQUIPMENT TIP

If you don't have an outdoor grill, you can use a grill pan on the stovetop to get the same effect.

CHANGE IT UP

Grill any kind of fruit that you can slice into thick pieces: apples, pears, peaches, or even whole figs!

Grilling sweet foods usually yields a delicious result—and these two beautiful, carb-rich foods are no exception.

1 butternut squash (2 1/2 to 3 pounds)

1/2 pineapple, peeled, cored, and sliced (1 inch thick)

1/4 cup butter, ghee (page 261), or coconut oil, melted

1 to 2 tablespoons Smoky Blend (page 256)

Sea salt

1/4 cup unsweetened shredded coconut, for garnish

Preheat the oven to 375°F.

Remove the skin from the butternut squash with a vegetable peeler, then slice the squash in half lengthwise and remove the seeds. Cut the squash into 1-inch-thick slices and place them on a rimmed baking sheet. Roast for 30 minutes, or until fork-tender.

When the squash is nearly done, preheat a grill to medium heat.

Brush the roasted squash and pineapple slices with the melted butter, season with the spice blend and a few pinches of salt, then place on the hot grill.

Grill the squash and pineapple for 3 to 5 minutes per side, until grill marks appear.

Serve warm, garnished with shredded coconut.

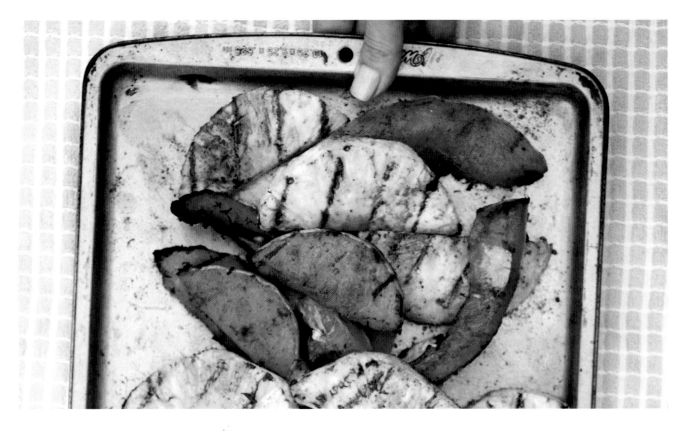

asparagus with lemon & olives

PREP TIME: 5 minutes | **COOKING TIME:** 10 to 15 minutes | **YIELD:** 4 servings

FODMAPS 21DSD QUICK & EASY FAMILY

Simply grilling, roasting, or steaming asparagus yields a delicious result, but topping asparagus with some citrus and olives takes it to a new level. Enjoy this dish as a side to the Lemon Rosemary Broiled Salmon (page 375) or with any simply grilled meat.

CHANGE IT UP
This recipe also works with green olives and orange zest.

1 pound asparagus

1 tablespoon butter, ghee (page 261), or coconut oil, melted

1/2 teaspoon garlic powder

Sea salt and black pepper

1 lemon

1 tablespoon extra-virgin olive oil

1/4 cup Kalamata olives, pitted and halved

Preheat the oven to 375°F.

Chop the ends off of the asparagus and rinse the spears under water. Place the asparagus on a rimmed baking sheet and toss with the melted butter. Sprinkle with the garlic powder and a few pinches each of salt and pepper. Roast for 10 to 15 minutes—less time for very thin asparagus or more time for very thick asparagus.

While the asparagus is roasting, use a Microplane grater to remove the zest from the lemon; set the zest aside.

When the asparagus is bright green and fork-tender, remove it from the oven. Drizzle with the olive oil and top with the lemon zest and halved olives.

crispy sweet potato coins

PREP TIME: 10 minutes | **COOKING TIME:** 20 to 30 minutes | **YIELD:** About 4 servings

`NUTS & SEEDS` `EGGS` `FODMAPS` `21DSD` `SPICE BLEND` `PARTY` `FAMILY`

NUT-FREE?

Use coconut flour.

EGG-FREE?

Dust the sweet potato coins with a smaller amount of the flour and spice blend, skipping the egg dip, and pan-fry or bake as desired.

CHANGE IT UP

If you prefer to bake your sweet potato coins, combine the flour mixture, eggs, and cooking fat to create a batter. Dip each coin in the batter, then place on a parchment paper–lined baking sheet. Bake at 350°F for 20 to 30 minutes, until golden brown on the outside and fork-tender.

If you're looking for a "fancier" way to prepare sweet potatoes, this is the recipe for you! By tossing the sliced potatoes in a "breading" of almond or coconut flour and mixing in your favorite spices, you can make this recipe a bit differently every time. Try different cooking fats as well for a varied flavor profile.

2 sweet potatoes, peeled

1/2 cup almond meal, almond flour, or sifted coconut flour

2 tablespoons spice blend of choice (pages 256 to 257)

1 or 2 large eggs (use 2 if your sweet potatoes are very large)

1/4 cup bacon fat, coconut oil, or ghee (page 261), or more as needed

Slice the sweet potatoes into 1/4-inch-thick coins. Place them on a rimmed baking sheet and set aside.

With a fork or whisk, combine the almond meal and spice blend in a bowl. In another bowl, beat the eggs. Set up a "station" and dip the sweet potato coins into the eggs, then into the flour mixture. After completing each coin, set it back on the baking sheet.

Heat the fat in a large skillet over medium heat. Use enough fat to cover the bottom of the skillet completely and come at least halfway up the sides of the sweet potato coins. Place some of the "breaded" sweet potato coins in the hot skillet and cook for 2 to 3 minutes per side, until golden brown. Remove from the skillet and set on paper towels to drain.

Repeat with the rest of the breaded coins, adding more fat to the skillet as needed so that the depth remains constant.

smashed potatoes with garlic & onions

PREP TIME: 10 minutes | **COOKING TIME:** 45 minutes | **YIELD:** 4 to 6 servings

`NIGHTSHADES` `FODMAPS` `21DSD` `PARTY` `FAMILY`

These smashed and roasted new potatoes are even easier to make if you boil the potatoes ahead of time and keep them handy in the refrigerator. They're so good that I recommend you make a double batch and simply reheat them in an oven or toaster oven to enjoy for a few meals—they're worth it!

2 to 3 pounds new potatoes

1 large onion

4 cloves garlic

3 tablespoons melted ghee (page 261) or butter

3 tablespoons extra-virgin olive oil

1 teaspoon dried oregano leaves (optional)

1/2 teaspoon sea salt

1/2 teaspoon black pepper

NIGHTSHADE-FREE?

Prepare this recipe with parsnips or turnips peeled and cut into large chunks instead of the potatoes. Line the baking sheet with parchment paper to prevent sticking.

Preheat the oven to 400°F.

Put the potatoes in a large pot, cover them with cold water, and bring the water to a boil. Continue boiling until the potatoes are fork-tender, about 15 minutes. When the potatoes are tender, remove the pot from the heat and drain the potatoes.

While the potatoes are boiling, slice the onion and chop the garlic, then toss them in a large mixing bowl with the ghee and olive oil. Season with the oregano (if using), salt, and pepper.

Place the boiled potatoes on a rimmed baking sheet, then smash each one flat with either a fork or a mallet. Toss the potatoes with the onion mixture, then spread everything evenly on the baking sheet.

Roast for about 30 minutes, until brown and crispy.

cilantro cauli-rice

PREP TIME: 20 minutes | **COOKING TIME:** 5 minutes | **YIELD:** 4 servings

FODMAPS 21DSD QUICK & EASY FAMILY

CHANGE IT UP

Instead of cilantro, use any fresh herb you like. Try basil or chives!

This rice replacement pairs well with any Mexican dish and is especially delicious under the Grilled Garlic Flank Steak with Peppers & Onions (page 334).

1 head cauliflower

1 tablespoon coconut oil, ghee (page 261), or butter

Sea salt and black pepper

1/4 cup minced fresh cilantro

Remove the outer leaves and core from the cauliflower, then chop the cauliflower into large chunks. Shred the chunks using a box grater or food processor.

In a large skillet over medium heat, melt the coconut oil. Place the shredded cauliflower in the skillet and season generously with salt and pepper. Sauté for about 5 minutes, until the cauliflower begins to become translucent, stirring gently to ensure that it cooks through.

Place the cooked cauliflower in a serving bowl and toss with the chopped cilantro before serving.

yellow cauli-rice

PREP TIME: 15 minutes | **COOKING TIME:** 5 to 8 minutes | **YIELD:** 4 servings

FODMAPS 21DSD QUICK & EASY FAMILY

1 large head cauliflower

1 tablespoon ghee (page 261), coconut oil, or extra-virgin olive oil

1 teaspoon turmeric powder

1 teaspoon granulated garlic

1/2 teaspoon sea salt

1/2 teaspoon black pepper

3 tablespoons currants

2 tablespoons chopped fresh cilantro or parsley (optional)

MAKE IT 21DSD

Omit the currants.

Remove the outer leaves and core from the cauliflower, then chop it into large chunks.

Use a box grater or food processor fitted with a shredder blade to shred the florets. Depending on the size of your food processor's bowl, and if your head of cauliflower is particularly large, you may need to shred the cauliflower in two batches.

Warm the ghee in a large skillet over medium heat, then add the cauliflower, seasonings, and currants to the hot pan. Sauté the cauliflower for 5 to 8 minutes, until cooked through but still holding its shape and not mushy. Serve topped with chopped fresh herbs, if desired.

roasted figs with rosemary

PREP TIME: 15 minutes | **COOKING TIME:** 10 to 15 minutes | **YIELD:** 4 servings

FODMAPS QUICK & EASY PARTY FAMILY

CHANGE IT UP
Wrap each bite of fig with some prosciutto and serve as an appetizer or snack.

Fresh figs are in season for only a couple of months each year—typically late summer into early fall in most parts of the United States. They have an entirely different taste and texture from dried figs, which are great in sauces like the Balsamic Fig Compote on page 372.

12 whole, fresh figs

2 teaspoons finely minced fresh rosemary

2 tablespoons extra-virgin olive oil

Coarse sea salt

Preheat the oven to 425°F.

Slice off the tips of the figs and cut them into quarters. Place the fig quarters on a rimmed baking sheet and sprinkle the finely minced rosemary over them. Roast for 10 to 15 minutes, until the edges of the figs are slightly browned.

Remove the figs from the oven. Serve warm or at room temperature, drizzled with the olive oil and sprinkled with some coarse salt.

candied carrots

PREP TIME: 10 minutes | **COOKING TIME:** 20 to 30 minutes | **YIELD:** 4 servings

FODMAPS   QUICK & EASY   FAMILY

These carrots are a bit of treat since they're cooked with dates. If you're watching your overall sugar or carb intake, you can reduce the number of dates or omit them altogether.

SERVE IT UP

With Balsamic Braised Short Ribs (page 332).

8 large carrots, peeled and sliced into 1/2-inch rounds

4 dates, pitted and chopped

2 tablespoons butter, ghee (page 261), or coconut oil, melted

Sea salt

Preheat the oven to 375°F.

Place the carrots and dates in a baking dish and top with the melted butter. Toss to coat, then sprinkle generously with salt.

Bake for 20 to 30 minutes, until the carrots are fork-tender.

roasted brussels sprouts

PREP TIME: 10 minutes | **COOKING TIME:** 30 minutes | **YIELD:** 4 servings

FODMAPS   21DSD   QUICK & EASY   FAMILY

CHANGE IT UP

Add chopped bacon to the pan to roast with the sprouts!

The easiest way to make Brussels sprouts is also the best: simply roast them with bacon fat, garlic, salt, and pepper. It doesn't take more than that to make these tiny cabbage-head-like vegetables taste fantastic.

4 cups Brussels sprouts (about 1 pound), ends trimmed

1 tablespoon bacon fat, ghee (page 261), butter, or coconut oil, melted

1/2 teaspoon granulated garlic

Sea salt and black pepper

Preheat the oven to 375°F.

Halve the Brussels sprouts, then place them on a large rimmed baking sheet (preferably stainless steel and not nonstick for the best browning). Toss them with the melted bacon fat.

Sprinkle the Brussels sprouts with the granulated garlic and a few pinches each of salt and pepper, then arrange them cut side down.

Roast for 30 minutes, or until the leaves begin to separate and become dark brown and crispy and the halves are cooked through and browned.

lemon roasted romanesco

PREP TIME: 10 minutes | **COOKING TIME:** 20 to 25 minutes | **YIELD:** 3 to 4 servings

FODMAPS 21DSD QUICK & EASY FAMILY

Romanesco can be a novelty, but whenever I see it, I pick it up for its unique look and color. Keep your cooking interesting by trying as many different kinds of vegetables as you can!

2 large heads romanesco (or 8 small heads if sold in palm-sized whole heads)

2 tablespoons butter, bacon fat, or coconut oil, melted

Sea salt and black pepper

1/2 lemon, very thinly sliced

CHANGE IT UP

Can't find romanesco in your grocery store or farmers' market? No problem! Substitute cauliflower or broccoli.

Preheat the oven to 375°F.

Remove and discard the outer leaves of the romanesco, then chop it into 2-inch pieces and place them on a rimmed baking sheet. Pour the melted butter over the romanesco and toss gently with your hands to coat the pieces evenly. Sprinkle with a few pinches each of salt and pepper and top with the lemon slices.

Roast for 20 to 25 minutes, until the romanesco is fork-tender and the edges are golden brown.

mashed faux-tatoes

PREP TIME: 10 minutes | **COOKING TIME:** 20 minutes | **YIELD:** 4 to 6 servings

FODMAPS · 21DSD · SPICE BLEND · QUICK & EASY · PARTY · FAMILY

NOTES

If you can't eat butter, try adding roasted garlic (see page 342) for more depth of flavor.

If you don't have a food processor, you can mash the cauliflower by hand with a potato masher.

SERVE IT UP

Try serving these with Chorizo Meatballs (page 322).

This is the most amazing alternative to mashed potatoes that you can make. My entire family was fooled when I served these up for Thanksgiving dinner a few years ago, and there were no leftovers!

1 head cauliflower

4 tablespoons butter, ghee (page 261), or coconut oil

1/2 teaspoon Herb Salt Blend of choice (page 258)

Black pepper

Chop the cauliflower into roughly 2- to 3-inch pieces. You should have about 4 cups.

Steam the cauliflower until it is fork-tender, then place it in a food processor. Add the butter, herb salt blend, and pepper to taste.

Puree until smooth and creamy.

whipped sweet potatoes

PREP TIME: 10 minutes | **COOKING TIME:** 10 minutes | **YIELD:** 4 to 6 servings

FODMAPS 21DSD QUICK & EASY PARTY FAMILY

This method for making sweet potatoes will quickly become your favorite because it just couldn't be any easier. Unlike starchier white potatoes, sweet potatoes can handle this treatment in a food processor and won't turn into a gummy mess!

FODMAP-FREE?
Omit the garlic powder.

2 pounds sweet potatoes, peeled and cut into 1 1/2-inch chunks

3 tablespoon ghee (page 261) or butter, divided

3 tablespoons full-fat coconut milk

1/2 teaspoon sea salt

1/4 teaspoon black pepper

1/4 teaspoon garlic powder

FOR GARNISH

Coarse sea salt and coarsely cracked black pepper

Ground cinnamon (optional)

Set a large steamer basket over 1 to 2 inches of boiling water. Place the sweet potato chunks in the steamer basket and cook for 10 minutes, until they are cooked through (they should be very soft and easily break apart with a fork). If you do not own a steamer basket, you can boil the sweet potatoes for 10 minutes or until cooked through.

Place the cooked sweet potatoes, 2 tablespoons of the ghee, coconut milk, salt, pepper, and garlic powder in a food processor and process until smooth, stopping the machine to scrape down the sides of the bowl once if necessary.

Garnish with the remaining 1 tablespoon of ghee or butter, coarse sea salt, cracked black pepper, and cinnamon (if using).

baked beets with fennel

PREP TIME: 15 minutes | **COOKING TIME:** 30 to 40 minutes | **YIELD:** 2 to 3 servings

`FODMAPS` `21DSD` `QUICK & EASY` `FAMILY`

FODMAP-FREE?

Bake carrots or parsnips with fennel instead of beets.

Beets are amazingly nutrient-dense and are recommended in nearly every meal plan in this book! Save some of these for a salad topping the next day.

2 large beets

1 fennel bulb

1/2 orange (optional)

2 tablespoons coconut oil, ghee (page 261), or butter, melted

Sea salt and black pepper

Preheat the oven to 375°F.

Peel the beets with a vegetable peeler and cut them into 1-inch cubes. Chop the tops (fronds) off the fennel bulb (save them for another use) and slice the bulb into 1/4-inch strips. Slice the orange (if using) into 1/2-inch pieces, or use segments if you prefer.

Top the beets, fennel, and orange pieces (if using) with the melted coconut oil, add a few pinches each of salt and pepper, and toss to combine. Spread evenly in a baking dish and bake for 30 to 40 minutes, until the beets are fork-tender.

sweet & savory potatoes

PREP TIME: 15 minutes | **COOKING TIME:** 30 minutes | **YIELD:** 2 servings

`FODMAPS` `21DSD` `QUICK & EASY` `FAMILY`

Sweet potatoes can be roasted and enjoyed simply with salt and pepper, but to kick them up, use a few different spices. The result is a whole new taste experience!

FODMAP-FREE?
Omit the onion and garlic powder and add 1/2 teaspoon dried rosemary leaves.

2 large sweet potatoes (about 1 pound)

1 teaspoon duck fat, bacon fat, ghee (page 261), or coconut oil, melted

1/2 teaspoon ground cinnamon

1/4 teaspoon garlic powder

1/4 teaspoon onion powder

Sea salt and black pepper

Preheat the oven to 375°F.

Peel the sweet potatoes and chop them into 1-inch pieces. (You should have 2 cups.) In a medium-sized mixing bowl, toss the sweet potato pieces with the melted fat to coat them evenly.

In a small mixing bowl, combine the cinnamon, garlic powder, onion powder, and a few pinches each of salt and pepper. Add the spice mixture to the sweet potatoes and toss again to distribute the spices evenly.

Spread the sweet potatoes in a single layer on a rimmed baking sheet and bake for about 30 minutes, until the sweet potatoes are fork-tender.

confit cherry tomatoes

PREP TIME: 5 minutes | **COOKING TIME:** 20 to 25 minutes | **YIELD:** 2 servings

NIGHTSHADES FODMAPS 21DSD QUICK & EASY FAMILY

Enjoy these tomatoes as a side dish or use them as a base for an easy sauce to pour over spaghetti squash. To make a sauce, puree the tomatoes with a few basil leaves, a clove of garlic, and some olive oil!

2 cups cherry tomatoes

1 tablespoon duck fat, bacon fat, or coconut oil, melted

Sea salt and black pepper

Preheat the oven to 400°F.

Place the tomatoes and duck fat in an oven-safe dish or pan and toss to coat. Season with a few pinches each of salt and pepper.

Place the dish in the oven and roast for 20 to 25 minutes, basting the tomatoes with the pan liquid every 10 minutes. The tomatoes are done when they appear soft and begin to burst open.

sautéed spinach with pine nuts & currants

PREP TIME: 5 minutes | **COOKING TIME:** 10 minutes | **YIELD:** 2 servings

NUTS & SEEDS   FODMAPS   21DSD   QUICK & EASY   FAMILY

One of my favorite tapas restaurants in San Francisco serves a spinach dish with golden raisins and almonds that's very similar to this one. I put my own twist on it by using pine nuts (pignoli) and currants.

2 tablespoons pine nuts (pignoli)

1 tablespoon butter, ghee (page 261), or coconut oil

4 cups baby spinach, washed

Sea salt and black pepper

2 tablespoons currants

MAKE IT 21DSD
Omit the currants.

CHANGE IT UP
You can make this recipe with chopped walnuts and raisins if you prefer.

In a large skillet over low heat, toast the pine nuts for about 5 minutes, tossing often to prevent burning. Set the toasted pine nuts aside.

Melt the butter in the skillet, then add the spinach and a few pinches each of salt and pepper. Cover and cook for about 2 minutes. Stir the spinach and continue to cook until it is wilted.

Place in a serving dish and top with the toasted pine nuts and currants.

bacon-wrapped party bites

PREP TIME: 20 minutes | **COOKING TIME:** 20 to 30 minutes
YIELD: 2 dozen bites (1 dozen of each kind)

FODMAPS   QUICK & EASY   PARTY   FAMILY

NOTE

Be very careful when biting into these little treats—right out of the oven, they'll be extremely hot in the center!

CHANGE IT UP

Use walnuts instead of pecans to stuff the dates.

Medjool dates are ideal for this recipe. If you can find only Deglet, they will work, but they may not be large enough for stuffing with pecans!

If you already follow a Paleo diet, you know that this is not only a classic pairing, but also a crowd favorite at parties. If you've never tried these before, watch out—they're addictive! The salty and sweet combination makes this dish a fantastic two-bite appetizer or dessert.

12 slices bacon

12 Medjool dates

2 dozen pecan halves

12 (1-inch) chunks fresh pineapple

Preheat the oven to 425°F.

Slice the bacon in half crosswise so that you have 24 pieces.

Slice the dates lengthwise down the center, then remove and discard the pits. Place a pecan half in the center of each date half (where the pit was) and press the date halves back together. Wrap a piece of bacon around each pecan-stuffed date and secure with a toothpick.

Wrap each pineapple chunk with the remaining pieces of bacon, 1 piece each, and secure with a toothpick.

Place the bacon-wrapped dates and bacon-wrapped pineapple chunks on a rimmed baking sheet and bake for 20 to 30 minutes, until the bacon is cooked to your liking.

simple baked kale chips

PREP TIME: 10 minutes | **COOKING TIME:** 20 minutes | **YIELD:** 4 servings

`FODMAPS` `21DSD` `QUICK & EASY` `PARTY` `FAMILY`

This recipe is a quick way to make use of a lot of kale. You'll find yourself making these chips often, as they go faster than you might expect. Kids especially enjoy these chips!

2 bunches curly kale or other variety

1 tablespoon coconut oil, melted

1/2 teaspoon garlic powder (optional)

Sea salt and black pepper

Preheat the oven to 350°F.

Rinse the kale leaves under cold water and pat them dry with a towel. Pull the leaves from the stalk by holding tightly onto the end of the stalk and running your hand up the sides. You can also just cut the stalks out. Discard the stalks or save them for juicing.

Roughly chop the kale into large pieces and place them in a large mixing bowl. Top the kale with the melted coconut oil and gently massage the oil into the kale, spreading it evenly over all of the pieces.

Arrange the kale in a single layer on two rimmed baking sheets and sprinkle with the garlic powder (if using) and a few pinches each of salt and pepper.

Bake for 10 minutes, then turn off the oven and leave the kale in the oven for an additional 10 minutes as the oven cools.

FODMAP-FREE?

Leave out the garlic powder; use other spices you like instead.

NOTE

Keep a close eye on the kale as it bakes—it can burn quite quickly if you're not paying attention!

CHANGE IT UP

Add any seasonings you like! This recipe is especially good with a few pinches of cayenne pepper or onion powder instead of garlic powder.

chicken liver pâté

PREP TIME: 15 minutes | **COOKING TIME:** 30 minutes | **YIELD:** 4 to 8 servings

FODMAPS 21DSD FREEZE ME

MAKE IT 21DSD

Omit the red wine.

CHANGE IT UP

Substitute apple cider vinegar or balsamic vinegar for the wine.

One bite of this pâté and I'm brought back to the age of twelve. More specifically, I'm brought back to the table in my great-grandmother's Upper West Side apartment in New York City. This recipe tastes exactly like the authentic pâté I ate back then, surrounded by my mother, grandmother, and great-aunts.

1 pound chicken livers (or other kind of liver)

1 small onion or 1/2 large onion, chopped

1/2 cup + 2 tablespoons butter or bacon fat, divided

1/2 cup red wine

2 to 4 cloves garlic, peeled and smashed with the side of a knife

1 tablespoon fresh lemon juice

1 teaspoon gluten-free Dijon mustard

2 sprigs fresh thyme

1 sprig fresh rosemary

Sea salt and black pepper

Sliced cucumbers, celery, carrots, bell peppers, or other vegetables of choice, for serving

In a large pot, sauté the chicken livers and onion in 2 tablespoons of the butter until the livers are browned and the onion is tender. Add the wine, garlic, lemon juice, mustard, thyme, and rosemary and cook, uncovered, until most of the liquid has evaporated. Remove the thyme and rosemary sprigs.

Transfer the mixture to a food processor and blend to a smooth paste, adding the remaining 1/2 cup of butter 1 tablespoon at a time until it develops a smooth, creamy consistency. Add salt and pepper to taste.

Put the pâté in a shallow dish and refrigerate before serving.

Enjoy this spread on sliced veggies.

creamy cauliflower hummus

PREP TIME: 15 minutes | **COOKING TIME:** – | **YIELD:** About 2 cups

NUTS & SEEDS | NIGHTSHADES | FODMAPS | 21DSD | QUICK & EASY | PARTY | FAMILY

NOTE

I used an orange cauliflower for this recipe. If you spot one in your store or market, use it instead of the white variety for a deeper-colored dip.

CHANGE IT UP

Substitute zucchini for the cauliflower, but shred and strain it first to remove most of its water content.

This twist on the traditional Mediterranean favorite tastes almost exactly the same as the chickpea (garbanzo bean) variety.

4 cups cauliflower florets, steamed

1/4 cup + 1 tablespoon extra-virgin olive oil

2 tablespoons tahini (sesame paste), raw or roasted

Grated zest and juice of 1 lemon (reserve zest for garnish)

Pinch of ground cumin

Sea salt and black pepper to taste

Pinch of paprika, for garnish (optional)

Sliced vegetables of choice, for serving

Olives of choice, for serving

In a food processor, combine the cauliflower, 1/4 cup of the olive oil, tahini, lemon juice, and cumin and process until smooth. Add salt and pepper to taste, along with more tahini or olive oil if you like.

Scoop the hummus into a serving dish and garnish with the reserved lemon zest, remaining tablespoon of olive oil, and paprika (if using).

Serve with sliced vegetables and olives.

dairy-free spinach artichoke dip

PREP TIME: 15 minutes | **COOKING TIME:** 20 minutes | **YIELD:** 3 cups

`NUTS & SEEDS` `NIGHTSHADES` `FODMAPS` `21DSD` `PARTY` `FAMILY` `FREEZE ME`

This spinach and artichoke dip is the perfect appetizer to make for your next party. Packed with flavor and seriously simple to throw together, this dip will become one of your go-to recipes for future get-togethers! Bring it to a New Year's Eve celebration, Super Bowl Party, or even a backyard BBQ—it's sure to be a hit, I'm telling you. You can serve this dip with crudités, Baked Potato Chips (page 430, as pictured), or Crispy Plantain Chips (page 431).

1 tablespoon extra-virgin olive oil

1 small yellow onion, chopped

2 large cloves garlic, grated or minced

1 tablespoon ghee (page 261) or butter

1 pound frozen spinach, thawed, with the water squeezed out

1 (14-ounce) can artichoke hearts, chopped

1 teaspoon granulated onion

1/2 teaspoon granulated garlic

1/2 teaspoon paprika

2 teaspoons sea salt

1/2 teaspoon black pepper

ALMOND CREAM

1 cup blanched almond flour

3/4 cup hot water

1/2 teaspoon sea salt

1/2 cup nutritional yeast

NUT-FREE?

To make this dip nut-free, make a sunflower cream instead of the almond cream. Simply blend together 3/4 cup of unsweetened sunflower seed butter with 1/2 to 3/4 cup of hot water (start with 1/2 cup and add more if it seems too thick) and a pinch of salt until a smooth cream forms.

SEED-FREE?

For a dip that is both nut-free and seed-free, puree an avocado with 1/4 cup of warm water and use it instead of the almond cream.

NIGHTSHADE-FREE?

Omit the paprika.

Heat the olive oil in a medium-sized sauce-pan over medium heat. Add the onion and garlic and cook for 10 minutes, stirring often.

Make a well in the onion mixture and add the ghee. Once the ghee has melted, turn the heat down to medium-low and add the spinach, artichoke hearts, granulated onion, granulated garlic, paprika, salt, and pepper and stir to combine. Continue to cook for 10 minutes, stirring often.

Meanwhile, make the almond cream: Blend together the almond flour, hot water, and salt in a food processor or high-speed blender until a smooth cream forms.

Once the spinach artichoke mixture has cooked for 10 minutes, remove the pan from the heat and add the almond cream and nutritional yeast. Stir to combine.

This dip can be served warm, chilled, or at room temperature and can be reheated in a preheated 350°F oven for 10 minutes. Store leftovers in an airtight glass container for up to a week. This recipe can be made up to a few days in advance of a party.

baked potato chips

PREP TIME: 10 minutes | **COOKING TIME:** 25 to 30 minutes | **YIELD:** 4 servings

NIGHTSHADES FODMAPS 21DSD SPICE BLEND QUICK & EASY PARTY FAMILY

FODMAP-FREE?

Use a FODMAP-free spice blend or just use sea salt.

EQUIPMENT TIP

I used the slicing blade and wider opening of my food processor to get even 1/8-inch potato slices for this recipe. Pushing slowly yields thinner slices, while pushing more quickly yields thicker slices. A mandoline would also work. If you choose to do the slicing by hand, make sure to use a just-sharpened knife!

CHANGE IT UP

You could season these chips with any of my other spice blends (pages 256 to 257)—the Diner or Greek Blend would be great—or simply use sea salt.

4 Yukon Gold potatoes (about 1 pound), peeled and sliced crosswise into 1/8-inch-thick rounds

1 tablespoon extra-virgin olive oil or melted coconut oil

2 teaspoons Smoky Blend (page 256)

Preheat the oven to 375°F. Line two rimmed baking sheets with parchment paper.

Toss the potato slices in the oil so that each slice is evenly coated. Divide the potato slices between the two pans and spread them out in a single layer. Sprinkle them evenly with the spice blend.

Bake for 15 minutes, then remove the pan from the oven and flip the potato slices. Bake for an additional 10 to 15 minutes, until the potatoes are golden brown and crispy. Serve warm.

Note: These chips are best when served immediately, as they may become quite soggy when stored. However, you can store them in an airtight container in the refrigerator for up to 5 days and re-crisp them in a preheated low oven or toaster oven (about 250°F) until warmed, about 5 minutes.

crispy plantain chips

PREP TIME: 10 minutes | **COOKING TIME:** 10 minutes | **YIELD:** 4 servings

`21DSD` `PARTY` `FAMILY`

Although you can find plantain chips in many grocery stores, you'll taste the difference when you make them at home! They're quite simple to make once you try. Choosing healthy cooking oils is critical to our health, and making these chips at home is a perfect way to keep the best fats in your diet. The flavor and texture of these chips are amazing—so fresh, and perfectly browned.

2 green plantains

2 to 3 tablespoons coconut oil, ghee (page 261), or lard

1 tablespoon coarse sea salt

Thinly slice the plantains with a sharp knife, making the slices about 1/8 inch thick. (If you have a food processor with a slicing blade or a mandoline, you may want to try using either of those if you aren't confident with your knife skills yet.)

Heat the coconut oil in a large skillet over medium heat; use enough oil to completely cover the bottom of the pan and create an even layer of oil. Add the plantains in a single layer, working in batches so as not to crowd the pan. Cook for 2 to 3 minutes on each side, until each chip is golden brown, flipping frequently to keep them from burning.

Place the plantains on a paper towel–lined plate and season immediately with salt. These are best eaten right away but can be stored for a day or two in an airtight container. To re-crisp, place in a low oven or toaster oven (about 225°F) for 10 minutes.

roasted garlic tahini sauce

PREP TIME: 10 minutes (not including roasted garlic) | **COOKING TIME:** −
YIELD: 3/4 cup (about 6 servings)

NUTS & SEEDS | FODMAPS | 21DSD | QUICK & EASY | PARTY | FAMILY

CHANGE IT UP

Substitute fresh garlic for the roasted garlic. Simply use 1 grated clove, adding it little by little to taste.

This simple sauce is delicious for dipping Lemony Lamb Dolmas (page 368), and it makes a nice burger topping or fresh vegetable dip as well.

1/2 cup extra-virgin olive oil

1/4 cup tahini (sesame paste), raw or roasted

4 cloves roasted garlic (see page 342)

Juice of 1 lemon

Sea salt and black pepper to taste

Whisk all of the ingredients together, or combine them in a small blender.

five kinds of salsa

PREP TIME: 30 minutes | **COOKING TIME:** – | **YIELD:** About 8 servings

NIGHTSHADES FODMAPS 21DSD QUICK & EASY PARTY FAMILY

Even if you don't eat tomatoes, there is no reason why you can't enjoy salsa! Simply swap out the traditional main ingredient for any of the other options in this recipe.

2 tablespoons minced fresh cilantro

1 shallot, minced

Juice of 1 to 2 limes (to taste)

1 tablespoon extra-virgin olive oil

2 cups of any of the following, or a combination, diced:

    Tomato

    Bell pepper

    Cucumber

    Mango

    Pineapple

Sea salt and black pepper

In a medium-sized mixing bowl, combine the base ingredients: the cilantro, shallot, lime juice, and olive oil.

Add the main ingredient(s) of your choice and stir to combine. Season with salt and pepper to taste.

NIGHTSHADE-FREE?
Use cucumber, mango, or pineapple for your salsa.

FODMAP-FREE?
Use tomato or cucumber for your salsa and replace the shallot with minced green onions.

MAKE IT 21DSD
Use tomato, bell pepper, or cucumber for your salsa.

CHANGE IT UP
Here are some suggested combinations: tomato + cucumber, pineapple + mango, bell pepper + mango, pineapple + cucumber.

salad dressings

YIELD: 1 cup per recipe

FOR ALL DRESSINGS:

Place all of the ingredients in a blender and blend on low for 10 to 20 seconds. You can also whisk the ingredients, but the texture of the dressing will not be as smooth. Taste the dressing and adjust the seasoning to your liking with salt, pepper, or more oil or vinegar/citrus juice.

Store the dressing in an airtight glass container or bottle in the refrigerator for up to 3 weeks.

BASIL SHALLOT VINAIGRETTE

2/3 cup extra-virgin olive oil

1/3 cup red wine vinegar

1/2 cup tightly packed fresh basil leaves

1 medium shallot (about 1 1/2 inches long), peeled

1 teaspoon honey (optional)

Sea salt and black pepper to taste

If you wish to make this dressing in a bowl, finely chop the basil and mince the shallot before adding them to the bowl along with the other ingredients, then whisk to combine.

DAIRY-FREE CAESAR DRESSING

2/3 cup extra-virgin olive oil

1/3 cup lemon juice (about 2 lemons)

2 tablespoons nutritional yeast

1 teaspoon grated or minced garlic (1 to 2 cloves)

1 to 2 anchovy fillets, minced, or 1 to 2 teaspoons anchovy paste (see Notes)

1/2 teaspoon gluten-free Dijon mustard

Sea salt and black pepper to taste

NOTE

If you prefer a saltier dressing, use 2 anchovy fillets or 2 teaspoons of paste.

ORANGE VINAIGRETTE

2/3 cup extra-virgin olive oil

1/4 cup fresh orange juice (about 1 juicy orange)

1 tablespoon apple cider vinegar

1 teaspoon gluten-free Dijon mustard

Pinch of garlic powder (optional)

Pinch of ground fennel seeds (optional)

Sea salt and black pepper to taste

FODMAP-FREE?

Leave out the garlic powder.

BALSAMIC VINAIGRETTE

2/3 cup extra-virgin olive oil

1/3 cup balsamic vinegar

1 teaspoon gluten-free Dijon
  mustard

1/2 teaspoon anchovy paste

Sea salt and black pepper to taste

HONEY MUSTARD DRESSING

2/3 cup extra-virgin olive oil

1/3 cup red wine vinegar

2 teaspoons whole-grain or spicy
  brown mustard

1 small shallot, minced (about
  1 teaspoon)

1 teaspoon honey

Sea salt and black pepper to taste

SPICY LIME DRESSING

2/3 cup extra-virgin olive oil

1/3 cup lime juice (about 3 limes)

1 teaspoon honey

1 teaspoon gluten-free Dijon
  mustard

1 teaspoon red pepper flakes

Sea salt and black pepper to taste

NIGHTSHADE-FREE?

Omit the red pepper flakes.

DRESS IT UP

*Save time and make extra of these dressing
to pour over salads in the near future.*

simple cranberry sauce

PREP TIME: 5 minutes | **COOKING TIME:** 15 minutes | **YIELD:** 2 cups

FODMAPS | QUICK & EASY | FAMILY | ONE POT | FREEZE ME

LOW-FODMAP?

Use maple syrup rather than honey.

SERVE IT UP

Spread this sauce over Pumpkin Cranberry Muffins (page 277).

CHANGE IT UP

To make a chunky cranberry sauce, add 1 cup of mandarin orange segments, drained; 1 cup of pineapple chunks (ideally fresh; check canned for additives, and get one without added sugar); and 1/2 cup of chopped walnuts.

Pair this sauce with Thanksgiving Stuffing Meatballs (page 326), use it to make Mom's Stuffed Cabbage Rolls with Tomato Cranberry Sauce (page 354), or simply add it to your own holiday recipe list.

1 (16-ounce) bag fresh cranberries

Grated zest and juice of 1 orange (omit if using the sauce to make Mom's Stuffed Cabbage Rolls)

1/4 cup water, plus more if needed (optional)

1 to 4 tablespoons honey or pure maple syrup (or more, according to taste and the sourness of your cranberries)

In a medium-sized saucepan, simmer the cranberries with the orange zest and juice until all of the berries have popped open and the texture is gelatinous. If you aren't using the orange juice, you may add water to the pan to help the sauce loosen a bit, starting with 1/4 cup and then adding 2 tablespoons at a time until the consistency is to your liking, noting that the sauce will firm up further once refrigerated. Stir in the honey.

Remove the sauce from the heat and allow it to come to room temperature before refrigerating for later use.

nightshade-free ketchup (AIP)

PREP TIME: 15 minutes | **COOKING TIME:** 20 minutes | **YIELD:** 2 cups

FODMAPS 21DSD QUICK & EASY FAMILY ONE POT

If you want a Paleo-friendly ketchup, there's an easy, sweetener-free recipe on my blog at balancedbites.com/recipes that you can try. However, if you need to make one without the tomatoes due to an allergy or intolerance, this one will be perfect for you!

1 pound carrots, peeled and cut into 2-inch chunks

8 ounces red beets, steamed, peeled, and chopped

1 1/2 teaspoons apple cider vinegar

1 teaspoon honey (optional)

3/4 teaspoon sea salt

1/2 teaspoon granulated garlic

1/2 teaspoon granulated onion

MAKE IT 21DSD
Omit the honey.

TIME-SAVING TIP
Buy precooked beets from your local grocery store.

Set a large steamer basket over 1 to 2 inches of boiling water. Place the carrots in the steamer basket and cook for 10 minutes, until they easily break apart with a fork. Alternatively, if you do not own a steamer basket, you can boil the carrots for 10 minutes, until cooked through.

Transfer the carrots to a dry, medium-sized saucepan and cook over medium-low heat for 5 minutes longer, stirring often so the carrots don't stick. Add the beets and cook for 5 more minutes, stirring often. This step releases excess moisture from the vegetables, helping to concentrate the flavor and maintain a proper ketchup consistency. If you skip this step, your ketchup will end up watery and will have a less robust flavor.

Transfer the carrots and beets to a blender, add the remaining ingredients, and blend until smooth. Store in an airtight glass jar in the refrigerator for up to 2 weeks.

paleo mayonnaise

PREP TIME: 15 minutes | **COOKING TIME:** – | **YIELD:** 3/4 cup

EGGS | 21DSD | QUICK & EASY | FAMILY

NOTE

Use this mayonnaise to make Bacon & Egg Salad (page 287).

EQUIPMENT TIP

You can also make Paleo Mayonnaise in a small blender, and you can double the recipe to make blending easier. Use the opening at the top of your blender to slowly stream in the avocado oil or bacon fat.

While more and more brands of mayonnaise made with healthier oils are available to buy, if you want to make your own or run out of the premade variety, this is a great option. And if you make a lot of Perfectly Baked Bacon (page 260), you will have plenty of bacon fat sitting in the refrigerator. When you make the effort to procure pasture-raised pork, you should absolutely save the fat that drips off during the baking process.

2 large egg yolks
1 tablespoon lemon juice
1 teaspoon gluten-free Dijon mustard

3/4 cup avocado oil or bacon fat, melted and cooled to room temperature, divided

In a medium-sized mixing bowl, whisk together the egg yolks, lemon juice, and mustard until blended and bright yellow (about 30 seconds). Add 1/4 cup of the avocado oil a few drops at a time, whisking constantly. Gradually add the remaining 1/2 cup of avocado oil in a slow, thin stream, whisking constantly, until the mayonnaise is thick and lighter in color.

Alternatively, you can place all of the ingredients in a tall, narrow jar and use an immersion blender to blend, beginning with the blade end submerged and slowly moving it upward as you hold the power on.

Store in a glass jar in the refrigerator for up to a week.

diane's magic green sauce

PREP TIME: 10 minutes | **COOKING TIME:** 45 minutes to 1 hour | **YIELD:** About 1 cup

`NIGHTSHADES` `FODMAPS` `21DSD` `QUICK & EASY`

I love to use this sauce as a marinade (see the steak bowl recipe on page 336), but it also makes a fantastic addition to mashed avocado for a quick guacamole, and it can be mixed 50/50 with Paleo Mayonnaise (page 438) for an amazing dip or sauce to put on meats or vegetables.

FOR A CREAMY VERSION

Mix the Magic Green Sauce 50/50 with my Paleo Mayonnaise (page 438)—note that this creamy version is not egg-free. For an egg-free creamy version of this sauce, mix it 50/50 with mashed avocado instead of mayonnaise.

2 poblano peppers

1 bell pepper (preferably yellow)

1 jalapeño or serrano pepper

1 bunch (8 to 10 stalks) green onions (scallions), green parts only

3/4 ounce fresh chives

1/2 cup tightly packed fresh cilantro leaves and stems (about 1/2 large bunch)

1 large clove garlic

Juice of 2 limes

Sea salt and black pepper

Preheat the oven to 375°F.

Roast all of the peppers for 45 minutes to 1 hour, until the skins have blackened on all sides, turning them every 15 minutes for even cooking.

Place the peppers in a bowl and cover with a lid or plastic wrap to allow the steam to loosen the skins. Remove the skins and stems from the peppers.

For a spicier sauce, leave the seeds and ribs (white portion) in the jalapeño; for a milder sauce, slice the ribs out of the jalapeño and discard the seeds. Take care not to touch your eyes or mouth after handling the hot pepper.

Place the peppers and the remaining ingredients, except the salt and pepper, in a blender or food processor and blend on high until smooth. Taste and add salt and pepper to your preference.

herbal tea gummies

PREP TIME: 10 minutes, plus time to chill | **COOKING TIME:** 10 minutes | **YIELD:** 4 servings

FODMAPS 21DSD QUICK & EASY FAMILY

MAKE IT 21DSD

Omit the sweetener and use an approved herbal tea.

TO YOUR TASTE

Fruit teas are an especially fun way to prepare this gelatin treat for kids! If you want a stronger flavor, simply use more tea.

If you're looking for the amazing gut-healing benefits of gelatin but want a change of pace from savory broth, make some herbal tea–infused gelatin. Use any kind of tea you like, sweetened or unsweetened; it's quite simple!

2 tablespoons loose herbal tea or 3 bags herbal tea

2 cups boiling water

1 tablespoon honey or pure maple syrup (optional)

6 tablespoons unflavored grass-fed gelatin

Steep the loose tea in a tea ball infuser or the bags in the water for about 5 minutes.

Whisk the honey (if using) into the steeped tea, then whisk in the gelatin.

Pour the mixture into a glass or ceramic baking dish, place in the refrigerator, and allow to set before cutting into cubes to serve.

cherry lemon gummies

PREP TIME: 10 minutes, plus time to chill | **COOKING TIME:** 5 minutes | **YIELD:** 4 servings

FODMAPS QUICK & EASY FAMILY

1 cup pitted and chopped cherries
(fresh or defrosted from frozen)

3/4 cup lemon juice (about 3 lemons)

2 tablespoons pure maple syrup

6 tablespoons unflavored grass-fed
gelatin

In a blender, pulse the cherries and lemon juice until no visible skins or large pieces of cherries appear.

In a small pot over medium-low heat, vigorously whisk the cherry lemon mixture with the maple syrup and gelatin until the gelatin is completely dissolved.

Pour the mixture into gummy molds or a glass or ceramic baking dish (about 6 by 9 inches) and place in the refrigerator until completely chilled and set, about 30 minutes. If you used a baking dish instead of molds, use a small cookie cutter to cut out different shapes simply cut the gummies into squares or rectangles. To release the gummies from the molds or baking dish, set the bottoms of the mold containers or baking dish in warm water.

SPECIAL EQUIPMENT (OPTIONAL)

Silicone gummy mold(s)

MAKE IT 21DSD

Omit the maple syrup and use an approved fruit like grapefruit or green apples to make the base instead of the cherries. If you make it with grapefruit, I recommend also omitting the lemon juice as they'll be extremely tart otherwise.

NOTE

If you use a baking pan to make the gummies, note that the smaller the pan, the thicker your gummies will be.

vanilla bean truffles

PREP TIME: 15 minutes, plus time to chill | **COOKING TIME:** – | **YIELD:** 1 dozen truffles

NUTS & SEEDS | FODMAPS | QUICK & EASY | PARTY

NUT-FREE?

Use 1 to 2 tablespoons of unsweetened shredded coconut in place of the sesame seeds as a coating.

HOW TO REMOVE VANILLA BEAN SEEDS:

To remove vanilla bean seeds, slice the bean lengthwise down the center, then run the back of your knife along the inside of one half of the pod to scrape out the seeds.

If you can't have nuts around your house due to allergies, this sesame seed–based recipe is a great option. These truffles are perfect for finishing off an Asian-flavored meal like the Beef & Veggie Stir-Fry on page 348 or the Seared Scallops with Orange Glaze on page 386.

1/4 cup coconut butter (also called coconut manna or coconut cream concentrate), softened

2 tablespoons tahini (sesame paste), raw or roasted

1 tablespoon unsweetened shredded coconut

1 to 2 teaspoons pure maple syrup

1/4 teaspoon ground cinnamon

Pinch of sea salt

Seeds from 1/2 vanilla bean pod or 1/2 teaspoon pure vanilla extract

2 tablespoons white or black sesame seeds, or a combination, for coating

In a mixing bowl, stir together the coconut butter, tahini, shredded coconut, maple syrup, cinnamon, salt, and vanilla seeds or extract until smooth. Freeze the mixture for about 15 minutes to firm up.

Using your hands, form the mixture into 1-inch balls, then roll each ball in the sesame seeds.

Set the truffles on a plate, flatten slightly, and refrigerate to solidify. Store in an airtight container in the refrigerator for up to 6 weeks.

easy chocolate truffles

PREP TIME: 25 minutes, plus time to chill | **COOKING TIME:** – | **YIELD:** 1 dozen truffles

`NUTS & SEEDS` `FODMAPS` `QUICK & EASY` `PARTY`

Impress guests with these super-simple truffles that look elegant but use ingredients you probably have lying around in your pantry.

TRUFFLE BASE

3 tablespoons coconut butter (also called coconut manna or coconut cream concentrate), softened

2 tablespoons coconut oil

2 tablespoons almond butter or other nut or seed butter of choice

1/4 teaspoon pure vanilla extract

MINT CHIP FLAVOR

2 teaspoons mint extract

1 teaspoon pure maple syrup

1 tablespoon cacao nibs

CHOCOLATE ORANGE FLAVOR

2 tablespoons unsweetened cocoa powder

2 teaspoons pure maple syrup

Grated zest of 1 orange (reserve 1 teaspoon for the coating)

TRUFFLE COATING

2 tablespoons unsweetened shredded coconut

SPICE IT UP

Add a pinch of cayenne pepper to the chocolate orange flavor to give it a kick!

DOUBLE YOUR PLEASURE

To make both flavors, either divide the truffle base in half and use half of the flavoring ingredients in each half portion of base, or double the base and make one full batch of each flavor.

Make the base: Place the coconut butter, coconut oil, almond butter, and vanilla extract in a mixing bowl and stir with a large spoon until smooth.

Add the ingredients for the truffle flavor of your choice to the base and mix thoroughly.

Place the mixture in the freezer for about 10 minutes, until it's firm enough to form into balls. If making the chocolate orange flavor, combine the shredded coconut for the coating with the reserved orange zest. Using your hands, roll the mixture into 1-inch balls, then roll each ball in the coating.

Set the truffles on a plate and refrigerate to solidify. Store in an airtight container in the refrigerator for up to 6 weeks.

Serve cold.

soft chocolate coconut cookies

PREP TIME: 20 minutes | **COOKING TIME:** 20 to 30 minutes | **YIELD:** 1 dozen cookies

`EGGS` `FODMAPS` `QUICK & EASY` `PARTY` `FAMILY`

NUT-FREE?

Leave out the almonds.

CHANGE IT UP

Add walnuts for more texture and crunch, or add chocolate chips to make these a bit more indulgent.

This cookie recipe is so easy that you can make it "to order" after dinner and enjoy the cookies warm from the oven. They're not super-sweet, but just right to hit the spot without overloading you with sugar.

2 large eggs

2 tablespoons butter, melted and cooled

2 tablespoons pure maple syrup (or more for sweeter cookies)

1/2 teaspoon pure vanilla extract

1 cup unsweetened shredded coconut

2 tablespoons unsweetened cocoa powder

Pinch of baking soda

1/4 cup sliced almonds (optional)

1/2 cup fresh raspberries (optional)

Preheat the oven to 350°F. Line a cookie sheet with parchment paper.

In a medium-sized mixing bowl, whisk together the eggs, melted butter, maple syrup, and vanilla extract. Mix in the coconut, cocoa powder, and baking soda until well combined. Fold in the almonds, if using. Refrigerate the dough for 10 minutes to allow it to firm up.

Scoop the dough into 12 equal-sized dollops on the lined cookie sheet and smooth them out with the back of a spoon. Bake for 20 to 30 minutes, until slightly firm to the touch.

If you wish to use raspberries, add one to the center of each cookie before baking.

creamy two-bite treats

PREP TIME: 15 minutes, plus time to chill | **COOKING TIME:** – | **YIELD:** 2 dozen treats

FODMAPS | QUICK & EASY | PARTY | FAMILY

Whip these delicious treats up any weeknight to enjoy, or bring them to a party. No one will ever guess that they're as simple to make as they are!

TREAT BASE

1/2 cup coconut oil

1/2 cup coconut butter (also called coconut manna or coconut cream concentrate)

ORANGE CREAM FLAVOR

1/2 teaspoon pure vanilla extract

Grated zest of 1 orange

2 teaspoons pure maple syrup

MINT FLAVOR

2 teaspoons chopped fresh mint

2 teaspoons mint extract

2 teaspoons pure maple syrup

DOUBLE YOUR PLEASURE

To make both flavors, either divide the treat base in half and use half of the flavoring ingredients in each half portion of base, or double the base and make one full batch of each flavor.

NOTE

Try adding your own favorite flavors to the base ingredients!

Place the treat base ingredients plus the ingredients for either the orange cream flavor or the mint flavor in a small mixing bowl and mix until smooth. Line a 24-well mini muffin tin with parchment paper liners, then spoon the mixture evenly into the lined cups, filling each about half full.

Place the pan in the refrigerator or freezer to set; serve cold. Store in an airtight container in the refrigerator for up to 3 weeks.

almond butter cups

PREP TIME: 40 minutes, plus time to chill | **COOKING TIME:** Less than 5 minutes
YIELD: 2 dozen small or 1 dozen large almond butter cups

NUTS & SEEDS | FODMAPS | PARTY | FAMILY

CHANGE IT UP

Use walnut or pecan butter in place of almond butter for the filling.

Peanut butter cups were a favorite of mine for many years. This updated version uses very little sweetener and more wholesome/natural ingredients.

DARK SHELLS

1/4 cup unsweetened cocoa powder

2 tablespoons coconut butter (also called coconut manna or coconut cream concentrate), softened

2 tablespoons coconut oil, melted

1 teaspoon pure maple syrup

1/4 teaspoon pure vanilla extract

Pinch of ground cinnamon

Pinch of sea salt

LIGHT SHELLS

3 tablespoons coconut oil, melted

3 tablespoons coconut butter (also called coconut manna or coconut cream concentrate), softened

1 tablespoon unsweetened shredded coconut

1 teaspoon pure maple syrup

1/4 teaspoon pure vanilla extract

Seeds from 1/2 vanilla bean pod (see page 442)

FILLING

3 tablespoons almond butter or other nut butter of choice

1 tablespoon coconut oil

1 teaspoon pure maple syrup

Pinch of sea salt

Line a 24-well mini muffin tin with parchment paper liners, as pictured, or line a standard 12-well muffin tin with parchment paper liners (the latter will create larger but flatter almond butter cups).

In a medium-sized mixing bowl, whisk together all of the ingredients for the dark shells. In another medium-sized mixing bowl, whisk together all of the ingredients for the light shells.

Spoon a 1/8-inch layer (about 1 teaspoon) of the dark shell mixture into half of the lined muffin cups, then spoon the same amount of the light shell mixture into the other half of the cups.

Place the pan in the refrigerator or freezer to set. While the first layer of the shells is setting, mix together all of the ingredients for the filling in a small mixing bowl. Transfer the filling mixture to a pastry bag or quart-sized plastic bag. If using a plastic bag, snip off a tiny corner of the bag with scissors.

Remove the shells from the refrigerator or freezer and pipe a small amount (about 1/2 teaspoon if making 24 mini cups or 1 teaspoon if making 12 standard-size cups) of the filling into the center of each one, leaving some of the edge visible. Once all of the shells have been filled, spoon in the remaining dark or light shell mixture until the filling is covered.

Place the pan back in the refrigerator or freezer to set; serve the almond butter cups cold or at room temperature.

Store in an airtight container in the refrigerator for up to 6 weeks.

pepita goji berry bark

PREP TIME: 15 minutes, plus time to chill | **COOKING TIME:** Less than 5 minutes
YIELD: 10 to 12 pieces

`NUTS & SEEDS` `NIGHTSHADES` `QUICK & EASY` `PARTY` `FAMILY`

SEED-FREE?

Omit the pepitas and use another type of dried fruit instead.

NIGHTSHADE-FREE?

Go with cherries or cranberries instead of goji berries.

Dark chocolate bark can be made with almost any combination of nuts and dried fruit. What I love about this recipe are the bright colors that pop within the rich, dark chocolate.

1 cup dark chocolate chips

1 teaspoon bacon fat or coconut oil

2 tablespoons roughly chopped goji berries (pictured), dried cherries, or cranberries

2 tablespoons roughly chopped pepitas (pumpkin seeds)

2 tablespoons roughly chopped walnuts (pictured), pecans, or other nuts of choice

Coarse sea salt

Line a rimmed baking sheet with parchment paper.

Melt the chocolate chips and bacon fat in a double boiler over low heat, stirring vigorously as it melts, or in the microwave in 10-second increments to prevent burning the chocolate, stirring after each 10-second interval, for 30 seconds total.

Stir in the goji berries, pepitas, nuts, and a pinch of coarse salt and spread the mixture on the lined baking sheet until it is 1/8 to 1/4 inch thick (depending on your preference). Sprinkle the top with another pinch or two of salt. Place in the refrigerator to chill and set.

Chop the bark roughly before serving. Store in an airtight container in the refrigerator for as long as it takes to finish the bark, which probably won't be too long.

nutty bacon bark

PREP TIME: 10 minutes, plus time to set | **COOKING TIME:** Less than 5 minutes
YIELD: 10 to 12 pieces

NUTS & SEEDS   QUICK & EASY   PARTY   FAMILY

There are few better ways to enjoy bacon than when it's combined with chocolate. This is a quick way to impress your guests with a delicious treat.

1 cup dark chocolate chips

1 teaspoon bacon fat or coconut oil

1/4 cup toasted hazelnuts or other nuts of choice

4 slices Perfectly Baked Bacon (page 260), chopped

1/2 teaspoon sea salt (smoked sea salt is ideal)

Line a rimmed baking sheet with parchment paper.

Melt the chocolate chips and bacon fat in a double boiler over low heat, stirring vigorously as it melts, or in the microwave in 10-second increments to prevent burning the chocolate, stirring after each 10-second interval, for 30 seconds total.

Spread the melted chocolate on the lined baking sheet until it is 1/8 to 1/4 inch thick (depending on your preference) and set aside to cool. Once the chocolate is nearly, but not entirely, set, sprinkle the nuts, bacon, and salt evenly over the top.

Chop the bark roughly before serving. Store in an airtight container in the refrigerator for as long as it takes to finish the bark, which probably won't be too long.

NUT-FREE
Omit the hazelnuts and use dried cherries instead for a fun sweet-and-salty combination.

MIXED NUTS
Use two or three kinds of nuts in this recipe—live on the edge!

dairy-free chocolate mousse

PREP TIME: 10 minutes | **COOKING TIME:** – | **YIELD:** 2 servings

`FODMAPS` `21DSD` `QUICK & EASY` `FAMILY`

MAKE IT 21DSD

Omit the sweetener and use green-tipped/underripe bananas (not optional, as they lend a bit of sweetness without adding anything else).

EQUIPMENT TIP

If you don't have a food processor, you can use an immersion blender to whip the ingredients together.

Eliminating dairy can seem daunting when making desserts, but this avocado-based mousse is surprisingly easy to make and so delicious that you won't miss the dairy one bit.

2 ripe avocados, cut in half and pitted

1/4 cup unsweetened cacao powder

2 to 4 tablespoons full-fat coconut milk (use less milk if omitting the banana)

1 ripe banana (optional)

1 to 4 tablespoons pure maple syrup or softened honey, or to taste (omit if including the banana and it is sweet enough)

1/2 teaspoon pure vanilla extract

Pinch of ground cinnamon

Pinch of sea salt

Cacao nibs, chopped toasted hazelnuts, or unsweetened shredded coconut, for garnish (optional)

Scoop the flesh of the avocados into a food processor. Add the cacao powder, coconut milk, banana (if using), maple syrup, vanilla extract, cinnamon, and salt and process until creamy, whipped, and well blended.

Serve in two individual dishes or bowls. Garnish with cacao nibs (pictured), toasted hazelnuts, or shredded coconut.

dairy-free pistachio mousse

PREP TIME: 10 minutes | **COOKING TIME:** – | **YIELD:** 2 servings

`NUTS & SEEDS` `FODMAPS` `21DSD` `FAMILY`

MAKE IT 21DSD

Omit the sweetener and use green-tipped/underripe bananas (not optional, as they lend a bit of sweetness without adding anything else).

EQUIPMENT TIP

If you don't have a food processor, you can use an immersion blender to whip all of the ingredients together.

A twist on the classic chocolate mousse, this recipe uses the natural color of the avocados for an entirely different taste combination.

2 ripe avocados, cut in half and pitted

1/4 cup full-fat coconut milk

1 large or 2 small ripe bananas

1 tablespoon pure maple syrup or softened honey, or to taste (omit if the bananas are sweet enough)

1 or 2 teaspoons pistachio or almond extract (use 1 teaspoon if the extract has an alcohol base or 2 if it has an oil base)

Pinch of sea salt

2 tablespoons chopped pistachios, for garnish

Scoop the flesh of the avocados into a food processor. Add the coconut milk, banana, maple syrup, pistachio extract, and salt and process until creamy, whipped, and well blended.

Serve in two individual dishes or bowls. Garnish with chopped pistachios.

raw raspberry tart

PREP TIME: 40 minutes, plus time to chill | **COOKING TIME:** –
YIELD: One 9-inch tart or four 4-inch tarts

`NUTS & SEEDS` `FODMAPS` `PARTY` `FAMILY` `FREEZE ME`

CHANGE IT UP

Substitute blueberries or strawberries for a different flavor. If you can't eat berries, use 1 1/2 cups (12 ounces by weight) mashed banana.

This raw recipe is fantastic for impressing dinner party guests or to serve at a barbecue. It's the perfect summertime treat since there's no need to turn on the oven and heat up your house.

CRUST

1 cup macadamia nuts

1 cup walnuts

4 large or 6 medium Medjool dates, pitted

FILLING

12 ounces fresh raspberries or other berries of choice

Juice of 1/2 lemon

2 tablespoons coconut butter (also called coconut manna or coconut cream concentrate)

1 tablespoon coconut oil, softened

4 or 6 Medjool dates (use 4 if your berries are very sweet or 6 if they are less sweet)

FOR GARNISH (OPTIONAL)

Strips of lemon zest and/or lemon slices

Make the crust: Place the nuts in a food processor and process until they are a very fine consistency, almost like nut flour. Add the dates and pulse until the mixture becomes sticky and forms a giant "ball" in the processor.

Press the crust mixture into one 9-inch round tart or pie pan or four 4-inch tart pans (lined with parchment paper if you have it) and place in the freezer to set.

Make the filling: Place the berries, lemon juice, coconut butter, coconut oil, and dates in the food processor and process until smooth. Taste to make sure you have added enough dates for your desired sweetness.

Remove the crust from the freezer and fill the pan with the berry mixture. Place the tart back in the freezer and chill it for at least 2 hours.

Remove the tart from the freezer a few minutes before serving to soften it slightly. Garnish with lemon zest or slices, if desired.

nut-free skillet peach crisp

PREP TIME: 10 minutes | **COOKING TIME:** 30 to 45 minutes | **YIELD:** 6 servings

FODMAPS   QUICK & EASY   PARTY   FAMILY

This is just about the easiest way to take fresh summer fruit and transform it into an impressive dessert that anyone can enjoy. When peaches aren't in season, frozen peaches will work beautifully, so you can enjoy this simple treat year-round.

FILLING

1/4 cup full-fat coconut milk

1 tablespoon pure maple syrup (optional, depending on how sweet your fruit is)

2 teaspoons arrowroot starch or tapioca flour

1 teaspoon pure vanilla extract

1/4 teaspoon ground cinnamon

6 fresh peaches, peeled and sliced, or 3 (10-ounce) bags frozen sliced peaches, defrosted

TOPPING

1 cup unsweetened finely shredded coconut

1/4 cup arrowroot starch or tapioca flour

1/2 teaspoon ground cinnamon

Pinch of sea salt

1/2 cup ghee (page 261), butter, or coconut oil

2 tablespoons pure maple syrup, coconut sugar, or maple sugar

Preheat the oven to 350°F.

In a large mixing bowl, whisk together all of the filling ingredients except the peaches until well combined. Toss the fruit in the mixture to coat well.

In a separate mixing bowl, whisk together the coconut, arrowroot starch, cinnamon, and salt until well combined. Using a large spoon, mix in the ghee and sweetener until everything is well incorporated (it's okay if there are some clumps; they will smooth out once baked).

Spread the filling evenly in a 10-inch cast-iron skillet or medium-sized baking dish (8-inch or 9-inch square will work). Cover the fruit with the topping, leaving the edges of the skillet exposed so you can see some of the fruit and to allow space for bubbling.

Bake for 30 to 45 minutes, until the topping is golden brown and the fruit filling is soft and bubbling.

fresh blueberry crumble

PREP TIME: 15 minutes | **COOKING TIME:** 30 to 40 minutes | **YIELD:** 6 servings

`NUTS & SEEDS` `QUICK & EASY` `PARTY` `FAMILY`

CHANGE IT UP

*Use any fruit you like;
bake just until you see the
juices bubbling and the top
becoming golden brown.*

*When you're looking for a quick and easy dessert, baking fruit with a nutty topping is
probably the easiest thing you can do.*

2 pints fresh blueberries

Juice of 1 lemon, divided

1 cup almond meal or almond flour

1/4 cup chopped macadamia nuts or
    walnuts

1/4 cup butter or coconut oil, melted

2 tablespoons pure maple syrup

1/4 teaspoon ground cinnamon

2 pinches of sea salt

Preheat the oven to 375°F.

Place the blueberries and half of the lemon juice in a 9-inch square baking dish. Toss
slightly to coat the blueberries with the juice.

In a mixing bowl, combine the almond meal, nuts, melted butter, maple syrup, remaining
lemon juice, cinnamon, and salt.

Spread the nut topping evenly over the blueberries and bake until the fruit is well cooked
and bubbly and the topping is golden brown, 30 to 40 minutes.

flourless dark chocolate brownies

PREP TIME: 20 minutes | **COOKING TIME:** 30 minutes | **YIELD:** 9 to 12 brownies

`EGGS` `FODMAPS` `PARTY` `FAMILY` `FREEZE ME`

NOTE

This recipe is much easier and more economical than other grain-free brownie recipes that call for a lot of almond butter!

FREEZE ME

Once completely cool, wrap well in parchment paper and then foil before freezing. Defrost overnight on the countertop.

CHANGE IT UP

For extra bacon-y brownies, use 1/4 cup of bacon fat in place of half of the butter.

Who needs flour when you can use cocoa powder, eggs, and butter to make brownies? Okay, this recipe involves a few more ingredients than that, but this is a very simple way to make a rich and delicious treat without grains!

4 ounces dark chocolate, melted and cooled

3 large eggs

1/2 cup butter, ghee (page 261), or coconut oil, melted and cooled slightly

3/4 cup pure maple syrup

1/2 cup plus 2 tablespoons unsweetened cocoa powder, plus extra for garnish

2 tablespoons very strong brewed coffee

2 tablespoons finely ground coffee

2 slices Perfectly Baked Bacon (page 260), chopped (optional)

Preheat the oven to 375°F. Line a 9-inch square baking dish with parchment paper.

In a medium-sized mixing bowl, mix together the melted chocolate, eggs, butter, and maple syrup until combined. Slowly sift the cocoa powder over the wet ingredients, whisking evenly. Add the brewed coffee and ground coffee and stir until well combined.

Pour the brownie batter into the prepared pan and top with the chopped bacon pieces, if using. Bake for about 30 minutes, until a toothpick inserted in the center comes out clean.

Garnish with a dusting of sifted cocoa powder.

Store refrigerated in an airtight container for up to a week.

Recommended Products

To shop my favorites, visit www.balancedbites.com/shop

BACON

APPLEGATE (applegate.com)
Most grocery stores

PETE'S PALEO
Online: petespaleo.com

VERMONT SMOKE & CURE
*Some stores and online:
vermontsmokeandcure.com*

WELLSHIRE FARMS
*Some stores and online:
wellshirefarms.com*

BROTH

BARE BONES BROTH
Online: amazon.com, barebonesbroth.com

BONAFIDE PROVISIONS: RESTORATIVE
BONE BROTH (formerly Real Bone Broth)
Online: bonafideprovisions.com

EPIC
*Whole Foods Market
Online: amazon.com, epicbar.com*

KETTLE & FIRE
Online: amazon.com, kettleandfire.com

PETE'S PALEO
Online: petespaleo.com

CHOCOLATE

DOMORI
Online: amazon.com, us.domori.com

EATING EVOLVED
*Some stores and online:
eatingevolved.com*

FRANÇOIS PRALUS
Online: amazon.com, chocolats-pralus.com

SOMA CHOCOLATEMAKER
Online: amazon.com, somachocolate.com

TAZA CHOCOLATE
*Some stores and online:
tazachocolate.com*

TCHO
Online: tcho.com

THEO CHOCOLATE
*Some stores and online:
theochocolate.com*

COCOA & CACAO POWDER

BIG TREE FARMS
Online: bigtreefarms.com

EQUAL EXCHANGE
*Online: amazon.com,
shop.equalexchange.coop*

WILDERNESS FAMILY NATURALS
Online: wildernessfamilynaturals.com

NAVITAS NATURALS
Online: amazon.com, navitasnaturals.com

SUNFOOD SUPERFOODS
Online: sunfood.com

COCONUT PRODUCTS

ARTISANA ORGANICS
*Some stores and online: amazon.com,
artisana.com*

BIG TREE FARMS
Some stores and online: bigtreefarms.com

COCONUT SECRET
COCONUT AMINOS
*Some stores and online: amazon.com,
coconutsecret.com*

EDWARD & SONS
*Online: amazon.com,
edwardandsons.com*

NUTIVA
*Some stores and online: amazon.com,
nutiva.com*

TRADER JOE'S COCONUT MILK
(canned)
traderjoes.com for locations

TROPICAL TRADITIONS
Online: tropicaltraditions.com

WHOLE FOODS STORE BRAND
COCONUT MILK
wholefoodsmarket.com for locations

WILDERNESS FAMILY NATURALS
Online: wildernessfamilynaturals.com

COCONUT WATER, SPARKLING WATER & OTHER BEVERAGES

CRIO BRU
Online: amazon.com, criobru.com

DRINK MAPLE - PURE MAPLE WATER
Online: drinkmaple.com

HARMLESS HARVEST
COCONUT WATER
*harmlessharvest.com for locations
Online: amazon.com*

HINT WATER
Online: amazon.com, drinkhint.com

INVO COCONUT WATER
*Some stores and online:
invococonutwater.com*

LA CROIX
Online: lacroixwater.com

TEAONIC
Online: teaonic.com

COFFEE

CHAMELEON COLD-BREW
Online: chameleoncoldbrew.com

EQUAL EXCHANGE
*Online: amazon.com,
shop.equalexchange.coop*

DELI MEATS

APPLEGATE (applegate.com)
Most grocery stores

FORK IN THE ROAD
*Whole Foods Market only
forkintheroad.com for locations*

DIPS & SAUCES

MT. VIKOS ROASTED EGGPLANT
SPREAD
mtvikos.com for locations

WHOLLY GUACAMOLE
*Whole Foods Market, Trader Joe's (as
store brand), Costco, local organic
grocers/co-ops
eatwholly.com for locations*

EGGS

VITAL FARMS
vitalfarms.com for locations

FATS & OILS

ARTISANA ORGANICS
*Some stores and online: amazon.com,
artisanaorganics.com*

CADIA
mycadia.com for locations

CALTON NUTRITION
Online: caltonnutrition.com

DR. BRONNER'S
Whole Foods Market, local grocers
Online: amazon.com, drbronners.com

EPIC
Online: amazon.com, epicbar.com

FATWORKS
Some stores and online: amazon.com,
fatworksfoods.com

KASANDRINOS INTERNATIONAL
EXTRA VIRGIN OLIVE OIL
Online: kasandrinos.com

KERRYGOLD BUTTER
Trader Joe's, Costco, Whole Foods
Market, local grocers
kerrygoldusa.com for locations

LA TOURANGELLE ARTISAN OILS
Some stores and online: amazon.com,
latourangelle.com

NUTIVA
Some stores and online: amazon.com,
nutiva.com

ORGANIC VALLEY / PURITY FARMS
Whole Foods Market, local grocers
Online: amazon.com, organicvalley.coop

PRIMAL KITCHEN AVOCADO OIL
Online: amazon.com, primalkitchen.com

PURE INDIAN FOODS GHEE
Whole Foods, local grocers
Online: amazon.com,
pureindianfoods.com

SMJÖR BUTTER
Whole Foods Market

SPECTRUM
Whole Foods Market, local grocers
(spectrumorganics.com for locations)
Online: amazon.com

TENDERGRASS FARMS
Online: amazon.com, tendergrass.com

TIN STAR FOODS GHEE
Online: amazon.com, tinstarfoods.com

TROPICAL TRADITIONS
Online: tropicaltraditions.com

WILDERNESS FAMILY NATURALS
Online: wildernessfamilynaturals.com

FISH SAUCE
RED BOAT FISH SAUCE
Whole Foods Market, local grocers
Online: redboatfishsauce.com

HOT SAUCE
ARIZONA GUNSLINGER
Selected retailers
Online: amazon.com, azgunslinger.com

FRANK'S REDHOT SAUCE
Local grocers
Online: amazon.com

OREGON BRINEWORKS HOT SAUCE
West Coast/Rocky Mountain local
organic grocers/co-ops
Online: amazon.com, azurestandard.com,
wildmountainpaleo.com

JERKY
BROOKLYN BILTONG
Online: amazon.com, brooklynbiltong.com

EPIC
Whole Foods, local grocers
Online: amazon.com, epicbar.com

NICK'S STICKS
Some stores and online: amazon.com,
nicks-sticks.com

HUNTED + GATHERED
Online: huntedandgathered.com.au

SOPHIA'S SURVIVAL FOOD
Online: grassfedjerkychews.com

STEVE'S PALEOGOODS
ORIGINAL JERKY
Online: stevespaleogoods.com

US WELLNESS MEATS
Online: grasslandbeef.com

KETCHUP
ANNIE'S
Whole Foods Market, local grocers
Online: amazon.com, annies.com

SIR KENSINGTON'S
Whole Foods Market, local organic grocers
Online: amazon.com, sirkensingtons.com

TRADER JOE'S
traderjoes.com for locations

KOMBUCHA
TOWNSHEND'S BREW DR. KOMBUCHA
brewdrkombucha.com for locations

GT'S
synergydrinks.com for locations

HEALTH-ADE KOMBUCHA
health-ade.com for locations

MAYONNAISE
PRIMAL KITCHEN
Some stores and online: amazon.com,
primalkitchen.com

MUSTARD
ANNIE'S
Whole Foods Market, local grocers
Online: amazon.com, annies.com

EDEN FOODS
Whole Foods Market, local grocers
Online: amazon.com, edenfoods.com

SIR KENSINGTON'S
Whole Foods Market, local organic
grocers/co-ops
Online: amazon.com, sirkensingtons.com

NUT & SEED BUTTERS
ARTISANA ORGANICS
Some stores and online: amazon.com,
artisanaorganics.com

BARNEY BUTTER
Some stores and online: amazon.com,
barneybutter.com

CADIA
mycadia.com for locations

JUSTIN'S NUT BUTTER
In stores and online: amazon.com,
justins.com

MARANATHA
maranathafoods.com for locations
Online: amazon.com

NUTIVA
Some stores and online: amazon.com,
nutiva.com

ONCE AGAIN
In stores and online: amazon.com,
onceagainnutbutter.com

PALEO MEENUT BUTTER
In stores (Calif. only) and online:
meeeatpaleo.com

SUNBUTTER (NUT-FREE)
In stores and online: amazon.com,
sunbutter.com

TRADER JOE'S
traderjoes.com for locations

TROPICAL TRADITIONS
Online: tropicaltraditions.com

WHOLE FOODS STORE BRAND
wholefoodsmarket.com for locations

WILDERNESS FAMILY NATURALS
Online: wildernessfamilynaturals.com

NUT & COCONUT MILKS

A-ROY D 100% COCONUT MILK
Online: amazon.com

MALK ORGANICS
malkorganics.com for locations

MYLK
almondmylk.com for locations (Calif. only)

NATURAL VALUE COCONUT MILK
Some stores and online: amazon.com

THAI KITCHEN
In stores and online: amazon.com, thaikitchen.com

THREE TREES ALMOND MILK
threetrees.com for locations (West Coast only)

SO DELICIOUS
sodeliciousdairyfree.com for locations
culinary coconut milk variety, contains guar gums

NUT, COCONUT & OTHER PALEO-FRIENDLY FLOURS

BOB'S RED MILL
Major grocery stores
Online: amazon.com, bobsredmill.com

EDWARD & SONS
Online: amazon.com, edwardandsons.com

HONEYVILLE
Online: amazon.com, honeyville.com

OTTO'S NATURALS
In stores and online: amazon.com, ottosnaturals.com

PALEO-FRIENDLY PRE-MADE MEALS

PETE'S PALEO
Online: petespaleo.com

PASTA SAUCES, TOMATO PRODUCTS & PUREED VEGETABLES

AMY'S (amys.com)
Most grocery stores
Online: amazon.com

BIONATURAE
Whole Foods Market, local organic grocers/co-ops (bionaturae.com for locations)
Online: amazon.com

CUCINA ANTICA
Whole Foods Market, local grocers
Online: amazon.com, cucina-antica.com

EDEN FOODS
In stores and online: amazon.com, edenfoods.com

FARMER'S MARKET FOODS
(farmersmarketfoods.com)
In stores and online: amazon.com

JOVIAL FOODS
In stores and online: amazon.com, jovialfoods.com

LUCINI
In stores and online: amazon.com, lucini.com

MARIO BATALI SAUCES
mariobatalisauces.com for locations
Online: amazon.com

MUIR GLEN ORGANIC (muirglen.com)
Most grocery stores
Online: amazon.com

POMI (pomi.us.com)
Whole Foods Market, local organic grocers/co-ops
Online: amazon.com

YELLOW BARN BIODYNAMIC
goodboyorganics.com for locations
Online: amazon.com

PROTEIN & COLLAGEN POWDERS

CALTON NUTRITION IN.POWER WHEY PROTEIN
Online: caltonnutrition.com

GREAT LAKES GELATIN
Online: amazon.com, greatlakesgelatin.com

VITAL PROTEINS
Online: amazon.com, vitalproteins.com

SALT, PEPPER & SPICES

MOUNTAIN ROSE HERBS
Online: mountainroseherbs.com

PRACTICAL PALEO SPICES
Online: amazon.com (limited selection), practicalpaleospices.com

PRIMAL PALATE SPICES
Online: amazon.com (limited selection), primalpalate.com

REAL SALT
Grocery stores nationwide
Online: amazon.com, realsalt.com

SIMPLY ORGANIC
In stores and online: amazon.com, simplyorganic.com

WILDERNESS FAMILY NATURALS
Online: wildernessfamilynaturals.com

SAUERKRAUT, PICKLES & OTHER FERMENTED ITEMS

BUBBIES SAUERKRAUT (bubbies.com)
Most grocery stores

FAB FERMENTS
Online: fabferments.com

FARMHOUSE CULTURE
(farmhouseculture.com)
Whole Foods Market, local grocers

OREGON BRINEWORKS
West Coast/Rocky Mountain local organic grocers/co-ops
Online: amazon.com, azurestandard.com, wildmountainpaleo.com

REAL PICKLES
Whole Foods Market, local organic grocers/co-ops
Online: realpickles.com

SONOMA BRINERY (sonomabrinery.com)
Midwest natural and local grocers

WILDBRINE (wildbrine.com)
Whole Foods Market, local organic grocers/co-ops
Online: amazon.com

SAUSAGE / HOT DOGS

AIDELLS
Whole Foods Market, local grocers
Online: aidells.com

FORK IN THE ROAD
Whole Foods Market only
forkintheroad.com for locations

TETON WATERS RANCH
tetonwatersranch.com for locations

SEAFOOD

BEAR & WOLF SALMON
Online: amazon.com, tridentseafoodsgifts.com/cans

SALTY GIRL SEAFOOD
Online: saltygirlseafood.com

VITAL CHOICE SEAFOOD
Online: vitalchoice.com

WILD PLANET
In stores and online: amazon.com, wildplanetfoods.com

SNACKS

ALIVE & RADIANT KALE KRUNCH
Online: amazon.com, aliveandradiant.com

ARTISAN TROPIC PLANTAIN & CASSAVA CHIPS
Online: amazon.com, artisantropic.com

BACON'S HEIR: PORK CLOUDS
Some stores and online: amazon.com, baconsheir.com

DOCTOR IN THE KITCHEN: FLACKERS
In stores and online: amazon.com, drinthekitchen.com

EDWARD & SONS
Online: amazon.com, edwardandsons.com

EPIC
Online: amazon.com, epicbar.com

GO RAW
In stores and online: amazon.com, goraw.com

INKA CHIPS (ENERGY MODIFICATION)
Online: amazon.com, inkacrops.com

JACKSON'S HONEST POTATO CHIPS
Some stores and online: amazon.com, jacksons-honest.myshopify.com

LIVING INTENTIONS: GONE NUTS!
Online: amazon.com, livingintentions.com

SEASNAX (seasnax.com)
Whole Foods Market, local grocers
Online: amazon.com

WONDERFULLY RAW GOURMET DELIGHTS
Online: amazon.com, mycocoroons.com

TEA

EQUAL EXCHANGE
Online: amazon.com, shop. equalexchange.coop

HONEST TEA (honesttea.com)
Local grocers

NUMI ORGANIC TEA
In stores and online: amazon.com, numitea.com

RISHI TEA
In stores and online: amazon.com, rishi-tea.com

TEAONIC
Online: amazon.com, teaonic.com

TRADITIONAL MEDICINALS
Whole Foods Market, local organic grocers/co-ops
Online: amazon.com, traditionalmedicinals.com

TORTILLAS & WRAPS

IMPROV'EAT: PURE WRAPS
Online: amazon.com, improveat.com

SIETE FAMILY FOODS
Whole Foods Market, local organic grocers/co-ops
Online: sietefoods.com

VINEGARS

BIONATURAE
Whole Foods Market, local organic grocers/co-ops (bionaturae.com for locations)
Online: amazon.com

BRAGG
Local grocers
Online: amazon.com, bragg.com

COCONUT SECRET
Some stores and online: amazon.com, coconutsecret.com

KASANDRINOS INTERNATIONAL PREMIUM BALSAMIC VINEGARS
Online: kasandrinos.com

MISCELLANEOUS

EMERALD COVE
Nori (dried seaweed)
Grocery stores, Asian markets
Online: amazon.com, great-eastern-sun.com

IF YOU CARE / PAPERCHEF
Parchment paper and other cooking/ baking liners
Whole Foods Market, local organic grocers/co-ops
Online: amazon.com

MEDITERRANEAN ORGANIC
Olives, other grocery items—read labels (mediterraneanorganic.com)
Local grocers and online: amazon.com

To shop my favorites, visit www.balancedbites.com/shop

Sources

Everything We've Been Taught About Good Nutrition Is Wrong

Anderson, Keaven M., William P. Castelli, and Daniel Levy. "Cholesterol and Mortality: 30 Years of Follow-up from the Framingham Study." *JAMA* 257, no. 16 (1987): 2176–80.

Carbohydrates and You, Part 1. Perf. Radhia Gleis. PsycheTruth, 2008. Web. www.psychetruth.net/nutrition_information_videos/diet-2/carbohydrates-you-part-1-advanced-nutrition-lecture/

Castelli, William. "Concerning the Possibility of a Nut . . . ." *Archives of Internal Medicine* 152, no. 7 (1992): 1371–2.

Eades, Michael R. "You Bet Your Life: An Epilogue to the Cholesterol Story." Blog post. *The Blog of Dr. Michael R. Eades, M.D.,* October 11, 2010. www.proteinpower.com/drmike/cardiovascular-disease/you-bet-your-life-an-epilogue-to-the-cholesterol-story/

Gaziano, J. M., C. H. Hennekens, C. J. O'Donnell, J. L. Breslow, and J. E. Buring. "Fasting Triglycerides, High-Density Lipoprotein, and Risk of Myocardial Infarction." *Circulation* 96, no. 8 (1997): 2520–5.

Knopp, Robert H., and Barbara M. Retzlaff. "Saturated Fat Prevents Coronary Artery Disease? An American Paradox." *American Journal of Clinical Nutrition* 80, no. 5 (2004): 1102–3. http://ajcn.nutrition.org/content/80/5/1102.full

Kresser, Chris. "Chris Masterjohn on Cholesterol and Heart Disease (Part 2)." Podcast episode. *The Healthy Skeptic,* September 8, 2011. https://chriskresser.com/episode-16-chris-masterjohn-on-cholesterol-heart-disease-part-2/

Kresser, Chris. "Vitamin K2: The Missing Nutrient." Blog post. *Chris Kresser,* May 6, 2008. http://chriskresser.com/vitamin-k2-the-missing-nutrient

Masterjohn, Christopher. "As the Cholesterol Consensus Crumbles, the Stance Against Saturated Fat Softens." *The Weston A. Price Foundation.* www.westonaprice.org/our-blogs/cmasterjohn/cholesterol-consensus-crumbles-stance-saturated-fat-softens/

Nestle, Marion. *Food Politics: How the Food Industry Influences Nutrition and Health.* Berkeley, CA: University of California Press, 2002.

Schurgers, L. J., and C. Vermeer. "Determination of Phylloquinone and Menaquinones in Food. Effect of Food Matrix on Circulating Vitamin K Concentrations." *Haemostasis* 30, no. 6 (2000): 298–307. www.ncbi.nlm.nih.gov/pubmed/11356998

Siri-Tarino, Patty W., Qi Sun, Frank B. Hu, and Ronald M. Krauss. "Meta-Analysis of Prospective Cohort Studies Evaluating the Association of Saturated Fat with Cardiovascular Disease." *American Journal of Clinical Nutrition* 91, no. 3 (2010): 535–46. www.ncbi.nlm.nih.gov/pubmed/20071648

Tang, Guangwen. "Bioconversion of Dietary Provitamin A Carotenoids to Vitamin A in Humans." *American Journal of Clinical Nutrition* 91, no. 5 (2010): 1468S–1473S. http://ajcn.nutrition.org/content/91/5/1468S.full

U.S. Department of Agriculture and U.S. Department of Health and Human Services. "Part D. Chapter 1: Food and Nutrient Intakes, and Health: Current Status and Trends." *Scientific Report of the 2015 Dietary Guidelines Advisory Committee.* http://health.gov/dietaryguidelines/2015-scientific-report/06-chapter-1/d1-2.asp

U.S. Department of Agriculture and U.S. Department of Health and Human Services. *Dietary Guidelines for Americans, 2015–2020. 8th Edition,* Washington, DC: U.S. Government Printing Office, December 2015. http://health.gov/dietaryguidelines/2015/guidelines/

Wallis, Claudia. "Hold the Eggs and Butter." *Time,* March 26, 1984.

Eat Whole Foods

"What Is the Meaning of 'Natural' on the Label of Food?" U.S. Food and Drug Administration, January 16, 2015. www.fda.gov/AboutFDA/Transparency/Basics/ucm214868.htm

Healing Digestion

Kresser, Chris. "Get Rid of Heartburn and GERD Forever in Three Simple Steps." Blog post. *Chris Kresser,* April 16, 2010. http://chriskresser.com/get-rid-of-heartburn-and-gerd-forever-in-three-simple-steps

Kresser, Chris. "The Hidden Causes of Heartburn and GERD." Blog post. *Chris Kresser,* April 1, 2010. http://chriskresser.com/the-hidden-causes-of-heartburn-and-gerd

Addressing Autoimmunity

Cojocaru, M., Inimiora Mihaela, and Isabela Silosi. "Multiple Autoimmune Syndrome." *Mædica* 5, no. 2 (2010): 132–134. www.maedica.org/jcm-vol-5-8-nr-2-2010/

Fasano, Alessio. "Zonulin and Its Regulation of Intestinal Barrier Function: The Biological Door to Inflammation, Autoimmunity, and Cancer." *Physiological Reviews* 91, no. 1 (2011): 151–75.

Fasano, Alessio. "Zonulin, Regulation of Tight Junctions, and Autoimmune Diseases." *Annals of the New York Academy of Sciences* 1258 (2012): 25–33. http://onlinelibrary.wiley.com/doi/10.1111/j.1749-6632.2012.06538.x/abstract

"Gastrointestinal Assessments: Intestinal Permeability Assessment." Genova Diagnostics. www.gdx.net/core/interpretive-guides/Intestinal-Permeability-Interp-Guide.pdf

Sequeira, Ivana R., Roger G. Lentle, Marlena C. Kruger, and Roger D. Hurst. "Standardising the Lactulose Mannitol Test of Gut Permeability to Minimise Error and Promote Comparability." *PLOS One,* June 5, 2014. http://dx.doi.org/10.1371/journal.pone.0099256

Managing Stress

Kharrazian, Datis. *Why Do I Still Have Thyroid Symptoms? When My Lab Tests Are Normal.* Carlsbad, CA: Elephant Press, 2010.

Wilson, James. *Adrenal Fatigue: The 21st Century Stress Syndrome.* Petaluma, CA: Smart Publications, 2001.

Frequently Asked Questions

Winter, Ruth. *A Consumer's Dictionary of Food Additives.* 7th ed. New York: Random House, 2009.

Ravnskov, Uffe. "High Cholesterol May Protect Against Infections and Atherosclerosis." *QJM: An International Journal of Medicine* 96, no. 12 (2003): 927–34. http://qjmed.oxfordjournals.org/content/qjmed/96/12/927.full.pdf

Meal Plans

Chahar, Maheep K., Neelu Sharma, Mahabeer P. Dobhal, and Yogesh C. Joshi. "Flavonoids: A Versatile Source of Anticancer Drugs." *Pharmacognosy Review* 5, no. 9 (2011): 1–12.

Disease Prevention and Treatment. 5th ed. Life Extension Media. LE Publications, 2013.

Murray, Michael. *Encyclopedia of Nutritional Supplements.* New York: Random House, 1996.

Scaglione, Francesco, and Giscardo Panzavolta. "Folate, Folic Acid and 5-methyltetrahydrofolate Are Not the Same Thing." *Xenobiotica* 44, no. 5 (2014): 480–8. www.ncbi.nlm.nih.gov/pubmed/24494987

Trivieri, Larry, and John W. Anderson, eds. *Alternative Medicine: The Definitive Guide.* 2nd ed. New York: Random House, 2002.

Quick Reference

Recipe	pg	NUTS & SEEDS	EGGS	NIGHTSHADES	FODMAPS	21DSD	SPICE BLEND	QUICK & EASY	LOW & SLOW MEAL	PARTY	FAMILY	ONE POT	FREEZE ME
signature spice blends	256				M	M							
lemon & herb salt blends	258					●		●				●	
mineral-rich bone broth	259				●	●			●			●	●
perfectly baked bacon	260					●		●			●	●	
clarified butter & ghee	261					●						●	●
raw probiotic sauerkraut	262			M	M	●		●				●	
paleo avocado "toast"	264		M	M	●	●		●	●		●	●	
breakfast fried "rice"	266	M	M	M	●	●		●	●			●	●
home fries & sausage skillet	268			M	M	●		●	●	●		●	●
swirly crustless quiche	270		●			●		●				●	●
zucchini pancakes	271		●			●	M	●				●	●
apple sage sausage	272				●	●	M	●	●			●	●
blueberry maple sausage	273				M	●		●	●			●	●
charlie's big fat italian frittata	274		●	●		●		●		●		●	●
lemon blueberry muffins	276		●			●		●		●		●	
pumpkin cranberry muffins	277		●			●		●		●		●	
carrot gingerbread muffins	278		●			●				●		●	
apple cinnamon egg muffins	280		●			M	M	●				●	
fluffy banana pancakes	282		●					●				●	●
pumpkin pancakes	284	M	●			●	M	●				●	●
sweet potato pancakes (burger buns)	285		M			M	●	●				●	●
pesto scrambled eggs	286	●	●				●	●				●	
bacon & egg salad	287		●				●	●				●	
n'oatmeal	288	M				●	M	●				●	
quick breakfast smoothies	289					●		●				●	
souvlaki kebabs	290			M	M	●	M	●			●	●	
citrus & herb whole roasted chicken	292				M	●	M	●				●	●
mediterranean baked chicken	294			M		●	●	●				●	●
lemon & artichoke chicken	296				M	●	M	●				●	●
bacon-wrapped smoky chicken thighs	298			M		●		●			●	●	
buffalo chicken lettuce wraps	299			M	M	●		●			●	●	
one-pot sausage & chicken sp. squash bake	300		M	●	●	●	●		●		●	●	●
slow-cooked salsa verde chicken	302			●	●	●	●			●	●	●	
dairy-free pepperoni chicken parm	304	●	●	●	●		M				●	●	●
orange & olive braised chicken	306				●	M			●	●	●	●	●
smoky buffalo wings	308			●	●	M	●	●			●	●	
honey garlic teriyaki wings	308	M			M			●			●	●	
spinach artichoke stuffed chicken	310	M		M		●		●			●	●	
restaurant-style lettuce cups	312	●		M	●	●		●			●	●	●
chicken satay sandwiches	314	●		M	●	●		●	●		●	●	
savory baked chicken legs	316	●		M	M	M	●	●				●	
mustard-glazed chicken thighs	317					●		●			●	●	
coffee BBQ rubbed pork	318			M	●					●	●	●	●
cumin-spiced pork tenderloin	320					M				●	●	●	
chorizo meatballs	322			●	●	●	●	●			●	●	●
grandma barbara's stuffed mushrooms	324			M	●	●	●	●			●	●	
thanksgiving stuffing meatballs	326	M			●	●	M				●	●	●
orange sesame meatballs	328	M			M	●					●	●	●
bacon & superfood meatloaf	330	M	M	M	●	●	●					●	●

● contains this allergen or is this type of recipe   M can be modified to be free of this allergen or to comply with this type of meal

Quick Reference

Recipe	pg	NUTS & SEEDS	EGGS	NIGHTSHADES	FODMAPS	21DSD	SPICE BLEND	QUICK & EASY	MEAL	LOW & SLOW	PARTY	FAMILY	ONE POT	FREEZE ME
balsamic braised short ribs	332				M	●	M	●			●	●	●	●
grilled garlic flank steak	334				M	M	●		●			●	●	
green sauce marinated steak & plantain bowl	336				●	●	●	●		●			●	●
spaghetti squash bolognese	338				M	●	M		●	●			●	●
meatball sandwich burgers with marinara	340	M	M		●	M	●	M				●	●	
indian spiced burgers	342		M	M	●	●	●					●	●	
prosciutto & caramelized onion burgers	343		M			●		●				●	●	
orange braised beef	344	●			●	M					●	●	●	●
hayley's skirt steak tacos	346				M	M	●		●			●		
beef & veggie stir-fry	348	M			M	M	●		●	●		●	●	
tangy taco salad	350				M	M	●		●	●		●	●	
mini mediterranean kebabs (kofta)	352				M	●	●		M			●	●	
mom's stuffed cabbage rolls	354				M	●				●		●	●	●
butternut cocoa chili	356				●	M	●		●	●	●	●	●	●
italian-style stuffed peppers	358				M	M	●	M				●	●	
bacon jalapeño burgers	360				●	●	●	M	●			●	●	
the easiest tacos (nightshade-free)	362					●	●	M	●	●	●	●	●	
slow-cooked mediterranean stew	364				M	●	●		●		●		●	
lamb chops with olive tapenade	366					●	●	●				●	●	
lemony lamb dolmas (stuffed grape leaves)	368					M	●	M				●	●	
lamb lettuce boats with avoziki sauce	370			M	M	●	M		●	●			●	
spiced lamb meatballs	372					M		M	●		●	●	●	●
quick & easy salmon cakes	374		●			M		●	●			●		
lemon rosemary broiled salmon	375						●	●	●				●	●
lemon & bacon scallops	376			M	M	●		M	●	●			●	
citrus macadamia nut sole	378	●				●	●		●				●	
pesto fettuccine with shrimp	380	M				M			●				●	
six-minute salmon bowls	382	M				M	M	●	●	●			●	
grilled tuna over fresh noodle salad	384						●		●	●				
seared scallops with orange glaze	386	M				M	●		●				●	
nori salmon handroll	388					●	●		●			●		
simple shrimp ceviche	389				M	●	●	●	●			●		
mexican chicken & avocado soup	390					M	●	M	●	●		●	●	●
broc-cauli chowder with bacon	392					●	●		●			●	●	●
butternut sage soup	394					●	●	●	●			●	●	●
dairy-free caesar salad	396				M	●	●			●		●	●	
winter kale salad	396	M				M	M		●		●	●		
italiano salad	398	M			M	M	M			●		●	●	
flank steak salad	399	M				M	M		●	●		●	●	
mixed greens salad	400					●			●			●	●	
prosciutto & berries salad	401					●			●	●		●	●	
greek salad with avoziki dressing	402				M	●	●	●	●			●	●	
summer squash caprese noodle salad	403				M	●			●			●	●	
rainbow red cabbage salad	404	●				●	M		●			●	●	
sautéed red cabbage	405					●	●						●	
acorn squash	406	M				●	M		●				●	
green beans with shallots	406					M	●					●	●	
smoky grilled squash & pineapple	408			●				●				●	●	
asparagus with lemon & olives	409					●	●		●				●	

● contains this allergen or is this type of recipe   M can be modified to be free of this allergen or to comply with this type of meal

Quick Reference

Recipe	pg	Nuts & Seeds	Eggs	Nightshades	FODMAPs	21DSD	Spice Blend	Quick & Easy	Low & Slow Meal	Party	Family	One Pot	Freeze Me
crispy sweet potato coins	410	M	M			●	●	●			●	●	
smashed potatoes with garlic & onions	411				M	●	●				●	●	
cilantro cauli-rice	412					●	●	●				●	
yellow cauli-rice	413					●	M	●				●	
roasted figs with rosemary	414					●		●			●	●	
candied carrots	415					●		●				●	
roasted brussels sprouts	416					●	●	●				●	
lemon roasted romanesco	417					●	●	●				●	
mashed faux-tatoes	418					●	●	●			●	●	
whipped sweet potatoes	419					M	●	●			●	●	
baked beets with fennel	420					M	●	●				●	
sweet & savory potatoes	421					M	●	●				●	
confit cherry tomatoes	422				●	●	●					●	
sautéed spinach with pine nuts & currants	423	●				●	M	●				●	
bacon-wrapped party bites	424					●		●			●	●	
simple baked kale chips	425				M	●		●			●	●	
chicken liver pâté	426					●	M						●
creamy cauliflower hummus	428	●				●	●	●			●	●	
dairy-free spinach artichoke dip	429	M			M	●	●				●		●
baked potato chips	430			●	M	●	●	●			●	●	
crispy plantain chips	431					●					●	●	
roasted garlic tahini sauce	432	●				●	●	●			●	●	
five kinds of salsa	433			M	M	M		●			●	●	
balsamic vinaigrette	434												
orange vinaigrette	434				M								
honey mustard dressing	434												
dairy-free caesar dressing	434												
spicy lime dressing	434				M								
basil shallot vinaigrette	434												
simple cranberry sauce	436					M		●			●	●	●
nightshade-free ketchup (AIP)	437				●	M		●			●	●	
paleo mayonnaise	438		●				●	●			●		
diane's magic green sauce	439			●	●	●		●			●		
herbal tea gummies	440				●	●	M	●				●	
cherry lemon gummies	441				●			●				●	
vanilla bean truffles	442	M			●			●			●		
easy chocolate truffles	443	●			●			●		●			
soft chocolate coconut cookies	444	M	●		●			●			●	●	
creamy two-bite treats	445				●			●			●	●	
almond butter cups	446	●			●						●	●	
pepita goji berry bark	448	M		M				●			●	●	
nutty bacon bark	449	M						●			●	●	
dairy-free chocolate mousse	450					●	M	●				●	
dairy-free pistachio mousse	450	●				●	M					●	
raw raspberry tart	452	●			●						●	●	●
nut-free skillet peach crisp	454				●			●			●	●	
fresh blueberry crumble	456	●						●			●	●	
flourless dark chocolate brownies	458		●		●						●	●	●

● contains this allergen or is this type of recipe   M can be modified to be free of this allergen or to comply with this type of meal

Recipe Index

Kitchen Basics

256
signature spice blends

258
lemon & herb salt blends

259
mineral-rich bone broth

260
perfectly baked bacon

261
clarified butter & ghee

262
raw probiotic sauerkraut

Breakfast

264
paleo avocado "toast"

266
breakfast fried "rice"

268
home fries & sausage skillet

270
swirly crustless quiche

271
zucchini pancakes

272
apple sage sausage

273
blueberry maple sausage

274
charlie's big fat italian frittata

276
lemon blueberry muffins

277
pumpkin cranberry muffins

278
carrot gingerbread muffins

280
apple cinnamon egg muffins

282
fluffy banana pancakes

284
pumpkin pancakes

285
sweet potato pancakes (burger buns)

286
pesto scrambled eggs

287
bacon & egg salad

288
n'oatmeal

289
quick breakfast smoothies

Poultry

290
souvlaki kebabs

292
citrus & herb whole roasted chicken

294
mediterranean baked chicken

296
lemon & artichoke chicken

298
bacon-wrapped smoky chicken thighs

299
buffalo chicken lettuce wraps

300
one-pot sausage & chicken spaghetti squash bake

302
slow-cooked salsa verde chicken

304
dairy-free pepperoni chicken parm

306
orange & olive braised chicken

308
smoky buffalo wings

308
honey garlic teriyaki wings

310
spinach artichoke stuffed chicken

312
restaurant-style lettuce cups

314
chicken satay
sandwiches with
blistered peppers

316
savory baked
chicken legs

317
mustard-glazed
chicken thighs

Pork

318
coffee BBQ
rubbed pork with
seared pineapple

320
cumin-spiced pork
tenderloin with
root vegetables

322
chorizo meatballs

324
grandma barbara's
stuffed mushrooms

326
thanksgiving
stuffing meatballs

328
orange sesame
meatballs

Beef & Bison

330
bacon & superfood
meatloaf

332
balsamic braised
short ribs

334
grilled garlic
flank steak with
peppers & onions

336
green sauce
marinated steak &
plantain bowl

338
spaghetti squash
bolognese

340
meatball sandwich
burgers

342
indian spiced
burgers

343
prosciutto &
caramelized onion
burgers

344
orange braised
beef

346
hayley's
skirt steak tacos

348
beef & veggie
stir-fry

350
tangy taco salad

352
mini mediterranean
kebabs (kofta)

354
mom's stuffed
cabbage rolls

356
butternut cocoa
chili

358
italian-style
stuffed peppers

360
bacon jalapeño
burgers

362
the easiest tacos
(nightshade-free)

Lamb

364
slow-cooked
mediterranean
stew

366
lamb chops with
olive tapenade

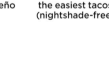
368
lemony lamb
dolmas

370
lamb lettuce boats
with avoziki sauce

372
spiced lamb
meatballs

Seafood

374 quick & easy salmon cakes

375 lemon rosemary broiled salmon

376 lemon & bacon scallops with roasted potatoes

378 citrus macadamia nut sole

380 pesto fettuccine with shrimp

382 six-minute salmon bowls

384 grilled tuna over fresh noodle salad

386 seared scallops with orange glaze

388 nori salmon handroll

389 simple shrimp ceviche

Soups, Salads & Sides

390 mexican chicken & avocado soup

392 broc-cauli chowder with bacon

394 butternut sage soup

396 dairy-free caesar salad

396 winter kale salad

398 italiano salad

399 flank steak salad

400 mixed greens salad with persimmons, asparagus & fennel

401 prosciutto & berries salad

402 greek salad with avoziki dressing

403 summer squash caprese noodle salad

404 rainbow red cabbage salad

405 sautéed red cabbage with onions and apples

406 acorn squash with cinnamon & coconut butter

406 green beans with shallots

408 smoky grilled squash & pineapple

409 asparagus with lemon & olives

410 crispy sweet potato coins

411 smashed potatoes with garlic & onions

412 cilantro cauli-rice

413 yellow cauli-rice

414 roasted figs with rosemary

415 candied carrots

416 roasted brussels sprouts

417 lemon roasted romanesco

418 mashed faux-tatoes

419 whipped sweet potatoes

420 baked beets with fennel

421 sweet & savory potatoes

422 confit cherry tomatoes

423 sautéed spinach

Snacks, Dips & Sauces

424
bacon-wrapped
party bites

425
simple baked
kale chips

426
chicken liver pâté

428
creamy cauliflower
hummus

429
dairy-free spinach
artichoke dip

430
baked potato chips

431
crispy
plantain chips

432
roasted garlic
tahini sauce

433
five kinds of salsa

434
balsamic
vinaigrette

434
orange vinaigrette

434
honey mustard
dressing

434
dairy-free
caesar dressing

434
spicy lime dressing

434
basil shallot
vinaigrette

434
simple
cranberry sauce

436

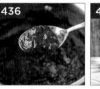
437
nightshade-free
ketchup (AIP)

438
paleo mayonnaise

439
diane's magic
green sauce

Treats & Sweets

440
herbal tea
gummies

441
cherry lemon
gummies

442
vanilla bean
truffles

443
easy chocolate
truffles

444
soft chocolate
coconut cookies

445
creamy
two-bite treats

446
almond butter cups

448
pepita goji berry
bark

449
nutty bacon bark

450
dairy-free
chocolate mousse

450
dairy-free
pistachio mousse

452
raw raspberry tart

454
nut-free skillet
peach crisp

456
fresh blueberry
crumble

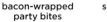

458
flourless dark
chocolate brownies

General Index